The several contributions to this landmark volume represent a variety of new and unique approaches to the joint study of the Nazi and Stalinist regimes.

Moshe Lewin and Ian Kershaw, prominent Russian and German experts respectively, have assembled a distinguished international team of historians and sociologists to examine the parallel aspects of totalitarianism. Although not explicitly comparative, these far-reaching essays provide the necessary foundation for a fuller comparative analysis and provide the means to deepen and extend research in the field. The essays are grouped into three selective areas of common ground between the systems. The first section highlights similarities and differences in the leadership cults at the heart of the dictatorships. The second section moves to the 'war machines' engaged in the titanic clash of the regimes between 1941 and 1945. A final area covered surveys the shifting interpretations of successor societies in Germany and Russia as they have faced up to the legacy of the past.

Stalinism and Nazism: Dictatorships in Comparison combines state-of-the art research with fresh perspectives on the most violent and inhumane epoch in modern European history. It will be essential reading for both students and specialists in the social and political sciences, international relations and transcultural studies.

Stalinism and Nazism:
Dictatorships in Comparison

Stalinism and Nazism:
Dictatorships in Comparison

EDITED BY

IAN KERSHAW

Professor of Modern History, University of Sheffield

AND

MOSHE LEWIN

*Professor-Emeritus of History, Department of History,
University of Pennsylvania*

CAMBRIDGE
UNIVERSITY PRESS

Published by the Press Syndicate of the University of Cambridge
The Pitt Building, Trumpington Street, Cambridge CB2 1RP
40 West 20th Street, New York, NY 10011-4211, USA
10 Stamford Road, Oakleigh, Melbourne 3166, Australia

First published 1997

Printed in Great Britain at the University Press, Cambridge

A catalogue record for this book is available from the British Library

Library of Congress cataloguing in publication data

Stalinism and Nazism: Dictatorships in Comparison/
edited by Ian Kershaw and Moshe Lewin.
p. cm.
ISBN 0 521 56345 3. – ISBN 0 521 56521 9 (pbk.)
1. Totalitarianism – Congresses. 2. Soviet Union – Politics and
government – Congresses. 3. Germany – Politics and
government – 1933–1945 – Congresses. I. Kershaw, Ian. II. Lewin,
Moshe, 1921– .
JC480.D53 1996
320.5'3–dc20   96-16150 CIP

ISBN 0 521 56345 3 hardback
ISBN 0 521 56521 9 paperback

Contents

CONTENTS

Contributors

IAN KERSHAW is Professor of Modern History at the University of Sheffield. A Fellow of the British Academy, Professor Kershaw is the author of *Popular Opinion and Political Dissent in the Third Reich*, *The Nazi Dictatorship* (now in its third edition), *The 'Hitler Myth': Image and reality in the Third Reich* and *Hitler: a Profile in Power*.

MOSHE LEWIN is Professor-Emeritus of History in the Department of History, University of Pennsylvania. He has also taught at the Ecole des Hautes Etudes en Sciences Sociales, Paris, and at the University of Birmingham. His many books include *Lenin's Last Struggle*, *Russian Peasant and Soviet Power*, *Political Undercurrents in Soviet Economic Debates*, *The Gorbachev Phenomenon* and *The Making of the Soviet System*.

RONALD GRIGOR SUNY is Professor of Political Science at the University of Chicago. His publications include *The Baku Commune, 1917–1918: Class and nationality in the Russian Revolution*, *The Making of the Georgian Nation*, *Looking toward Ararat: Armenia in Modern History*, and *The Revenge of the Past: Nationalism, Revolution and the Collapse of the Soviet Union*.

HANS MOMMSEN is Professor of History at the Ruhr University, Bochum.

MICHAEL MANN is professor of Sociology at the University of California, Los Angeles. He has written two volumes of a major global survey of *The Sources of Social Power*.

OMER BARTOV is Associate Professor of History at Rutgers University. His most recent publications include *Hitler's Army: Soldiers, Nazis and War in the Third Reich* and *Murder in our midst: the Holocaust, Industrial Killing, and Representation*.

BERND BONWETSCH is Professor of East European History, Ruhr University, Bochum.

JACQUES SAPIR is Vice-Professor in Economics at the Ecole des Hautes Etudes en Sciences Sociales, Paris. His many books on Soviet and Russian economic and military affairs include *The Soviet Military System* and *Problèmes monétaires et financiers dans la transition en Russie.*

MARK VON HAGEN researches at the Harriman Institute of Columbia University.

GEORGE STEINMETZ is Assistant Professor of Sociology at the University of Chicago. He is the author of *Regulating the Social: The Welfare State and Local Politics in Imperial Germany.*

MARY NOLAN teaches European, German and Women's History at New York University. She is the author of *Social Democracy and Society: Working-Class Radicalism in Düsseldorf, 1890–1920* and *Visions of Modernity: American Business and the Modernisation of Germany.*

Preface

This book had its genesis in a conference (of which Moshe Lewin was the principal organiser) that took place in Philadelphia in September 1991. Fifty scholars from five countries – France, Germany, Russia, the United Kingdom, and the United States – took part. The aim of the conference was to explore similarities and differences in the development of Russia and Germany during the twentieth century. The Cold War had not encouraged comparison outside the framework of the totalitarianism concept and its assumption that comparison assumed similarity. The conference accepted no such imperative and ranged across the century, tackling a broad array of topics – some widely couched, others more narrowly focused – that reached back into the monarchical systems before the First World War and forward to the demise of the Soviet system. The wide thematic and chronological range of the comparison, the conceptual framework of the enquiry, and the fact that it could take place without the ritual ideological posturing which had existed in the era of the Cold War, meant that the conference was breaking new ground. The participants shared the view that comparison offered the nearest the historian could come to the laboratory experiment of the natural scientist, but that there is no single prescribed or specific method to undertake comparative history. The methods and approaches must remain eclectic and pragmatic in comparative history, as in any other kind of historical analysis.

The conference produced 27 papers and 18 prepared commentaries. The initial intention was to publish not only these, but in addition transcripts of the recorded discussions that flowed unabated for three days. It became clear, however, that to publish the full proceedings of the conference would not have served the interests of a wider, non-specialised, readership. Moreover, several volumes and a number of additional editors would have been necessary to accommodate the extensive material. With some reluctance, therefore, we opted for

concentration on a more limited period, but on one where the comparative issues posed themselves particularly clearly, and could be delin-
eated with some precision. In some instances the initial conference
papers were considerably revised. In addition, it was necessary to solicit
a number of new contributions on topics which had not been covered at
the conference itself. The debt which the editors and authors of the
papers in this volume owe to the conference participants whose papers
did not fit the narrower confines of the theme of this volume, and which
could not, therefore, be included is considerable indeed. Most of these
contributions, it is gratifying to note, have in any case meanwhile
appeared in print.

This description of the genesis of the present volume is sufficient to
indicate that it has not been conceived as a systematic or comprehensive
comparative history of Russia and Germany in the Stalinist and Nazi
periods. 'Perspectives', as noted in the title of the Introduction, aptly
summarises what was intended. The selection of subject areas might
easily have been a quite different one. Even so, we believe that this
volume serves as a modest pointer to numerous promising avenues for
research, reflection, and debate on a subject of self-evident importance.

The editors would like to offer their warmest thanks to the National
Council for Soviet and East European Research in Washington DC,
which supplied most of the funding needed to stage the conference, and
to the School of Arts and Sciences of the University of Pennsylvania
which contributed the residue. The Department of History at the
University of Pennsylvania offered important administrative support.
Special thanks are also owing to James Heinzen and David Kerans,
doctoral students at the time of the conference and by now qualified as
PhD, for splendid assistance in organisational matters.

Ian Kershaw
Moshe Lewin

Introduction

The regimes and their dictators: perspectives of comparison

Ian Kershaw and Moshe Lewin

The need to compare

The starting-point of comparative history is invariably the impression, realisation, or certainty that two (or more) societies have sufficient in common to invite – even demand – analysing them as a part of a single set of questions. Normally, it is a problem common to both societies or the historical interaction of those societies which prompts recourse to the comparative method.

Alongside the many exhortations to undertake comparative analysis are the many warnings of its pitfalls. A conventional theoretical objection to comparison is embodied in the claim that historical knowledge is derived from unique, non-repeatable events – in contrast to those fields of knowledge which relate to phenomena capable of repeating themselves, about which generalisations can be drawn and conceptual constructs erected. However, the dichotomy is a false one. The categories are not mutually exclusive. Each individual, for instance, has a unique personality. But we do not presume that the uniqueness of the individual prevents us from comparing individuals, using concepts like 'humanity', or generalising about 'society' and the 'systems' or 'structures' underpinning that society. For societies are not simply agglomerates of individuals. They could not exist, and could not have existed in the past, without creating and recreating discernible patterns allowing that modicum of predictability without which human activity would be impossible. For this to be so, individual 'personality', though unique, has also to be seen as a social product. And once this is admitted, we can theorise; and we can and should compare. In fact, it is self-evident that only comparison allows an understanding of uniqueness. Nietzsche's conclusion that 'only things without a history are definable'[1] could be stood on its head: in human

---

[1] Friedrich Nietzsche, *Use and Abuse of History* (Indianapolis–New York 1959), pp. 59, 61, 70.

affairs *only* entities with a history are subject to theorisation, and are thus definable.

In some senses, all historical enquiry is comparative, even if unwittingly so. Like Molière's Monsieur Jourdain, who did not know that he was using prose, we engage in comparison without always realising it. The study of lengthy stretches of history even of a single country, for example, involves a comparison of different periods in the past. Equally, any study of extensive geographical areas (such as Western Europe) or deployment of concepts in historical explanation (for example, capitalism, or nationalism) is by definition comparative, even if this is not always claimed or even realised. By contrast, some studies purporting to be comparative are in reality describing separate histories in parallel. In other cases, historians might claim similarities for phenomena whose superficial likeness is deceptive on account of the greatly differing historical environment in which the phenomena occurred. In any case, the obvious point needs to be reiterated: comparison does not consist of seeking similarity. It is at least equally important to seek out and explain fundamental differences, to understand not just what common ground there might be between the societies or systems compared, but also their specific and unique features. To keep these aims in view requires constant questioning of the validity of the comparison, and of the historical method deployed to explore it. No patent or ready-made methodology is to hand. Comparison is fraught with difficulties. But not to compare leaves us blind to the past – and to the past's implications for the present and future. For knowing just one society may often amount to a poor understanding of even that single society.

One way of approaching the past of the two countries examined in this volume has proved influential, but contains a fallacy which is not immediately evident. Seeking to explain the respective 'anomalies' of the historical development of Germany and Russia, some scholars have turned to liberal-bourgeois western societies and their political systems as a model and blueprint. The absence of such a development has then been taken to explain the growth of National Socialism in the one case, Leninism and Stalinism in the other. Looking to 'the West' and the mechanisms of its political and social development as the paradigm seemed to offer the key to what was missing east of the Rhine. As critics, particularly specialists on Germany, have said, it sometimes amounted to studying what did not happen, rather than what actually did take place.[2] The French ethnographer and political sociologist Pierre Clastre thought this a more broadly shared fallacy among social scientists. He

---

[2] See David Blackbourn and Geoff Eley, *The Peculiarities of German History* (Oxford 1984), esp. p. 283.

complained that in some studies of 'primitive societies', such societies 'were determined negatively, under the guise of what was missing', allowing them to be portrayed as societies without states, without literacy, and without history, incapable of creating a market or acquiring surpluses, and thereby of developing into 'advanced' societies.[3] This 'ethnocentric' approach, positing an inexorable evolution (or prevention of such an evolution), hindered real understanding of these societies. Moreover, the evolutionary determinism of such 'ethnocentrism' is of self-evidently limited value if two societies within a specific socio-economic system followed quite different paths. Deducing Nazism and Stalinism from the failure of Germany and Russia to develop like Britain raises the obvious objection: not every country with weak capitalism (even in the absence of parliamentary government) produced an equivalent of Stalinism; not every country with a vibrant capitalist system (even where authoritarian structures of rule prevailed) engendered an equivalent of Nazism. Once the 'ethnocentric' fallacy is avoided, however, comparison – including comparison with the West – is often illuminating.

Even so the question arises: why compare countries with such different history, geography, social structures, and levels of development as Germany and Russia (subsequently the Soviet Union)? The framework we have imposed upon this volume suggests three strands of an answer, though these are certainly not the only possibilities.

One reason is certainly that for much of this century Germany under Nazi rule and the Soviet Union *have* been openly compared, by bracketing them together through the concept of 'totalitarianism' – a comparative concept *par excellence*. Here we had comparison with a vengeance, positing a high degree of similarity between two different, and opposed, systems of rule. (This is itself somewhat unusual, since comparative political science tends to look for affinities rather than opposites, for groups of intrinsically similar systems, such as liberal democracies, or fascist regimes.) Criticism by many scholars about the usability of the concept in comparative analysis, and about the superficiality of the purported similarities of the two supposed 'totalitarian states', has not dented the continued, in recent years even strengthened, usage of the term both in common parlance and in academic analysis.

Above all, it was the way in which the totalitarianism concept was used as an ideological tool in the service of the Cold War – often distorting reality and intellectually dishonest – which disqualified it in the eyes of numerous scholars. Indeed, the comparison did often contain all too obvious ideological or propagandistic aims. By claiming

---

[3] Pierre Clastre, *La société contre l'état* (Paris 1974), p. 162.

3

an essential 'sameness' between Nazism and Stalinism, though they had been in mortal combat with each other, it used the evils of the dead Hitler regime to condemn the Soviet system which was still very much alive. However, the ideological abuse of a comparative concept does not in itself invalidate genuine historical comparison. Scholarly analysis of comparative fascism, for example, has never been regarded as invalid – though some dispute the applicability of the term 'fascism' to German National Socialism – despite the fact that the concept of 'fascism' has been at least as commonly abused as 'totalitarianism' for propagandist and ideological purposes.

Another objection was that Stalinism and Nazism were wholly different phenomena, arising from totally different types of society, thereby rendering comparison otiose. Like had to be compared with like, the argument ran; to compare fundamentally dissimilar societies and systems was futile. This objection, it will be noted, is based upon an *a priori* determination of dissimilarity. It is, of course, impossible to evaluate the extent of difference, or of similarity, without comparison. It is as well, therefore, to make such a comparison explicit.

When comparison is a method of scholarly enquiry, not of propaganda, there can be no logical objection to it, even if the conclusions emphasise differences more than similarities. Comparative analysis welcomes both sameness and difference. It can work with nuances of analogy, parallelism, identity, and polarity. In two different societies, or even in two very different periods in the history of one society, nothing is ever actually very similar, let alone identical. That does not invalidate comparison. Comparing two societies demands the search for the 'specific' in each case, while acknowledging the common features when and if they can be ascertained.

In fact, looking for 'common ground' is more fruitful than the search for 'sameness'. After all, very different species can form part of the same genus. Elements of the historical development of the two countries which are our concern here also speak in favour of the 'common ground' approach, even where the differences and contrasts are obvious. Before the First World War, both countries had authoritarian monarchies, which were forced into concessions to parliamentarism (of an extremely curtailed kind in the Russian case). Both had powerful bureaucracies, and strong military traditions. Both possessed powerful landowning classes, but also experienced strong economic modernising drives and rapid industrialisation (intense, if geographically very circumscribed, in Russia). Both countries were expansionist powers with imperialist ambitions, in which the contested territories of central and eastern Europe figured prominently. The countries clashed militarily in the First World War, but both felt the trauma of defeat and

4

revolution (if of very different kinds). Germany went on to experience what has been described as a fourteen-year 'latent civil war'[4] (in which the 'model' of the Soviet Union posed as a bogy figure in the intensifying ideological confrontation of bolshevism versus nationalism). Russia's experience was of a near-genocidal actual civil war of the utmost brutality, leaving behind a baleful legacy. Alongside the fragile pluralism of Weimar democracy, eventually collapsing to open the door to the Hitler dictatorship, it is even possible to see a form of 'authoritarian pluralism' during the 1929s, when Soviet Russia conducted the so-called New Economic Policy (often abbreviated as NEP), before this gave way to Stalin's dictatorship.

The 'common ground' approach, based upon recognition of crucial differences, offers pointers towards explaining how such easily equated dictatorships, though fundamentally different in so many respects, were produced almost simultaneously in countries with sharply contrasting profiles. Multi-layered systemic crisis is certainly a key element. It helps, too, in focusing attention on the historical background to the acute ideological struggle of the two regimes during the 1930s and to the titanic clash of the Nazi and Stalinist systems during the Second World War, which forms the second strand of our volume. In 1941, lines of historical development which had mainly seemed to run parallel to each other converged and clashed with the utmost violence. The extremity of clashes in war offers the most direct comparison of all.

The Second World War determined, of course, the total eradication of one of the dictatorships, while the other, following the death of Stalin, attempted to distance itself from the atrocities of his regime and, partially metamorphosised, lived on for almost four decades. During this time the existence of the German Democratic Republic, the most loyal Soviet satellite, was the clearest expression of the continued intertwined histories of Germany and the Soviet Union.

The end of the Soviet system has revealed in all openness a trait largely concealed, despite Krushchev's famous denunciation of 1956, before the Gorbachev era: the problem of confronting the Stalinist past. This parallels the continuing problem in Germany of coming to terms with the Nazi past, and of locating the past in a wider German historically-shaped identity. It is a problem acutely felt since 1945, one that came into full focus in the Fischer controversy of the 1960s and especially the *Historikerstreit* of the 1980s, and resurfaced once more in the aftermath of Unification. This further common ground for a comparison between the two countries forms the third strand of enquiry in this volume.

---

[4] The term is Richard Bessel's. See his *Germany after the First World War* (Oxford 1993), p. 262.

The national debates about the fate and identity of the respective countries are invitations to compare those very debates. For 'facing the past' involves, in these cases, questioning identities with roots extending beyond the era of the two dictatorships themselves. They are questions with deep political and ideological implications, as is made evident in the analyses offered in this section of the volume. This can, perhaps, be most vividly illustrated by a further example, drawn from an area which is not part of the sustained comparison offered in the contributions which follow: the denial of the Holocaust.

The perversity of the denial that the Holocaust actually happened has psychological underpinnings that echo the perversity of mind of the Nazi perpetrators themselves. Implied by the denial is that the Jews themselves invented the horror stories of the death-camps. Thus the victims are once more vilified as the perpetrators are exonerated. While some of those swallowing the denial claims might – charitably – be regarded as no more than naive, the main promoters of such ideas cannot but be well aware of what the Nazis did to the Jews, and must even approve of their actions. They share the antisemitic fury of the Nazis themselves, illustrated by the lengths to which they are prepared to go to revile Jews by attempting to turn the Jewish tragedy into a Jewish invention.

An attenuated or 'indirect' version of the Holocaust-denial occurred in the Soviet Union with the suppression by the Stalinist regime – and for some time under Stalin's successors – of information on the destruction of the Jews in the Ukraine. Though the Soviet regime had not itself perpetrated the killing of the Ukrainian Jews, the slaughter had involved the active participation of many local pro-Nazi collaborators. And it had probably met with tacit acquiescence among broader strata resting on support and connivance to be found in the deeply chauvinistic and antisemitic atmosphere permeating influential party circles under, and after, Stalin. The conspiracy of official silence was only broken by Yevtushenko's courageous poem *Babij Yar* – dealing with the notorious massacre of 33,371 Jews on 29–30 September 1941. The poem was later set to music by Shostakovitch and performed in concert halls.[5]

The distortion of history in the attempt to salvage historical identity is seldom as crude as in the Holocaust denial stories. But parallels exist in both countries of the misuse of comparison for such purposes. An example is provided by one strand of the *Historikerstreit* in Germany in the mid-1980s, depicting Nazi racial genocide as the *reaction* to the earlier

---

[5] Krushchev ferociously attacked Yevtushenko's poem in 1961 for the implied insult to the Soviet people in depicting the loneliness of the Jews' fate – Gerald Reitlinger, *The Final Solution* (Sphere Books end, London 1971) pp. 248–9.

'class genocide' of the Bolsheviks.[6] In attributing prime guilt to Soviet Communism – still a going concern at the time – this interpretation overlooked the evidence in Hitler's own early writings and speeches. This indicated that anti-bolshevism was a later insertion into an already present virulent, latently genocidal anti-Jewish myth which had been prevalent on the *völkisch* Right long before the Russian Revolution, and long before Hitler's entry into the political arena.[7] Hitler's own antisemitic prejudices were probably formed, or accentuated, during his time in pre-war Vienna, as he claimed in *Mein Kampf*. But the first clear evidence that whatever feelings he had about the Jews had been 'rationalised' into an antisemitic ideology dates from September 1919. Strikingly, this first antisemitic statement, concluding that the final aim of antisemitism must be 'the uncompromising removal of Jews altogether', does not mention Bolshevism or Russia.[8] Anti-capitalism à la Gottfried Feder, not anti-Bolshevism, was the basis of this and Hitler's other early attacks on the Jews, portrayed as racketeers, war profiteers, speculators, and exploiters of 'interest slavery'. Anti-bolshevism was only included in the armoury some months later, around April 1920. It was summer 1920 before it became a frequent vehicle for his anti-Jewish tirades. It gave Hitler a further propaganda weapon. And it provided him with yet greater certainty in the correctness of his 'world view'. But it did not cause that intrinsically genocidal 'world view' in the first place.

In the Soviet case, many defenders of Stalinism, from the beginnings of *perestroika*, either denied that gross atrocities had taken place or continued to voice the view advanced by the regime at the time that those arrested and executed under Stalin were indeed traitors and enemies of the country, who had deserved their punishment. A rich crop of such statements, which, in addition, accused the critics of denying the Stalinist regime's enormous achievements and, above all, its victory over the Nazis to save humanity from slavery, could still be found in the post-Soviet press. Unlike the German attempt to salvage the past by eliding Hitler from it as a kind of aberration produced by an understandable response to a worse evil in Soviet Communism, the Russian apologetics amounted to an attempt to save the past by rehabilitating Stalin.

6 See Ernst Nolte, 'Zwischen Geschichtslegende und Revisionismus?', in *'Historikerstreit'. Die Dokumentation der Kontroverse um die Einzigartigkeit der nationalsozialistischen Judenvernichtung* (Munich 1987), p. 32.
7 Hitler's antisemitic rantings in his early speeches drew eclectically on a variety of tracts by well-known anti-Jewish writers, including Houston Stewart Chamberlain, Adolf Wahrmund, and, especially, Theodor Fritsch. All, of course, pre-dated anti-Bolshevism. See Reginald Phelps, 'Hitler's "grundlegende" Rede über den Antisemitismus', *Vierteljahreshefte für Zeitgeschichte*, 16 (1968), pp. 390–420, here esp. pp. 395–9.
8 Eberhard Jäckel and Axel Kuhn (eds), *Hitler. Sämtliche Aufzeichnungen 1905–1924* (Stuttgart 1980), pp. 88–90.

7

A final example of politically motivated distortions of comparison in the continuing reappraisal of the recent past of both countries returns us to the Holocaust and what one might call the 'atrocity toll' of each regime. Not only German nationalists and apologists for Nazism, but also vehemently anti-communist Russian nationalists, emphasise the extent of Stalinist terror, the one tendency in order to point out that Stalin claimed even more victims than Hitler (as if that excused anything in the horrors perpetrated by Nazism), the other to appropriate to Stalinism genocide of a comparable or even worse kind than that of the Nazis in order to stress the evil they see embodied in Communism itself.

Stalinist terror does not need to be played down to underline the uniqueness of the Holocaust – the only example which history offers to date of a deliberate policy aimed at the total physical destruction of every member of an ethnic group. There was no equivalent of this under Stalinism. Though the waves of terror were massive indeed, and the death-toll immense, no ethnic group was singled out for total physical annihilation. A particularly heavy toll among Stalin's victims was, of course, exacted from the state and party apparatus.

The application of the term 'Holocaust' to the Stalinist system is inappropriate. The best way to reveal the pathology and inhumanity of Stalinism is by scholarly attention to the evidence, and not by abusing the methods of comparative history through the loose – and often far from innocent – misleading transplantation of terms imbued with deep historical significance.

II. Comparative approaches

As already noted, this volume makes no pretence at offering a systematic comparison of Stalinism and Nazism. It sets out to be suggestive, not definitive. It is, of necessity, rigorously selective in the themes chosen for comparison. For instance, we do not have a contribution – surprising as it might at first sight seem – which offers an explicit comparative analysis of terror in 'the two great slaughterhouses of the twentieth century' (Michael Geyer). Yet, implicitly, the terroristic aspect of the two regimes figures in almost every contribution. No other aspect of the Nazi and Stalinist regimes has been the subject of so many studies.[9] Perhaps for this very reason, no paper specifically on terror was offered to the conference from which this volume emanates. Our volume in this important case, as in others, can offer pointers to a

---

[9] Standard works include Hans Buchheim et al., Anatomie des SS-Staates, 2 vols. (Olten–Freiburg in Breisgau 1965); and Robert Conquest, The Great Terror (London 1968) (with findings updated in the new edition of 1990).

full-scale comparison.[10] But it cannot provide the systematic comparison which still awaits its historian. Another crucial theme, comparison of the 'war machines' of the two regimes, is a parallel omission. The literature on the armed forces in each of the two countries is vast. But systematic comparison is hard to undertake and, as a result, is hard to find. We thought we had the prospect of such a comparison for this volume. But, ultimately, it did not materialise. What remains once more is a series of pointers towards a comparison – building bricks rather than the fabric itself. A third area where the gulf between the relative state of empirical research in Germany and in the former Soviet Union hinders what would be an important comparison is the impact of the regimes on attitudes and behavioural patterns of 'ordinary' citizens. Here, the volume is perhaps regrettably but necessarily one-sided. Germany is simply far better researched than is the Soviet Union under Stalin in this respect. The uneven historiographical base makes systematic comparison extremely difficult, if not at present impossible.

It would be expecting too much, therefore, to look to overt comparison in all or even in most of the papers of the volume. In more cases than not, analysis centres upon one or other of the regimes in question, though inviting in every case direct comparison with the counterpart regime. The eclectic approaches reflected in the volume are aimed in most cases at suggesting fruitful possibilities of comparison, rather than providing the finished product. This was also the aim of the conference underlying the volume: it saw itself as an experimental laboratory testing possible ground for comparison, rather than attempting to produce a refined product which the raw materials would not yet sustain. It is our hope that, on this basis, the papers presented on the three areas chosen make a collective contribution in providing just such raw materials out of which systematic comparison can begin to be constructed. One promising area of comparison is that of the leadership cult in the two regimes.

Both the Stalinist and the Nazi regimes represented a new genre of political system centred upon the artificial construct of a leadership cult – the 'heroic myth' of the 'great leader', no longer a king or emperor but a 'man of the people'. The first section of the volume highlights similarities and differences in the menacing new cult-driven form of authoritarianism.

In the first essay in the volume Ronald Suny explores the basis of

---

[10] A number of comparative reflections on Stalinist and Nazi terror are brought together in the 'Afterthoughts'. See also Ian Kershaw, 'Totalitarianism Revisited: Nazism and Stalinism in Comparative Perspective', *Tel Aviver Jahrbuch für deutsche Geschichte*, 23 (1994), pp. 23–40. Charles Maier, *The Unmasterable Past* (Cambridge, Mass. 1988), pp. 71–84, provides some perceptive comments.

Stalin's personal autocracy, how he was able to sustain his authority. Though Suny does not explicitly deal with it, there is a resonance here of the 'intentionalist' versus 'structuralist' (or 'functionalist') debates about the role of Hitler in the National Socialist regime.[11] Suny rejects an exclusive focus on terror and propaganda as the explanation of Stalin's power, arguing that terror itself rested on widespread support and collaboration. He emphasises Stalin's centralisation drive, and aim to monopolise decision-making, though demonstrates the practical effect this had of building up local power bases run by 'little Stalins'. Concentration of power at the top thus led inevitably at the same time to its diffusion through a multiplicity of agents, dependent upon Stalin for their careers and even for their physical survival, and not surprisingly anxious to do his will. (There are parallels here to the readiness of Nazi functionaries to 'second-guess' Hitler and anticipate his presumed wishes, as emphasised in Kershaw's essay below.)

Suny also points to the social groups who were on the receiving end of Stalin's 'Big Deal', and wedded through material improvement to the 'order created by Stalin'. He singles out 'a new Soviet middle class . . . with its own form of "bourgeois values"', 'Stakhanovite workers, with their newly acquired bicycles and wristwatches, . . . factory managers and their wives'. For there is no doubt, in Suny's view, that Stalin *did* create 'Stalinism', that his personal role was crucial. The functionalist argument for Suny – and here there are clear parallels to the German debates – reaches only so far, as he points out in the context of the debates among Soviet specialists on the causes of Stalinist terror: 'neither arguments from social context nor functionalist deductions from effects to causes have successfully eliminated the principal catalyst to the Terror, the will and ambition of Stalin'.

One of the most important features of the Soviet system was its bureaucratic character. This can be seen as one reflection of what Trotsky (reformulating Marx's concept of 'uneven development') called 'combined development' – the merging of the most modern with the most archaic traits in systems attempting rapid modernisation.[12] By the end of the Civil War a huge, 'pre-modern' peasantry was ruled over by a new, centralised state with the full command of whatever modern means of control and administration were available. The potential was provided, therefore, for a rapid expansion of 'statism'. In what came to be known as 'the Stalin Revolution', the state monopoly, especially with

---

[11] Ian Kershaw, *The Nazi Dictatorship. Problems and Perspectives of Interpretation* (3rd edn, London 1993), offers an evaluation of these debates.

[12] Leon Trotsky, *The History of the Russian Revolution* (1st edn 1932; New York 1980), pp. 3–15. Trotsky did not try to apply this to Stalin's Russia, probably because Stalinism was insufficiently crystallised at the time he was writing in 1930.

regard to economic reconstruction, opened up an enormous bureaucratisation of all walks of life. With that came, naturally, growing power of the bureaucracy as the main carrier of the state's activities. The term – 'bureaucratic absolutism' – used to characterise the grip on power of the bureaucracy in the USSR after Stalin's death, had originally been deployed with reference to the Prussian bureaucracy in the eighteenth century. This itself serves as a pointer that the extensive literature available on the history of bureaucracy in Prussia/Germany presents obvious avenues for opening up comparison with the role of the bureaucracy in the Soviet state.

The history of the Soviet bureaucracy illustrates the stages of its development as well as its social composition. Soviet bureaucrats in the middle and higher rungs of the hierarchy enjoyed power and privilege, though until Stalin's death the path to the emergence of the bureaucracy as a genuine ruling class was blocked by the dictator's despotic and arbitrary exercise of power. Before 1953, the upper tiers of the bureaucracy had to be content to be 'ruling serfs'. After Stalin's demise, the way was clear for a new stage to begin in the bureaucracy's collective hold on power.

Moshe Lewin's first contribution to the volume singles out the vital contradiction at the heart of the Stalinist system hinted at in the previous remarks: the indispensability of state bureaucracy, yet its incompatibility with arbitrary personalistic despotism. As Lewin succinctly puts it: 'Despotism depends on bureaucracy but cannot trust it.' Bureaucracy once instituted, as Max Weber commented, is as good as impossible to destroy. The waves of Stalin's purges, bloody as they were, could not achieve this. On the contrary: Lewin provides evidence for a remarkable growth of officialdom throughout the very period when the purges were at their height. As long as Stalin was alive, bureaucracy, ever-present though it was, could not take over the system. Rather, it had to cope with the arbitrariness and insecurity which are the antithesis of efficient administration. The despot, for his part, could destroy a 'little Stalin', but ended up by having to replace him. Centralisation produced a proliferation of localised bureaucracies. But 'system' was impossible to create and sustain as long as bureaucracy's own rules were overridden by the whim of the despot. The central contradiction in Stalinism therefore casts grave doubt over its reproductive capacity as long as the despotic element prevailed. Following Stalin's death, the real heyday of bureaucracy commenced. It could now form a fully fledged ruling class. It could, as Lewin concludes, replace 'the cult of Stalin' by 'the cult of the state'.

The theme of intrinsic structural contradiction – and consequently inherent self-destructiveness – is echoed in Hans Mommsen's contribution. Mommsen highlights the Nazi regime as one where the regulative

11

power of state bureaucracy is undermined and corroded by arbitrary and despotic power nevertheless incapable of supplanting and replacing an expanding bureaucracy. He sees a causal relationship between, on the one hand, the escalating radicalisation, external expansionism, and what he calls the ultimate 'running amok' of the regime, and, on the other hand, the fragmentation and disintegration of the governmental and administrative apparatus of the state. National Socialism, he insists, certainly unleashed enormous energy, ruthlessly channelled into accomplishing short-term aims. But it was incapable at any point of creating a coherent institutional framework of government. Rather, it took over the existing institutional framework of the Weimar state, exploiting that framework where it was useful, but otherwise simply bypassing it or erecting new organisations which often stood in competition with the formal organs of government. The result was increasing organisational chaos, a 'war of all against all'.

The 'culmative radicalisation' of the regime, with ever fewer constraints on the exercise of its power within Germany and above all in the occupied territories, could not be halted, argues Mommsen, because there were no institutions able to take on overall responsibility and block the catastrophic course which the Nazi leadership had set in train. This 'structural' explanation is more persuasive in Mommsen's eyes than explanations which put ideological commitment above the mobilisation of base social resentments and prejudices and the consequent collapse of 'civilised' behavioural norms. It is also more satisfactory, he claims, than explanations stressing the personal role of Hitler as the main reason for the inability to restrain the regime's radical dynamic and limit its aims. The destruction of the Third Reich came about, therefore, in Mommsen's view, not simply because Hitler unleashed a world war which could only lead to Germany's defeat, but because self-destructiveness was immanent to Nazism. Purely parasitic, the Hitler regime was incapable of reproducing itself – a contrast in this respect, in Mommsen's eyes, with Stalinism.

Ian Kershaw's contribution develops the comparison between the Stalinist and Nazi dictatorships. Despite superficial similarities, he argues, the regimes were fundamentally different – a difference residing directly in the character of leadership under Stalin and Hitler. The Nazi movement, he contends, was a classic charismatic leadership movement; the Soviet Communist Party was not – a key difference which had a bearing on the self-reproductive capacity of the two regimes. He explores a number of points of contrast in the character of the Stalin and Hitler dictatorships. Where Hitler's style was wholly unbureaucratic, Stalin immersed himself in bureaucratic detail. Whereas Stalin was highly interventionist, Hitler remained largely aloof from government administration. While Stalin ruled through the insecurity of his underlings and purges directed at his closest collaborators, Hitler operated through a contrived and cultivated *Nibelungentreue* – quasi-feudal bonds of loyalty with his paladins and chieftains. Where Stalin's cult was superimposed on an existing ideological orthodoxy, Hitler *was* ideological orthodoxy, and the 'Hitler myth' the very pivot of National Socialism. While Stalin's rule, for all its horror, was nevertheless compatible with limited rational goals, Hitler's was not. Where, therefore, Stalinism had the capacity to reproduce itself – once the despot seemingly bent on the destruction of anything resembling systematic rule was dead – Nazism was innately both systemless and self-destructive. These tendencies were embedded in the incompatibility of 'charismatic rule', the essence of the 'system', with the bureaucratic rule it overlaid but could not replace. Kershaw goes on to suggest how the disintegration of 'ordered' government and administration was related to the gathering momentum of radicalisation, and how Hitler's ideological imperatives became transformed into practical policy options. He singles out a key mechanism in the way wielders of political and social power 'worked towards the Führer', anticipating his presumed intentions without any regular string of precise directives from above.

In a second essay, Moshe Lewin explicitly uses comparison in deploying the more extensively developed historiography on the Hitler dictatorship as a mirror to cast reflection on Stalin. He shows how the Stalin cult – though artificially created (directly under Stalin's own supervision) and not in existence at all before 1928 – was easily able to exploit social and psychological preconditions arising from the post-revolutionary and post-Civil War turmoil. In the construction of the differing facets of the cult surrounding him, Stalin tapped various traditions – not least the tsarist heritage – and erected a form of personal rule with a wholly different base to Lenin's and accomplished by a thorough perversion of Bolshevik ideology. In Lewin's interpretation, the Stalin cult had, indeed, to be constructed as a form of justification or internal legitimation – an 'alibi' to camouflage the fact that Stalin had been merely one of the claimants (and a disputed one at that) to the mantle of Lenin, and had betrayed the real Bolshevik heritage. The 'Stalin myth' – the analogy with the 'Hitler myth' is plain here – was, states Lewin, indispensable to Stalin's rule. But, he adds, the rapid demise of the 'myth' after Stalin's death demonstrates that it was not indispensable to the Soviet system or to the party – a point of contrast to Nazism.

Close comparison with the German dictatorship is drawn by Lewin, however, in his remark that 'not unlike Hitler and his self-identification with the function of Führer, Stalin actually became the system and his personality acquired therefore a "systemic" dimension'. Lewin brings out further similar as well as contrasting traits in the portrayed images and personalities of the two dictators, and in the style and character of their rule. One could be highlighted here: the intense inhumanity and detachment from the sufferings of their own peoples of both dictators as revealed by their wartime leadership; the way they refrained from contact with ordinary soldiers and civilians; the manner in which they directed the fates of dehumanised masses remote from the reality of their actual experiences and actions; the readiness to turn their own failings into the most brutal wrath towards those they regarded as 'guilty'. At the end, while Hitler, in the isolation of the bunker, was deserted by some of his closest henchmen, most prominently Göring and Himmler, Stalin's increasing self-isolation, as Lewin points out, was accompanied by such pathological derangement that he felt betrayal and treachery all around him, and with practically his last gasp had a group of mainly Jewish doctors arrested and tortured into confessions of plotting to kill Kremlin leaders.

The paper by Michael Mann, which closes the first section, offers an analysis of the Stalinist and Nazi systems not from the position of a specialist on German or Russian history, but from the comparative perspective of a sociologist. In contrast to those (including, in this volume, Mommsen and Kershaw) who are critical of the 'totalitarianism' concept and emphasise the differences between the two systems, Mann, while not wedded to the particular term 'totalitarianism' (though he sees it as so deeply implanted in scholarly and popular language that it is inescapable), states at the outset that 'the two regimes belong together' and that 'it is only a question of finding the right family name'. 'What was common to the Nazi and Stalinist regimes, *and to no others*', Mann emphasises, 'was their persistent rejection of institutional compromise' in favour of 'the frontal violent assault of continuous revolution'. The 'continuous revolution', the essence of each of the systems in Mann's interpretation, had, of course, different goals – the 'class' and 'nation-statist' revolutionary aims representing the two major power actors of modern times. The administrative methods which Mann detects in each of the systems – internalised divide-and-rule strategies, 'working towards' the despot, reliance on comradeship, and local party mobilisation – produced fluidity and violence, not bureaucratic regularity. Mann is not prepared (in contrast to Mommsen) to see in what he regards as a *relative* administrative disorder and lack of bureaucratic coherence a total lack of coherence in the system, nor the root of its self-destruction. However, he accepts a point raised in a number of contributions about the innate self-destructiveness of each of the systems. In Mann's articulation: 'Neither regime could in the long run reproduce itself. Both were destroyed by the contradiction between institutionalising party rule and achieving the party's goal, continuous revolution.'

The second section of the volume takes us to the heart of the 'deadly clash' between the Nazi and Stalinist regimes between 1941 and 1945. The victims of this clash numbered tens of millions. The consequences left Germany in ruins and divided in a Europe riven by the Iron Curtain and plunged into forty-five years of the Cold War. In a century whose hallmark has been unprecedented violence, destruction, and inhumanity, these four years of war in eastern Europe stand out in their horror even more than the trenches of the First World War, the atomic bombs on Hiroshima and Nagasaki, the Vietnam War, or the killing fields of Cambodia.

In the first paper in this section, Omer Bartov examines how images of the *Blitzkrieg*, which had its culmination and dénouement in 'Operation Barbarossa', were related to reality. An underlying premise of this paper is a revision of the distinction usually drawn between *Blitzkrieg* and 'total war'. In contrast to some long-held historiographical positions, he argues, '*Blitzkrieg* was not practised *instead* of total war, but was rather a new manner of deploying and employing forces without giving up the notion of total mobilisation.' Moreover, the attempt to minimise the cost of war to the German population was coupled with the unleashing of a genocidal policy directed at the subject populations, and in this way, too, an aspect of total war. It was, therefore, 'merely a tactical innovation, not a new strategy'. It 'cannot be divorced from total war as a phenomenon of modern industrialised society', but has to be seen as an attempt to make total war more effective. Bartov points out how the success of the propagated image of the 'lightning war' in creating the impression of invincibility led to an over-confidence that blinded the Germans to the limitations of their own strategy, leading to catastrophe in the final *Blitzkrieg* of 'Barbarossa' and, ironically, to a reversion to the very 'total war strategies' reminiscent of 1914-18 which they had set out to avoid. Once this stage was reached, adds Bartov, Germany had no prospect of competing successfully against its enemies, despite the significant improvements in weapon technology and armaments production in the last war years.

Despite the catastrophic course of the actual *Blitzkrieg*, Bartov argues that the *image* of *Blitzkrieg* has been enduringly successful – and dangerously so – in depicting modern warfare as fast, heroic, and glamorous. In speculating upon such images of *Blitzkrieg* and the indifference bred by present-day news coverage of live war and violence, Bartov suggestively concludes that *Blitzkrieg* was 'part of a

15

process in the development of modern humanity which perfected our capacity . . . to observe with fascination and yet remain indifferent'. As is well known, when the Soviet Union encountered the initial might of the German *Blitzkrieg* on 22 June 1941, it was caught completely unawares. Bernd Bonwetsch's paper begins by seeking to explain the débâcle which, as he shows, took place in a country that had been expecting war and preparing for it since the mid-1930s. In the parlance of German historiography, his account would be regarded as a largely 'intentionalist' one, which nevertheless builds in important strands of a 'structuralist' explanation, inviting comparison with the far more thoroughly researched relationship between Hitler and the German military leadership during the Second World War.[13]

Bonwetsch unequivocally sees Stalin's actions as decisive. However, he also clearly shows not only how those actions directly destroyed the army command in the pre-war purges, how Stalin's personal shock and corresponding *inaction* following the German invasion contributed to the Soviet military paralysis, and how his repeated interventions and those of other military 'illiterates' contributed massively to the setbacks of the Red Army. He adds to this the 'atmosphere of suspicion, intimidation, and irresolution' which Stalin's rule had created, and which 'severely impaired the professional self-confidence' of the army command. This in turn, he goes on to illustrate, together with the genuine intimidation and repression exerted even against high-ranking officers, produced a cowed and supine military leadership, unwilling to stand up to Stalin even when his absurd orders flew in the face of all military logic. Genuine opposition to Stalin in the military command, he claims, did not exist. Stalin could count upon the consent, by whatever means it had been manipulated, of his officers. Bonwetsch indicates the corrosive perversity of Stalinism in the action of the relatively indepen-dent-minded Marshal Zhukov – echoing Stalin's *leitmotiv* of the early war period that any thought of war on Soviet soil or contemplation of retreat was 'defeatism' – reprimanding the Commander of the Kiev District for taking routine military precautions 'which under normal conditions would have been self-evident'. Ultimate blame for the repeated refusal to confront the reality of the situation lay, however, for Bonwetsch in one place only: in Moscow, where Stalin remained the prisoner of his illusions, his paranoia demanding the ruthless search for scapegoats for defeats which his own actions had rendered certain.

Bonwetsch sees the change in Soviet military fortunes from Autumn

---

[13] See the still incomplete multi-volume series, edited by the Militärgeschichtliches Forschungsamt, *Das Deutsche Reich und der Zweite Weltkrieg* (Stuttgart 1979–), for the most thorough analyses. The attack on the Soviet Union is the subject of the fourth volume.

1942 onwards as heavily influenced by the increased reliance upon professional military judgement, and prevention of interference by the military 'illiterates'. This decisive shift, too, he attributes directly to Stalin. Though his power remained absolute, Stalin was prepared for the rest of the war to give his commanders greater leeway. Even so, Soviet losses of men and equipment were far higher than those of the Germans. The human and material cost accorded with the practice of Stalinism long before the war began. Bonwetsch can therefore conclude that 'however Stalin changed during the war, the victory had been achieved with genuine Stalinist methods'.

Jacque Sapir's analysis of the Soviet war economy, approaching the issue from the perspective of an economist, offers quite a different interpretation to that of Bonwetsch. Certainly, Sapir explicitly accepts that Stalin himself, already 'a pathological case' by the later 1930s, has largely to be blamed for the disasters of 1941. Responsibility cannot be removed from the Soviet dictator, who destroyed his own armed forces, believed Hitler's promises, and took all the key decisions. Even so, Stalin scarcely figures in Sapir's paper, whereas he dominates in Bonwetsch's. Turning away from a concentration on the dictator and the decision-making process, Sapir concentrates on the structural problems of Soviet military thought, armaments production, and economic mobilisation. He sets out to explain the economic implications of Soviet military planning – leading to what has been described as a 'war economy' before the war – and the economic transformation needed once the Soviet Union was embroiled in a war that did not fit pre-war conceptions.

Sapir outlines a specific conceptualisation of warfare, developed in the interwar years by the Soviet military establishment. It demanded an all-embracing mobilisation of economy and society even in peacetime, and provided rigid prescriptions for wartime mobilisation and military strategy. In the turmoil of the 1930s, the military conception changed from emphasis upon a lengthy, but defensive, war under full mobilisation, to a short but total, mechanised war, with all military resources immediately available and deployed in combined operations, though without the earlier requirement of prior complete economic mobilisation. Sapir shows that this led to a notable increase in weapons production and massive stockpiling. But the weapons were of low quality, the economic cost was very heavy, and technological innovation was neglected. Military and technological conservatism, despite attempts to adjust in the light of the German *Blitzkrieg* successes in 1939–40, left the Soviet armed forces ill-equipped to meet the onslaught when it came in 1941.

Out of the catastrophic defeats of 1941 and 1942 emerged, however, a

17

profound restructuring of the armed forces alongside the traumatic relocation of industry. The need to readjust to fighting a protracted defensive war paid no heed to the scale of human or material losses. The 'extensive' use of men and weapons which Bonwetsch also emphasised, had been, as Sapir shows, a hallmark of Soviet military planning even before 1941. Military success was attained at terrible cost.

Despite serious flaws in military and economic planning before 1942, Sapir argues that the reconstruction from 1942 onwards shows an underlying soundness in Soviet military thought that was absent in a Nazi system predicated upon a strategic gamble without genuine economic mobilisation. The comparison, he comments, reveals 'the difference between pathological interference and a pathological process from the outset'. This applies, in his view, also to a comparison of military-industrial economics and 'technological culture' in the two countries. He suggests that the differences between the Soviet and Nazi economies in the 1930s have often been overdrawn. Even so, in the military-industrial sector the differences were significant and growing. This was especially the case in the technological sophistication and superiority of German weaponry, though, Sapir remarks, this was 'an irrational answer to the problem of war production in a protracted conflict'. In a suggestive comment which could possibly be extended to a comparison of the Nazi and Stalinist systems as a whole, he states: 'Whereas organisational and institutional pathologies were limited to crisis conditions in the USSR, they were a norm of social behaviour in Germany'.

Sapir goes on to ask how the complete concentration of Soviet industrial output on munitions production was compatible with economic reproduction, since the economy had been already so heavily mobilised before the war, and so squeezed thereafter, that it was almost at breaking-point. He offers a threefold explanation. The specialisation of the Soviet war industry and the benefits of the US Lend-Lease Programme form two strands. The third, most fundamentally, he locates in the far-reaching economic reforms which, paradoxically, *demobilised* the economy in part by introducing individual initiative together with market and financial mechanisms that had largely been replaced by administrative *fiat* before the war. Sapir concludes by asking whether an opportunity was not lost in the post-war era, with its return to brutal Stalinist policies, of continuing the incorporation of elements of the market within a centrally planned economy. The war experience shows, he suggests, that there was nothing to have prevented this from developing fruitfully. There was, in other words, nothing systemic in the incapacity of the Soviet system to adapt. But from a position at the end of the war analogous, in its mix of market

18

mechanisms and central planning, to present-day China, the Soviet system reverted to a rigidity which helped to ensure the failure of *perestroika* at precisely the same juncture that Chinese reform was proving successful.

Mark von Hagen's first paper in this collection deals with the shifting interpretations of the Soviet wartime experience that have developed since the end of the Cold War, as Russian scholars have been able to operate openly with normal methods of historical scholarship and proper access to sources. He shows how the need for regime legitimation, encapsulated in the very appellation 'the Great Fatherland War', has thereby succumbed to the more descriptively named 'Second World War', reflecting the move to critical analysis of the USSR's war effort. Even after Krushchev's denunciation of Stalin in 1956, he points out, conservative forces rallied to the traditional interpretation – and the defence of Stalin – in support of their own vested interests. Apart from the brief interlude of the Krushchev era, serious debate about the war only commenced in 1987. Von Hagen describes the revisionism which then began in earnest, its harshest form regarding the wartime failures and even the pre-war purges as the most radical reflection of a system which had been both intrinsically inhumane and fundamentally flawed since 1917. He also outlines a third 'alternativist' approach, standing between this fundamentalist revisionism and the revamped orthodoxy, that of 'an anti-Stalin Leninist tradition'. The familiar line here is of a genuine socialism derailed by a Stalinist clique, breaking the true Soviet military tradition. The attack on Stalinism has meanwhile been so frontal, he goes on to show, that even the 'alternativist' approach is heavily on the defensive, while revisionism has not only recognised non-Soviet scholarship but has adopted many of its arguments.

The way is now open, therefore, he suggests, for a genuinely international scholarship on the basis of a vastly increased range of sources. This will enable not only a deepened understanding (as represented in this volume by the papers of Bonwetsch and Sapir) of the decision-making, military planning, and the direction of the war. It will also encourage the exploration of the complex and varied social experience of the war – a field left completely unexamined in Soviet historiography because of the ideological insistence upon monolithic treatment of the 'heroic struggle of the Soviet people'. This in turn, suggests von Hagen, will demand research into and reevaluation and comparison of social mobilisation and experience in the First World War and the Civil War. Von Hagen ends, however, on a cautionary note, looking to the likely impact of new nationalisms in the USSR's 'successor states' in ensuring that the Second World War will form part of a continuing ideological and political struggle over interpretations, as has proved to be the case in Germany since 1945.

Von Hagen's paper is a reminder, then, of the point we have already noted, that both Germany and the successor states to the USSR share a common problem, though of course quite differently manifested, in facing up to the legacy of the past. In Germany, the term invented soon after the War and still enjoying some currency today was *Vergangen-heitsbewältigung* ('mastery of the past'). It is a somewhat awkward concept. Presumably no past, not even a less troubled one than that of Germany, can in any comprehensible sense be 'mastered'. But 'coping with', 'facing up to', or 'confronting' a past burdened with a large and quite obvious moral, political, and ideological freight is broadly what is meant. Confronting the Soviet past raises many obvious parallel issues, though serious attempts to do so within Russia have only been possible since the Gorbachev era. The short duration of the reassessment of the Soviet past means that in some respects the ideological colouring, as von Hagen showed, is more garish than in Germany, where greater nuance has arisen from five decades of unabated and often rancorous debate of the Nazi past. But in one sense, there is perhaps a position still possible in the ex-USSR which has no tenable parallel in the German case: of seeing some good in the system despite Stalin. In Germany, there is no voice worth listening to which could divorce Hitler from Nazism as an 'aberration', seeing some good in it despite the faults in its leader. The totality of the denunciation of Nazism from moral standpoints that range from socialism to conservatism may well differ, therefore, from the post-Soviet experience. Whether this is the case or not, the 'battle of interpretations' provides further common ground for comparison between our two countries. It provides the framework for the last section of the volume.

The argument for the uniqueness of Nazism has always rested upon the notion of the exceptionality of Germany's path to modernity. George Steinmetz, from a sociological perspective, puts a different gloss on the well-established historiographical positions on the German *Sonderweg* ('special path'). Steinmetz outlines the varied articulations of the case for German exceptionalism – those before 1933 generally approving of an alleged deviation from the standard 'western' path of liberal development, and especially the 'new orthodoxy' of critical stances towards the purported social backwardness hampering the growth of a liberal state and society. He goes on to summarise the numerous strands of the 1980s criticism of the *Sonderweg* thesis, heavily emphasising the modernity of state and society in pre-Nazi Germany, and rejecting its supposed non-synchronised development. In this, the critics were arguing that there was nothing *structurally* exceptional about German

20

development. The problem, in Steinmetz's view, is that both *Sonderweg* proponents and critics alike fall victim to fallacious assumptions about social development: that societies can be broken down into cohesive political, economic, and cultural levels with a uniform pattern of development in any one of them, let alone in all of them together; that it is normal to have reached an equivalent level of development in each simultaneously; and that the lack of simultaneity leads to fascism. He argues that 'where general trends or shared discourses exist across fields, this is the result of "hegemonic" articulatory practices and not an automatic, natural historical development'. This means that the empirical establishment of social and political power structures, rather than generalisations about 'backwardness' or 'modernity', is necessary in order to understand the uniqueness which Steinmetz, though rejecting the 'exceptionalist' theory, insists upon in characterising Nazism. For he concludes that, ironically, it is the emphasis upon the exceptionality of pre-determined spheres of German development which prevents full recognition of 'the role of contingency and unique constellations of causes' – hence 'uniqueness' – in the Nazi case. He ends by showing, however, that, academically discredited though the *Sonderweg* thesis now is, it continues to flourish as a legitimation of the current post-Unification German state, justifying images of Germany since 1949 – since it was also claimed for the old Federal Republic – as now 'a functional western democracy'. In Steinmetz's view, however, if a form of *Sonderweg* thesis has any validity, then it is as a depiction of a present-day Germany whose inheritance from Nazism has made it more, rather than less, difficult to become simply another European country, just another western democracy.

There is no strict equivalent to the German *Sonderweg* thesis in the heated historical debates which have sprung up since the advent of *glasnost* in the former USSR. Even so, as Mark von Hagen's second contribution to the volume points out, some sort of echo can be heard in the question of social, economic, cultural, and political modernisation in pre-revolutionary Russia, which has naturally surfaced as the search for the roots of Stalinism turned inevitably to considerations of Russia's backwardness. In a muted echo of the German 'historicisation' debate, notes von Hagen, 'developmental or modernisation theories appear to their critics to "historicise" or even "normalise" Stalinism by making the phenomenon more comprehensible'.[14] As these remarks show, the recent reevaluation of the past in the successor states has raised issues which are redolent in certain ways of the German *Historikerstreit* (whose implications are touched upon in Mary Nolan's paper). These centre

---

[14] For a summary of the German debate, see Kershaw, *The Nazi Dictatorship*, ch. 9.

upon the place of Nazism in German history, the construction of a sense of historical identity, and the relative singularity or comparability of Nazism.[15] The last of these considerations invokes once more, if in new fashion, the totalitarianism concept – a term also used in recent debates in the former Soviet Union. Unsurprisingly, these debates in Russia, compared with those on Nazism, are still for the most part relatively unsophisticated and, of course, fought out in extremely heated, ideologically loaded, and morally charged terms. Moreover, the empirical base for studies of Stalinism is, of course, still quite underdeveloped in comparison with that provided by a vast array of thoroughly researched monograph literature on Nazism. Even so, the debates on Stalinism, comments von Hagen, have in a remarkably short time replicated the most important debates that had already taken place among Soviet scholars outside the former USSR, and produced a 'rich and innovative' agenda for future research.

Above all, as von Hagen's analysis brings out plainly, it is the German 'intentionalist' and 'structuralist' debates that have the clearest application to recent attempts at reevaluating Stalinism. These have placed personalistic against structuralist interpretations. On the one hand, Stalin has been blamed for the terrible rupture of what had allegedly been an otherwise healthy development derived from Leninism – shades here of the early post-war German demonisation of Hitler – and has been seen as more or less single-handedly responsible for all the Soviet Union's ills. On the other hand, von Hagen can point to a variety of structuralist analyses that have stressed with differing degrees of radicality the deep-seated problems in pre-Stalinist society which produced Stalin and conditioned the nature of his rule. At present, the 'intentionalists' seem to be carrying the day – a not unnatural turn to human agency after decades of a type of extreme 'structuralist' interpretation in orthodox Marxist-Leninist accounts. As von Hagen remarks, 'the moral stakes in the debate are such that authors still risk being charged as "soft on Stalinism" if they tread too far away from the intentionalist mainstream'.

The final section of von Hagen's paper, on the 'national question', points to perhaps the most worrying trends in historical writing on the territory of the former Soviet Union – though most of what he is

---

[15] There is in the meantime an extensive literature on the *Historikerstreit*. Good analyses are provided by: Charles Maier, *The Unmasterable Past*, and Richard J. Evans, *In Hitler's Shadow* (New York 1989). Peter Baldwin (ed.), *Reworking the Past* (Boston, Mass. 1990), contains English translations of some important contributions, as well as a valuable introduction by the editor. Some of the initial, controversial articles are also available in *Yad Vashem Studies*, 19 (1988). The German texts of all the relevant contributions were gathered together in: *'Historikerstreit'. Die Dokumentation der Kontroverse um die Einzigartigkeit der nationalsozialistischen Judenvernichtung* (Munich, 1987).

describing here is not scholarly historical writing, but ideology, or history abused for ideological purposes (now of an anti-Soviet kind). National chauvinism, xenophobia, and antisemitism are, he shows, commonplace components in the new extreme anti-Soviet (and, outside Russia, anti-Russian) interpretations of history. Messianic utopianism and chauvinistic myth-making are the order of the day in the writing of nationalist history. Even so, von Hagen is not altogether pessimistic. At least there is now a pluralism of interpretations, with post-Soviet historians operating as part of a world of international scholarship.

The final paper in the volume, by Mary Nolan, takes us into territory for which, as we noted earlier, there is no comparable historiography on any scale to date on Stalinism, despite some fine pioneering work by western scholars. Mark von Hagen has already pointed to the absence of empirical research on Soviet society as a major *lacuna* in the historiography of Stalinism, given the obvious limitations on such work under the Communist regime.

Nolan sets out to assess the balance of two decades of research and debate on a number of central aspects of the social history of the Third Reich: work, gender, and everyday life. She evaluates first the recent studies on the labour process in the Third Reich which mark a shift away from the earlier emphasis upon the oppositional behaviour of the working class. The focus has been on the ways in which 'National Socialism picked up on, continued, and partially distorted processes of rationalisation that were initiated in the mid-1920s and continued into the Federal Republic and German Democratic Republic'. A key consequence of rationalisation, sharply enhanced during the Third Reich, she notes, was the fragmentation of the industrial working class and the accompanying promotion of individualistic and instrumental attitudes towards work – a feature of the post-war *Wirtschaftswunder* in the Federal Republic. However, she singles out racism as 'the specific Nazi contribution to the reconceptualising of work and the restructuring of the working class'. Not 'achievement' alone, but racial 'fitness', was the key to the hierarchisation of a labour force increasingly dependent during the war upon 'foreign workers'.

The second strand of Nolan's enquiry covers the unfolding literature on women and gender in Nazi Germany. Research here has concentrated upon the impact of Nazi ideology and policy on women's work and reproduction; on gender and Nazi racial-eugenic policies; and on the extent of women's complicity on Nazi rule. On the first area, Nolan concludes that the Nazi regime 'failed to reverse long-term secular trends in women's work', but 'did mix racism and labour-market policies in ways that were new'. As regards women's reproductive role, race and purported eugenic value were decisive, class relatively

23

insignificant. Studies of the relationship between eugenics and gender, she shows, have even prompted the bizarre assertion that the solution to the *Frauenfrage* ('woman question') was for the Nazis just as important as the solution to the 'Jewish question'. But more balanced views would surely still see gender issues as wholly subordinated to racial and eugenics imperatives in the Third Reich. Finally, while the debate on complicity has also sometimes shed more heat than light, Nolan pleads for disaggregated, empirical investigation. This ought to bring out the particular experiences of specific groups of women, rather than simply resorting to broad – and thereby unsatisfactory – generalisations about women as a whole.

The last part of Nolan's survey, on 'everyday life', deals with the way research has developed on the issue of Nazi encroachment on 'the private sphere'; that is, the extent to which a 'normality of everyday life' detached from the inroads of Nazi ideology could continue in the Third Reich. The upshot of recent studies in a number of varied fields has been, she comments, to move away from earlier interpretations of 'everyday life' which emphasised the continuation of such a relatively impervious 'private sphere'. Newer approaches have emphasised the internalisation of Nazi ideas, especially on race, leading to the conclusion that 'the private was transformed and politicised much more than memory claims'.

Nolan's paper, surveying a rich scholarship that has developed since the 1970s on German society under the Nazi regime, might be seen as offering an agenda for a future major research programme on equivalent themes in the history of Soviet society under Stalinism. The fields are not totally *terra incognita* in the case of the USSR. In particular, the labour process under Stalinism has been extensively studied. However, knowledge of popular cultures and counter-cultures is far less advanced, and the key questions of support and opposition are only now beginning to be systematically addressed as the study of *byt* – the Russian equivalent of *Alltagsgeschichte* ('history of everyday life') – starts to gain ground. When it is undertaken, this work will surely discover – as, indeed, is already becoming apparent – that extensive sub-cultures retained a level of autonomy despite the pressures of the system; that certain partial immunities (*Resistenz* in the German parlance) to regime penetration persisted. The prospect of such work being carried out on Stalinist society, and benefiting in the process from the methods and approaches developed in the more established German historiography, is indeed an exciting one.

As we have already noted, this volume certainly does not claim to offer any more than a number of pointers towards a comparative history of the USSR under Stalin and Germany under Hitler. Apart from the necessary selectivity of themes which has determined the shape of this volume, the varied stages of development of the historiography in almost every aspect of research would mean that such an enterprise would be in some ways premature and unbalanced. However, the papers presented here amount both to a summary of the current state of research in some key areas of comparison, and to an invitation to deepen and extend that research – and in so doing to amplify and enrich the basis of the comparison. The German specialist, though working in historiographically well-ploughed fields, will find much in the analyses of Stalinism in this volume which will provoke a rethink of positions on Nazism. For the Soviet expert, there is the prospect of exploiting the German historiographical debates as, in Lewin's phrase, a 'mirror of the other'. And for historians of either society, the explicitly comparative contributions to the volume offer the potential stimulus of fresh perspectives and conceptualisation on the most violent and inhumane epoch in modern European history.

Studying the history of inhumanity, perpetrated on such a vast, unprecedented scale, has an emotional and psychological cost.[16] It is not like studying the history of philosophy, the Renaissance, or the age of the cathedrals. The subject matter is less uplifting than almost any other conceivable topic of historical enquiry. But it is history all the same. And it *is* important. The emotional involvement has to be contained, even where the very effort to arrive at some balanced and reasoned interpretation seems an affront. 'Interpretation' consists in any case of the attempt to find a rationale for actions which scarcely seem to warrant the term. Hence, there remains the need to master the irrational, the illogical, and the psychologically deranged in order to explain the level of pathological debauchery accepted, approved of, and sustained by masses of people – including highly intelligent ones – and coming to be regarded as normal and justifiable practice. Admitting the irrational in past human behaviour as a legitimate object of study is vital – even at the risk of succumbing to the notion that the irrational is the reality which is bound to prevail. There is nothing else for it than to adhere to scholarly methods in the hope that knowledge might inform action to prevent any conceivable repetition of such political pathologies as characterised Stalinism and Nazism.

[16] Jane Caplan in *Radical History*, 49 (1991), p. 88, citing Tim Mason.

1

Stalin and his Stalinism: power and authority in the Soviet Union, 1930–53

Ronald Grigor Suny

The deceptively simple question to be answered in this essay is: how did Stalin rule? How did he maintain his authority while establishing a personal autocracy? His extraordinary and brutal political achievement was to act in the name of the Communist party and its central committee against that party and central committee, while remaining the unchallenged head of party and state and, evidently, a vastly popular leader. At the end of the process his absolute grip on power allowed him to declare black white and completely reverse the foreign policy of the Soviet Union and the line of the Comintern by embracing Nazi Germany in a non-aggression pact. The colossal and costly destruction he brought upon the country on the eve and in the early days of the Second World War gave rise to no organised opposition, and the centralised apparatus of control that he had created was not only able to weather the Nazi invasion but to organise a victory that would preserve the essence of the system he forged for another half-century.

The simplest, though inadequate, answer to the question, would be that Stalin's power was maintained through the exercise of terror and monopolistic control of the means of communication throughout society. Though certainly an important part of the answer, an exclusive focus on terror and propaganda does not explain how Stalin won his authority within the party in the 1920s and maintained it among his own supporters even before the advent of the Great Terror. Once initiated, terror operated through collaboration, and Stalin's associates almost never attempted to free themselves from the source of their fears. Terror was supported by many within and outside the party who believed that extraordinary means against vicious and hidden enemies were required. Tens of millions regarded Stalin as the indispensable leader of

The author wishes to express his gratitude to Lewis Siegelbaum and Moshe Lewin for their careful and critical readings of earlier drafts.

the 'socialist' camp, perhaps someone to be feared as was Ivan *groznyi*, a leader who filled the hearts of enemies with awe.[1]

I *Power and persuasion in the 1920s*

The paradox of the October Revolution was that the Bolsheviks possessed the physical power to overthrow the Provisional Government and disband the Constituent Assembly but did not yet have either a popular mandate to rule all of Russia (let alone the non-Russian peripheries) or an unassailable legitimising myth to sanction their claim to govern. Even as they successfully built a new state during the years of Civil War, the Bolsheviks were (as Lenin usually admitted) a minority party that needed to justify its hold on power. The Bolsheviks required more than passive acquiescence in the new order; they wanted active support that could be mobilised toward heroic goals. One of the central dilemmas of the Communists in the first two decades of their rule was to move from an exercise of power through force toward creating a base of support through the construction of a widely accepted, hegemonic understanding of the historical moment.

Whatever benefits military victory, the practice of state terror, or the repression of opposition might bring a regime in the short term, 'authority-building is necessary to protect and expand one's base of political support'.[2] As George Breslauer has written about a later period in Soviet history, 'Authority is legitimized power', and Soviet leaders had to legitimise their power and policies by demonstrating their competence or indispensability as rulers.[3] In their own search for legal authority in the 1920s, the Bolsheviks could rely neither on tradition (associated with the *ancien régime*) nor on religious faith. They sought – in Weber's terms – a 'value-rational' 'belief in the absolute validity of the order as the expression of ultimate values'.[4] Over time legal authority was supplemented (and compromised) in Stalin's USSR by charismatic authority in which the 'charismatically qualified leader . . . is obeyed by virtue of personal trust in his revelation, his heroism or his exemplary qualities so far as they fall within the scope of the individual's belief in his charisma'.[5]

---

[1] Michael Cherniavsky, 'Ivan the Terrible as Renaissance Prince', *Slavic Review*, 27, 2 (June 1968), pp. 195–211.

[2] George W. Breslauer, *Khrushchev and Brezhnev as Leaders: Building Authority in Soviet Politics* (London: George Allen Unwin 1982), p. 10.   [3] Ibid., p. 4.

[4] Max Weber, *Economy and Society: An Outline of Interpretive Sociology*, edited by Guenther Roth and Claus Wittich (Berkeley and Los Angeles: University of California Press 1968), p. 33. 'In the case of legal authority, obedience is owed to the legally established impersonal order. It extends to the persons exercising the authority of office under it by virtue of the formal legality of their commands and only within the scope of authority of the office' (pp. 215–16).   [5] Ibid., p. 216.

Yet even as they attempted to construct a legitimising cultural and political hegemony, the Communists steadily narrowed the political field, centralising power and eliminating dissent. One of the most 'democratic' (in the sense of grassroots popular participation) polities in the world (in the revolutionary years 1917–18) rapidly turned step by step into a dictatorship of a single party. First the establishment of Soviet power and the dissolution of *zemstva*, dumas, and the Constituent Assembly eliminated the upper and middle classes, as well as the clergy, from the *pays legal*. When, in the months before the Civil War began, the coalition partners of the Bolsheviks, the Left Socialist Revolutionaries, resigned from the Sovnarkom, the Bolsheviks ruled alone in a one-party government. During the Civil War the vitality and autonomy of local soviets declined, as the working class of 1917 itself fragmented and dissolved.[6] Agents of the central government, along with Red Army officers and soldiers, the police and the party officials, increased their power at the expense of local committees and soviets. Manipulation of elections, coercive practices, indifference and apathy of voters, all in the context of the vicious fratricidal warfare of 1918–21, steadily weakened the power and legitimacy of the local soviets and eroded the rival political parties.[7] A new state power emerged from the war, under the control of Communists imbued with habits of command and ready to use violence to maintain their political monopoly.[8]

By 1922 interparty politics were an historical memory, and the only arena for political discussion and infighting was within the Communist party. The ban on factions in 1921, the progressive elimination of political oppositions through the 1920s, and the steady accumulation of power by a single faction reduced the political arena even further, until a handful of influential figures decided the course for the rest of the party.[9] Within the party political manipulation, Machiavellian intrigues, and a willingness to resort to ruthlessness were certainly part of

[6] William G. Rosenberg, 'Russian Labor and Bolshevik Power after October', *Slavic Review*, 44, 2 (Summer 1985), pp. 212–38; and the discussion with Moshe Lewin and Vladimir Brovkin, pp. 239–56.

[7] Vladimir Brovkin, *The Mensheviks After October: Socialist Opposition and the Rise of the Bolshevik Dictatorship* (Ithaca, NY: Cornell University Press 1987).

[8] Leonard Schapiro, *The Origin of the Communist Autocracy: Political Opposition in the Soviet State: First Phase, 1917–1922* (Cambridge, Mass: Harvard University Press 1955); Robert Service, *The Bolshevik Party in Revolution: A Study in Organizational Change, 1917–1923* (New York: Macmillan 1979); T. H. Rigby, *Lenin's Government: Sovnarkom 1917–1922* (Cambridge: Cambridge University Press 1979); Orlando Figes, *Peasant Russia, Civil War: The Volga Countryside in Revolution, 1917–1921* (Oxford: Oxford University Press 1989); Mark von Hagen, *Soldiers in the Proletarian Dictatorship: The Red Army and the Soviet Socialist State, 1917–1930* (Ithaca, NY: Cornell University Press 1990).

[9] Robert Vincent Daniels, *The Conscience of the Revolution: Communist Opposition in Soviet Russia* (Cambridge, Mass: Harvard University Press 1960).

Stalin's repertoire, but he also managed to position himself in the immediately post-Lenin years as a pragmatic centrist supportive of the compromises and concessions of the New Economic Policy and unwilling to risk Soviet power in efforts to promote elusive revolutions abroad.

In the post-October scramble to hold on to the reins of government, Lenin and the Bolsheviks had justified their actions by reference to a variety of historic claims – that they represented the vanguard of the proletariat organised in the soviets; that they were the only party able to bring peace and order to the country and willing to give the land to the peasants; that the transition to socialism was at hand and the weakest link in the capitalist chain had been broken. Russia's second revolution would receive its ultimate sanction in the rising of the European working class, and all talk of the prematurity of the Bolshevik seizure of power would cease. The Civil War provided a new justification for holding power – the fight against enemies domestic and foreign, the preservation of the victories of 1917 and the prevention of a restoration. As unpopular as the Communists were in many parts of the country, they were accepted as the lesser of evils, and acquiescence to, if not positive acceptance of, Lenin's government spread through different social strata and groups – workers, many peasants, intellectuals, certain nationalities, like the Jews, who were particular victims of White antisemitism. 'As long as the peasants feared the Whites, they would go along, feet dragging, with the demands of the Soviet regime ... Thus the Bolshevik dictatorship climbed up on the back of the peasant revolution.'[10] Without a proletarian victory in the West (without which, according to Lenin, socialism was impossible in Russia), millenarian rhetoric was supplemented with a hardnosed reliance on force, terror, armed might, organisation and new kinds of propaganda.

Particularly effective were Lenin's concessions to the non-Russian peoples. Originally opposed to a federal structure for the post-revolutionary state, Lenin quickly readjusted his views after the October seizure of power. For both Lenin and Stalin, who soon emerged as the key players in the formation of the multinational Soviet Union, nationality policy was a temporary tactical adjustment, not unlike the party's agrarian policy and New Economic Policy, to deal with problems that would be resolved once the international proletarian revolution occurred. But far more than most other party members, Lenin promoted the concept of national self-determination, even to the point of separation from Russia. In 1922 Lenin and Stalin fought over the relationship between the Russian republic and the other fledgling socialist states of

---

[10] Figes, *Peasant Russia, Civil War*, p. 354.

the periphery. Stalin favoured a much more centralised arrangement, with the formally independent states reduced to autonomies within the RSFSR, whereas Lenin proposed that the republics remain powerful members of a new federation, the USSR. As his own power increased, Stalin consistently shifted the emphasis in Lenin's nationality policy until it became an ideology for a new, disguised form of empire in which the centre and Russia emerged superordinate and the non-Russian peripheries fell into a state of tutelage.

II *Building the* apparat

In his pre-revolutionary career Stalin had been a *komitetchik* (committee man), a party operative rather than an activist among the workers.[11] Never gifted in theoretical analysis and synthesis, so prized by party intellectuals, Stalin was a *praktik*, a man who got things done, a skilful political infighter able to sense when he needed to retreat or keep silent and when he could act with impunity. Whatever his personal predilections for unchallenged power, his inability to accept frustration or criticism, and his visceral suspiciousness directed even at those close to him, Stalin was also the product of the particular political culture and internal party practices of Bolshevism. Disputes were fierce and often personal; subordination to higher authorities within the movement was required; force and repression were available to be used in the service of socialism, which was eventually defined in Stalin's mind as identical to his own policies and preservation of his personal position. Once he had reached his exalted position as chief oligarch, he spoke in the name of the party and the Central Committee without consulting anyone else. And he moulded his own version of Leninism as an effective weapon against pretenders.

In the early months of Soviet rule Stalin worked at the very centre of power, in Smolny, close to Lenin, constantly in contact with party members and state officials by telegraph.[12] Over time, like other high party leaders, Stalin took on a wide range of assignments – from People's Commissar of Nationalities (Narkomnats) (from 1917 to 1923), People's Commissar of State Control (from 1919) and Worker-Peasant Inspection (Rabkrin) (1920–2), to membership in the Military-Revolutionary Soviet of the Republic, the Politburo and the Orgburo (from their creation in March 1919), to political commissar of various fronts in the

---

[11] Ronald Grigor Suny, 'A Journeyman for the Revolution: Stalin and the Labour Movement in Baku, June 1907–May 1908', *Soviet Studies*, 23, 3 (January 1972), pp. 373–94; 'Labor and Liquidators: Revolutionaries and the "Reaction" in Baku, May 1908–April 1912', *Slavic Review*, 34, 2 (June 1975), pp. 319–40.

[12] This is clear from working through Stalin's personal archive in the Rossiiskii Tsentr Khraneniia i Izucheniia Dokumentov Noveishei Istorii (RTsKhIDNI), f. 558, op. 1.

Civil War and participant in a variety of commissions set up to solve specific problems.[13] In what at the time seemed to many to be a trivial appointment, the Eleventh Party Congress in the spring of 1922 elected Stalin a member of the party Secretariat with the title 'general secretary'.[14]

By the time of Lenin's incapacitation in 1923, Stalin was fast becoming indispensable to many powerful figures. He combined with his political allies, Grigorii Zinoviev and Lev Kamenev, to prevent the growth of influence of Trotsky. On the eve of Politburo meetings, this *troika* would meet, at first in Zinoviev's apartment, later in Stalin's Central Committee office, ostensibly to approve the agenda. In fact, they decided what positions they would take on specific issues and what roles each would play in the meeting.[15] In 1924–5 the group was expanded to seven (the *semerka*) and included Stalin, Zinoviev, Kamenev, Nikolai Bukharin, Aleksei Rykov, Mikhal Tomskii, and Valerian Kuibyshev.[16]

The Secretariat was supposedly subordinate to the Orgburo, which in turn was subordinate to the Politburo, but by statute any decision of the Secretariat that was not challenged by the Orgburo became automatically the decision of the Orgburo. Likewise, any decision of the Orgburo unchallenged by a member of the Politburo became the decision of the Politburo. A decision by the Politburo might be challenged by a member of the Central Committee, but unless a plenum of the Central Committee annulled that decision it remained in force. No strict division was maintained between political and organisational questions.[17]

In general, the Politburo was to decide on policy, and the Orgburo was to allocate forces – under the authority and guidance of the Central Committee. But both of these small committees met more frequently and proved more effective in day-to-day decision-making than the larger, more unwieldy Central Committee. From the earliest years of the

---

[13] The Central Committee worked through a system of commissions, among the most important of which was the Instructional Commission, which prepared the text of directives to be sent to local party organisations. In the early 1920s, Molotov or Kaganovich presided over this commission (Boris Bazhanov, *Bazhanov and the Damnation of Stalin*, trans. and commentary by David W. Doyle (Athens, OH: Ohio University Press 1990), p. 17).

[14] Stalin was overburdened to the point that his health suffered. In the summer of 1922, the Politburo ordered Stalin to spend three days a week out of the city at his dacha (*Izvestiia TsK KPSS*, no. 4 (1989), pp. 185–6).

[15] Bazhanov, *Bazhanov and the Damnation of Stalin*, pp. 34–5.

[16] 'Pis'ma I. V. Stalina V. M. Molotovu (1925–1936 gg.)', *Izvestiia TsK KPSS*, no. 9 (1990), p. 185.

[17] As Lenin had told the Eleventh Party Congress, 'It is impossible to differentiate a political question from an organisational one. Any political question might be organisational, and vice versa. And only the established practice that any question can be transferred from the Orgburo to the Politburo has made it possible to get the work of the Central Committee going correctly . . .' (*Odinnadtsatyi s'ezd RKP (b)*, p. 143).

RONALD GRIGOR SUNY

Soviet government, small overlapping groups of high officials made the most important and wide-reaching decisions, and Stalin was the only person who was a member of all of these groups. Even more important-ly, with his complete dominance over the Orgburo, Stalin was able to use this institution to make appointments throughout the party and to work out his own policies. For example, many of the documents concerning Stalin's 'autonomisation' plan for the new Soviet federation initially emerged from discussions in a special commission of the Orgburo.[18]

Each of the top party institutions had its own secretariat, for example, *Sekretariat Politburo*, *Sekretariat Orgburo*, and *Sekretariat Tsentral'nogo komiteta*. The Secretariat of the Central Committee in turn had a Bureau, established on 12 September 1921, which was replaced by the so-called *Sekretnyi otdel* in March 1926.[19] All the while, Stalin, as the leading member of both the Orgburo and the Central Committee Secretariat, built up his own staff, which soon amounted to a personal chancellery. Despite his suspicious nature and his intellectual limitations (certainly exaggerated by political rivals and opponents), Stalin was able to attract a number of loyal subordinates, whose fortunes would rise with him. Most important were Viacheslav Molotov, with whom he worked from 1917; his comrades from the Caucasus, Anastas Mikoyan and 'Sergo' Orjonikidze; and his civil war associate, Kliment Voroshilov.[20] Among Stalin's assistants within the apparatus of the Central Committee were: Amaiak Markovich Nazaretian, his secretary in 1923; Boris Grigorevich Bazhanov, secretary of the Politburo and assistant to Stalin for Politburo affairs; Ivan Pavlovich Tovstukha, who would remain Stalin's secretary almost until his death in 1935; Lev Zakharovich Mekhlis, Stalin's personal secretary; Grigorii Kanner, secretary for matters dealing with the police; Giorgii Maximilianovich Malenkov, who replaced Bazhanov as secretary of the Politburo; and eventually Aleksandr Nikolaevich Poskrebyshev, who rose from clerk in the Central Committee mailroom to replace Tovstukha as Stalin's principal secretary.[21] In 1928 Pos-

---

[18] *Izvestiia TsK KPSS*, no. 9 (1989), pp. 191–218.

[19] RTsKhIDNI, f. 17 (Central Committee), op. 84; documents from the *Biuro Sekretariata* and the *Sekretnyi otdel* can also be found in op. 85 and 86.

[20] 'Molotov was the only member of the Politburo whom Stalin addressed with the familiar pronoun *ty* . . . Molotov, though impotent without Stalin's leadership, was indispensable to Stalin in many ways. Though both were unscrupulous in their methods, it seems to be that Stalin selected these methods carefully and fitted them to circumstances, while Molotov regarded them in advance as being incidental and unimportant. I maintain that he not only incited Stalin into doing many things, but that he also sustained him and dispelled his doubts . . . it would be wrong to underestimate Molotov's role, especially as the practical executive' (Milovan Djilas, *Conversations with Stalin* (New York: Harcourt, Brace & World 1962), pp. 62, 70–1).

[21] Bazhanov, *Bazhanov and the Damnation of Stalin*, pp. 34–40.

32

krebyshev became the head of the *Osobyi sektor Sekretariata TsK*. This 'special section' of the Central Committee's secretariat was in charge of security matters and secret communications within the party apparatus. Receiving information from the state security service, the *Osobyi sektor* oversaw a hierarchy of 'special sections' at the regional and local level.[22] Eventually, by 1934, the *Osobyi sektor* replaced the *Sekretnyi otdel*, and Poskrebyshev moved into the position held formerly by Tovstukha.[23] Stalin's relationship with all of them was never one of partnership or equality but of subordination. He usually addressed them with the formal *vy*, with exceptions made for Nazaretian, Orjonikidze, Voroshilov (who in turn called him 'Koba'), and later Molotov.[24]

Before 1926, no voting member of the Politburo owed his position to Stalin, and Stalin did not use his influence in the Central Committee to force changes in the Politburo. As T. H. Rigby argues, Stalin employed the Central Committee to keep his shifting majority in the Politburo in power.[25] Only after the routing of the Zinoviev-led Opposition in December 1925 did close supporters of Stalin join the Politburo. Kamenev was demoted to candidate member, and Molotov, Voroshilov, and Kalinin were elevated to the highest party body. In July 1926, Rudzutak replaced Zinoviev, and in October, Trotsky and Kamenev both lost their seats. In the next month, Orjonikidze joined the Politburo. By December 1927, Stalin had an absolute majority, and as the crisis over grain collection strained Stalin's alliance with Nikolai Bukharin, Stalin changed 'from being the soul of caution and moderation' to becoming 'intransigence itself'.[26] By 1930, he removed the so-called 'Right', those unwilling to follow him unreservedly through collectivisation, and revamped the apparatus of the Central Committee. With the fall of Bukharin, Rykov, and Tomskii, Stalin had established an unchallenged oligarchy with himself as chief oligarch.

Stalin insisted that all important decisions be made at the highest level. In 1925 he was concerned about the loss of direct control over economic matters by the Politburo, as he indicated in a letter to Molotov.

> The business with the STO [the Council of Labour and Defence] is, of course, not very good . . . The Politburo itself is in an uncomfortable position, as it is cut off from economic matters. Look at *Ekonmicheskaia zhizn'* [an economic journal] and you will under-

22 Niels Erik Rosenfeldt, *Knowledge and Power: The Role of Stalin's Secret Chancellery in the Soviet System of Government* (Copenhagen: Rosenkilde and Bagger 1978), pp. 86–92.
23 Rosenfeldt, *Knowledge and Power*, p. 177.
24 Bazhanov, *Bazhanov and the Damnation of Stalin*, p. 37; Djilas, *Conversations with Stalin*, p. 62.
25 T. H. Rigby, *Communist Party Membership in the U.S.S.R., 1917–1967* (Princeton: Princeton University Press 1968), p. 113.   26 Ibid.

stand that our funds are being distributed by Smilga and Strumilin plus Groman [all of whom were working in Gosplan, the principal planning agency], and the Politburo . . . has been turned from the leading organ into a court of appeals, something like a 'council of elders'. Sometimes it is even worse – Gosplan is not leading, but the 'sections' of [bourgeois] specialists of Gosplan . . . Business can only suffer from this, of course. I see no way out except a restructuring [*perestroika*] of STO with members of the Poliburo there in person.[27]

Early in the 1930s Stalin pushed hard for the end of any duality between party and state, urging Molotov in a series of private letters to end Prime Minister Rykov's tenure and take the job himself.[28]

The top (*verkhushka*) of our central soviet [apparatus] [STO, SNK (Council of People's Commissars), the conference of deputy com- missars] is sick with a fatal disease. STO has turned from a businesslike and fighting organ into an empty parliament. SNK is paralysed by the wishy-washy and, essentially, anti-party speeches of Rykov. The conference of deputy commissars, which was earlier the staff of Rykov, As, and Sheiman, now has the tendency to turn into the staff of Rykov, Piatakov, Kviring or Bogolepov (I see no great difference between the latter and the former), setting itself up against the Central Committee of the party. It is clear that this can continue no further. Fundamental measures are needed. I will discuss what kind when I return to Moscow.

A week later he urged the dismissal of Rykov and Schmidt and the dissolution of 'their entire bureaucratic consultative, secretarial appar- atus'. By securing the premiership for Molotov, one of the few he seems to have trusted through the 1930s, Stalin sought to prevent the development of a state apparatus that could rival the party. Any *razryv* (schism) between party and state was unacceptable, and discussion in the Sovnarkom that delayed the carrying out of his policies had to end. All decision-making was to be concentrated within a loyal Politburo. 'With this combination we will have full unity of the soviet and party summits (*verkhuski*) that will undoubtedly double our strength.[29]

Overall Stalin's organisational project was aimed at monopolisation of decision-making at the highest possible levels. Yet his drive for centralisation and the reduction of local power, in fact, often had the opposite effect, fostering local centres of power, 'family circles', *atamanshchina*, and low-level disorganisation. 'Little Stalins' were cre-

[27] 'Pis'ma I. V. Stalina V. M. Molotovu (1925–1936 gg.)', *Izvestiia TsK KPSS*, no. 9 (1990), p. 187.
[28] 'Pis'ma Stalina Molotovu', *Kommunist*, no. 11 (1990), pp. 102–5.   [29] Ibid., p. 105.

ated throughout the country, and in the national republics ethnopoliti-cal machines threatened the reach of the central government.[30]

III   Building hegemony in the 1930s

Though the relative peace, stability, and economic improvement of the NEP years, in contrast to the preceding seven years of war, revolution, and civil war, had given the Leninist state a degree of acceptance and authority in the eyes of many, that acceptance was fragile and based on the compromises and limits of what the Communists almost invariably saw as a transitional period, a temporary retreat from socialism. The launching of the Stalin revolution, first in the countryside and then in industry, destroyed the basis of the regime's fragile relationship with the great majority of the population (the *smychka*) and created a new crisis of legitimacy and authority.

By ending NEP and almost all private production and trade, Stalin created the first modern non-market, state-run economy, one that simultaneously eliminated rival sources of power and resistance to the will of the central authorities. 'Industrialists' no longer held property in the means of production. Workers could no longer effectively organise in order to raise the price of labour. Farmers could no longer withhold grain to affect market prices. Yet all of these groups devised ways within the command economy to exercise limited degrees of power, autonomy, and resistance. Workers, to take one example, were able to undermine harsh factory regimes by taking their skills, so desired by managers, to another workplace. Bosses, caught between demands from above for higher productivity, had to satisfy, however inadequately, some of the needs and demands of their workers and even permit a degree of worker autonomy on the shop floor.[31] Much of the time and effort of Soviet officials was concerned with raising output and productivity, and successive state strategies required accommodations and conces-sions as often as additional pressure and repression.[32] Thus, while power was actively being concentrated at the top by Stalin, it was being diffused downward and outward throughout the economic and politi-cal systems by thousands of *vintiki* (little screws) who had their own

[30] Merle Fainsod, *Smolensk Under Soviet Rule* (Cambridge, Mass: Harvard University Press 1958), pp. 48–61; Ronald Grigor Suny, *The Making of the Georgian Nation* (Bloomington and Stanford: Indiana University Press and Hoover Institution Press 1988), pp. 260–91.
[31] Hiroaki Kuromiya, *Stalin's Industrial Revolution: Politics and Workers, 1928–1932* (Cambridge: Cambridge University Press 1988).
[32] Much of the work of Lewis Siegelbaum has explored the various strategies by which the regime attempted to raise productivity. See, for example, his 'Soviet Norm Determina-tion in Theory and Practice, 1917–1941', *Soviet Studies*, 36 (1984), pp. 48–67; and *Stakhanovism and the Politics of Productivity in the USSR, 1935–1941* (Cambridge: Cambridge University Press 1988).

requirements for survival and 'making out'. The state grew; in Moshe Lewin's sense, it 'swallowed' society; but at the same time it was unable to realise the vision presented by totalitarian theory of complete atomisation of society. The limits of state power were met when people refused to work efficiently, migrated from place to place by the millions, or informally worked out ways to resist pressure from above.

Stalin came to power in the absence of a broad consensus on the legitimacy and necessity of his personal rule. Using the instruments of state power to mobilise people in a grand programme of social transformation, the regime confidently conceived of itself as possessing a popular and historically sanctioned mandate and worked assiduously to increase support for itself through education and propaganda, leadership cults, election campaigns, broad national discussions (e.g., on the constitution), public celebrations (like the Pushkin centennial of 1937), show trials, and political rituals.[33] Most importantly, the party/state made real concessions to the populace and satisfied the ambitions and aspirations of many (certainly not all) for social mobility and an improved living standard. Peasants who became workers and workers who became managers and party bosses were moving up, while many of their envied social 'betters' of the past were experiencing an enforced downward mobility.[34]

In the Stalinist formulation the 'revolution from above' of the 1930s, though initiated by the state, was supported from below by millions of peasants and workers struggling to create a new society based on collective farms and socialist industry. The state-initiated industrialisation of the 1930s mobilised millions of men and women into the most mammoth building project in modern times, and a romance of dams and powerstations, new cities on the steppe and in Siberia, created enthusiasts among the new workers and managers. The enormous difficulties that the breakthrough into 'socialism' entailed – resistance from farmers, famine, economic bottlenecks and breakdowns – were seen as the work of enemies and saboteurs, rather than inherent in the party's policies or a by-product of popular recalcitrance and massive coercion. Though the disjuncture between these forced images of imagined harmony and purpose and the hardships and dislocations of actual worksites created unease among many who attempted to govern a vast country, the sheer scale of the transformation and its construction as a human epic engendered the broad

[33] Christel Lane, *The Rites of Rulers: Ritual in Industrial Society – the Soviet Case* (Cambridge: Cambridge University Press 1981).
[34] Social mobility has been a frequent theme in the work of Sheila Fitzpatrick. See, for example, *Education and Social Mobility in the Soviet Union, 1921–1934* (Cambridge: Cambridge University Press 1979); and 'Stalin and the Making of a New Elite, 1928–1939', *Slavic Review*, 38, 3 (September 1979), pp. 377–402.

social support that the regime had sought for two decades.[35]

The naked exercise of unrestrained power was key to Stalin's victory, but his regime simultaneously worked to create authority and acceptance, borrowing from and supplementing the repertoire of justifications from Lenin's day. While appropriating the mantle of Lenin and much of the rhetoric of Bolshevism, however, Stalin revised, suppressed, and even reversed much of the legacy of Lenin. Internationalism turned into nationalism; the *smychka* between the workers and the peasants was buried in the ferocity of collectivisation; radical transformation of the family and the place of women ended with reassertion of the most conservative 'family values'. And in the process almost all of Lenin's closest associates fell victim to the self-proclaimed keeper of the Leninist flame.

Within ten years of his dispute with Lenin, Stalin transformed nationality policy from a series of concessions to non-Russians into a powerful weapon of imperial state-building. He reversed Lenin's focus on 'Great Russian chauvinism' as the principal danger in nationality relations and emphasised instead the dangers from the nationalism of non-Russians. In 1923, he turned on M. Kh. Sultan-Galiev, a former associate in Narkomnats and a spokesman for the aspirations of Muslim Communists, accused him of *national-uklonizm* (national deviationism), had him 'tried' before a party conference, arrested, and expelled from the party.[36] Five years later, the state police 'discovered' a new plot, the 'Sultan-Galiev counter-revolutionary organisation', and in the next decade the OGPU and its successor, the NKVD, 'unmasked' dozens of conspiratorial groups promoting nationalism from Ukraine to Central Asia.[37] In a letter to Levon Mirzoian, first secretary of the Kazakh

[35] As the Harvard Project interviews in the early 1950s demonstrated, and as Donna Bahry has emphasised in a recent study, 'one of the cardinal values defining the Soviet system's claim to legitimacy was industrial transformation . . . [R]apid industrialization appeared to have near-universal backing' (Donna Bahry, 'Society Transformed? Rethinking the Social Roots of Perestroika', *Slavic Review*, 52, 3 (Fall 1993), p. 524).

[36] *Tainy natsional'noi politiki TsK RKP: 'Chetvertoe soveshchanie TsK RKP s otvetstvennymi rabotnikami natsional'nykh respublik i oblastei v g. Moskve 9–12 iiunia 1923 g.': Stenograficheskii otchet* (Moscow: Insan 1992); N. Tagirov, 'Sultan-Galiev: Pravda i domysly', *Kommunist Tatarii*, no. 9 (September 1989), pp. 68–76; 'Shchitaem svoim revoliutsionnym dolgom', *Kommunist Tatarii*, no. 6 (June 1990), pp. 51–5; Alexandre A. Bennigsen and S. Enders Wimbush, *Muslim National Communism in the Soviet Union: A Revolutionary Strategy for the Colonial World* (Chicago: University of Chicago Press 1979); Stephen Blank, 'Stalin's First Victim: The Trial of Sultangaliev', *Russian History/Histoire Russe*, 17, 2 (Summer 1990), pp. 155–78; Douglas Taylor Northrop, 'Reconsidering Sultan-Galiev', in *Selected Topics in Soviet Ethnopolitics*, eds. Gail Lapidus and Corbin Lydey (Berkeley: University of California 1992), pp. 1–44.

[37] 'V komissii Politbiuro TsK KPSS po dopolnitel'nomu izucheniiu materialov, sviazannykh s repressiiami, imevshimi mesto v period 30–40-kh i nachala 50-kh godov', *Izvestiia TsK KPSS*, no. 9 (1990), pp. 71–6; 'O tak nazyvaemom "national-uklonizme"', *Izvestiia TsK KPSS*, no. 9 (1990), pp. 76–84.

kraikom, in 1933, Stalin called for intensifying the struggle against local Kazakh nationalism 'in order to create the conditions for the sowing of Leninist internationalism'.[38] Five years later, after having carried out purges against Kazakh intellectuals and 'deviationist' party members, Mirzoian himself was arrested and executed.[39]

Stalinism was both a revolutionising system, unwilling to accept backward Russia as it was (and here it differs from many traditionally authoritarian dictatorships), and a conservative, restorative one, anxious to reestablish hierarchies, affirm certain traditional values like patriotism and patriarchy, and create political legitimacy based on more than victorious revolution.[40] The revolution and the restoration were both evident in the 1930s, with the former powerfully present in the First Five-Year Plan period and the latter dominating in the middle 1930s. The unresolved tensions between those aspects of Stalinism that extended the revolutionary egalitarian, participatory impulses of 1917 and those that resurrected stratification and authoritarianism remained in irresolvable tension with one another.

The ultimate 'man of the machine', Stalin was one of the least likely candidates for charismatic hero. Short in stature, reticent in meetings and on public occasions, neither a talented orator like Trotsky or Zinoviev, nor an attractive and engaging personality, like Lenin or Bukharin, Stalin did not himself project an image of a leader – until it was created for him (and by him) through the cult. First the promotion of a cult of Lenin, which Stalin actively encouraged, then his identification as a loyal Leninist, and eventually his merger with and substitution for the image of Lenin were important props for Stalin's authority both within the party and in society.[41] All this was accomplished in a political culture based on the pre-revolutionary Bolshevik traditions in which emphasis on personality, the exaggerated import-

[38] Ibid., p. 79.

[39] Boris Levytsky (comp.), *The Stalinist Terror in the Thirties: Documentation from the Soviet Press* (Stanford: Hoover Institution Press 1974), pp. 176–9; Martha Brill Olcott, *The Kazakhs* (Stanford: Hoover Institution Press 1987), pp. 218–19.

[40] Nowhere was this more evident than in the state's shifting strategies toward women and the family. See Wendy Z. Goldman, 'Women, Abortion and the State, 1917–36', in *Russia's Women: Accommodation, Resistance, Transformation*, eds. Barbara Evans Clements, Barbara Alpern Engel, and Christine D. Worobec (Berkeley–Los Angeles: University of California Press 1991); and her *Women, the State and Revolution: Soviet Family Policy and Social Life, 1917–1936* (Cambridge: Cambridge University Press 1993).

[41] Robert C. Tucker, 'The Rise of Stalin's Personality Cult', *American Historical Review*, 84, 2 (April 1979), pp. 347–66. A key role in the effort to link Stalin with the legacy of Lenin was played by Stalin's assistant, Tovstukha, who worked in the Lenin Institute from 1924 to 1926, helped edit the first two volumes of Lenin's collected works, edited the first nine editions of Stalin's collection of articles *Problemy leninizma*, and wrote the first official Soviet biography of Stalin (1927) (Rosenfeldt, *Knowledge and Power*, pp. 170–4; *Pravda*, 10 August 1935, pp. 1, 3; I. B. Rusanova, 'I. P. Tovstukha. K 80-letiiu so dnia rozhdeniia', *Voprosy istorii KPSS*, no. 4 (1969), pp. 128–30).

ance of the leader, and the attendant sacral notions of infallibility were all alien. The ideological props of the Stalin dictatorship were both a radically revised Marxism and a pro-Russian nationalism and etatism. Class warfare was seen as inevitable and intensifying rather than diminishing as the country approached socialism. As long as the country was surrounded by hostile capitalist states, it was claimed, state power had to be built up. When the Soviet Union was declared to be socialist by Stalin in 1936, the positive achievement of reaching a stage of history higher than the rest of the world was tempered by the constant reminders that the enemies of socialism existed both within and outside the country, that they are deceptive and concealed, and must be 'unmasked'. Repeated references to dangers and insecurity and to the need for 'vigilance' justified the enormous reliance on the 'steel gauntlets of Ezhov'.

IV   Inventing opposition

The enthusiasm for industrialisation was tempered by much less support for Stalin's agrarian revolution. The open resistance to collectivisation among the peasants was reflected in less dramatic form by quiet forms of opposition within the party. The oligarchy that carried out the Stalin revolution was a very narrow political elite but not one that had effectively closed the party to debate and consideration of alternatives. Between the fall of Bukharin in 1928–9 and the death of Kirov in December 1934, Stalin-faction rule produced and reproduced oppositions and potential oppositions. The real disagreements with the General Line of rapid industrialisation and full collectivisation and dekulakisation were fuelled by the evident failures and costs of implementing these policies. In his own statements Stalin refused to accept any blame for the economic chaos or the famine. Because 'the last remnants of moribund classes', some of whom had 'even managed to worm their way into the party', were actively sabotaging the building of socialism, more repression was needed.

> The abolition of classes is not achieved by the extinction of the class struggle, but its intensification . . . We must bear in mind that the growth of the power of the Soviet state will intensify the resistance of the last remnants of the dying classes.[42]

In a letter replying to the Cossack writer Mikhail Sholokhov's protests against the systematic brutality of the grain collection, Stalin took a hard line:

[42] Originally this was an idea put forth by Trotsky. I. V. Stalin, 'Itogi pervoi piatiletki: Doklad 7 ianvaria 1933 g.', Sochineniia, 12, pp. 211–12.

One must take into account . . . the other side. And that other side amounts to the fact that the respected corn-growers of your region (and not only your region) have gone on a sit-down strike (sabotage!) and shown no concern about leaving the workers, the Red Army, without grain. The fact that the sabotage was peaceful and outwardly bloodless in no way alters the realities – that the respected grain-growers have in essence carried out a 'peaceful' war with Soviet power. A war by starvation (*voina na izmor*), dear Comrade Sholokhov.[43]

The growing gap between the public statements and images put forth by the state, on the one hand, and the real destruction in the countryside, on the other, prompted prominent party members to resist the cover-up of the failures. Already in late 1930 some in the leadership of the RSFSR and the Transcaucasian federation expressed misgivings, which in turn were interpreted by the Stalin centre as a widespread and united oppositional tendency (the Syrtsov–Lominadze Right–Left Bloc).[44] Swift retribution (demotion in these cases) did not deter a number of other critical foci from emerging, notably the Riutin Platform and Appeal (1932) and the Smirnov, Tolmachev, and Eismont opposition (1932). Within the Central Committee and the Politburo more moderate elements opposed the rapid tempos in industry and proposed a more conciliatory attitude toward society, particularly the peasantry.

The short-lived attempt to organise opposition to Stalin by Martem'ian Ivanovich Riutin never went further than a few meetings of like-minded party members, the formation of an organisation – the Union of Marxist-Leninists, the discussion of Riutin's report, 'Stalin and the Crisis of the Proletarian Dictatorship', and an appeal to party

---

[43] Quoted by Khrushchev, 8 March 1963; *Pravda*, 10 March 1963; Jonathan Haslam, 'Political Opposition to Stalin and the Origins of the Terror in Russia, 1932–1936', *The Historical Journal*, 29, 2 (1986), p. 403.

[44] R. W. Davies, 'The Syrtsov–Lominadze Affair', *Soviet Studies*, 33, 1 (January 1981), pp. 29–50. Indicative of the mood in the party is a conversation with Lominadze reported by a friend: 'When I saw him, with another of his friends, in 1931, he was boldly critical of Stalin's leadership. Now that opposition from both Left and Right had been suppressed, he thought the next logical step was a radical reform of the Party and its personnel.

"What about the General Secretary?" asked his friend.

"If there is a spring cleaning, every piece of furniture has to be removed, including the biggest one."

"But who could replace him?"

"That's up to the Congress." It was time for younger men to take a share of the responsibility – men who had some practical experience but had been less involved in the struggle between the factions.

Needless to say, this was extremely risky talk. It even occurred to me that Lominadze saw himself as a suitable successor to Stalin' (Joseph Berger, *Shipwreck of a Generation: The Memoirs of Joseph Berger* (London: Harvill Press 1971); American edition: *Nothing But the Truth* (New York: John Day 1971), p. 166).

members to join their efforts. Riutin condemned Stalin's emerging dictatorship as the negation of the collective leadership of the Central Committee and the principal cause of the growing disillusionment of the people with socialism. He believed that the only way to save Bolshevism was to remove Stalin and his clique by force. If Riutin was right that 'the faith of the masses in socialism has been broken, its readiness to defend selflessly the proletarian revolution from all enemies weakens each year', then the regime had either to move immediately toward conciliation and the rebuilding of confidence or turn to even more radical and repressive measures.[45]

Riutin's circle is an unusual instance of coherence and organisation among those who opposed Stalin.[46] Much more evident was a broad, inchoate discontent with Stalin's rule that permeated political and intellectual circles. Several loyal Stalinists, like Kaminskii, Kosior, Vareikis, and Bauman, harboured serious doubts about Stalin's agricultural policies. Others, like Mykola Skrypnyk, a co-founder of the Ukrainian Communist Party who had sided with Stalin in the 1920s and early 1930s, were critical of the growing ethnocentrism in the party and state and the evident pro-Russianness of Stalin's nationality policies.[47] Perhaps most ominously, tensions arose between the Red Army commander, Mikhail Tukhachevskii, who called in 1930 for expansion of the armed forces, particularly aviation and tank armies, and Stalin and Voroshilov, who opposed what they called 'Red militarism'.[48] During the

---

[45] On Riutin, see: 'Stalin i krizis proletarskoi diktatury' [Platform of the Union of Marxist-Leninists (the Riutin Group)], *Izvestiia TsK KPSS*, no. 8 (1990), pp. 200–7; no. 9, pp. 165–83; no. 10, pp. 191–206; no. 11, pp. 161–86; no. 12, pp. 180–99, with commentary, pp. 200–2; M. Riutin, 'Ko vsem chlenam VKP (b)', reprinted in *Osmyslit' kult Stalina*, ed. Kh. Kobo, (Moscow: Progress 1989), pp. 618–23; 'O dele tak nazyvaemogo "Soiuza Marksistov-Leninistev"', *Izvestiia TsK KPSS*, no. 6 (1989), pp. 103–15. See also, the biography of Riutin by B. A. Starkov in *Izvestiia TsK KPSS*, no. 3 (1990), pp. 150–63, followed by Riutin's letters, pp. 163–78.

[46] The members of the Riutin group were arrested a few weeks after their first meeting. Riutin had been expelled from the party in 1930, and his seventeen associates were expelled by the Central Control Commission on 9 October 1932, for 'having attempted to set up a bourgeois, kulak organization to re-establish capitalism and, in particular, the kulak system in the USSR by means of underground activity under the fraudulent banner of "Marxism-Leninism"'. A number of accounts hold that Stalin demanded the death penalty for Riutin but was thwarted by Kirov and other moderates (Boris I. Nicolaevsky, *Power and the Soviet Elite: 'The Letter of an Old Bolshevik' and Other Essays* (New York: Frederick A. Praeger 1965), pp. 3–65; Arkadii Vaksberg, 'Kak zhivoi s zhivymi', *Literaturnaia gazeta*, 29 June 1988; Lev Razgon, 'Nakonets!' *Moskovskie novosti*, 26 June 1988; Dmitrii Volkogonov, *Triumf i tragediia: Politicheskii portret I. V. Stalina*, I, part 2 (Moscow: Novosti 1989), pp. 85–6). Riutin was sentenced to ten years' solitary confinement. On 10 January 1937, he was secretly tried and shot.

[47] Skrypnyk committed suicide in 1933, as Ukrainian national communists were systematically being purged.

[48] R. W. Davies, *The Industrialisation of Soviet Russia, 3: The Soviet Economy in Turmoil, 1929–1930* (Cambridge, Mass: Harvard University Press 1989), pp. 446–7. In May 1932 Stalin apologised to Tukhachevskii and endorsed some of his proposed reforms.

famine in Ukraine high military officers, like Iakir, angered Stalin by reporting their upset at peasant resistance, which, they felt, could spread to the troops, and by demanding that more grain be kept in the region.[49]

Even among Stalin's closest supporters there were fractures, though their precise nature remains mysterious. The open disagreement at the Seventeenth Party Congress (January–February 1934) between Orjonikidze and Molotov over industrial targets was a rare public sign of a deeper split between moderates and radicals.[50] The popular Kirov, the only real rival left to Stalin by 1932, was in all his public and political appearances completely loyal to the General Secretary, though he often emphasised the need for 'revolutionary legality', which was understood to be a lessening of repressive measures.[51] Stalin still represented for the majority of party members the militant turn toward socialism – collectivisation, rapid industrialisation, the destruction of organised political opposition. However, his personal proclivity toward the use of force seemed to some to have gone beyond the broad bounds of Bolshevik practice.

The private letters from the vacationing Stalin to his closest comrade Molotov (from 1930 and 1933) reveal in a striking way the less public characteristics of the dictator and his methods of rule. He wrote short, terse memoranda to Molotov on the important matters that were before the Politburo, and apparently did the same with Kaganovich, Orjonikidze, and others. 'From the boss (*khoziain*) we are receiving regular and frequent directives', Kaganovich wrote to Orjonikidze in 1932.[52] While he preferred to work through his own narrow circle of friends – Molotov, who was his principal executor, Voroshilov, Mikoyan, Orjonikidze, Kaganovich – Stalin was quick to turn on any of them if he felt challenged. In 1933 he severely criticised Orjonikidze for objecting to remarks by Vyshinskii that attacked those working in the industrial and agricultural ministries: 'The behaviour of Sergo (and Iakovlev) in the story of the "completeness of production" is impossible to call anything else but anti-party, because it has as its objective goal the defence of reactionary elements of the party *against* the CC VKP(b).'[53] Because Kaganovich had sided with Orjonikidze, he too fell under Stalin's wrath. Nothing came of this dispute at the time, nor of the more serious accusations made against Mikhal Kalinin.

[49] Eventually some grain was sent to Ukraine in January 1933 along with the new party boss, Postyshev.

[50] Kendall E. Bailes, *Technology and Society under Lenin and Stalin: Origins of the Soviet Technical Intelligentsia, 1917–1941* (Princeton: Princeton University Press 1978), pp. 275–80; J. Arch Getty, *Origins of the Great Purges* (Cambridge: Cambridge University Press 1985) pp. 13–17.

[51] S. Kirov, *Stati i rechi, 1934* (Moscow 1934).   [52] 'Pis'ma Stalina Molotovu', p. 94.

[53] Ibid., p. 94.

The OGPU was carrying out investigations in 1930 into a series of anti-Soviet 'parties' made up of former Mensheviks, industrial specialists, and Ukrainian activists.[54] Stalin received regular reports from Iagoda and insisted that Molotov circulate them among the members of the Central Committee and the Central Control Commission, as well as among 'the more active of our *khoziaistvenniki* (economic managers)'. He told Molotov that he was convinced that these conspiratorial elements were linked with the Rightists within the party.

> It is absolutely essential to shoot Kondrat'ev, Groman and a pair of the other bastards (*merzavtsy*) . . . It is absolutely essential to shoot the whole group of wreckers in meat production and to publish this information in the press.[55]

He personally demanded the arrests of the former Menshevik Sukhanov, his Communist wife (who, he says, must have known what was going on in their home), Bazarov, Ramzin, and others. The concocted stories of anti-Soviet conspiracies were fed throughout the top bureaucracy and created an atmosphere of suspicion that justified the use of precisely the kinds of harsh measures that Stalin advocated.

Fear and the need for vigilance, which were created both by the police findings and by the real and imagined weaknesses and insecurities of the Soviet Union, bound the Communists together around the leader who projected an image of Bolshevik toughness. At the same time the Stalinist settlement involved the creation of a highly hierarchical system of rewards and privileges, of access to information and influence, that effectively disenfranchised the great mass of the population and privileged a small number of party and state officials, intellectuals, and managers. The end of rationing in 1934–5 forced everyone below the privileged upper levels of society to forage in government stores and peasant markets for what they could afford. Social inequalities grew in an economy of permanent shortages where money talked less effectively than one's position and personal connections. A 'ruling class without tenure', in Lewin's phrase,[56] grew increasingly dependent on being in favour with those even higher up. They were under a constant threat of demotion, expulsion from the party, arrest and even death. Their success required absolute and unquestioning obedience, enforcement of the decisions from the top with determination, even ruthlessness, on those below, and a willingness to acquiesce and participate in what can only be considered criminal activity (denunciations of the innocent, approval of lawlessness, collaboration with a regime based on

[54] Ibid., p. 103.   [55] Ibid., p. 103.
[56] Moshe Lewin, 'The Social Background of Stalinism', in *Stalinism: Essays in Historical Interpretation*, ed. Robert C. Tucker, (New York: W. W. Norton 1977), p. 130.

43

deception).[57] Their dilemma was that it was dangerous for them to be anything but responsive to the top, and yet their position and requirements to increase production and satisfy the demands of the top and the centre pulled them toward making arrangements with the bottom and the periphery.

V Conservative revolutionary

Neither a consistent moderate nor radical, Stalin himself shifted from centre-right (during his alliance with Bukharin in the mid-1920s) to left (during the period of the so-called 'cultural revolution' at the end of the 1920s and the early 1930s) and then back to a more moderate position around 1931–2. Responding to a growing mood among party leaders concerned with industry, Stalin announced in June 1931 a major change in the party's wage policy (the end of *uravnilovka*, levelling the wages, and the introduction of greater differentials between skilled and unskilled workers in order to end labour migration) and a much more tolerant and supportive policy toward the technical intelligentsia.[58] Whether or not this policy shift was imposed on Stalin or corresponded to a genuine reevaluation of his position, during the next half-decade he steadily began to reverse the more radical policies of the end of the 1920s and the early 1930s and pull back from egalitarianism and collectivism toward a promotion of hierarchy, cultural traditionalism, and social conservatism that has come to be known as the 'Great Retreat'.

On a variety of fronts the Stalinists retreated from their forward positions of just a few years earlier. Though the collective farms remained firmly under the tutelage of the state and continued to operate essentially as grain-collection apparatuses,[59] a series of decisions allowed the collective-farm peasants to possess some livestock, to sell their surpluses on the market, and to own their houses and work household plots. While workers were increasingly restricted in their movements through the 1930s, an essentially 'bourgeois' system of remuneration

---

[57] Roi Medvedev, *Oni okruzhali Stalina* (Moscow 1990); English translation: *All Stalin's Men* (Garden City, NY: Doubleday 1984).

[58] I. V. Stalin, 'Novaia obstanovka – novye zadachi khoziaistvennogo stroitel'stve', *Sochineniia*, 13 (Moscow: Gosudarstvennoe izdatel'stvo politicheskoi literatury 1951), pp. 51–80. Bailes shows how this conciliatory move was initiated by Orjonikidze and others involved in industrial production (*Technology and Society*, pp. 144–55).

[59] Moshe Lewin, '"Taking Grain": Soviet Policies of Agricultural Procurements Before the War', *The Making of the Soviet System: Essays in the Social History of Interwar Russia* (New York: Pantheon 1985), pp. 142–77. 'Peasants in Stalin's times were indeed legally bound to their place of work, submitted to a special legal regimen, and – through the kolkhoz – to a form of collective responsibility with regard to state duties. They were transformed, not unlike as in pre-emancipation times, into an estate placed at the very bottom of the social ladder' (p. 176).

was created: 'from each according to his ability, to each according to his work'. Workers were encouraged to compete with one another in order not only to maximise output, but to win material rewards, and various collective forms of organising work and payment were eliminated.[60] Progressive piece-work was introduced in the spring of 1934, and while real wages fell for most workers a significant number of *udarniki* (shock workers) and *stakhanovtsy* participated in the more 'joyous' life that Stalin had promised.[61] Worker power declined and that of managers and technicians increased.[62] 'The Party wanted the bosses to be efficient, powerful, harsh, impetuous, and capable of exerting pressure crudely and ruthlessly and getting results "whatever the cost" . . . The formation of the despotic manager was actually a process in which not leaders but *rulers* were made.'[63] In the words of Mikhail Kaganovich, 'The ground must shake when the factory director enters the plant.'

The severe economic crisis of the winter of 1932–3, as well as the coming to power of Hitler in Germany, helped accelerate the swing toward state policies that favoured the educated and ambitious and eased the pressure on others. By the middle of the year arrests and deportations declined; production targets for the Second Five-Year Plan were reduced; and consumer goods were given higher priority. As one historian sums it up:

> In the mid-1930s Soviet society struck a balance that would carry it through the turmoil of the purges, the Great War and reconstruction. The coercive policies of the Cultural Revolution [1928–31] were replaced or supplemented by the use of inducements. Benefits were quickly apparent: education opened professional opportunities; a stable countryside improved dietary standards; increased production and income encouraged consumerism. A lightened mood swept the nation. Women wore make-up; young people revived ballroom dancing. Life, as Stalin said, and Lebedev-Kumach's popular song repeated, had become better and happier.[64]

A new Soviet middle class developed with its own form of 'bourgeois values'. More attention was paid to private life. From Stakhanovite

[60] Lewis H. Siegelbaum, 'Production Collectives and Communes and the "Imperatives" of Soviet Industrialization, 1929–1931', *Slavic Review*, 45, 1 (Spring 1986), pp. 65–84.

[61] Lewis H. Siegelbaum, *Stakhanovism and the Politics of Productivity in the USSR, 1935–1941* (Cambridge: Cambridge University Press 1988), particularly chapter 6, 'Stakhanovites in the Cultural Mythology of the 1930s'.

[62] Hiroaki Kuromiya, *Stalin's Industrial Revolution*, pp. 50–77.

[63] Moshe Lewin, 'Society, State, and Ideology during the First Five-Year Plan', in *Cultural Revolution in Russia, 1928–1931*, ed. Sheila Fitzpatrick (Bloomington: Indiana University Press 1978), p. 74.

[64] James van Geldern, 'The Centre and the Periphery: Cultural and Social Geography in the Mass Culture of the 1930s', in *New Directions in Soviet History*, ed. Stephen White, (Cambridge: Cambridge University Press 1992), p. 62.

workers, with their newly acquired bicycles and wristwatches, to factory managers and their wives, who were on the receiving end of Stalin's 'Big Deal', a certain level of security and material improvement, 'a sense of pride and participation', wedded them to the order created by Stalin.[65]

James van Geldern emphasises how Soviet citizens were turned into spectators in the 1930s, rather than active participants. Formal, meaningless voting, viewing the leaders atop Lenin's mausoleum, were 'rituals of participation', public observations of political spectacles.[66] New heroes, from aviators to polar explorers, and extended public dramas – like the rescue of downed female fliers and ice-bound sailors – riveted public attention and reinforced the values of the modernising party/state. An empire was created disguised as a voluntary federation of free peoples, with a reconstructed Moscow at its centre, and festivals of reaffirmation, like the Moscow Olympiad of Folk Music, periodically reminding people of the unbreakable unity of a diverse, continent-size country. Ideas of progress – the conquest of recalcitrant nature, the overcoming of peasant 'darkness' and the isolation of remote villages, the building of the Moscow Metro – enhanced the heroic nature of Soviet leaders and the efforts of the Soviet people. Sacrifice and vigilance went along with pride in *nashi dostizheniia* (our achievements). The image of the motherland (*rodina*) was revived, gradually displacing that of the international community of proletarians, until in 1943 Stalin cavalierly dissolved Lenin's Third International. In 1939, he had proposed, as a joke to Ribbentrop: 'Let's drink to the new anti-Cominternist – Stalin!'[67]

In his public rhetoric of these years Stalin maintained his severity and toughness, qualities that had long been part of Bolshevik culture, but showed that under pressure he could be more flexible and accommodating. He seemed not only a competent commander to many but indeed an indispensable leader in a time of political stress and economic crisis. A high party official, Barmin, wrote about this period (1932): 'Loyalty to Stalin was based principally on the conviction that there was no one to take his place, that any change of leadership would be extremely dangerous, and that the country must continue in its present course, since to stop now or attempt a retreat would mean the loss of

[65] Ibid., Siegelbaum, *Stakhanovism and the Politics of Productivity*, pp. 210–46. The idea of the 'Big Deal', Stalin's exchange of material goods and security for loyalty, is the theme of Vera Dunham, *In Stalin's Time: Middleclass Values in Soviet Fiction* (Cambridge: Cambridge University Press 1976).

[66] Van Geldern, 'The Centre and the Periphery', p. 71.

[67] *Sto sorok besed s Molotovym: Iz dnevnika F. Chueva* (Moscow: Terra 1991), p. 19; *Molotov Remembers: Inside Kremlin Politics: Conversations with Felix Chuev*, ed. Albert Resis (Chicago: Ivan R. Dee 1993), p. 12.

everything.'[68] Rumours that Stalin had suggested that he resign (probably after the suicide of his second wife, Nadezhda Allilueva, in November 1932) were embellished by reports of his associates rallying around him.[69]

The years of upheaval and uncertainty of the early 1930s were clearly coming to an end by the opening of the Seventeenth Party Congress in late January 1934. Though the full story has yet to be told, there appears to have been a movement at the Congress to replace Stalin with Kirov, but Kirov's differences with Stalin were not great enough for the Leningrad leader to repudiate the General Secretary as many others wished. Though many still feared the trend toward personal autocracy by Stalin, the oligarchic bureaucratic system seemed more secure than ever; oppositions had been rendered impotent; and a new emphasis on 'revolutionary legality' seemed to promise a more orderly, procedural, less disruptive mode of governance. But, as Lewin notes:

> Stalin was not ready to accept the role of just a cog, however powerful, in his own machine. A top bureaucrat is a chief executive, in the framework of a constraining committee . . . But Stalin had had the power, and the taste for it – for ever more of it – since he had led the early stage of the shattering breakthrough and gotten full control over the state in the process. At this point, the traits of his gloomy personality, with clear paranoid tendencies become crucial. Once at the top and in full control, he was not a man to accept changes in the pattern of his personal power . . . He therefore took the road of shaking up, of destabilising the machinery and its upper layers, in order to block the process fatally working against his personal predilection for autocracy.[70]

VI Terror and autocracy

The half-dozen years before the murder of Kirov (December 1934) might be seen as the prehistory of Stalinism, the period of formation of the political structures and social conditions that created the possibility for

---

[68] A. Barmin, *One Who Survived* (New York, 1945). When the Menshevik Fedor Dan asked Bukharin in 1936 why he and other communists had so blindly trusted Stalin, Bukharin answered, 'You don't understand this; it is completely different. It is not he who is trusted but a man whom the party trusts; it happened that he became a kind of symbol of the party, [and] the lower ranks, the workers, the people believe in him; maybe this is our fault but that is how it happened, that is why we all climb into his mouth . . . knowing for sure that he will eat us. And he knows this and only chooses the right moment' ('On pozhret nas', from the archive of L. O. Dan in the Institute of Social History, Amsterdam, published in *Osmyslit' kult Stalina*, ed. Kobo, p. 610).

[69] On Stalin's relationship with his second wife, see '"Nadezhde Sergeevne Alliluevoi, lichno ot Stalina" (Perepiska 1928–1931 godov)', *Istochnik: Dokumenty russkoi istorii*, no. 0 (1993), pp. 9–22.   [70] Lewin, 'The Social Background of Stalinism', pp. 130–1.

a regime of extreme centralisation of power, overwhelming dominance of a weakened society, and particular ferocity. The unlimited despotism of Stalinism was the product of the Great Purges, which simultaneously eliminated all possible resistance and created a new and more loyal elite with which the tyrant could rule.

There is no consensus among scholars as to the motivations behind the Purges. Interpretations range from the idea that purging was a permanent and necessary component of totalitarianism in lieu of elections (Zbigniew Brzezinski) to seeing the Great Terror as an extreme form of political infighting (J. Arch Getty).[71] Dissatisfaction with Stalin's rule and with the harsh material conditions was palpable in the mid-1930s, and the regime was faced with the difficulties of controlling the family circles and local feudatories (particularly in the union republics). One of the effects of the Purges was the replacement of an older political and economic elite with a younger, potentially more loyal one.[72] The largest number were promoted workers and party rank-and-file, young technicians, who would make up the Soviet elite through the post-Stalin period until the early 1980s.[73] 'Stalin – and, for that matter, the majority of Soviet citizens', writes Sheila Fitzpatrick,

> saw the cadres of the mid-1930s less in their old role as revolutionaries than in the current role as bosses. There is even some evidence that Stalin saw them as Soviet boyars (feudal lords) and himself as a latter-day Ivan the Terrible, who had to destroy the boyars to build a modern nation state and a new service nobility.[74]

Yet neither arguments from social context nor functionalist deductions from effects to causes have successfully eliminated the principal catalyst to the Terror, the will and ambition of Stalin. The Great Purges have been seen traditionally as an effort 'to achieve an unrestricted personal dictatorship with a totality of power that [Stalin] did not yet

---

71 Getty, *Origins of the Great Purges*, p. 206. For a range of views on the purges, particularly of the so-called 'revisionists', see J. Arch Getty and Roberta T. Manning (eds.) *Stalinist Terror: New Perspectives* (Cambridge: Cambridge University Press 1993).

72 A. L. Unger, 'Stalin's Renewal of the Leading Stratum: A Note on the Great Purge', *Soviet Studies*, 20, 3 (January 1969), pp. 321–30; Bailes, *Technology and Society*, pp. 268–71, 412–13; Sheila Fitzpatrick, 'Stalin and the Making of a New Elite, 1928–1939', *Slavic Review*, 38, 3 (September 1979), pp. 377–402.

73 Bailes criticises Fitzpatrick for not distinguishing between those who rose into the intelligentsia through formal education, many of whom were workers (the *vydvizhentsy*), and the *praktiki*, who were elevated through their work experience ('Stalin and the Making of a New Elite: A Comment', *Slavic Review*, 39, 2 (June 1980), pp. 286–9).

74 Sheila Fitzpatrick, *The Russian Revolution* (Oxford: Oxford University Press 1982), p. 159. Comparisons to the Russian past – autocracy, the service nobility, the collective-farm peasantry as serfs – are used metaphorically by Moshe Lewin and are central to the analysis of Robert C. Tucker in *Stalin in Power: The Revolution from Above, 1928–1941* (New York: W. W. Norton 1973).

possess in 1934.'[75] Stalin guided and prodded the arrests, show trials, and executions forward, aided by the closest members of his entourage: Molotov, Kaganovich, Zhdanov, Malenkov, Mikoyan, and Ezhov.[76] Here personality and politics merged, and the degree of excess repression was dictated by the peculiar demands of Stalin himself, who could not tolerate limits on his will set by the very ruling elite that he had brought to power.[77]

Whatever his authentic political aspirations, Stalin was marked by his deep suspiciousness and insecurity. As Bukharin told the old Mensheviks Fedor and Lydia Dan, Stalin

> is even unhappy because he cannot convince everyone, and even himself, that he is greater than everyone, and this is his unhappiness, perhaps the most human feature in him, perhaps the only human feature in him, but already not human. Here is something diabolical: because of his great 'unhappiness' he cannot but avenge himself on people, on all people, but especially on those who are somehow higher, better than he . . .[78]

The Purges destroyed primarily those in power. 'It is one of the mysteries of Stalinism', Lewin summarises,

> that it turned much of the fury of its bloody purges against this very real mainstay of the regime. There were among the *apparaty*, probably, still too many former members of other parties or of the original Leninist party, too many participants and victors of the civil war who remembered who had done what during those days of glory. Too many thus could feel the right to be considered founders of the regime and base on it part of the claims to a say in decisions and to security in their positions. Probably, also letting the new and sprawling administration settle and get encrusted in their chairs and habits could also encourage them to try and curtail the power of the very top and the personalised ruling style of the chief

---

[75] Robert C. Tucker, 'Introduction', in *The Great Purge Trial* eds. Tucker and Stephen F. Cohen (New York 1965), p. xxix. This is essentially the argument of the second volume of his Stalin biography, as well as the view of Robert Conquest in *The Great Terror: Stalin's Purge of the Thirties* (New York: Macmillan 1968); *The Great Terror: A Reassessment* (New York: Oxford University Press 1990).

[76] Boris A. Starkov, 'Narkom Ezhov', in *Stalinist Terror*, eds. Getty and Manning, pp. 21–39.

[77] Stalin's personal involvement in the details of the Terror has been indisputably demonstrated by archival documents released in the late 1980s and early 1990s. One such note to Ezhov will suffice to give the type of intervention that the *vozhd'* engaged in. In May 1937, he wrote: 'One might think that prison for Beloborodov is a podium for reading speeches, statements which refer to the activities of all sorts of people but not to himself. Isn't it time to squeeze this gentleman and make him tell about his dirty deeds? Where is he, in prison or in a hotel?' (*Dialog* (Leningrad), no. 4 (1990), p. 21; cited in Starkov, 'Narkom Ezhov', p. 29).   [78] 'On pozhret nas', p. 610.

of the state – and this was probably a real prospect the paranoid leader did not relish.[79]

Stalin's initiation and personal direction of the Purges was the catalyst to thousands of smaller settlings of scores.[80] In the context of deep and recurring social tensions the state gave the green light to resentments against the privileged, the intelligentsia, other ethnicities, outsiders. The requirement to find enemies, to blame and punish, worked together with self-protection and self-promotion (and plain sadism) to expand the Purges into a political holocaust. At the end the Soviet Union resembled a ruined landscape, seriously weakened economically, intellectually, and militarily, but at the same time dominated by a towering state apparatus made up of new loyal *apparatchiki*, disciplined by the police, and presided over by a single will.

VII Victory and decline, finale and conclusion

By the outbreak of the Second World War the central government, the military, the republics and local governments, the economic infrastructure had all been brutally disciplined. Obedience and conformity had eliminated most initiative and originality. Ruling through his likeminded lieutenants, Stalin relied on specialists whenever he needed expertise or greater competence. After decimating the high command of the armed forces, his control over his military was greater than Hitler over his, at least at the beginning of the war. He intervened and interfered in both minute and major decisions, and was often abrupt and threatening, yet he was more willing to rely on his generals than was Hitler, who became progressively more involved with operational command and more contemptuous of the military leaders. 'Hitler's generals', writes Severyn Bialer, 'exercised less influence on the decisions of their High Command at the moment they were most able to act effectively; Stalin's generals exercised more'.[81] Stalin stood at the centre of all strategic, logistical, and political decisions. He was chairman of the State Defence Committee, which included the highest party officials (Molotov, Beria, Malenkov, Voroshilov, Kaganovich, and later Voz-

[79] Moshe Lewin, 'Grappling with Stalinism', *The Making of the Soviet System*, pp. 308–9.
[80] Sheila Fitzpatrick, 'How the Mice Buried the Cat: Scenes from the Great Purges of 1937 in the Russian Provinces', *Russian Review*, 52, 3 (July 1993), pp. 299–320.
[81] Severyn Bialer, *Stalin and His Generals* (New York: Pegasus 1969), p. 43. 'As supreme head of army command, Hitler was centrally involved in the formulation of day-to-day tactics in a way which occupied no other head of state during the Second World War. For the German army, this was catastrophic. The command structure which he had devised placed him in charge of both the general management of military campaigns and its detailed tactics' (Ian Kershaw, *Hitler* (London and New York: Longman 1991), p. 175).

nesenskii and Mikoyan); the chairman of Stavka, the supreme military headquarters; General Secretary of the party and chairman of the Politburo; chairman of the Council of Ministers and People's Commissar of Defence. Real business often took place in late-night meetings at Stalin's apartment or dacha, and the exigencies of total war reinforced and accelerated the centralisation of power.[82]

Official propaganda convincingly identified the victory over Nazism with the superiority of the Soviet system, its organic link with *rodina* (the motherland), and the personal genius of Stalin. The triumph over fascism provided the Communists with another source of legitimation and authority. New Russia and the Soviet Union were melded into a single image. Patriotism and accommodation with established religious and national traditions, along with the toning down of revolutionary radicalism, contributed to a powerful ideological amalgam that outlasted Stalin himself. In the post-war decades the war became the central moment of Soviet history, eclipsing the revolution and the *velikii perelom* of the early 1930s.[83] And though there would be sporadic uses of repression and terror against individuals or groups (the 'Leningrad Affair' of 1947, the 'Doctors' Plot' of 1953), as well as a series of ethnic deportations of repatriated Armenians, Kurds, Meskhetian Turks, and others, no massive terror on the scale of 1937 was employed after the war.

Whatever benefits accrued to the Soviet system from the unity of decision-making at the top must be weighed against the costs of overcentralisation and the resultant paralysis lower down in the apparatus. In the years of the Cold War, as Stalin deteriorated physically and mentally, the entire country – its foreign policy, internal politics, cultural life, and economic slowdown – reflected the moods of its leader and was affected by his growing isolation, arbitrariness, and inactivity. No one could feel secure. The ruling elite was concerned with plots, intrigues, and rivalries between Stalin's closest associates, the rise and fall of clients and patrons. 'All of us around Stalin', writes Khrushchev, 'were temporary people. As long as he trusted us to a certain degree, we were allowed to go on living and working. But the moment he stopped trusting you, Stalin would start to scrutinize you until the cup of his distrust overflowed.'[84] In his last years Stalin turned against Molotov and Mikoyan, grew suspicious of Beria, Voroshilov, Kaganovich, and Malenkov. Khrushchev overheard him say, 'I'm finished. I trust no one, not even myself.'[85]

[82] Djilas, *Conversations with Stalin*, passim.
[83] Nina Tumarkin, 'The Great Patriotic War as Myth and Memory', *Atlantic Monthly*, 267, 6 (June 1991), pp. 26, 28, 37, 40, 42, 44.
[84] *Khrushchev Remembers*, trans. and ed. Strobe Talbott (Boston: Little, Brown and Co. 1970), p. 307.   [85] Ibid.

The Stalinist system was restored and consolidated after the devastation of the war years. As a single political cultural synthesis became hegemonic and the more disruptive violence of the pre-war period receded, pervasive fear, which disciplined people into obedient silence, coexisted with genuine acceptance of the system. The figure of Stalin stood symbolically for ideal behaviour in an ideal society. Enemies were still omnipresent; a single simplified reading of historical reality was at hand in the *Kratkii kurs* (the short history of the Communist party) and the official biography of Stalin; and the USSR was still the future in the present.

2

Bureaucracy and the Stalinist state
Moshe Lewin

In a nutshell

Bureaucracy, as a problem or historical factor, did not play much of a role in the thinking of the Bolsheviks. The analysis of the Bolsheviks was conducted mostly in terms of social classes whereas bureaucracy was not considered a class – or was not supposed to be one. The appearance of bureaucracy as a problem (at first as 'bureaucratism' rather than bureaucracy) came with accession to power – and muddled the concepts as well as the realities.

An interplay of perceptions in ideological terms with changing political realities (facts of life) is our story, as well as that of the Soviet system at large.

We need to consider two key stages. The first involved the discovery of the apparatus – and its crucial force – when ex-tsarist government officials went on strike in 1918 against the new regime.

In stage two the state apparatus became a must – and the cooperation of specialists (experts), obviously from the previous regime, was a painful need and precondition for making the state machinery work.

Class composition seemed to be the biggest worry – notably because officials of the old regime, 'alien' both ideologically and in terms of class, were known to epitomise bureaucratism.

This was why acquiring 'their own cadres' – with the right class origin and ideology to be formed in the regime's own educational institutions – became for the Bolsheviks a crucial task ahead.

Although such a 'class approach' in dealing with the bureaucratic phenomenon continued to be applied, the problem was obviously 'bifocal': 'proletarisation' of the apparatus or not, inefficiency and bureau-pathology were growing and so were the numbers (and costs) of the administrations and their officials. 'Bureaucratism' (and 'bureaucratisation') was becoming over the years a huge problem per se, but the party line attributing bureaucratism to the legacy of the tsarist past and the country's backwardness hindered the emergence of a more potent analysis of *bureaucracy* as a social and political phenomenon. 'Proletarisation' of the apparatus as the ideologically correct remedy against 'bureaucratism' was proving to be ineffectual. The bureaucratic phenomenon has its own thrust and complexity that could not be expressed by just listing its much-deplored malfunctions. Many problems were not just due to inefficiency and backwardness – they stemmed from previously misunderstood social realities, past and present.

A better analysis and better-thought-out policies were needed but this was not achieved (nor was it seriously attempted) to the very end of the regime.

Opposing factions battled against bureaucratisation, especially inside the party: the party apparatus seemed to be taking over the party and thereby deeply changing its character. This kind of discovery led those who studied western writings or read historical works on the tsarist government to the awareness of a worrisome political feature inherent in bureaucracy, namely its propensity to become a contender for power. The leadership, willy-nilly, had to yield some ground. This was done, at first, by a slow process of offering some categories of officials rights previously reserved only for industrial workers. By the late 1920s an average official already earned much more than the average worker and top officials earned much more than the best-paid workers. In the 1930s, 'a status revolution' took place. As the state became the central tenet of Soviet socialism, the orientation of the regime switched from workers to officials. The class of state servants, the natural *carriers of the state principle*, moved to the foreground in ideology, in pace with their growing power in the state.

Full monopolisation of power by the bureaucracy would be the last stage in this process, that would take several decades to take its final shape. But, as just stated, ideology had already begun to follow reality in the 1920s, by trying to put a veil on the real processes at work. This required many manipulations, 'loans' from other ideologies and an eventual dumping of the founders' creed; concepts such as socialism, Marxism-Leninism and communism tended to become simply, especially in the 1930s, coextensive with whatever the system was doing at any given time. Many of the system's chief practitioners already used other, more convenient languages and rationales – and not just in private. Finally, class explanations were pushed aside, in substance, almost entirely. The enemy was now sought (and found) 'within', serving foreign 'intelligence services' from inside the party and its strongholds. Class origin stopped being a defence: doubting – let alone opposing, defending somebody whom 'the organs'[1] accused, or just formulating things differently, became heretical activities. As class concepts died, they were replaced by the 'demonisation principle'. Hence the prevailing method stopped practising social analysis of any kind, and turned instead to exorcism, to promoting a 'cult' and to uprooting undesirables by terror. We are, of course, talking about Stalinism.

Was Stalinism an emanation of bureaucracy, as was often claimed, notably by Trotsky? There was in Stalinism a considerable ambiguity in this respect: it was undergirded by bureaucracy, yet it considered bureaucracy both indispensable (hence the pampering of their upper layers) and unreliable (hence the repressions).

Research and studies conducted worldwide recognised bureaucracy as an immensely complicated phenomenon. It is known that bureaucratic layers possess their own autonomous aspirations (despite an image of impartial servants of the state they tend to propagate about themselves), that manifest themselves in their ability to mind and fight for their interests and their proven capacity to head off measures undertaken against them. This is why, despite their growing numbers, cost and often glaring inefficiencies, they seem to defy policies and measures of control, however severe. Moreover, on an even grander scale, state bureaucracies often succeeded in 'taming' the absolutism and despotism of rulers by making them follow bureaucratic procedures and routines. Making top bureaucrats out of capricious autocrats would be the aspiration of a bureaucracy behind which was also lurking its potential to become a contender to a share if not the fullness of political power in the state.

Stalin must have been aware of such problems. He studied the experience of the tsars, and the tendency of bureaucracies to 'regulate' absolutism could not have escaped his attention. He was certainly determined not to allow this to happen to him – and was, to some extent, successful on this score. Stalinism, in fact, made it impossible for the upper layers of bureaucracy to become a fully fledged ruling class. The essence of Stalin's policy consisted in ensuring his own and his system's security, by transforming his aims into the cornerstone of a specifically Stalinist mythology. Security agencies were called upon to uproot, en masse, presumed or potential enemies – notably, from amidst the regime's main levers, namely the state and party administrations. This was the quintessential Stalinist strategy which actually deprived the ruling party of its power and treated the state bureaucracy as a main

---

[1] 'The organs' referred to the Russian term 'organy bezopasnosti', i.e. security services. The public called them simply *organy* – with an unmistakable ironic connotation.

suspect of an unending web of sabotage activities against the regime, even if they actually *were, or were becoming, the regime.*

The Stalinist method of bloody purges looked like the ultimate weapon against the unstoppable growth, power, greed and malfunctions of the bureaucracy. But we will be able to demonstrate the futility of 'the ultimate weapon'. Purges, however bloody, were entirely useless as a method for changing bureaucracy's way of being. Weber maintained that, once created, bureaucracy was very difficult to destroy, or even – one can add – just to make change some of its ways. This was especially true in Soviet conditions of bureaucratic monopoly over the implementation of policies all over the system. Stalin realised, maybe before others, that the bureaucracy only looked like some transparent pyramid, awaiting assignments and easy to control from the top. In fact, it tended to split into powerful, difficult-to-coordinate bureaucratic fiefdoms, each aiming at full control over its respective domain and tending, if unopposed, to tear apart the state system, rendering planning not just indispensable but actually not feasible. In sum, though, it was a monopoly over the whole Soviet system that they harboured, not so much by design initially, but by a spontaneous thrust. When Soviet bureaucracy, after Stalin's death, finally achieved its goals, it became apparent that it was not capable of planning. At best, it was just 'administering', in fact rather 'overadministering' the domains under its tutelage. The moment it succeeded in becoming *the system* its thrust for a 'total' bureaucratisation turned out actually to have been a utopia, at least as far as the Soviet model went.

In any case, a full takeover of the system by the bureaucracy (even if it kept breeding plenty of little Stalins) was not possible, as long as Stalinism under Stalin himself still existed. Stalin's image – and shadow – were so powerful, both within and outside the USSR, that most observers abroad did not imagine this system being able to function without some Stalin replica at the helm. In fact, Stalin and Stalinism were replaced by a profoundly bureaucratic model, leading to a possible confirmation of the idea that Stalin himself must have been 'a creature of bureaucracy'.

Trends and stages

The society that Lenin inherited and was burdened with after the Civil War was more primitive than the tsarist one had been. In the desperate situation, compounded by the failure of revolutions in the West, the ground was ready, whatever 'ism' the central government embraced, to reproduce another version of an 'agrarian despotism'.

The idea of 'socialisation', central to any concept of the socialist ideology, took on the form of 'nationalisation', without reservations and nuances. Once this happened, one could observe – some even predicted – that the elites at the head of backward countries were condemned to becoming bureaucracies. In a devastated Russia after the Civil War, concentrating scarce material and intellectual resources at the centre and next (hopefully) spreading the experience and competence lower down looked like the obvious strategy to follow. But it was also a prescription for the scarce intellectual forces of the country to get sucked into the governmental process and to become part of a hierarchy that had a propensity toward metastatic growth. Something quite contrary to both democratisation and socialisation did occur, and persisted despite the development of industry and of large-scale schooling at a somewhat later stage.

Lenin must have realised this potential of his system quite early in the regime's history. He tried to escape the trap first by launching in early 1918 his idea of 'state capitalism', which might, by implication, have turned around the danger of an 'Asiatic' or 'agrarian' variety of despotism. The Civil War interrupted this line of thought, to be replaced by the NEP experiment which Lenin initially saw as another version of state capitalism. In any case, Lenin now began to formulate a new strategy best expressed by the slogan: no third revolution!

He was, in particular, extremely worried by phenomena of bureaucratisation in the new state. It was, probably, one of the factors that made him tell the Eleventh Party Congress that 'the car does not drive at all in the direction the driver steers it'[2] – this already in 1922! The Bolsheviks were still newcomers to the power game but unlike many of his collaborators, he had the courage to admit that the state and its *apparaty* were poorly understood and had a potential of dragging the new regime into uncharted and unwanted territory. Notably, they threatened to carry the regime back to the features of the past which seemed to penetrate the new system through many visible or barely visible capillaries, despite the resolve to destroy the old governmental machinery and build a new one. In fact, under Lenin and after him, the trends in the administrative machineries continued to move 'elsewhere', either spontaneously or as wanted from above, by the ever more powerful new 'driver'.

The making of the Soviet bureaucratic self, as presided over by the party, was full of painful rifts. The experts of the previous regime (the 'bourgeois specialists') were indispensable, especially in the highest and most sensitive administrations – but could not be trusted. The trustworthy rulers with good party credentials were not competent

---

[2] Lenin, *Sochineniia*, 5th edn, vol. 45, p. 86.

enough. They could suppress but they were dependent on the expertise of their 'bourgeois' subordinates and advisors in coping with their job requirements. Both sides, mostly, hated this situation. This kind of 'dual power' should have subsided in due course through the creation and promotion of Soviet-made cadres, but this, as we shall see, failed to materialise. The suspicion of 'antiparty' tendencies in the administrations continued unabated despite the fact that the bourgeois specialists were replaced, especially during the 1930s, by small and big bosses of a more reliable class origin. The previous (now diminishing) internal rift was compounded or replaced by a new one: in the key administrative *apparaty*, where higher specialisation and education were crucial, even the new bosses would still tend to be of 'non-proletarian', especially from intellectual or white-collar, origin. On the face of it, this vexing problem should have been solved by a full 'rehabilitation' of these non-proletarian but still 'soviet-made' officials. An ideological promotion of this attitude actually did begin, quite aggressively, in the 1920s, initially in relation to the party's own apparatus, notably in the form of defending party bureaucrats against the attacks by the intra-party oppositions: they were declared by the ruling majority to be the heart of the party, and an attack against the apparatus was presented as an attack on the party, whatever the social background of the officials.

This, of course, was not a problem of just defending them from the 'calumnies' of the critics (which had a valid point when railing against the bureaucratisation of the party). It reflected – as was already argued – a growing trend, early on in the Soviet experience, toward the making of an administrative class, ever more the real carrier, inside and outside the party, of, first, the 'nationalisation' principle as socialism par excellence and, second, of the state as the sole guarantor of the socialist system. The redefinition of the role of the party apparatus would be followed, in due course, by a similar 'rehabilitation' of the state apparatus at large, thus 'catching up' with a powerful objective trend.

In the meantime, already in the 1920s and more impetuously during the 1930s, governmental agencies and their bureaucracies were growing in complexity, evolving elaborate and numerous ranks and categories and an intricate maze of hierarchies. An equally intricate scaffolding of institutions was erected to control the spontaneous trends in the *apparaty* and to try to boost the very low level of their performance.

When RKI, a government inspectorate[3] was instructed in the 1920s to study the lower *apparat* and help improve their performance in the provinces, they realised that they knew next to nothing about these

---

[3] RKI stands for Raboche-Krest'ianskaia Inspektsiia (Workers' and Peasants' Inspection), a state agency for controlling and studying the state administrations.

administrations and how to go about doing this job. How were they going to 'reorganise' it? Ia. A. Iakovlev, the new head of RKI, admitted to being inexperienced: for example, he did not know that edicts from the centre were not implemented by the lower bodies, as long as they had not received a clear order from their direct supervisor. His pal Mikoian, the savvy head of Narkomtorg, already practised this art very skilfully and confided in Iakovlev how this was done.[4] Still, Iakovlev already knew enough to complain that the *apparat* resembled an 'organised barbarity'.[5]

Particularly critical was the level of the lower agencies. Krinitsky, from the party's organisational department, told a conference of the Union of State Employees that these agencies – including their planning departments – had no professional preparation whatsoever. And they were the ones that fed their superiors with their ignorant reporting.[6]

There are, incidentally, plenty of hair-raising stories about such reporting that could be found in the files of the central governmental agencies. Narkomfin, for example, deplored the fact that 'the state of reporting from the lower local echelons [was] catastrophic.'[7]

Despite such 'catastrophic' reporting, the pressure from above to report was equally bewildering. The matters that the wretched *nizovka* (local bureaucrats) were asked to report about were ridiculous and the task was virtually impossible. Consequently, the requests from above were mostly disregarded, pointing to the obvious conclusion that the top was not capable of getting its act together in coordinating the proliferating summits (*golovki*) of Moscow's offices. The development of a whole system of *uchraspredy* (personnel department) in the state agencies aimed at training and controlling their personnel, was one answer to the predicament. A description by Commissar of Labour Tsikhon of his own 'personnel sector' and its 'nomenklatura' (list of offices and officials under his Commissariat's autonomous jurisdiction), discovered in TsGAOR,[8] shows how intricate the organisation of such a sector was. The system of nomenklatura – with its complexities, routines and absurdities – was another maze. The task of defining, classifying the staffs (the so-called *shtatnoe raspisanie*) for the whole administration, looks like a Sisyphean one. Frequent reorganisations and dismissals of the officials (*chistki* or purges), and countless measures to curtail, make cheaper, prohibit proliferation, and simplify, amount to an agitated history that has not yet been written. A short

---

[4] TsGAOR, f. 374, e. khr. 320. pp. 91–2. These were minutes of an inter-departmental consultation concerning the lower rungs of the state apparatus.
[5] *Partiia v bor'be s biurokratizmom*, (Moscow 1928) p. 44.
[6] TsGAOR, f. 7709, 1, 2, pp. 305–7, April 1931.
[7] TsGAOR, f. 374, 6, 316, p. 23, on a meeting of Narkomfin with RKI officials, 2 February 1931.   [8] TsGAOR, f. 5515, 36, 6, pp. 71–3.

outline may offer enough of a glimpse: through the 1920s and early 1930s different departments were established to watch over staffing – finally (in 1935) the task was handed over to a 'special sector' in Narkomfin, in tandem with the STO (Council of Labour and Defence, no less) – to ensure that no administration hired more employees and paid them more than was allocated to its *shtat*.[9]

The controls, surveys, commissions and task forces were particularly preoccupied with the leading personnel (*Otvetrabotniki*), especially the very top (*rukovodiashchii sostav*) of, first, the top leadership in state administration and, next, the higher ranks in economic institutions. The policy of simultaneously pestering and pampering these echelons finally degenerated into both a massive destruction and an equally massive promotion of replacements. This was a desperate policy that contributed to the flux that pervaded the bureaucracies, and was more intense than in the social structure at large – itself in the throes of a set of upheavals – a key feature of the social landscape of the 1930s.

The other key feature – which was new – was the policy of promoting into the administration, through the party or otherwise, many people of popular extraction. This certainly increased support for the regime among the population, but also caused increased fluidity in the ranks, as well as lowering of the already very low educational standards, especially in the politico-administrative agencies. This made all the more painful the dependence on experts 'of alien ideology', in particular in the most crucial sectors of state activity where a high level of professionalism was needed but did not exist in the party ranks.

Dispatching instructors, plenipotentiaries and special envoys, mostly in the framework of one extraordinary endeavour after another (dubbed by critics 'campaign style' – *kampanejshchina*), was all part of the usual way of conducting national affairs in those years. Special task forces, under powerful trouble shooters from the Central Committee or the Politburo who wanted to see things done 'whatever the cost', were presented as the epitome of the party's administrative prowess. The same applied to 'extraordinary organs' (*politotdely*) recurred to in 'emergencies' – a strictly military conception, paralleling 'shock units' (*udarny gruppy*) – ordered to apply 'shock methods', which became the prevailing way of handling urgent tasks. This explains why so many things were, in fact, done 'on the double' – pointing, indirectly, to the leaders' dissatisfaction with the performance, or rather indolence, of the routine-oriented regular administrative agencies.

The handling of recruitment policies into the (swelling) administra-

---

[9] TsGANKh, f. 7733, 14, 1043, pp. 62 *et seq.*

tive machinery is in itself a good example of the tensions and contradictions that permeated policies during 'the big drive'. The government was constantly preaching that 'a Bolshevik order' should be imposed in the sphere of personnel (*shtaty*), their salaries and overhead costs. Rationalisation, simplification, curtailment of paperwork, mechanisation and introduction of piece-work in many offices were prodded to make the 'machinery' work systematically and smoothly.

What the Central Government was dreaming of transpires from a draft of a decree by the Council of Commissars (September 1929),[10] that requires officeworkers to achieve the following: 'A firm configuration of jobs, firm composition of staffs, firm salaries for each confirmed post.' The predominant term is 'firm' (*tverdyj*) – an aspiration obviously reacting to the flux and the spontaneity in the work of administrations that proved so difficult to handle. But it was an impossible dream. Routine work was inefficient and slothful, whereas political campaigns and shake-ups, although wasteful, seemed to achieve something. This points to the following feature of the 1930s: two models were operating simultaneously in the political arsenal, denoting the inherent 'split personality' of a state system, whose 'choleric' part tried to jolt its opposite that strived for predictability and settling down.

More 'realistic' for the longer run was the 'pampering' side of the policies, as opposed to the repressive measures. The 'status revolution' in favour of officials, reversing the preferential treatment accorded the workers earlier in the regime's history, continued through the 1930s.

Officially, the policy was presented as an 'innocently' sounding 'equalisation' of the living standards of soviet officials with workers, notably in offering equal access to lodging, social benefits and schools and, finally, in conditions of acceptance to party membership. In reality, and eventually in ideology, the trend was quite obviously not about 'equalising' but about producing a privileged layer and adapting ideology to the reality of the power that the strata of top and medium-ranking officials actually exercised. Making the state the centrepiece of the ideology opened the door to putting in the centre of things the main state (and party) servants – the leading cadres of higher state bodies. It became officially admitted already in the later 1920s that the top crust of the *apparaty* – by now 'proletarianised' and socially reliable (Soviet produced) – were to be called 'the leading cadres' and hostility toward them was to be treated as hostility to the state. The policy reached its predictable threshold, when it was at least semi-formally declared in the mid-1930s that there was no reason any more for the trade unions to engage in wage bargaining with management. Wage policies were

[10] TsGAOR, 5515, 26, 31, a file of the Commissariat of Labour (Narkomtrud).

firmly and, supposedly, safely lodged in the reliable hands of the economic management itself. Wages, an important tool of productivity, became in fact an almost exclusive and legitimate preserve of management. Nor were the unions to fuss any more about distortions of proletarian policies by administrators, as had often been ascertained by the trade unions and officially acknowledged by the party in the 1920s. Such distortions, the new official line ordered, were now successfully overcome, and the trade union should not defend workers but deal with social benefits, cultural activity and so on, as Stalin enjoined them to do.[11]

The less visible part of the policy was also pursued aggressively, often in secret, and consisted in offering privileges to the same 'leading cadres', in the form of high salaries, sizeable premiums, thirteen months' salary, hidden perks and supplies – and enormous power over their subordinates. These layers were all very strictly controlled, but they also had their own ways of amassing additional power and incomes, through a skilful manipulation of loopholes and structural features of the system. They suffered from the controls, but they also learned how to outmanoeuvre many of those, including the famous system of *nomenklatura*[12] that was supposed to be the ultimate controlling device. Nevertheless, the worst in arbitrary despotism made them, in particular their very top layer, into those uniquely powerful slaves, always on the brink of catastrophe. Their power and privileges were shadowed by a constant *memento mori*; until they got rid of the nightmare that hung over their heads.

1937–9: Kill them any way you like still . . .

Table 2.1 showing the growth of officialdom during the years 1928–39 provides only a tentative computation of a few selected indicators – but the growth factor is quite obvious. One source estimated a 15 per cent annual growth for the 1930s, but it was not clear from this source what categories were included. The numbers used in the tables come from population censuses for 1926 and 1959 (the latter contains data from the unpublished 1939 census) and from articles in *Statisticheskoe Obozrenie*.[13]

[11] E. Evreinov, *O svoeobraznom krizise profsoiuzov i ob ikh novykh zadachakh* (Moscow 1936), pp. 27–8.

[12] *Nomenklatura* related to a system of nominations where each layer of leadership – from the Central Committee, through the ministries and to heads of departments – is assigned responsibility for either direct nomination of or just the right to confirm candidates presented by the lower echelons. The party's control of the top layer of officials cannot be overestimated but many observers overlooked the complexity of the whole system, its numerous countervailing trends that often frustrated the wishes of the controllers, in this as in many other spheres of the bureaucratic realm.

[13] *Statisticheskoe Obozrenie*, especially No. 5 (1928), pp. 92–4.

Table 2.1 *The growth of officialdom, 1928–39*

	Admin. personnel	Leading officers	Total white-collar workers	
1928	1,451,564	600,000	3,974,836	(4.8%)*
1939	7,505,010	1,557,983	13,821,452	(15.5%)*

*The percentages in parentheses show the share of all white-collar workers in the total labour force.

The figures should be used only as indicators of trends, not as statistically warranted givens.

I have tried to single out the category of 'administrative personnel' from the broader category of 'officials' or – better – blue-collar employees (*sluzhashchie*) that also included teachers, scientists, and medical personnel who certainly do not qualify as 'bureaucrats' or 'administrators'. *Sluzhashchie* include all white-collar employees drawing a salary. 'Bosses' (*rukovodiashchie rabotniki*) include the higher or leading ranks of the bureaucratic or administrative offices.

The table shows the number of those employed in 'administrative offices', (*unchrezhdeniia*), the number of bosses among them, and the total number of white-collar workers in the labour force.

In the table, the figures for 'Admin. personnel', as said, do not include medical, pedagogic, and scientific personnel whom Soviet statisticians included in the *sluzhashchie* category. Neither do the figures include engineers and technicians employed in the economy who qualify for the category of 'white-collar' but not of 'bureaucrats' or 'administrators', although many of them certainly worked in 'offices' and held administrative (managerial) jobs. Hence, we are focusing on administrative jobs in the governmental machinery, meaning mostly the administrators (and their staffs) of central and local state agencies, who do not directly produce goods (like factories) or dispense services (like schools, hospitals and stores). The administrators of the latter institutions, though state employees in the Soviet conditions, did not belong to the state apparatus that we are trying to pinpoint. Calculations can also be made of the number of employees in central ministries and other top agencies, as well as in regional ones. Further classifications of the personnel into leading-administrative echelons and personnel who assisted the latter – those being subdivided into 'operative' (middle-level) managers and 'auxiliary clerical personnel' – are also possible, because there are figures for each of these categories. But they are rarely comparable. Most of the available data are not stating clearly what categories of officials were included at different points in time.

Whatever the statistical reliability of the data[14] for the later 1930s (1937–9) they were particularly alarming for the party leadership: general employment in the economy rose by 10.3 per cent (mainly in commerce, education, and health), the overall salary fund rose 41 per cent. But the number of officials in administrative-managerial positions in the different government offices rose (between March 1937 and September 1939) by 26.6 per cent, the central offices of the USSR, of the republics and lower down to the districts, showed a particularly alarming growth of more than 50 per cent in numbers of officials. Their salary fund grew by 66.5 per cent.

Even more pronounced was the increase in the number of officials in the personnel of trusts, procurement and supply bureaus, numerous so-called cost-accounting agencies (*khozraschetnye* – servicing the economic enterprises); they grew by 35.6 per cent. General employment in industry grew only 2.1 per cent, whereas numbers of employees in those *khozraschet* organisations serving industry increased by 26.3 per cent. In construction enterprises the overall number of personnel declined, their service bureaus grew by 29.8 per cent. The numbers of establishments of direct trade grew by 16.1 per cent but their employees expanded by 39.3 per cent.

The general cost of such *khozraschet* organisations grew 50 per cent: all in just about two years.

The continuing growth of the economy during the 1930s necessitated the breaking up of large ministries into smaller ones and of the older vast administrative units of the state into new smaller districts, to allow for more flexible management. But all these indispensable measures resulted, again, in more growth of staffs and overhead costs, rather than in outputs and efficiency. A disquieting inflation of staffs (*razduvanie shtatov*) occurred because the new small agencies (*narkomaty*) or smaller districts (*raiony, oblasti*) replicated automatically the old top-heavy, complicated multi-tier structures. This in turn entailed an enormous splintering (*drobimost'*) of supply and marketing offices (the notorious (*snaby i sbyty*), and the appearance of all kinds of superfluous segments of *apparaty* and a plethora of far-fetched jobs, with an ensuing growth of their salaries. The 'swelling' was smaller in management offices of production units than in the rest of the officialdom, but even in those managerial offices – as well as in designer and project organisations, in the transportation sector, in urban development and so on – overemployment and imbalances among different sectors took on menacing proportions. In 1940 another effort was undertaken to reduce the

---

[14] E. Vasil'ev, *Planovoe Khoziajstvo*, 9 (1940), pp. 27–8.

number of officials, notably by increasing the working hours in offices. This was decreed by the Government on 16 July 1940 and was seen as a chance to curtail the staffs and make them more flexible. The war, quite naturally, reduced numbers of officials but after the war, and even after the 'departure' of the dictator, centralisation remained and with it the heavy weight of bureaucracy. By then, even the serious improvements in standards of education – low standards having been an important factor in the earlier formative stages – did not arrest the ailments that kept wrecking the state agencies: among them 'institutional inflexibility', comparable to the hardening of arteries in human beings,[15] or the proverbial *vedomstvennost'* – the fierce departmental 'patriotism' of the agencies.

The efforts to contain, make cheaper and curtail the officialdom through different control methods and mass purges proved to be of no avail, and the pertinent sources paint a pathetic state of affairs: beginning with the early pronouncements of Lenin, through those of Orjonikidze in 1932, Bukharin in 1934, and a wealth of publications, appearing notably just before the war – all express bewilderment and helplessness.

The enormous and unjustified growth, cost, proliferation, inefficiency, nepotism, narrow-mindedness, false reporting, inflexibility and arbitrariness defied all party and other controls.

One is tempted to derive 'the big purges' – Stalin's recourse to the ultimate method of camps and killings – from this impotence in overcoming the bureaucratic maze and their skilful dodging of most government controls and injunctions. But physical elimination of officials did not eliminate the sociology of this layer: no purges could have done this. The material quoted earlier from *Planovoe Khoziaistvo* illustrates this point convincingly. The purges were a policy that had nothing to do with any serious analysis or relation to reality. The inner tendencies of higher and lower layers of the *apparaty* continued, although the quality of their performance dropped sharply as did their morale. Their ethical world and their psychological equilibrium were certainly impaired, because so many of them were demoted, exiled, arrested or executed. Still their numbers kept growing and this is why I could present my figures without bothering about the complex problem of the scale of the 'turnover' inside bureaucracy that the purges inflicted on them.

These traits of the bureaucracy, whatever its resemblance, in many ways, to the tsarist one, could not be ascribed any more to 'the past'. They grew from the conditions inherent in the Soviet system: wholesale

---

[15] Marshall E. Dinnick, in *Reader in Bureaucracy*, eds. Robert K. Merton *et al*, (New York–London 1952), p. 402.

nationalisation, elimination of markets and of diversified sectors in the economy and society, predominantly administrative methods in planning.

Older thinkers and Soviet realities

A few ideas, borrowed from western students of bureaucracy, can enrich the reflection on the trends we describe. Max Weber[16] maintained that domination is inherent in any organisation, especially in the big ones. Smaller and simpler organisations allow democratic forms, but once they grow and get complex a fight for power begins and direct democratic forms lose their character. Political parties are created, but those are about domination, by definition; and this trend too tends to subvert democracy. A special structure of professional administration appears 'which of necessity means the exercise of domination' and may become 'monocratic', so that all the functionaries are integrated into a hierarchy culminating in one single 'head'.[17] When reading such ideas it becomes clear that we do not need to live under any 'Leninism' to encounter phenomena like this.

Similar lessons can be learned from 'the iron law of oligarchy' which was formulated by Robert Michels (1915), later documented nicely in the early 1930s by Max Adler[18] who examined trends in the social-democratic parties and confirmed Michels' findings: the leadership (administration) is needed because of growth and complexity; in due course enough wealth and power gets amassed to be worth preserving and this weighty fact discourages policy-makers from risking damaging losses. Next comes the stage when[19] the tool gets transformed into an ideal, or an aim per se – thus actually leading to a dumping of the ideal, although lip service may still be paid by using some quite radical formulae.

Turning to Weber again, we borrow from Wolfgang Mommsen quotes from Weber's *Wirtschaft und Gesellschaft* in which he stated that 'a bureaucracy, once it is fully implanted, belongs to the range of social formations that are most difficult to destroy'.[20] A British student of bureaucracy emphasised that bureaucracy was a work environment for millions of people. Work being formative of the very identity of individuals, the bureaucratic world is a powerful social milieu that

---

[16] Max Weber, *On Law And Society* (New York 1954, pbk 1967), pp. 333–7.

[17] Ibid., p. 334.

[18] T. Bottomore and P. Goode (eds.), *Austro-Marxism* (Oxford 1978), pp. 229–39.

[19] Cf. Jacques Elliot, *A General Theory of Bureaucracy* (London–New York 1977) and *passim*, but also the dangers of bureaucratisation, p. 344.

[20] I cite from the French translation of Wolfgang Mommsen's *Max Weber et la politique allemande* (Paris 1985), p. 219.

shapes human beings as a mass. Other authors contended that giant bureaucracies are on the level of governments: they are not really part of the national competition but more of the domain of national economic planning.[21]

These are only a few examples from western thinkers that point to phenomena observed in the West, anticipating, or partly in common with those observed in the Soviet case.

But in the Soviet conditions, some of the same processes went much farther: unlike in the West, bureaucracy did become *the polity*. Hence, the bureaucratic mentality became even more powerful a factor in shaping all or most human relations. Also relevant to the Soviet experience is Weber's observation that the absolute dictator 'is often completely in the power of his bureaucracy since . . . he has no means of discovering whether his policies are being enforced'.[22] This does not contradict the argument about Stalin's anti-bureaucratic urges. Instead, it actually anticipates much of the essence of Stalinism, leading to my idea of 'institutional paranoia' writ large – a sense of powerlessness, developing in the narrow leadership apex, and later in the one-man apex, that increases or persists as more power is amassed and centralised. Moreover, taking a clue from Weber again,[23] Soviet bureaucracy was not 'modern' as some were elsewhere. 'A real bureaucracy' was normally paid in cash. In the Soviet case, the hidden privileges and supplies were actually payments *in natura* – like in ancient subsistence economies – making them into some kind of an in-between formation.

It is also worth reflecting on Soviet bureaucracy's 'retardation' from another angle: the bureaucrats were the guarantor and main tool in the lifting of a devastated country from misery. They also helped to build a state system and its services – all run by bureaucracies. This monopoly over implementation of policies was a key problem, only temporarily camouflaged by the supposed control by the party, the presumed sovereign, hence 'employer', of these bureaucracies. The ideological claim of workers' supervision in the 'workers' state' lost any credibility quite early in the regime's history. The monopolistic manager of all of the state's resources was following its inner thrust to develop the country. But by denying enough freedom of action to autonomous agents – factories, organisations, movements, institutions – this 'manager' was saddled with the direct control over the whole economy–policy–society complex. This was bound to lead well beyond its capacity to cope effectively with a job like that. In a system where everything is done by government agencies, not much or nothing,

[21] Kenneth Galbraigth, quoted by Elliot, *General Theory of Bureaucracy*, p. 329.
[22] In Hans Gerth and Mills Wright, *From Max Weber* (New York 1944), p. 234.
[23] Cf. Ibid., pp. 204 *et seq.*

except in the making of 'malfunctions' comes from below. Operating on such a scale without an appropriate societal input was a mighty source of backwardness in itself. It is symptomatic that in the industrial sphere, even when machines, such as excavators, were available and could have alleviated the burden of primitive toil, it was reported that workers did not want to use them and managers preferred to resort to a crude labour force. The fact was noted, for example, by Central Committee member Ian Rudzutak's in his speech to the Seventeenth Party Congress.[24] He spoke of construction works but a similar and widespread anti-mechanisation trend could be observed in industry, culminating in a powerful thrust inside industry, from below and from above, against innovation and modernisation of equipment and administrative practices. Similar tendencies could be observed, in many ways, all over the bureaucracy.

In this context, it could be illuminating to realise the enormous weight and numbers of *praktiki*, or cadres promoted on the job to run administrations or take up engineering positions on railroads, with trusts and in factories, without adequate professional training. They composed, for example, 40 per cent of the whole leading apparatus of the railroads by the end of 1938, at a time when well over three-fourths of those *apparaty* were just freshly promoted to replace the thousands of purged functionaries and specialists.[25] For such cadres, except for the most gifted among them, assimilating only the most superficial routines then in practice was a major challenge of a life-time.

These trends had a boomerang effect also on the party apparatus. The crucial party apparatus that was also growing larger and more complicated during the 1930s exhibited the same, seemingly incongruous development of 'power lines': on one hand was the growing personal power of Stalin who decided on everything he wanted, in all the meetings of all the bodies. On the other was the swelling (*razbukhanie*) of the party apparatus which became unwieldy and inefficient,[26] in its efforts to shadow and thereby duplicate the government machinery. The apparatus of the Central Committee was endowed in 1939 with large-scale administrative departments, such as the one for 'Propaganda and Agitation' or 'the Department for Cadres' which, under Malenkov, had forty-five subunits.

Also in the same 1939, the apparatus of the Central Committee of the Ukraine alone employed 222 'responsible functionaries' and 90 techni-

[24] *Semnadsatyj s'ezd VKP (b)* (Moscow 1934), pp. 284–5.
[25] *Zhelezodorozhnyj transport v gody industrializatsii SSSR (1926–1941)* (Moscow 1970), pp. 309–10.
[26] Data on the party are taken from V. G. Kolychev in *Trsidtsatye gody: vzgliad iz segodnia*, ed. D. A. Volkogonov (Moscow 1990), p. 24.

cal workers. Unfortunately, the source of these data did not provide global figures for the party apparatus of the USSR. This was, as we know, a period when the number of ministries and so-called higher Agencies in the government was growing from 10 in 1924, to 18 in 1936, with a leap to 41 in 1940 (plus state committees with a Commissariat status like Gosplan, Grain Procurements, Higher Education, Artistic Affairs – again, with proliferating staffs).[27] To match its controlling ability, the party organisations below the central level also created in their own *apparat* numerous branch departments with growing numbers of heads, instructors and technical services.

The parts of the sprawling administrative machinery were not enjoying delegation of powers to do the things they were created for. The opposite was true. In internal affairs everything was not just centralised but even concentrated in a tight-fisted way (*zatsentralizovano*). The Politburo meetings would deal with hundreds of items – obviously, not in any depth – which included minutiae that did not belong to such a high level of decision-making and sometimes not to the next lower ones.

We see therefore a phenomenon with a Catch-22 quality to it: the growing Stalinist centralisation has as its counterpart, unavoidably, the growth (overgrowth) of party and state *apparaty*, proverbially inefficient. But it also worked the other way round: the growth of large, inefficient bureaucracies seems to call for . . . more centralisation.

These data and trends underscore again the essential feature specific to the Soviet system: because of the state's involvement in running the economy, the bulk of its officials in state and party administrations, the overwhelming majority of whom were party members, were engaged in the economy. We can find here the seeds of future trouble. Since the elimination of the NEP, collectivisation of agriculture and the big industrialisation drive, the takeover of the economy by ministerial machineries was complete. This allowed the system to achieve, initially, important targets. But this was management without responsibility for results (except before the party). And it caused the administrations to be forever glutted by functions that these kinds of agencies were not designed for.

As long as there was a Stalin at the top, he could use fear to force people to work – but not to work efficiently. His terror was arbitrary, not really a retribution for anything particular or predictable, and even the best performance was no shield against repressions.

The monopoly and supposed cohesion that the popular totalitarian model implied was, in many ways, a fiction in these conditions: the

---

[27] Numbers of ministries (*narkomaty*) are from an unpublished paper by the Russian historian V. P. Naumov that was presented to our conference on Germany and Russia.

specialised, functional administrations became a basis for the crystal-lisation of powerful departmental vested interests and the overall system turned out extremely refractory to effective coordination. The perennial bargaining and infighting actually blocked the system's capacity to act – despite the illusion that a strong top leadership in a dictatorship can always have things its way; except for some areas considered to be of top priority, mostly in the realm of security.

Leroi-Beaulieu already knew how important independent courts could be for the taming of bureaucracy and, maybe, for containing some of its worst features.[28] Checking of *apparaty* by other *apparaty* could be counterproductive. There is enough evidence to maintain that the key agency for such controls in the early 1930s – the RKI – was itself afflicted by bureaucratisation. The idea of having independent courts, in addi-tion to internal administrative inspectors, was a plausible one during the NEP. The reliance though on the party as controller of the *apparat*, with the hoped-for help from the masses, was nearer to the hearts of a number of Bolshevik leaders.

But Bolshevism was not there any more, once the relations of power transformed the party itself into an agency badly in need of being supervised by somebody.

Stalin and bureaucracy

I doubt that Stalin was 'the creature of bureaucracy', as Trotsky claimed, though he built bureaucratic structures and used them as best he could. But he may have been their creature by 'negation', in the same sense that he was, to a large extent, dominated psychologically by the image of Trotsky and thus was Trotsky's creature. Stalin can be seen as the anti-Christ of bureaucratic structures – and, in this sense, their product. They were 'dedicated' to him, no doubt, but this does not change the underlying momentum of their development which went against his system.

Stalin was rather the creature of his party which he himself helped shape as its general secretary and a master of its *apparat*. Although he was not the party's founder, he overwhelmed the small group of top leaders, most of whom supported him, to become a despot dominating his associates.

In this situation the problem of 'taking over' and taming the despot by

---

[28] Anatole Leroi-Beaulieu, *L'empire des tsars et les Russes*, I–III (Paris 1881–9), still an astonishingly valid work. Volume II deals with the institutions of the state, the judicial reforms of 1884 being described in book 4, chapter 1. The bureaucracy hated these reforms because they gave the courts an independence which could effectively block or thrust back bureaucratic arbitrariness and power.

the bureaucracy proved impossible. The same conditions that made society fluid induced the same fluidity into the administrations and constrained their ability to solidify and defend their interests. The enormous structural shifts and a cascade of crises in the early 1930s worked in the opposite direction: they favoured the establishment of the new autocracy rather than a bureaucratic countermodel.

Another factor deepened further the oppressive-despotic features of the political system: the state that 'owned and ran' the industry and the rest of the economy. The efforts in the economic field were permeated by a prevalence of state power and the spread of networks of its officials. Markets and civil society of the short-lived NEP having been pushed out, two further models of Soviet history emerged: first Stalin's version of an 'agrarian despotism' in the shorter run, followed by 'a state-bureaucratic monopoly', after the two had coexisted unhappily for a time. 'The dual model' inside Stalinism that grew from the enormous tasks and the prevalence of the mobilisational methods it required was not and could not have been to the bureaucracy's taste. Brought to a paroxysm under Stalin much of its fury was directed against party and state administrations.

Bureaucracy as a stratum and a powerhouse weathered this ordeal and came out victorious, in the longer run, although it still managed to obtain small victories under Stalin, when it clipped the wings of some shock campaigns, such as Stalin's preferred Stakhanovism that actually aimed at shaking up the bureaucrats by unleashing – so Stalin hoped – the initiative and pride of workers. In conditions of Soviet state ownership, bureaucracy was not replaceable. If a problem emerged and was acknowledged, the method was generally the same: send powerful trouble shooters to solve problems. But they too would end up creating yet another office with officials, carriers of the routine-oriented model. This combination of contradictory pulls in the monopolistic state was at the root not only of Stalinist supercentralisation but also of its nemesis, namely the reproduction of the centre's arbitrariness (Stalinism was *this* by definition), by the multiplication from below of Stalin replicas at all levels of the administration ('the little Stalins'). This process reveals the paradoxical, 'impossible' side in Stalinism: the capricious supercentraliser was giving away power by default. Each 'little Stalin' could be destroyed but was immediately replaced.

The reflection on the 'impossible Stalinism' should point to a broader and peculiar set of paradoxes at work: despotism cannot operate without shock methods (*udarnost''*). Bureaucracy cannot work with them. Despotism develops hierarchy but hierarchy cannot support despotism which denies the very importance of hierarchy. Despotism works arbitrarily and spreads its effects over the system, corrupting the *apparaty* and destroying their self-importance and their capacity to act as bodies and as powerholders. Despotism depends on bureaucracy but cannot trust it. Stalinism's numerous 'paradoxes' were actually an expression of this model's 'impossibility': it stopped solving vital tasks of state. Instead, it found itself at odds with the better results of its own developmental drive, but also incapable of tackling the negative ones.

Borrowing from Hans Rosenberg

We have already made the point that much of what was going on in the Soviet *apparaty* was universal. But producing Stalinism was another matter. When reading Hans Rosenberg's *Bureaucracy, Aristocracy and Autocracy*, one is tempted to apply to the Stalinist phase a variation on this theme, namely: 'Bureaucracy, Partocracy and Despotism'.

But as we study the processes at work under this heading, and the subsequent transition into the second, post-Stalinist stage, we can revert to another of Rosenberg's terms – 'bureaucratic absolutism' – that expresses well the model that was to replace Stalinism and was already emerging earlier, despite the powerful muzzle put on it by the 'mobilisational' methods. Although interwoven, the two were nevertheless distinctive and, finally, contradictory processes and models of a polity. After Stalin's death the key features of personal despotism were dismantled.

In the course of over half a century, preceding and following Stalinism and maturing under Brezhnev, bureaucracy went from a suspect and barely tolerated layer, through a partly rehabilitated one, to highly privileged but again suspect and terrorised congeries of 'powerful serfs'.

'The third avenue' – neither working class nor party – was in these conditions still just a potentiality, often actually denied by some marxists for whom a bureaucracy could never become a ruling class. In fact, they could not yet become a solid and stable layer capable of an open and efficient defense of their rights against the party leadership. Surreptitious, though less directly challenging ways were available but more meaningful changes began to appear soon after Stalin's death.

His despotism brought back an old trait of the erstwhile Moscovite princes as owners of all the state's lands (which are given to servants, making them into a gentry or nobility). Stalin's rule did make him into a de facto owner of all land and of the other resources, including the labour force. Once he disappeared the collective ownership of the hierarchy's summit appeared quite clearly – but without an individual or group appropriation by key players at the top (except as manifestations of corruption, mostly as misappropriations of consumer goods). The power over the labour force also changed its character considerably and 'the agrarian despotism' period was over. The bureaucracy now blossomed into a fully fledged ruling class. An elite is only part of it – mostly composed of the top layers of the bureaucracy. A class is a larger and more complex social construct, where the elite's power is backed by numerous lower ranks or layers inside the framework and by different social groups in the population outside it. At the same time, in the Soviet case, there was no doubt about who ran and actually owned the national economy: few other ruling classes in modern times have had this kind of monopoly.

The takeover of real power in the system by the bureaucracy went hand-in-glove with its de facto emancipation from the party, including the 'neutralisation' and co-optation by the bureaucracy of the *nomenklatura* system that was devised to control it. This happened thanks to the fact that the tool of control was also a two-way street: the controlled, as insider, can take over the tool from the controller.[29]

The new stage that began with the elevation of Khrushchev started by reinvigorating the system and engendering a new dynamism in society and the polity and still larger intra-systemic changes seemed imminent. But the ruling bureaucratic power grid, on its way to its own pinnacle, stalled reforms. It replaced 'the cult of Stalin' by the 'cult of the state' and further consequences of this change unfolded inexorably. The bureaucracy successfully eliminated the most unpalatable elements of Stalinism – notably all those that were damaging to itself – but it also succeeded in disarming the party, by making it into its own 'ruling servant'. Once this was achieved a super-monopoly ensued – a system of 'bureaucratic absolutism' Soviet style, quite unprecedented in the twentieth century. Yet, this moment of supreme power also revealed that this class was not able any more to handle any business except protecting its privileges. It had no serious leaders and it was ideologically vacuous, demoralised

---

[29] The Soviet bureaucracy, although a mainstay and key feature of the system, did not attract enough attention from scholars and there are very few monographs to help produce a broader synthetic picture. This is why the pioneering works that appeared rather recently (and some of the older ones) should be greeted. In William G. Rosenberg and Lewis H. Siegelbaum (eds.), *Social Dimensions of Soviet Industrialization* (Bloomington and Indianapolis 1993), the reader will find five chapters by R. W. Davies, Don K. Rowny, Hiroki Kuromiya, Lewis Siegelbaum and David Shearer, on different echelons of the industrial administration. Prof. Don K. Rowny, a pioneer in this sphere, deals here with the new industrial commissariats. In his earlier book *Transition to Technocracy: The Structural Origins of The Soviet Administrative State* (Ithaca, New York 1989) he studied Soviet bureaucracy till 1928. Important pioneering works were offered much earlier by Armstrong and by T. H. Rigby. The latter used the concept of 'mono-organisational Society' and applied it to the Soviet system. See his paper in *Stalinism: Essays in Historical Interpretation*, ed. Robert C. Tucker (New York 1977). Rigby also produced a study of the Sovnarkom under Lenin.

and often corrupt. The era of *perestroika* was a logical outcome of this situation.

Addendum

Eric Olin Wright's summary of Weber's 1917 essay on 'Parliament and Government in Reconstructed Germany'[30] is a good source to borrow ideas from when studying the causes of Soviet bureaucracy's demise. One of the crucial factors would be the party's loss of ability to produce strong and effective leaders. This would square with the broader statement (my own thesis) about the party having lost its political role and becoming just a part of the bureaucracy itself. In this case Weber's thesis as to why a bureaucracy is incapable of producing political leaders (who are supposed to be adept at formulating global policies and mobilising the population in support of it) is valid in the Soviet case too. Also missing in the Soviet case was answerability of the leadership to an electorate or to an established institutional setting, this being a precondition of its being 'political' that is, being capable, among other tasks, of reining in the pernicious potentials of bureaucracy and imposing on it the implementation of political programmes. Weber postulated the need for leaders (who also run the bureaucracy) to be answerable to parliament: but according to Olin (who agrees on this point with Lenin) this is not enough. The class composition (of the parliament), which Weber disregarded in this context, may prevent real popular answerability. The latter was not Weber's aim. Weber was interested in powerful leadership, not in the parliamentary body per se. Parliaments were for him mainly a school from which leaders can appear – not the depositories of popular sovereignty. Weber's leaders would be 'charismatic' – hence, sovereign by definition. Obviously, 'a charismatic bureaucrat' would be a contradiction in terms.

The party could have played (and actually did play) the role of a 'school of leadership' that Weber saw mainly in parliaments, and it also could – to some extent – exercise control over bureaucracy as long as it still preserved its supra-bureaucratic (political) role, in the sense of being run by institutions that enjoy a modicum of democratic procedures in their work. We know that this feature was dwindling fast, especially during the later 1920s. It would be interesting to explore in some other context whether and when Soviet leaders were still 'politicians' and when did they become 'bureaucrats'.

[30] Eric Olin Wright, 'To Control or Smash Bureaucracy: Weber and Lenin on Politics, the State and Bureaucracy', *Berkeley Journal of Sociology*, 19 (1971–5), pp. 69–108.

3

Cumulative radicalisation and progressive self-destruction as structural determinants of the Nazi dictatorship

Hans Mommsen

The National Socialist regime is in many respects a peculiar phenomenon which does not fit theories of comparative government. There have been numerous attempts to arrive at a consistent description of the Nazi state, among them Franz Neumann's model of the 'Behemoth' state, alluding to Thomas Hobbes,[1] and Ernst Fraenkel's theory of the 'dual state', distinguishing between a normative and an arbitrary sector of state power.[2] Both depicted only the early stages of Nazi dictatorship, while the diversity of explanations based on the concept of totalitarianism, including the assumption that Nazism was essentially 'Hitlerism', as Hans Buchheim claimed, accentuated the personal aspects of Hitler's rule.[3] All these patterns of explanation tend to omit the point that the Nazi dictatorship was characterised by an inherent tendency towards self-destruction. It did not so much expand governmental prerogative through bureaucratic means as progressively undermined hitherto effective public institutions through arbitrary use of power. An accelerating fragmentation of the administrative apparatus was increasingly accompanied by the formation of new independent administrative bodies controlled by the party and promoting their own agendas. While this procedure of creating new ad hoc agencies increased the regime's short-term efficiency, it ultimately led to a dissolution of the unity and authority of the government. In some respects, Nazi expansionist policy accelerated the process of internal dissolution, because the methods of rule in the occupied territories were subsequently transferred to the Reich itself and contributed to the progressive destruction of public administration, which became more and more controlled by party functionaries.[4]

---

[1] Franz Neumann, *Behemoth* (London 1942); cf. Ernst A. Menze, *Totalitarianism Reconsidered* (London 1981).   [2] Ernst Fraenkel, *The Dual State* (London 1981).
[3] Hans Buchheim, *Totalitäre Herrschaft, Wesen und Merkmale* (3rd edn, Munich 1964).
[4] Cf. Dieter Rebentisch, *Führerstaat und Verwaltung im Zweiten Weltkrieg* (Stuttgart 1989), pp. 175–6.

Thus, National Socialism, by exploiting all the elements of a fully shaped modern state, eventually developed into the opposite of one, and formed an anti-state. This development, however, could not be visualised when Hitler came to power. In fact, the Dictator avoided any open break with the Weimar Constitution and in 1935 rejected the proposal of Wilhelm Frick, the Reich Minister of the Interior, to replace the Enabling Act by a constitution for the German Reich, since he regarded this as a revolutionary step which he wanted to avoid.[5] Nor did Hitler formally replace the republican state apparatus, whose foundations had been laid in preconstitutional Prussia, despite the expectations of his followers that he would grant the executive functions to the Nazi Party in line with the assurance in *Mein Kampf* that the 'transfer of National Socialist ideas of law' to the state would be achieved.[6]

Contrary to such expectations of the party radicals, represented especially by Ernst Röhm and the SA-leadership, Hitler did not give the Nazi Movement immediate access to executive functions. He transferred the party leadership to the weak but loyal Rudolf Hess, who acted as his Deputy Leader and entered the cabinet as minister without portfolio. It took several years, however, until Hess could secure for his staff a certain amount of control and an effective veto power over the legislative process. In general, the party rank and file felt pushed into the background by an ever more self-confident state administration.[7]

The influence of the party was exerted rather by frequent cases of personal union on the level of the *Oberpräsidenten* and minister in *Länder* administration. But in principle the Reich government remained independent of the political organisation of the NSDAP, which had merely informal control. The role of Rudolf Hess and, until June 1934, of Ernst Röhm as ministers without portfolio in the cabinet was insignificant. As a mass organisation, the party's prerogatives were restricted to a certain influence at the municipal level, control over ordinary citizens, and propaganda tasks.

This changed during the later war years when party agencies achieved an increasing influence at the regional and municipal levels

[5] See Martin Broszat, *Der Staat Hitlers. Grundlegung und Entwicklung seiner inneren Verfassung* (Munich 1969), pp. 316–2; cf. Günter Neliba, *Der Legalist des Unrechtsstaates: Wilhelm Frick, Eine politische Biographie* (Paderborn 1992), pp. 155 ff.
[6] Adolf Hitler, *Mein Kampf* 67th edn (Munich 1933), p. 657.
[7] Symptomatic are the complaints by the *Hoheitsträger* at their meeting with Hess at the end of the party rallies; cf. Hans Mommsen, "Hitlers Stellung im nationalsozialistischen Herrschaftssystem', in *Der 'Führerstaat': Mythos und Realität, Studien zur Struktur und Politik des Dritten Reiches*, eds. Gerhard Hirschfeld and Lothar Kettenacker (Stuttgart 1981), p. 44.

and the *Gauleiter*, in their function as Reich Defence Commissioners, took over substantial parts of the internal administration. Before that, party-controlled agencies such as the police apparatus, the Four-Year Plan, and, not least, the Reich Propaganda Ministry extended their spheres of control at the cost of the traditional ministries of state. In contrast to Stalin, who in 1936 proclaimed the Soviet Constitution, Hitler avoided any institutional changes that could restrict his unlimited political power. He rejected Frick's proposal to bring about a comprehensive restructuring of the Nazi state, to be reflected in a new constitution. He preferred to prolong the Enabling Law despite the fact that it had been repeatedly violated and partly disrupted through the merger of the office of the Reich President with that of the Reich Chancellor. Surprisingly, as one of his last acts before his suicide, Hitler decided again to separate the offices of the Reich President and the Reich Chancellor.[8]

The political process was affected by a continuous erosion of inherited institutional patterns through increasingly informal modes of decision-making. This started with Hitler's apprehension about cabinet meetings, at which he disliked debate with ministers on political issues, thereby exposing him to their specific expertise regarding legislative measures. Hence, he induced them to settle interdepartmental conflicts before a matter was to be presented in cabinet, which therefore functioned merely as an affirmatory board for legislative proposals put forward by individual government departments. Hence, the cabinet lost its function of coordinating competing departmental interests, and consequently ceased to be a means of political integration.[9]

Hitler lost all interest in cabinet meetings, therefore, and they were eventually abolished and replaced by a less formalised legislative procedure based on written communication between the departments involved. This proved to be extremely slow, and for urgent matters special meetings of the undersecretaries of state sought, by replacing the cabinet, to achieve the necessary coordination. The most notable example of such routine meetings is the Wannsee Conference in January 1942 to coordinate the measures for the deportation of the European Jews.

While institutionalised political integration at the level of the ministries became almost exceptional, their coordinating function was not

---

[8] Cf. Reimer Hansen, *Das Ende des Dritten Reiches. Die deutsche Kapitulation 1945* (Stuttgart 1966), pp. 93–4; Marlis G. Steinert, *Die 23 Tage der Regierung Dönitz* (Düsseldorf 1967), pp. 19–20.
[9] See Lothar Gruchmann, 'Die "Reichsregierung" im "Führerstaat". Stellung and Funktion des Kabinetts im nationalsozialistischen Herrschaftssystem', in *Klassenjustiz und Pluralismus, Festschrift für Ernst Fraenkel*, eds. Günther Doecker and Wilfried Steffani (Hamburg 1973), pp. 187–223.

replaced by party agencies. In complete contrast to what took place under Communist regimes, Hitler prevented the formation of any mechanism to achieve integration within the party. Especially when they refounded the NSDAP in 1925, following its temporary prohibition on account of the Putsch of November 1923, Hitler and his intimate followers within the Munich organisation were resolved to extinguish any surviving element of democracy within the party, enforcing the unrestricted leadership principle. The authoritarian rule of the Munich local party organisation implied the prohibition of the election of subleaders, who were installed from above. Functionaries on all levels were nominated by the central apparatus in Munich. The totalitarian party structure achieved by this measure, however, also precluded any debate on political issues within the party.

The motive for these organisational provisions was the prevention of any internal party opposition to the predominant Munich local party, which was deeply committed to Adolf Hitler. The long-term consequence was the elimination of any institutionalised means of conflict-regulation within the party apparatus, except for the party courts. While securing the unlimited impact of the leadership principle, the prohibition of any collective decision-making, or even exchange of views (other than in an informal fashion) on controversial issues, resulted in an extreme personalisation of politics, with the inevitable consequence that political controversies turned into personal feuds among the subleaders.

During the crucial period of the movement's growth after 1929, Gregor Strasser, then Reich Organisation Leader, had tried to integrate the expanding party apparatus by creating central steering agencies and by nominating inspectors (*Landesinspektoren*) for the different party regions, whose task was to control the local and regional party organisation. Without the highly bureaucratised party leadership established by Gregor Strasser – by far the most talented subleader of the NSDAP – the party would never have gained its spectacular successes during the election campaigns between 1930 and 1932.

Strasser failed, however, to eliminate the direct relations between the individual *Gauleiter* and Hitler, who regarded his provincial leaders as his personal chieftains and rejected Strasser's attempts to establish an uninterrupted line of command between the local organisations and the top leadership. Thus, Strasser had to accept the intermediate role of the group of the *Gauleiter*. And after Strasser's decision to resign his party offices on 8 December 1932, Hitler did not hesitate to withdraw the former's organisational reforms and to replace the office of the Reich Organisation Leader by a weak leadership structure divided between Rudolf Hess as head of the party organisation and Robert Ley as head of a newly established central party commission.[10] Consequently, following the seizure of power the party lacked a strong and efficient leadership, while Hitler was no longer preoccupied with party affairs. Hence, Jeremy Noakes' observation that, following Hitler's intervention to undermine Strasser's organisational planning, the NSDAP consisted virtually of thirty-two fairly autarkic Gau organisations, is crucial for any understanding of the Nazi regime.[11] Not before Hess's spectacular flight to Britain and the establishment of the Party Chancellery under Martin Bormann, who had been the head of administration in Hess's department and acted as Hitler's private secretary, were serious attempts undertaken to restore a central leadership over the party's rank and file.[12] Despite Bormann's assiduous endeavours to reestablish an efficient party control, however, he was never strong enough sufficiently to curtail the influence of those *Gauleiter* who had direct access to the Dictator.[13]

Although the leading figures in the party were eager to usurp state offices in order to strengthen their personal position, they had no respect for the inherited framework of public administration and especially no inclination to preserve the formal legality of administrative procedures. Their mentality was rather reflected in a predilection for what was called the principle of '*Menschenführung*' (literally, 'leadership of men') over '*Verwaltung*' ('administration'), which was based on fixed legal rules and was now denounced as purely bureaucratic and politically sterile.[14]

The reduction of politics to a matter of purely personal allegiance had been quite efficient during the period of the party's fight for power, the so-called '*Kampfzeit*' when all its energies could be concentrated on continuous election campaigning and mass mobilisation. But these qualities were far less necessary once the NSDAP had achieved political power and the average functionary had to fulfil primarily administra-

[10] See Peter D. Stachura, ''Der Fall Strasser'': Gregor Strasser, Hitler and National Socialism', in *The Shaping of the Nazi State*, ed. P. Stachura (London 1978), pp. 88–130; Udo Kissenkœtter, *Gregor Strasser und die NSDAP* (Stuttgart, 1978), pp. 178 ff.

[11] Jeremy Noakes, *Government, Party and the People in Nazi Germany*, Exeter Studies in History (Exeter 1980), p. 15.

[12] See Peter Longerich, *Hitlers Stellvertreter. Führung der Partei und Kontrolle des Staatsapparats durch den Stab Hess und die Partei-Kanzlei Bormann* (Munich 1992), pp. 166 ff.

[13] See Peter Hüttenberger, *Die Gauleiter. Studie zum Wandel des Machtgefüges in der NSDAP* (Stuttgart 1969), pp. 195 ff; Peter Diehl-Thiele, *Partei und Staat im Dritten Reich. Untersuchungen zum Verhältnis von NSDAP und allgemeiner innerer Staatsverwaltung*, 2nd edn (Munich 1971), pp. 34 ff.

[14] See Dieter Rebentisch and Karl Teppe, *Verwaltung contra Menschenführung im Staat Hitlers. Studien zum politisch-administrativen System* (Göttingen 1986), pp. 25 ff and Jane Caplan, *Government without Administration, State and Civil Service in Weimar and Nazi Germany* (Oxford 1988), pp. 325 ff.

tive tasks. Moreover, in the long run this mentality could not be reconciled with any governmental continuity and coordination.

However, after the seizure of power and the *Gleichschaltung* ('coordination') of public and private institutions, the NSDAP did not change its specific political approach which had emerged from the organisational patterns of the 'time of struggle' and was primarily characterised by the absolute dominance of the leadership principle on all levels. Hitler strongly supported the relative autonomy of the subleaders while securing their unrestricted personal loyalty. During the election campaigns before 1933 that system of combining charisma and factionalism increased the dynamism of Nazi politics. After 1933, extended to the entire political system, it necessarily contributed to widespread antagonism and rivalry within the party.[15]

The virtual absence of any interest representation within the party organisation intensified conflict and inefficiency. The informal leadership structure was retained after the seizure of power and transferred to the political system as a whole. Already during the Weimar era party rallies had been reduced to merely propagandistic mass meetings without any exchange of opinion of discussion and programmatic issues. During the early years of the regime, they became gigantic celebrations of the party's growth and the omnipotence of the Führer, symbolising the complete aesthetisation of politics.[16]

Nor did the Reich Leadership (*Reichsleitung*), founded in 1932, ever function as a steering body, remaining purely decorative and confined to propaganda functions. Despite repeated promises by Hitler, the Party Senate, which could have been the counterpart of the Fascist Grand Council that deposed Mussolini in July 1943, never came into being (though a Senate Hall was created for it in the 'Brown House': in Munich). Initiatives by Wilhelm Frick or Alfred Rosenberg, aimed at establishing at the very least a body responsible for selecting the future leader after Hitler's death, did not find the Dictator's approval. The rare meetings of the *Gauleiter* or, in the first years, of the *Reichsstatthalter* (Reich Governors), were not institutionalised, and in any case were largely confined to a forum for a speech by Hitler but without any platform for political consultation.[17] The increasing informality of political decision-making in the Third Reich was for Hitler first and foremost a matter of personal convenience which exonerated him from

[15] CF. Wolfgang Horn, *Führerideologie und Parteiorganisation in der NSDAP (1919–1933)* (Düsseldorf 1972), pp. 220 ff.: Joseph Nyomarkay, *Charisma and Factionalism in the Nazi Party* (Minneapolis 1967), pp. 76 ff.
[16] See Hamilton T. Burden, *The Nuremberg Party Rallies 1933–1939* (London 1967).
[17] See Martin Broszat, *Der Staat Hitlers. Grundlegung und Entwicklung seiner inneren Verfassung* (Munich 1969), p. 262: Dieter Rebentisch, *Führerstaat und Verwaltung im Zweiten Weltkrieg* (Stuttgart 1989), pp. 422–3.

the tasks of day-to-day administration. It corresponded, however, to his concept of politics, since he saw the task of the statesman as the setting of visionary goals rather than the handling of detailed matters of government. Thus, he did not support Strasser's attempts to prepare in concrete fashion for participation in government and to outline a future legislative programme.[18] Consequently, apart from a few preliminary studies by Strasser's *Reichsleitung*, and Hitler's notions of a huge Reich Propaganda Ministry to function as a coordinating agency above the traditional departments,[19] only vague ideas for a governmental programme of the NSDAP existed. This reveals Hitler's overwhelmingly propagandistic understanding of politics which, as David Schoenbaum has pointed out, often led him to confuse ends with means.[20]

The informalisation of politics relied partially upon Hitler's predilection not only for avoiding regular office hours, but increasingly, too, for avoiding taking decisions. The influence of non-official advisers on his decisions curtailed, therefore, almost all attempts of the Reich Chancellery under Hans-Heinrich Lammers to guarantee the previously indispensable participation of the responsible departments. In many cases, the ministerial bureaucracy was outflanked by high-ranking party leaders, especially by Goebbels, Himmler and Ley. By using their direct access to Hitler, such figures deliberately circumvented the Reich Chancellery, which was officially in charge of coordinating Hitler's legislative activity.

The struggle among leading chieftains to obtain Hitler's approval in controversial issues led to the disruption of any controlled decision-making process at the head of the regime. Apart from the fragmentation of legislation, leading to an ever increasing number of ordinances decreed without sufficient coordination between the different ministries of state, there was as good as no systematic communication among the leading elite. Even this situation deteriorated under wartime conditions, when Hitler disappeared into his field headquarters. Otto Ohlendorf, a sectional head within the *Sicherheitsdienst* (SD, Security Service of the police), tried to compensate for the lack of official information through editing the so-called 'Reports from the Reich' (*'Meldungen aus dem Reich'*), based on the systematic monitoring of rumours, public reactions to events, and the like. But this did not stop the growing flight from reality among leading officials.

Originally, the widespread lack of communication among the leaders

[18] See Hitler's December 1932 'Memorandum on the internal reasons for the measures to increase the striking power of the Movement' (BA Koblenz NS 22/110).
[19] See Joseph Goebbels, *Die Tagebücher von Joseph Goebbels*, ed. Elke Fröhlich, vol. II (Munich 1987), pp. 218–19 (entry for 9 August).
[20] See David Schoenbaum, *Die Braune Revolution. Eine Sozialgeschichte des Dritten Reiches*, 2nd edn (Cologne 1968), p. 26.

of the Nazi regime emanated from Hitler's inclination to provide his subleaders only with the fragmentary information necessary to fulfil their specific functions. The splintering of governmental bodies magnified this tendency. Thus, even those with high standing had increasing difficulties in obtaining a realistic picture of the Reich's political and military situation, quite apart from the fact that they acquired only informal knowledge of secret operations, such as policies of genocide.

The assumption that the fragmentation of politics arose from a deliberate divide-and-rule strategy on Hitler's part is, however, misleading. Rather, this was a reflection of the social-darwinist conviction that the best man would ultimately prevail. The consequent technique of operating through special emissaries promised short-run efficiency, but meant in the long run that a great deal of energy was dissipated in personal feuds and taken up by increasing inter-departmental rivalries, as well as between party and state agencies. These mechanisms were, however, of the utmost importance for the internal development of the regime. This social-darwinist struggle led to an escalating ruthlessness in pursuit of the extreme goals of the movement, and thus to a process of cumulative radicalisation. Owing to the lack of institutional guarantees, individual chieftains felt compelled to fight competitors with all the means at their disposal. Each office-holder tried to gain the special sympathies of the Führer by appearing as a fanatical fighter for the realisation of the visionary and extreme goals of the *Weltanschauung*.

This tendency was interwoven with a 'selection of the negative elements' of the Nazi *Weltanschauung*, as Martin Broszat observed, since 'positive' objectives generally encountered resistance from vested interests. Jews, Gypsies and other target groups became declared enemies once Communists and Socialists had been eliminated as a political threat. Hence, the destructive impetus of Nazi ideology was continuously on the increase while more moderate targets were dropped or postponed.[21] Above all, anti-Jewish policy, culminating in the systematic liquidation of European Jewry, pushed competing interests completely into the background. In the treatment of the occupied countries, a similar radicalisation was evident, blocking any path to a modus vivendi with the subjugated peoples.

The structural inability of the Nazi regime to accept political compromise instead of pursuing visionary 'final goals' (*Endziele*) prevented any consolidation of its rule over continental Europe and made it impossible to achieve any lasting arrangements, at least with France and the Benelux countries. Consequently, Hitler prohibited for the time being any deliberation about the future restructuring of the European conti-

---

[21] Martin Broszat, 'Soziale Motivation und Führer-Bindung des Nationalsozialismus', in: *Nach Hitler. Der schwierige Umgang mit unserer Geschichte* (Munich 1986), pp. 11–33.

nent and wanted to postpone any decision on this until the 'final victory'.[22] This attitude implied a dramatic over-extension of the available economic and manpower resources, leading ultimately to military defeat.

The progressive fragmentation of the Nazi political system was closely connected with territorial expansion. In the annexed and occupied territories, party and SS representatives were able to shrug off any restraint by public law and administrative regulation and exercise an arbitrary rule that attempted to enforce the total compliance of the subjugated population through repeated use of violence and terror. Hitler expressly welcomed the new type of leadership, characterised by harshness and unbureaucratic methods, that was emerging in the East.[23]

The arbitrary power structures which developed in the former Soviet territory and the General-Gouvernement were taken by Hitler as a model for a future German Reich. Robert Koehl coined the term 'Neo-Feudalism' to describe the conditions in the occupied eastern territories which led to a total personalisation of the politics and gave the local commanders unrestricted power.[24] Consequently, growing corruption emerged within their entourage, preventing efficient administration. When the Wehrmacht was eventually forced to retreat and the now superfluous civil administrators withdrew from the occupied territories, the atavistic political style which they represented was transferred to the 'Old Reich'.

To what extent this decay of modern statehood had a parallel in the Soviet Union is an open question. Unlike the Stalinist system, the Nazi regime did not try to enlarge its political base through the restoration of its former alliance with the traditional elites, as Stalin attempted to do by proclaiming the 'Great Patriotic War'.[25] Though exploiting conservative-Prussian traditions and invoking their nationalistic elements to the very end, the Nazi leadership, confronted with pending defeat, cut all its ties to the conservative elites and returned to its socio-revolutionary origins and aims, which for tactical reasons had been pushed aside after the seizure of power.

From now on, the party deplored the fact that it had ended the revolutionary process in 1933 and had accepted a compromise with the conservative elites and the higher civil service. In 1944, the so-called 'Gitter-Aktion' ('Iron Bars Action') led to the arrest of several thousand

---

[22] Hans Werner Neulen, *Europa und das 3. Reich. Einigungsbestrebungen im deutschen Machtbereich 1939–45* (Munich 1987), p. 163.

[23] Rebentisch, *Führerstaat und Verwaltung*, pp. 26–7 and 312.

[24] Robert Koehl, 'Feudal Aspects of National Socialism', in *Nazism and the Third Reich*, ed. Henry Turner (New York 1972), pp. 151–74.

[25] See Ronald Suny, 'Stalin and his Stalinism', in this volume pp. 26–52.

people regarded as sympathisers with the Weimar Republic and potential political opponents.[26] The Nazi elite was convinced that the absence not only of racial, but also of ideological, homogeneity was the very source of Germany's military crisis and political backlash. In accordance with this assumption, Nazi chieftains retained the illusion that only a complete take-over of public administration by the party could turn the tide and secure Germany's final victory.

Symptomatic of this mentality was the continual reference in propaganda to the 'time of struggle' ('*Kampfzeit*') and, especially to the abortive Munich Putsch in November 1923, seen as proof that the party had mastered severe crises in its history and that it would be able to overcome the military crisis if it took things in hand. The memory and myth of the '*Kampfzeit*' served, therefore, to conceal the prospect of a bleak future. At the same time, the legacy of the War of Liberation against Napoleon and the Fridericus Rex (Frederick the Great) myth were reactivated by Goebbels' propaganda in order to strengthen the 'stick-it-out' mentality.

Under the impact of the battle of Stalingrad, Goebbels, Bormann, and Ley realised that the survival of the regime depended on the reform of the NSDAP and that it was crucial to improve its public prestige, which has been profoundly damaged by the widespread corruption of party functionaries. To what extent the attempts to renew the party's revolutionary spirit through a wave of party rallies, propaganda marches and public demonstrations succeeded, is difficult to assess. But Bormann and Ley were successful in mobilising the party apparatus behind the shattered regime. At the same time, the functions of the *Gauleiter* in their role as Reich Defence Commissioners were massively extended. Most of the municipal administration, and also police functions, were handed over to the local and regional party organisations. To this extent, the process of 'partification', which had been interrupted in summer 1933 in conjunction with the stoppage of the 'national revolution', was renewed.[27]

The most outstanding example of the mobilisation campaign at the final hour was the establishment of the *Volkssturm* – a mass militia embracing virtually all citizens. Though perceived as a military formation, its commanding officers were meant to be drawn from the local and regional party organisation – an absurdity since the party did not have adequately trained troop commanders. Nevertheless, it was not

---

[26] Cf. Walter Hammer, *Die "Gitteraktion" vom. 22. 8. 1944*, Freiheit und Recht 8/9 (1959), pp. 15 ff.

[27] See Karl Teppe, 'Der Reichsverteidigungskommissar. Organisation and Praxis in Westfalen', in *Verwaltung contra Menschenführung*, pp. 294–5.; Dietrich Orlow, *The History of the Nazi Party*, vol. II: *1933–1945* (Pittsburg 1973), pp. 345 ff.

the reserve army, which in 1944 stood under the command of Heinrich Himmler, but the Party Chancellery under Martin Bormann which bore the responsibility for the *Volkssturm* – conceived as a representation of the true 'people's community' and as 'the unified deployment of the entire people united in the idea of National Socialism'.[28]

Even before the creation of the *Volkssturm*, the Party Chancellery had won Hitler's approval for the introduction of the National Socialist 'Leadership Officer' (*Führungsoffizier*), a direct copy of the much disdained Soviet *politruk*. In the long run, this was directed at the complete nazification of the army after the war – an ambition that had been the primary goal of Ernst Röhm in 1934.[29] To this extent, the party returned to its very origins, promulgating total ideological fanatisation as a pledge for final victory, and believing in the 'cult of the will' which would ultimately force Germany's enemies to retreat in the face of the superior principle of National Socialism.[30]

These deliberations show that, while the party's active elements underwent a process of continuous radicalisation, the Nazi regime entered an irreversible phase of internal decay which ultimately destroyed its very foundations. Attempts by the Ministry of the Interior, by Goebbels, and by others, to restore the unity of government, either by reactivating the Reich Defence Council under the authority of Göring or by establishing new institutions such as the 'Three Men's Committee' (*Dreierausschuß*), were of limited success, while the installation of Goebbels as 'Plenipotentiary for Total War Mobilisation' was also a failure. In the depths of the bunker below the Reich Chancellery, Hitler was in the final phase no longer able to keep the reins of government in his hands. But no one among his entourage – with the possible exception of Albert Speer – dared confront him with military and economic reality.

There were numerous similarities and parallels between the Stalinist and Hitler dictatorships – not least in each case the mounting loss of any sense of reality. Both Hitler and Stalin constantly ignored unwelcome truth and lived in an increasingly fictitious world. Both tended to turn night into day, and to prefer informal advisers to competent professionals in government departments. The deep distrust of their subordinates felt by both dictators induced them repeatedly to dismiss their military leaders.

But there were also obvious differences which emerged from contrasting political backgrounds and structures. Despite the progressive

---

[28] *Zeitschriftendienst/Deutscher Wochendienst*, ed. by Reichsministerium für Volksaufklärung und Propaganda, vol. 154 (Berlin 20 October 1944).
[29] See Volker Berghahn, 'NSDAP und "geistige Führung" der Wehrmacht 1939–1944', *Vierteljahreshefte für Zeitgeschichte* 17, 1969; Arne W. G. Zoepf, *Wehrmacht zwischen Tradition und Ideologie. Der NS-Führungsoffizier im Zweiten Weltkrieg* (Frankfurt 1987).
[30] Cf. J. P. Stern, *The Führer and the People* (London 1975).

'partification', the internal splits within the Nazi regime, and the virtually complete elimination of any administrative unity, the system inclined towards an ever-increasing political *anomie* that ended in the complete collapse which accompanied military defeat. The inability, too, to end an already lost war, as well as the emerging mass terror now directed at the German population itself, signified this process of dissolution. In comparison, the Soviet system preserved its ability to adapt itself to shifting challenges and changing situations, revealing a higher level of stability despite also relying on escalating terror.[31]

The NSDAP differed structurally from Communist parties through the predominance of the leadership principle and the exclusion of any political discourse within the party apparatus. Above all, the National Socialists failed to create new and lasting foundations of rule capable of transcending the continuous indoctrination, terror, and the relentless improvisation and dynamic that kept the population in line and prevented it from recognising the myths of Nazi propaganda. In this respect, the Nazi Movement differed from the Soviet Communist Party since, instead of revolutionising the inherited state and German society, it restricted itself to a mere simulation of social change. It effectively exploited the potential for protest of sectors of German society which, in Ernst Bloch's terms, had 'non-synchronised' (*nicht gleichzeitigen*) – partly modern, partly pre-modern – interests, in order to create a mass base.

Nazi politics unleashed an unbridled political, economic, and military dynamic with unprecedented destructive energy, while proving incapable of creating lasting political structures. Significant for the primarily destructive character of the Nazi regime is the fact that the quasi-revolutionary goal of reshaping the ethnic map of great parts of Europe in conjunction with the so-called 'General Plan for the East' (*Generalplan-Ost*), while only partially accomplished, was indeed attained in anti-Jewish policy, culminating in the deaths of around five million people.[32] All the related aims, especially the huge settlement projects in eastern Europe, of which the genocide against the Jews was but a part, remained unfulfilled.

The assumption that the Thousand-Year-Reich was anything more than a facade of modernity, that it achieved a real modernisation of Germany, takes the results of destruction as positive values and

---

[31] For post-war developments in Germany see Klaus-Dietmar Henke, *Die amerikanische Besetzung Deutschlands* (Quellen und Darstellungen zur Zeitgeschichte, Bd. 27, Munich, 1995), pp. 78 ff.
[32] Cf. Götz Aly, *"Endlösung". Völkerverschiebung und der Mord an den europäischen Juden* (Frankfurt 1995), pp. 397–8. Götz Aly and Susanne Heim, *Vordenker der Vernichtung. Auschwitz und die deutschen Pläne für eine europäische Ordnung* (Hamburg 1991), pp. 121–2, 485 ff.

overlooks the regime's basic political sterility.[33] The very essence of the Nazi regime lay in its parasitical character, its purely destructive nature, that excluded any ability to create a positive future for the German people, let alone for the millions of repressed and exploited citizens of the occupied or aligned countries. It seems to me that this essential substance of Nazism does not match the Stalinist system, whatever the latter's totalitarian and terroristic traits.

[33] For the recent debate on Modernisation see my article on 'Nationalsozialismus und Modernisierung', in *Geschichte und Gesellschaft*, vol. 21 (1995), pp. 391–402.

4

'Working towards the Führer': reflections on the nature of the Hitler dictatorship*

Ian Kershaw

The renewed emphasis, already visible in the mid-1980s, on the intertwined fates of the Soviet Union and of Germany, especially in the Stalin and Hitler eras, has become greatly intensified in the wake of the upheavals in eastern Europe. The sharpened focus on the atrocities of Stalinism has prompted attempts to relativise Nazi barbarism – seen as wicked, but on the whole less wicked than that of Stalinism (and by implication of Communism in general).[1] The brutal Stalinist modernising experiment is used to remove any normative links with humanising, civilising, emancipatory, or democratising development from modernisation concepts and thereby to claim that Hitler's regime, too, was – and intentionally so – a 'modernising dictatorship'.[2] Implicit in all this is a reversion, despite the many refinements and criticisms of the concept since the 1960s, to essentially traditional views on 'totalitarianism', and to views of Stalin and Hitler as 'totalitarian dictators'.

There can be no principled objection to comparing the forms of dictatorship in Germany under Hitler and in the Soviet Union under Stalin and, however unedifying the subject matter, the nature and extent of their inhumanity.[3] The totalitarianism concept allows comparative analysis of a number of techniques and instruments of domination, and this, too, must be seen as legitimate in itself.[4] The underlying assump-

---

* An earlier version of this essay first appeared in the journal *Contemporary European History*, and I am grateful to the editors for permission to reprint.

[1] Ernst Nolte's contributions to the *Historikerstreit* (see *'Historikerstreit'. Die Dokumentation der Kontroverse um die Einzigartigkeit der nationalsozialistischen Judenvernichtung* (Munich 1987) pp. 13–35, 39–47, and his book *Der europäische Bürgerkrieg 1917–1945* (Frankfurt am Main Berlin 1987), reflect this tendency.

[2] See, for instance, the recently published essay collection produced by Michael Prinz and Rainer Zitelmann (eds.) *Nationalsozialismus und Modernisierung* (Darmstadt 1991), especially the editors' foreword (pp. VII–XI) and Zitelmann's own essay, 'Die totalitäre Seite der Moderne' (pp. 1–20).

[3] See on this the thoughtful comments of Charles Maier, *The Unmasterable Past. History, Holocaust, and German National Identity* (Cambridge, Mass.–London 1988), pp. 71–84.

[4] The Deutsche Forschungsgemeinschaft is currently investigating the structures of

tion that both regimes made total claims upon society, based upon a monopolistic set of ideological imperatives, resulting in unprecedented levels of repression and of attempted indoctrination, manipulation, and mobilisation – giving these regimes a dynamic missing from more conventional authoritarian regimes – again seem largely incontestable. But the fundamental problem with the term 'totalitarianism' – leaving aside its non-scholarly usage – is that it is a descriptive concept, not a theory, and has little or no explanatory power.[5] It presumes that Stalinism and Hitlerism were more like each other than different from each other. But the basis of comparison is a shallow one, largely confined to the apparatus of rule.[6]

My starting point in these reflections is the presumption that despite superficial similarities in forms of domination the two regimes were *in essence* more *unlike* than like each other. Though seeing greater potential in comparisons of Nazism with other fascist movements and systems rather than with the Soviet system, I would want to retain an emphasis upon the unique features of the Nazi dictatorship, and the need to explain these, alongside those characteristics which could be seen as generic components of European fascism in the era following the First World War, through the specific dominant features of German political culture. (In this I admit to a currently rather unfashionable attachment to notions of a qualified German *Sonderweg*.)[7]

Sometimes, however, highlighting contrasts can be more valuable than comparison of similarities. In what follows I would like to use what, on an imperfect grasp of some of the recent historiography on Stalinism, I understand to be significant features of Stalin's dictatorship to establish some important contrasts in the Hitler regime. This, I hope, will offer a basis for some reflections on what remains a central problem of interpretation of the Third Reich: what explains the gathering momentum of radicalisation, the dynamic of destruction in the Third Reich? Much of the answer to this question has, I would suggest at the outset, to do with the undermining and collapse of what one might call

differing authoritarian systems in twentieth-century Europe in a major research project, 'Diktaturen im Europa des 20. Jahrhunderts: Strukturen, Erfahrung, Überwindung und Vergleich'.

[5] I argue this case in chapter 2 of my *Nazi Dictatorship, Problems and Perspectives of Interpretation* (3rd edn, London 1993).

[6] The comparison becomes even more shallow where the focus shifts from Stalin's own regime to later 'Stalinist' systems. The revelations of the extent of repression in the German Democratic Republic have, for example, promoted simplistic notions of essential similarities between the Honecker and Hitler regimes. See on this the comments of Eberhard Jäckel, 'Die doppelte Vergangenheit', *Der Spiegel*, 23 (Dec. 1991), pp. 39–43.

[7] On the *Sonderweg* debate, see the sensible comments of Jürgen Kocka, 'German History before Hitler: the Debate about the German *Sonderweg*', *Journal of Contemporary History*, 23 (1988), pp. 3–16.

'rational' structures of rule, a system of 'ordered' government and administration. But what caused the collapse, and, not least, what was Hitler's own role in the process? These questions lie at the centre of my enquiry.

First, however, let me outline a number of what appear to me to be significant points of contrast between the Stalinist and Hitlerist regimes.[8]

- Stalin arose from *within* a system of rule, as a leading exponent of it. He was, as Ronald Suny puts it, a committee man, chief oligarch, man of the machine,[9] in Moshe Lewin's phrase 'bureaucracy's anti-Christ', the 'creature of his party',[10] who became despot by control of the power which lay at the heart of the Party, in its secretariat. In a sense, it is tempting to see an analogy in the German context in the position of Bormann rather than Hitler. Is it possible to imagine Stalin echoing Hitler's comment in 1941: 'I've totally lost sight of the organisations of the Party. When I find myself confronted by one or other of these achievements, I say to myself: "By God, how that has developed!"'?[11]

At any rate, a party leader and head of government less bureaucratically inclined, less a committee man or man of the machine, than Hitler is hard to imagine. Before 1933 he was uninvolved in and detached from the Nazi Movement's bureaucracy. After 1933, as head of government he scarcely put pen to paper himself other than to sign legislation put in front of his nose by Lammers. The Four Year Memorandum of 1936 is a unique example from the years 1933 to 1945 of a major policy document composed by Hitler himself – written in frustration and fury at the stance adopted during the economic crisis of 1935–6 by Schacht and some sectors of business and industry. Strikingly, Hitler gave copies of his memorandum only to two persons – Göring and Blomberg (much later giving a third copy to Speer). The Economics Minister himself was not included in the short distribution list! Business and industrial leaders were not even made aware of the existence of the memorandum.[12]

Hitler's way of operating was scarcely conducive to ordered government. Increasingly, after the first year or two of the dictatorship, he

---

[8] I have elaborated on some of the following points in my essay 'Totalitarianism Revisited: Nazism and Stalinism in Comparative Perspective', *Tel Aviver Jahrbuch für deutsche Geschichte*, 23 (1994), pp. 23–40. Some further valuable comparison is provided by Alan Bullock, *Hitler and Stalin, Parallel Lives* (London 1991), ch. 10.

[9] See Ronald Suny's essay in this volume.

[10] See Moshe Lewin, 'Bureaucracy and the Stalinist State', in this volume.

[11] Werner Jochmann (ed.) *Adolf Hitler. Monologe im Führerhauptquartier* (Hamburg 1980), p. 158; trans. *Hitler's Table Talk* (introd. H. R. Trevor-Roper) (London 1953), p. 153.

[12] Dieter Petzina, *Autarkiepolitik im Dritten Reich* (Stuttgart 1968), pp. 48–53; Peter Hayes, *Industry and Ideology. IG Farben in the Nazi Era* (Cambridge 1987), pp. 164–7.

reverted to the habits of a lifestyle recognisable not only in the Party leader of the 1920s but even in the description of the indolent youth in Linz and Vienna recorded by his friend Kubizek.[13] According to the post-war testimony of one of his former adjutants:

> Hitler normally appeared shortly before lunch, quickly read through Reich Press Chief Dietrich's press cuttings, and then went into lunch. So it became more and more difficult for Lammers [head of the Reich Chancellory] and Meißner [head of the Presidial Chancellory] to get him to make decisions which he alone could make as head of state . . . When Hitler stayed at Obersalzberg it was even worse. There, he never left his room before 2.00 p.m. Then, he went to lunch. He spent most afternoons taking a walk, in the evening straight after dinner, there were films . . . He disliked the study of documents. I have sometimes secured decisions from him, even ones about important matters, without his ever asking to see the relevant files. He took the view that many things sorted themselves out on their own if one did not interfere.[14]

As this comment points out, even Lammers, the only link between Hitler and the ministries of state (whose heads themselves ceased definitively to meet around a table as a cabinet in early 1938), had difficulty at times with access to Hitler and the extraction of decisions from him. Lammers himself, for example, wrote plaintively to Hitler's adjutant on 21 October 1938 begging for an audience to report to the Führer on a number of urgent matters which needed resolution and which had been building up since the last occasion when he had been able to provide a detailed report – on 4 September![15]

Hitler's increasing aloofness from the State bureaucracy and the major organs of government marks, it seems to me, more than a difference of style with Stalin's *modus operandi*. It reflects in my view a difference in the essence of the regimes, mirrored in the position of the leader of each, a point to which I will return.

- Stalin was a highly interventionist dictator, sending a stream of letters and directives determining or interfering with policy. He chaired all important committees. His aim appears to have been a monopolisation of all decision-making and its concentration in the Politburo, a centralisation of state power and unity of decision-making which would have eliminated party–state dualism.[16]

[13] See August Kubizek, *Adolf Hitler, mein Jugendfreund* (5th edn, Graz–Stuttgart 1989).
[14] Fritz Wiedemann, *Der Mann, der Feldherr werden wollte* (Kettwig 1964), p. 69; trans. Jeremy Noakes and Geoffrey Pridham (eds.), *Nazism, 1919/1945. A Documentary Reader* (Exeter 1984), vol. II, pp. 207–8 (hereafter N & P).
[15] Institut für Zeitgeschichte, Munich, Nuremberg Document No. NG-5428; trans. N & P, vol. II, p. 245.   [16] See Suny's contribution to this volume.

Hitler, by contrast, was on the whole a non-interventionist dictator as far as government administration was concerned. His sporadic directions, when they came, tended to be delphic, and conveyed verbally, usually by the head of the Reich Chancellory Lammers or, in the war years (as far as civilian matters went), increasingly by Bormann.[17] Hitler chaired no formal committees after the first years of the regime, when the Cabinet (which he hated chairing) atrophied into non-existence.[18] He directly undermined the attempts made by Reich Interior Minister Frick to unify and rationalise administration, and did much to sustain and enhance the irreconcilable dualism of Party and State which existed at every level.[19]

Where Stalin appeared deliberately to destabilise government (which offered the possibility of a bureaucratic challenge),[20] Hitler seems to have had no deliberate policy of destabilisation, but rather, as a consequence of his non-bureaucratic leadership position and the inbuilt need to protect his deified leadership position by non-association with political infighting and potentially unpopular policies, to have presided over an inexorable erosion of 'rational' forms of government. And while the metaphor of 'feudal anarchy' might be applied to both systems, it seems more apt as a depiction of the Hitler regime, where bonds of personal loyalty were from the beginning the crucial determinants of power, wholly overriding functional position and status.[21]

- Personalities apart, Hitler's leadership position appears to have been structurally more secure than Stalin's. If I have followed the debates properly, it would seem that there may initially have been some

---

[17] Dieter Rebentisch, *Führerstaat und Verwaltung im Zweiten Weltkrieg* (Stuttgart 1989), has clearly shown that Hitler involved himself in civilian affairs to a far greater extent than was once thought. However, when he intervened it was usually at the prompting of one of the few favoured Nazi leaders graced with regular access to his presence, and providing him with one-sided information on specific issues of concern to them. He remained at all times alert to any extension of their power which could undermine his own. Other than this, there was nothing in his haphazard interventions to indicate any systematic grasp of or clear directives for coherent policy-making. In military matters and armaments production, from the middle of the war onwards, Hitler's involvement was on a wholly different scale. Here, his interventions were frequent – at daily conferences – and direct, though his dilettante, arbitrary, and intransigent interference was often disastrously counter-productive. See Helmut Heiber (ed.), *Hitlers Lagebesprechungen. Die Protokollfragmente seiner militärischen Konferenzen 1942–1945* (Stuttgart 1962), and Willi A. Boelcke (ed.), *Deutschlands Rüstung im Zweiten Weltkrieg. Hitlers Konferenzen mit Albert Speer 1942–1945* (Frankfurt am Main 1969).

[18] See Lothar Gruchmann, 'Die "Reichsregierung" im Führerstaat', in *Klassenjustiz und Pluralismus*, eds. Günther Doecker and Winfried Steffani, (Hamburg 1973), p. 192.

[19] See Peter Diehl-Thiele, *Partei und Staat im Dritten Reich* (Munich 1969), pp. 61–9.

[20] See Suny's paper in this collection.

[21] See Robert Koehl, 'Feudal Aspects of National Socialism', *American Political Science Review*, 54 (1960), pp. 921–33.

rational basis for Stalin's purges even if the dictator's paranoia then took them into wholly irrational realms of fantasy.[22] As the exponent of one Party line among several, one set of policies among a number of alternatives, one interpretation of the Marx-Lenin arcanum among others, Stalin remained a dictator open to challenge from within. Kirov, it appears, posed the potential of a genuine rival leader in the early 1930s, when dissatisfaction and discontent with Stalin's rule were widespread.[23] Stalin's exaggerated feeling of insecurity was then – at any rate at first – to some measure grounded in reality. The purges which he himself instigated, and which in many instances were targeted at those closest to him, were above all intended to head off a bureaucratic challenge to his rule.

Hitler thought Stalin must be mad to carry out the purges.[24] The only faint reflections in the Third Reich were the liquidation of the SA leadership in the 'Night of the Long Knives' in 1934, and the ruthless retaliation for the attempt on Hitler's life in 1944. In the former case, Hitler agreed to the purge only belatedly and reluctantly, after the going had been made by Himmler and Göring, supported by the army leadership. The latter case does bear comparison with the Stalinist technique, though by that time the Hitler regime was plainly in its death-throes. The wild retaliation against those implicated in the assassination attempt was a desperation measure and aimed essentially at genuine opponents, rather than a basic technique of rule.

Down to the middle of the War, Hitler's position lacked the precariousness which surrounded Stalin's leadership in the 1930s.[25] Where Stalin could not believe in genuine loyalty even among his closest supporters, Hitler built his mastery on a cultivated principle of personal loyalty to which he could always successfully appeal at moments of crisis.[26] He showed a marked reluctance to discard even widely disliked

[22] My main orientation was gleaned from the debates in *The Russian Review*, 45–46 (1986, 1987), as well as from J. Arch Getty, *Origins of the Great Purges* (Cambridge 1985); Moshe Lewin, *The Making of the Soviet System* (New York 1985); Robert C. Tucker ed., *Stalinism: Essays in Historical Interpretation* (New York 1977); and the contributions to this volume by Ronald Suny and Moshe Lewin.   [23] See Suny's essay in this volume.

[24] Elke Fröhlich (ed.), *Die Tagebücher von Joseph Goebbels* (Munich 1987), vol. III, p. 198 (entry for 10 July 1937).

[25] Hitler nevertheless had the acutest antennae for any move which might threaten or weaken his absolutism. He also had an elaborate security system constructed. See Peter Hoffmann, *Hitler's Personal Security* (Basingstoke–London–Cambridge, Mass. 1979). Even so, several attempts were, of course, made on his life, whereas none, it seems, was made on the life of Stalin.

[26] A good example was his successful appeal to his old comrades, the *Gauleiter*, to close ranks at the moment of deep crisis following the sudden departure of Gregor Strasser in December 1932. See N & P, vol. I, pp. 112–14 (the translation of an unpublished post-war account by Heinrich Lohse held in the Forschungsstelle für die Geschichte des Nationalsozialismus, Hamburg).

and discredited satraps like Streicher, who had in Hitler's eyes earned his support through indispensable loyalty and service in the critical early years of the Movement.[27] And he was in the bunker visibly shaken by news of Himmler's treachery – the 'loyal Heinrich' finally stabbing him in the back.[28]

A dangerous challenge to Hitler, especially once Hindenburg was dead, could effectively only come from within the armed forces (in tandem with an emergent disaffected, but unrepresentative, minority among the conservative elites), or from a stray attack by a lone assassin (as came close to killing Hitler in 1939).[29] Even in 1944, the leaders of the attempted coup realised their isolation and the lack of a base of popular support for their action.[30] Hitler, it has to be accepted, was, for most of the years he was in power, outside the repressed and powerless adherents of the former working-class movements, sections of Catholicism, and some individuals among the traditional elites, a highly popular leader both among the ruling groups and with the masses.

And within the Nazi Movement itself, his status was quite different from that of Stalin's position within the Communist Party. There are obvious parallels between the personality cults built up around Stalin and Hitler. But whereas the Stalin cult was superimposed upon the marxist-leninist ideology and Communist Party, and both were capable of surviving it, the 'Hitler myth' was structurally indispensable to, in fact, the very basis of, and scarcely distinguishable from, the Nazi Movement and its *Weltanschauung*.

Since the mid-1920s, ideological orthodoxy was synonymous with adherence to Hitler. 'For us the Idea is the Führer, and each Party member has only to obey the Führer', Hitler allegedly told Otto Strasser in 1930.[31] The build-up of a 'Führer party' squeezed heterodox positions on to the sidelines, then out of the Party. By the time the regime was established and consolidated, there was no tenable position within Nazism compatible with a fundamental challenge to Hitler. His leadership position, as the fount of ideological orthodoxy, the very epitome of Nazism itself, was beyond question within the Movement. Opposition

---

[27] See Jochmann (ed.), *Monologe im Führerhauptquartier*, pp. 158–60; trans. *Hitler's Table Talk*, pp. 153–6.

[28] H. R. Trevor-Roper, *The Last Days of Hitler* (Pan Books edn, London 1973), p. 202.

[29] See Anton Hoch, 'Das Attentat auf Hitler im Münchner Bürgerbräukeller 1939', *Vierteljahreshefte für Zeitgeschichte*, 17 (1969), pp. 383–412; and Lothar Gruchmann (ed.), *Autobiographie eines Attentäters. Johann Georg Elser* (Stuttgart 1970).

[30] See Hans Mommsen, 'Social Views and Constitutional Plans of the Resistance', in *The German Resistance to Hitler*, eds. Hermann Graml *et al.* (London 1970), p. 59.

[31] N & P vol. I, p. 46. Though Otto Strasser is an unreliable source, Hitler did not challenge his published account of their meeting in May 1930, prior to Strasser's expulsion from the Nazi Party. The reported comments also match those expressed on other occasions around that time by Hitler about the inseparability of leader and 'idea'.

to Hitler on fundamentals ruled itself out, even among the highest and mightiest in the Party. Invoking the Führer's name was the pathway to success and advancement. Countering the ideological prerogatives bound up with Hitler's position was incompatible with clambering up the greasy pole to status and power.

● Stalin's rule, for all its dynamic radicalism in the brutal collectivisation programme, the drive to industrialisation, and the paranoid phase of the purges, was not incompatible with a rational ordering of priorities and attainment of limited and comprehensible goals, even if the methods were barbarous in the extreme and the accompanying inhumanity on a scale defying belief. Whether the methods were the most appropriate to attain the goals in view might still be debated, but the attempt to force industrialisation at breakneck speed on a highly backward economy and to introduce 'socialism in one country' cannot be seen as irrational or limitless aims.

And despite the path to a personalised dictatorship, there was arguably no inexorable 'cumulative radicalisation'[32] in the Soviet Union. Perhaps it is possible to speak there of 'despotic radicalisation', to underline the degree to which the developments mirrored the dictator's own increasing irrationality. But despite Stalin's growing detachment from reality, there was even a 'great retreat' from radicalism by the mid-1930s and a reversion towards some forms of social conservativism before the War brought its own compromises with ideological rectitude.[33] Whatever the costs of the personal regiment, and whatever the destructiveness of Stalin in the purges of the Party and of the military, the structures of the Soviet system were not completely broken. Stalin had been a product of the system. And the system was capable of withstanding nearly three decades of Stalin and surviving him. It was, in other words, a system capable of self-reproduction, even at the cost of a Stalin.

It would be hard to claim this of Nazism. The goal of national redemption through racial purification and through racial empire was chimeric – a utopian vision. The barbarism and destructiveness which were immanent to the vain attempt to realise this goal were infinite in extent, just as the expansionism and extension of aggression to other peoples were boundless. Whereas Stalinism could 'settle down', as it effectively did after Stalin's death, into an undynamic, even conservative, repressive regime, a 'settling down' into the staid authoritarianism

---

[32] The term is that of Hans Mommsen. See his article, 'Der Nationalsozialismus: Kumulative Radikalisierung und Selbstzerstörung des Regimes', in *Meyers Enzyklopädisches Lexikon*, vol. 16 (1976), pp. 785–90.
[33] See Suny's essay in this collection.

of a Francoesque kind is scarcely conceivable in the case of Nazism. Here, the dynamic was ceaseless, the momentum of radicalisation an accelerating one incapable of having the brakes put on – unless the 'system' itself were to be fundamentally altered.

I have just used the word 'system' of Nazism. But where Soviet communism in the Stalin era, despite the dictator's brutal destabilisation, remained recognisable as a *system* of rule, the Hitler regime was inimical to a rational order of government and administration.[34] Its hallmark was *systemlessness*, administrative and governmental disorder, the erosion of clear patterns of government, however despotic.

This was already plain within Germany in the pre-war years as institutions and structures of government and administration atrophied, were eroded, or were simply bypassed and faded into oblivion. It was not simply a matter of the unresolved Party–State dualism. The proliferation of 'special authorities' and plenipotentiaries for specific tasks, delegated by the Führer and responsible directly to him, reflected the predatory character and improvised techniques immanent to Nazi domination.[35] Lack of coherent planning related to attainable middle-range goals; absence of any forum for collective decision-making; the arbitrary exercise of power embedded in the 'leadership principle' at all levels; the Darwinistic notion of unchecked struggle and competition until the winner emerged; and the simplistic belief in the 'triumph of the will', whatever the complexities to be overcome: all these reinforced each other and interacted to guarantee a jungle of competing and overlapping agencies to rule.

During the War, the disintegration of anything resembling a state *system* rapidly accelerated.[36] In the occupied territories, the so-called Nazi 'new order' drove the replacement of clearly defined structures of domination by the untrammelled and uncoordinated force of competing power groups to unheard of levels. By the time Goebbels was writing in his diary, in March 1943, of a 'leadership crisis'[37] – and speaking privately of a 'leader crisis'[38] – the 'system' of rule in which Hitler's leadership was both absolutely pivotal and at the same time utterly incompatible with a rational decision-making process, or with a coherent, unified administration and the attainment of limited goals,

---

[34] This may be to underestimate the 'systemlessness' of Stalinism. Even so, I would still see an important difference. Whatever erosion of systematic government and administration took place under Stalin was largely attributable to the dictator's deliberate actions, the inroads of his personal despotism. Under Nazism, the process was intrinsic to the nature of the regime. See my article, 'Totalitarianism Revisited', pp. 36–7.

[35] See Martin Broszat, *Der Staat Hitlers* (Munich 1969), esp. ch. 8–9.

[36] The internal government of Germany during the War has now been systematically examined by Dieter Rebentisch, *Führerstaat* (see reference in note 17 above).

[37] Louis D. Lochner, ed., *Goebbels Tagebücher aus den Jahren 1942–43* (Zürich 1948), pp. 242, 274, 296.   [38] Albert Speer, *Erinnerungen* (Frankfurt am Main–Berlin 1969), p. 271.

was unrescuable, its self-destructive capacity unmistakable, its eventual demise certain.

Hitler was irreplaceable in Nazism in a way which did not apply to Stalin in Soviet Communism. His position was, in fact, irreconcilable with the setting up of any structures to elect or select a successor. A framework to provide for the succession to Hitler was never established. The frequently mooted Party senate never came about.[39] Hitler remained allergic to any conceivable institutional constraint, and by 1943 the deposition of Mussolini by the Fascist Grand Council ruled out once and for all any expectation of a Party body existing quasi-independently of the Leader in Germany. Though Göring had been declared the heir apparent, this became increasingly nominal as the Reich Marshal's star waned visibly during the War. None of the other second-rank Nazi leaders posed as a serious alternative candidate to succeed Hitler. It is indeed difficult to see who could have taken over, how the personalised rule of Hitler could have become systematised. The regime, one is compelled to suggest, was incapable of reproducing itself.

The objection that but for a lost war there was nothing to prevent this happening seems misplaced. The War was not accidental to Nazism. It lay at its very core. The War had to be fought, and could not be put off until a more favourable juncture. And by the end of 1941, even though the War dragged on a further three and a half years, the gamble for 'world power' was objectively lost. As such, the dynamism of the regime and its self-destructive essence could be said to be inseparable.

This bring me back to the questions I posed at the beginning. If my understanding of some of the recent discussion on Stalinism is not too distorted, and if the points of contrast with the Hitler regime I have outlined above have some validity, then it would be fair to conclude that, despite some superficial similarities, the character of the dictatorship, that is, of Stalin's and Hitler's leadership positions within their respective regimes, was fundamentally different. It would surely be a limited explanation, however, to locate these differences merely in the personalities of the dictators. Rather, I would suggest, they should be seen as a reflection of the contrasting social motivations of the followers, the character of the ideological driving force, and the corresponding nature of the political vanguard movement upholding each regime. The Nazi Movement, to put the point bluntly, was a classic 'charismatic' leadership movement; the Soviet Communist Party was not. And this has a bearing on the self-reproducing capacity of the two 'systems' of rule.

---

[39] See Broszat, *Staat*, pp. 262, 361–2; Rebentisch, *Führerstaat*, pp. 101, 421–2.

The main features of 'charismatic authority' as outlined by Max Weber need no embroidering here: perceptions of a heroic 'mission' and presumed greatness in the leader by his 'following'; tendency to arise in crisis conditions as an 'emergency' solution; innate instability under the double constant threat of collapse of 'charisma' through failure to meet expectations and 'routinisation' into a 'system' capable of reproducing itself only through eliminating, subordinating, or subsuming the 'charismatic' essence.[40] In its pure form, the personal domination of 'charismatic authority' represents the contradiction and negation of the impersonal, functional exercise of power which lies at the root of the bureaucratic legal-rational authority of the 'ideal type' modern state system.[41] It cannot, in fact, become 'systematised' without losing its particular 'charismatic' edge. Certainly, Max Weber envisaged possibilities of institutionalised 'charisma', but the compromises with the pure form then become evident.

The relevance of the model of 'charismatic authority' to Hitler seems obvious.[42] In the case of Stalin it is less convincing. The 'mission' in this latter case resides, it could be argued, in the Communist Party as the vehicle of marxist-leninist doctrine. For a while, it is true, Stalin hijacked the 'mission' and threatened to expropriate it through his personality cult. But this cult was a gradual and belated product, an excrescence artificially tagged on to Stalin's actual function. In this sense, there was a striking contrast with the Hitler personality cult, which was inseparable from the 'mission' embodied in his name practically from the beginning, a 'mission' which from the mid-1920s at the latest did not exist as a doctrine independent of the leader.

Max Weber's model of 'charismatic authority' is an abstraction, a descriptive concept which says nothing in itself of the content of any specific manifestation of 'charismatic authority'. This is determined by the relationship of the leadership claim to the particular circumstances and 'political culture' in which it arises and which give shape to it. The essence of the Hitlerist 'charismatic claim' was the 'mission' to achieve 'national rebirth' through racial purity and racial empire. But this claim was in practice sufficiently vague, adaptable, and amorphous to be able to mesh easily with and incorporate more traditionalist blends of nationalism and imperialism whose pedigree stretched back to the

[40] Max Weber, *Economy and Society*, ed. Guenther Roth and Claus Wittich (Berkeley–Los Angeles 1978), pp. 241–54, 266–71, 1111–57.
[41] See André Gorz, *Farewell to the Working Class* (London 1982), pp. 58–9, 62–3.
[42] The model is interestingly deployed by M. Rainer Lepsius, 'Charismatic Leadership: Max Weber's Model and its Applicability to the Rule of Hitler', in *Changing Conceptions of Leadership*, ed. Carl Friedrich Graumann and Serge Moscovici, (New York, 1986). My own attempt to use it is in my recent short study *Hitler. A Profile in Power* (London 1991).

Kaiserreich.[43] The trauma of war, defeat, and 'national disgrace', then the extreme conditions of a state system in a terminal stage of dissolution and a nation wrecked by chasmic internal divisions offered the potential for the 'charismatic claim' to gain extensive support, stretching way beyond the original 'charismatic community', and for it to provide the basis for an altogether new form of state.

In a modern state, the replacement of functional bureaucracy through personal domination is surely an impossibility. But even the coexistence of 'legal rational' and 'charismatic' sources of legitimacy can only be a source of tension and conflict, potentially of a seriously dysfunctional kind. What occurred in the Third Reich was not the supplanting of bureaucratic domination by 'charismatic authority', but rather the superimposition of the latter on the former. Where constitutional law could now be interpreted as no more than 'the legal formulation of the historic will of the Führer' – seen as deriving from his 'outstanding achievements'[44] – and where Germany's leading constitutional lawyer could speak of 'state power' being replaced by unrestrained 'Führer power',[45] the result could only be the undermining of the basis of impersonal law on which modern 'legal-rational' state systems rest and the corrosion of 'ordered' forms of government and institutionalised structures of administration through unfettered personal domination whose overriding source of legitimacy was the 'charismatic claim', the 'vision' of national redemption.[46]

The inexorable disintegration into 'systemlessness' was, therefore, not chiefly a matter of 'will'. Certainly, Hitler was allergic to any semblance of a practical or theoretical constraint on his power. But there was no systematic 'divide-and-rule' policy, no sustained attempt to *create* the administrative anarchy of the Third Reich. It was indeed in part a reflection of Hitler's personality and his style of leadership: as already pointed out, he was unbureaucratic in the extreme, stayed aloof from the daily business of government, and was uninterested in complex matters of detail. But this non-bureaucratic style was itself more than just a personality foible or eccentricity. It was also an inescapable product of the deification of the leadership position itself,

---

[43] For the imperialist traditions on which Nazism could build, see Woodruff D. Smith, *The Ideological Origins of Nazi Imperialism* (Oxford 1986). The ways in which Nazism could exploit 'mainstream' nationalism are stressed by William Sheridan Allen, 'The Collapse of Nationalism in Nazi Germany', in *The State of Germany*, ed. John Breuilly (London 1992), pp. 141–53.

[44] Hans Frank, *Im Angesicht des Galgens* (Munich–Gräfelfing 1953), pp. 466–7; trans. N & P, vol. II, p. 200.

[45] Ernst Rudolf Huber, *Verfassungsrecht des Großdeutschen Reiches* (Hamburg 1939), p. 230; rans. N & P, vol. II, p. 199.

[46] For a compelling analysis of 'national rebirth' as the essence of the fascist doctrine, see Roger Griffin, *The Nature of Fascism* (London 1991).

and the consequent need to sustain prestige to match the created image. His instinctive Darwinism made him unwilling and unable to take sides in a dispute till the winner emerged. But the need to protect his infallible image also made him largely incapable of doing so.

It was not in itself simply the undermining of 'rational' structures of government and proliferation of chaotic, 'polycratic' agencies that mattered. It was that this process accompanied and promoted a gradual realisation of ideological aims which were inextricably bound up in the 'mission' of the 'charismatic' Leader as the 'idea' of Nazism, located in the person of the Führer, became translated between 1938 and 1942 from utopian 'vision' into practical reality. There was, in other words, a symbiotic relationship between the structural disorder of the Nazi state and the radicalisation of policy.

The key development was unquestionably the growth in autonomy of the authority of the Führer to a position where it was unrestrained in practice as well as theory by any governmental institutions, or alternative organs of power, a stage reached at the latest by 1938.[47] After the Blomberg–Fritsch affair of February 1938 it is difficult to see where the structures or the individuals capable of applying the brakes to Hitler remained. By this date, the pressures unleashed in part by the Dictator's own actions, but even more so by diplomatic and economic developments beyond his control, encouraged and even conditioned the high-risk approach which was in any case Hitler's second nature.

Meanwhile, in conjunction with the expansion into Austria and the Sudetenland in 1938, race policy too, moved up a gear. The *Reichskristallnacht* pogrom in November, initiated by Goebbels not Hitler, though carried out with the latter's express approval,[48] was the culmination of the radicalisation of the previous year or so, and ended by handing over effective centralised coordination of the 'Jewish Question' to Heydrich.

Territorial expansion and 'removal of the Jews', the two central features of Hitler's *Weltanschauung*, had thus come together in 1938 into sharp focus in the foreground of the picture. The shift from utopian 'vision' to practical policy options was taking shape.

It would be mistaken to look only or even mainly to Hitler's own actions as the source of the continuing radicalisation of the regime. Hitler was the linchpin of the entire 'system', the only common link of its various component parts. But for the most part he was not directly needed to spur on the radicalisation. What seems crucial, therefore, is the way in which 'charismatic authority' functioned in practice to

[47] See Broszat, *Staat*, ch. 8.
[48] The recently discovered, formerly missing, parts of Goebbels' diaries make explicitly clear Hitler's role in approving the most radical measures as regards both the pogrom itself and its aftermath. See the extracts published in *Der Spiegel*, No. 29 (1992), pp. 126–8; an abbreviated version of the diary entry for 10 Nov. 1938 is available in Ralf Georg Reuth (ed.), *Joseph Goebbels. Tagebücher* (Munich 1992), vol. III, pp. 1281–2.

dissolve any framework of 'rational' government which might have acted as a constraint and to stimulate the radicalisation largely brought about by others, without Hitler's clear direction.

The function of Hitler's 'charismatic' Führer position could be said to have been threefold: that of unifier, of activator, and of enabler in the Third Reich.

As *unifier*, the 'idea' incorporated in the quasi-deified Führer figure was sufficiently indistinct but dynamic to act as a bond not only for otherwise warring factions of the Nazi Movement but also, until it was too late to extricate themselves from the fateful development, for non-Nazi national-conservative elites in army, economy, and state bureaucracy. It also offered the main prop of popular support for the regime (repeatedly giving Hitler a plebiscitary basis for his actions) and a common denominator around which an underlying consensus in Nazi policy could be focused.[49]

As *activator*, the 'vision' embodied by Hitler served as a stimulant to action in the different agencies of the Nazi Movement itself, where pent-up energies and unfulfilled social expectations could be met by activism carried out in Hitler's name to bring about the aims of Leader and Party. But beyond the Movement, it also spurred initiatives within the state bureaucracy, industry, the armed forces, and among members of the professions such as teachers, doctors, or lawyers where the motif of 'national redemption' could offer an open door to the push for realisation of long-cherished professional or career aims, felt to have been held back or damaged by the Weimar 'system'.[50] In all these ways, the utopian 'vision' bound up with the Führer – undefined, and largely undefinable – provided 'guidelines for action'[51] which were given concrete meaning and specific content by the voluntary 'push' of a wide variety of often competing agencies of the regime. The most important, most dynamic, and most closely related to Hitler's ideological imperatives of these was, of course, the SS, where the 'idea' or 'vision' offered the scope for ever new initiatives in a ceaseless dynamic of discrimination, repression, and persecution.

Perhaps most important of all, as *enabler* Hitler's authority gave implicit backing and sanction to those whose actions, however inhumane, however radical, fell within the general and vague ideological remit of furthering the aims of the Führer. Building a 'national community', preparing for the showdown with Bolshevism, purifying

---

[49] I have attempted to present the evidence in my study *The 'Hitler Myth'. Image and Reality in the Third Reich* (Oxford 1987).

[50] For an excellent study of how the medical profession exploited the opportunities offered by national socialism, see Michael H. Kater, *Doctors under Hitler* (Chapel Hill–London 1989).

[51] Martin Broszat, 'Soziale Motivation und Führer-Bindung des Nationalsozialismus', *Vierteljahreshefte für Zeitgeschichte*, 18 (1970), p. 405.

the Reich of its political and biological or racial enemies, and removing Jews from Germany, offered free licence to initiatives which, unless inopportune or counter-productive, were more or less guaranteed sanction from above. The collapse in civilised standards which began in spring 1933 and the spiralling radicalisation of discrimination and persecution that followed not only met with no blockage but invariably found legitimation in the highest authority in the land.

Crucial to this 'progress into barbarism'[52] was the fact that in 1933 the barriers to state-sanctioned measures of gross inhumanity were re-moved almost overnight. What had previously been unthinkable suddenly became feasible. Opportunities rapidly presented themselves; and they were readily grasped.

The Sterilisation Law of July 1933 is an early instance of such a dropping of barriers, as ideas long cherished in eugenics circles of biological-social engineering found all at once a climate in which they could be put into practice without constraints still taken for granted in proposals – in themselves inhumane enough, but still confined to *voluntary* sterilisation – for legislation put forward by the German Doctors' Association just weeks before Hitler's takeover of power.[53]

By 1939 the erosion of civilised values had developed far enough to allow for the possibilities of liquidating as 'useless life' those deemed to be harmful to the propagation of 'healthy comrades of the people'.[54] And, illustrating how far the disintegration of the machinery of government had progressed, when written authorisation was needed it took the form not of a government law or decree (which Hitler expressly ruled out), but of a few lines typed on Hitler's private headed paper.[55] The few lines were enough to seal the fate of over 70,000 mentally sick and physically disabled persons in Germany by mid-1941 in the so-called 'euthanasia action'.

After 1939, in the parts of Poland annexed by Germany and incorpor-ated into the Reich, prompted by Hitler's exhortation of brutal methods in a 'racial struggle' which was not to be confined by legal consider-ations,[56] the constraints on inhumanity towards the Polish population, and of course towards the Jewish minority in Poland, disappeared com-pletely. Hitler needed to do nothing to force the pace of the rapidly escalating barbarism. He could leave it to his satraps on the spot.

[52] Michael Burleigh and Wolfgang Wippermann, *The Racial State. Germany 1933–1945* (Cambridge 1991), back cover.
[53] See Jeremy Noakes, 'Nazism and Eugenics: the Background to the Nazi Sterilisation Law of 14 July 1933', in *Ideas into Politics*, eds. R. J. Bullen *et al.* (London–Sydney 1984) pp. 75–94, esp. pp. 84–5.
[54] See the documentation by Ernst Klee, *'Euthanasie' im NS-Staat. Die 'Vernichtung lebensunwerten Lebens'* (2nd edn, Frankfurt am Main 1983).
[55] Klee, *'Euthanasie'*, pp. 100–1.
[56] Martin Broszat, *Nationalsozialistische Polenpolitik 1939–1945* (Frankfurt am Main 1965), pp. 11, 25.

Characteristically, he said he asked no more of his *Gauleiter* in the east than that after ten years they should be able to announce that their territories were completely German.[57] The invitation was in itself sufficient to spark a competition in brutality – though allegedly this was the opposite of what Hitler wanted – between the arch-rival provincial chieftains Albert Forster in West Prussia and Arthur Greiser in the Warthegau to be able to report to the Führer in the shortest time that the 'racial struggle' had been won, that complete Germanisation had been achieved.[58]

The licence which Hitler as 'enabler' offered to such Party bosses in the east can be illustrated graphically through the 'initiative' taken by Greiser in May 1942 recommending the liquidation of 35,000 Poles suffering from incurable tuberculosis.[59] In the event, Greiser's suggestion encountered difficulties. Objections were raised that it would be hard to maintain secrecy – reference was made here to the impact of the earlier 'euthanasia programme' in Germany itself – and was likely, therefore, to arouse unrest among the Polish population as well as presenting foreign propaganda with a gift. It was regarded as necessary to consult Hitler himself if the 'action' were to go ahead. Greiser's enlightening response ran: 'I myself do not believe that the Führer needs to be asked again in this matter, especially since at our last discussion with regard to the Jews he told me that I could proceed with these according to my own judgement'.[60] This judgement had already in fact been to recommend to Himmler the 'special treatment' (that is, killing) of 100,000 Jews in the Warthegau – the start of the 'final solution' there.[61]

Greiser thought of himself throughout as the direct agent and instrument of the Führer in the crusade to create his 'model Gau'. Any hindrance was met by the claim that his mandate to germanise the Warthegau rested upon plenipotentiary powers bestowed upon him personally by the Führer himself.[62]

The relationship between the Führer, serving as a 'symbol' for

---

[57] Broszat, *Polenpolitik*, p. 200 n. 45.　　[58] Broszat, *Polenpolitik* p. 122.

[59] The correspondence between Greiser and Himmler on the subject, dated between 1 May and 3 December 1942, is in the personal file of Arthur Greiser in the Berlin Document Center (hereafter BDC). For a more extended discussion, see my article, 'Improvised Genocide? The Emergence of the "Final Solution" in the "Warthegau"', *Transactions of the Royal Historical Society*, 6th Series, 2 (1992), pp. 51–78, here pp. 71–3.

[60] BDC, Personal File of Arthur Greiser, letter of Greiser to Himmler, 21 Nov. 1942.

[61] BDC, Personal File of Arthur Greiser, letter of Greiser to Himmler, 1 May 1942.

[62] Examples in the Archive of the Polish War Crimes Commission, Ministry of Justice, Warsaw, Greiser Trial Documents, File 11, Fol. 52, File 13, Fol. 15. According to the post-war testimony of one of the heads of regional administration in the Warthegau, Greiser never missed an opportunity in his speeches to insist that he was 'persona gratissima' with the Führer – File 36, Fol. 463. Another contemporary commented that his gratitude knew no bounds once Hitler had granted him this special plenipotentiary authority. See Carl J. Burckhardt, *Meine Danziger Mission 1937–1939* (Munich 1962), p. 79. I have contributed a short pen-picture of Greiser to Ronald Smelser *et al.* (eds.), *Die braune Elite und ihre Helfer*, vol. II (Darmstadt 1993), pp. 116–27.

actionism and ideological radicalisation, and the drive 'from below' on the part of so many agencies, non-Nazi as well as Nazi, to put the 'vision' or parts of it into operation as practical policy is neatly captured in the sentiments of a routine speech of a Nazi functionary in 1934:

> Everyone who has the opportunity to observe it knows that the Führer can hardly dictate from above everything which he intends to realise sooner or later. On the contrary, up till now everyone with a post in the new Germany has worked best when he has, so to speak, worked towards the Führer. Very often and in many spheres it has been the case – in previous years as well – that individuals have simply waited for orders and instructions. Unfortunately, the same will be true in the future; but in fact it is the duty of everybody to try to work towards the Führer along the lines he would wish. Anyone who makes mistakes will notice it soon enough. But anyone who really works towards the Führer along his lines and towards his goal will certainly both now and in the future one day have the finest reward in the form of the sudden legal confirmation of his work.[63]

These comments hint at the way 'charismatic authority' functioned in the Third Reich – anticipation of Hitler's presumed wishes and intentions as 'guidelines for action' in the certainty of approval and confirmation for actions which accorded with those wishes and intentions.

'Working towards the Führer' may be taken in a literal, direct sense with reference to Party functionaries, in the way it was meant in the extract cited. In the case of the SS, the ideological executive of the 'Führer's will', the tasks associated with 'working towards the Führer' offered endless scope for barbarous initiatives, and with them institutional expansion, power, prestige, and enrichment. The career of Adolf Eichmann, rising from a menial role in a key policy area to the manager of the 'Final Solution', offers a classic example.[64]

But the notion of 'working towards the Führer' could be interpreted, too, in a more indirect sense where ideological motivation was secondary, or perhaps even absent altogether, but where the objective function of the actions was nevertheless to further the potential for implementation of the goals which Hitler embodied. Individuals seeking material gain through career advancement in Party or State bureaucracy, the small businessman aiming to destroy a competitor through a slur on his 'aryan' credentials, or ordinary citizens settling scores with neighbours by denouncing them to the Gestapo, were all, in a way, 'working

---

[63] Niedersächisches Staatsarchiv, Oldenburg, Best. 131, Nr. 303, Fol. 131v, speech of Werner Willikens, State Secretary in the Ministry of Food, 21 Feb. 1934; trans. N & P, vol. II, p. 207.   [64] See Hannah Arendt, *Eichmann in Jerusalem* (London 1963).

towards the Führer'. Doctors rushing to nominate patients of asylums for the 'euthanasia programme' in the interests of a eugenically 'healthier' people; lawyers and judges zealous to cooperate in the dismantling of legal safeguards in order to cleanse society of 'criminal elements' and undesirables; business leaders anxious to profit from preparations for war and once in war by the grabbing of booty and exploitation of foreign slave labour; thrusting technocrats and scientists seeking to extend power and influence through jumping on the bandwagon of technological experimentation and modernisation; non-Nazi military leaders keen to build up a modern army and restore Germany's hegemony in central Europe; and old-fashioned conservatives with a distaste for the Nazis but an even greater fear and dislike of the Bolsheviks: all were, through their many and varied forms of collaboration, indirectly at least 'working towards the Führer'. The result was the unstoppable radicalisation of the 'system' and the gradual emergence of policy objectives closely related to the ideological imperatives represented by Hitler.

Time after time, Hitler set the barbaric tone, whether in hate-filled public speeches giving a green light for discriminatory actions against Jews and other 'enemies of the state', or in closed addresses to Nazi functionaries or military leaders where he laid down, for example, the brutal guidelines for the occupation of Poland and for 'Operation Barbarossa'. But there was never any shortage of willing helpers, far from confined to Party activists, ready to 'work towards the Führer' to put the mandate into operations. Once the War – intrinsic to Nazism and Hitler's 'vision' – had begun, the barbarism inspired by that 'vision' and now unchecked by any remnants of legal constraint or concern for public sensitivities plumbed unimaginable depths. But there was no prospect, nor could there have been, of the 'New Order' settling into a 'system' of government. Competing fiefdoms, not structured government, formed the grim face of Nazi rule in the occupied territories. The rapaciousness and destructiveness present from the start within Germany now became hugely magnified and intensified with the conquered peoples rather than the Germans themselves as the main victims.

Through the metaphor of 'working towards the Führer', I have tried to suggest here that the 'vision' embodied in Hitler's leadership claim served to funnel a variety of social motivations, at times contradictory and conflicting, into furthering – intentionally or unwittingly – Nazi aims closely associated with Hitler's own ideological obsessions. The concept of 'charismatic authority' in this interpretation can be taken as useful in helping to depict the bonds with Hitler forged by various social and political forces, enabling the form of personalised power which he represented to free itself from all institutional constraints and to legitimise the destructive dynamic intrinsic to the Nazi gamble for European hegemony through war.

The model of 'charismatic authority', which I have suggested is applicable to the Hitler but not the Stalin dictatorship, not only helps to characterise the appeal of a quasi-messianic personalised form of rule embodying national unity and rebirth in the context of the collapse of legitimation of the democratic system of Weimar, but also, given the irreconcilable tension between 'charismatic authority' and bureaucratic rule in the Third Reich, offers insights into the inexorable erosion of anything resembling a *system* of domination capable of reproducing itself.

Within this 'Behemoth' of governmental disorder,[65] 'working towards the Führer' amounted to a selective push for the radicalisation and implementation of those ideological lines most closely associated with Hitler's known broad aims, which could gradually take shape as policy objectives rather than distant goals.

Above all, the 'charismatic' model fits a form of domination which could never settle down into 'normality' or routine, draw a line under its achievements and come to rest as conservative authoritarianism, but was compelled instead to sustain the dynamism and push ceaselessly and relentlessly for new attainments in the quest to fulfil its chimeric goal. The longer the Hitler regime lasted, the more megalomaniac the aims, the more boundless the destructiveness became. But the longer the regime went on, the less it resembled a governmental *system* with the capacity to reproduce itself.

The immanent instability of 'charismatic authority' in this manifestation – where the specific content of the 'charismatic claim' was rooted in the utopian goal of national redemption through racial purification, war, and conquest – implied then not only destructiveness, but also self-destructiveness. Hitler's own suicidal tendencies could in this sense be said to accord with the inbuilt incapacity of his form of authoritarian rule to survive and reproduce itself.

[65] See Franz Neumann, *Behemoth. The Structure and Practice of National Socialism* (London 1942).

5

Stalin in the mirror of the other

Moshe Lewin

This chapter is based, to a large extent, on one of the insights that comparative history can offer: helping oneself to the rich historiography of Germany and to a much better knowledge about Hitler and his regime, in the hope of generating new ideas and questions about the less-known Stalin and his regime. The exercise consists then, in a sense, in holding the German mirror to Russia's face – or rather to its history. In this case, we limit ourselves only to the two dictatorships – although the same method could be applied to other periods and areas too. The reader will realise that our aim here is to learn more about Stalin, not to try to contribute to the knowledge of Hitler.

It is also quite revealing that many students of Germany use interpretative constructs, specifically concepts that can be or are already being usefully employed in interpreting the Russian historical processes at different periods. Ideas like 'Gleichzeitigkeit des Ungleich-zeitigen' (E. Bloch) or 'combined development' (Trotsky), 'legacy of the pre-capitalist past' (Wehler), 'crisis of modernity' (Peukert), are 'strategic' ones in the battle of interpretations concerning the dictatorships in question.[1]

Stalin's cult-autocracy

The making of Stalin's autocracy, amidst an enormous construction effort, was permeated by destructive policies: abundance of terror, magic and rituals testified to and covered up for a deep cultural and political regression and a mighty cultural counter-revolution, as destructive as the other aspects of Stalinism. The enormous schooling effort, with its unavoidably half-baked products, contributed to the

---

[1] See on this David Blackbourn and Geoff Eley, *The Peculiarities of German History* (Oxford–New York 1987), pp. 239–41 and *passim*.

damage, even as it lifted a multitude of people to new positions and chances in life. All these traits were preconditions for the launching and results of the successful imposition of a 'cult figure' who filled out the socio-psychological and political space of a country in turmoil, impressed the minds of the population, and was widely accepted as indispensable. Replacing Stalin seemed unimaginable.

The cult fitted the given circumstances quite naturally. There was no cult of Stalin, of any kind, before 1928: it was fabricated, as in Nazi Germany, with ever-growing doses of terror. Unlike Germany though (except for the purge of the SA in 1934), the Nazi party itself was not ruled internally by terror, though it was deeply authoritarian and disciplinarian. Stalin applied mass terror in the party on an unheard-of scale. And, unlike Hitler, he also terrorised his entourage: all the top leaders, from the Politburo down, were either actually executed, or knew that they were candidates for the gallows at a moment's notice. This may underscore the point that the party, per se, was not a natural carrier of the Stalin cult – or, at least, Stalin did not believe it was. There was no Lenin cult in the upper ranks of the party during his lifetime. Had there been one, no one would have been able to engage in polemics and ideological battles with a cult figure. Yet it is a fact that most of the important leaders, and many lesser figures, did not hesitate to challenge Lenin when they believed they should. Parallel to Ian Kershaw's reflection on the Hitler myth, Stalin's myth was deliberately created by Stalin himself or under his direct, supercilious supervision. He personally edited his biography in an effort to produce a new form of legitimacy, not just in the population but, initially, even more so inside the party. That was indispensable because the mutation into 'Stalinism' consisted in abandoning the historical ideology and replacing it by another that better fitted the reality and aims of a regime that was by now 'moving elsewhere' very rapidly, away from marxism and socialism, away from ideals of popular sovereignty and rule of law – the list is longer – while still denying that the change was occurring. What better than a deified autocracy for minds that were still mostly rural, or were just freshly from the countryside, shaped by tsarist traditions and a religious mentality with a deeply seated psychological need for a strong figure in times of stress? Or so runs the argument quite often.

Charisma, a helpful term for leaders who were cult figures, may not be the proper term to apply to Stalin, unless we redefine it. In Weber's concept charisma did not come with an office (like the Pope's) but had to be conquered. Neither did his concept have any place for terror. It was up to the leader to prove himself over and over again to his followers. There was adoration among the believers, followed either by abandonment of the charismatic leader once the spell failed, or by his 'routinisation'.

Terrorising the followers would not fit the whole concept. Stalin, at the height of his power, was hidden from his followers, and he kept people around him under the threat of death. They had constantly to prove something to him rather than the other way round. They had, all too often, to prove the impossible – that they were not 'enemies'. The German historical experience has examples of techniques that authoritarians used – for similar needs. Hans Ulrich Wehler, a key theoretician of the thesis commonly called 'the German *Sonderweg*',[2] speaks about Bismarck (and others) whose policy was based on what he calls 'negative inspiration': when the ability to offer positive inspiration is missing, creating images of 'enemies of the Empire' (liberals, Catholics, socialists, Jews) and of other, non-existent dangers, is often successfully used to shore up the power and mobilising capacities of the regime. Wehler also mentions 'structural hostility towards democracy' that characterised many nationalisms, ideologies and some churches which engaged in spreading their 'negative inspirations' notably to serve their 'structural hostility'. These were, unfortunately, all too often very effective policies. In view of these, as well as Russian precedents, it turns out that what Stalin practised was actually a political 'classic'. His earlier 'enemies' (foreign encirclement, capitalist hostility) were more realistic – but the later 'enemies of the people' were internal, not concrete, extremely vague and deliberately broad – anyone could fit in. This fact squares with another element of this all-purpose 'strategy' (my term) that Burckhardt (quoted in Wehler) described as creating 'a stage of a quiet siege' as a way of ruling: which is precisely what Stalin's regime 'accomplished'.

The creation and use of an image of *vozhd* (best translated by the Latin term 'dux', just 'leader' would not do), based on Lenin's position and role but with considerable bending of the historical truth about the founding father, served as a stepping-stone for Stalin's 'cult'. This was an important part of Stalin's ruling technique – he projected over the years more than one image of himself. There was one, or barely one, until the end of the civil war, another in NEP (without Stalinism as yet), another during 'the cult' and what some called 'high Stalinism'. In any case, he was no *vozhd* in those earlier years and even after Lenin's death the party's activists heard from Kamenev – previously no lesser a leader than Stalin – 'our party does not need a *vozhd*'. So there were some steps Stalin had to climb before being able to bestow on himself the coveted chasuble.

[2] Hans Ulrich Wehler, *The German Empire, 1871–1918* (Leamington–Hamburg–New York 1985), pp. 90–4.

Behind the changing Stalin images ran different stages in the history of the system, which eventually harboured some alternative roads that could be taken. They could be deduced from obstacles that Stalin had to overcome on his way to full power. The question whether there was, say, 'a Lenin state', however short-lived, before it became Stalin's, can be answered by Stalin's use of a cult as the centrepiece of the political edifice – but also other features of his system which I call an 'agrarian despotism'. If I am correct in using it in relation to Stalinism, this notion could not be applied to the NEP period and its state system. It was a deeply agrarian society but it had no despotic cult figure at the centre of its political life, and however authoritarian the regime, it was nobody's 'agrarian despotism'. This had to be created, or recreated, first.

Nepian Russia, as it emerged from the Civil War, became again a peasant ocean, dominated by communal (*obshchinnye*) institutions which were made possible by the disappearance of capitalism during the revolutionary storm. The traditional traits of *muzhik* Russia were thereby accentuated in the early Soviet system. But on the other had they now had to face a state endowed with a new vigor. One of the aims of Stalin's policies, once he was firmly at the helm of this state, was to force the peasants to shed precisely the features that their own recent revolution had enhanced. What followed was a tortured interlacing of 'traditional' and 'modern' features, the so-called most advanced inter-mingling with the most backward, even barbarian ones. Furthermore, this intermingling happened in the process of 'a leap forward' – a special strategy, undergirded by the gap between the social base, from which a leap started, and a state that could and did decide to use all its power to overcome a crisis, with the party tipping the scale towards a policy of a *ryvok* – a dash! The scale could have been tipped towards a different strategy, but once the choice was made, the Bolsheviks themselves, as a party, followed the Liberals, Mensheviks and the SRs 'into the dustbin of history'. The 'combined development' thesis, or 'Gleichzeitigkeit des Ungleichzeitigen', as Ernst Bloch called it, is tailor-made for this situation.

The strategies of the *ryvok* turned out to be, to a large extent, an all-out war against the peasants (they were the bulk of the nation) – thus a 'revolution' but not anti-capitalist as claimed. Anti-petty bourgeois then? Not even this. Whatever our class analysis of the peasantry, the upshot was momentous: with coercive methods applied to the majority of the nation to keep it working, especially in *kolkhozy*, a forceful intrusion of a dynamic force into a more traditional, deeply rural (agrarian) society took place.

These then were the circumstances in which an autocratic, personally despotic system reappeared – even if absolutism was already very considerably watered down in the last stages of the tsarist state. It manifested itself in many of the traits of the Stalinist state, all flowing from the basic premisses – not just a controlled and constrained environment but one that was still very 'traditional'. The depth of the cult's success in people's minds, hence the weight of the tsarist past as one of the preconditions, without which, presumably, the fabrication would have remained hanging in the air, is still a matter of conjecture.

The very making of Stalinism implies an ideological transformation, including a return to forms of nationalism from before the revolution and even to more ancient imperial themes and symbols – a perfectly fitting requirement for an agrarian despotism seeking to legitimise itself in a very shifty and explosive situation. 'Socialism' would not do the trick. Magic, rituals, and, finally 'demonisation' of ubiquitous, subversive enemies – all equally 'archaic' ingredients although not at all rare apparitions and not exclusively Russian phenomena – were the indispensable ideological and emotional crutches. The dogmatic canonisation of thought and of a leader who controlled the terms of praise that are showered on him closes the list.

The inadequacy of Leninism for the needs of the Stalinist era is illustrated by the effort the regime undertook to mobilise ideological resources entirely foreign to the initial creed. It is obvious that Stalin tried to tap political traditions, several of them simultaneously or at different times: he wanted to put to his use the aura of the great, successful, mostly 'imperial' tsars; he also wanted the glamour of the traditional state (with its auxiliary borrowing of church iconography for its own splendour); and, finally, he wanted to partake of the personal charisma of an anointed *tsar-batiushka* but magnified well beyond the tsar's reach. '*Rodina-Mat*' – a peculiarly Russian over-emotional term for 'motherland', later the more politically expressive but equally emotive and mythical '*Velikaia Rus*', (best translated as 'Russia the Magnificent') – all were taken from the tsarist-Russian heritage, of obvious right-wing inspiration, and used by Stalin in an effort to gain a historical over-insurance for himself and his system. This over-insurance or 'alibi' problem is worth exploring further.

The evanescent 'alibi'

If somebody could have extracted it from him, Stalin would have had a lot of explaining to do as to why, having reached the top without internal terror and any 'cult' around his persona, he became a bloody oppressor, found it necessary to resort to massive distortions and silencing of any criticism, destroyed social thought and Marxism with it – but still keeping some elements of it and mingling them with archaisms of all kinds. He was no founder of the party and had quite a problem with it, until he finally did produce a system, a genuine product of his own. But this was done at the expense of perverting the ideology of the founders, destroying the whole original setting of Bolshevism, in fact, betraying it. A whole system of lies had to be erected to cover up these facts. He did not and could not remain faithful in earnest to the initial gospel. His was, by the tenets of the founding ideology, a counter-revolution. Such a tortuous itinerary had to have convoluted and destructive effects – notably, what we call 'an alibi problem'.

It is doubtful whether building a violence-crazy superstate already existed as a hidden agenda in Stalin's mind at some early stage in his political life. He certainly had aspirations and ideas of his own at the stage of his career when he was already at the top of the party but was not yet its chief. We are not yet sure how far he intended to go at that time. But there are some well-known facts that emerge as we study nationalities and nationalism in Russia. We know from Hitler's biography that his soldiering in World War I exercised a powerful, formative influence on his personality and thinking. The most formative period for Stalin as a politician must have been the Civil War. It is here that his personal ruthlessness seemed to have shown its weight as an excellent political expedient. It is in this terrible crucible that Stalin learned the secret of victorious politics in the most daunting situation: state coercion was the secret of success, mobilisation, propaganda, military might, terror – such were the ingredients of power. It must have become for him synonymous with success in political leadership on a large historical arena. The debates about the way of incorporating the different nationalities of the empire into a common state show how those lessons of the Civil War were assimilated by Stalin and made into guidelines for his political choices. He was ready to make some verbal concessions – but the bottom line had to be a highly centralised, unitary state that would not broach any interference with its will from some spurious 'sovereignties'. In these conditions the discussions about 'building socialism in one country' were mostly a way of intimating that he actually assimilated the old Russian great power syndrome and his intention to lift it to unprecedented heights – in more than just his own country. It is on this plane that he clashed quite sharply with Lenin and turned against him. But Lenin, even when already mortally ill, was still too formidable a foe to be challenged very openly. This is why Stalin was still taking precautions and biding his time. It is true that the dying Lenin finally saw through his game – but by now it was too late.

Let us now glean some ideas from Hitler's biographies that could be used to cast a better light on aspects of Stalin's personality and leadership.

We know that the strands of Hitler's ideological development were coming together at the end of his writing of *Mein Kampf* in 1924–5 – and never changed thereafter.[3] At the same time, the main force of his appeal, and his personal insight in recognising the key feature of mass psychology, were also in place and rehearsed during his Munich rabble-rousing demagoguery. The lesson he learned and practised was one: masses do not understand complex ideas; what moves them is hatred. This is what he based his techniques on.

We do not yet know that much about the stages of Stalin's political development – except for his statism which we discussed earlier. Whipping up fear and hatred was certainly not yet of central import-ance in Stalin's methods and image at the time he became general secretary – he was to invent or reinvent these elements later. But he had to consolidate his power first, for he was far from firm in his saddle in the early 1920s. Hitler's fate too was still decided by others in 1932 and early 1933, mainly by those who were the players around Hindenburg. He would play with those who gave him power for some time – but would emancipate himself quickly. A similar stage in Stalin's biography occurred much earlier. His career for a time depended on Lenin and next lay briefly but precariously in the hands of the Central Committee, with a casting vote in the hands of Kamenev and Zinoviev – all around the bequest of the already deceased Lenin who had advised the party to remove Stalin from his post. Stalin liberated himself from this cloud over his head earlier than he understood – but he still fought this past 'dependence' for quite a time. And he didn't just outsmart those who helped him. He never forgave his past 'dependence' on them or any debt to them.

Whatever the timing of such innermost intentions of Stalin, he did build his vision on the future system around his person and that had to be done at the expense of his movement's original ideology and leadership. He must have been driven by an enormous psychological urge for personalised power – a quest he himself was probably discovering as he went along in playing the power games as nobody else around him did.

---

[3] William Carr, *Hitler: A Study in Personality and Politics* (New York 1973) is an important source for me, especially on the personal features of Hitler that I use more often than I acknowledge. I had no time to read the whole of Alan Bullock's impressive *Hitler and Stalin: Parallel Lives* (New York 1992) at the time I was working on this essay. Bullock provides a vast panorama covering the lives and times of the two dictators, without attempting systematically to compare them. He correctly stated in the title of the book that he is running 'parallel lives', in paired chapters devoted to each man separately at approximately the same period. There is enough there for anyone who wishes to use the material for comparative exercises.

Obviously, this kind of thirst for power had to be concealed from the party's top layers – and Stalin was an accomplished master of deception. His was an image of moderation and simplicity for most of the NEP. It worked very well for him. Internal terror, though intense, was probably less important in the making of Hitler's image but as the integrating power of the Hitler image declined in the later stages of the war, terror was increasing. Yet, miseries and terror were endured – the population, the army, the acolytes remained faithful to the very end because, according to Carr, 'in the Führer most people found a point of identification and a point of hope'.[4] In another context Carr also speaks of fear of the Russian conquest, dedication to the common ideological ground of a Greater Germany, shaking off Versailles, and so on.

At a time when Hitler was offering exactly what he promised and what the Germans adopted, to a large extent, as their own, he used and hyperbolised Germany's pre-existing nationalist, racist and militarist traditions, worked them into a specific war and expansion-oriented ideology – the Nazi one – and acted upon it. In this process he degraded the developed country he took over and destroyed millions of people, in the service of mythical dreams. He was a real founder of his party and destroyed it too but only in the sense that his policies were self-defeating. Otherwise, except for the 1934 purge, he did not slaughter either his party or his collaborators.

Hitler was – or became – confident and over-confident in his and his country's possibilities and in the dedication of his collaborators. Stalin had a tendency to test the loyalty toward him not only among the collaborators around him but also, more broadly, of the country's population. His distrust was certainly cast over the whole nation (certainly not a small burden to carry) and that is borne out by his belief in the hosts of 'enemies' which his secret services were constantly instructed to keep ferreting out. This must have been actually a need, because it provided a reassurance, however fleeting. No wonder that he, notably, underestimated his country's capacity to fight, allowing us to say that they fought and won 'despite him'. It all stemmed, in part, from the traits of his psyche and his mind which could not accept reality. Most notably, he was not historically the founder of this movement and he was taking the country in a direction he had to lie about: instead of the hoped-for ever-broadening emancipation, there was Stalinism. 'Betrayal' must have been an outrageously terrible thing for him to admit and it was none other than Trotsky, the only one among the leaders of the revolution to do so, who directly accused Stalin of being 'the gravedigger of the revolution'. This is why 'betrayal' had to be

---

[4] Carr, *Hitler*, pp. 160–1.

made into everybody else's fault. This is why he needed to test the strength and moral fibre ('moral', according to his own definition) of his entourage and the people at large – notably by the dubious test of dedication to his persona. The glorification of his greatness, genius, and, above all, his 'great simplicity', in so many speeches and writings, is known to have been 'commissioned' and the very terms used were screened in advance by Stalin himself. Strong leadership could be offered by a strong government – without a deified despot – without this kind of Stalin. We can speculate that this thought occurred to Stalin too. This is why it can be surmised that the 'need' in his kind of deified leadership, though it turned out acceptable to the masses, emanated not so much from them, not even from the party, but from the top group in power – and mainly from Stalin himself. Thus terms of adulation were one of the tests he conceived for his close collaborators. They knew it and competed in inventing ever newer superlatives in their speeches; some were really good at that. But lack of such praise (in Marshal Tukhachevsky's speeches, for example) could be and was fatal. Even a sparseness of adulatory expressions was an indication of an impending or actual 'betrayal'.

Thus, despite Stalin's unaccountability as leader, he was driven by an internal need for justification and a compelling alibi problem. We can deduce this from his method of supervising the ingredients of his cult and, not less convincingly, from his drive to destroy anyone who knew him or might have thought he knew him in a light that was different from what became his self-image. Thus the cult was not just a ruling device that some dictators might have seen, 'instrumentally', as the only way to rule 'these people'. One can safely say that here was not just a calculated *arcanum imperii* to be offered to the masses so that they would behave as expected. It was generated by the psyche of a man whose vanity was unsatiable (Volkogonov), coupled with a constant worry about his own security. It must have become part of the 'alibi' strategy – a deeply seated psychological urge. Stalin's strategy of 'producing enemies' (Hitler, of course, also used this device in a phantasmagoric and murderous manner) was all turned inward, more than outward. The 'sabotage' myth created the desired all-encompassing insurance policy against having to be liable for any damages. The obvious internal culprit was ever ready (vaguely attached to 'foreign intelligence'), credible enough to be charged with all possible treason, and account-able for Stalin's failures. When needed, 'the enemy' would just confess to anything. But these phantasms could hit all and any institutions and personalities of the regime. The whole action was conducted in a warlike style. When in the course of war Hitler needed slave labour, he ordered that people be hauled from conquered territories outside

115

Germany. Stalin's conquered territory was inside his own country, and this was where he created and used his pool of slave labour. His power inside and over his country was more absolute than Hitler's, but he still never felt that he had enough of it.

The cult capped this hallucinatory insurance policy which served psychological as well as systemic needs. It was a unifier and symbolic reassurance, and both dictators practised it. But Stalin's was created by him and for him years after he was already in power; Hitler had it, at least inside the party, almost from the beginning. Hitler's was also the unifying glue and mobiliser – and his image as the 'heroic' leader that seems to be expected in tough times, was 'fabricated' by Goebbels and Hitler himself. Hitler though, as we know, did it all on his own terms: a Hitler myth as he defined it himself originally. He did not hide the essence of what he was up to. His deification served a country in crisis and, even if his militaristic-conquering thrust was initially kept in abeyance, it was present all the time and clear to anyone who wanted to know. Hitler did not need an alibi. He did not perceive his aims as being treasonable in any way. Despite this circumstance there is enough evidence that Hitler took care and was preoccupied with the degree of his popularity among the people.

In Russia, the cult (deification) was pushed on the country from above in times of stress and fragmentation caused by the imposition of a forceful and spasmodic industrialisation. There was enough fuel there to worry the leaders. Was there any relation between popularity rates and Stalin's politics of purges? We have no good data so far to answer this question, but the powerful need in 'overinsuring' is, in itself, a very telling fact.

Nazism was impossible without the Hitler myth; it went with the other mythological aims that Nazism was all about. Nazi rule could not have functioned without it, as convincingly shown by Ian Kershaw.[5] The Stalin myth was indispensable to Stalin's rule. The fact that the myth could rather easily switch to 'collective leadership' after Stalin's death shows that this myth was not indispensable to the system or to the party. Its importance was a post-hoc rationalisation and it stayed much longer than Stalin himself in the minds of not only the citizens but also many foreign observers. But as long as Stalin was in power, his rule was strong. He did not need, like Hitler, to produce military exploits constantly. He could be content with – real or, again, mythical – achievements on the internal front, the term 'front' being symptomatic in this context: the internal 'offensive' was conducted as a set of planned military campaigns against mythical enemies. A more

[5] I have made systematic use of Ian Kershaw's *The Hitler Myth: Image and Reality in the Third Reich* (Oxford–New York 1987) as well as his later *Hitler* (London–New York 1991).

116

'normal' authoritarianism that came after his death showed how wasteful had been the regime that was so mightily mobilised to assure the safety of its dictator.

There is no need to prove that the inner dynamic of the Nazi party and of Hitler – war being its essence – was destructive. The same cannot be said however, about the pre-Stalin and post-Stalin ruling party. Stalin's war against his own was an interlude but as long as it lasted – and the same applied to Hitler almost until his very end – both personal dictatorships and myths were strong. There was plenty of support for and fascination with these leaders in both countries and that can be measured by simple, well-documented facts. When people in Germany were dissatisfied with some of the regime's doings, they still reacted widely and wishfully by saying' 'If only the Führer knew . . .' Likewise in Russia even sophisticated people thought during the deadly heat of the purges that Stalin did not know about these and would have stopped them if he had found out, or even that the accused must have been guilty at least of something. In both cases the dictators were actually exempted from responsibility.

Stalin's biographer Robert Tucker points out in the second instalment of his work[6] that solving great state problems by killing a leader was alien to the Bolshevik Marxists and none of them was using this method. 'The only Old Bolshevik capable of "individual terror" was Stalin.' Tucker wrote this in connection with Stalin's visit to Tomsky, the demoted old Bolshevik leader who reacted to this visit quite aggressively: he expelled Stalin from his house, cursing as he did so – and then committed suicide. Tucker goes on: 'The whole world would have changed in many ways for the better had Tomsky shot his visitor instead of or along with himself.' Obviously, Stalin was not worried about a thing like that. He knew an Old Bolshevik wouldn't do this to him. But he himself was different. And, as we said, he needed this additional psychological game to prove to himself his superiority over those 'meek' ex-comrades.

A civilisation amidst low literacy

Data on the cultural level of Russia and of its cadres, which I produced in an earlier work (*The Making of the Soviet System*, 1985, 1995) cast light on the stage that the country had reached. We offer here some additional eye-openers on this important subject. At the end of the 1920s and in the early 1930s 'in the majority of cases, the peasants were entering the ranks of labour being semi-literate or illiterate' according to three Soviet

---

[6] Robert C. Tucker, *Stalin in Power* (London 1991), pp. 374–5.

analysts writing in 1988. They quote a 1936 study of Stakhanovite combine drivers that showed that most of them 'never read books other than manuals of their machines'.[7] The authors claim (do they still claim it some years later?) that there was a development in the countryside of a 'socialist spirit' (*idejnost*) but in the 1930s 'this new socialist spirit overlaid a quite meagre cultural soil (2–3 years of elementary schooling in the best of cases) and it acquired, unavoidably, dogmatic and vulgar features'. The official Stalinist propaganda made things even worse. Still, even in those primitive forms, the *kolkhozniks* learned to think in terms broader than just their own district – they learned to think about the whole state.[8]

We can interject that there is nothing socialist about this – but this is just an aside.

New sources discovered by O. V. Khlevniuk shed more light on the state of the cadres: Malenkov, the Secretary responsible for cadres at that time, prepared a background brief for Stalin who needed it for the March–April plenum in 1937. He reported that among regional party secretaries only 17.7 per cent had higher education and 70.4 per cent had only elementary schooling. Respective figures for city secretaries were 12.1 and 80.3 per cent. Lacking adequate knowledge and culture, many local leaders made do through political resourcefulness and dexterity. They surrounded themselves with grey and pliant people – as a base for their own elevation. Stalin noticed this, says the author, but actually encouraged precisely this kind of personnel policy.[9] Such data were symptomatic of the cultural-moral background in the country – and among the cadres. This is important for interpreting Stalinism. But aren't we reading too much into such data? Hitler's cult grew in an educated country with plenty of excellent high-level professionals, some of them along the world's best. We know from reliable authorities that the professional academics – notably lawyers, judges, and, equally, the scions of nobility – flocked into the institutions of the regime and offered excellent, dedicated service. It is especially interesting to note that many educated 'generalists' – often excellent administrators – were particularly active in the Gestapo, the SS, and other parts of the security apparatus – many were active in planning and implementing the '*Endlösung*'. That such a large segment of the elite flocked into the top of the SS helped 'ennoble' this 'elite' by considering them as an elite service in the first place. They played a visible role in the repressive organs in

---

[7] P. S. Kabytov, V. A. Kozlov and D. G. Litvak, *Russkoe Krest'ianstvo-etapy dukhovnogo osvobozhdeniia* (Moscow 1988). All quotations are taken from pp. 208–10.

[8] Ibid., p. 209.

[9] O. V. Khlevniuk, *1937-oi* (Moscow 1992), pp. 78–9. He quoted from the party archives, Ts. P. A., f. 17, op. 2, d. 773, 1. 127. Khlevniuk is a fine scholar and publicist who produces very reliable work based on solid archival research.

the occupied territories, served not only in the SS-Führerkorps, but also in the Allgemeine-SS. And even if some of them, in private, were not really loyal to the regime, they gave the regime prestige and their talents.[10] This cannot but raise important questions concerning the relation between the level of education and political leanings.

Soviet Russia did not have at its disposal anything like Germany's intellectual resources. It had to rely, initially, on an often politically unsympathetic (and relatively small) layer of professionals and intellectuals who were not flocking into the system and especially not into the security agencies (in which they would, probably, not have been accepted). Later on, layers of their own intelligentsia would appear and serve the system and their quality would improve, quite slowly, but they too went through some stages in their attitude towards the regime. Once this intelligentsia was produced (by the regime, with some help of the older cadres, especially the army) it served loyally in all the agencies, accepted the 'cult', the myths, the lies, helped spread them and produced a huge layer of (more or less) educated Stalinists. Critical, sceptical, internal émigrés and outright open dissidents appeared much later in some numbers, but the vast majority served and enjoyed privileges until the last stages of the regime – again, even as growing numbers were ever more sceptical, critical, or hostile to it.

Russia's lack of culture and of cadres was insufficient for the country to have its 'leap forward' and socialism at the same time. It leapt into something else instead. Germany did not need to industrialise in the first place. The Germans went for a racist-nationalistic drive for conquest, and, it turns out, high levels of development do not give any immunity against the contagious power of such ideologies. One does not need a low-literacy country to see it adopt and spread a wave of barbarism. In Germany's case, the high level of development afforded enormous destructive possibilities for unleashing murderous myths onto the world. In Russia's case low literacy, in a sense, imposed very large tasks but limited the possibilities of accomplishing them. This is a kind of historical bind that enhanced the role of the state but also atrociously disfigured the regime.

The subject needs more thought, because a vast improvement of educational standards did continue to play a role in considerably softening many of the Soviet regime's oppressive features and actually did prepare the ground for this regime's demise. The earlier stages of the Soviet regime – that is, the post-World War I period – belonged to an era of dictatorships all around Russia. Studying them all comparatively could yield important insights into the genesis of such systems, at least

[10] All these data are from Gunnar C. Boehnert, in *The Führer State*, eds. Gerhard Hirschfeld and Lothar Kettenacker (Stuttgart 1981), pp. 361–73.

in the given broad area. The personal aspect – that is, the role of the dictator, his cult (charisma), and so on – was a key function in all such regimes and provided some glue for the state machinery and often, probably, for the bulk of the population whom the leader helped rally behind the state. Still, Hitler's Germany and Stalin's Russia stood out quite clearly as two, in some ways, 'pure' and most extreme dictatorial models and great powers.

Hitler and Stalin – images and myths

In *The Hitler Myth*, Ian Kershaw shows that this myth – or rather 'the Führer principle' – was crucial for the system, and Hitler used it as he 'transformed himself into a function, the function of Führer'.[11] Kershaw's aim was to contribute to the understanding of this key component of the system and to add something new to the already extensive knowledge of Hitler's personality.

All we know about Stalin, however, is the myth and mythmaking. We have little empirical knowledge about the functioning of the system, the wheels of his personal political staff – and even less about his personality. Volkogonov's biography added a lot of data previously unknown (though his use of sources demands a considerable vigilance from the reader)[12] – but we still are in the dark on many points. We do know fairly well, though, that, not unlike Hitler and his self-identification with the function of Führer, Stalin actually *became the system* and his personality acquired therefore a 'systemic' dimension. Kershaw's study of 'the Hitler myth' was by implication an invitation to compare, not only to find common personal traits – there were more than a few – but to explore the whole politics of mythmaking in both countries, the eventual differences, as well as the scholarly debates on such themes.

Hitler tried to project an image of being above the fray, aloof and uninvolved in governmental dross, but somehow all-powerful and talking to the nation in a *mise en scène* conceived for a pagan deity. In contrast, Stalin's image was one of simplicity and, as the Soviet novelist Simonov attested in his autobiography,[13] of a leader deeply interested in

---

[11] Kershaw, *The Hitler Myth*, pp. 2–4, citing Tim Mason in Hirschfeld and Kettenacker, *The Führer State*, p. 35.

[12] Dmitrij Volkogonov, *Triumf i Tragediia: Politicheskij Portret I. V. Stalina* (Moscow 1989). This was the first Soviet biography of Stalin that was based on a vast amount of archival material previously never seen, though the author's ideas and ways of using the data are often controversial. An English translation is available. It is in two books and four parts but all citations here are taken from the Russian edition.

[13] Konstantin Simonov, *Glazami cheloveka moego pokoleniia* (Moscow 1990). This is an excellent source on Stalin: the writer participated in a number of meetings with Stalin in his capacity as editor and members of the leadership of the Writers' Union. We will rely on his impressions about Stalin as war leader and as the 'engineer' of literature.

and involved with people's life (although both Stalin and Hitler were equally detached and insensitive to human fate). Stalin managed to transform his lack of rhetorical power into an enormous asset: the brevity of his utterances seemed to convey depth, self-confidence and wisdom – and this became an image deeply believed by many observers.

It is also quite revealing that both dictators distanced themselves from the party (and officialdom) so that the blame for poor policies – even disasters – could be absorbed by others. This distance from the party was their common technique of rule. Hitler built his image at the expense of his party, as did Stalin, but also at the expense of the whole bureaucracy. The same was true of Stalin. In this sense they actually did it at the expense of the pillars of their own systems. Hitler gained a lot from his first bloody purge, which was actually tiny compared to Stalin's but it did occur before Stalin's big ones. In this case it could have been Stalin who borrowed from Hitler rather than the other way around. On the other hand, Hitler saw Stalin's purge of the generals as an utterly stupid action, and he never committed anything like that. He found other ways to bury his army and his country.

For both Hitler and Stalin, dissociation from officialdom and party was a calculated move to ground their own power better in people's minds, and it was, in fact, widely accepted by the general public in both cases. In Hitler's case there were also initially enormous successes, or events seen as such – plus a sense that he moved forward without war. In fact, the racial-imperialist part in Hitler was not initially perceived fully outside the Nazi party. But as his power rose above the party, government and state, his innermost aims of conquest and hegemony could go into action.[14]

Both cases offer different versions of a 'deconstruction' of the state as a rational-legal, administrative, and normally policed organisation and its replacement by some kind of 'privatisation' of the state (Kershaw's term). In Hitler's case his personal bodyguard became the main power behind the cult whereas, in Stalin's case, the state's security services became his personal bodyguards and the principal base of his power. The arbitrariness of these reactions and results was in both cases a 'normal' feature of an 'abnormally' personalised state in which the despot himself became a crucial institution – a one-person institution, to be sure, but a linch-pin of a dictatorial system that spun many myths but was in itself real enough.

Still, differences between the two abound. Stalin's essential drive had nothing to do with racialism or racial superiority, with deindustrialisa-

---

[14] Ian Kershaw, 'The Führer Image and Political Integration', in *The Führer State*, p. 156.

tion of 'inferior' nations, with wiping out of their intelligentsia, or with war. The regime's pathologies were reserved for the internal 'front' which was dominated – with well-known ups and downs – by a terroristic large-scale war against presumed enemies, who happened to be the country's peasants, many of its officialdom, and the best of the military, the party and the management.

On the other hand, again unlike the case of Hitler, Stalin possessed a powerful drive to develop his country, to bring it up to a different age. Despite the basic incompatibility between mass slaughter of the country's elites and this building drive under Stalin, the system had yet another important act to play on the historical arena after the dictator's death. Stalin conducted his policy in a military fashion and his terror inside his country was much broader in scale than Hitler's. Therefore, eliminating some of the self-defeating murderous features of Stalinism gave the post-Stalin regime an important additional stimulus.

Stalin himself though ended his career living in a bunker, believing only in the security apparatus, and becoming increasingly deranged. His state of mind was clearly dominated at this stage by a paranoic fear of his country and a view of people as unreliable and dangerous. The reason probably lies in the character of his superstate: it was – and was to stay – deeply bureaucratic, yet Stalin did not relish this reality. He felt in the bureaucrats, including those nearest to him, a force that could not like despotism. He was wrong, in the sense that no one ever tried to kill him, but he was right in a sociological sense: they did want to do things differently and to acquire for themselves both better conditions and, finally, the fulcrum of power. Very few of Stalin's suspects were actually criminally guilty of anything. He struck on the basis of a pathological sociology that suggested to him where the enemies might come from. This was one of the internal traps laid for Stalin by Stalinism. Unfortunately, the whole country found itself sharing with him the same trap for a time.

Stalin: personality and power

The dictators we are studying were, as said, one-man institutions of power. In such cases personality traits and the political game the dictators play merge quite unavoidably. Nevertheless, when we study their regimes with the aim of exploring the systems they presided over and the broad political strategies they adopted, the personality issue remains backstage. Yet, when we turn to the personal portrait, details of intimate aspects come up, but the political activity does not get relegated to the back seat. Politics was their main preoccupation and obsession. Therefore the style and much of the substance of their politics could not but be deeply permeated by their psyches and characters.

Moreover, with regard to style, preferred stratagems and mannerisms, chapters of Hitler's and of Stalin's biographies reveal numerous similarities.

One of them was the predilection for histrionics that was practised by both men. Stalin's biographers noted that he indulged in elaborate histrionic scenes and today we have enough detailed testimonies actually to illustrate this particular side of his personality. An excellent source for these (and many other features of Stalin's persona) is the autobiography of K. Simonov who often confirmed or expanded on Volkogonov, as well as other memoirists. Stalin clearly relished playing 'scenes' of, say, magnanimity and thoughtfulness, accompanied by dramatic, supposedly 'sudden' decisions and gestures – all prepared in advance and delivered in a deliberate, slow and (according to Simonov) masterly way. Simonov gives an example of a meeting in Stalin's office when people of the rank of Malenkov or Molotov denounced a person, actually present at the meeting, but Stalin offered himself a moment of thought and decided against the accusers. The man's life was saved – but Stalin was only pretending not to have heard of the accusation before the meeting.

Or, in a story with a different outcome, Stalin deliberately minimised an incident in a display of good, 'paternal humour', but the culprit nevertheless disappeared the next day. Simonov testified that 'being a great actor was an intricate part of Stalin's political gift'.

We know that Hitler also played scenes for the audience which, we must add, was a captive one that could do no other. Hence the acting talent of the two dictators would not necessarily pass the test of a free public.

But there was also, in both men, another face – the darker side of the moon, when self-control would give way to terrifying outbursts of rage which were often described and feared, especially in the case of Stalin. Even more terrible for those present, according to Simonov's account of one such incident, were cases when Stalin, in the throes of an outburst, managed to control his rage with great difficulty, as was visible from his grimaces. The apparent effort to restrain himself, in fact, already presaged a terrible punishment for the 'perpetrator'. It is plausible that before Stalin acquired virtual omnipotence, he had managed to control those fits, but the effort must have been ravaging his psyche. Once on top and beyond control, the brakes were off – unless there was some political or personal interest to keep them on. Those cases might have occurred when a particular meeting was convened with an audience he wanted to impress for some reason, like representatives of the literary elite, or foreign diplomats. Often the self-control was simply a part of his

123

preferred form of revenge which he must have been hatching patiently. Another case worth reporting (from Simonov) concerned a young air-force general. At a meeting that was convened in order to investigate the causes of numerous flight accidents of military planes, he said openly that it all happened because 'we are forced to fly in coffins'.

Stalin, who felt himself to be the target of the general's comment, controlled his rage, uttered some deliberately short remark ('You should not have said this, General') – and had him killed the very next day. It is also said about Stalin that he liked to kill some people slowly.[15] He must have relished it or experienced some kind of psychological relief in those games that he played with his victim and waited for the moment when he wanted to strike. As far as is known, Stalin played such a game with Bukharin. Larina, Bukharin's wife, gave a vivid picture of Bukharin's slow assassination, deliberately conducted by Stalin against the already broken man.[16]

Likewise, Komsomol secretary Kosarev heard many compliments from Stalin, until one day Stalin whispered something into his ear that turned Kosarev's face livid. Stalin did something similar to Tomsky, who then angered Stalin by committing suicide, 'before his time'. Stalin also destroyed the whole family and the associates of Orjonikidze, one by one, but in the process of doing this he kept coming to the man's apartment for a chat and a drink. But loud shouts were overheard when the fiery Orjonikidze reacted to the chicanery. After one such 'friendly visit' Orjonikidze, like Tomsky, killed himself.

There was yet another Stalin stratagem of 'testing' his closest collaborators – Kaganovitch, Molotov, Poskrebyshev, and many others – by having their wives (or relatives) arrested for 'hostile activity', probably making some of them sign or co-sign the order of arrest. He would tell his collaborator – who did not always manage to preserve a stony face – that he, Stalin could not intervene because everything was in the reliable and 'impartial' hands of the NKVD. We can add this faked innocence to the histrionic proclivities of the *vozhd*. Volkogonov[17] claimed that Stalin did not care that a figure like Ezhev (head of the Secret Police, 1936–8) was a brutish sadist who personally 'interrogated' prisoners or was a morally rotten creature. But he supposedly hated weaklings, especially drinkers, and Ezhev was one of those. Stalin preferred, in his perverse way, strong-willed people (*volevye*), which meant that they could be absolutely devoted and ready to do anything for him. We can surmise that arresting or destroying a family member of his 'co-ruler' from the Politburo without the latter protesting or even

[15] Simonov, *Glazami cheloveka*, pp. 187–8.
[16] See, Anna Larina, *This I cannot Forget* (New York 1993).
[17] Volkogonov, *Triumf I Tragediia*, I-2, pp. 180–1.

uttering a murmur was such a test of 'character'. If Molotov, Kaganovich or Poskrebyshev had tried to defend their relatives, this would have meant they were 'weak'. The fact that Stalin destroyed his own wife's entire family, which was his family too, is telling evidence of a pathological mind that is best left to the expertise of experienced psychiatrists.

A very different facet emerges when we study Stalin's working day. He had a capacity for long hours of hard work, followed by late-night libations with a few of his top lieutenants. He did not like a vast entourage. He read quite a lot, though mostly working files – and Volkogonov's study of his personal files showed that he filtered 100–200 dossiers a day.[18] His phenomenal memory and mastery of details were impressive. But his odd hours of work and sleep – the privilege of a despot – kept the whole governmental machine on alert, especially at night. A top official was present the whole night in any important governmental agency and Stalin used to call in the small hours of the morning and ask for the chief bureaucrat. This was particularly damaging during World War II when a very tired army commander tried to catch an hour of badly needed rest before an offensive.

The warlord

During the war years the features of the system and the traits of the persona blended as never before in Stalin's role as warlord and reached their full and final shape.

Soviet armament at the end of the 1920s and the beginning of the 1930s was still on the level of the Civil War. Russia would not have had a chance if a clash with Western armies had occurred at that time. The weakness of the industrial base was the main problem. It had no branches for aircraft, tank, car, machine building and for other facilities needed for producing arms. Russia was also short of metal[19] and this was an ominous handicap. The ways of overcoming such a weakness produced heated debates and the strategies to be adopted hinged, to a large extent, on differing assumptions concerning the character of future wars. Marshal Tukhachevsky's views on a mobile technological war became the source of a deep-seated conflict with the narrow-minded Voroshilov, the Commissar of Defence, against whose views Tukhachevsky was known to have reacted in the early 1930s, in a sharply worded letter. But this was also an unmistakable gibe against Stalin[20] that was neither forgotten nor forgiven. The destruction of the

---

[18] Volkogonov, *Triumf i Tragediia*, II-1, p. 340.
[19] V. M. Kuritsyn, in D. Volkogonov (ed.), *Tridtsatye Gody* (Moscow 1990), p. 78.
[20] Volkogonov, *Triumf i Tragediia*, I-2, p. 76.

leadership of the armed forces in 1937–8 which killed or imprisoned many thousands of high-ranking officers, might have grown from this or some other set of impulses and previously concealed rancours and umbrages. It was an unprecedented destruction of military cadres by their own commander-in-chief. The armed forces' backbone and brain – its strategists, theoreticians, industrial managers and constructors – were broken on the very threshold of World War II. It goes without saying that this carnage contributed heavily to the terrible losses of the Red Army in the first years of the war. It is true that a certain number (unknown so far) of officers and technicians were released before and during the war, but many more arrests and executions continued well into the war. Stalin's pathological vindictiveness and diffidence were probably even exacerbated as his fortunes as a war leader reached their nadir.

The problem was not however only in this unbelievable destruction of some of the best military men in Europe – Stalin's own. The counterpart of the gloomy suspiciousness was a 'trimphalism'[21] which was a case of self-deception (the Russian term *samoodurachivanie* sounds stronger) of maniacal proportions. Soviet military thinking under Stalin was forced to orientate itself to a quick counter-attack, followed by an 'unavoidable' crushing of the enemy on his own territory. No professional military nor anybody else could afford so much as a sigh about the power of the enemy or the recognition that the army's lack of preparation for defensive action, even retreat, meant suicide. And suicide would have been the route for anyone who might have dared to warn Stalin about what lay ahead. Stalin underestimated the German army's strength and did not pay attention to his (often excellent) intelligence services (he cut them down no less than the other branches of the security system); and although he had worked very hard before the war to overcome the retardation in armaments and the relevant economic branches, these efforts too were marred by inconsistencies and by his preference for cronies from the Civil War and for their advice, rather than that of better qualified and abler people. His 'pact diplomacy' with Nazi Germany might have been unavoidable. He was not ready for war, and the prospect of a war on two fronts (including against Japan) was a nightmare, which he actually avoided (as Hitler fell into the trap). But the way Stalin played his game with Germany was lamentable and the story is by now quite well known in its main aspects. Suffice it to say here that his stubborn refusal to allow the military units on the frontiers, in the rear, or anywhere else, to take the slightest precautions to get ready for the imminent attack 'in order not to provoke

Germany', makes for very depressing reading. His self-serving confidence in his ability to outmanoeuvre others and to avoid ever experiencing the same, was probably the reason for the state of shock and paralysis of will that struck him for about a week at the beginning of the war when he realised that all his strategies and prognostications had failed and that the Germans were already conquering enormous territories of Russia. There was at least this price to pay for the arrogant overconfidence of a man who was entirely spoiled by a political function without having to face any political contradiction. The rumours that Stalin and Molotov discussed 'a new Brest', or partial surrender to Hitler, as Beriia claimed after he was arrested by pro-Khrushchev generals, may not have been true. Stalin quickly got hold of himself. But the story of the next stages of the war – until the Stalingrad victory – is one of an army that still had to learn how to fight under a 'teacher' who committed blunder after blunder, of a strategic, operational, and even tactical character. He meddled heavily and in excruciating detail in ongoing war operations, persisted in notions harking back to the Civil War (the creation of a useless Cossack cavalry was one of those) and stuck to an obtuse and characteristic gigantism that caused incredible abuse and losses in manpower.

Stalin struggled to come to grips with the situation and master a global picture of the war fronts. As Zhukov, Volkogonov and others asserted, he was capable and did learn quite a lot about warfare. He even softened some of his 'Stalinism' appreciably during the second, more successful, part of the war. In essence, though, the man and his system continued their routine: a relentless pressure to engage in offensives without time to prepare them, identification of retreat with treason (later softened down somehow), crude, voluntaristic and repressive methods, the tendency to explain failure by sabotage and the incredible cruelty in treating the supposed culprits. Moreover, special penal battalions, barrages (*zagradotriady*), and cleansing operations in the Red Army's rear, mounted by the security units which otherwise rarely participated in frontline battles – the whole arsenal and paraphernalia of a security state – were mobilised against the army that was winning the war. Having been attenuated during part of the war, the Stalinist internal war machine persisted and swelled into a new draconian wave toward the end of the war with new, elaborate chicaneries: special 'filtering' concentration camps for the military who were captured, or just encircled, by the enemy even if they fought their way out, suspicion against anyone who lived under the German occupation – all contributed to an enormous pool of potential suspects for the secret police. The Commander-in-Chief suspected and fought his own no less fiercely than he fought the enemy.

The study of the two dictators as warlords reveals numerous features that they shared. The policy that identified retreat with treason was one of them – but it was particularly costly for Russia's soldiers and for many of its civilians. In both cases 'retreat' was taken by the two personally, as an act of defiance, a personal insult for which they were ready to settle accounts with millions of people. The two did not see themselves either as leaders or as servants of the state: they were the state. Hitler expressed this clearly to a confidant on 27 January 1944 : 'if the German people are not prepared to stand up for their own preservation, fine. Let them perish.'[22]

Stalin did not leave any open statement to this effect, but the 'discovery' of so many enemies tells the story. His policies clearly underestimated, and therefore also blocked, Russia's capacity to fight. He was – or rather became – essentially a *karatel'*, a Russian term difficult to translate that pertains to somebody whose main business is to punish. His ignominious orders at the beginning of the war – like number 270 (issued on 16 August 1941) which authorised the arrest of family members of officers who 'betrayed' the country and which deprived of aid and state benefits the families of soldiers who fell into captivity, belong to this category. Yet he presented himself to the country as a caring father. The people of the USSR thus had to endure a double calamity. They managed to fight off the invader, but they could not get rid of the enemy behind their backs and above their heads. Their adulation for their leader is another baffling testament to the power of myths which the dictators learned to use very successfully.

The figures on 'the cost of victory' are a good occasion to reflect on a leadership whose moment of glory was also the height of its inner rottenness. The disproportion between the losses of both sides – in lives and property – is a measure of the 'extensive' character of the Russian historical effort that Stalinism pushed to the limit. The lack of consideration for human losses paralleled the attitude to the labour force in general that is best summed up by the de facto distinction between the attitude towards the 'workforce' (*rabsila*) – a sociological reality – as opposed to 'working class', which was used as an ideological fetish.

In this context, Stalin's way of running the war points to his personal inhumanity – that also went deep into the heart of his system. He operated with rather dehumanised ideas of numbers, of abstract blocks of 'a workforce' or 'fighting forces' without the faintest idea about the reality of their work and action. He visited very few places where real people acted and he never saw and never wanted to see the front and to realise what people did and how people functioned in real military

---

[22] A. Hillgruber, *Germany in the Two World Wars* (London 1981), p. 96.

units and headquarters. There were, I believe, only two cases of presumed visits to the front line – but they were phoney. Stalin kept himself at a safe distance and remained aloof, never seeing or speaking to his soldiers.

To this should be added that the industrial thrust that was so crucial for the war effort was as skewed by the methods of 'planning' as the politics were distorted by overcentralisation and the very essence of despotism. The key here lies in debilitating imbalances: armaments factories were built but in areas that were the nearest to the future front. Defence was extolled, but 'strategy' was 'mythologised', with only the offensive allowed to be considered – so there was no need to worry when military aircraft plants and most airfields were located too near to the frontier. With defence and retreat 'forbidden', there was no argument against the dismantling of powerful fortification a short time before the war – which is what was done.

Moreover, not unlike what was happening throughout the imbalanced economy, armaments industries produced weapons, but not enough ammunition or spare parts for them. An endless stream of similar disparities forced administrators and chiefs to get things done by running after a tail without a head, or perhaps after a head that had lost its tail. The toll this took on the cadres cannot be quantified. We cannot miss the occasion to state here that there were plenty of exemplary achievements in these and other fields – but all of this required a superhuman effort not only because of the inherent complexity of the task but also because of this system's inability to plan.

The other interesting feature that became particularly blatant during the war was Stalin's eagerness almost to 'suck in' all the key functions and positions of the state directly into his own jurisdiction. The plenitude of power he already held was not enough. He needed a direct institutional takeover on a much larger scale than Hitler was interested in. All the departmental boundaries between war-related agencies became so blurred that the participants in one or another 'council' – all very high ranking officials – never knew what body they were attending. Stalin alone would decide at the end of the session whether the body that was deliberating was the Supreme State Council, the Council of Commissars, General Headquarters, the Politburo or something else again. For Stalin these were all the same – as long as he was the boss.[23]

The megalomaniac urge for fullness of power drove Stalin to become not only boss of all the bodies just cited but also the Supreme Commander and Commissar (later Minister) of Defence. Taking on

---

[23] Volkogonov, *Triumf i Tragediia*, II-1, p. 271.

anything more would have gone beyond the ridiculous. At the same time, Stalin's readiness to assume the title of Generalissimo (not without a fake show of anger against the idea, followed by an acceptance of it) fully justifies Bukharin's snide characterisation of Stalin (in October 1929) as a 'petty oriental despot'[24] – a quite justified quip in many ways despite the fact (maybe because of the fact) that Stalin personally called himself *'Velikij'* – 'The Great' – that is. Modestly, he never said this himself in public, but forced the media to hail him in such terms.

This feature of subsuming the key administration of the government as Stalin's personal property meant that institutions could not offer any independent initiative or, in fact, do a decent job. Government leaders were paralysed by the fear of Stalin's retribution. In principle, nothing could be done without him. Others never contradicted him even if they knew that his assessment or decision was totally wrong. Contradicting or correcting him could mean death or a prison camp. Simple demotion would have been an act of charity. A leadership engaged in amassing so much power could not but abuse it, almost by definition. This also was a predictable impediment to grasping reality. This offers an additional illustration of the idea proposed elsewhere that the takeover of power after Stalin's death by the bureaucracy brought, curiously enough, a quite meaningful emancipation of the state apparatus, in the first place, and meaningful improvements for the population. The story of the preparedness – or lack of it – for the war, the lamentable policies of forbidding any action to counter the imminent German attack, a persistent mania for staging offensives without any good strategic reason or enough time for preparations, the terroristic and dishonest punishing of officers for Stalin's own failures, and the mass persecution of 'deserters' or war prisoners or simply people who got out of an encirclement, is both a deeply depressing tale and an indictment of Stalin's regime. How people lived through all this is an equally grim story. The people, the army, and the generals were all 'guilty' by definition; hence the key method of treating the soldiers, not unlike the labour force, was *silovaia* – that is coercive, punitive, brutal, and ugly. Stalin believed in the glitter of his cult and in his infallibility and through a seeming political miracle made the masses and many of the elites believe in it too. Even the terrible price of his failures did not shatter this image. Critics of Stalin knew that they would have no chance with the public, much less with his security agents. The regime's security was therefore foolproof and the enormous security apparatus and precautions were, to a large extent, superfluous. When we eventually get data on the number of people in the security services, it may turn

---

[24] Volkogonov, *Triumf i Tragediia*, I-2, p. 41 – but his source is not stated clearly.

out again that even in this domain Hitler's regime was much more 'economical' in terms of the number of secret service agents per thousand inhabitants. Stalin, who not only personified but privatised the system's institutions, was losing control over his actions and his mind as he was succumbing to the folly of trying to control everything.

The overlord of the arts (literature)

Our main source here is, mainly, the autobiography of the novelist K. Simonov. A fine and honest person, and an avowed and naive Stalinist, Simonov illustrated in his self-searching memoirs the depth of dedication to Stalin and an almost total disregard for the most monstrous aspect of Stalin's leadership among a whole generation of Soviet intellectuals. This was despite the fact that many of them, including Simonov himself, knew from personal experience that their position was extremely fragile and that they could be crushed at a moment's notice. The liberation from Stalin's spell that began only after his death was a painstaking path that Simonov described in his memoirs. They remain an important document about this sinister spell and the difficulty many honest people experienced when trying to shed it. The breathtaking building-sites (strojki), the victories in war, and the credible and desirable vision of a great man ('warts and all') were important factors in the acceptance by people such as Simonov. Another powerful contributor to make people succumb to Stalin's cult was the massive phenomenon of social promotion that the regime engendered including the ascension to national glory by many unassuming but bright lads – Simonov being one such case. These people did not yet know or understand the Stalinism we are talking about. When Stalin was already an acknowledged leader, Simonov's cohorts were fifteen and when Stalin died, they were 38 years old. The images and the ethos that were propagated by the regime had nothing to do with massive slave labour or other iniquities. Instead, the young followers saw and experienced an impressive ethos of building the country and serving the upward movement of an awakening giant, in a spirit of romanticism and moral integrity. It was therefore painfully dispiriting to them to discover that this ethos had its much darker counterpart.

The frequent meetings with Stalin on problems of literature in which Simonov participated together with other leaders of the Writers' Union (he recorded the content of those meetings by making personal notes immediately after each one) give an excellent picture of this aspect of Stalin's activity. Stalin showed an amazing knowledge on all aspects of literary affairs, including a detailed mastery of the content of novels. This was a degree of expertise that Simonov called 'bewildering'.[25] The meetings with the representative of the Writers' Union, Simonov surmised, helped Stalin – who did not go out very much, if at all – to gauge the moods of the intelligentsia. He also meddled in minutiae of literary life and discussed who should get prizes, premiums, blame, and censures. He personally nominated leaders and editors (and their deputies) of literary journals, 'commissioned' novels and plays on specific subjects, demanded that authors make changes and unhesitatingly told writers when he thought their work was no good.

Simonov himself had to write a novel on a specified theme. Stalin needed a prestigious author to help him promote after the war his policy 'against kneeling before the West' – a seemingly widespread attitude among intellectuals that Stalin considered dangerous. Simonov obliged and got a Stalin prize for it, but he later viewed this as a moral low in his life.

Since Simonov gave us a sense of what Stalin liked or criticised and expected from literature, we can gain an additional inkling into Stalin's political methods. He wanted to control minds personally and to instill ideas, by dictating how history and literature should be written, how films and, as we know, also music, should be made. According to Volkogonov's biography of Stalin,[26] a personal assignment of this type – a novel, a play and, we could add, also Stalin's own biography or the noisily trumpeted *Short Course of the History of the Communist Party of the USSR* – was one of Stalin's methods in shaping the spiritual development of the nation in the direction he wanted, especially in terms of constant readiness to battle 'the enemies of the people'. But literature certainly played here a special role.

This type of supposedly sophisticated personal leadership (which was also so destructive of cultural life) had no parallel, to my mind, in Hitler's actions. His regime also dominated culture, without detailed or, perhaps, any personal interference from Hitler. Ideology and censorship were probably enough for him, and he relied on associates to deal with such matters. The task was self-evident for the members of the Nazi creed.

The Old Tyrant

World War II devastated Russia, but it legitimised – or re-legitimised – Stalin's rule. At the same time, the backward-looking traits (essentially the inability to move the country out of its rut) and deep obscurantism of his regime were thickening. This can best be illustrated by the obscurantist 'cultural' policies of the years 1946–8 that came to be known as

---

[25] Simonov, *Glazami cheloveka*, p. 142.
[26] Volkogonov, *Triumf i Tragediia*, II-2, pp. 32–3.

Zhdanovism. Stalin's imposition on a multinational country of a chauvinist anthem extolling *Velikaia Rus'* (best translated as 'Rus' the Magnificent') – was the last chapter of his and his system's degeneration. The fact that it went with a virulent display of antisemitism makes the character of his rule quite transparent.

Hitler was destroyed by the war, but the economic system of Germany was preserved, although not intact. Post-war Germany could climb up (with Western help) and rebuild a supermodern economy (as did Japan). Fifty years later Germany (and again Japan) seemed almost to have won their lost war. Self-sustained growth and an ability for renovation were the secret. In contrast, the Soviet system managed to create a backward superpower – a very Russian historical syndrome.

As we already know, Stalin was reacting viscerally after the victory in the war to any sign of 'toadying to the West' among his citizens. He certainly perceived it as a blow to his prestige and a real defeat in victory, insofar as millions of his soldiers saw the conquered live so much better than the victors. Stalin needed his intellectuals (many of whom he suspected of getting contaminated) and he mobilised people like Simonov and Ehrenburg to battle this scourge.

The victory in the war 'froze' Stalin and his system. He was not ready to change anything.[27] Becoming a victorious world leader had a 'mummifying' effect on him – exactly as reaching a superpower position and boasting of other big achievements had a numbing effect on his successors. The *karatel'* in Stalin came now mightily to the fore again. In January 1948, Stalin personally ordered the making of new camps for 'Trotskyites'. He also required 'prisons for special tasks' and other high-security institutions. Volkogonov, who studied Stalin's personal files, says that his attention was concentrated mainly on security agencies. As usual, he dealt with these matters in great detail, and he pampered and extolled, decorated and promoted security personnel (especially the NKVD and NKGB).[28]

He did not write diaries, but there might have been a file that Beriia eventually snatched from his office when Stalin lay in a coma.[29] Doctors were not called to help him thanks to a Beriia manoeuvre: Stalin supposedly listened to Beriia's advice about some home-made remedies for his illness.

Beriia probably sensed that Stalin were plotting against the old guard, including Beriia himself. It is also quite obvious that the 'security'-obsessed, aging and ever more deranged and antisemitic Stalin (who, on

---

[27] Volkogonov, *Triumf i Tragediia*, II-2, pp. 20–3.   [28] Ibid., p. 132.

[29] Volkogonov, *Triumf i Tragediia*, II-2, p. 45 and *passim*. The story of Beriia's moves during the last hours of Stalin's life is not yet convincingly documented in Volkogonov or elsewhere.

top of this, refused to see doctors), let Beriia control details of Stalin's life more than ever before. Beriia even managed to convince Stalin that his two most faithful servants – Poskrebyshev (personal political secretary) and Vlasik (head of his body guard) – had to be fired. Beriia had tried hard before because these two were certainly informed enough to make Stalin suspicious of Beriia's manipulations. Stalin's emphasis on the security agencies now allowed Beriia to have it his way. But this place of choice among Stalin's top lieutenants could easily turn into a bog for anyone, especially for those at the very top.

Simonov described Stalin's last appearance at the Central Committee Meeting on 16 October 1952, where he shocked the audience by savagely attacking Molotov and Mikoian, hinting that they would not be reliable and staunch successors to him. When the same Central Committee adopted another Stalin idea – a new and much larger Praesidium of the party – it was immediately apparent that the members of the old Politburo were a minority in the new ruling body and this was a possible sign of Stalin's intention to eliminate the old guard altogether in his next move. A Beriia did not need anybody to tell him what was brewing.

During the same session (he spoke for one and a half hours in a session that lasted two and a half hours) Stalin played his last histrionic number by offering his resignation, which was duly rejected by a unanimous vote.[30]

In the last of his nightmarish concoctions he ascribed to a group of mostly Jewish doctors a plot to kill Kremlin leaders. The doctors were arrested and tortured to make them confess to the crime. This was a telling testimony to the old dictator's derangement and the flotsam of a decomposing regime – the last gasp of a deranged and hating execu-tioner. Self-isolation was part of the final period in old Stalin's life. And the same Beriia who listened to Stalin's speech against the old guard was still responsible for his well-being and security.

[30] Simonov, *Glazami cheloveka*, pp. 211–16.

6

The contradictions of continuous revolution
Michael Mann

Introduction: labels and models

Both the Hitler and Stalin regimes were one-party states under dictators. But so were many interwar states. Their ruling parties were
ideological and mobilised for mass action. This was rather rarer. Yet
quite uniquely these two regimes repressed, enslaved, and then killed
millions of their subjects. The recent German debate about the comparability of the two regimes, the *Historikerstreit*, could only suggest one
other comparably murderous regime, that of Pol Pot in Cambodia. True,
Nazis and Stalinists denied their regimes were similar. Each viewed the
other as its veritable Anti-Christ. Much twentieth-century theory has
strongly contrasted 'left' communism and 'right' fascism. There were
major differences – the Bolsheviks abolished capitalism, the Soviet
Union was bigger, less industrialised and modern, more secular and
ethnically diverse, and women were more equal. Their prior histories
and seizures of power also differed. So did the two dictators: Hitler was
a lazy charismatic, Stalin a dull workaholic. Nonetheless, despite all
this, to a non-specialist like myself, as to their victims and probably to
most of humanity, the two regimes belong together. It is only a question
of finding the right family name.

'Totalitarian', 'dictatorships', 'party dictatorships', 'party despotisms', 'authoritarian', have all been popular family names. All have
disadvantages. The two regimes were authoritarian, despotic and
dictatorial, but so were many blander regimes of the period. These
labels conceal the unparalleled terrorism of these two. 'Party dictatorship' does better, since the Nazi and Communist Parties dominated the
state (especially the Communist Party) as in no other country. Yet it
suggests too institutionalised a state. It conforms to Soviet ideology (i.e.
'the dictatorship of the proletariat' under 'the leading role of the party')
yet ignores the absence of responsible party institutions in either

regime. 'Party despotism' does convey the sense of a regime and ruler without law. Yet they ruled more as a fluid, continuing revolutionary movement than as an institutionalised state. I label them here 'regimes of continuous revolution' and delineate their structures, dynamics and contradictions. I identify two main sub-types, one driven by revolutionary class ideology, exemplified by the Stalinist regime, the other driven by what I shall call a revolutionary 'nation-statist' ideology, exemplified by Nazism.

But the most common label and model has been the contentious word *totalitarian*. Totalitarian theorists believed twentieth-century states wielded two crucial new powers. They might exploit the revolutions which had smashed down traditional restraints on state *despotic* power. Hitherto even absolute monarchs had ruled according to law, respecting the customs and privileges of the community. Yet post-revolutionary regimes could dispense with the law which could be subordinated to their ideological goals. They also acquired new *infrastructural* powers – ability to penetrate the practices of civil society routinely – created by industrialisation, urbanisation, and modern technology. Wielding new despotic and infrastructural powers totalitarian states had abolished all significant autonomy lying within civil society. And though various regimes (Mussolini, Franco and post-war Eastern European Communist) have been termed totalitarian, the exemplary cases were Nazism and Stalinism. They were believed to share three characteristics.

(1) *A revolutionary ideology* claiming the right to transform society totally. The source of their unparalleled terrorism lay in this ideological ambition: the entire society and the entire human being were to be remoulded or eliminated so that 'Socialist Man' or 'the pure Aryan' might emerge.

(2) *A party* implementing this transformation. Party institutions infiltrated every central and local government agency and most voluntary organisations. The armed forces, for example, were constrained by party cells, commissars, paramilitaries and, finally, by entire party divisions (the Waffen SS and the NKVD). Rival power blocs survived, especially in Germany, where Churches, the army, and capitalists largely ran their own affairs (in the Soviet Union large capitalists had not survived, churches were emasculated, and only the army retained autonomy). But they were subordinated to Nazi goals.

(3) *A bureaucracy* – a single, centralised, hierarchical state, maximised routinised top-down dictatorial control over society. Party and bureaucracy together generated 'total' power.

Totalitarian models are not nowadays favoured by specialists on the two regimes. German scholars often deny that the Nazis were revolutionaries. But most fire has been concentrated upon bureaucracy: We find a smoothly functioning and hierarchical bureaucracy in the pages of Orwell's *1984* or Huxley's *Brave New World*, but not in Nazi or Soviet reality. However, we must not throw out the baby with the bathwater. Totalitarian theorists correctly identified the first two elements of these regimes but drew the wrong conclusion from them. Instead of revolutionary ideology and party institutions smoothly combining to produce a totalitarian bureaucracy, they undercut each other to produce a less institutionalised, more dynamic and arbitrary despotism. Between revolutionary ideology and party institutions lay a contradiction, leading to an internal regime dynamic and ultimately to downfall. Yet the two regimes were not at the same point in this self-destructive dynamic at the same time, and this led to important differences between them.

From bureaucracy to chaos

Nobody ever argued that the Nazi or Stalinist regime constituted a perfectly functioning bureaucracy. Totalitarian theorists had noted struggles between party and state as well as the proliferation of surveillance organisations seeking to control both. Critics began mildly, labelling the Soviet Union as 'inefficient totalitarianism', noting 'polycracy' among the Nazis. Then others stressed 'unwritten pacts' between the Nazis and other power blocs, and 'anarchic competing fiefdoms' among Nazi leaders. Soviet specialists perceived Stalin exercising only limited control over the many levels and agencies of party and government. Many purges and forced collectivisations, they say, were local, even popular, initiatives which Stalin and his henchmen could not control.

A comparative sociologist like myself can support such criticisms in two ways. First, totalitarian theorists depicted an unreal level of coherence for *any* state. Modern states are a long way short of Hegelian or Weberian rational bureaucracy and they rarely act as singular, coherent actors. Normally regimes are factionalised; in an unpredictable world they stumble along with many foul-ups. Second, we should remember Weber's essential point about bureaucracy: it kept politics out of administration. Political and moral values ('value rationality') were settled outside of bureaucratic administration, which then limited itself to finding efficient means of implementing those values ('formal rationality'). Contrary to totalitarian theory, the twentieth-century states most capable of such formally rational bureaucracy were not the dictatorships but the democracies. This was already evident by 1900. Since the British and French parliaments were sovereign, value-conflicts were fought out there. Responsible collective Cabinets articulated the result into a legislative programme, implemented by relatively bureau-cratic administrations. Yet in more authoritarian Germany and Russia, sovereignty was divided and contested between monarch, court, minis-tries, the military, and (in Germany) parliaments. Politics and adminis-tration could not be separated and so civil servants played essentially political roles (Mann, *The Sources of Social Power*, vol. II: Chapter 21).

In 'totalitarian' regimes formal sovereignty was vested in a single ruling party and ultimately in the person of its Supreme Leader. Hitler was unchallenged, Stalin became so. Yet this fostered less bureaucracy than *despotism*. Like any Roman Emperor the leader's power was arbitrary. If power is rule-governed, then bureaucratised party or ministerial institutions can administer them. Neither despot nor their party entourages wanted this and so they dispensed with the laws and administrative rules necessary to bureaucracy. As Lewin notes here (cf Caplan, *Government without Administration*, on the Nazis), Soviet and Nazi administrations remained politicised. The term 'bureaucracy' meant to the Bolsheviks (Lewin makes clear), not the entire state or party structure, but only officials pursuing their own interests, thwart-ing the regime's. Only modern democracies have centralised sover-eignty sufficiently to bureaucratise their administrations.

Thus it is no surprise that critics of totalitarianism revealed fierce Nazi and Bolshevik power struggles between party, state, and para-military institutions, resulting in 'satraps', fiefdoms', and 'departmental patriot-isms'. The centre was factionalised, far more so than in the democracies. True, the Soviet Politburo had formal collective responsibility for policy. No such supreme body existed in Nazi Germany after 1938, when the Reich Cabinet last met. Yet the Politburo was largely supine under Stalin.

But however active Hitler, Stalin or Politburos might have been, they still faced a second power limitation: the difficulty of penetrating routinely into the everyday infrastructures of provincial and local administration. As Lewin notes, Stalin was forced to resort to 'shock-methods' administered from above – a violent but not very effective form of control. These two great infrastructural restrictions on despotic power – political factionalism and local insulation – are analysed in this volume by Kershaw, Lewin, and Suny. Fiefdoms and local autonomies modified by violent but erratic shock-tactics were necessary since there were no final laws or administrative rules regulating administrators. Both despots, just like any Roman Emperor, encouraged subordinates' rivalries as part of a 'divide-and-rule' strategy (discussed later). Like many Emperors, Stalin (though not Hitler) developed Lewin's 'institu-tional paranoia' or what in Rome I diagnosed as 'imperial schizo-phrenia' (Mann, *The Sources of Social Power*, Vol. I) – the supposedly

138

supreme despot's realisation that he cannot break through the obfuscations and autonomies of the 'little Caesars' (or 'little Stalins') below. Since these are not routinely controllable or even knowable, the despot easily assumes they are plotting against him.

Critics of totalitarianism see violence as proof of a weak not a strong regime. The Smolensk archives, says Getty, reveal a 'technically weak and politically divided party whose organisational relationships seem more primitive than totalitarian' (*Origins of the Great Purges*: 6). Once the party turned upon itself, says Rittersporn, 'the country was submerged in a chaotic struggle of all against all' ('Rethinking Stalinism': 353). Caplan, Kershaw, and Mommsen also portray the Nazi state as chaotic and inefficient: administrative 'systemlessness' was part of a dynamic of self-destruction. Mommsen has catalogued Nazi failures – 'administrative anarchy', 'temporarily well-organised chaos', exhibiting 'increasing fluidity and chaos' and 'escalating wastage'. He concluded, 'It would be difficult to describe this "rule" by spasmodic and unsystematic intervention in the political workings of the Third Reich as "governing"'; 'The Nazi system of rule completely lacked internal coherence' ('Hitler's position' 170–8, 186). Caplan has written: 'The subversion of the civil service was piecemeal and *ad hoc*, the effect of incompetence, impatience and neglect rather than the pursuit of a clear alternative . . . If this was an example of Nazi social Darwinism in practice, its effect was one of negative selection, the survival of the unfittest' (*Government without Administration*: 322–3). All these argue that the end came not only from the Allies: the state also disintegrated from within. Anything less like the rigid top-down bureaucracy of totalitarian theory is hard to imagine.

But just because the Nazi and Stalin regimes lacked bureaucratic coherence, did they lack *all* coherence? It makes one wonder how either could have ever got its act together to conquer so many countries or to liquidate so many enemies. There may be a further problem underlying this: how to analyse *evil*. Germans, Russians, conservatives, and Marxists have found it especially hard to comprehend the evil that perverted their countries and ideologies. It may console to describe the perpetrators of evil as mad and their regimes as chaotic: evil is removed from our normal world and attributed to a sudden descent into a abyss of madness and chaos. In contrast I try to give the evil of these regimes a precise twentieth-century social location and structure. And, though I borrow considerably and gratefully from these critics of totalitarianism, I emphasise perhaps more than they do the extent to which regimes of continuous revolution possessed both coherent administration and internal dynamism.

Revolutionary goals

We all readily appreciate the revolutionary utopian tradition represented by Marxism and Bolshevism, and can agree that Stalinism intensified and perverted this tradition. Yet to call the Nazis 'revolutionary' is contentious. In this volume Mommsen argues that the Nazi regime 'radicalised', yet (as do most liberal or socialist Germans) he refuses to label it 'revolutionary'. Since liberal and Marxian ideologies won the two World Wars, they are familiar to us. We readily understand ideological promises and betrayals concerning social classes – indeed, for too long we viewed fascists through Marxian and liberal eyes, as covert or perverted spokesmen for class interests. Yet there have been *two* major power actors of modern times, classes and nation-states, and so there have been *two* great types of modern social ideology: that analysing society in terms of classes and that analysing it in terms of nation-states. Because extreme *'nation-statist'* ideologists like the Nazis were defeated, their ideas now have little resonance. We have difficulty understanding their revolutionary aspirations.

The Nazis were certainly not class revolutionaries. They suppressed socialists and trade unions, believed strongly in managerial hierarchies, and received (discreet) support from reactionary elites. But, along with most nation-statists, they had little interest in classes or economics. Their economic programme was a rag-bag of incompatible bribes to different social groups. In office they devised a quasi-Keynesianism which enjoyed shortrun success, but was really a byproduct of something else they valued, rearmament. Yet they were revolutionary nation-statists. Their vision was not of a world of classes but of nation-states founded essentially on races, struggling for absolute domination. 'Order' could only be imposed violently, first on Germany and then on other inferior races and nations. A strong nation-state provided the order, indeed the moral basis, of society. That is what I mean by 'nation-statism'.

Thus, though Hitler himself was uninterested in economics, he intervened actively in diplomacy, military issues, armaments, racial matters, propaganda, and architecture. These (minus architecture) had been his concerns in *Mein Kampf*. The Nazis' central concern was to make Germany strong again, forcibly to restore order within and to force enemies to give ground (literally) abroad. The most recent research on party members and voters shows that the Nazis were, as they claimed, a national party, a *Volkspartei*, drawing support from all social classes for their supposedly national goals (e.g. Mühlberger, *Hitler's Followers*: 207; Fischer, *The Rise of the Nazis*).

Nazi ideology appalls us. But it was only an extreme version of a whole family of early twentieth century rightist ideologies centring the supposed virtues of order, hierarchy, and militarism on the nation-state. There were major differences of interpretation amongst them. Conservative authoritarians (especially those actually controlling the state) emphasised the state more than the (potentially uncontrollable) nation. Fascists reversed this emphasis, since they mobilised a popular party yet lacked control of the older parts of the state. But they all believed moral order was to be imposed on the world by some degree of fusion of nation and state. Most endorsed far less racism and violence than the Nazis. Many claimed they sought only to 'restore' a traditional social and moral order, now undermined by liberalism, socialism, regional dissidents, and foreigners. But since this tradition was largely mythical, its implementation involved major social restructuring. 'Restore' national unity by eliminating divisive regionalists, 'Bolsheviks', and 'anarchists' (i.e. all worker and peasant militants) and then regulate class and regional conflict with 'organic', 'corporatist' or 'integral' state institutions. 'Restore' a corporate moral order by eliminating corrupt parliamentary parties and selfish individualism. 'Restore' national honour with strong armed forces, usually pursuing expansionist goals. Such ideas swept interwar central, eastern and southern Europe, modifying social catholicism, antisemitism, and militarism. As conservatives changed into authoritarian nationalists and fascists, they defeated liberals and socialists across the south and east. They usually received most support from the upper classes, especially landowners, but they picked up much of the intelligentsia, the middle class, peasant farmers, and even (in more particular circumstances) many workers.

Fifty years after their defeat nation-statist ideas seem bizarre. Reading *Acción Española*, an influential journal of the 1930s (see Morodo, *Los orígines ideológicos*), produces an eerie sense of an alien culture. Many educated Spaniards then seriously believed the defects of their Republic could be cured by a return to *Hispanidad*, Spain's divine (yes, divine) mission in the world, exemplified in the values of the Catholic Kings and the Inquisition of the fifteenth to the seventeenth centuries and a centralised, hierarchical state. This would eliminate the 'anti-España' of socialists, anarchists, and regionalists, and restore the true 'España' to its integral, imperial, and most catholic greatness. Only the handful of corporatists among them would seem to the modern reader to understand much of how a modern society or economy actually works. I chose this example because their ideas strike us now as crazy rather than evil. I could choose other examples, for example virulent antisemitism among German, Austrian or Romanian politicians, which might strike us as rather more sinister. It is a world we in the liberal-democratic West have forgotten, but which we should try to reconstruct imaginatively – since it might return. It is not very likely a nazi, even a fascist, regime might return. It is far more likely we (or more precisely the east of the continent) will face a new offspring of the nation-statist family. Without this reconstruction we forget that fascist and nazi ideologies existed amid a much broader penumbra of nation-statist ideas, and we are prone to brand them as the work of isolated 'madmen' and their regimes as 'chaotic'. The Nazis were simply the most extreme of many movements entering the 1920s or 1930s advocating nation-statist transformation.

Nazi goals were 'revolutionary' – provided this term is denuded of all positive value-judgements. A revolution is a sudden overturning of the power structure of society. The Nazis sought new racial nation-statist principles of stratification, overturning Europe's geopolitical order and subjugating and 'eliminating' 'inferior races'. This was far more revolutionary than Stalinist geopolitical goals. As class revolutionaries, Stalinists were obsessed by class, uninterested in foreign policy. Their 'socialism in one country' was only pragmatic isolationism. Stalin took only a sporadic interest in foreign policymaking, which Haslam (*The Soviet Union*: 52–3) declares was 'ramshackled'. Stalin's blindness toward Hitler's invasion of 1941 (he refused to believe it for a day even after it happened) was devastating proof of his neglect. Domestically, Nazis were not as revolutionary as the Bolsheviks. Yet even kulaks and Crimean Tartars did not suffer oppression as murderously systematic as did Jews, gypsies, and the mentally and physically handicapped; while racism also pervaded many Nazi social and economic policies – property inheritance, agricultural subsidies, child allowances, public housing projects, and educational provision for the poor (Burleigh and Wippermann, *The Racial State*). Class drove forward Bolsheviks, nation-statism drove forward Nazis. The regimes were not opposites – and thus it conceals much to describe one as simply 'left', the other as 'right'. But the revolution that one concentrated hard on, the other neglected. Both were revolutionary, though in different ways.

The politics of continuous revolution

The two regimes were also revolutionary in a second, perhaps more important sense: they practised the politics of continuous revolution (sometimes expressed as a 'permanent' or 'one thousand year' revolution or regime). Revolutionary goals involve a wholesale transformation of society. Yet even where the masses at first offer considerable support, their social practices must be transformed. A few thousand revolutionary militants cannot easily do this without the support of innumerable local notables – schoolteachers, clerics, civil servants, magistrates, employers, leaders of voluntary associations, mayors, village headmen, etc. Revolutionaries need allies, and these may waver or pursue their own goals. The purists face dissent not with compromise but with a continuing revolution, implemented with frontal force. As Huntington ('Social and institutional dynamics') puts it, they simply *eliminate* rival political constituencies.

In this second sense, the opposite of a revolution is institutionalised compromise. In modern societies multi-party democracy is the most institutionalised form of compromise between opposed power actors. 'Social democracy', where most compromising socialists ended up, is an especially institutionalised regime. The ideals of a one-party Bolshevik democracy or of a fascist syndicalist corporatism would be also examples of institutionalised compromise, though mainly among revolutionary allies. Yet these ideals were not realised in practice. Indeed, *none* of the thirty-plus authoritarian regimes of left and right in Europe between the 1920s and 1980s developed a coherent constitution, embodying institutional compromise, to which it actually adhered. Instead they developed informal 'semi-institutionalised', less principled compromise between allies, involving dividing the spoils with local notables and settling back into a non-constitutional, less ambitious one-party rule, implicitly abandoning revolutionary goals. The contradiction between institutions and revolutionary ideology was resolved in favour of institutions.

Take Mussolini, for example. In the 1920s his fascist party contained a more coherent fascist (i.e. nation-statist revolutionary) programme than we find among the Nazis. Yet the Mussolini regime came to rest on an institutional compromise (never written into the constitution) between fascist factions and other power blocs. These were separately represented in the state right up to the highest levels, the Fascist Grand Council and the Council of Ministers. Regime policy emerged through explicit and implicit horsetrading between a number of rough equals – fascists, monarchy, Catholic Church, armed forces, and big capital. This made unrealisable most of the regime's fascist goals. Whatever Mussolini's own (probably declining) fascist proclivities, they were restrained by his realistic assessment of the power of these rival actors (de Grand, *Italian Fascism*).

The Franco regime is a second example. Franco seems to have believed in most of the ideals of *Acción Española*, and his personal despotism (once established) was unchallenged. Perhaps this was because of his caution and pragmatism since he carefully distributed his ministries among the distinct regime 'families' – fascist *falangistas*, Alfonsin monarchists, Carlists, Catholic leaders, the armed forces, and industrial and agrarian capitalists. The rules governing this compromise were informal and clientelistic. Ideological arguments among

143

ministers were discouraged and might result in the dismissal of both. His belated constitution failed to formalise power relations, since it inserted a limited monarchy into a constituent dictatorship! Franco was content to repress his Civil War opponents and then to survive, accommodating, bending under international pressures, without seeking real social transformation (Linz, 'Falange'; Jerez Mir, *Elitas políticas*). This was not a regime of continuous revolution – better perhaps to label it 'reactionary despotism', says Giner ('Political economy').

Mussolini and Franco also compromised by broadening their fascist parties to include all the regime 'families'. As Franco and perhaps Mussolini intended, this undermined the genuinely revolutionary fascists and made the enlarged party fairly irrelevant to real decision-making. Here the contradiction between revolutionary ideology and institutional compromise was resolved decisively, inside the party, in favour of compromise. This was even truer of other regimes drawn from the same ideological stable. The earlier Primo de Rivera dictatorship in Spain had even brought socialist unions into its institutional compromise, while the Horthy regime in Hungary bargained with the socialist party (at least in the cities). During the 1920s and 1930s there were many varied compromises of the nation-statist movement. They saved many regimes from committing more than moderate evil.

What was common to the Nazi and Stalinist regimes *and to no others* (except perhaps the 'cultural revolution' phase of Maoism, the short-lived regime of Pol Pot, and the very short-lived regimes of the communist Bela Kun in Hungary and the fascist Szalasi in Romania) was their persistent rejection of institutional compromise with enemies and allies alike. They strove to overcome disagreement by the frontal violent assault of continuous revolution. This derived substantially from their violent, militaristic origins. The Bolsheviks had accomplished a street revolution and then won a protracted, bloody, and merciless civil war. They came to believe, not only in the necessity of violence, but also in some of its 'virtues'. The Nazi regime more enthusiastically embraced military virtues, inherited from the morale of frontline troops in World War I, from the *Freikorps* and other reactionary paramilitaries, and from its own streetfighting days. The Röhm purge stands as an exception to Nazi politics of continuing revolution. Then Hitler killed some of his own shock-troops to appease his conservative allies (though the purge also enabled him to remove his main Nazi rival). Thereafter the regime chose more radical, uncompromising policy alternatives. At first it trod warily with rival power blocs (big business, the Catholic Church, and the army), but they were increasingly subordinated to Nazi goals, especially during the War (see Kershaw, *The Nazi Dictatorship*, Chap 3). And though Stalin long hesitated before choosing purges over institutional compromise within the party and with the peasantry, his rule then escalated terror up until his last years.

This reveals the main source of the unique genocidal tendencies of the two regimes: they embarked on a continuous revolution, refusing compromise with allies and enemies. Hungarian 'Whites' in 1919–20, Italian *squadristi* in the early 1920s, Spanish Republican and Nationalist extremists in 1936 and Nationalists in 1939–41, Maoists during the cultural revolution, all began to kill their opponents. But they were then all reined in, usually by their more moderate allies. Only Nazis and Stalinists remained on the path of continuous revolution, of escalating, exponential evil. The Nazis committed premeditated genocide. The Stalinists usually confined mass killing to adult males from among their 'class opponents', and this is not quite true genocide. But this is a quibble when we contrast them to all other regimes. *Why* they, and they alone, embarked upon the path of continuous revolution is largely outside of my scope here, but *that* they did is the essence of their similarity, their unparalleled evil. By what methods did they accomplish it?

Methods of rule in regimes of continuous revolution

Some regime insiders did advocate the centralised and bureaucratic state described by totalitarian theorists. Albert Speer planned a bureaucratic and centralised German war economy. Wilhelm Frick, the Minister of the Interior, produced blueprints for a comprehensive *Reichsreform*, establishing a clear division of labour between the civil service and the Nazi party, with the former centralised and bureaucratic (Caplan, *Government without Administration*). Walter Buch sought impersonal rules governing the behaviour of party officials so that the party courts under his direction could fairly try leaders suspected of abuses (McKale, *The Nazi Party Courts*). All their efforts were frustrated. Speer could not control SS institutions, nor prevent them from disrupting war production by killing essential *Untermenschen* workers. Frick was undermined by jealous Nazi barons, and Buch by Hitler's preference for arbitrary despotism.

At stake in all these disputes was a contradiction between revolutionary politics and administrative institutionalisation, as Caplan (*Government without Administration*: 337) has noted. She argues that since the Nazis subordinated administration to politics (instead of regarding both as necessary), theirs was a deeply inefficient state. Yet the Nazis faced the customary problem of revolutionaries, unable to trust functionaries to carry out their policies. Though many civil servants were authoritarian conservatives, fewer endorsed the racial revolution. Even

145

Nazi party officials might not be trusted, since they comprised the usual assortment of revolutionaries, eccentrics, time-servers, and opportunists. Thus revolutionary purists interfered with orderly administration (whether of state or party), to prevent it settling back into unambitious institutional compromises with other power blocs and local notables. Frick could not be allowed his rational administration nor Buch his rule-governed party courts. Bureaucrats do not implement revolutions.

Were there alternative, *revolutionary* administrative methods, or was there merely the chaos of 'competing fiefdoms'? The answer is a bit of both. The Nazi regime was indeed polycratic and Hitler was slow to arbitrate disputes among his barons. Kershaw describes him as a 'laissez-faire' leader, Mommsen even as a 'weak' one. Russian memoirs seem not to agree about how active and interventionist Stalin was. But there was method in Hitler's laid-back style, and much of it was also practised by Stalin. I will identify four administrative methods of regimes of continuous revolution, all of which veered between a rule-governed institutionalisation and a revolutionary fluidity.

First, both despots divided and ruled (as many scholars have noted). This is not specific to revolutionary regimes but common to despotism ancient and modern. Stalin shifted his support between the 'left' and 'right' factions in the years around 1930. As his own despotism consolidated, he still did not let lieutenants feel secure in his affections. Both men cultivated informal, personalistic networks around them, which meant that official rank counted for little unless reinforced with influence over the despot or one of his confidants. But Hitler let rivalries flower more than is common among despots. This was not just tactics or laziness (though it contained both). It also entwined with his revolutionary Social Darwinism. He believed it to be a sign of the Aryan dynamism of Ley, Frick, Hess, Himmler, Bormann, and others that they sought to extend their own fiefdoms and undermine others. A *Gauleiter* observed in a memorandum on Nazi administration that 'The principle of letting things develop until the strongest has won is certainly the secret of the really remarkable development and achievements of the movement' (Noakes and Pridham, *Documents on Nazism*: 261). Yet Hitler rarely expected any contender to defeat his rivals comprehensively. He would let all of them struggle and mobilise their alliances. Then word would leak out from his cronies as to his own views and the rivals (if sensible) would begin an upward-looking reorientation of their strategy. A final decision might emerge somewhat tardily, or not even emerge at all, but this method kept rivalries fluid and personalistic. They did not solidify into ideological factionalism. Nor in either regime could any single institution rest confident in its power: the limits of party, state, military, and surveillance-organisation power were left undefined.

This was not only a strategy of Hitler or Stalin. The leadership principle enshrined it right down the Nazi Party, just as 'Little Stalins' imitated Stalin's cult of personality. Geyer ('The State') adds that Nazi divide-and-rule was not just a top-down strategy. It was internalised by all the power rivals: politics did not really aim at a final cooperation or resolution of competition between them, but rather at continuous negotiation to maintain their mutual autonomy. That could also apply to Stalinism.

In this volume, as in his earlier book (*The Nazi Dictatorship*, 1993), Kershaw identifies a second administrative method of the Nazi regime: administrators did not enforce rules but tried to 'work towards' Hitler, second-guessing his intentions from his speeches and from gossip about his conversations and preferences. Many Soviet officials did the same with Stalin. Party members looked upward for hints as to desired policy, and these were usually to radicalise. In the absence of information, they complied with their superior's orders if they recognised that his connections with higher-ups were better than theirs. In a despotism success comes by pleasing one's superiors.

Third, the revolutionary parties were value-driven, containing normative solidarity and comradeship, nourished under conditions of physical danger, in clandestine agitation, streetfighting, revolution, and civil war. The revolution and civil war indicated that the Bolsheviks had developed more cohesive morale based on comradeship than had the Whites, Mensheviks or SRs. Allen (*Nazi Seizure of Power*) shows that the Nazis were more committed, self-sacrificing grassroots activists than were the members of the bourgeois or socialist parties. Both movements constantly referred to 'discipline' and 'comradeship' (or 'national comradeship' in the case of the Nazis). Nazis expounded at great length about comradeship in their contributions to Theodore Abel's (1938) remarkable essay competition (*Why Hitler Came to Power*). Both movements gave status and privileges to 'old fighters' and 'old Bolsheviks', and leaders wore military tunics and used metaphors drawn from mass infantry formations to describe revolutionaries – stormtroopers, fortress-storming, shock-troops, campaigns, labour brigades, etc. Thus both sets of leaders had a certain confidence in the revolutionary elan of their 'shock-troops' against enemies and compromisers. Hitler's confidence lay partly in the Nazi Party, partly in an idealised conception of the German nation, the two merging into the notion of the 'true Aryan'. German foreign policy tended to be swallowed up by Hitler's broader revolutionary optimism. Plunge Aryans into the fray (rather as Rosa Luxemburg argued plunging in the working class) and the 'people's vital will' would overcome all odds. Extraordinary confidence in the will of the nation was common among nation-statist movements, influenced by Nietzschean notions of the Superman and the power of Will. Yet it was also echoed by the Bolsheviks: comrades or Stakhanovites could move mountains. Hitler's and Stalin's architecture and statuary graphically depicted such Supermen.

Fourth, the parties developed new mobilisation techniques, unknown in prior societies, little used in democracies. The technology of the mass party provided less than totalitarian theory has suggested. Only now, in the age of computers and video cameras, is surveillance technology moving potentially into the scenarios depicted by Orwell and Huxley. Propaganda techniques then centred on mass meetings, radio, and newspapers, and allowed only limited penetration of the population. Yet they did better with a narrower audience like the party itself – as at the Nuremberg Rallies – or with impressionable minds in the youth movement. They were also potent in the armed forces where Nazi and military values of nationalism, discipline, and morale overlapped, reinforced by strict discipline.

Nazis and Bolsheviks mobilised parties based on the cell, an essentially early-twentieth-century organisation presupposing the technological achievements of that era. A cell might have a radio receiver (occasionally a transmitter), a telephone, a motorbike, a truck, and a printing machine at its disposal. A hundred party militants could broadly supervise workplaces and the public activities of neighbourhoods and they could propagandise and coerce at street level. A few hundred Hitler Youths or Young Communists could be effectively prepared for this role and penetrate some non-party households. Collectivisation sought to compensate for Russian backwardness. The rural population were herded into large farms hopefully controllable by party cells.

Yet the cell strengthened the local party more than the centralised hierarchy. It gave some reality to the 'democracy' of the Communist Party and to the 'direct action orientation' of the Nazis. Thus some of their supposed 'chaos' may be better described as strong party localism, capable of continuously mobilising militants to achieve local goals, often at odds with the party or state hierarchy. Regional party bosses also had autonomy as brokers between the centre and the local party. Those at the centre who wished to institutionalise the regime reacted with alarm to the autonomy of locality and region, and sought to impose greater hierarchical controls. But revolutionary purists at the centre reacted with ambivalence. On the one hand, many local and regional party activists might be opportunists and place-seekers, wanting little more than to institutionalise relations with local notables to share in the spoils. But, on the other hand, many were purists of the nation-statist or class revolution. Hitler and Stalin wanted to let them rip yet still control their energy and violence. They could not do both, consistently. But they could zig-zag across the dilemma, sometimes prodding local and regional parties forward with 'shock-methods', sometimes trying to rein them in (as in Stalin's 'Dizzy with Success' article of 1930).

Combined, these four administrative methods – internalised divide-and-rule, 'working towards' the despot, reliance on comradeship, and local party mobilisation – generated not bureaucracy, but fluidity and violence. It seems chaos if contrasted to the ideal-type bureaucratic states depicted by Hegel or Weber or even to actual democracies or to despotisms like Franco's. Yet such methods enabled the dominant leadership faction, party militants, and non-party sympathisers to achieve not quite permanent, but certainly continuing, revolution.

The revolutionary process

The Stalinist revolution proceeded the more uncertainly. The Bolshevik factions went with much wrangling and opposition toward forced industrialisation and collectivisation. The purges and massacres came suddenly and erratically thereafter. Some scholars doubt whether the various purges up to even 1937 were a singular process or whether they comprised a number of separable reactions to distinct opponents. Nonetheless, once the policy of 'frontal assault' on the economy was beginning to win the argument (by 1930), this required continuing revolution and violence, even if the party purges need not have gone so far.

The Nazi drive toward a distinctively racial nation-statist revolution was more consistent. It was there from beginning to end. It was laid out in *Mein Kampf*, written in 1924; its racial expansionism became more explicit in Hitler's 'Second Book' of 1928 and became regime policy, as we see in the Hossbach Memorandum of 1937 (Noakes and Pridham, *Documents on Nazism*: 502–7, 521–9). True, the Nazis downplayed racism and antisemitism in favour of more conventional nationalism at election times and when negotiating with other power blocs. Had such allies retained their powers – as in all other nation-statist movements – the revolution would have been derailed into compromise. True, Broszat and Mommsen have shown that the Nazi leaders did not systematically plot their way to the Final Solution, and that the slogan of 'elimination' came to have a different, and far more terrible, meaning only amid the contingent opportunities of war. But let us not take revisionist tendencies too far. The 'elimination' of the Jews, the 'purification' of the German/Teuton/Aryan race and the 'clearing' of *Lebensraum* in the East had been ubiquitous in Nazi rhetoric. Until the war these terms probably signified mass expulsion rather than mass murder. Yet as Nazi autonomy from other power blocs increased, this

149

changed. The concentration camps and the extermination programmes against the more helpless *Untermenschen* expanded. Nearly 100,000 people, mostly mentally handicapped, were systematically murdered between 1939 and 1941, in a kind of trial run for what was to come. Of course, this programme was stopped – the one case in which opposition from a rival power bloc, the Catholic Church, helped derail an important aspect of the revolution. The Nazis did not change their revolutionary goals. What changed was opportunity, defined only by the degree of opposition. When nobody protected the 'impure', they were killed.

Most Nazis knew that in some sense this was the movement's, and especially Hitler's, goal. More than a million Germans, not all of them Nazis, 'worked towards' the Holocaust partly because they believed in it, partly because they knew it was the preferred policy and the regime and of Hitler. Some might take the Führer's calls to 'eliminate' Jews more literally than others; wartime economic exigencies also deflected the extermination drive. The brighter the prospects of victory, the more radically the Nazis implemented full 'racial cleansing'; the worse the military situation (except at the very end), the greater the 'compromises' using *Untermenschen* merely as forced labour (Herbert, 'Labour and extermination': 192). Thus the Holocaust emerged erratically rather than by concerted executive action – a not uncommon political process. But the Holocaust was no accident. It was the highly probable outcome if the Nazis under Hitler remained on top – just as Russian mass killings were highly probable if the Bolsheviks under Stalin remained on top.

The Nazi revolution was broader than just the Holocaust. Its second goal was to eliminate Slavs from central and eastern Europe and to create a *Lebensraum* for Aryans. This also proceeded by fits and starts, influenced by the fortunes of war. But it did proceed. As Bartov (*The Eastern Front; Hitler's Army*) shows, it barbarised the German armies on the eastern front. Most of their three million men, from generals to ordinary soldiers, helped exterminate captured Slav soldiers and civilians. This was sometimes cold and deliberate murder of individuals (as with Jews), sometimes generalised brutality and neglect. No less than 58 per cent of Russian POWs held by Germany died, compared to a tiny 4 per cent of Anglo-American POWs! German soldiers' letters and memoirs reveal their terrible reasoning: Slavs were 'the Asiatic-Bolshevik' horde, an inferior but threatening race. Only a minority of officers and men were Nazi members. Yet in nation statism Nazi propaganda blended well with military values, so that patriotism and respect for discipline merged imperceptibly into an authoritarian racism which viewed the Russians as *Untermenschen*. Officers increasingly used Nazi terms in their orders and objected to atrocities only when they feared discipline might be undermined. Bartov observes that this genocide was committed by an army whose high command was now integrated into the regime, and whose soldiery was now representative of German males.

Since my essay offers support to the *Historikerstreit* revisionist thesis that the crimes of Nazis and Stalinists were comparable, I should make clear that I totally reject its other main thesis. The main motivation of the German army of the east in fighting grimly to the end was not to protect German civilians from the advancing Russians (as revisionists claim). If the soldiers shared the vision of a 'demonic invasion' by Asiatic Bolsheviks, this resulted from their internalising Nazi ideology and their realisation that there was no retreat from the evil they themselves had committed.

This raises the question of whether the two regimes' revolutionary goals and evil deeds were endorsed by the people. Whereas totalitarian theorists saw revolutionary ideology as confined within the party, revisionist historians of Russia have stressed its broad popularity and partial autonomy from central control. Cohen (*Rethinking the Soviet Experience*) Fitzpatrick ('New perspectives on Stalinism') and Getty ('The Politics of Stalinism') conclude that, though Stalin and other leaders set in motion the purges and forced collectivisations and remained responsible for many crimes, nonetheless the ferocity also had popular aspects. In many towns and villages ancient populism, reinforced by the class hatreds of the Revolution and the Civil War, then legitimised by Stalin, stimulated a massive proletarian and peasant settling of scores against the rich, the kulaks, bourgeois specialists, officials, and other intelligentsia both outside and inside the Party. Often, when top or regional party officials wanted to stop the violence, they could not. A 'bottom-up' revolutionary process (as well as a top-down stimulus) was evident in the purges and forced collectivisations. Evil was not simply imposed from above: class conflict, if made continuous and uncompromising, could itself become evil.

German historians have not identified a comparable popular pressure for Nazi revolutionary goals. They agree that Hitler enjoyed an extraordinary personal popularity until well into the war, and that up to 1940 the restoration of German prosperity and international prestige was widely welcomed. Yet they argue most Germans neither wanted war nor endorsed, much less initiated, murderous antisemitism or racism. Nonetheless, since Nazi ideology flourished amid a much broader penumbra of nation-statism, some of its revolutionary ideas were widely shared. It resonated in German Lutheranism, though not much in Catholicism. Its militarism, shared by all nation-statist movements of the period, conferred moral worth on disciplined violence and on the esprit de corps and comradeship of fighters. Geyer ('The State') reminds us that militarism was not confined to upper-class groups: it had a mass base throughout central, eastern, and southern Europe. The Nazis recruited heavily from ex-front-line troops of all ranks in World War I, while the SS officer corps recruited disproportionately from military and civil-service families. Less extreme antisemitism predated the Nazis and permeated non-Nazi institutions. Nation-statism appealed strongly to youth, as elsewhere. The Nazis took over (fairly democratically) the German student movement around 1930, and the Hitler Youth became popular among all classes. As the Nazi leadership aged, the rank-and-file swelled with young people who had grown up accepting National Socialism merely as German patriotism. The Nazis also recruited foreign idealists, as collaborators and as volunteers to fight the 'Asiatic-Bolshevik horde' on the Eastern Front. The Charlemagne, *Azul*, and other divisions were typical nation-statist revolutionaries, young men drawn quite widely across the class spectrum, seeking to find a new, more vigorous, communitarian and corporatist society. So though the worst evils (Jewish deathcamps and other massacres) were half-concealed by the regime because they believed they would not be popular, the penumbra of nation-statism, in Germany with strong racial overtones, found much popular support.

Thus the core of these regimes was a fluid alliance between tens of leaders, thousands of party purists, and millions of ordinary German and Soviet citizens among whom the penumbra of class or nation-statist revolutionary ideas resonated. But since all three groups had to deal with more pragmatic compromisers (and with opponents), the regimes could not develop rule-governed practices to secure their cooperation. This means that both regimes were fluid and sometimes verged on the chaotic.

Yet it also means that the Nazi regime self-destructed more because of the policy choices of millions of Germans sharing revolutionary racial nation-statism, than because of the 'chaos' of intra-Nazi rivalries. 'Cumulative radicalisation' did destroy them, as Mommsen argues, but not through the mechanism of regime chaos. As an extreme nation-statist Hitler distinguished only two macro-actors, 'us', the Aryan people, and 'them', the enemies surrounding and infiltrating Germany. Thus he tended to take 'them' all on at once and he had little ability to divide his enemies. As his racial policies 'radicalised' into barbarity, they totally alienated all enemies. How could Russians now forgive Nazi treatment of Slavs? How could the West compromise with Holocaust-dealers in Hitler's projected anti-Communist pact? The British archives show British hostility was not at first to the Holocaust but to a broader nation-statism, especially to a militarism they identified as 'Prussian'. For them evil was not primarily the fate of the *Untermenschen* but having to fight repeated world wars. As happens only very rarely in wars, the allies demanded unconditional surrender and total destruction of the Nazi state. They had the military might to achieve it. Under the strain of a two-front war, mass bombing and armies haemorrhaging to death, the regime did indeed disintegrate into chaos from perhaps late 1944. In Hitler there was also what we conventionally call 'madness', since he deliberately chose doom for himself and his Aryan nation rather than compromise and survival. Yet even this was influenced by early twentieth-century nation-statist values – sacrifice, heroic death, and the cleansing power of destruction – which we find in other examples of near-suicidal violence (like that of the Iron Guard Legionaries in Romania). There were both methods and goals in the Nazi evil and madness. With Stalin there was rather more survival-oriented pragmatism. There was also luck: his continuous revolution also might have led to utter destruction, but it was stopped from outside by a war that he did not start.

Regime dynamic cycles

In the 1930s and early 1940s the two regimes differed greatly because they were at different points in the dynamic cycle I wish now to identify. Between the Röhm purge and the 1944 assassination attempt the Nazis remained a strikingly solidary group. Of the one hundred or so *Reichsleiter* and *Gauleiter* – drawn from extraordinarily varied social backgrounds – during the whole existence of the NSDAP only about ten resigned or were dismissed, and only two or three were murdered. Their collective loyalty was extraordinary. They might embezzle on a mass scale, engage in sexual practices considered deviant, they might beat, imprison or kill the wrong people or fail to beat, imprison or kill the right people. But they survived in power. Buch's party courts, active in disciplining lower Nazis, never developed the law by which the barons could be disciplined independently of Hitler's will.

By contrast the Bolshevik comrades did fall out, from 1928 and with gathering momentum through Stalin's purges. Figures have been presented which are strikingly opposite to the Nazi experience – 80 per cent of the Central Committee members of 1934 arrested by 1938, almost all of them killed![1] The Nazis turned their violence outward, beyond the party. Stalin made little distinction between party and society. The difference derived partly from Stalin's paranoia, partly

---

[1] Ideas expressed at the 1991 conference, the papers from which are not reproduced in this volume.

from the different domestic objectives of Bolsheviks and Nazis. Though the Nazis were revolutionary in their foreign and racial policies, these were not central to the everyday life of most Germans. Once the Nazis had suppressed open opposition, they could settle back into domestic rule that – outside of the racial sphere – was less ambitious and more self-enriching. It did not evoke massive ideological disagreements within the party. The Bolsheviks did the opposite, abandoning their revolutionary foreign policy but with severe factionalism over domestic policy through the late 1920s. This provoked massive opposition to the official line in both party and country – hence the purges and massacres.

Yet as the purges ended, and then again with the death of Stalin, the regime settled down into less ambitious, less revolutionary, institutionalised rule – into 'the Great Retreat' of collective self-reproduction by the *nomenklatura apparatchiki*. During the Cold War the military-industrial complex joined them. Similar tendencies have been shown within Communist East Germany,[2] where the regime did what the Nazis had been unable to do: settle back into relaxed, collectivist, semi-institutionalised rule, merging party and state. The Chinese communists seem to have had short, alternating bursts of both – perhaps the best survival technique!

Thus there was a dynamic contradiction between institutional compromise and revolution in both regimes. They could semi-institutionalise their rule into the state by backtracking on their revolutionary ideologies. They could achieve a few of their goals, destroy hardcore opponents and cow the rest. In such phases the party elites abandoned the notion of continuous revolution and shared power fairly amicably among themselves, allowing each other and some non-party notables administrative autonomy. Huntington ('Social and institutional dynamics') refers to this as 'corporate pluralism' – a label which might apply to the Soviet Union for some of the 1920s and increasingly through the 1950s, and (less well) to the Nazis in the mid-1930s. Huntington argues that a dynamic toward 'corporate pluralism' was endemic to such regimes since multi-group representation becomes necessary as society becomes more modern and complex. I doubt this. Germany in 1939–41 was probably more modern and complex than the Soviet Union ever became, yet the Nazis were then finally abandoning the temptation of 'corporate pluralism' for continuing revolution. Rather, outcomes emerged from political struggles. Bukharin and other advocates of a more rule-governed 'corporate pluralist' party lost out to Stalin, just as Frick and Buch lost out to Hitler. This was not some

---

[2] Ideas expressed at the 1991 conference, the papers from which are not reproduced in this volume.

general logic of modernisation, but the effect of political struggles which might have gone otherwise.

And the principal driving force remained the party's continuing revolutionary zeal. The Nazis drove themselves to geopolitical and racial evil that was suicidal. The Soviet Communists were twice driven toward self-destruction by the revolutionary aspirations of party militants. Their transformative goals led to bitter factionalism in the early 1930s. Collectivisation and the purges might have destroyed them, but the World War saved the regime. But enough of them remained more wedded to socialist transformation (and thus to outperforming Western capitalism) than was good for their own semi-institutionalised self-preservation. This time intense factionalism over how to achieve it was not saved by a Great Patriotic War. The regime broke apart from the top.

The Nazi dynamic related more to geopolitics, the Soviet to domestic politics. But the same contradiction arose between the revolutionary and the party institutionalising elements which totalitarian theorists had assumed were mutually reinforcing. One-party despotism could become partly institutionalised, though with fewer bureaucratic or centralised institutions than totalitarian theorists had envisaged. But this was undermined by goals of continuous revolution resonating inside the party. Neither regime could in the long run reproduce itself. Both were destroyed by the contradiction between institutionalising party rule and achieving the party's goal, continuous revolution.

I have indicated my preference for the term 'regime of continuous revolution'. But labels are not that important. In the present conjuncture of world-history, it is doubtful whether we can remove the term 'totalitarian' from scholarly or popular discussions. Perhaps my title should have been 'The contradictions of totalitarianism'.

Totalitarian theorists correctly identified the two central features of such regimes, though they failed to see that the two undermined each other. The power totalitarian theorists believed to be 'total' was instead contradictory and self-destructive – luckily for Germany, for Russia, and ultimately for the world. We have seen the back of these two regimes of continuous revolution – indeed fascist regimes will probably not reappear, nor will communist regimes trouble us much longer. But the ideological families from which they sprang will surely endure. Classes and nation-states remain the most significant actors in the world today and revolutionary parties may be expected to reemerge, attributing crises and their solutions to them. Once in power, most would again surely compromise. But it only needs one or two to pursue continuous revolution, and evil deeds – again paradoxically legitimated by ideologies of hope – might again stalk the world.

155

Bibliography

Abel, T. 1938 *Why Hitler Came to Power*. New York: Prentice-Hall.

Allen, W.S. 1965 *The Nazi Seizure of Power: The Experience of a Single German Town, 1930–1935*. Chicago: Quadrangle Books.

Bartov, O. 1985 *The Eastern Front, 1941–45, German Troops and the Barbarisation of Warfare*. London: Macmillan.

1991 *Hitler's Army, Soldiers, Nazis and War in the Third Reich*. Oxford: Oxford University Press.

Burleigh, M. and Wippermann, W. 1991 *The Racial State: Germany 1933–1945*. Cambridge: Cambridge University Press.

Caplan, J. 1988 *Government without Administration: State and Civil Service in Weimar and Nazi Germany*. Oxford: Clarendon Press.

Cohen, S. 1985 *Rethinking the Soviet Experience: Politics and History Since 1917*. New York: Oxford University Press.

de Grand, A. 1982 *Italian Fascism: Its Origins and Development*. Lincoln, Neb.: University of Nebraska Press.

Fischer, C. 1995 *The Rise of the Nazis*. Manchester: Manchester University Press.

Fitzpatrick, S. 1986 'New perspectives on Stalinism', *Russian Review*, Vol. 45.

1987 *Russian Review*, Vol. 46, no. 4.

Getty, J.A. 1985 *Origins of the Great Purges: The Soviet Communist Party Reconsidered, 1933–1938*. Cambridge: Cambridge University Press.

1992 'The politics of Stalinism', in *The Stalin Phenomenon*, ed. A. Nove. New York: St Martins Press.

Geyer, M. 1984 'The state in National Socialist Germany', in *Statemaking and Social Movements*, eds. C. Bright and S. Harding. Ann Arbor, Mich.: University of Michigan Press.

1989 'The militarization of Europe, 1914–1945', in *The Militarization of the Western World*, ed. J.R. Gillis. New Brunswick, NJ: Rutgers University Press.

Giner, S. 1985 'Political economy, legitimation and the state in Southern Europe', in *Uneven Development in Southern Europe*, eds. R. Hudson and J. Lewis. New York: Methuen.

Haslam, J. 1984 *The Soviet Union and the Struggle for Collective Security in Europe, 1933–39*. New York.

Herbert, U. 1992 'Labour and extermination: economic interest and the primacy of *Weltanschauung* in National Socialism', *Past and Present*, No. 138.

Huntington, S. 1970 'Social and institutional dynamics of one-party systems', in *Authoritarian Politics in Modern Society*, eds. S. Huntington and C. Moore. New York: Basic Books.

Jerez Mir, M. 1982 *Elitas políticas y centros de extracción en España, 1938–1957*. Madrid: CIS.

Kershaw, I. 1993 *The Nazi Dictatorship*. London: Edward Arnold.

Linz, J. 1970 'From falange to movimiento-organizacion: The Spanish single party and the Franco regime, 1936–1968', in *Authoritarian Politics in Modern Society*, eds. S. Huntington and C. Moore. New York: Basic Books.

Mann, M. 1986 *The Sources of Social Power*. Vol. I: *A History of Power from the Beginning to 1760 A.D.* Cambridge: Cambridge University Press.

1993 *The Sources of Social Power*. Vol. II: *The Rise of Classes and Nation-States, 1760–1914*. Cambridge: Cambridge University Press.

Manning, R. 1987 'State and society in Stalinist Russia', *The Russian Review*, Vol. 46.

McKale, D.M. 1974 *The Nazi Party Courts. Hitler's Management of Conflict in His Movement, 1921–1945*. Lawrence, Kansas: University Press of Kansas.

Mommsen, H. 1991 'Hitler's position in the Nazi system', in his *From Weimar to Auschwitz*. Princeton, NJ: Princeton University Press.

Morodo, R. 1985 *Los orígines ideológicos del franquismo: Acción Española*. Madrid: Alianza.

Mühlberger, D. 1991 *Hitler's Followers*. London: Routledge.

Noakes, J. and Pridham, G. 1974 *Documents on Nazism, 1919–1945*. London: Jonathan Cape.

Rittersporn, G.T. 1984 'Rethinking Stalinism', *Russian History*, Vol. 11.

7

From *Blitzkrieg* to total war: controversial links between image and reality

Omer Bartov

The German *Wehrmacht* conducted two distinct, though not unrelated and at times overlapping types of warfare between 1939 and 1945. One was based on massive, concentrated, and well-coordinated attacks along narrow fronts, leading to encirclements of large enemy forces and aimed at achieving a rapid military and political disintegration of the opponent by undermining both his logistical apparatus and psychological determination at a minimum cost to the attacking force. The other constituted a stubborn and costly defence, along huge, static, or gradually retreating fronts, normally launching only local attacks and counter-attacks with relatively limited elements of the armed forces, and relying increasingly on fortifications and doggedness rather than on speed and daring. The first type, which came to be known as *Blitzkrieg*, or lightning war, since it assumed a brief, though intense military confrontation, called for the preparation of limited stocks of armaments (without any major, long-term changes in the economy) needed for the implementation of such shock tactics, namely tanks, armoured personnel carriers, motorised artillery, and anti-aircraft guns, as well as fighter planes and tactical support light and medium bombers. The second type, generally called total war, and closely related to the experience of 1914–18 (whose repetition so many European countries, and especially Germany, had hoped to avoid), necessitated a much more profound restructuring of the economy and the industrial organisation of the nation, as well a greater participation of, and a heavier burden on, the population, so as to be able to produce the endless quantities of *matériel*, to use most efficiently the existing material resources, and to mobilise the largest possible numbers of men and women, in order to satisfy the voracious appetite of total industrial warfare.[1]

[1] On *Blitzkrieg* and the economy, see T. Mason, 'Some Origins of the Second World War', and 'Internal Crisis and War of Aggression, 1938–1939', in *Nazism, Fascism and the Working Class*, ed. J. Caplan (Cambridge 1995), pp. 33–52 and 104–30, respectively; A. S.

As long as Germany pursued political and military goals which could be achieved by resorting to a series of brief, albeit highly brutal, *Blitzkrieg* campaigns, it remained victorious. Once it moved beyond these relatively limited goals (by continuing the war with Britain and attacking the Soviet Union), Germany found itself increasingly embroiled in a total, world war which it had no hope of winning, due to the much greater industrial and manpower capacities of its opponents. Hence we can say that the transition from *Blitzkrieg* to total war spelt the end of German military and political hegemony in Europe, even though at the time there were those in Germany (including such rational technocrats as Albert Speer) who argued that only a truly total mobilisation of the nation would save it from defeat.[2] There is, however, controversy over the *nature*, *degree*, and *implications* of German military preparation. Whereas one school claims that the Nazi regime launched a *Blitzkrieg* campaign due to the domestic economic, social, and political cul-de-sac into which it had manoeuvred itself, the opposing thesis holds that the regime was motivated by foreign political and expansionist ambitions, showed no signs of anxiety over any alleged domestic crisis, did not seem unduly worried about its popularity, and was all along preparing for a total war rather than a *Blitzkrieg*, a war it finally launched not because it felt constrained to do so but because it seized what seemed to be the best opportunity.[3]

Debates over the nature and meaning of *Blitzkrieg*, not only as a military tactic, but also a type of war favoured by certain kinds of regimes and hence a strategic concept to be understood only as a combination of political, economic, and military factors, have to a large extent been moulded by the images it has produced ever since its

Milward, *The German Economy at War* (London 1965), and his *War, Economy, and Society 1939–1945* (Berkeley 1977). For criticism of this literature, see below, note 3. For a highly detailed discussion, see W. Deist *et al.*, *Das Deutsche Reich und der Zweite Weltkrieg* (Stuttgart 1979), Vol. I, esp. parts 2–4 (H.-E. Volkmann, W. Deist, M. Messerschmidt); and W. Deist, *The Wehrmacht and German Rearmament* (London 1981). On *Blitzkrieg* doctrine, see B. R. Posen, *The Sources of Military Doctrine* (Ithaca 1984), esp. chaps. 3 and 6. On pre-1914 military strategy, see J. Snyder, *The Ideology of the Offensive* (Ithaca 1984), esp. chaps. 2–5.
[2] A. Speer, *Inside the Third Reich*, 5th edn (London 1979), pp. 269–367, esp., e.g., pp. 299–314, 351–6. Detailed analysis in B. R. Kroener *et al.*, *Das Deutsche Reich und der Zweite Weltkrieg* (Stuttgart 1988), Vol. V/1, esp. parts 2–3 (R.-D. Müller and B. R. Kroener). A more general case for the relationship between economy and hegemony, in P. Kennedy, *The Rise and Fall of the Great Powers*, 2nd edn (New York 1989), esp. chap. 6.
[3] R. J. Overy, 'Germany, "Domestic Crisis" and War in 1939', and 'Hitler's War and the German Economy: A Reinterpretation', in his *War and Economy in the Third Reich* (Oxford 1944), pp. 205–32 and 233–56, respectively; 'Debate: Germany, "Domestic Crisis" and War in 1939', comments by D. Kaiser and T. W. Mason, reply by R. J. Overy, *Past & Present* 122 (1989), pp. 200–40. See also G. L. Weinberg, *The Foreign Policy of Hitler's Germany* (Chicago 1980), and D. Kaiser, *Politics and War* (Cambridge, Mass. 1990), pp. 370–92, esp. 375–84.

inception. Images, in the case of *Blitzkrieg*, have been especially important, since the very success of this type of war has depended to a large extent on the image it projected, just as much as on its reality. Indeed, it would be more accurate to say that the image of *Blitzkrieg* was *part* of its reality, though precisely for that reason it is, nevertheless, important to distinguish between the more quantifiable facts of specific *Blitzkrieg* campaigns and their perception by contemporaries and later generations.[4] Such an analysis may tell us more about the relationship between the material aspects of war, on the one hand, and the power of myth and psychological suggestion, on the other.

In this chapter I will discuss several aspects of this issue. First, I will point out some of the implications of the disparities between the facts of *Blitzkrieg* as it was conducted by the *Wehrmacht* in the initial phases of the Second World War, and the impression it made not only on those subjected to its violence but also on its practitioners. Second, I will present some of the main controversies over the nature and meaning of *Blitzkrieg* and note their wider implications for the historiography of the Third Reich. Finally, I will briefly examine the images of *Blitzkrieg* both during the war and following the collapse of the Nazi regime, and remark on some of the more problematic and disturbing manifestations of the representation of the German war machine.

I Realities and impressions

The concept of *Blitzkrieg* was developed as an attempt to avoid the recurrence of a static, costly, and, especially for Germany, unwinnable war such as the Western Front of 1914–18. In order to prevent a similar stalemate along well-defended lines of trenches and fortifications, new types of weaponry and tactics were needed. Such ideas were already emerging during the latter part of the Great War, and during the interwar period they were widely discussed and in some cases put into practice. All European nations were intrigued by the new technologies developed during the period and the manner in which they could be put to military use. But their conclusions as to organising their armed forces and rethinking their strategic and tactical concepts differed greatly. While there is no doubt that the major European powers, namely the Soviet Union, Germany, France, and Britain, recognised the importance

---

[4] On the powerful impact of the war on contemporaries and the manner in which its image distorted their understanding of reality, see, e.g., M. Bloch, *Strange Defeat. A Statement of Evidence Written in 1940* (New York 1968), pp. 25–125, esp. pp. 25–6, 51–4, including the notes. See also such accounts as J. Green, *La fin d'un monde: Juin 1940* (Paris 1992); H. Habe, *A Thousand Shall Fall* (London 1942); J.-P. Sarte, *Les carnets de la drôle de guerre* (Paris 1983), and his *Iron in the Soul* (Harmondsworth 1984 [1949]); C. Malaparte, *Kaputt* (Milano 1979 [1943]).

of using modern tanks and aircraft in any future war, for a variety of reasons, which had to do both with their different experience during the war and with the domestic and foreign conditions in each country, it was only the newly established *Wehrmacht* which ultimately practised the new form of *Blitzkrieg* warfare in the initial phases of the Second World War.[5]

From the very beginning, it was clear to all those involved in conceptualising and planning *Blitzkrieg* that this type of warfare depended to a large extent on the impression it made on the opponent, since it was aimed just as much at demoralising the enemy as at destroying him. And, while the enemy was to be given the *coup de grâce* after he had been debilitated by a combination of deep thrusts into his rear, thereby severing the contact between his combat elements and logistics, as well as by bombing of control centres and civilian targets, one's own troops were expected to be greatly energised by the constant, if ultimately exhausting, momentum of the fighting. Hence *Blitzkrieg* was intended to create the impression of an invincible army both among its enemies and among its own soldiers.[6]

In this the Germans were highly, perhaps even dangerously success-ful. While the campaign in the West culminated in one of the greatest, and cheapest, victories in modern warfare, it created a new and vastly more confident perception of the German capacities for war among those *Wehrmacht* generals who had previously been somewhat reluctant to accept the risks of *Blitzkrieg*. The result was that the Western campaign was not analysed clearly enough, and those aspects of the fighting which might have turned a great German victory into a disastrous defeat were neglected or ignored. Nor did the failure of the

---

[5] The prophets of armoured warfare included J. F. C. Fuller and B. H. Liddell Hart in England, Charles de Gaulle in France, Heinz Guderian in Germany, and Marshal Tukhachevsky in the Soviet Union. See brief discussion in M. Howard, *War in European History*, 2nd edn (Oxford 1977), pp. 130–5. The British rejected these ideas, the French preferred the Maginot Line, and Tukhachevsky was executed by Stalin in 1937. Guderian, however, became one of Hitler's darlings. See further in Charles de Gaulle, *Vers l'armée de métier* (Paris 1934); B. H. Liddell Hart, *The Tanks*, 2 vols. (London 1959); J. F. C. Fuller, *Memoirs of an Unconventional Soldier* (London 1936); J. Erickson, *The Road to Stalingrad*, 2nd edn (London 1985), pp. 12–20, 30, 44–9 (on Tukhachevsky); and Heinz Guderian, *Panzer Leader*, 4th edn (London 1977), esp. pp. 18–46. On French strategy, see J. M. Hughes, *To the Maginot Line* (Cambridge, Mass. 1971); and R. J. Young, *In Command of France* (Cambridge, Mass. 1978).

[6] German *Wochenschauen* of the period, often reproduced in post-war films, provide a vivid picture of both the reality and the image of *Blitzkrieg*, especially in France. A highly intimidating German film on the *Blitzkrieg* in Poland was shown widely in European capitals. See T. Taylor, *The March of Conquest* (New York 1958), p. 10. The panic and confusion on the French side has also been the subject of numerous representations. One of the most outstanding is the opening scene of René Cléments 1952 film 'Forbidden Games', which depicts the perverting impact of war on children. See also the outstanding novel, C. Simon, *La route des Flandres* (Paris 1960).

Battle of Britain deter German military leaders from planning an even vaster, and much riskier campaign in the Soviet Union, where precisely those elements which had formed the potential Achilles' Heel of the Germany army's western campaign were greatly accentuated. To make matters worse, the industrial output of military wares remained far below the rate needed by such an unprecedented operation, so that in terms of the ratio between space and material, the German Eastern Army was actually weaker than its Western counterpart of the previous year.[7]

The irony of this turn of events is obvious. While the Germans drew the correct military conclusions from the Great War, and prepared themselves better than anyone else for the fighting in the first part of the Second World War, it was their victories during those early campaigns that blinded them to the limitations of their own strategy. Hence their final and greatest *Blitzkrieg* ended in catastrophe, and had to be followed by a reversion to total war strategies highly reminiscent of 1914–18, with the unavoidable conclusion of a complete and total German defeat. The impression created by the swift victories and tremendous energies unleashed by *Blitzkrieg* therefore debilitated not only the enemy, but also the minds of those who had launched it. From being a means to preventing total war it came to be seen as a magic formula for German victory, and found its own nemesis in bringing about precisely what it had been intended to thwart. The concentration of forces at a given point, which formed the essence of *Blitzkrieg*, appeared to both sides as reflecting total strength, rather than relative power limited to a specific time and space.[8]

The fact that Germany chose *Blitzkrieg* in the first place was, of course, related to its severe industrial and manpower constraints, which were not fully appreciated abroad and were forgotten in the flush of early victory by the Germans themselves. We will have occasion to discuss the debates on this issue in the next section, but for now let us examine the relative strengths of the armies and armaments industries of the major powers involved in the Second World War.

It is now generally accepted that contrary to the image disseminated (for different reasons) by both the Germans and their foes at the time, and indeed popularly accepted for a long time after the end of the war, the *Wehrmacht*'s armoured forces during its most successful *Blitzkrieg* operation were in fact numerically, and in some respects also qualitatively, inferior to those of its opponents. Germany attacked in the West with some 2,500 tanks, while the combined forces of the

---

[7] H. Boog *et al.*, *Das Deutsche Reich und der Zweite Weltkrieg* (Stuttgart 1983), Vol, IV, esp. part 1, chap. 3 (Müller).

[8] Further on the planning of 'Barbarossa', see ibid., part 1, chaps. 1 and 4 (J. Förster, E. Klink, and H. Boog).

Allies had about 3,400 machines. Moreover, only 700 German tanks had the speed, armour, and calibre of guns to be effective against the heavier types of enemy machines. However, whereas most French tanks were subjugated to the infantry and the few existing tank formations were lacking both training and support, the Germans concentrated their tanks in large and well-integrated Panzer divisions. These divisions were then organised in powerful Panzer groups which could be used to punch through the enemy's front and thrust deep into his rear, dislocating and isolating his forces from their logistical support. Hence it was thanks to a combination of innovative (but not entirely unknown) organisational and tactical concepts that the *Wehrmacht* overwhelmed its enemy. Nevertheless, the impression created was of overall numerical preponderance and technological superiority.[9]

This impression was enhanced by the much more highly developed air doctrine of the *Luftwaffe*, which in this case also enjoyed a numerical and technological advantage, as well as being able to deploy types of aircraft best suited for its strategy (but not for later phases of the war such as the Battle of Britain and the strategic bombing of Germany). Facing the *Luftwaffe's* 4,000 operational aeroplanes were about 3,000 Allied machines, including those aircraft stationed in Britain. And, compared to the *Luftwaffe's* crucially important 1,500 bombers, the Allies had only 700 mostly obsolete machines. Nevertheless, in this case too it was largely the use made of air power which decided the issue, rather than its numbers and quality. The fact that by the end of the campaign the French air force had more aircraft on the ground than it had had at the beginning of the fighting, testifies to the timidity and incompetence with which existing aeroplanes were employed at a time when their proper use could have made a crucial difference. The *Luftwaffe*, on the other hand, used its aircraft as 'flying artillery', and due to good planning, training, and cooperation with the ground units, achieved its goal of unhinging the enemy's front, disorienting his command, sowing chaos in his logistical system, and demoralising both the front and the rear, thus greatly contributing to his rapid military and political collapse. The much-hailed Maginot Line, where a high proportion of the numerically superior Allied artillery was to be found, played no role in the fighting, apart from tying down large numbers of inactive French troops.[10]

[9] K. A. Maier, *Das Deutsche Reich und der Zweite Weltkrieg* (Stuttgart 1979), Vol. II, part 6 (H. Umbreit), esp. pp. 268 and 282 for figures. See also the excellent discussion in Posen, *Military Doctrine*, esp. chap. 3 (slightly different figures cited on p. 83).

[10] See Maier, *Deutsche Reich*, II, pp. 244–59, 282–307 (Umbreit), and p. 282 for figures; and Posen, *Military Doctrine*, esp. chaps. 4 and 6 (slightly different figures on p. 84, and statement on more operational French aircraft on the Armistice than on 10 May 1940, p. 133, citing the commander of the French Air Force, General Joseph Vuillemin).

In spite of the initial impression created by the swiftness and decisiveness of the German victory, it would be a mistake to view it as inevitable. First we should note that only some 7 per cent of the German force was truly modernised (10 Panzer out of a total of 141 mostly infantry divisions). Second, and as a consequence of the previous observation, the kind of breakthrough demanded by *Blitzkrieg* tactics necessitated the concentration of almost all tank formations along a very narrow front, and the exploitation of the initial penetration further called for a growing gap between the armoured thrust and its infantry and logistical support. Hence, while the Germans did manage to drive a wedge into the Allied Force, the Allies were in a position to do the same to the Germans by driving a wedge between the nine Panzer divisions rushing to the Channel and the mass of the German army trudging far behind. To a large extent, then, the success of the German *Blitzkrieg* in the West depended both on its novelty and on the incompetence of the other side's command. Had the Allies understood the essence of *Blitzkrieg* tactics (an example of which had been already given them in Poland), had they organised their existing manpower and *matériel* appropriately, and, had they shown a slightly greater degree of cooperation and tactical skill, the *Wehrmacht* would have had a much harder time confronting their forces.[11]

Because the Germans were taken in by their representation of their own successes in the West as inevitable, and due to their prejudices about the nature of both the Russians in general and the Bolsheviks in particular, they had little doubt that a *Blitzkrieg* against the Soviet Union would lead to an even greater victory than the campaign just won in the West. This hope proved to be an illusion. Indeed, within a few weeks of fighting it became clear that the *Wehrmacht* could not conduct a war on the mammoth scale demanded by the Soviet Union using the same tactics and equipment of the Western campaign. Here both the ratio between manpower and machines on the one hand, and space on the other, as well as between the German and Soviet armed forces, was much less favourable than in the West. The tremendous victories achieved nevertheless by the *Wehrmacht* in the initial phases of 'Barbarossa' were thus not only a tribute to the tactical ability of the German officers and the fighting skills of their soldiers, but could also be attributed to the incompetence of the Soviet commanders and the lack of training (but not of determination) among their troops. It should be noted that while the *Wehrmacht* attacked Russia with 3,600 tanks (of

[11] The risks involved are nicely articulated in Howard, *War in European History*, p. 132. For the German divisional structure on the eve of the attack, see Maier, *Deutsche Reich*, IV, p. 254 (Klink). For an account of the fighting from the perspective of the German tank formations, see Guderian, *Panzer Leader*, pp. 89–117. On the French side, see G. Chapman, *Why France Collapsed* (London 1968); A. Goutard, *The Battle of France 1940* (London 1958); Bloch, *Strange Defeat*, esp. chap. 2.

which only 450 could confront modern Soviet armour), the Red Army in the West had 15,000 tanks (of which close to 2,000 were excellent modern machines). The *Luftwaffe* deployed only 2,500 aircraft in the East, significantly fewer than during the Western campaign, while the Red Army deployed 9,000 admittedly mostly inferior aircraft. It is interesting to point out that in fact the Red Army had a better ratio between men and machines than the *Wehrmacht*, that is, it was more modern, since it had only 2.9 million soldiers along the Western front of the Soviet Union as opposed to the 3.6 million attacking German (and allied) troops.[12]

The attempt to repeat its *Blitzkrieg* tactics over a vastly larger space than in the West compelled the *Wehrmacht* to split its relatively limited forces into even smaller groupings, and to allot its modern elements to each of these separate bodies with the result of further weakening its punch. Worse still, in the central sector of the front, the huge tracts of land to be covered meant that the *Wehrmacht*'s armour had to be split once again in order to encircle the large Soviet forces in Belorussia. Meanwhile, as the Germans drove ever deeper into Russia, the front tended to extend, so that by late fall 1941 it had doubled in length, from 800 to 1,500 miles, while supply lines stretched 1,000 miles to the rear. Insufficient motorisation of the *Wehrmacht*'s logistical apparatus, the primitive road infrastructure of the Soviet Union, and the different gauge used by the Russian railroad, all made for growing chaos and eventually totally paralysed the German *Blitzkrieg*. The fact that about half of the German divisions deployed in Soviet Russia relied solely on horse-drawn wagons for their provisions, meant that even when supplies arrived at the railheads, it was difficult to bring them to the front. Considering these factors, as well as the shortage of spare parts for the modern elements of the army, and the lack of replacement horses for the more backward formations, one can only wonder how the *Blitzkrieg* got as far as it did.[13]

Once *Blitzkrieg* failed, production, industrial capacity, material and manpower resources, organisation and technical skill, all became more important than tactics, training, and courage. Of course, *Blitzkrieg* itself depended on technology, indeed, it made a fetish of modern fighting machines. But now technological innovation had to be paralleled by

---

[12] For figures, see Boog, *Deutsche Reich*, IV, pp. 56–76 (J. Hoffman), and 168–89, esp. 184–8 (Müller). On prejudices and ideological determinants concerning Russians and Bolsheviks, see ibid., pp. 18–25, 413–47 (Förster).

[13] On operations, see ibid., pp. 451–712 (Klink) for the German side, pp. 713–809 (Hoffman) for the Soviet side. On the collapse of the economic '*Blitzkrieg* strategy', see pp. 936–1029 (Müller). Also see M. van Creveld, *Supplying War*, 3rd edn (New York 1980), pp. 142–80; H. Rohde, *Das Deutsche Wehrmachttransportwesen im Zweiten Weltkrieg* (Stuttgart 1971); W. Zieger, *Das deutsche Heeresveterinärwesen im Zweiten Weltkrieg* (Freiburg i.Br. 1973).

quantities produced, while the initial psychological impact of mass (but spatially and temporally limited) use of modern weaponry lost much of its force. In this area Germany had no chance of competing successfully with its enemies. One interesting consequence of this change was a transformation of the image of the war, to be discussed in the last section of this chapter. But this change took time, and although in retrospect one could find its origins in the pre-war period, it became increasingly obvious only during the latter part of the war.

The growing gap between Germany and the Allies can be gauged from some revealing figures. Between 1940 and 1941 Germany's tank production rose from more than 2,000 to well over 5,000. Consequently the *Wehrmacht* doubled the number of its armoured divisions, but reduced the number of tanks per division by a third. Nevertheless, this expansion of the armoured forces was insufficient in view both of the growing amounts of *matériel* on the Soviet side, and the immense losses of equipment suffered by the Germans. It is indicative, for instance, that while in 1940 fewer than 400 modern tanks were built in the Soviet Union, in the first half of 1941 alone their number rose to 1,500. Even more impressively, in the second half of that year, and in spite of the loss of Russia's primary industrial regions, almost 5,000 advanced models were turned out.[14] At this point Germany was apparently still not committed to fighting a total war, since between 1940 and 1941 its expenditure on war production hardly rose (although this may be partly explained by its previously high investment in armaments). During the same period the expenditure on armaments in Great Britain, the Soviet Union, and the United States put together almost doubled; even more significantly, this total was already three times larger than that of the Reich, although the United States was certainly not close to the peak of its war effort.[15]

In the wake of the terrible fighting of winter 1941–2, Germany greatly expanded its armaments production, and over the next few years also made significant improvements in the technology of its weapons. But by this point the nature of the fighting had already changed irreversibly. While in the West it had been possible (though not without risks) to maintain military effectiveness with a few well-equipped divisions followed by the great bulk of infantry formations, in the East, due to the vast spaces which had to be occupied, the infantry proved unable to keep up with the armour over such long distances. This meant that the

---

[14] Figures in Boog, *Deutsche Reich*, IV, pp. 62–75, 734 (Hoffman) on the Soviet side, 183–5 (Müller) on the German side. See also Erickson, *The Road to Stalingrad*, pp. 93, 322; and Ploetz, *Geschichte des Zweiten Weltkrieges*, 2nd edn (Würzburg 1960), pp. 122–7.

[15] Boog, *Deutsche Reich*, IV, p. 183 (Müller). For a somewhat different calculation, see Posen, *Military Doctrine*, p. 20. See also, H. Schustereit, *Vabanque: Hitler's Angriff auf die Sowjetunion 1941 als Versuch, durch den Sieg im Osten den Westen zu bezwingen* (Herford: Germany 1988).

armour had either to wait for the infantry, or to operate independently from its support (and logistical apparatus). Both options meant the end of *Blitzkrieg*, since the first dictated loss of momentum, and the second weakened the power of the punch by dispersing the forces and exposing them to constant threat of encirclement and annihilation. *Blitzkrieg* operations could have been resumed only if the *Wehrmacht* had been motorised on a scale which was far beyond the capacities of the Reich. Hence, as a more or less stable front emerged in the East, it became clear that it had to be held by the *Wehrmacht*'s ill-equipped infantry forma-tions, joined now by a growing number of armoured divisions which had lost most of their tanks over the winter and could no longer be replenished. Some elite army and Waffen-SS units were, of course, constantly supplied with modern fighting machines, but attempts to bring about fundamental changes in the overall situation repeatedly failed. Thus, while the summer offensive of 1942 already limited itself to the southern sector of the Eastern Front (where it met with disastrous defeat), the summer offensive of 1943 (the last time the Eastern Army took the initiative) was limited only to the area of Kursk and was stopped within a few days without any hope of success. Similarly, the winter offensive of 1944 in the West relied chiefly on surprise and cloud cover, and once more had to be given up shortly after it was launched. Consequently, during most of the years of fighting on the Eastern Front (where the bulk of the German army was engaged), conditions became increasingly similar to those on the Western Front of the Great War. However, while the *Wehrmacht* had to contend with a growing de-modernisation of its frontline forces, the Red Army was rapidly modernised as it prepared for its own *Blitzkrieg* to the West.[16]

A few figures will suffice to demonstrate that in spite of Germany's tremendous efforts to increase armaments production, it had little chance of catching up with its foes. If by 1944 the Third Reich had raised the annual production of tanks to 27,000, already in 1943 the Soviet Union had reached an annual production rate of 30,000 tanks, while the British produced 36,000 tanks in 1942–3, and the total American tank production by the end of the war reached 90,000. Similarly, while Germany produced 40,000 aircraft in 1944, the Soviet Union was already producing aircraft at an annual rate of 30,000 in the last years of the war, and the United States put out a total of 100,000 fighters and 90,000 bombers, many of which were strategic four-engined aircraft of a type Germany was unable to produce. Add to this the four million vehicles of

---

[16] On the experience of German soldiers on the Eastern Front, see O. Bartov, *Hitler's Army: Soldiers, Nazis and War in the Third Reich* (New York 1991), and T. Schulte, *The German Army and Nazi Policies in Occupied Russia* (Oxford 1989). On the failure of the Wehrmacht to replenish its manpower and matériel, see Kroener, *Deutsche Reich*, V/1, parts 2–3 (Müller and Kroener).

all kinds put out by the American motor industry, and we can see that Germany stood little chance of winning the war once it had been transformed into a total world confrontation.[17]

II Controversies and historiography

Two main controversies have developed around the concept of *Blitzkrieg*, its causes, consequences, and implications. One has to do with the relationship between domestic pressures and foreign policy, especially the decision to go to war.[18] The second concerns the relationship between war and the implementation of criminal policies by the Nazi regime, especially the decision on the 'Final Solution'.[19] Both controversies are of crucial importance not merely for our understanding of the wider implications of *Blitzkrieg* but, more importantly, for the analysis of the nature of the Third Reich, and, even more generally, the relationship between modern war and the state.

For the first two decades following the end of the Second World War it was generally believed that *Blitzkrieg* had been simply utilised as the most fitting strategy for the Third Reich to accomplish its policy of military expansion. There was no appreciation of the fact that this might have been a way to resolve or prevent domestic tensions, or to wage war without further exacerbating popular discontent. Because Germany had reaped such amazing successes in its first military campaigns in Poland, Scandinavia, the West, South-East Europe, and the initial phases of 'Barbarossa', it was deemed natural that it had prepared a military machine most suitable for such battles, and that it was only due to unforeseen natural and political factors, as well as blunders by the political leadership of the Reich, that this series of triumphs finally turned into defeat. In the mid-1960s, however, this convention was challenged by a number of historians who claimed, on the basis of either new evidence, or new interpretations of old evidence, that in fact both the timing of the German decision to go to war, and the nature of the war

---

[17] Ploetz, *Geschichte*, pp. 448–53, 471, 499, 593–4, 613; Boog, *Deutsche Reich*, IV, p. 734 (Hoffman). Somewhat different figures are cited in Milward, *War, Economy, and Society*, p. 74.

[18] For the initial phase of the controversy, see esp. the contributions by T. Mason and A. J. P. Taylor in *The Origins of the Second World War*, ed. E. M. Robertson, 5th edn (London 1979); A. J. P. Taylor, *The Origins of the Second World War* (1976 [1961]); Mason, 'Internal Crisis'. For its later development, see Overy, 'Domestic Crisis' and 'Hitler's War'; 'Debate', Kaiser, *Politics and War*, esp. pp. 375–82.

[19] Most importantly, see C. R. Browning, *Fateful Months: Essays on the Emergence of the Final Solution* (New York 1985), chap. 1, and his *The Path to Genocide: Essays on Launching the Final Solution* (New York 1992), part 2, esp. chap. 5; A. Mayer, *Why Did the Heavens Not Darken?* (New York 1989); R. Breitman, *The Architect of Genocide* (Hanover, N.H. 1991); M. R. Marrus, *The Holocaust in History* (New York 1989 [1987]), esp. chap. 3; G. Fleming, *Hitler and the Final Solution* (Berkeley 1984), including the introduction by S. Friedländer.

conducted by the *Wehrmacht*, were anything but a matter of choice. Rather, they argued, the Nazi leadership was compelled to follow this course by a combination of economic constraints, popular pressures, and political anxieties, along with the better-known aspirations of conquest and expansion. Surveys of the condition of the German economy during the initial phases of the war seemed to indicate that the Reich had not at all been as totally mobilised as had been assumed up to then. While it did build up an impressive military machine, and produced modern armaments for a portion of the armed forces, Germany failed to create the economic basis necessary to sustain a long-term military commitment, but rather used only certain sectors of industry, and even those could be shifted to peacetime production relatively rapidly. The question thus arose, what were the reasons for this obvious lack of preparation in a country apparently set upon waging a large-scale war, indeed, a war which it had itself initiated? Further examination of economic conditions in Germany on the eve of the war appeared to show that a major transformation had taken place from a state of widespread unemployment in the early 1930s to severe shortages of labour and resources by 1938. It was also noted that the Nazi leadership, and Hitler in particular, were profoundly anxious about the possibility of popular anger and unrest in case the regime attempted to make the same demands on the population associated with the Great War, namely both blood sacrifices and domestic economic hardship and privation. The German public, not unlike the population of France and England, was anything but enthusiastic about the prospect of another war, knowing full well the horrific toll it would take on each and every member of the nation (even if some suffered more than others).[20]

Combining all these findings together, a new interpretation of the relationship between domestic and foreign policy in Nazi Germany was proposed.[21] According to this thesis, by 1938 Hitler realised that

[20] Apart from works by Mason and Milward cited in note 1, see also T. Mason, 'The Workers' Opposition in Nazi Germany', *History Workshop Journal* 11 (1981), pp. 120–37, and his *Social Policy in the Third Reich: The Working Class and the 'National Community'* (Providence 1993); S. Salter, 'Class Harmony or Class Conflict?', in *Government, Party, and People in Nazi Germany*, ed. J. Noakes (Exeter 1980), pp. 76–97; Deist, *Das Deutsche Reich*, Vol. I, part 1 (W. Wette).

[21] It is interesting to note that at about the same time several important works were published dealing with the relationship between domestic crisis and Germany's role in the unleashing of the First World War. See F. Fischer, *Germany's War Aims in the First World War* (London 1967 [1961]), and his *War of Illusions* (London 1973 [1969]); H.-U. Wehler, *The German Empire 1871–1918* (Leamington Spa 1985 [1973]); V. R. Berghahn, *Germany and the Approach of War in 1914* (New York 1973). This approach, whose origins are to be found in E. Kehr, *Battleship Building and Party Politics in Germany* (Chicago 1973 [1930]), was somewhat qualified, though not wholly undermined, by G. Eley, *Reshaping the German Right* (New Haven 1980), and his *From Unification to Nazism* (London 1986); D. Blackbourn, *Class, Religion and Local Politics in Wilhelmine Germany* (New Haven 1980), and his *Populists and Patricians* (London 1987); D. Blackbourn and G. Eley, *The Peculiarities of German History* (Oxford 1984).

he was faced with the choice of either slowing down the rapid rearmament of Germany, for which he had neither sufficient man-power nor resources, or unleashing a war which would bring in more (slave) labour and (requisitioned) resources from newly conquered territories. The first option entailed giving up, or at least greatly postponing, his plans for expanding Germany's territories, an idea with which he was obsessed and therefore could in no way agree to give up, quite apart from the political repercussions such a decision might have had on his own stature and the Nazi regime in general.[22] The second option, however, meant that Germany would have to go to war before it had completed its rearmament programme and hence at a point at which it was unready for a full-scale, potentially two-front confrontation.[23] Moreover, while discontent, especially among the working class, was already troubling the Nazi regime, it was feared that total war would greatly increase such manifestations of opposition, to the point of threatening the stability of the regime.[24] The choice was therefore made, not untypically for Hitler, to unleash a limited, but ferocious war, against selected targets and along specific fronts, while doing all that was possible to keep other nations out of the conflict until it was too late to intervene. This was to be carried out at a minimum cost to the population, without mobilising the whole industrial infrastructure of Germany for war, but rather by producing, in certain sectors of industry, only those types of military hardware deemed necessary for the campaign. Hence, the idea was to fight a victorious war without paying the price Europeans had come to expect since 1914–18.[25]

This plan worked until the collapse of the German invasion of Russia in winter 1941–2. At that point it became clear that if Germany wished to stay in the war, it had to strive in all earnestness for a total

[22] This could also be related to the tendency of the regime toward what has been termed 'cumulative radicalisation', and for its need to move constantly forward, generated at least in part by Hitler's sense of mission and fears regarding his approaching physical and mental decline. See H. Mommsen, 'The Realization of the Unthinkable', in *The Policies of Genocide*, ed. G. Hirschfeld (London 1986), pp. 93–144; A. Bullock, *Hitler, A Study in Tyranny*, 2nd edn (New York 1964), e.g. pp. 525–6, 568–9, 755–6; and J. Fest, *Hitler* (Harmondsworth 1982 [1973]), pp. 607–21, for an acute analysis of Hitler's psychological motives in unleashing the war.

[23] For the controversy over the Hossbach memorandum outlining Hitler's plans for war and Germany's state of preparation for the conflict, see the various contributions in Robertson, *The Origins*. For the document itself, see J. Noakes and G. Pridham, *Nazism 1919–1945* (Exeter 1988), I, pp. 675–92, esp. 680–8.

[24] Mason, 'The Workers' Opposition'; Salter, 'Class Harmony or Class Conflict?'

[25] For Mason's last essay on and reexamination of this debate, see his 'The Domestic Dynamics of Nazi Conquests'; for revisionist interpretations, see P. Hayes, 'Polycracy and Policy in the Third Reich'; and H. James, 'Innovation and Conservatism in Economic Recovery', all in *Reevaluating the Third Reich*, ed. T. Childers and J. Caplan (New York 1993), pp. 161–89, 190–210, 114–38, respectively.

mobilisation of its resources. Paradoxically, just as Hitler's natural inclination to avoid such measures, motivated by his fear of unpopularity, was overcome, and total war was both declared and eventually also practised, the fate of Germany was sealed.[26] This was not, however, due to unrest among the German population, as Hitler had feared, nor to any attempted 'stab in the back' but rather to the fact that the Reich could only hope to win in a series of *Blitzkriege*, a type of warfare which, ironically, had initially been chosen for reasons of domestic constraints, not strategic calculation. Not uncharacteristically for the murderous absurdity which increasingly dominated the Reich, it was now such cool, rational technocrats as Albert Speer who insisted on making ever greater efforts for total mobilisation of the nation's resources, and thereby simply prolonged the war and the suffering and destruction it entailed without being able to prevent Germany's ultimate defeat, an outcome already anticipated by far less brilliant minds no later than winter 1941/42.[27]

This complex analysis of the wider implications and underlying motives of *Blitzkrieg* has been accepted by a large number of scholars, and has served as an important interpretative tool in explaining both the domestic and foreign/military policy of the Reich. Only in recent years have the data on which it was established come under increasing scrutiny and criticism. The argument has been made that there was no such widespread opposition to the regime among the working classes as had been previously assumed, that the labour and resources shortage was not as severe as it had been depicted, and that Germany had actually done its very best, under the circumstances, to mobilise as totally as it could. Hence *Blitzkrieg* was not practised *instead* of total war, but was rather a new manner of deploying and employing forces without giving up the notion of total mobilisation. In other words, *Blitzkrieg* was merely a tactical innovation, not a new strategy. The timing of the war, it has been said, had to do much more with the opportunities Hitler felt he had been presented with, than with the alleged domestic crisis, which in fact never existed,

---

[26] Total war was of course declared only after the débâcle in Stalingrad in early 1943, which was also seen at the time as the beginning of the end for the Reich. But pressure toward total mobilisation came during the first winter in Russia, just as the recognition of a possible defeat began to surface in many people's minds. The most detailed, best documented, and most reliable analysis of the transformation from *Blitzkrieg* to *Weltkrieg* and its military, economic, and manpower implications, is to be found in volumes IV, V/1, and VI of *Das Deutsche Reich und der Zweite Weltkrieg* issued by the Militärgeschichtliches Forschungsamt, formerly in Freiburg, currently in Potsdam, Germany, with well over 3,000 pages of tightly printed text, along with maps, charts, and graphs.

[27] Speer, *Inside the Third Reich*, parts 2–3. See also R. J. Overy, *Goering, The "Iron Man"*, 2nd edn (London 1987).

or at least was not perceived as such by the Nazi leadership.[28]

The criticism of the 'domestic crisis' thesis is of some importance not only because it questions several of the basic contentions about the nature of *Blitzkrieg*, but also since it constitutes part of a larger trend in recent scholarship on the Third Reich. The previous Marxist-oriented interpretation of *Blitzkrieg* had rejected the Nazi notion of *Volksgemeinschaft* as a mere propagandistic myth, and strove to document the workers' adherence to their interests and consequent opposition to the regime. While this view of society under the Nazi regime appears now to have resulted, at least in part, more from wishful thinking than from a balanced analysis, recent interpretations have similarly questioned the *Volksgemeinschaft* as a social reality, preferring for their part to concentrate more on passive resistance to the regime by widespread (often middle-class) sectors of society, or on non-conformist fringe groups made up mainly of youths of both middle- and working-class origins.[29] From another perspective of inquiry, the insistence on the primacy of domestic factors, typical of Marxist interpretations, was also shown to be at least not as foolproof as it had seemed in the past.[30] Finally, *Blitzkrieg* has always remained for many political and military historians, soldiers, and intelligent laymen, a military tactic rather than the outcome of complex forces and pressures and the expression of a totalitarian regime in crisis.[31] To be sure, this criticism, persuasive as it is

[28] The chief criticism in the economic sphere is by Overy; see above, notes 3 and 27. See also articles by James and Hayes, above, n. 25. For the increasingly more nuanced interpretations of German society under Nazism, see I. Kershaw, *The "Hitler Myth." Image and Reality in the Third Reich* (Oxford 1987), and his *Popular Opinion and Political Dissent in the Third Reich* (Oxford 1983); D. J. K. Peukert, *Inside Nazi Germany* (New Haven 1987 [1982]); R. Gellately, *The Gestapo and German Society* (Oxford 1990).

[29] On passive resistance, everyday life, and youth, see, e.g., M. Broszat and E. Fröhlich, *Alltag und Widerstand* (München 1987); D. J. K. Peukert, 'Edelweisspiraten, Meuten, Swing. Jugendsubkulturen im Dritten Reich', in *Sozialgeschichte der Freizeit*, ed. G. Huck (Wuppertal 1980), and his 'Alltag und Barbarei', in *Ist der Nationalsozialismus Geschichte?*, ed. D. Diner (Frankfurt/M 1987); D. J. K. Peukert and J. Reulecke (eds.), *Die Reihen fast geschlossen* (Wuppertal 1981); L. Niethammer (ed.), *Lebensgeschichte und Sozialkultur im Ruhrgebiet 1930–1960*, 3 vols. (Berlin/Bonn 1983–5); A. Klönne, 'Jugend-protest und Jugendopposition', in *Bayern in der NS-Zeit*, eds. M. Broszat *et al.* (Munich 1979–81) V, pp. 527–620; A. Klönne, *Jugendkriminalität und Jugendopposition im NS-Staat* (Münster 1981), and his *Jugend im Dritten Reich* (Düsseldorf 1982).

[30] However, see T. Mason, 'The Primacy of Politics. Politics and Economics in National Socialist Germany', in Mason, *Nazism*, pp. 53–76. Apart from works of criticism noted above, there had always been a trend which insisted on the centrality of foreign policy. See, e.g., in K. Hildebrand, *The Third Reich*, 4th edn (London 1987); A. Hillgruber, *Germany and the Two World Wars* (Cambridge, Mass. 1981); his *Endlich genug über Nationalsozialismus und Zweiten Weltkrieg?* (Düsseldorf 1982), and his *Zweierlei Untergang: Die Zerschlagung des Deutschen Reiches und das Ende des europäischen Judentums* (Berlin 1986).

[31] Note, among innumerable examples, the popular book by L. Deighton, *Blitzkrieg* (London 1979), which was, e.g., issued in a Hebrew translation by the publishing house of the Israeli Ministry of Defence in 1986. For a different angle on relations between the military and the regime, see the excellent study by K.-J. Müller, *Army, Politics, and*

in many ways, has not been able to demolish altogether the previous interpretation, and has left untouched many of the more intricate and subtle connections drawn between war, society, totalitarian regimes, and economic preconditions. What is most important in this critique for our own argument, however, is that it blurs the distinction between *Blitzkrieg* and total war, and presents the former only as a version or elaboration of the latter, without denying that it was a crucial aspect of the Nazi state.

In the meantime, the importance of the ties between war and domestic policy has been highlighted from a different, even more disturbing, but nevertheless related perspective. In the course of debating the origins of the so-called 'Final Solution of the Jewish Question', it was suggested by some scholars that the decision to initiate mass murder had been taken only after the invasion of the Soviet Union. Consequently it was argued that the realisation of genocide might well be related to the progress of the Russian campaign. The various versions of this interpretation belonged, generally speaking, to what has been called the 'functionalist', or 'structuralist' school, a term coined, interestingly enough, by the same scholar who had insisted on the relationship between the decision to go to war and domestic policy.[32] Conversely, the so-called 'intentionalist' school viewed operation 'Barbarossa' at best as the occasion, but certainly not the cause of or impetus for, the plan of genocide. Rather, the 'intentionalists' argued that the plan had been conceived years earlier, perhaps even long before Hitler came to power.[33]

Society in Germany, 1933–45 (New York 1987). It is interesting that some of the criticism of Fischer's and Wehler's theses bears similar marks, in that it both seeks to undermine the notion of manipulation from above by investigating popular trends, and, from the opposite extreme, lays more stress on foreign policy and strategic calculations. Apart from the literature cited above, see, e.g., V. R. Berghahn and M. Kitchen (eds.), *Germany in the Age of Total War* (London 1981); W. Deist, *Militär, Staat und Gesellschaft* (Munich 1991).

[32] T. Mason, 'Intention and Explanation: A Current Controversy about the Interpretation of National Socialism', in Mason, *Nazism*, pp. 212–30. The best available introduction to interpretations of Nazism is I. Kershaw, *The Nazi Dictatorship*, 3rd edn (London 1993). An example of 'intentionalist' interpretation is K. D. Bracher, *The German Dictatorship* (New York 1970 [1969]); and of a 'functionalist' one: M. Broszat, *The Hitler State* (London 1981 [1969]). Recent analyses of these two schools can be found in: Browning, *Fateful Months*, chap. 1, and his *The Path to Genocide*, chap. 5; and S. Friedländer, 'Reflections on the Historicization of National Socialism', in S. Friedländer, *Memory, History, and the Extermination of the Jews in Europe* (Bloomington 1993), pp. 64–84.

[33] The foremost representative of the 'intentionalist' school as regards the Holocaust is L. S. Dawidowicz, *The War Against the Jews 1933–1945*, 3rd edn (New York 1986 [1975]); see also her historiographical survey in *The Holocaust and the Historians* (Cambridge, Mass. 1981). Other important 'intentionalists' are, e.g., Fleming, *Hitler and the Final Solution*; E. Jäckel, *Hitler's World View*, 2nd edn (Cambridge, Mass. 1981 [1969]). Useful introductions to interpretations of the 'Final Solution' include: Marrus, *The Holocaust in History*; and F. Furet (ed.), *Unanswered Questions: Nazi Germany and the Genocide of the Jews* (New York 1989 [1985]); D. Cesarani (ed.), *The Final Solution: Origins and Implementation* (London 1994).

The 'functionalists', however, precisely because they rejected such teleological interpretations, needed to find the point at which a decision *was* reached by the top echelons of the regime. Alternatively, since the more extreme representatives of this school maintained that genocide was first begun as a series of local initiatives from the middle ranks in the field and only then adopted and expanded as a general policy by the regime, it became necessary to provide the chronological and geographical context within which this process took place (the assumption being that there had in fact never been a specific decision on the 'Final Solution').[34] Since there was no doubt that the killing of Jews by mass shootings began only following the invasion of Russia, and since the construction of death camps began only in the fall of 1941, with the first installations being put into operation in winter 1941/42 and spring 1942, it seemed likely that there was some connection between the military operations and the 'Final Solution'.[35] But while it is clear that the occupation of a huge territory, and the vicious nature of the fighting in the East, provided the context in which genocide could be carried out, partly concealed and, more importantly, made acceptable to perpetrators and bystanders already brutalised by war, some scholars maintain that the course of the *Blitzkrieg* campaign in the Soviet Union had a much more direct and specific effect on the decision to implement the 'Final Solution'.

Two contradictory interpretations of the relationship between *Blitzkrieg* and genocide have been suggested. The first argues that the Nazi regime chose to carry out mass murder following its realisation that the *Blitzkrieg* in the East, and therefore in the long run the war itself, had been lost. The recognition of the failure to defeat Bolshevism was of crucial importance, since the Nazi regime had unleashed its campaign in the East as a crusade against what it perceived to be the enemies of humanity and culture (at least its Aryan representatives). Hence the immense sense of frustration felt by the Nazis. It was this frustration of having been unable to complete the task they had set themselves, rather than any premeditated plan to annihilate the Jewish people, which made Germany turn against the Jews, the one 'enemy' they were capable of destroying. Thus the failure of the *Blitzkrieg* in Russia is

---

[34] See, esp. H. Mommsen, 'The Realization of the Unthinkable', and his 'National Socialism: Continuity and Change', in *Fascism: A Reader's Guide*, ed. W. Laqueur, 2nd edn (Harmondsworth 1982); M. Broszat, 'Hitler und die Genesis der "Endlösung"', *Vierteljahreshefte für Zeitgeschichte* 25 (1977), pp. 753–5. See also Broszat's polemical essay on the need for a revision of German history and decentring of Auschwitz: 'A Plea for the Historicization of National Socialism', in *Reworking the Past: Hitler, the Holocaust, and the Historians' Debate*, ed. P. Baldwin (Boston 1990), pp. 77–87.

[35] The best discussion is in Browning, *Fateful Months*, chap. 1, and his *The Path to Genocide*, chap. 5. See also Marrus, *The Holocaust in History*, chap. 3; and the authoritative R. Hilberg, *The Destruction of the European Jews*, 3 vols., rev. edn (New York 1985).

presented as being at the root of the 'Final Solution'. Had the campaign against the Soviet Union succeeded, genocide might not have taken place at all, and the Jews could have been expected to be simply pushed further East, expelled from the German-occupied parts of Russia.[36] This interpretation, in spite of its Marxist origins, has the curious characteristic of partly overlapping with a conservative revisionist thesis on the German war against Russia and the origins of the 'Final Solution'. In the latter interpretation, the argument is made that the Nazis waged war against Bolshevism out of fear, since they were certain that otherwise Stalin and his 'Asiatic Hordes' would overrun and destroy Germany. Having been informed of the atrocities committed by Stalin against his own people, the Nazi and military leadership simply adopted (or 'copied') his methods as what they believed to be self-defence measures. This revisionist thesis itself is of course anything but original, since it is closely related to the Nazis' own presentation of reality. Moreover, it both implies, and in some places clearly asserts, not merely a seemingly logical connection between the war against Bolshevism and the genocide of the Jews, but also an apparently reasonable course of action on the part of the Germans, since it claims that the 'Final Solution' was not 'original', but only an imitation of the real or perceived acts of the Bolsheviks, who were, after all, seen by the Nazis as identical with the Jews. Hence we are presented with a process whereby the Nazis both took an example from the enemy, and, having associated their victims with the same enemy from whom they had allegedly learned these methods, felt they had a licence to destroy them.[37]

Both the left-wing and the right-wing revisionist interpretations which view the 'Final Solution' as a 'by-product' of either the failure of *Blitzkrieg* or the nature of Stalinism are exceedingly problematic, since to a large extent they do not correspond to the evidence.[38] Thus the

[36] This is the central argument of Mayer, *Why Did the Heavens Not Darken?*.

[37] This argument was made by Ernst Nolte, whose main articles on this issue are now to be found in an English translation, in *Forever in the Shadow of Hitler?* (Atlantic Highlands, N.J. 1993). Nolte has also argued that it was reasonable for Hitler to view the Jews as enemies and to treat them as prisoners of war (or internees), since Chaim Weizmann allegedly declared war on Germany. See also contributions by Michael Stürmer, Klaus Hildebrand, Joachim Fest, and Andreas Hillgruber. Related to this was Hillgruber's above-cited book, *Zweierlei Untergang*. On the connection between revisionist texts of the 1980s and their Nazi origins, see: O. Bartov, 'Historians on the Eastern Front: Andreas Hillgruber and Germany's Tragedy', in his *Murder in Our Midst: The Holocaust, Industrial Killing and Representation* (New York 1996), pp. 71–88. The best discussions of the *Historikerstreit*, the German historians' controversy which set the context for these arguments, are: C. S. Maier, *The Unmasterable Past* (Cambridge, Mass. 1988); H.-U. Wehler, *Entsorgung der deutschen Vergangenheit?* (Munich 1988); R. J. Evans, *In Hitler's Shadow* (London 1989); Baldwin, *Reworking*.

[38] On differences between 'Stalinism' and 'Hitlerism' see the chapter by I. Kershaw, '"Working Towards the Führer". Reflections on the Nature of the Hitler Dictatorship', in this volume.

contrary thesis points out that the killing of the Jews began well *before* the *Wehrmacht* had suffered major military reverses. Hence it has been argued that rather than deciding on the 'Final Solution' out of a sense of frustration, the decision on the genocide of the Jews was taken precisely at the point when Hitler felt that the war against the Soviet Union had been won and that therefore Germany's energies could be diverted to the next important mission, purging the world of the Jews. And, once that policy had been decided on and the first steps leading to its implementation were taken, there was no going back, due to the nature of the regime and to its previous fixation on the 'Jewish Question'.[39]

It should be pointed out, of course, that some interpretations reject such clear-cut connections between *Blitzkrieg* and the 'Final Solution'. Thus, for instance, while the 'frustration' thesis tends to push the decision on genocide to as late as winter 1941/42, and the 'height of victory' thesis places it in the summer months of 1941, yet another thesis, though not necessarily 'intentionalist', tends to predate the decision on genocide to before the attack on Russia. Nevertheless, even this interpretation has to concede that the actual *killing* began only after the launching of 'Barbarossa'. Hence, while there is no consensus on the nature of the tie between the *decision* on mass murder and the course of the *Blitzkrieg* in Russia, there is almost complete unanimity on the connection (but not on the *nature* of that connection) between *Blitzkrieg* and the *implementation* of genocide.[40]

This bring us, however, to yet another aspect of the relationship between war and genocide. *Blitzkrieg*, as we have seen, has been presented by some scholars as a determined attempt to avoid total war. However, there can be little doubt as to the ties between total war and the Nazi version of genocide, namely, industrial killing. It was, after all, the so-called 'Great War', the first modern, industrial, total war, which introduced the notion and practice of killing of millions of soldiers over

---

[39] This is the main argument of Browning, *The Path to Genocide*, chap. 5. In chap. 4 of this book Browning criticises Mayer's view of the Holocaust as a 'by-product'. See also O. Bartov, Review of Mayer's *Why Did the Heavens Not Darken?*, in: *German Politics and Society* 19 (1990), pp. 55–7. There is a different 'by-product' interpretation of Nazi genocide policies, whereby these are seen as part of a general trend of perverted science, or even as inherent to the nature of 'normal' modern science. See, e.g., D. J. K. Peukert, 'The Genesis of the "Final Solution" from the Spirit of Science', in Childers, *Reevaluating the Third Reich*, pp. 234–51; M. Biagioli, 'Science, Modernity, and the "Final Solution"', in *Probing the Limits of Representation*, ed. S. Friedländer (Cambridge, Mass. 1992), pp. 185–205; M. H. Kater, *Doctors Under Hitler* (Chapel Hill 1989); R. Proctor, *Racial Hygiene: Medicine Under the Nazis* (Cambridge, Mass. 1988); R. J. Lifton, *The Nazi Doctors: Medical Killing and the Psychology of Genocide* (New York 1986).

[40] The main argument on a pre-'Barbarossa' decision is made by Breitman, *The Architect of Genocide*. In the 17th Annual Conference of the German Studies Association (1993), Browning and Breitman debated the issue at the panel 'The Nazi Decision to Commit Mass Murder', and their positions seem now to have come somewhat closer.

a relatively short span of time. The death camps of the Second World War would seem inconceivable without the mechanical slaughterhouse of the Western Front between 1914–18. Hence, I would argue that while it is important to recognise the ties between the strategic, political, and ideological aspects of *Blitzkrieg*, on the one hand, and the nature of totalitarian regimes, domestic policy, and genocide, on the other, we must also emphasise that this type of warfare cannot be divorced from total war as a phenomenon of modern industrialised society. Rather, *Blitzkrieg* should be viewed as an aspect, or offshoot, of total war, an attempt to revise it or to make it more effective without doing away with those features of the original deemed crucial to the conduct of modern war. In this sense it can be argued that while Nazi Germany attempted to avoid total war in the military and economic sense, it certainly did all it could to accomplish a total psychological mobilisation of the population, just as much as it strove for a total elimination of its real and perceived enemies. The limits on war were to be set only as far as the suffering of the population at home and the German soldiers at the front were concerned. The foe could expect either complete subjugation or total annihilation.[41]

The Nazi *Blitzkrieg* was therefore not an alternative to total war, but rather an attempt to adapt modern war to existing domestic and foreign conditions, as well as to Germany's expansionist aims and ideological ends. The Nazi conception of war predicated total domination and ruthless extermination. Hence the still-present admiration for the Nazi war machine, even when allegedly focused only on its purely military aspects, is especially disturbing, since it carries within it an implicit fascination with mass killing and total destruction. It is this issue which I would like to address in the final section of this chapter.

---

[41] In this context see the important chapter by M. Geyer, 'The Militarization of Europe, 1914–1945', in *The Militarization of the Western World*, ed. J. R. Gillis, (New Brunswick, N.J. 1989). A good introduction to the First World War is, M. Ferro, *The Great War 1914–1918*, 2nd edn (London, 1987 [1969]). On total mobilization see, e.g., J. W. Winter, *The Great War and the British People* (Cambridge, Mass. 1986); J.-J. Becker, *The Great War and the French People* (Leamington Spa 1984 [1973]). On cultural aspects of the first industrial war, see P. Fussell, *The Great War and Modern Memory* (Oxford 1975); R. Wohl, *The Generation of 1914* (Cambridge, Mass. 1979); E. J. Leed, *No Man's Land* (Cambridge 1979); M. Eksteins, *Rites of Spring: The Great War and the Birth of the Modern Age*, 2nd edn (New York 1990 [1989]); S. Hynes, *A War Imagined: the First World War and English Culture* (New York 1991). On the fascist personalities forged by the war and its aftermath, see the fascinating work by K. Theweleit, *Männerphantasien*, 2 vols., 2nd edn (Reinbeck bei Hamburg 1987 [1977]). The writings of Ernst Jünger, and the cinema of Fritz Lang, are both essential to understanding the post-1918 European mentality. I thank Anton Kaes for his illuminating paper on this issue, 'War, Media and Mobilization', delivered at the October 1993 New York University conference 'War, Violence, and the Structure of Modernity'.

III   Images and representation

The image of the quick, lethal, almost clinical German *Blitzkrieg*, that combination of roaring tanks and screaming dive bombers, brilliant staff officers and healthy, smiling troops singing as they march to victory, was first propagated among both the German public and the Reich's neighbours, friends and foes alike, during the initial phases of the war. It was a powerful and persuasive image, for it closely corresponded to events as they were experienced by the various parties involved in the conflict, even if their radically different implications depended on one's loyalties. Indeed, the perceived congruity between the propagandistic image of war as disseminated in films, newsreels, photographs, leaflets, radio programmes, etc., and its reality was perhaps the most shocking aspect of *Blitzkrieg* for a public grown sceptical about the correspondence between image and reality. For in reality, just as on the silver screen, the tanks roared, the Stukas screamed, and the *Wehrmacht*, though perhaps not made of smiling soldiers, marched on into victory.[42]

While Nazi propaganda produced such images of *Blitzkrieg* with the clear intention of both intimidating its enemies, prospective allies, and neutrals, and uplifting the spirits of a German public initially quite anxious about a possible repetition of the 1914–18 ordeal, other nations found this image just as useful in explaining their own experience of the war. Thus the French, for instance, tried to justify or rationalise their humiliating 1940 débâcle by grossly exaggerating the overwhelming numerical and technological superiority of the *Wehrmacht*, drawing what seemed to a public just recovering from the actual manifestations of *Blitzkrieg* highly convincing sketches of endless streams of tanks and aircraft, followed by invincible, not to say superhuman Aryan troops (feared, even hated, but occasionally also envied and admired[43]), all

[42] See notes 4 and 6, above. Further on the French attitude to war during the *drôle de guerre* and the subsequent shock and bewilderment following the German attack, see, e.g., J.-L. Crémieux-Brilhac, *Les Français de l'an 40*, 2 vols. (Paris 1990); H. Amouroux, *Le peuple du désastre 1939–1940* (Paris 1987 [1976]); P. Rocolle, *La guerre de 1940*, 2 vols. (Paris 1990); R. Bruge, *Les combattants du 18 juin*, 3 vols. (Paris 1982); J.-P. Azéma, *1940 l'année terrible* (Paris 1990); P.-A. Lesort, *Quelques jours de mai–juin 40: Mémoire, témoignage, histoire* (Paris 1992); P. Richer, *La drôle de guerre des Français* (Paris 1990). A mere look at the covers of these books suffices to evoke the sense of fear, confusion, shock and anxiety to escape the enemy with which such works are concerned. A good popular account in English is A. Horne, *To Lose a Battle: France 1940*, 2nd edn (London 1988 [1969]).

[43] Ambiguous portrayals of fascists and Nazis can be found, e.g., in M. Tournier, *The Ogre* (New York 1972 [1970]); J.-P. Sartre, 'The Childhood of a Leader', in his *Intimacy* (Frogmore, UK 1977 [1949]), and his trilogy *Les Chemins da la liberté*, published in English as *The Roads to Freedom*. Ambiguity in portraying Nazis and fascists is of course

descending in an unstoppable flood upon France's fair fields and towns, shrugging aside the courageous, amiable, but outnumbered and technologically outdated French *poilus* (who by implication had been betrayed by the corrupt republic). This utilisation of Nazi propagandistic images was an easy way out for incompetent generals and weak or opportunistic politicians whose lack of insight, indecisiveness, and outright blunders had had much more to do with the defeat than any material, numerical, or innate superiority of the enemy. Nevertheless, since this image proved to be so useful in explaining what would have otherwise been difficult to accept, it was generally taken at face value at the time and lingered long after the end of the war.[44]

As the war went on, and *Blitzkrieg* receded in the face of a more total, and much less swift and glorious war, its German image became increasingly ambiguous, until finally it was transformed, indeed revers-ed, with the wielders of technology now playing the role of inhuman automatons, while those lacking *matériel* but rich in courage taking up the posture of the superman. Thus whereas in 1940 it was the *Wehrmacht* which won cheap victories with modern fighting machines, by 1944 it was the enemy who was flying and driving even more sophisticated machines against the increasingly (at least in relative terms) ill-equipped troops of the *Wehrmacht*. Consequently Nazi propaganda now changed its tune, presenting the war as a struggle between the German spirit and the cold, inhuman technology of the enemy (symbolised by the strategic bomber, that one item of technology not produced by the German armaments industry). Thus whereas in 1940 spirit and machine were welded together into the German *Blitzkrieg*, in

not confined to French writers, and has, for instance, featured in many post-war films, such as Cavani's 'The Night Porter', Visconti's 'The Damned', Bertolucci's '1990', Malle's 'Lacombe, Lucien', Fassbinder's, 'Lili Marleen', Syberberg's 'Hitler', Kluge's 'The Patriot', Wertmuller's 'Seven Beauties', etc. The bizarre obverse side of this tendency was Hitler's expression of admiration for Stalin, whom he called 'one of the most extraordinary figures in the world history', and 'a hell of a fellow!' See *Hitler's Table Talk 1941–44*, 2nd edn (London, 1973 [1953]), pp. 8, 587.

44 On lingering images from Vichy, H. Rousso, *The Vichy Syndrome: History and Memory in France since 1944* (Cambridge, Mass. 1991). On France's soldiers, their self-representation, role in the débâcle, and subsequent conduct and views, see P. -M. de la Gorce, *The French Army* (London 1963); J. S. Ambler, *Soldiers Against the State*, 2nd edn (Garden City, NY 1968 [1966]); P. C. F. Bankwitz, *Maxime Weygand and Civil-Military Relations in Modern France* (Cambridge, Mass. 1967); R. O. Paxton, *Parades and Politics at Vichy* (Princeton, NJ 1966). On the realities of opinion, images, and collaboration in Vichy, see, e.g., P. Ory, *Les collaborateurs 1940–1945* (Paris 1976); J.-P. Rioux, *La vie culturelle sous Vichy* (Brussels 1990); P. Laborie, *L'Opinion française sous Vichy* (Paris 1990). On the attempts and failures to purge France of the collaborators and to recreate an acceptable image of an indigestible past, see P. Novick, *The Resistance Versus Vichy: The Purge of Collaborators in Liberated France* (London 1968); R. Aron, *Histoire de l'épuration* (Paris 1967); P. Assouline, *L'Épuration des intellectuels* (Brussels 1990).

1944 the German spirit confronted the alien machine, and the *Geist* was naturally bound to win in this newly christened *Materialschlacht*.[45]

This, of course, never happened. Nor did the previous image ever totally vanish, since the great heroes of the latter years of the war still remained to a large extent both the *masters* of machines, such as the *Luftwaffe* pilots, the submarine crews, and the *Panzertruppen*, and the machines themselves, the superheavy 'Tiger' and 'Panther' tanks, the first jet planes such as the Messerschmitt 262, and, most of all, the V-1 and V-2 rockets, those wholly depersonalised weapons, the epitome of technological war, the *Wunderwaffen* which failed to bring about that change of fortune and total transformation of modern war itself finally accomplished in a different part of the world by the atom bomb.[46] Hence, when the war ended, the Germans (but many other participants in the conflict as well) were left with two competing images of their war. The first, closely related to the end-phase of the fighting, portrayed hordes of well-equipped enemies attacking the Reich from every conceivable direction, East and West, air and sea, held back by desperately tired but courageous troops, ill fed, sorely lacking in modern armaments, tough and cynical and proud.[47] The second evoked

[45] This is one of the central arguments of my book, *Hitler's Army*, where I make use of various types of evidence such as letters, diaries, and propaganda. For letters, see also W. and H. W. Bähr, (eds.), *Kriegsbriefe gefallener Studenten 1939–1945* (Tübingen/Stuttgart 1952); and H. F. Richardson (ed.), *Sieg Heil! War Letters of Tank Gunner Karl Fuchs 1937–1941* (Hamden, Conn. 1987). For youthful images of the war, see A. Heck, *A Child of Hitler*, 3rd edn (Toronto 1986); R. Schörken, 'Jugendalltag im Dritten Reich', in *Geschichte im Alltag–Alltag in der Geschichte*, ed. K. Bergmann and R. Schörken (Düsseldorf 1982), pp. 236–46. For soldiers' post-war representations of their experience, see, e.g., G. Sajer, *The Forgotten Soldier*, 2nd edn (London 1977); H.-U. Rudel, *Stuka Pilot*, 2nd edn (Maidstone 1973). On propaganda, see, e.g., J. W. Baird, *The Mythical World of Nazi War Propaganda, 1939–45* (Minneapolis, Minnesota 1974), and his *To Die for Germany: Heroes in the Nazi Pantheon*, 2nd edn (Bloomington 1992); E. K. Bramsted, *Goebbels and National Socialist Propaganda, 1925–45* (London 1965); Z. A. B. Zeman, *Nazi Propaganda* (London 1964); D. Welch (ed.), *Nazi Propaganda: The Power and the Limitations* (London 1983), his *Propaganda and the German Cinema, 1933–1945* (Oxford 1983), and his *The Third Reich: Politics and Propaganda* (London 1993). For German reception of propaganda, see M. G. Steinert, *Hitler's War and the Germans* (Athens, Ohio 1977).

[46] This search for the heroic individual even in mass technological war is addressed in O. Bartov, 'Man and the Mass: Reality and the Heroic Image in War', in his *Murder in Our Midst*, pp. 15–32. Representatives of this tendency in Germany, on very different intellectual levels, are, e.g., Ernst Jünger, Hans Ulrich Rudel, and the film 'Das Boot'. Jünger's revived popularity among intellectual circles in Europe and the United States is especially interesting in this context. These are examples of depoliticised, rather than depersonalised, technological warfare, and of team spirit in a 'war is hell' situation where one accepts the rule that *à la guerre comme à la guerre*. See esp. E. Jünger, 'Der Erste Weltkrieg: Tagebücher 1', Vol. I of *Sämtliche Werke* (Stuttgart 1978), including his *In Stahlgewittern* (1920), *Das Wäldchen 125* (1925), *Feuer und Blut* (1925), and *Kriegsausbruch 1914* (1934).

[47] This was the image sketched by Hillgruber in his *Zweierlei Untergang*, but of course, it is a common one in popular post-war literature and divisional chronicles. See, e.g., H. Spaeter and W. Ritter von Schramm, *Die Geschichte des Panzerkorps Grossdeutschland*, 3

better times, and compared the orderly, efficient, neat victories of German arms with the messy, destructive, chaotic defeat. Naturally, this image was derived from the German perspective, whereby the destruction of Warsaw or Rotterdam was part of a swift triumph, while that of Hamburg and Berlin served as proof of the enemy's steamroller techniques and over-destructiveness. But it was a powerful and enticing image, which cast the winner in an inferior moral role, allowing him only superiority of numbers and production capacity, not of human virtues and technological quality. Moreover, both images could to a large degree be disseminated rather easily in the West, since they played on liberal guilt feelings regarding the terror bombing of Germany and the conquest and political subjugation of Eastern Europe and eastern Germany by the Red Army as an ally of the West. Both images also relied on the assumption, widely held in Germany and generally accepted in the West, that there was no correlation between the German soldier, who conducted a professional, 'fair' war, and the criminal policies of the regime carried out by the SS and its various agencies.[48]

Hence the image of *Blitzkrieg* continued to play an important role in the post-war period as well. Yet this role was not confined to Germany. Indeed, precisely because *Blitzkrieg* was always both a military tactic and an image, both a reality and a manner of representing that reality, it became, in a sense, the ideal (of) modern war. Thus anyone who imagined war, propagated it, represented it in film or art or fiction or conscription brochures, could draw upon this available image of *Blitzkrieg*. Although, as I have argued, in reality *Blitzkrieg* was merely a version of total war, it came to serve as a highly potent counter-image to that other memory of industrial, modern total war, that of the mechanical slaughter of the Western Front in 1914–18, and while the latter was to be avoided at all cost, the former remained horribly (whether perversely or naturally) attractive, especially to those young men of

---

vols. (Bielefeld 1958), esp. Vol. III. There is, however, a clear distinction between the Western Allies, portrayed mainly as carriers of deadly, inhuman technology, and the Red Army, portrayed more as barbarous hordes. The former are infantile, playing irresponsibly with dangerous toys, and stupidly indoctrinated into seeing all Germans as Nazis; the latter are primitive, savage, innumerable, irrational, but individually can be more easily pacified, especially with alcohol. Fundamentally both are inferior to the Germans, being less cultured and sophisticated, less mature and responsible.

[48] On the images and reality of the German army in the Second World War, see: M. Messerschmidt, *Die Wehrmacht im NS-Staat: Zeit der Indoktrination* (Hamburg 1969); C. Streit, *Keine Kameraden: Die Wehrmacht und die sowjetischen Kriegsgefangenen, 1941–1945*, 2nd edn (Bonn 1991); H. Krausnick and H.-H. Wilhelm, *Die Truppe des Weltanschauungskrieges: Die Einsatzgruppen der Sicherheitspolizei und des SD, 1938–1942* (Stuttgart 1981); G. R. Ueberschär and W. Wette (eds.), *"Unternehmen Barbarossa"* (Paderborn 1984); J. Förster, 'The German Army and the Ideological War against the Soviet Union', in *The Policies of Genocide*, ed. Hirschfeld; O. Bartov, *The Eastern Front 1941–45* (London 1985), and his *Hitler's Army*.

181

numerous nationalities and several generations who, given the opportunity, were always likely to try and reenact it. This is, after all, the popular image of war as portrayed in countless war films and novels. It is a heroic, fast, dangerous, exhilarating, glorious, and sensuous representation of a paradoxically fifty year-old futuristic war.[49]

This transformation of *Blitzkrieg* into the good war, that is, the kind of war everyone prefers to fight, at least if fighting cannot be avoided, is not only the domain of over-enthusiastic teenagers, but also of sober (though ambitious) generals. The Israeli tank General Tal, for instance, is said to have likened the 1967 Israeli desert war against Egypt to a *Blitzkrieg* and to have compared himself with Guderian.[50] Similarly, one cannot help feeling that the American General Schwarzkopf was portrayed (not unwillingly, one would assume) as the leader of a 1990's-style *Blitzkrieg*, which contained all the necessary elements of few losses, immense quantities of sophisticated *matériel*, quick results, and massive destruction to the enemy. But while the good war has thus come down to us in German (blissfully ignoring of course those essential components of this type of warfare such as terrorising the population by concentrated bombing of open cities), we are now experiencing yet another disturbing transformation of *Blitzkrieg* into a media spectacle.

Since *Blitzkrieg* is essentially part image and part reality, its two fundamental components are military action and media representation. Propaganda was always crucial for the success of *Blitzkrieg* campaigns, just as harmless but frightening sirens formed an inherent element of dive bombers whose demoralising effect was much greater than their destructive power. *Blitzkrieg* itself was to some extent a frenzied, yet well planned, murderous spectacle in which the actors were supplied with live ammunition. But nowadays, since the introduction of live media coverage, we are experiencing another kind of theatre. Now we can watch battles at close range, in real time, without knowing what their outcome will be, indeed, sharing the confusion of the battle scene with the participants. This is a play without a script, and while the reporting is live, the dead really die, and the blood really flows. Yet we view all this at an immense distance from the event, and though we

---

[49] On the creation of the new American hero as a counter-image of the failed Vietnam venture, see S. Jeffords, 'War, Gender, and Identity: "Rambo", "Terminator", "Robo Cop"', unpublished paper (1993). It should also be noted that antiwar films are often viewed, especially by young men, as exciting war films. See J. W. Chambers II, 'All Quiet on the Western Front (1930): the Antiwar Film and Image of the First World War', *Historical Journal of Film, Radio and Television*, 14/4 (1994), pp. 377–411.

[50] On the Israeli '*Blitzkrieg*' see, e.g., M. Handel, 'Israel's Political-Military Doctrine', in *Occasional Papers in International Affairs*, No. 30, Center for International Affairs (Cambridge, Mass. 1973); and on its nemesis in 1973, see H. Bartov, *Dado: 48 Years and 20 Days* (Tel-Aviv 1981).

know that it is happening just as we observe it, there is absolutely nothing we can do about it, not even give a drink of water to the wounded, or bandage a bleeding child. If *Blitzkrieg* was the first war which blended modern images and technology, which sold itself as a media event, war in the post(modern)war age has become even more immediate and direct, happening right in front of our eyes, yet simultaneously reinforcing our sense of complete detachment from the events unfolding on the screen, since they are, precisely due to their being broadcast in real time, so far from us that they can never touch our actual existence. Hence live reporting breeds indifference, not compassion, detachment, not empathy. We take it as a given that the war out there and our own reality are connected *only* through the television screen, and that the connection can be severed at any moment we choose by pressing a button.

By way of conclusion I would thus like to emphasise the links between the various aspects of *Blitzkrieg* discussed in this chapter. We have noted that while *Blitzkrieg* could have been motivated by a desire to minimise the price of war as far as one's own population was concerned, it was simultaneously closely related to the unleashing of a policy of genocide toward other populations. That is, while trying to be a limited war domestically, it was a total war *vis-à-vis* real and perceived enemies. We have also seen that *Blitzkrieg*'s reliance on images was not only a necessary precondition for its success, but has also played a role in perpetuating its fascination for post-war generations. Thus we may say that there is a link between the anaesthetised image of *Blitzkrieg* disseminated in the popular media, and the current 'real-time' reporting on war and violence whose effect seems to be detached curiosity and indifference, rather than compassion and political mobilisation. In recognising these links, we would be justified to feel profound unease about the potentialities of our own civilisation. To take just one hypothetical example, how would we react today to a live CNN report from Auschwitz, showing us the gas chambers in operation, the smoking crematoria, the arrival of new transports, all in real time? How would that reality affect our own? We think of the real-time reports from Bosnia, Somalia, India, China, Russia, as well as the inner cities of the United States, and we know the answer. In this sense we can perhaps argue that *Blitzkrieg* was much more than a new strategy, for it was part of a process in the development of modern humanity which perfected our capacity to participate and yet remain detached, to observe with fascination and yet remain indifferent, to focus on an extraordinary explosion of energy and passion, and then calmly switch it off and go about our business. Perhaps *this* is the essence of *Blitzkrieg*, since it was, after all, an attempt to wage destructive war while pretending that nothing of importance (at least for the domestic population) was actually going on. In this sense we may even argue that *Blitzkrieg* was the perfect manifestation of modernity, since it presupposed normality as a simultaneous and essential component of atrocity, or, in our own terms, it anticipated the phenomenon of the 'real-time' report, the symbol of contemporary humanity's indifferent acceptance of, and detached fascination with, death and destruction.

8

Stalin, the Red Army, and the 'Great Patriotic War'

Bernd Bonwetsch

The German attack on 22 June 1941 came as a total surprise to the Soviet Union, although war had been expected already since the mid-1930s. The 'new imperialist war' had become a 'fact' as Stalin told his audience at the 18th Party Congress in March 1939, pointing to the conflicts in Africa and East Asia.[1] At this time 'war' had already penetrated the daily language as had the theme of 'capitalist encirclement' and the metaphor of the Soviet Union as a 'besieged fortress'.[2] Psychologically, though not only psychologically, the Soviet people already lived in a state of war. Militarily they actually were being prepared for war. It is striking to see that Soviet military expenditure in the 1930s was high as Germany's.[3] The workforce was being transformed, step by step, into a mobilised working army. Freedom of movement and free choice of workplace, already restricted by 'work-books' and internal passports, were formally abolished on 26 June 1940, when a law was passed that turned the relationship at the place of work into a military one. On 19 October of the same year workers were finally mobilised. Not only could they no longer freely leave their place of work, but they could be transferred without their consent to different ones. Additionally, at the request of the trade unions, as was made public, and without wage compensation, the working day was extended from seven to eight hours and the working week from five to six days, with Sunday again as the common day of rest.[4]

At the same time the Red Army grew continuously. Its size quad-

---

[1] J. W. Stalin, *Works*, German edition, Vol. XIV (Dortmund 1976), p. 185.

[2] For example: P. Lisovskii, *SSSR i kapitalisticheskoe okruzhenie* (Moscow 1939).

[3] J. Sapir, *Les fluctuations économiques en URSS 1941–1985* (Paris 1989), p. 47.

[4] W. Hoffmann, *Die Arbeitsverfassung der Sowjetunion* (Berlin 1956), pp. 102–6, 140–4; H. Schwartz, *Russia's Soviet Economy* (New York 1954), pp. 524–5; S. M. Schwartz, *Arbeiterklasse und Arbeitspolitik in der Sowjetunion* (Cologne 1953), pp. 114–24.

rupled from 1.1 to 4.2 million soldiers between January 1937 and January 1941 and reached almost 5.4 million in June that year.[5] Consequently, the armaments production had to be increased enormously, the peak being reached in 1940 when, compared with 1939, it had risen by one third.[6] Owing to these endeavours the Red Army had at its disposal in June 1941 more tanks than all other armies in the world taken together. Among these tanks were already 1,861 of the new models T34 and KV which proved in many respects superior to the German tanks. Furthermore, the Red Army had more than 20,000 older tanks. Of course, not all of them were outdated in the sense that they were useless on the battlefield. They still represented a formidable force.[7]

Even more important was the fact that the Soviet armament production capacity had not only steadily increased but had partially been transferred to the eastern regions (Volga, Urals, Siberia) during the years preceding the war. The Stalingrad and Chelyabinsk tractor plants, for instance, had changed to tank production already in 1940.[8] This was not in expectation of a German invasion far behind the Soviet border but in order to help equip the nine newly formed mechanised corps in 1940 and another twenty in 1941, each of them to consist of 1,031 tanks. This increase and eastward transfer of armament production capacity – by June 1941 almost 20 per cent of it already was located in the East[9] – made it possible for the Soviet Union not only to produce 5,500 tanks in 1941 but during the second half of 1941, despite all handicaps, still to produce more tanks than Germany in all of 1941. On the basis of the pre-war increases the Soviet Union outran the German weapons production during the war by far.[10]

Artillery and planes presented a similar picture: guns and mortars were produced in huge quantities. The production of fighter planes and bombers was increased almost irrespective of costs once war in Europe had begun. In 1939 the construction of nine new aircraft and seven motor plants was instigated. In 1949 another seven plants of the metal industry changed their production to aircraft. The result was a 70 per cent increase of production capacity. According to a directive of 16 November 1940, the factories had to report their production figures

[5] *Sovetskaya voennaya entsiklopediya*, Vol. II, pp. 348–9; 'Pomnit' uroki istorii', in *Voenno-istoricheskii zhurnal* (hereafter abbreviated as *VIZh*), (1988), p. 5.

[6] *Izvestiya TsK KPSS*, 5 (1990), pp. 181–2; L. G. Ivashov, 'V poslednye predvoennye', *VIZh*, II (1989), pp. 12–18

[7] J. Erickson, *The Road to Stalingrad* (London 1975), p. 32. The Red Army had a total of 23,457 tanks on 22 June 1941 (Ivashov, 'V poslednye', p. 14).

[8] *Izvestiya TsK KPSS*, 2 (1990) pp. 181–2, 202–4. For the 'pereprofilirovaniye' of many Moscow-based industrial plants after January 1940, see: 'Stalin ne pomyshlyal sdavat' Moskvu' *VIZh*, 10 (1991), p. 36.

[9] V. Anfilov, 'Na izlome ispytanii', *Vozhd', khozyain, diktator* (Moscow 1990), p. 357 (cf. *Osteuropa* 1989, p. A456).   [10] Sapir, *Fluctuations*, p. 51.

daily to the Central Committee, that is to Stalin. Suppliers had to consign highest priority to aircraft orders as had the People's Commissariat for Transport. State controller Lev Mekhlis, an overseer of sorts, was put in charge of the surveillance of these directives. All this brought about a real explosion of production. From 1 January 1939 to 22 June 1941, almost 18,000 new aircraft were delivered to the Red Army, among them 3,719 of the newest models.[11]

There can be no doubt that the Soviet economy on the eve of the war was a 'mobilised economy' or a 'war economy in peace times' as Jacques Sapir has called it.[12] Nor can there be any doubt that as regards equipment and strength the Red Army had nothing to fear. The question that remains, then, is: what was made out of this fighting force? The answer is: not what could have been made of it, to say the least. We all know that the leading personnel of the Red Army had been liquidated since 1937. The exact number of victims of 'Stalin's war against the Red Army' (Pavlenko) has not been established to date. There are figures in circulation that put the number of officers who underwent repression at 40,000 for 1937/38 and another 40,000 for the years 1939–1941.[13] But these figures are by no means final and are being debated. Particularly puzzling are the figures given by the Administration of Leading Personnel of the Red Army for the reinstatement of officers originally expelled from the army.[14]

Whatever the exact figures, the Red Army was 'decapitated'. The higher the rank, the greater was the rate of 'losses'. At the level of generals, for instance, Stalin's 'war' cost many more lives than Hitler's. About 80 per cent of the generals (before 1940 the corresponding 'commanders') suffered repression. Most of them were shot. Only a few, such as the later Marshal Rokossovskii, survived and were rehabilitated before the war. But repression did not end with the war's beginning. In October 1941, for instance, at the height of the battle of Moscow, numerous high-ranking officers – 300 according to Marshal Zhukov[15] – were shot after having been imprisoned since before the war. In fact, the

---

[11] *Izvestiya TsK KPSS*, 2 (1990), pp. 183–4, 194–6. G. K. Zhukov, *Vospominaniya i razmyshleniya* (Moscow, 10th edition, 1990), Vol. I, chapter 9, ('On the Eve of the Great Patriotic War') gives a good picture of Soviet military preparations.

[12] Sapir, *Fluctuations*, p. 46.

[13] N. Pawlenko, 'Stalins Krieg gegen die Rote Armee', *Moscow News*, German edition, 6 (1989), p. 6. Cf. B. Bonwetsch, 'Die Repression des Militärs und die Einsatzfähigkeit der Roten Armee im "Großen Vaterländischen Krieg"', in *Zwei Wege nach Moskau. Vom Hitler–Stalin-Pakt zum 'Unternehmen Barbarossa'*, ed. B. Wegner (Munich 1991), pp. 404–4.

[14] A rather optimistic picture is given by F. B. Komal, 'Voennye kadry nakanune voiny', *VIZh*, 2 (1990), pp. 21–8. Cf. among other articles: 'O masshtabakh repressii v Krasnoi Armii v predvoennye gody', *VIZh*, 1 (1993), pp. 56–63; 2, pp. 71–80.

[15] A. Mirkina, 'Marshal pishet knigu', *Ogonyok*, 16 (1988), p. 13. See also: 'Sud'by general'skie', *VIZh*, 10–12 (1992), 1–2 (1993).

Red Army had enormous problems in supplying its units with qualified officers since not only those who had been arrested had to be replaced, but at the same time there was need for additional officers on account of the considerable expansion of the army.

The consequences of this double demand were clear: on the eve of the war the officers of the Red Army were seldom trained according to their rank and often held a position above their rank. There were instances where captains, who previously had commanded only a company, found themselves within weeks not only at the head of battalions and regiments but even of divisions. Promotions more than doubled: from nearly one-fifth to a quarter of all officers in 1935–7 to five or six out of ten in 1938–9.[16] The shift of commanding personnel resembled a merry-go-round. There was barely a commanding post that did not see several personnel changes. But despite all this, the Red Army was not left without officers, because training programmes and facilities were increased to the utmost. The schools released 70,000 new officers into the army in the first half of 1941. In 1939 the figure had been 101,000 for the whole year.[17] Germany's war with England seemed to grant the necessary time to train still more officers until war, finally, reached the Soviet Union.

On Sunday 22 June 1941, around half past three in the morning, this belief of Stalin proved a miscalculation, although he himself for some hours still refused to realise this, believing that the whole affair was a provocation by German generals who had acted without Hitler's knowledge and consent. For until this deadly proof of the opposite, Stalin clung unshakably to his conviction, that Hitler was not 'such a fool' as to open a second front voluntarily.[18] Yet Hitler was. And since dawn the three concentrated German army groups, supported by three air force 'fleets' and forces of the German allies, proceeded to drive wedges into the totally unprepared Soviet forces in the border zones. Within a few weeks the Germans advanced deep into the western areas of the Soviet Union. No wonder that Colonel-General Halder noted in his war diary on 3 July 1941 that 'this war has been won within two weeks'.[19]

Here Halder erred deeply. But in the beginning the 'Russian campaign' looked like another lightning victory (*Blitzsieg*). The German tank wedges closed like pliers in the rear of Soviet armies, forming the famous 'pockets'. Encircled at Bialystok, Smolensk, Kiev, and Vyazma-Bryansk, the Red Army lost whole armies and thousands of tanks,

[16] *Izvestiya Tsk KPSS*, 1 (1990), pp. 186–92; Anfilov, 'Na izlome', pp. 352–5; O. F. Suvenirov, 'Vsearmeiskaya tragediya', *VIZh*, 2–4 (1989).   [17] Komal, 'Voennye kadry', p. 27.
[18] Zhukov, *Vospominaniya*, Vol. I, p. 366, Vol. 2, pp. 9–10.
[19] Generaloberst Halder, *Kriegstagebuch*, Vol. III (Stuttgart 1963), p. 38.

aircraft, and guns by early October. About three million soldiers fell into German captivity; about the same number of Red Army soldiers were wounded or killed.[20] The Red Army did everything to try to compensate for these losses. Before the end of June five million men were mobilised and 2.5 million already sent to the front by the end of July. But in spite of a steady stream of newly formed units sent to the fronts, the number of soldiers facing the Germans fell to 2.3 million in October 1941, the lowest figure during the war.

However, the defeats seemed to have no end. Leningrad was encircled by the end of August, and the city was prepared for surrender;[21] Kiev was lost in September; Moscow faced the same fate in early October when the Germans took the Soviet High Command by surprise. The destruction of several Soviet armies at Vyazma left 'almost a vacuum', as Marshal Rokossovskii commented, between them and Moscow, and Marshal Zhukov stated that 'on the evening of October 7th all the gates to Moscow stood open' to the Germans.[22] Indeed, German advance forces reached the city borders on 16 October. Except for water supply and sewerage everything of importance was prepared to be blown up or otherwise destroyed – more than 1,100 objects. Foreign diplomats, many government and other institutions, were evacuated; Stalin, who had ordered all this in his capacity of chairman of the State Defence Committee, had also ordered the evacuation of 'Comrade Stalin'.[23] The main evacuation road, by some strange coincidence named 'Highway of Enthusiasts', was jammed with fleeing representatives of the party and state, abused by gathering crowds. The city of Moscow presented a picture of disorder and even panic. For some days the Stavka seemed ready to surrender the Soviet capital. Beriia, People's Commissar for Internal Affairs, according to one of the participants of a GKO meeting during the night of 19 October was the main proponent of this idea. Stalin, cautious as ever, had the silent members of the State Defence Committee give their opinion one by one before he gave his own. So no one, including Beriia, pleaded for abandoning Moscow. It was decided to hold out. On 19 October, the state of siege was declared for the next day and order was reestablished in the city with the usual

[20] Maksudov, 'Pertes subies par la population de l'URSS 1916–1958', *Cahiers du monde russe et soviétique*, 18 (1977), p. 260. Cf. the much lower figures in *Grif sekretnosti snyat. Poteri Vooruzhennych Sil SSSR v voinakh, deistviyakh i voennykh konfliktakh* (Moscow 1994), p. 143.

[21] G. A. Kumanev, 'V ogne tyazhelykh ispytanii (iyun' 1941-noyabr' 1942 g.)', *Istoriya SSSR*, 2 (1991), p. 16.

[22] K. K. Rokossovskii, 'Soldatskii dolg', *VIZh*, 6 (1989), p. 53; Zhukov, *Vospominaniya*, Vol. II, p. 208.

[23] *Izvestiya TsK KPSS*, 12 (1990), pp. 210–12, 217; D. Volkogonov, *Stalin, Triumph and Tragedy*, German edition (Düsseldorf 1989), p. 595; *Moskva voennaya, 1941–1945. Memuary i arkhivnye dokumenty* (Moscow 1995), pp. 87–93, 100–6.

brutality; the military commandant reported almost 400 persons shot and thousands arrested between 10 October and 13 December 1941.[24]

During these critical days not only the fate of the Soviet capital with all its symbolic meaning, but even the basic question of whether to continue or discontinue the war, was at stake. True, the Stavka on 27 September had advised the Western Front of the possibility of a German attack. But when it started three days later no one in Moscow believed that this was already the expected attack.[25] For several days there was no adequate reaction. The reports from the front about the destruction of several Soviet armies at Vyazma and Bryansk and the German breakthrough towards Moscow were considered fruits of panic. Stalin and Molotov took these reports to be a 'provocation'.[26] Beriia threatened those commanders who insisted that their reports were true with being placed before a war tribunal. Only when two operational groups of the State Security, sent out by Beriia, confirmed the threat was it taken seriously.[27]

Stalin was in a state of shock during these days. Colonel-General Konev, then commander of the Western Front, wrote that Stalin gave no sign of understanding and reaction when, on 4 October, he reported on the situation and made suggestions for the rescue of his troops. Stalin seemed to be utterly depressed.[28] Army General Zhukov got the same impression when, in the afternoon of 7 October, he arrived in the Kremlin to where he had been ordered directly from Leningrad. Zhukov later related to others that he met a Stalin who was even ready to consider concluding a separate peace, ceding large territories to Germany. Beriia was to sound out German peace terms and indeed he did try to use the mediation services of the Bulgarian minister in Moscow, Stamenov.[29]

[24] *Izvestiya TsK KPSS*, 4 (1991), pp. 209–21. 'Stalin ne pomyshlyal sdavat' Moskvu', p. 39; K. I. Bukov, 'Trevozhnyi oktiabr' 41-ogo', *Kentavr*, 10 (1991), p. 75. CF. A. N. Mertsalov, '"Molniyenosnaya voina" i "aktivnaya oborona" 1941 goda', in *Istoriki otvechayut na voprosy*, Vyp. 2 (Moscow 1990), pp. 320–34; R. Medvedev, *Let History Judge. The Origins and Consequences of Stalinism* (Oxford 1989), pp. 759–64.

[25] K. F. Telegin, *Voiny neschitannye versty* (Moscow 1988), pp. 45, 47; Zhukov, *Vospominaniya*, Vol. II, p. 207; Erickson, *Road*, pp. 213–14.

[26] *Izvestiya Tsk KPSS*, 4 (1991), p. 217 (Pronin statement); Rokossovskii, 'Dolg', pp. 52–4.

[27] *Izvestiya Tsk KPSS*, 2 (1991) pp. 210–11; Telegin, *Versty*, pp. 47–60; K. F. Telegin, 'German Breakthrough', in *Stalin and His Generals*, ed. S. Bialer (London 1970), pp. 272–6; Erickson, *Road*, pp. 216–17.

[28] I. S. Konev, 'Vospominaniya', *Znamia*, II (1987), pp. 40–2; 12, p. 100.

[29] There are two versions of Zhukov's words. One comes from Viktor Anfilov, in *Literaturnaya gazeta*, No. 12, (22 March 1989), p. 11 (cf. my German language translation in *Osteuropa* (1989), p. A458). The other, more drastic version, comes from Nikolay Pavlenko: 'Istoriya voiny eshche ne zapisana', *Ogonyok*, 25 (1989) p. 7; idem, 'Stalins Krieg', p. 6 (where the name of the Bulgarian minister in Moscow is erroneously given as Stotenov). Volkogonov, *Stalin*, pp. 564–5, relates a report by Marshal Moskalenko that would confirm Pavlenko's more drastic version. But he refers this episode to June

Nothing substantial sprang from this initiative which was kept secret until recently. There were no 'peace talks'. Nevertheless, it demonstrates that the will to continue fighting the Germans was broken for some days. This will obviously returned when Zhukov was appointed Commander of the Western Front on 10 October. The cancellation of the Central Committee Plenum one day before it was due to meet on 9 October, when the majority of the Committee's members and candidate members had already gathered in Moscow, certainly has to be seen in this context as has the original convocation of the plenum by Stalin on 2 October. The real meaning of this mysterious plenum, which was first mentioned by Khrushchev in his secret speech, has yet to be revealed.[30] But there can be no doubt that something quite extraordinary must have triggered Stalin's decision to summon the meeting, as it was clearly not his habit to convoke Central Committee plena. The next one was to gather on 27 January 1944, for quite special purposes.

In October 1941 the Red Army succeeded in warding the *Wehrmacht* off Moscow and the Germans had to cancel something that they had already announced – victory celebrations in Moscow. They narrowly escaped a military catastrophe during the winter offensive of the Red Army. That did not yet mean victory to the Soviet Union. But despite the enormous setbacks in 1942 that allowed the Germans to advance still further, to the Volga and the Caucasus, no such deep crisis as in October 1941 recurred in Moscow. After the serious defeats of the Germans in the winter of 1941/42 Stalin underrated their fighting ability and already expected victory in 1942.[31] However, the scales did tip steadily in favour of the Soviets as far as the balance of forces at the front as well as armament production were concerned. On the battlefield, the Red Army could increasingly bring its numerical superiority to bear. And in the rear the munitions production, once the difficulties of the first half-year had been overcome, reached such levels that the Germans never had a chance to match it. It gave the Red Army a comfortable superiority in all kinds of weaponry.

Nobody had expected such a turn of events. In the second half of 1941 munitions production had even partially decreased because of losses and evacuation problems. The situation worsened especially as regards aircraft and ammunition. But even rising production in other sectors in 1941 could not keep pace with the rise in demand. There was, for

1941. The same is true for Khrushchev who confirms Pavlenko's version as well, but dates the episode vaguely to 1942 – obviously an error (*Khrushchev Remembers. The Glasnost Tapes* (Boston 1990), p. 65). The sheer fact of Stalin's order to Beriia in October 1941 is not to be doubted, in any case.

[30] Kumanev, 'V ogne', pp. 19–20; Khrushchev's secret speech 'O kul'te lichnosti i ego posledstviyakh', *Izvestiya TsK KPSS*, 3 (1989), pp. 136, 167 note 8.

[31] A. M. Wassilewski, *Sache des ganzen Lebens* (Berlin 1977), p. 177.

example, a serious shortage of rifles caused by the loss of war reserves stored closely behind the border and, therefore, lost during the first weeks of the war. Such losses amounted to 30 per cent of all ammunition and 50 per cent of all fuel and food reserves.[32] The militia units (*narodnoe opolchenie*), for example, which were formed in all haste in October 1941 in Moscow, lacked rifles. The newly formed regular units of the Red Army could only be equipped with 30 per cent of the necessary quantities. For training purposes the use of wooden rifles under these circumstances was a rule rather than an exception.[33]

However, the Red Army overcame these difficulties as well as the military setbacks of spring and summer 1942. In November of that year it was able to encircle and later destroy a whole German army at Stalingrad. That was the first incontestable victory over the enemy. After the successful defence against the German summer offensive at Kursk, which turned out to be the last German one in the East, the Red Army finally took the initiative and added offensive on offensive and victory on victory. The Germans were given no respite and the Red Army finally conquered Berlin on 2 May 1945. The repetition of the German capitulation of Reims on 8 May in Karlshorst at the seat of the Soviet Command in Germany paid tribute to this prominent role of the Red Army in the victory over Nazi Germany.

Neither the great successes of the Red Army after Stalingrad nor its catastrophic defeats before autumn 1942 can be questioned. The question to be answered, however, is why all this could happen. An explanation for the early defeats cannot be found in numerical inferiority at the start of the war. Although this was maintained by Soviet scholars until recently, it never existed. On the contrary, there are now realistic figures which demonstrate that at the Western Front, taking the main thrust of the German attack, the balance of forces was even, that at the North-Western Front the Germans had a slight superiority, and that at the South-Western Front, where the main drive of the *Wehrmacht* had been expected, the Red Army enjoyed considerable superiority but was unable to make use of it.[34] Therefore, the main reason for the Soviet defeats in the initial phase of the war was not lack of but improper use of disposable forces, as Viktor Anfilov has correctly stated.[35]

---

[32] 'Die Sowjetunion am Vorabend des Krieges', *Osteuropa* (1989), p. 215; Zhukov, *Vospominanya*, Vol. 1, pp. 337–8.

[33] Telegin, *Versty*, p. 19; B. L. Vannikov, 'Zapiski narkoma', *Znamia*, 2 (1988), p. 152; D. V. Pavlov, 'Iz zapisok narkoma', *Novaya i noveishaya istoriya*, 6 (1988), p. 111.

[34] M. I. Meltiukhov, '22 iyunia 1941 g.: tsifry svidetel'stvuyut', *Istoriya SSSR*, 3 (1991), pp. 16–28; B. N. Petrov, 'Voennye deistviya na severo-zapadnom napravlenii v nachal'nyi period voiny', *VIZh*, (1988), p. 45; A. A. Gurov, 'Boevye deistviya sovetskikh voisk na jugo-zapadnom napravlenii v nachal'nyi period voiny', *VIZh*, 8 (1988), p. 36; V. A. Semidetko, 'Isoki porazheniya v Belorussii', *VIZh*, 4 (1989), p. 30. Cf. N. Pavlenko, 'Razmyshleniya o sud'be polkovodtsa', *VIZh*, 11 (1988), p. 26.

[35] Anfilov, 'Na izlome', p. 365.

The surprise caused by the German attack was, of course, to the disadvantage of the Red Army. But this can only account for setbacks during the first days or weeks, since strategically the country was prepared for war. Another explanation is that the 'decapitation' of the Red Army caused the defeats. There is, of course, some truth in this. Lack of experienced upper-echelon personnel was a fact. However, the behaviour of all such personnel, experienced or not, shows that the repression – and Stalinism generally – caused psychological damage far more serious than purely numerical damage. An atmosphere of suspicion, intimidation, and irresolution had developed that severely impaired the professional self-confidence of the military.

The writer Konstantin Simonov pointed as long as three decades ago to this most important consequence of Stalinist repression: any 'military illiterate' (*voennyi bezgramotnyi*) felt free to meddle with the business of the military.[36] What Simonov had in mind was particularly the case of the former *Pravda* editor Lev Mekhlis, head of the Main Political Administration of the Red Army in 1941. Already before the war Mekhlis had played an ugly role in the 'purges' among the military. After 22 June 1941, he lived up to his notoriety. Like many others in Moscow he never hesitated to attribute failures rather to the lack of will, to the activity of 'enemies of the people' and 'parasites' or even traitors than to lack of capability and forces. He treated the military accordingly, read them lectures or even effected their persecution. And Stalin, as is well known, was always ready to lend an ear to this kind of reasoning. But of course, the problem was not the individual Mekhlis, but the system. And there were many 'illiterates', beginning with Stalin and ending with less important party leaders and functionaries who were fulfilling their obligations as representatives of the Headquarters (*Stavka*) or the State Defence Committee (*Gosudarstvennyi komitet oborony*/GKO), as – political – members of 'Military Soviets' of fronts and armies or, after their reintroduction on 16 July 1941, as war commissars.

There was rarely a member of the military who could free himself of this influence of 'illiterates'. This is valid also for the pre-war period. Only this can explain why Stalin, putting aside the conclusions of the then Chief of Staff Shaposhnikov, could claim that the main thrust of the German *Wehrmacht* was to be expected in the Ukraine. Stalin was convinced that Hitler, for reasons of the war economy, would above all try to conquer the Ukraine, while the General Staff had come to the conclusion that the main German effort would be directed against the western frontier. However, nobody stood up to Stalin. As a result, the main forces of the Red Army were concentrated in the Ukraine. Even

---

[36] K. Simonov, *Glazami cheloveka moego pokoleniya* (Moscow 1988), pp. 291–306.

when Stalin's error became clear in 1941 through further military intelligence, nobody dared inform him. Only minor concealed attempts were made to redirect some units from the Ukraine northwards into the Smolensk region.[37]

There were other disastrous effects of Stalin's interference with military affairs, particularly his strict prohibition of any of the precautionary measures considered necessary by the military in view of the German preparations for attack. The People's Commissar for Defence Timoshenko and his new Chief of Staff Zhukov together with the commanders of the Military Districts and of the units at the border were all, under threat of severe consequences, forbidden to do what seemed necessary. The People's Commissar for Internal Affairs Beriia had his agents secretly control the observance of this prohibition. The border troops, belonging to his People's Commissariat, were also used to keep a watch on the military. As late as 21 June he demanded the recall and punishment of the Soviet minister in Berlin, Dekanozov, because, as he complained to Stalin, Dekanozov would not stop 'bombarding' him with 'disinformation' about an impending German attack on the Soviet Union.[38]

Everyone who dared put the units under his command into readiness for combat was threatened with punishment. Measures secretly taken had to be revoked. Stalin considered those measures as a provocation which he thought could serve as the only reason for Hitler to start a war against the Soviet Union as long as he had not yet finished with the British in the West. By being friendly towards Germany, Stalin not only hoped but was convinced that war with Germany could be avoided, at least for 1941.[39] What he himself intended to do in this case is still open to debate.[40]

Nobody on the Soviet side could prove for sure that Stalin was not right in his conviction. But the paradox was that Stalin also prohibited precautionary measures directed towards a more defensive disposition of the Soviet troops which could not have provoked Hitler. Not even the mobilisation reserves were allowed to be stored farther to the rear. All suggestions of this kind were condemned as signs of mistrust in the capability of the Red Army. All those who suggested similar measures,

---

[37] Anfilov, 'Na izlome', p. 360; N. Pavlenko, 'Na pervom etape voiny', *Kommunist*, 9 (1988), p. 90; Wassilewski, *Sache*, pp. 89–94; Zhukov, *Vospominaniya*, Vol. I, pp. 331–2.

[38] 'Svodka no. 8', *Argumenty i fakty*, 4 (1989), p. 7; Zhukov, *Vospominaniya*, Vol. I, pp. 368–9; Kumanev, 'V ogne', p. 10.

[39] Zhukov, *Vospominaniya*, Vol. I, pp. 350–3; 'Svodka, no. 8', p. 7; Simonov, *Glazami*, pp. 435, 449–51; Kumanev, 'V ogne', p. 9. Even the commander of the Western Special Military District D, V. Pavlov, was not that stupid and ignorant of the danger as he is often depicted. Cf. L. M. Spirin, 'Stalin i voina', *Voprosy istorii KPSS*, 5 (1990), pp. 99–100.

[40] Cf. V. D. Danilov, 'Stalinskaia strategyia nachala voiny: plany i real'nost', *Otechestvennaya istoriya*, 3 (1995), pp. 33–43.

including the preparation of partisan warfare, were reproached with 'cultivating the spirit of retreat'. Even military war games that took retreat into consideration underwent this verdict. Any thought of war on Soviet soil was called 'defeatism'. Offensive strategy was the only alternative left for military thinking and action.[41]

Everyone around Stalin accepted his bizarre views, whether from conviction or fear. They in turn forced others to accept these views as the only ones possible. Marshal Zhukov, for example, by no means felt at ease with the situation. But he did not hesitate, on 10 June 1941, to reprimand severely the commander of the Kiev Special Military District Kirponos who had anxiously ordered greater preparedness and the advance to combat position for some units. Of course, the military system of order and obedience left almost no room for a different handling of the affair. But Zhukov's reprimand lacked even the slightest hint of sympathy for an officer who did what under normal conditions would have been self-evident and what to postpone would have constituted a grave neglect. Instead, Zhukov himself took a typical Stalinist ploy: he ordered those guilty to be named and threatened with severe punishment.[42]

After 22 June, when chaos was total and the *Wehrmacht* advanced with breathtaking speed, this forced ignoring of reality had costly results, since the commanders continued to substitute wishful thinking for realistic analyses. Their reports as a rule anticipated or repeated what was expected from 'above'. And Moscow expected the Red Army to stop the Germans and drive them back within a few days. Less optimistic reports would have been considered fruits of panic. During the first twenty-four hours of the war, therefore, no front commander dared give a picture of the real situation, nor confess that the general chaos made it impossible to know what was really happening at the front. Instead, the commanders gave assurances without any basis that the enemy would be 'destroyed'. Only such assurances can account for an order such as that of the evening of 22 June to all fronts demanding decisive counter-offensives and the destruction of the enemy.[43]

This ignoring of the real situation continued and led particularly at the Western Front to catastrophic results. General Pavlov, Commander in Minsk, passed on to his front commanders the orders from Moscow,

[41] Zhukov, *Vospominaniya*, Vol. I, pp. 289, 291, 323; Volkogonov, *Stalin*, p. 547; D. Volkogonov, 'Stalin als Oberster Befehlshaber', in *Zwei Wege*, ed. Wegner, p. 489; 'Die Sowjetunion am Vorabend des Krieges', pp. 215–16.

[42] Anfilov, 'Na izlome', p. 362; Kumanev, 'V ogne', p. 10.

[43] Anfilov, 'Na izlome', p. 367. The general chaos at the front is depicted by Rokossovskii, ('Dolg', No. 4, pp. 55–7, pp. 59–60) and – dryly, but impressively – by L. M. Sandalov (*Pervye dni voiny* (Moscow 1989)).

not caring whether they still corresponded to the situation or indeed reached their addressees. When his deputy objected, he rebuked him rudely. What counted most for him was the impression he made in Moscow, namely that everything had gone in accordance with the orders. Anyone objecting to meaningless orders for attack that would only have assisted the Germans was silenced by the handy reproach of panic-mongering. That happened for instance to the Chief of Staff of the South-Western Front Lieutenant-General Purkaev on 22 June. The political member of the Military Soviet of the Front, Corps Commissar Vashugin, silenced him with the panic reproach when he objected to a militarily senseless order from Moscow.[44] Front Commander Kirponos did not support his chief of staff. He preferred to follow 'blindly the orders of the general staff and the Stavka although they were out of date and no longer corresponded to the situation at the front which rapidly changed', as Major-General Rokossovskii saw it. Rokossovskii, Commander of the 16th Army, had the impression in the middle of July that Kirponos 'was afraid of facing the facts'. He ordered decisive counterstrokes, for instance, 'without caring whether the units concerned could or did execute these orders at all'.[45] Here, as at the Western Front, wishful thinking and lack of realism prevailed.

The causes of this disastrous behaviour lay in Moscow, with Stalin. Only on 28 June, when the Germans had taken Minsk, did he grasp that things were not going according to expectations. But instead of parting with his illusions, Stalin looked for scapegoats. He, or rather his authorised agent Mekhlis, found them in the command of the Western Front. Within a few days after his dispatch to the front on 30 June, Mekhlis 'discovered' that General Pavlov and his officers had acted as 'criminals' if not 'traitors'. In all, eight generals were put before a court-martial, sentenced to death, and executed. Stalin used this brutal incident to intimidate the military still further. In an order of 16 July, he deplored the behaviour of the generals and announced that the State Defence Committee, in the future, too, would suppress 'with an iron hand' any sign of cowardice. This order was read to all officers of the Red Army on 27 July.[46]

Shortly afterwards, Stalin's Order No. 270 of 16 August 1941 declared surrender to the enemy or flight generally to be desertion and breaking of the oath of allegiance, the occurrence of which had to be punished with execution on the spot. This order, also read to the entire army, declared millions of soldiers captured by the *Wehrmacht* to be traitors. As was usual in Stalin's Soviet Union, relatives of these 'traitors'

[44] Bonwetsch, 'Repression', p. 418.
[45] Rokossovskii, 'Dolg', No. 5, pp. 60, 62; K. Rokossowski, *Soldatenpflicht* (Berlin 1973), p. 30.   [46] Anfilov, 'Na izlome', pp. 367–8; Bonwetsch, 'Repression', pp. 413–14.

underwent persecution as well, particularly relatives of officers. Under these circumstances the threat of court-martialling became part of the ordinary issue of orders. It is no wonder that fear spread in the army, that the atmosphere of 1937/38 arose anew.[47]

As a result, the lack of professional independence and self-confidence could not have been greater. Induced from Moscow, the reality of the powerful German advance continued to be ignored. Retreat did not officially exist even when German pressure made it not only reasonable but unavoidable. Instead, as Marshall Rokossovskii mentions in his memoirs, the units at the fronts continued to receive 'bombastic, vigorous directives that did not take into consideration whether they could be carried out in reality. They were the reason for unnecessary losses and for the fact that the fronts, one after another, retreated in full flow.'[48]

Neither strategical nor tactical defensive measures nor retreat were considered, even though this considerably increased the German successes and the Soviet losses during the first months of the war. But even losses and failures on this scale did not bring Stalin and his entourage to their senses. They continued to attribute the catastrophes to lack of will and to treason. Any hint of the necessity to retreat was qualified as an expression of panic. Under such conditions the front commanders did not object even to the most foolish orders. Instead they passed them on to their subordinates. Obviously, it seemed to be much easier to face destruction and the loss of whole armies than Stalin's reproaches and abuse. Thus the fateful events of Kiev could take place where in September 1941 the Germans could take more than 600,000 Soviet soldiers as prisoners.[49] Chief of Staff Zhukov had been the only one who, already on 29 July, had declared to Stalin that retreat behind the Dnepr was necessary in order to avoid a catastrophic encirclement. But instead of military consequences Stalin drew personal ones – he dismissed Zhukov as Chief of Staff.[50]

Stalin put his trust instead in Lieutenant-General Eremenko who promised what Stalin wanted to hear, namely that he would destroy the 'scoundrel Guderian' and his tank forces. 'This is the man we need in such a difficult situation', commented Stalin with such self-confi-

---

[47] Bonwetsch, 'Repression', p. 414.   [48] Rokossovskii, 'Dolg', No. 6, p. 52.
[49] A. Seaton, *Der russisch-deutsche Krieg 1941–1945* (Frankfurt 1973), p. 112. The German figure of 665,000 captured Red Army soldiers is cited by Anfilov ('Na izlome', p. 368). The Soviet figure, 452,720 is cited by Kumanev, ('V ogne', p. 17). On different bases, they may be both 'correct'. The question of losses, which Russian historians are now taking up, is a highly controversial one. *Grif sekretnosti sniat*, p. 166, puts the 'irreplaceable' loss (including deaths) of the entire Kiev defensive operation from 7 July to 16 September 1941 at 616,000.
[50] Zhukov, *Vospominaniya*, Vol. II, pp. 118–22; Simonov, *Glazami*, pp. 218, 360–61.

dence. Zhukov did not trust these assurances supported only by the desire to please the Supreme Commander. Therefore, on 19 August Zhukov repeated his warnings against the approaching disaster. But he remained isolated. His successor as Chief of Staff, Marshal Shaposhnikov, shared his apprehension but openly contradicted Stalin neither at this nor on other occasions. The same is true for those in command of the South-Western Front, Colonel-General Kirponos and his attached members of the Military Soviet, in the beginning of the war Khrushchev, later Burmistenko, second secretary of the Ukrainian CP. Despite better knowledge and earlier requests, the command rejected up to the bitter end any thought of retreat when confronted with Stalin. Quite the contrary, they confirmed his illusion that Kiev could be defended.[51]

In a similar vein to their denials of reality were those of Stalin and his Chief of Staff. Whatever reservations Shaposhnikov may have had, as Vasilevskii suggests, he concealed them successfully from Stalin, even after Zhukov insisted for a third time on 9 September on the necessity to surrender Kiev. As late as 11 September, Stalin could still point to the opinion of his Chief of Staff who supposedly considered a withdrawal of the front 'premature'.[52] Khrushchev, now Member of the Military Soviet of the 'Southwestern Direction', and Budennyj, its commander, seem to have asked again after 11 September for a decision to pull back the front. The same is said of Kirponos. But according to the evidence in other cases, it is realistic to assume that none really dared to insist on this demand and resist Stalin, if a clear demand was made at all. The discrepancy between Khrushchev's statements in his memoirs about his actions during the disastrous Kharkov offensive in May 1942 and the documentary evidence is quite revealing.[53]

But of course, Stalin's reactions were dangerous. Even hints about the possibility of retreat were punished. Budennyi, who had supported the original request for withdrawal by Kirponos, was dismissed as Commander of the South-Western Direction and Timoshenko appointed in his place on 13 September. Kirponos was a broken man and no longer dared make suggestions at all. When his chief of staff, Major-General Tupikov, drew up a realistic report for the Stavka, concluding that Kiev could no longer be defended, he refused to sign it. He exposed his chief of staff to Stalin's reprimand, which followed immediately. In an order dictated by Stalin, Chief of Staff Shaposhnikov had to qualify Tupikov's

[51] Zhukov, *Vospominaniya*, Vol. II, pp. 127–33; Wassilewski, *Sache*, pp. 118–32; I. Kh. Bagramjan, *So begann der Krieg* (Berlin 1979), pp. 337–44.
[52] Zhukov, *Vospominaniya*, Vol. II, pp. 143–47; Anfilov, 'Na izlome', p. 369.
[53] Seaton, *Krieg*, p. 111. Cf. *Chruschtschow erinnert sich* (Reinbek 1971), pp. 188–95; S. F. Begunov *et al.*, 'Vot gde pravda, Nikita Sergeevich!" *VIZh*, 12 (1989), 1990, Nos. 1–2.

report as panic-mongering and to repeat the strict order to hold the front.

No wonder that nobody dared take upon himself the responsibility for a decision to retreat. When Timoshenko could finally no longer suppress his own judgement on 16 September, he only gave this order orally to Colonel Bagramyan, operations officer at the South-Western Front. As could almost be expected, the Commander at the Front Kirponos refused to act 'without a written order' and insisted on confirmation of this order by Stavka. Only in the night of 18 September did Stalin give permission to surrender Kiev, and only then did Kirponos and Burmistenko give the order for retreat.[54] While the broken armies were desperately struggling eastwards, Moscow continued to ignore reality. Three days before the total destruction of the South-Western Front on 26 September, with the entire front command among the dead, Kirponos received advice from Shaposhnikov to show 'more decisiveness and calmness'. 'Success is certain', he continued. 'Against you stand minor enemy forces . . . I repeat, more decisiveness, calmness and energy in action . . .'[55]

Indeed, more than calmness was required in order to overcome such catastrophes. Stalin himself did not possess such qualities. When Colonel-General Konev, Commander of the Western Front, a few days later on 4 October, reported the seriousness of the situation and asked permission to retreat since the enemy had already broken through the neighbouring fronts, Stalin did not react at all. Or, rather, he reacted strangely. He did not take a military decision but, according to Konev, 'almost hysterically' asserted that 'comrade Stalin is not a traitor' but an 'honourable man'.[56] This is to be doubted. While he himself was ready to end the war by concluding a separate peace with Germany, he aggravated Konev with a commission of the State Defence Committee. Its task, according to the tested pattern, was to restore order and declare a number of persons guilty. Molotov, head of the commission and a military 'illiterate', did not understand what was going on, as Konev notes.[57] But nevertheless he was ready to execute Stalin's order and to certify the responsibility of the front command for the situation. Zhukov succeeded in dissuading Stalin from putting Konev before a court-martial but the fact remained that Molotov continued to supervise the new front commander Zhukov. Only two days after his appointment to his new post, Molotov threatened Zhukov with a court-martial because he was not content with the latter's actions.[58]

---

[54] Bagramjan, *So begann*, pp. 347–56; Wassilewski, *Sache*, pp. 130–1.
[55] Volkogonov, *Stalin*, pp. 585–6.   [56] Konev, 'Vospominaniya', No. 12, p. 100.
[57] Ibid. No. 11, p. 42.
[58] Simonov, *Glazami*, pp. 364–5, 398; Zhukov, *Vospominaniya*, Vol. II, p. 215; V. Sokolov, 'Slovo o marshale Zhukove', in *Marshal Zhukov. Kakim my ego pomnim* (Moscow 1988). pp. 222–3.

Zhukov did not tolerate this and answered in a sharp manner. But not every commander had the stature of Zhukov. The interference of military 'illiterates' in the affairs of the military continued. The most spectacular case of such interference was during the battle on the Kerch peninsula in May 1942, where the Red Army suffered one of its most humiliating defeats. This was above all due to the activities of Lev Mekhlis. As one of the most self-confident and unflagging 'illiterates', he acted there as the representative of the Stavka and meddled with the duties of Lieutenant-General Kozlov, the front commander. Mekhlis insisted on the implementation of his bizarre ideas that were meant to demonstrate courage. Kozlov, an experienced officer, complied against his better judgement and thus allowed the Germans with far inferior forces to achieve a success they had not expected. Konstantin Simonov has related intriguing reports of the bizarre situation on Kerch peninsula where Kozlov, according to Stalin, 'feared Mekhlis more than the Germans'.[59]

This defeat in the Crimea represented only part of the meddling of civilians in military affairs which characterised the entire strategic and operational planning of the Red Army during 1942. As in 1941, for instance, the miscalculation of German strategic intentions originated with Stalin. The latter expected the main strike to be against Moscow. Although the General Staff had shared this opinion originally, they changed their mind when enemy intelligence made it clear that the *Wehrmacht* was concentrating its forces in the south. But Stalin brushed this knowledge aside and persisted in his original conviction. As a result, the main forces of the Red Army and almost all Stavka reserves were deployed around Moscow.[60] In the south-west there were no reserves at hand when the German summer offensive started. Thus, as in 1941, the Red Army was not concentrated in accordance with the real situation, since Stalin again presumed to know better than his intelligence people what the Germans were going to do. No one knows what made him so sure. But with everybody, even in the light of better knowledge, submitting to Stalin's conviction no rational decision could be made.

Another grave mistake originating with Stalin was the dissipation of the Soviet forces in spring 1942. The Chief of Staff had suggested preparation for an 'active strategic defence' because of lack of sufficient forces and sources for offensive operations. Stalin nominally concurred with this view. But in fact he pressed for 'single' offensive operations.

---

[59] Simonov, *Glazami*, pp. 301–2; 366, 431–3. c.f. Wassilewski, *Sache*, pp. 185–8; Erickson, *Road*, pp. 347–50; Zhukov, *Vospominaniya*, Vol. II, pp. 279–80.

[60] A. Seaton, *Stalin As Warlord* (London 1976), pp. 143–8; Wassilewski, *Sache*, p. 183; L. Trepper, *Die Wahrheit* (Munich 1975), pp. 126–7; Erickson, *Road*, pp. 338–42.

And even this was to hide, as Zhukov has remarked, the fact that Stalin was the 'advocate of offensive operations on all fronts' in order to wear down the enemy.[61] Zhukov was the only one who raised serious objections. He pleaded for only one offensive, west of Moscow. For all other fronts he recommended a defensive approach. Otherwise, he was afraid that not the enemy but the Red Army would be worn down. Yet Stalin made it quite clear that he did not think much of 'keeping the hands in the lap and waiting on the defensive until the Germans commit the first strike'. At a big conference of the Stavka in the end of March 1942, he declared Zhukov's suggestion to be only 'half a measure'.[62]

In this question, too, Stalin's view prevailed because no one except Zhukov dared to oppose him. Many a commander even hurried to propose what Stalin would like to hear. When Nikolai Voznesenskii, responsible for economic affairs, made some sceptical remarks, Beriia sharply rebuked him: 'What do you presume, comrade Voznesenskii? Do you call in question the intentions and plans of comrade Stalin?' To all present the threat in this servile rebuke was only too obvious. Even General Zhukov, otherwise imperious and self-confident enough, stopped making critical remarks about Stalin in order not to let Beriia hear them.[63] Nobody wanted to expose himself to such rebukes, as their consequences were never to be foreseen. Therefore it sounds close to reality when Zhukov states that hardly one of the leading commanders consented actively to Stalin's ideas. The consent that Stalin met with consisted mainly of lack of any sign of opposition.[64]

In any case, the big Stavka conference at the end of March 1942 was by no means a collective search for a decision. Rather, its aim was the inclusion of others into the responsibility for decisions Stalin already had long favoured or had already taken. Stalin had often used this method before, and he did so again this time. This became clear when Chief of Staff Shaposhnikov approached Zhukov after the meeting. He confessed to the bewildered general that the latter had struggled in vain because the decision about the offensive of the South-Western Front which Zhukov opposed had already been taken before the convening of the conference. Stalin acted, as he used to do, 'behind the back of the Stavka' (Erickson), in this particular case in consultation with Marshal Timoshenko, the Commander of the South-Western Direction. That explains Timoshenko's behaviour at the Stavka conference. Sure of Stalin's applause, he energetically suggested the offensive of the South-Western Front, although the negative attitude of the Chief of Staff

[61] Zhukov, *Vospominaniya*, Vol. II, pp. 275–6; Pavlenko, 'Na pervom etape', p. 92.
[62] Zhukov, *Vospominaniya*, Vol. II, pp. 277–8; Sokolov, 'Slovo', pp. 227–9.
[63] Sokolov, 'Slovo', pp. 229–30.   [64] Zhukov, *Vospominaniya*, Vol. II, p. 278.

was no secret to him.[65] Stalin may well have induced him to suggest this offensive. Shtemenko's remark that it was the initiative of Timoshenko and Khrushchev and that the plans for the offensive were indeed presented by the South-Western Direction to Stavka in mid-March, 1942 are no proof to the contrary.[66]

Thus, the Stavka conference turned out to be a sham. It is quite appropriate that Dmitrij Volkogonov has depicted Stalin in his biography as a 'great actor' with whom pretence had become second nature. Stalin could simply have ordered and everybody would have obeyed. However, he did not only want his will executed, but was always cautious not to act alone and to share responsibility for his own will with others.[67] Therefore, he often practised this method of staging collective decision-making by using his undeniable charm, joviality, and flattery, by taking advantage of fear, vanity, envy of the commanders or other persons around him and, not the least, by taking advantage of their desire to be in favour with the 'Supreme' (*Verkhovnyi*), as Stalin was called.[68]

One of the unwritten laws of Stalin's 'theatricals' was that everybody played his part. If someone broke this rule by opposing Stalin, infrequent as this was, he had to be prepared for serious consequences. In any case, Zhukov was dismissed as commander of the 'Western Direction' and of the Kalinin Front as soon as he returned from the Stavka conference to his command post. He felt this was the price he had to pay. The 'Supreme' did not shut his eyes to his criticism, nor forget that Zhukov continued to cling to his opinion, which finally proved to be right when Timoshenko's offensive in May 1942 culminated in disaster.[69] Even in this phase of developments, Stalin again practised his method of playing off a front command against his general staff. This happened when the Chief of Staff on 18 May suggested discontinuing Timoshenko's offensive towards Kharkov because the Germans were already threatening to turn the latter's flanks. Stalin, after consultation with Timoshenko and Khrushchev, ordered the continuation suggested by them. But it is quite obvious that they knew what Stalin would like to hear and answered accordingly. The responsibility for the disastrous continuation of the offensive lay clearly with Stalin, as Zhukov notes. But again, it was

[65] Sokolov, 'Slovo', p. 230; Zhukov, *Vospominaniya*, Vol. II, pp. 278–9; Erickson, *Road*, pp. 335–8.

[66] S. M. Schtemenko, *Im Generalstab* (Berlin 1975), Vol. II, pp. 545–6; Belgunov *et al.*, 'Vot gde pravda', No. 12; *Chruschtschow erinnert sich*, pp. 188–95.

[67] Concerning the repressions of the 1930s F. Burlazki mentions this as a habit of Stalin (*Chruschtschow. Ein politisches Porträt* (Düsseldorf 1990), p. 98).

[68] G. Zhukov describes the method of playing the commanders off against each other ('Korotko o Staline', in *Marshal Zhukov. Kakim my ego pomnim*, pp. 393–5).

[69] Zhukov, *Vospominaniya*, Vol. II, pp. 278, 280.

formally at least a shared responsibility if not the front command's alone.[70]

Under Stalinism such interference by Stalin and other 'military illiterates' in the business of the military was obviously not to be avoided. This would have required real opposition to Stalin as well as to his methods. But such opposition had only existed in Stalin's paranoic mind and had produced those legions of 'enemies of the people'. Although Stalin had the power to define the rules and, if necessary, to enforce their observance, he never had to resort to this power because he could count on consent achieved by more subtle means.

Under these conditions, not the military but Stalin alone was in a position to stop or at least to reduce the interference of 'illiterates' in military affairs. And indeed this happened, beginning in autumn 1942 after the enormous setbacks the German summer offensive had brought. This gradual turn of events had announced itself with the demotion of Lev Mekhlis because of his striking failure on the Kerch peninsula in May 1942, and particularly with his removal as head of the Main Political Administration of the Red Army in June of the same year.[71] The abolition of the war commissars on 9 October 1942 was the final turning point. There remained the system of shared command on the level of fronts and armies. But in general the military was encouraged to adopt a much more self-confident attitude than before. The formal rules and institutions had always had less significance than the political will emanating from Moscow and taking decisions on the basis of the actual situation. And what became visible in Moscow in autumn 1942 was trust in the professional self-reliance of the military.

This change expressed itself in a reintroduction of tsarist traditions in the army which were now increasingly placed in the foreground, although they were not entirely new. As a reflection of insecurity and search for orientation, it had been a phenomenon since the outbreak of war. It manifested itself, for example, in the reaction to the supply problems of the Red Army that arose immediately after 22 June. Those problems were, in fact, quite normal in such a situation of surprise and general confusion. But as usual, Stalin and his entourage reacted with hasty organisational reforms, many of which sooner or later proved failures. If someone made such a reform suggestion it was always an advantage, as Marshal Voronov has noted, to have a 'historical basis' for the proposal, a pre-revolutionary one, of course.[72] This prerequisite was satisfied when Lieutenant-General Khrulev in early July 1941 proposed the reorganisation of the supply system of the Red Army to Anastas Mikoyan. It was a simple transcript of the 'Regulation of the Field

[70] Wassilewski, *Sache*, pp. 190–91; Zhukov, *Vospominaniya*, Vol. II, pp. 280–3.
[71] Erickson, *Road*, p. 349.   [72] N. N. Voronov, *Na sluzhbe voennoi*, Moscow 1963, p. 192.

Administration of the Army in War-Time' of July 1914. In fact, Khrulev handed over to Mikoyan a copy of the original 'Regulation' to convince him. With this document he not only convinced the people's commissar responsible for the supply of the army, but above all Stalin. Literally overnight Stalin consented to the reorganisation of the supply system of the Red Army according to the regulation of 1914 and confirmed, on 1 August 1941, the formation of a 'Main Administration of the Rear Services of the Red Army' against the explicit vote of his Chief of Staff Zhukov.[73]

Much more was introduced according to this pattern, such as, for instance, the title 'guards unit'.[74] In January–February 1943 a further step was taken when the name 'officer' instead of 'commander' was reintroduced together with golden shoulder-pieces and stripes. All these and other measures served to strengthen the self-reliance of the military, for the experience of 1942 had shown that even extreme rigour could not bring about the impossible, could not turn wish into reality. The interference of 'military illiterates' in the business of the military subsided, as did the frequent resort to court-martials. In the first phase of the war the threat of court-martialling was part of the mechanism that brought about the elimination of the power of judgement and of independent thinking of the military. Also in this sphere many mechanisms not only worked at the top but continued to work at lower levels. Even Zhukov, who objected to being denied of his own judgement, treated his own subordinates as he was treated. While he repelled the court-martialling threats of the Stavka representative Molotov, he himself used the same means unrelentingly. For example, when Army Commander Rokossovskii reported to him realistically in October 1941 about the enemy strength, Zhukov reproached him with panic-mongering. According to Rokossovskii's impression, even Zhukov wanted to substitute wish for reality. He refused to allow Rokossovskii to withdraw to a more favourable defence line and ordered him not to go 'a single step backward' and to 'fight to the last drop of blood'. Since even this did not prevent the Germans from advancing, it was Zhukov's turn to send a commission to Rokossovskii's 16th Army with the task of establishing those guilty for the retreat and calling them to account. The purpose of all this according to Rokossovskii was Zhukov's wish to exculpate himself in Stalin's eyes.[75] Major-General Golubev, commander of the 43rd Army, confirms this conduct of Zhukov in a report to

[73] A. V. Khrulev, 'Stanovleniye strategicheskogo tyla v Velikoi Otechestvennoi voine', *VIZh*, 6 (1961), pp. 67–9.
[74] This happened already on 18 September 1941, but the decision was published only much later (Kumanev, 'V ogne', p. 17).
[75] Rokossovskii, 'Dolg', No. 6, pp. 52–5; idem, *Soldatenpflicht*, pp. 115–16.

Stalin of 8 November 1941. He asks Stalin to stop using a 'policy of the big stick' on him. Since his arrival at the front five days previously, the Commander of the Western Front Zhukov had threatened him daily with execution on the spot or with court-martial. This was not in the least helping him to do his duty better than without those threats but instead caused anxiety and undermined the commander's authority.[76]

It took Stalin some time until he realised the fruitlessness of a rigour that demanded under the disguise of 'discipline' the self-sacrifice of officers and men even when absolutely senseless in military terms; it took some time until he realised that will and self-sacrifice alone could not make up for bad military strategies and tactics. In his notorious Order No. 227 of 28 July 1942, known under its leitmotif 'Not a Step Backward', Stalin again tried to attribute Soviet defeats to cowardice, treason, and panic-mongering; he attempted to enforce the necessary 'discipline' by threatening commanders with court-martialling, by forming 'punishment battalions' for officers and 'punishment companies' for soldiers, by posting heavily armed 'blocking detachments' (*zagraditel'nye otriady*) immediately behind the front line.[77] But it is not usually noticed that this order and the military situation in which it was issued already indicated a fundamental change: In contrast to earlier orders of this kind the categorical 'No step backward!' is for the first time not unconditional, but is completed by 'without order'. Orders for timely retreat had simply not existed before. It was given for the first time when Rostov was surrendered just a few days before the Order No. 227 was issued. The course of the battle at Rostov obviously had demonstrated to Stalin the advantage of a *retreat on order* compared to the *forced retreat* that had prevailed before. For the first time the Red Army had not assisted the German tactics of encirclement by trying to hold the front at any cost. Quite on the contrary: the German victory, despite the space the Germans had won, was not the kind of success they had hoped for, because Colonel-General Malinovskii had given the timely order to the Southern Front to withdraw behind the Don.[78]

This was actually a quiet sensation and marked the turn that fully materialised only in 1943. The military were given not only golden shoulder-pieces but greater freedom to enable them to act professionally. That was clearly a concession which could be withdrawn at

[76] *Izvestiya TsK KPSS*, 1991, No. 3, p. 221.
[77] 'Prikaz narodnogo komissara oborony Soyuza SSR No. 227, 28 iyul'ia 1942 g.', *VIZh*, 8 (1988), pp. 73–75. The 'blocking detachments', supposedly introduced by this order, were nothing new. They were established already during the Finnish 'Winter-War', and were again introduced right after the beginning of the war. C.f. B. Bonwetsch, 'Der "Große Vaterländische Krieg" und seine Geschichte', in *Der Umbau der Sowjetgeschichte*, ed. D. Geyer (Göttingen 1991), p. 173; Kumanev, 'V ogne', p. 7; 'Kogda rodina zvala v boi', *VIZh*, 11 (1992), p. 4.   [78] Erickson, *Road*, p. 371; Seaton, *Krieg*, p. 209.

any time. But as long as it existed, military decisions were taken much more rationally. This change originated with Stalin who no longer wanted only confirmation and shared responsibility for decisions he himself favoured or had already taken. Stalin remained the absolute 'Supreme' who also in this second period of the war could force his opinion upon his commanders even when they did not agree with him. But the 'Supreme' made less use of this possibility. The defensive tactics the general staff and the front commanders applied in expectation of the German summer offensive in 1943 made this change in Stalin's attitude clear. He urged them several times not to wait for the Germans to attack, but yielded to the arguments of the military and did not 'stage-manage' their consent.[79]

Moreover, Stalin revised his underestimation of the Germans which resulted in the severe setbacks of 1942 and at Kharkov and Belgorod in March 1943. The circumspection of the Soviet offensives since July 1943 originated in those experiences. Although Stalin, even in the phase of Soviet victories, continued to urge for offensives under all circumstances,[80] he was now more open-minded towards objections. Nevertheless, not only the Soviet defeats but also the victories cost dearly. A comparison of human and material losses on the Eastern Front shows that in all phases of the war the Red Army suffered more casualties and material losses than did the enemy. It fought 'extensively', so to speak.

Stalin never hesitated to sacrifice his men. He never felt the urge to save them, as Dmitrij Volkogonov has pointed out.[81] His advice of late May 1942 to learn 'how to fight with little blood' (voyevat' maloi krov'yu), that is to save lives as the Germans do, given to the command of the struggling South-Western Front,[82] was rather a justification for refusing them fresh troops than a change of military thinking. Soviet tactics were always 'expensive in terms of human life' compared with German ones, as Earl Ziemke has stated.[83] According to the calculations of Boris Sokolov the ratio of human losses (deaths) on the Eastern Front was 3.7 to 1 to the disadvantage of the Red Army. Even during the last year of the war he puts the ratio at 2 to 1.[84] These figures are certainly not mathematically precise. But generally speaking they give an adequate picture. According to the latest figures made public by the Russian Defence Ministry, the Red Army lost 8.7 million soldiers during 1941–5,

---

[79] Wassilewski points to this change in Stalin's behaviour (Sache, pp. 286–311). Cf. also Pavlenko, 'Na pervom etape', p. 93.

[80] Cf. as a typical example Volkogonov, 'Oberster Befehlshaber', pp. 486–7.

[81] Ibid., p. 488. Cf. Sokolov, 'Slovo', p. 219.   [82] Danilov, 'Stalinskaia strategiya', p. 43.

[83] E. F. Ziemke, Stalingrad to Berlin. The German Defeat in the East, 1968, p. 500.

[84] B. V. Sokolov, 'O sootnoshenii poter' v liudiach i boevoi technike no soevetsko-germanskom fronte v khode Velikoi Otechestvennoi voiny', Voprosy istorii, 2 (1988), No. 2, pp. 119–20.

civilian partisans not included.[85] The German *Wehrmacht* lost approximately 4 million men during 1939–45.[86] Of course, these figures do not represent only losses at the Eastern Front and are not to be compared without adjustments. But an enormous discrepancy to the disadvantage of the Red Army remains a fact under all circumstances.

The same could be said about material losses. The Red Army, for instance, lost 96,500 tanks and self-propelled guns between 1941 and 1945, many more than the Germans produced in total between 1939 and 1945.[87] A closer look at losses of other war material produces a similar impression. It is obvious that the Soviet conduct of war entirely accorded with the wasteful use of human and material resources that had become the habit in Stalin's Soviet Union since long before the war. Costs did not matter and were, consequently, high – very high. However Stalin changed during the war, the victory had been achieved with genuine Stalinist methods.

[85] 'Tsena pobedy', *VIZh*, 3 (1990), p. 14; *Grif sekretnosti sniat*, p. 129.
[86] B. Mueller-Hillebrand, *Das Heer 1933–1945*, Vol. III: *Der Zweitfrontenkrieg. Das Heer vom Beginn des Feldzuges gegen die Sowjetunion bis zum Kriegsende* (Frankfurt 1969), pp. 261–3. For losses on the Eastern Front see G. Ueberschaer, W. Wette (eds.), *'Unternehmen Barbarossa'. Der deutsche Ueberfall auf die Sowjetunion 1941* (Paderborn 1984), p. 402. Some Russian historians tend to let the losses look more equal. 'Tsena pobedy' gives a figure of 5.5 million Germans killed in action (p. 14). *Grif sekretnosti sniat* gives a loss ratio of only 1:1.3 in favour of the Axis powers, including prisoners of war (pp. 392–3). Cf. J. Erickson, 'Soviet War Losses. Calculations and Controversies', in *Barbarossa. The Axis and the Allies*, J. Erickson and D. Dilks eds. (Edinburgh 1994), pp. 255–77.
[87] 'Tsena pobedy', p. 15; Sokolov, 'O sootnoshenii', pp. 123–6; G. F. Krivosheyev, 'Voina broni i motorov', 4 (1991), pp. 36–41. For German production of tanks cf. Sapir, *Fluctuations*, p. 51.

9

The economics of war in the Soviet Union during World War II

Jacques Sapir

It is not surprising that the functioning of the Soviet economy during the Second World War has long fascinated historians. A large literature has arisen on this topic, aimed mainly at showing how the USSR mustered the resources necessary to defeat the German war machine.[1] The primary aim of the present chapter is not to compete with this literature, but rather to analyse the relationship between the war and the economy from the other direction – namely, to elucidate how the evolution of Soviet military doctrine helped to shape the economic system. Thus posed, the topic inevitably raises far-reaching questions concerning the flexibility of the economic system over the whole of the Stalin period. For, while the Soviets began earnestly to prepare for the war early in the 1930s, creating a central planning system that has been called a war economy *sui generis*,[2] the roller-coaster evolution of Soviet military doctrine shortly before and during the war combined with the dislocations attendant upon the territorial losses of 1941–2 prompted major transformations in the economic system. Did wartime changes amount to a continuation and deepening of pre-war practices, or did they represent new departures and transformations? Were the wartime transformations harbingers of a radical reform towards a version of market socialism, a reform that could only be thwarted by virulent Stalinist reaction in the immediate post-war years?[3]

---

[1] See, among others, J. Erickson, *The Road to Stalingrad* (London, Harper and Row 1975); J. Erickson, *The Road to Berlin – Continuing the History of Stalin's War with Germany* (Boulder, Co., Westview Press 1983). M. Harrison, *Soviet Planning in Peace and War* (London, Cambridge University Press 1985). S. J. Linz, (ed.), *The Impact of World War II on the Soviet Union* (London–New York, Rowan and Allanheld 1985). A. Nove, *An Economic History of the USSR* (London, Penguin 1980 (1969)). E. Zalesky, *La Planification Stalinienne* (Paris, Economica 1984).

[2] The term is O. Lange's, *Papers in Economics and Sociology*, (Warsaw and London, PWN and Pergamon Press 1970), pp. 101–2.

[3] The author began discussion of this aspect of the present theme in two earlier publications: 'Le système économique stalinien face à la guerre', in *Annales ESC*, no. 2

With this agenda in mind, we begin with an analysis of the Soviet art of warfare in its historical development.

I. The economic implications of the Soviet art of warfare

A Before the war

Early Soviet military theoreticians themselves established a clear link between military art and economic policies. They recognised the significance and intricacy of this link while trying to absorb the lessons of the Civil War and the First World War. The first task before Soviet military thinkers of the 1920s was to refine the terms used to describe the complexities of war arising from both technological and doctrinal innovations. They took what was for the time a pioneering perspective in approaching this task, concentrating on the ground between tactical doctrine and strategic postures, a ground now known in the Western literature as 'operational art'. Operational art includes the theory and practice of large-unit operations aimed at achieving strategic results in specific theatres of military operations.[4] Since in this time period the invention of tanks, parachute infantry, trucks, armoured personnel carriers, and self-propelled artillery were providing armies with an ever-expanding menu of alternative large-unit organisations, the elaboration of operational art took on tremendous significance. An army's operational art would govern not only its battlefield tactics, but also its economic strategies in the pre-war period (the requisite weaponry could not necessarily be produced at short notice in the event of a approaching crisis). Thus the character of Soviet preparations for the Second World War depended on the operational art the military theoreticians would create.

A. Svechin, N. Varfolomeev, and V. Triandafilov were the first theoreticians – Soviet or otherwise – to make major advances concerning operational art, by elaborating the concept itself and establishing its connection to the strategy of waging war. Focusing on the battlefront arena of war, Svechin described tactics as the material of this operational art, which was itself the material of the overall strategy of war.[5] He saw operational art as the principles, doctrine, and professional skills used to combine material and human resources for the conduct of battle operations. In turn, the character of operational art was governed

---

(1989), March–April, pp. 273–97; and *Les Fluctuations Economiques en URSS: 1941–1985* (Paris, Editions de l'Ecole des Hautes Etudes en Sciences Sociales 1989), chs. 2, 3.

[4] For more on the meaning of the term, see V. E. Savkin, *Osnovnye printsipy operativnogo isskustva i taktika* (Moscow, Voenizdat 1972); and V. G. Kulakov, 'Operativnoe iskusstvo', in *Sovetskaia voennaia entsiklopediia*, vol. VI (1978), p. 53.

[5] A. Svechin, *Strategiia*, 2nd edn. (Moscow 1927), p. 14.

by the nation's strategic posture. In peacetime, the strategic posture was the product of perceptions of future war and assessment of the nation's means. Svechin defined two competing strategic postures: 'annihilation' and 'attrition'.[6]

N. Varfolomeev focused on the conduct of operations of annihilation. He stressed the need to combine breakthrough and deep pursuit so as to destroy the enemy forces throughout their entire depth. Such a combination implied a sequence of successive deep operations, which would put tremendous strain on the army's supply structure. Thus logistics would assume a critical importance, and would have to become an integral part of operational art.[7] This is the first link between operational art and economic policy. The USSR was seen as dominated by a backward economy and a 'peasant rear'. In contrast, the capitalist Western countries were highly industrialised and able to mechanise their forces.[8] Against such foes, the USSR could survive only by preparing for a long war and preserving the so-called workers–peasants alliance.

V. K. Triandafilov was among the best-known Soviet strategists to address the problem of global mobilisation in a backward economy.[9] In case of a protracted war, he wanted to combine shock armies, as exemplified by Frunze in the Civil War, with an echelon of forces for the exploitation of breakthroughs. In peacetime, therefore, he advocated a kind of 'high–low' mix of forces, which would reduce military expenditures and ease economic development within the framework of NEP.[10]

Alongside Triandafilov's focus on a protracted war scenario, the development of the notion of operational art was closely linked to the concept of successive operations, as developed by Varfolomeev and Tukhachevsky. The latter was a strong proponent of the idea of a continuous campaign, waged in a stream of successive operations along the entire battlefront and throughout its depth.[11] But to be able to achieve anything like this, the Red Army badly needed an infusion of modern technology on a scale incompatible with the current level of economic development. It is no wonder, then, that Tukachevsky began to campaign for a quick development of military-related industries.

[6] Svechin, *Strategiia*, pp. 6–26.
[7] N. Varfolomeev, 'Dvizhenie presleduiushchei armii k poliu reshitel'nogo szarheniia', in *Voina i revoliutsiia*, no. 13 (1921), pp. 69–96; and his 'Strategiia v akademicheskoi postanovke', in *Voina i revoliutsiia*, no. 11 (1928), pp. 83–4.
[8] V. Triandafilov, 'Vozmozhnaia chislennost' buduschchikh armii', in *Voina i revoliutsiia*, no. 3 (1927), pp. 14–47.
[9] Triandafilov, 'Vozmozhnaia chislennost' and his *Kharakter operatsii sovremennykh armii*, 1st edn. (Moscow 1929).
[10] Triandafilov, 'Vozmozhnaia chislennost'.
[11] M. N. Tukhachevsky, 'Voprosy sovremennoi strategii', 'Voina', and 'Novye voprosy voiny', in (Coll.) *Voprosy strategii i operativnogo iskusstva v sovetskikh voennykh trudakh* (Moscow, Voenizdat 1965), pp. 90–114.

Early in 1928 he wrote a report stressing the urgent need for re-equipment and technical expansion.[12] Nonetheless, the times were not ripe for such a policy. The military establishment was itself strongly divided, and a majority of high-ranking officers were supporting Triandafilov's views about the need to preserve NEP.[13] For a time it seemed that this opinion would prevail.[14]

With the 'Great Turn' of forced collectivisation and industrialisation, the evolution of military doctrine proceeded more quickly.[15] The unreliability of the 'peasant rear' was exposed,[16] and it seemed necess-ary to protect the military effort from social and political turmoil by establishing a separate economic sector.[17] Having concentrated up to this point on the likelihood of a protracted defensive war with full-scale mobilisation, Soviet operational art now anticipated a short war scen-ario. If it were to deliver an immediate, decisive blow, the Soviet Union would need to have all of its military resources available as soon as war broke out.[18] The Red Army would have to take to the offensive quickly with a combination of airborne and ground forces, backed by massed armoured and mechanised units.[19]

By the time the Field Regulations of 1933 supplanted those of 1929, the new emphasis on immediate offensive operations had found termino-logical expression in the replacement of the more tactical formula 'penetration battle' by the more strategic-scale concept of 'deep oper-ations'. The new concept's emphasis on the offensive contradicted some of Svechin's tenets. But Tukhachevsky's faith in a large, mechanised, standing army induced Soviet leaders to believe that covering forces could undertake an offensive of their own before the enemy was able either to complete the mobilisation and deployment of its forces or to undertake defensive measures. Thus, during the fateful years of the First Five-Year Plan Soviet military thinking shifted away from concern with the problem of defence and the repelling of aggressors. Under the shield of defensive slogans and statements, the Soviet military forgot

[12] This report has been reprinted in *Voenno-istoricheskii zhurnal*, no. 5 (1983).
[13] M. V. Boetticher, 'Soviet Defence Policy and the First Five-Year Plan', unpublished working paper, West European Conference on Soviet Industry and the Working Class in the Inter-War Years, University of Birmingham, June 1981.
[14] That did not stop Tukhachevsky from campaigning, however, even after being demoted to Commander of the Leningrad Military District in May 1928. His theses on mechanised armies were even censored as 'red militarism'.
[15] On the consequences of collectivisation for the military establishment and its internal debates, see J. Sapir, *The Soviet Military System* (Cambridge, Polity Press 1991), pp. 228–9.
[16] L. S. Degtiarev, *Politrabota v Krasnoi Armii* (Moscow 1930), p. 29.
[17] S. Botner, 'Voennaia podgotovka imperialisty i problema oborony SSSR v svete osushchestvleniia piatiletke', in *Voina i revoliutsiia*, no. 12 (1930).
[18] Sapir, *The Soviet Military*, pp. 229–30.
[19] G. S. Isserson, *Evoliutsiia operativnogo iskusstva* (Moscow 1932), p. 3.

some of Svechin's lessons about defensive operations, and prepared itself to conduct offensive operations, even pre-emptive strikes.[20] The emergence of Tukhachevsky was the result of this far-reaching shift in Soviet strategy. At the same time, Tukhachevsky's brilliance did much to shape the contours of the new Soviet operational art. Far from mimicking crude *Blitzkrieg* theories – which he even went so far as to criticise as the tenets of professional armies,[21] Tukhachevsky was able to introduce a full range of new concepts into Soviet military culture. His 1936 *Field Regulations for the Red Army*, for example, placed heavy emphasis on a mechanised war where decisive attacks, relentless pursuit, massed application of tanks and mobile units, and close cooperation with the air force would bring victory.[22]

It was, then, the combination of a brilliant intellect and a process of massive social and political transformation, bringing with it both political instability and new industrial capacity during the first half of the 1930s, which led the Soviet Union to commit itself to a future war scenario that stressed readiness for military action without awaiting full mobilisation. By a fateful irony, this evolution closely paralleled that in Germany.[23]

At the same time, the intention to employ tanks, aeroplanes, and mechanised formations *en masse* had important economic implications. First, maintaining such formations in readiness would impose a heavier burden on the Soviet economy than had been planned. Secondly, in the trade-off between quality, quantity, and lag, emphasis on a high quantity of production in the shortest possible time would entail a sacrifice of quality. Only equipment that could be expected to mature quickly from prototype to the production stage was accepted. The military became relatively conservative towards technological innovations. This approach, which could be relevant in a short war, was a major mistake in peacetime.

The armament production policy of the early 1930s could be criticised on other grounds as well. Building huge stocks of weapons during a period when the world's major powers were experimenting with rapid and wide-ranging technological innovations meant freezing the technological level of Soviet forces' equipment. The backwardness of the industrial base, itself to some extent the result of this strategy oriented towards instant action, precluded major qualitative advances in tech-

---

[20] Col. D. M. Glantz, *Soviet Military Operational Art* (London, Frank Cass 1991), pp. 77–8.
[21] M. N. Tukhachevsky, 'Predislovie k knige Dzh. Fullera', *Reformatsiia voiny*, in *Izbrannye proizvedeniia* (Moscow, Voenizdat 1964), vol. II, p. 152.
[22] Narodnyi Komissariat Oborony, *Vremennyi polevoi ustav RKKA – 1936* (Moscow, pp. 9–16.
[23] M. Geyer, 'German Strategy in the Age of Machine Warfare, 1914–1945', in *Makers of Modern Strategy*, ed. P. Paret (Princeton, University Press 1986).

Table 9.1 *Weapons production during the first half of the 1930s*

	1 October 1930 to 31 December 1931	1932	1933	1934
Tanks and light tanks	740	3,038	3,509	3,565
Artillery pieces	1,966	3,574	4,638	4,123
of which, smaller pieces	1,040	972	2,884	2,521
Fighter aircraft	120	74	336	570
Bomber aircraft	100	72	291	392

Sources: *Istoriia vtoroi mirovoi voiny, 1939–1945*, 12 vols. (Moscow 1973–82), vol. I, p. 214; *Voenno-istoricheskii zhurnal*, no. 12 (1964), p. 7.

nology. This is not to say that Soviet designers were not innovative. On the contrary. But they were forced to compromise radical designs (like Polikarpov's I-16, BT-5, and BT-7 tanks) because of low-quality components and the backwardness of certain branches of industry (as in the fields of light alloys or chemical production). In retrospect, a policy of building prototypes and enhancing war mobilisation capacities would have been wiser. Such an approach would have allowed the USSR swiftly to expand production of up-to-date models in case of a crisis.

The cost of maintaining large stocks of military hardware (see table 9.1) was a huge burden on the overstretched military budget. In the classic trade-off between stock and flow, the Soviet leadership had clearly chosen the first, with all its military, technological, and economic implications. This was a complete reversal of the policy of the 1920s. Critics immediately pointed out how World War I had proved the irrelevance of stockpiling. They emphasised the need to prepare a thorough industrial mobilisation, which would enable the economy to sustain itself despite massive rates of wartime attrition by generating large flows of equipment.[24] As late as 1930, the chairman of Gosplan's Defence Commission, K. Mekhonochin, had argued that it would be a grievous mistake to establish a major military-industrial sector in peacetime, as this would slow down the economic growth rate and undermine mobilisation capabilities thereafter.[25] But arguments like

[24] P. Dybenko, 'Motorizatsiia SSSR: Krasnaia Armiia', in *Voina i tekhnika*, no. 7 (1928), p. 89. Svechin, *Strategiia*, p. 67. S. Ventsov, *Narodnoe khoziaistvo i oborona SSSR* (Moscow 1928), p. 30.
[25] K. Mekhonochin, *Oborona v piatiletke* (Moscow 1930), p. 30.

these fell on deaf ears. Military equipment accumulated rapidly (see table 9.2).

The tangled evolution of Soviet mobile forces doctrine would take yet another strange twist in the late 1930s, thanks on the one hand to Stalin's purges, and on the other hand to the misunderstanding of lessons from the limited wars of the period. The purges killed thousands of officers, including Tukhachevsky and other generals and marshals who stood at the heart of Soviet military development. The repression effectively terminated innovative thinking in the armed forces. In the 1960s, the then Chief of Staff, Marshal M. Zakharov, offered this perspective:

> [the repression of 1937] adversely affected the development of military-theoretical thought. Study of the problems of military science became narrowly focused . . . In the military academies, strategy was no longer studied as a science and an academic discipline . . . Military theory became essentially a mosaic of Stalin's military expressions. But since Stalin had never had much to say on such matters, and since the initiator [of prevalent Soviet military theories] had been labelled an 'enemy of the people', the theory of 'deep operations' fell into disrepute . . . Independent employment of mechanized and cavalry formations in advance of the front and in the depth of the enemy defence was even called sabotage . . . This signified an about face in military theory, a retreat to the linear form of combat at the operational level.[26]

This regress can be traced at least in part to the Soviets' failure to understand the lessons of the limited wars in Spain and the Far East. It is true that, in 1937–8, operations in the Spanish Civil War were reminiscent of the trench warfare of World War I. But neither on the Nationalist nor the Republican side were units and commanders equipped and trained for mobile warfare. Nonetheless, the German General Staff was able to test some of its concepts during this conflict. Thus, from the operations of the armoured force under General Ritter von Thoma they came to realise the overarching significance of combined arms cooperation.[27] In Spain the Germans also came upon the possibility of offensive use of anti-tank guns, which would become one of their major tactical innovations. The Soviets, meanwhile, mistakenly took the vulnerability of lightly armoured tanks to anti-tank guns and mines to signify the incapability of armoured formations to achieve breakthroughs.[28]

It could be argued that, at least until 1943, the Germans owed their battlefield superiority not to their emphasis on tanks per se, but rather to

---

[26] M. N. Zakharov, 'Predislovie', in *Voprosy strategii i operativnogo iskusstva*, p. 13.

[27] H. Guderian, *Panzer Leader* (London, Michael Joseph 1952), pp. 43–50.

[28] J. Weldon, *Machine Age Armies* (London, Abelard-Schulman 1968).

Table 9.2 *Soviet armament stockpiling during the first half of the 1930s*

	1-1-1928	1-1-1932	1-1-1935
Tanks and light tanks	92	1,401	10,180
of which, light tanks	0	348	2,547
Aircraft in Air Force	1,394	3,285	6,672
Artillery pieces of 76 mm and over	6,645	10,684	13,867

Source: *Istoriia vtoroi*, vol. I, p. 270.

their advanced concepts of close cooperation between combined arms, as exemplified in Panzer divisions.[29] The Soviets would not properly understand these concepts before suffering bitter defeats at their hands. Even under Tukhachevsky, Soviet armoured units were top-heavy with tanks.[30] This imbalance made it difficult for them to attain the level of coordination that their own operational concept demanded. It is true that the rapid growth and hasty training of the armoured forces in the early 1930s made harmonious functioning of these units an elusive goal. But the root of the problem lay in technical imbalances that planners had not foreseen. In speeding up tank production, other branches, especially communications, were neglected. Few Soviet tanks had radios, and the logistical tails of Soviet units did not have the mobility to follow the forces they were supposed to support. For all its other achievements, the General Staff under Tukhachevsky had allowed the creation of a deep contradiction between operational concepts and equipment on the one hand, and command and control practices and facilities on the other hand.

The limited conflicts in which Soviet forces took part in 1939–40 did not serve to remedy the situation. Military theorists were not able (or did not dare) to generalise from the experience of battles like Lake Khasan, Khalkin-Gol, or the Winter War.[31] By November 1939, large mechanised corps were abolished, and tanks were dispersed throughout the army.[32] Both armour and aviation were now reduced to the role of supporting the infantry, which was expected to be the dominant arm

[29] H. B. C. Watkins, 'Only Movement Brings Victory – The Achievements of German Armour', in *Armoured Fighting Vehicles of Germany – World War II*, ed. D. Crow (London, Barrie & Jenkins 1978).

[30] A problem which Tukhachevsky appears to have understood belatedly as in one of his last published papers he stressed deficiencies in all-arms cooperation and insisted that its achievement should be the top priority for Soviet commanders (*Avto-bronetankovyi zhurnal*, no. 8 (1936)).

[31] Glantz, *Soviet Military*, p. 27.

[32] A. Ryzhakov, 'K voprosu o stroitel'stve bronetankovykh voisk Krasnoi Armii v 30-e gody', in *Voenno-istoricheskii zhurnal*, no. 8 (1968), pp. 105–11.

in future battles.[33] Already in the next year the German successes against France made the injudiciousness of this reorganisation clear. In commenting on the battles in France, an article in a leading military publication conceded that '. . . in order to achieve a decisive victory and destroy an enemy army, operations require . . . the cooperation and massive employment in new forms of tanks, motorised infantry, parachutists, and aviation'.[34]

The USSR responded to the *Blitzkrieg* in the West with a crash programme on rehabilitation of mechanised units.[35] But it was too late. The country had paid the economic price of building up a large armoured and mechanised army, only to be deprived of the benefits by the combination of the purges, technological backwardness, conceptual conservatism, and the muddle of a full-fledged reorganisation on the eve of the German onslaught. As one observer later put it '. . . commanders and staffs were not fully familiar with all deep operation theories, and various shortcomings with respect to equipment hindered the application of these theories in any event.'[36]

To a large extent, it is possible to attach personal blame to Stalin for all of the disasters of 1941. But it must be recognised that structural problems within the Soviet army ran very deep at this time. The material and human costs of the inconsistent and inaccurate application of Tukhachevsky's operational art over the course of the 1930s had been dramatic. By 1941, the Soviet army's relationship to its mechanical stocks resembled that of a child in premature possession of a complicated toy.[37] Inevitably, constant breakdowns in Command and Control combined with very poor coordination at all unit levels to plague Soviet efforts to stem the tide of Barbarossa in 1941.[38]

B Operational art and the economic cost of defeat in 1941–2.

Soviet losses in 1941–2 were staggering. More than half of the Soviet troops killed in action in World War II fell in these two years – 27.8 per cent in 1941 and 28.9 per cent in 1942.[39] In the first five months of the war

---

[33] I. Begerchuk, 'Vzaimodeistvie pekhoti, tankov i artillerii v nastupatel'nom boi', in *Avto-bronetankovyi zhurnal*, no. 7 (1939).

[34] A. Konenko, 'Boi v Flandrii', in *Voenno-istoricheskii zhurnal*, no. 3 (1941), p. 25.

[35] Ryzhakov, 'K voprosu', M. V. Zakharov *et al.*, *50 let vooruzhennykh sil SSSR* (Moscow, Voenizdat 1968), pp. 235–8.

[36] Kulakov, 'Operativnoe iskusstvo', p. 55.

[37] D. M. Glantz, 'Toward Deep Battle: The Soviet Conduct of Operational Manoeuvre', in *Transformation in Russian and Soviet Military History*, ed. Col. C. W. Reddel (Washington DC, USAF Academy 1990), p. 184.

[38] The battle around Smolensk was a particularly clear case of this. See, e.g., I. Kh. Bagramian (ed.), *Istoriia voin i voennogo iskusstva* (Moscow, Voenizdat 1970), pp. 144–5.

[39] G. F. Krivosheev, 'V pervykh strazheniiakh', in *Voenno-istoricheskii zhurnal*, no. 2 (1991), pp. 10–16.

alone the USSR lost an estimated 17,500 of its 24,000 tanks.[40] Meanwhile, territorial losses deprived the nation of a significant part of its war potential. While the army swelled to 10.9 million people by 1942, the non-military workforce that supplied them dropped from 66 million in 1940 to just 33.5 million in 1942.[41] Despite the wholesale mobilisation of adolescents into factory jobs, the workforce in the industrial sector shrank from 11 million to 7.2 million over the same period.[42] Adolescents and women were rushed in to replace the male workers siphoned away by conscription.[43] But disorganisation of production was pandemic as enterprises struggled to integrate so many new, untrained hands. The much ballyhooed evacuation of factories to the east did not simplify the economic landscape. The evacuation was unplanned, at best. 2,593 enterprises were relocated to Central Asia, the Urals, and points beyond, 5.9 million workers going with them.[44]

Structural flaws in the Soviet Army clearly contributed to the early defeats, and the correction of these flaws would drive the price tag of the defeats up even higher. With respect to Soviet command and control in particular, the disastrous summer of 1941 revealed critical shortcomings that are traceable to the political and intellectual effects of the purges. Commanders were unaware of the ways in which they might employ their forces, or at least reluctant to use them otherwise than in strict adherence to the 1939 field regulations. The 1939 regulations advocated, for example, the assignment of tanks to infantry close support missions. This explains why Soviet tanks began the war so heavily supplied with high-explosive shells (for use against soft targets) and so under-supplied with armour-piercing shells(with which to fight German armour). Meanwhile, command and logistic chains broke down chronically, thanks to the shortage of communication and transport equipment.[45]

In response to these problems the Soviets reorganised their armoured

[40] J. Millsom, *Russian Tanks – 1900–1979* (London, Arms & Armour Press, Lionel Leventhal Ltd. 1970), p. 61.

[41] M. Harrison, *Soviet Planning in War and Peace* (London, Cambridge University Press 1985), p. 162.

[42] A. V. Mitrofanova, *Rabochii klass SSSR v gody velikoi otechestvennoi voiny* (Moscow, Nauka 1971), pp. 182, 439–4.

[43] In industry the percentage of women employed rose from 41 per cent in 1940 to 53 per cent in 1943. The ascendance of women in the labour force was most pronounced in the *sovkhozy*, where 61 per cent of the employees were women in 1943, as compared to just 34 per cent in 1940. Mitrofanova, *Rabochii klass*, p. 445.

[44] S. K. Kerimbaev, *Sovetskii Kirgizistan v velikoi otechestvennoi voiny (1941–1942 gg)* (Frunze, Illim 1980). *Istoriia velikoi otechestvennoi voiny Sovetskogo Soiuza 1941–1945 gg* (Moscow IVOVSS 1965), vol. II, p. 498.

[45] A. Begishev, 'Primenenie tankov dlia neposredstvennoi podderzhki pekhoty v nastupatel'nykh operatsiiakh velikoi otechestvennoi voiny', in *Voenno-istoricheskii zhurnal*, no. 6 (1962).

units in the autumn of 1941. In essence, they returned to the old-style, tank-heavy units. The process was nearly complete by December 1941, when the army had in the field 7 tank divisions (quite understrength), 79 tank brigades, and 100 tank battalions.[46] The new structure helped the Soviets to win important actions around Rostov and Moscow in late 1941. But the units took heavy losses, usually because of a lack of support from other units and deficient logistics. Further, the reorganisation of the armoured units did not cure Soviet tactical commanders of the habit of dispersing their tanks among infantry units:

> Tank brigades and separate tank battalions . . . were often employed in small groups and uniformly distributed among rifle regiments and divisions . . . During the Moscow counter offensive, all 50 tanks supporting the 33rd Army on the Western Front were equally allocated to the five rifle divisions. The divisional commanders then redistributed these tanks to their front-line regiments. As a result, tank density was only three per kilometre of front . . .[47]

The reorganised formations proved unable to transform tactical successes into larger victories. Firepower was too limited, and logistics were too weak, to permit deep operations. The Soviets' failure to exploit breakthroughs was particularly glaring during the Moscow counter-offensive in the winter of 1941–2 and the Kharkov offensive in May of 1942.[48] Despite all the lessons learned at such cost, more than 60 per cent of the armour was allocated piecemeal to the rifle units in this period.[49] Not surprisingly, in mobile operations old-fashioned cavalry units remained quite important to the Soviets well into 1942. By December 1941 the army had formed 80 cavalry divisions.[50]

The armoured units' consistently inferior performance in offensive operations soon prompted a further reorganisation, involving the formation of larger, more complex units. This reorganisation began at the brigade level in May–June 1942, expanded to the division level by July, and led to the creation of large tank and combined armies during the last quarter of the year. However, thanks in part to the continuous loss of experienced commanders, and in part to the dislocations consequent to the reorganisation process itself, the goal of concentrating the armoured forces in battlefield situations remained elusive. Tanks continued to be doled out to the infantry for close support.[51]

[46] I. V. Pavlovskii, *Sukhoputnye voiska SSSR* (Moscow, Voenizdat 1985), pp. 108–10.
[47] Begishev, 'Primenenie tankov'.
[48] I. Kh. Bagramian, *Tak nachinalas' voina* (Moscow, Voenizdat 1975), pp. 433–69. F. Tamanov, 'Primenenie bronetankovykh voisk v bitve pod Moskvoi', in *Voenno-istoricheskoi zhurnal*, no. 1 (1967), pp. 14–23.
[49] Begishev, 'Primenenie tankov'.   [50] Zakharov *et al.*, *50 let*, pp. 269–71.
[51] Begishev, 'Primenenie tankov'. Figures for tank densities slightly different from Begishev's appear in A. I. Radzievskii, *Tankovyi udar* (Moscow, Voenizdat 1977), p. 40.

Although the recurring reorganisations of mechanised units helped the Soviets to achieve some limited successes in offensive operations, they were not sufficient to repair the unfavourable ratio of Soviet to German losses in armour. The Soviets continued to take heavy losses despite the technological superiority of their tanks to the Germans'. Until the introduction of the Panther tank in June 1943, the German tanks were both outgunned and underarmoured in comparison to their Soviet opponents.[52] The Germans achieved a decisive tactical superiority through clever manoeuvring, engineer warfare, and a thorough commitment to anti-tank artillery (especially the assignment of the notorious 88 mm anti-aircraft guns to anti-tank duty).

Under tremendous strain to replace the huge losses of armour, Soviet industry registered remarkable achievements. Various simplifications – including, for instance, foregoing the rubber rims on tank wheels – enabled the factories to speed up production. In 1942 they turned out 12,553 T-34s, as compared to just 1,886 during the last six months of 1941.[53] Automobile factories were easily converted to produce large numbers of light tanks. 6,000 T-60s came out in 1942, and more than 8,000 T-70s from early 1942 to autumn 1943.[54] Not only did these figures represent a remarkable success in the face of terrible difficulties, but they dwarfed the contemporary German production effort. The two German tanks capable of challenging the T-34, the Pz IV and the models of the Pz III equipped with the 50mm/L60 gun, appeared in much smaller numbers: 480 of the former and 40 of the latter in 1941, 964 and 1,907 in 1942.[55]

In retrospect, it was less the case that Operational Art had undergone a process of adaptation to the economic consequences of defeat than that the economy had had to adapt to an Operational Art generated by a defensive posture. The human and material losses of 1941–2 had not pushed Soviet planners to a policy oriented towards quality. Employment of men and weapons *en masse* was the keyword, as it had been before 1941.

C Operational art and the cost of victory

The building of balanced, large-scale Soviet forces began before the victory at Stalingrad, as early as September 1942. At that time, new

---

[52] The German Pz IV tank did not begin to receive the 'long' 75 mm gun until the spring of 1942, meaning that the Germans generally had to rely on the Pz III's 50 mm gun – more or less the equivalent of the 45 mm weapon of the much more numerous Soviet BT5/7 and T-26 light tanks. The Germans' old Pz II with its 20 mm gun and the Czech tanks with their 37 mm cannon were helpless against the Soviets' T-34 and KV-1 tanks.
[53] S. Zaloga and J. Grandsen, *T34 in Action* (Carrollton, Tx., Squadron/Signal Publications 1981), pp. 13–17.   [54] Milsom, *Russian Tanks*, pp. 93–5.
[55] W. J. Spielberger, 'Panzerkampfwagen III', and 'Panzerkampfwagen IV', in *Armoured Fighting Vehicles*, ed. Crow, pp. 37, 76.

mechanised corps, with a mix of motorised infantry, artillery, and tanks, were created. At full strength, these corps contained 13,600 men and 175 tanks. Twenty-four tank corps and eight mechanised corps were in the field by the end of 1942, in addition to two full tank armies.[56] These units were able to deploy powerful concentrations of artillery and tanks – from 30-40 guns and mortars, and 10-14 tanks per kilometre of front at the close of 1942.

Despite their firepower, the new mechanised corps continued to struggle to exploit breakthroughs achieved in offensive operations. Technological shortcomings accounted for some of the difficulties. The Soviets did not have true infantry combat vehicles, like the American and German halftracks. Nor did their tank forces have enough radios – clearly a result of the unbalanced development before the war. The Soviets' weak communications exacerbated their command and control problems, which in turn allowed the German forces to deal separately with isolated columns. Even the Soviets' conceptual innovation of assigning specific rifle divisions with special equipment to support tank corps on the offensive (that is, kind of operational manoeuvre group) failed to live up to its promise because of weak inter-unit coordination.[57]

These disappointments on the battlefield prompted the Soviets to enlarge and diversify their mechanised formations yet again, this time with more success, in 1943 and 1944. More tank armies were created, and all mechanised forces received additional complements of the valuable supports units (such as engineers, communications, bridging, special weapons, etc.). By 1944, tank corps (with 12,000 men and 228 tanks) and mechanised corps (16,300 men and 183 tanks) made up the backbone of the army's striking forces.[58] These units attained formidable densities of weapons during offensive operations: up to 250 guns plus 70–80 tanks and self-propelled guns per kilometre of front.[59]

The tremendous success of the summer offensive of 1944 (Operation Bagration) vindicated the 1943–4 composition of mechanised formations and testified to the quality of the commanders in the field at this time. The campaign involved the conduct of simultaneous and successive enveloping manoeuvres, which the Soviets executed very well.[60] Indeed, at the level of operational command, Operation Bagration represented a greater achievement than either Kursk or Stalingrad.

---

[56] Radzievskii, *Tankovyi udar*, p. 24.
[57] *Sbornik materialov po izucheniiu opyta voiny*, no. 8 (August–October 1943), (Moscow 1943). A. V. Kuzmin and I. I. Krasov, *Kantemirovsty: boevoi put' gvardeiskogo tankogo Kantemirovskogo ordena Lenina krasnoznamennogo korpusa* (Moscow, Voenizdat 1971), pp. 50–60. [58] Radzievskii, *Tankovy udar*.
[59] I. Kh. Bagramian, *Istoriia voin*, p. 418.
[60] For which, see, A. M. Samsonov (ed.), *Osvobozhdenie Belorussii 1944* (Moscow, Voenizdat 1974).

Quite apart from the ongoing reorganisations of the large mechanised units which we have followed up to this point, the Soviets were also making significant modifications at the tactical level. In essence, these modifications proceeded along one line of evolution: as manpower resources shrank, firepower increased. The weight of a full artillery salvo of a rifle division strikingly illustrates this evolution. Whereas in July 1941 the weight of such a salvo was 548 kg, it rose to 1,086 kg just one year later, and reached 2,040 kg by war's end – almost a fourfold increase in just four years.[61]

So long as the army remained on the strategic defensive, bolstering the infantry units' firepower remained relatively inexpensive, and required no industrial re-tooling. The army simply relied on growing numbers of easily produced smoothbored mortars (which represented 57.6 per cent of a rifle division's firepower in July 1942, up from 36.5 per cent a year earlier).[62] However, while these inexpensive weapons were excellent for defensive support, they were far less effective in supporting units moving forward. After the Soviets grasped the strategic initiative in 1943 their successes owed much to their factories' ability to produce large numbers of more technologically complex guns, like the 122 mm field guns and 152 mm howitzers. Meanwhile, not only did the factories have to produce larger numbers of shells, but these munitions had to be transported farther to the west as the front shifted. This put a tremendous strain on fuel supplies. The 1st Tank Army, for example, used 2,961 tons of fuel in the Belgorod-Kharkov operation in 1943, but 5,045 tons in the L'vov-Sandomir operation a little over a year later.

Despite the tremendous cost, therefore, the fuel, the shells, the artillery pieces, and the tanks did get to the front. And the *matériel* did enable the army to string together an almost uninterrupted sequence of victories over the last two years of the war. But a close view of the war at the tactical levels reveals that these operational and strategic-level victories usually came through a costly succession of micro-defeats. On average, Soviet tank armies lost 5.3 per cent of their tanks and self-propelled guns on each day of offensive operations. Even considering that two-thirds of this equipment was salvaged in repairable condition, the losses were extremely heavy. Over time, the percentage of armour lost per campaign shrank somewhat.[63] But the reduction in

---

[61] C. N. Donnelly, 'The Soviet Use of Military History for Operational Analysis: Establishing the Parameters of the Concept of Force Sustainability', in *Transformations in Russian*, ed. Reddell, pp. 248–9.   [62] Donnelly, 'The Soviet Use', p. 258, table 9.

[63] Whereas in 1943 the 1st, 2nd, and 4th Tank Armies lost (permanently) about 40 per cent during the Belgorod-Kharkov and Orel operations, the 2nd, 3rd, and 4th Tank Armies lost just 15 per cent during the Vistula-Oder advance in 1945 (Donnelly, 'The Soviet Use', pp. 264–5, tables 16, 17).

percentage of losses was more the result of a massive increase of initial forces than of improved tactical competitiveness. Even towards the end of the war the Soviets suffered colossal casualties. The 5th Tank Army lost 72 per cent of its armour in just 25 days in the East Prussia operation.[64] Human casualties declined somewhat for two years after 1942, but they reached a crescendo in 1945 – according to official statistics 22.7 per cent of the battle casualties came in the last four months of fighting.[65]

The Soviets' persistently high losses in men and *matériel* testify to the fact that their operational art did not reach maturity during the Second World War. While the organisation and armament of their units improved, command and control continued to be their weak link. Means of communication were still inadequate and primitive, especially at the tactical level. Inevitably, therefore, tank units and other support formations did not combine together harmoniously:

> It proved to be very difficult to assign tank units revised tasks during the course of a battle. Tank brigades and regiments were either completely unable to rejoin their corps, or did so only after two or three days' delay, thus greatly reducing [the corps'] effectiveness.[66]

Already by 1943 the Soviets' superiority in *matériel* allowed them to sustain offensive operations despite the discoordination of their units. They applied their massive superiorities not in ways that would reduce losses, but rather in ways that increased the tempo of their attacks. Even the deep and highly mobile operations of 1944 and 1945 usually amounted to a kind of attrition warfare carried on at an accelerated tempo.

The consequences for the labour-deprived economy are obvious. Mass production was at a premium. Women, the young, the old, and the disabled had to carry the labour load.[67] Production processes had to be simplified, and innovations in weapons design foregone. In turn, this technological climate found reflection on the battlefield. If the USSR's tanks began the war with an edge in both armour and firepower, they lost this edge by 1943, never to regain it.[68] The Soviet Air Force achieved a kind of parity by 1943, but only by specialising in close support capabilities and accepting severe penalties in radius of action and armaments. The Soviets could achieve local air superiority, but only at a terrible cost. The Soviet Air Force was not equipped to strike at the

---

[64] Donnelly, 'The Soviet Use', pp. 264–5, tables 16, 17.
[65] Krivosheev, 'V pervykh', p. 13.   [66] Begishev, 'Primenenie tankov'.
[67] Sapir, 'Le système économique', pp. 280–2.
[68] Even the impressive JS-II with its 122 mm gun was less effective than the German King Tiger, whose long 88 mm gun had superior armour-piercing capability.

logistical system of the German war machine. Both in the Army and the Air Force, therefore, the slogan 'everything for the front' had to be taken at face value. The USSR focused its entire war effort on achieving superiority along the narrow strip of the front line.

D Soviet operational art in perspective

Viewing the pre-war and war periods as a whole, it is very difficult to arrive at a final assessment of the influence of Soviet operational art on the nation's economic development and the army's ability to wage war. It would certainly be a mistake to deride Soviet military thinking in its entirety on account of the Red Army's poor showing in the Winter War and the initial phase of the struggle against Germany. So too would it be improper to exaggerate the conceptual achievements of Tukhachevsky and his fellow officers by assigning all the blame for the defeats to a leader, Stalin, who had by the second half of the 1930s clearly become a pathological case. It is beyond doubt that the concept of deep operations as imagined first by Varfolomeev and Triandafilov was an outstanding one, and that its refinement by the Soviet general staff was very thorough and adroit. But this does not mean that its adoption was a realistic proposition for the USSR. As we shall now see, the brilliance of Tukhachevsky's exposition camouflaged some troublesome questions arising from the concept of deep operations.[69]

To begin with, we should consider the issue of the mobility of the Red Army relative to its prospective Western opponents. In deep operations battles the attacker must maintain an advantage in mobility for the duration of the campaign, and the logistical nightmare of supplying the spearhead formations during such a campaign compounds the difficulty. It was not sensible for Soviet generals in the 1920s and 1930s to presume either that the Red Army could soon surpass a developed Western nation's army in mobility or that they would soon develop the requisite resupply capacities. It should have been clear from the outset, in the early 1930s, that the Red Army could not count on the rail network during offensive breakthrough operations, and would need a huge fleet of trucks for resupplying spearheads. But nothing was done to prepare for this. Deep penetrations became possible only in 1944, thanks to the availability of US-made trucks.[70]

---

[69] In fairness one must take into account a recent work of two Russian historians indicating that, by 1936, Tukhachevsky was having second thoughts about the Red Army's ability to crush a Western army in a lightning strike (V. Rapoport and Iu. Alekseev, *High Treason – Essays on the History of the Red Army, 1918–1938* (Durham, NC, Duke University Press 1985)).

[70] Tailoring the first-echelon units in such a way as to limit the logistical drain was an option the Soviets employed in the 1945 Manchurian campaign. What made this possible, however, was the Japanese weakness in armour and anti-tank guns.

Secondly, the Soviet proponents of deep operations did not fully appreciate the importance of command and control. The combined use of tanks, mechanised infantry, cavalry, long-range artillery, and ground-support aviation demands efficient and secure communications. It also demands that tactical commanders exercise virtually complete autonomy. As Martin van Creveld put it in his study of war: 'The critical importance of command in armoured warfare cannot be exaggerated, and is equalled only by the lack of systematic attention paid to it by most military historians'.[71]

Rigidities in troop control, linked to both the institutional character of the Stalinist regime and the low level of education and training of a draft army (compounded by the lack of a professional NCO corps) certainly threatened to undermine the application of the deep operations concept.[72] So did the underdevelopment of means of transport and communications, which was a consequence of industrial priorities.

Thus Svechin was right: the fateful choice of 1930 to embrace the deep operations concept was militarily unsound. But was it not economically unsound as well, as Mekhonochin argued? If the Soviet Army had no other option when waging offensive operations than to fight a succession of breakthrough battles, then it could never hope to win a major war quickly and easily. The USSR would have to rely on the mobilisational capacity of its economy, not on its standing army. In the sequel, the massive build-up of mechanised forces imposed a considerable burden on the quickly-developing, fragile industrial sector, leading to serious imbalances. The build-up also produced a false sense of security, as well as social tensions (both inside and outside the military establishment) that were instrumental in the pathological development of the purges. One can only wonder whether, if Stalin and his military associates (Voroshilov, Timoshenko) had understood that the stockpiling and parading of weapons was not giving them military superiority in Europe, they would have dared to emasculate the Red Army as they did. But, in military as well as economic affairs, Stalinist culture was prone to a kind of 'fetishism of capital'.[73]

However, no critical assessment of Tukhachevsky's doctrine can remove from Stalin's shoulders the lion's share of the responsibility for the disaster of 1941–2. Stalin was, ultimately, the one who took the decision to destroy his own armed forces, and who believed blindly in Hitler's promises. The painful process of reorganising the armed forces

[71] M. van Creveld, *Command in War* (Cambridge, Mass., Harvard University Press 1985), pp. 193–4.
[72] On the pervasiveness of these problems for the Soviet Army during the 1970s and 1980s, see Sapir, *The Soviet Military*.
[73] B. Chavance, *Le Capital Socialiste – Histoire critique de l'économie politique du socialisme* (Paris, Le Sycomore 1980).

during the war proved that the mistaken programmes of the 1930s were correctable. Until the purges, the intellectual process in the armed forces remained vital. Without Stalin's terror, corrections, adjustments, and innovations would have been possible before it was too late.

When viewed in the Soviet mirror, Germany's operational art – the famous *Blitzkrieg* – reveals some interesting comparisons and contrasts. That German officers had mastered the tactical and operational implications of mobile, mechanised warfare is clear. That the German military attained a balanced array of forces (including the mechanisation of arms slated to support the tank units) and that they had devoted an appropriate amount of attention to problems of command and control in this style of warfare is equally clear.[74] But, for all its successes, the *Blitzkrieg* doctrine was doomed from the outset. As M. Geyer demonstrated, operational and tactical innovation replaced strategic thinking in Germany: German officers knew how to fight battles, but they did not understand how to wage a long-term war. This lacuna can be linked to the very nature of the Nazi system, for which '. . . war was war for the sake of social reconstruction through the destruction of conquered societies', and in which officers competed with each other in arriving at ever more daring campaign plans. In this atmosphere coherent strategic thinking disappeared, and strategic planning collapsed.[75] Eventually, and inevitably, the result was a deep contradiction between the military doctrine and the nation's economic capabilities. Until 1942 Nazi leaders resisted any true economic mobilisation despite engaging in strategic gambles on a scale that would have overwhelmed even a fully mobilised German economy. It is therefore no surprise that officers and officials in charge of strategic planning were as disdainful of their Nazi masters as they were admiring of Soviet planning.[76] Such were the differences between pathological interference (as in the USSR) and a process pathological from the outset.

II. From a 'mobilisation economy' to war economics

A The evolution of Soviet planning in a comparative perspective

Protracted wars have a tremendous impact upon economies. Not only do military operations exert a constant pressure for more men and equipment, but the economy as a whole has to be reorganised. The potential of any economy in a wartime setting is not a simple derivative of its peacetime wealth. It depends on the ability to resolve or surmount

---

[74] R. Simpkin, *Tank Warfare* (London, Brassey's Publishers 1979), pp. 38–48.
[75] M. Geyer, 'German Strategy', pp. 566, 575, 587.
[76] B. Carroll, *Design for Total War: Arms and Economics in the Third Reich* (The Hague, Mouton 1968).

the administrative frictions and social tensions that conversion to a war footing generates.[77] Even for countries not dedicated to a vision of war as apocalyptic as that of Nazi Germany, major armed conflict spurs economic and social transformations to a point which affects economic and social dynamics themselves. As far as the economy of Stalin's USSR is concerned, two different questions arise regarding the shift to a war economy. First – with respect to a topic we have already begun to explore – what transformations did Soviet operational art generate in the economy? Secondly, how did these transformations fit the specificities of the Soviet economic system, which has been described as a kind of 'mobilisation economy' on the same lines as the 'mobilisation state' concept D. Okimoto uses to describe present-day Japan.[78]

To begin with, we should point out that the term 'mobilisation' does not necessarily imply any kind of militarisation, but rather describes the directing of economic potential by institutional means.[79] Having said that, however, it must be conceded that the similarities between Soviet planning and the management of a war economy were numerous.[80] Indeed, Soviet-type economies in the USSR and Eastern Europe experienced a dynamic of economic fluctuations in the 1950s and 1960s that was extremely close to the kind of economic cycle Germany knew in the period 1916–18.[81] O. Lange has gone so far as to call the Soviet economy a war economy *sui generis*.[82]

But the Soviet system, if clearly linked to war economies, was not strictly speaking an economy geared to war. The development of a large

[77] A. S. Milward, *War, Economy, and Society 1939–1945* (Berkeley, California University Press 1977), chap. 2; K. Knorr, *The War Potential of Nations* (Princeton, NJ, Princeton University Press 1956).

[78] Sapir, *L'économie mobilisée – Essai sur les économies de type soviétique* (Paris, La Decouverte 1990); D. I. Okimoto, T. Sugano, and F. B. Weinstein, *Competitive Edge* (Stanford, CA, Stanford University Press 1984), p. 48.

[79] Thus the concept of a 'mobilisation economy' is not far removed from the 'growth oriented statehood' concept by which Hungarian sociologists characterise Soviet-type societies. Each term provides a useful framework for understanding economic institutions that give birth to a seller's market and a shortage economy, both of which are well-documented characteristics of Soviet-type economies. G. Szoboszlai, 'Bureaucracy and Social Controls', in *Politics and Public Administration in Hungary*, ed. G. Szoboszlai (Budapest, Akademiai Kiado 1985), pp. 16–164.

[80] Many authors have perceived as much. See, e.g. V. I. Lenine, 'Sur l'Infantilisme de Gauche', in *Oeuvres Complètes*, ed. V. I. Lenine (Moscow, Editions du Progrès 1971), vol. 27, p. 354; and W. Rathenau, *La Mécanisation du Monde* (Paris, Aubier-Montaigne 1972), pp. 34, 77.

[81] G. D. Feldman, *Army, Industry, and Labor in Germany: 1914–1918* (Princeton, NJ, Princeton University Press 1966); J. Sapir, 'Rythmes d'Accumulation et Modes de Regulation de l'Economie Soviétique – Essai d'interpretation des cycles d'investissement et de main d'oeuvre en URSS de 1941 a nos jours', PhD (these d'Etat), Université, de Paris-Nanterre, 1986, 3 vol., vol. I, pp. 97–111.

[82] O. Lange, 'The Role of Planning in a Socialist Economy', in *Papers in Economics and Sociology* (Warsaw and London 1970), pp. 101–2.

military-industrial sector was, to repeat, the product of political choice and not of systemic necessity. As far as the Soviet military-industrial sector is concerned, three kinds of legacy can be traced. A growth path had its share, generating a very peculiar economic situation indeed. But military policy, or what the Soviets call 'construction of the armed forces' ('stroitel'stvo vooruzhennykh sil'), was also at the heart of what we can now call military irreversibilities. Then the institutional framework which was both designed to cope with and was the product of the deep turmoil of those fateful years was generating its own long-ranging effects. The decision-making process was largely shaped by institutional networks built during the 1930s.[83] Soviet military doctrine under Tukhachevsky was committed, as we have seen, to manoeuvre and attack. But this commitment demanded a tremendous upsurge in arms production.[84] That it was achieved is beyond doubt.[85] However, this achievement has to be put in the perspective of the general upsurge of industrial production that took place in the wake of the First Five-Year Plan.[86]

The traditional Soviet view of the connection between economic growth and military potential focuses upon aggregate indicators of specific items like steel, fuel, or electricity outputs.[87] The 1930s could then be seen as a time when the roots of military power and potential were laid. But the 'big turn' brought more than an invaluable industrial upsurge.[88] It also induced a switch to a new style of economy, the so-called shortage economy.[89]

The model of the shortage economy implies a self-induced shortage situation generated by soft budget constraints, disorganisation of logistical links, automatic selling rules, and the systematic employment of a priority system. The economic turmoil and supply disruptions prevalent in the 1930s only exacerbated the shortage situation. At the microeconomic level, managers responded by setting up a semi-closed system: they discouraged interference from above, withheld informa-

[83] See J. F. Hough, 'The Historical Legacy in Soviet Weapons Development', in *Soviet Decision-Making for National Security*, eds. J. Valenta and W. Potter (London, Allen and Unwin 1984), pp. 87–115.

[84] *Voprosy strategii i operativnogo iskusstva v sovetskikh voennykh trudakh* (Moscow, Voenizdat 1965), pp. 14–17. See also S. A. Tiushkevich et al., *Sovetskie vooruzhennye sily – istoriia stroitel'stva*, Moscow, Voenizdat, vol I, chap. 6.

[85] J. Cooper, 'Defence Production and the Soviet Economy, 1929–1941', CREES Discussion Paper, University of Birmingham, 1976.

[86] Sapir, *The Soviet Military*, pp. 227–31.

[87] See A. I. Pozharov, *Ekonomicheskie osnovy oboronnogo mogushchestva sotsialisticheskogo gosudarstva* (Moscow, Voenizdat 1981), pp. 91–104.

[88] The value of which is beyond doubt. See J. Sapir, *Les fluctuations économiques*, chap. 2.

[89] For a theoretical discussion, see C. Davis and W. Charemza (eds.), *Models of Disequilibrium and Shortage in Centrally Planned Economies* (London, Chapman and Hall 1989). With respect to discussion on the shift, see Sapir, *L'économie mobilisée*.

tion, and adopted a very conservative approach to innovation.[90] This kind of economic behaviour has survived until the present day.

Obviously the priority system helped the military-industrial sector. However, as C. Davis has pointed out, the very scale of military output induces such a demand that even a very potent priority system is unable to cope with it.[91] In the event, priorities did not bring a golden age for the defence industry, but they did create a real gap in some civilian sectors, related to weapon production. Enterprises 'internalised'[92] on a massive scale, leading to severe problems when times were ripe for a mobilisation of civilian potential.[93]

The Soviet growth path cannot, however, be described simply as one of shortages and priorities. Very serious interbranch imbalances had been developing for a while. The chemical industry was underdeveloped, as was non-ferrous metallurgy. Even within high-priority sectors like ferrous metallurgy, the emphasis was more on the quantity of the output than on quality.[94] The Soviet defence industry had no choice but to use low-grade components, and was engaged in forced substitution to make good shortages of some basic components (an imbalance that persists today).[95] Last but not least, and a further legacy of the 1930s, as a consequence of both shortage economics (internalisation and conservative innovation) and interbranch imbalances, a very specific technological culture blossomed in the Soviet defence sector.

A technological culture describes the way designers try to solve problems related to technical specifications on the one hand, and economic and technological constraints on the other hand. It is linked to the operation of a factory as a place where informal knowledge is both accumulated and shared, giving birth to a kind of collective knowledge.[96] The plant acts here as a semi-closed system processing information from the outside world. Thanks to the complexity of some technical

[90] P. Hare, 'The Economics of Shortage in the Centrally Planned Economies', in *Models of Disequilibrium* eds. Davis and Charemza, p. 61.

[91] C. Davis, 'Interdependence of the Defense and Civilian Sectors in the Contemporary Soviet Economy: Concepts, Problems, and Reform', paper presented at the AAASS Convention, Chicago, November 1990, pp. 25–7.

[92] 'Internalisation' signifies the striving of a given organisation, be it an enterprise or a production ministry, to produce whatever it needs – by its own means and at any cost – rather than relying on procurements through other organisations.

[93] N. E. Nosovskii, 'Nadezhnyi arsenal vooruzheniia', in *Voprosy istorii*, no. 11 (1970), p. 125.

[94] On interbranch imbalances, see E. Zaleski, *Stalinist Planning and Economic Growth, 1933–1952* (Chapel Hill, NC, University of North Carolina Press 1980).

[95] Many memoir accounts develop this point. See, for instance, I. M. Danishevskii (ed.), *Byli industrial'nye (ocherki i vospominaniia* (Moscow, Politizdat, 2nd edn, 1973); M. M. Lobanov, *My – voennye inzhenery* (Moscow, Voenizdat 1977); V. Emelianov, *O vremeni, o tovarishchakh, o sebe* (Moscow, Sovetskaia Rossiia, 2nd edn, 1974).

[96] D. C. Mowery, 'Economic Theory and Government Technology Policy', in *Policy Sciences*, no. 1 (1983), pp. 27–33.

information, which prevents price mechanisms from functioning freely, this process is not specific to a planned economy, but is general to industrial production.[97] Nonetheless, constraints specific to a Soviet-type economy gave the technological culture a greater role than in a market economy.

In effect, technological culture is very often nothing other than bitter memories of previous failures, frozen into a way of thinking which affects people working in design offices.[98] In the USSR, this technological culture settled for:

- clever use of low-grade components;
- emphasis on immediate as opposed to sustained performance;
- cutting corners to cope with the burdens induced by low-grade components;
- achieving reliability by redundancy of systems and not redundancy within the system (i.e., producing a multiplicity of relatively simple but complementary weapons systems in place of a small number of versatile – but complex and expensive – systems).

The notion of a technological culture raises the issue of the comparability of the Soviet and the Nazi economies in conceptual terms. One long-established line of argument begins with the assertion that political will replaced or overrode economics in both countries.[99] The volitional dimension was so central, continues the argument, that it transcended the differences between the two nations and rendered two inherently similar economies. According to another old school of thought, on the other hand, the visible hand of Soviet planning made their economy fundamentally distinct from the chaotic Nazi economy.[100] Recent scholarship has substantially diluted the persuasiveness of this view – it is now clear that Soviet planning amounted more to a system of priorities (with frequent conflicts) than to true

[97] J. L. Gaffard, *Economie industrielle et de l'information* (Paris, Dalloz 1990); B. J. Loasby, *Choice, Complexity, and Ignorance. An Inquiry into Economic Theory and the Practice of Decision-Making* (Cambridge, Cambridge University Press 1976); E. Penrose, *The Growth of the Firm* (Oxford, Basil Blackwell 1968).

[98] J. Sapir, *La culture technologique: le cas des matériels militaires soviétiques*, Cahier de recherche no. 3 – Analyse des choix technologiques, Université de Technologie de Compiègne, 1990.

[99] K. Korsch, P. Mattick, A. Pannekoek, O. Ruhle, and H. Wagner, *La Contre Revolution Bureaucratique*, UGE 10/18, Paris, 1973, (papers written between 1934 and 1939); B. Rizzi, *L'URSS, collectivisme bureaucratique* (Paris, Champs Libres 1976) (first published in 1939); R. Hilferding, 'Capitalisme d'Etat ou économie d'état totalitaire', posthumous paper published by *La Révue Internationale*, no. 18 (Octobre 1947); O. Nathan, *The Economic System* (Durham, NC, Duke University Press 1944); L. Hamburger, *How Nazi Germany has Controlled Business* (Washington, DC, The Brookings Institution 1943).

[100] F. Neumann, *Behemoth* (New York, Praeger 1944); C. Bettelheim, *L'économie allemande sous le nazisme*, PCM Maspero, 2 vols., Paris 1971, (first published in 1945).

229

planning.[101] In that case, what were the salient similarities between the two economies? Much remains to be learned, clearly, from a comparative study of the two economies.

If we consider the similarities of the technological culture, as we have defined the term, in Nazi Germany and the Soviet Union, we find that price controls and the liberal application of coercion enabled Nazi administrators to achieve comparable results to the state ownership system of the Soviet Union.[102] At the same time, implicit bargaining flourished under the Soviet system, with the proliferation of 'pushers' (*tolkachi*, a position very much akin to the Second World War 'expediter' in the USA), and the multiplication of parallel and overlapping authorities.[103] There was plenty of common ground:

> It is a mistake to think that the Soviets were in control of their economy, while the Nazis were not. Both economies were subject to the confusion that follows from implementing new and untried ideas.[104]

But the differences between the two countries' technological cultures outstripped the similarities. The most glaring contrast was German technology's emphasis on the sophistication and complexity of the product. It is well known that German tanks, planes, and ships tended to be better built and more complex than their Soviet or even British counterparts. However, this sophistication frequently brought with it both a high price tag and unreliability in the field.[105] In the end, Germany was outstripped in production not only by the USSR and the USA, but also by a dwindling industrial power like Great Britain. On a one-to-one basis, German weapons were often (but not always) superior. But the margin of qualitative superiority was never sufficient to compensate for the numerical inferiority.

The strain that numerical inferiority in advanced weapons put on the German armed forces increased over the course of the war. Most of the complex equipment demanded highly trained crews if it was to be used efficiently. While the equipment got more complex over time,

---

[101] J. Millar, 'Soviet Planners in 1936–37', in *Soviet Planning, Essays in Honor of Naum Jasny* eds. J. Degras and A. Nove (Oxford, Basil Blackwell 1964), p. 120.

[102] C. W. Guillebaud, *The Economic Recovery of Germany from 1933 to the Incorporation of Austria in March 1938* (London, Macmillan 1939); P. Hayes, *Industry and Ideology: IG Farben in the Nazi Era* (Cambridge, Cambridge University Press 1987).

[103] Sapir, *Les Fluctuations*.

[104] P. Temin, 'Soviet and Nazi Economic Planning in the 1930s', Working Paper no. 554, Department of Economics, MIT, Cambridge, Mass., May 1990, p. 2.

[105] With respect to cruisers and destroyers, for example, see M. J. Whitley, *German Destroyers of World War Two* (Annapolis, Maryland, Naval Institute Press 1991); and the same author's *German Cruisers of World War Two* (London–New York, Arms and Armour Press 1985).

casualties reduced the qualifications of the personnel. Thus German technological culture proved quite ill-suited to the problem of war production in a protracted conflict. If Soviet technological culture was distorted by an unbalanced and underdeveloped economy, pervasive shortages, and an underqualified work force, German practices hardly evolved more rationally. This was no accident – on the contrary, it says a great deal about the socio-political environment in Nazi Germany. The social disintegration that followed upon Nazi rule created an unruly, competitive environment in the domain of technological culture where every institution was fighting its counterparts. This situation yielded extremely advanced products, just as competition between Nazi commanders yielded some extremely daring and innovative operations on the battlefield. But in military and economic affairs alike, the innovations ran against the grain of the country's strategic requirements.

In retrospect, it seems that Nazi Germany behaved very much like the Soviet Union did under exceptional circumstances, as during the 1936–8 purges. Whereas in the USSR organisational and institutional pathologies were limited to crisis conditions, they were the norm in Germany, swamping what was left of bureaucratic rationality inside economic, administrative, and military establishments.

B Systemic implications of the Soviet Union's productive effort
Given the trying circumstances in which the Soviet economy functioned during the war, the volume of weapons and ammunition output that the industrial sector turned out was truly impressive.[106] Inevitably, however, in straining to provide their armies with the requisite firepower Soviet industry had to drop almost everything not perceived as immediately essential for the front.[107] The weight of machine-building and metalworking production began to dwarf all other branches of industry. In Omsk *oblast'*, for example, machine-building and metalworking accounted for 84.7 per cent of industrial output by 1944, as opposed to 39.6 per cent in 1940.[108] The hyper-intensive channelling of resources into heavy industry during the war raises a very important question for anyone attempting to conceptualise the Soviet economy over the course of the whole Stalin period. How could the economic

---

[106] For instance, the Soviets produced 88,000 tanks from June 1941 to December 1945, as against 23,500 for Germany from 1939 to 1945 (Sapir, 'Le Système économique', p. 287); by 1944 Soviet munitions output was as much as 4.6 times that of 1940 (M. Harrison, 'The Volume of Soviet Munitions Output, 1937–1945: a reevaluation', in *The Journal of Economic History* 50, no. 3 (1990), p. 585, table 7).

[107] Sapir, 'Le Système économique', p. 288; Lobanov, *My – voennye*.

[108] G. A. Dokuchaev, *Sibirskii tyl velikoi otechestvennoi voine* (Novosibirks, Nauka 1968), p. 282.

system created in the 1930s accomplish this without destroying the economic reproduction process? Making weapons requires a steady flow of electricity, metals, and machine-tools. Workers must be fed, even if badly. Increasing production requires building new factories or enlarging old ones, and this demands construction materials. Could the 1930s economy remain recognisable while doing this?

To begin to answer this question, let us consider the implications of a protracted war on a 'mobilised' economy such as the Soviet Union in the pre-war period. In contrast to Western economies, a 'mobilised' economy is already, before any war, stretched to very nearly 100 per cent of its productive capacity. With the war acting to decrease national income and increase military consumption, ever fewer re-sources were available for investment. Investment fell from 19 per cent of the national income in 1940 to 7 per cent in 1943. The war exacerbated the shortages that not only disrupted production (energy shortages stalled production in Frunze *oblast'* for nearly half of the working time in January 1942),[109] but also conditioned the production-limiting micro-economic behaviour discussed above with respect to Soviet technological culture. Furthermore, the manpower losses of 1941 and 1942 deprived Soviet enterprises of reliance on the labour market to overcome shortages of technical and mechanical inputs. Not even the agricultural sector could be raided for workers, so closely did collapse loom there as well. When we add to this mix the imbalances that pre-war Soviet operational art had generated in the military-industrial structure, we see how remarkable were Soviet industry's achievements during the war.

Three factors accounted for these achievements. The first factor was the streamlining of the Soviet weapons inventory. Unlike the other major combatants in the Second World War, including Germany, the USSR virtually abandoned the production of complex naval vessels.[110] With respect to air forces, the Soviets concentrated all of their efforts on short-range, low-altitude fighters and ground-attack planes. The Soviets did not have to expend any resources on heavy bombers, high-altitude interceptors, or night fighters.[111] For the ground forces, the Soviets never introduced armoured troop carriers, and they made do with a much smaller repertoire of self-propelled artillery systems than their German enemy.

Even within the smaller and simpler repertoire of weapons systems they produced, Soviet industry was under such pressure that it could

---

[109] Kerimbaev, *Sovetskii Kirgizistan*, p. 62.

[110] With respect to Soviet warship production in general, see S. S. Berezhnoi, *Korabli i suda VMF SSSR, 1928–1945* (Moscow, Voenizdat 1988).

[111] R. A. Belyakov and J. Marmain, *MIG 1939–1989* (Paris, Editions Lavrière 1991).

not develop all weapons components evenly. We have already noted the paucity of Soviet electronics and communications equipment and pointed to the consequences of this weak link on the battlefield. Anti-aircraft defences suffered for the same reason – the Soviets had developed their first two radar systems before the war, but wartime priorities postponed research and development until after the war.[112] The country had to make do without radar.

The second factor permitting industry to keep pace with the armed forces' tremendous appetite for weapons and munitions was the Lend Lease programme. Aid from the USA and Great Britain made itself felt not so much at the front lines, in the form of tanks, guns, and aeroplanes, as in the rear, where it helped to shore up the gaps in Soviet production. The USA provided over 360,000 trucks, 43,000 jeeps, 2,000 locomotives, and 11,000 railroad cars, as well as supplementary electronic and communication equipment.[113] Lend Lease brought in critical raw materials, industrial equipment, and foodstuff. It is very probable that without Lend Lease, average food consumption for the civilian population would have declined by a third. With Lend Lease curing many of the imbalances produced by the past as well as those arising out of the circumstances of war, Soviet planners were free to focus on arms production without having to fear a possible breakdown of the industrial apparatus.

But the combination of industrial specialisation and Lend Lease was not enough by itself to carry the economy through to victory. The third piece of the puzzle was the application of what, in retrospect, appears to have been a far-reaching, multi-sided economic reform. A range of relaxations were permitted throughout the economy, beginning in 1942. Price mechanisms were allowed to govern a very large portion of retail trade, controls over the agricultural sector receded, and financial policy responded to the emerging reality of market mechanisms within the economic system.[114]

With respect to budgeting, the Soviet government's usual practice both before and after the war was to rely on non-financial means as far as possible. This is not to imply that budgetary flows were mere shadows of physical ones. There was a budgetary policy as well as a monetary policy, even if these were relatively unimportant, and difficult to trace.[115] With the war, and the retreat, some revenues were lost; at

---

[112] M. M. Lobanov, *Razvitie sovetskoi radiolokatsionnoi tekhniki* (Moscow, Voenizdat 1982).
[113] A. C. Sutton, *Western Technology and Soviet Economic Development*, vol. III, 1945–65 (Stanford, CA, Hoover Institution Press 1973), pp. 11–12; and H. P. van Tuyl, *Feeding the Bear* (Westport, Conn., Greenwood Press 1989), table 10, p. 157.
[114] See on this Sapir, 'Le Système économique'.
[115] R. Hutchings, *The Soviet Budget* (London, MacMillan 1983). See also the discussion on the relevance of monetary flows in Sapir, *Les Fluctuations*, chaps. 1, 3.

the same time, expenditures had to grow quickly. The government then had no option but to run a large budget deficit, the amount of which is still a matter of discussion.[116] This deficit was paid for mainly by credit and cash emissions – according to one Soviet source cash increased during the war years by as much as 380 per cent.[117]

The significance of the Soviets' employment of credit and cash emissions during the war is obvious: if planning were to be carried out only on the basis of material balances there would be no point in adopting a kind of Keynesian policy relying on inflation. The role of material balances in Soviet planning receded in favour of increased employment of market mechanisms. It is true, as James Millar has pointed out, that Soviet leaders haltingly and unenthusiastically employed financial instruments in directing the economy.[118] Nonetheless, they had to use them, and in so doing they reversed pre-war trends.[119]

The relaxation of central controls over the economy found further reflection in the distribution of administrative authority in the USSR, with local and regional officials acquiring more autonomy.[120] It is paradoxical, but only superficially so, that a 'mobilisation economy' had to be at least partially 'demobilised' to achieve war mobilisation. This is not to say that the Soviet government did not use direct levers of control during the war. But to be able to concentrate on some tasks like arms production and evacuation, it had to rely on individual initiative and market mechanisms to a greater extent than before the war. By employing economic mechanisms rather than administrative will to rule the system, Soviet leaders gained more freedom to implement economic policies under hard constraints.

In large part, the economic and administrative adjustments of the war anticipated the debate of the 1950s and 1960s on Market Socialism. Indeed, the diffusion of administrative authority prompted much heated discussion in the Soviet Union between 1946 and 1948.[121] But these discussions were short-lived. Already by 1947/48 the monetary reform and a brutal return to Stalinist practices (particularly in Ukraine) reestablished the pre-war state of affairs.[122]

[116] Different estimates can be found in Sapir, 'Le système stalinien', pp. 282–3; and J. Millar, 'Financing the Soviet Effort in World War II', in *The Soviet Economic Experiment* ed. S. J. Linz (Urbana–Chicago, University of Illinois Press 1990), pp. 139–43.
[117] Z. V. Atlas (ed.), *Denezhnoe obrashchenie i kredit SSSR* (Moscow, Gosfinizdat 1957), p. 122; and Sapir, 'Le système stalinien', p. 283.
[118] Millar, 'Financing the Soviet Effort', p. 151.
[119] Millar, 'Financing the Soviet Effort', p. 151.
[120] See especially J. Hough, *The Soviet Prefects. The Local Party Organs in Industrial Decision-Making* (Cambridge, MA, Harvard University Press 1969), p. 218.
[121] Sapir, *Les Fluctuations*, chap. 3.
[122] Sapir, *Les Fluctuations*, chap. 3.

C Adapting to the war in retrospect

Once some steps had been taken toward a partial 'demobilisation' of the system, the Soviet planning system proved its capacities to react and adapt efficiently in the most difficult circumstances. Since a war economy has a two-pronged task, i.e. producing goods where quantities matter more than prices, and at the same time assuring the reproduction of the economic system as a whole, a combination of command and market is the natural solution. This is exactly the road the Soviets took, with considerable help from Lend Lease. Along the way, Soviet planning did not impair the innovation process. The war created a socio-political situation where the combination of incentives and loyalty to a system demonstrating its ability to defend the country enabled innovations to flow and to be controlled. In contrast, in Germany, where competition and institutional infighting escalated because of the social characteristics of the Nazi system, innovation proceeded wildly, sometimes nonsensically (some projects were pure science fiction or obviously technologically unsound), and could never be placed in a strategic perspective.

Facing both human and material resource constraints, the Soviet leadership chose to maintain a maximum volume of production throughout the war rather than to optimise the quality of weapons systems. Imbalances in the pre-war industrial sector excluded a high-technology approach for the USSR, in contrast to Germany. But, if industrial specialisation and strict control over innovations in order to maximise the volume of production were the only ways to win the war, they were not so easy to implement. The stress on the productive system could have led to an economic collapse but for the adroitness of the partial 'demobilisation' policies and the critical supplies coming in through Lend Lease.

And so the Soviet forces got the weapons and munitions they needed to speed up offensive operations and to defeat the Germans. If the wartime management of the economic system had been less precise, the army would surely have been stuck on the strategic defensive for much longer, probably well into 1944, if not later. But the style of warfare with which the Soviet Army capitalised on its strategic initiative carried its own consequences for the economic system. For reasons we have already detailed, Soviet offensive techniques amounted to mobile attrition warfare. Casualty rates were so enormous as to become a self-reproducing process. Units were decimated before achieving the proficiency that comes with the experience of combat; training was curtailed in the rush to replace losses; equipment had to be tailored for use by inexperienced troops; and commanders were forced to use less sophisticated – and more costly – battlefield tactics.

The vicious circle continued to turn all the way to the end of the war, and it froze industrial and economic imbalances to the point that the Soviets emerged victorious with nearly obsolete military forces. The huge, formidable Soviet armoured forces that rolled into Eastern Europe in 1944–5 epitomised to Western eyes the USSR's military and political power. However, by war's end these forces were unfit to compete with their most likely enemy in the future: the USA, which enjoyed naval, amphibious, and strategic air forces on a massive scale. The Soviets' combination of strengths and weaknesses would do much to shape both Western and Soviet perceptions and misconceptions in the years that followed.

While acknowledging all of the drawbacks to the Soviets' attrition warfare, we must also acknowledge that this warfare did succeed in defeating the German army. As time went by, the German units were increasingly made up of young recruits unable to make the best use of the ever more sophisticated weapons that German industry was providing for them. While her scientists were building the weapons of the next war, Germany's soldiers were overwhelmed on the battlefields of the present war.

10

From 'Great Fatherland War' to the Second World War: new perspectives and future prospects

Mark von Hagen

The history of the Soviet Union in World War II has begun to be transferred from the realm of the regime's ideologues to the domain of professional and amateur historians. The post-Soviet rewriting of the wartime experience is part of a larger international process of reinterpretation that has coincided with the end of the Cold War and the transformation of the power relationships that the post-war settlement had for so long held in place. In the Cold War version that dominated in the 'free world', erstwhile enemies like Germany, Italy, and Japan became allies while recent allies, notably the Soviet Union and China, were refigured as cosmic enemies.[1]

Because of the central place that the wartime victory had occupied in

---

[1] Nearly all the major belligerents wrote their histories of the war to legitimise post-war political settlements. Although the German case received the most attention from the beginning with the victors' prosecution of the Nuremberg Tribunal, after the establishment of the Federal Republic of Germany the *Wehrmacht* and German people were quickly recast as the bulwark of the West against the Soviet-dominated East. Only with the *Historikerstreit* were these chapters of the wartime past reopened for scrutiny. (See the essay by Omer Bartov in this volume.) Japanese history was similarly rewritten to omit the atrocities of the occupation regimes in Asia and the Pacific after the war-crime trials there, with Japan and China eventually changing roles after Mao's triumph in 1949 (Carol Gluck, 'The Past in the Present', in *Postwar Japan as History*, ed. Andrew Gordon, University of California Press 1993). Elsewhere, French historians have been reluctant to treat the Vichy Regime and the subject of collaboration, and even British historians rarely diverge from a highly favourable account of Churchill's leadership and the reaction of the citizenry to the hardships of war. See the controversies provoked by Robert Paxton's *Vichy France* (New York, Knopf 1972) and the film *The Sorrow and the Pity*; and Angus Calder, *The Myth of the Blitz* (London, Jonathan Cape 1991). For those countries that had been occupied by the Axis powers (notably France, China, the German Democratic Republic, and Yugoslavia), the histories of resistance movements that often succeeded to state power became the hegemonic narrative that shaped historians' agendas. See the recent conference, 'Resistance and Collaboration in Europe, 1939–1945: Experience, Memory, Myth, and Appropriation', held at the Institute for Human Sciences, Vienna, 2–5 September 1993.

the Soviet state's legitimating ideology, the version of the war that had been available in monographs and in popular accounts was the story of an heroic and popular struggle waged by a talented military leadership under the guidance of the all-knowing Communist Party. The very fact that Soviet historians wrote not about the Second World War, but about the 'Great Fatherland War', a specifically Soviet war virtually removed from the rest of humanity's experience of that conflict and elevated to mythical status, set the parameters for the largely didactic genre of writing. The general focus of this historiography, narrow and constrained as it was by Party and military censors and self-censors, was to elaborate the 'sources of victory'[2] and thereby to help legitimate various aspects of the Stalinist and, later, post-Stalinist regime. In addition to 'justifying' the Soviet domination of Eastern Europe through the Warsaw Pact and Comecon, among the institutions whose place in the Soviet political order benefited from this prescribed narrative were the armed forces, the military-industrial complex and the Stalinist planned economy generally, and the multinational character of the Soviet state.[3]

As a consequence, for all the considerable literature devoted to the war, including memoirs of the leading participants published during the 1970s and 1980s, crucial questions about the origins and consequences, the impact of the war on politics and society, and the behaviour of both elites and rank-and-file citizenry, were not posed, let alone answered; furthermore, that literature was remarkably void of specific context and of any sense of genuine human agency. Much as the genres of Soviet 'social history' failed to convey anything of the life or politics of the workers, peasants, or intelligentsia who were the ostensible objects of the multi-volume studies, so too the slogan 'spiritual unity of the Soviet people' produced formulaic hagiographies of heroism and highly depersonalised narratives, which most closely resembled the faceless histories of the Communist Party and Soviet Union that were written by collective authors following Khrushchev's denunciations of Stalin in 1956. Only in belles-lettres, theatre and film were human beings depicted with more of their complexities, failings, and virtues. Despite vigilant efforts by the Party ideological watchdogs and the reigning Director of Armed Forces' Political Administration,

---

[2] One of the last contributions to this genre was edited by an erstwhile 'dean' of Soviet study of the war, Georgii Kumanev, *Istochniki pobedy sovetskogo naroda v Velikoi otechestvennoi voine, 1941–1945* (Moscow, Nauka 1985).

[3] These 'postulates' were formulated by Stalin himself immediately after the war. See his speeches collected in *O Velikoi Otechestvennoi voine Sovetskogo Souiza*, 5th edn (Moscow 1946). For a critical analysis of Soviet historiography, see Vasilii Kulish, 'O nekotorykh aktual'nykh problemakh istoriografii Velikoi Otechestvennoi voiny', in *Istoriia i stalinizm* (Moscow, Politizdat 1991), pp. 298–349.

writers, playwrights, and filmmakers occasionally challenged the wooden stereotypes.[4]

During the Khrushchev era, a small space was briefly opened for breaking some of the Stalin-era taboos because Khrushchev himself made Stalin's wartime failures a centrepiece of his campaign of de-Stalinisation. Historians could mention the initial wartime disasters, the devastating impact of the purges on the army's performance, and Stalin's stubborn refusal to believe the steady stream of military intelligence warning him of the imminent German invasion.[5] But even before Khrushchev's ouster, the institutions who felt their interests threatened by the historical revisionism mobilised 'their' historians in defense of orthodoxy; the result was the Nekrich affair. The late Boston-based expatriate Soviet historian Aleksandr Nekrich placed the blame for the unpreparedness squarely on Stalin, but, when the conservative forces reconsolidated their hold over the social sciences shortly after Khrushchev's ouster from power, he was quickly and loudly drummed out of the historical establishment.[6] In the aftermath of the counter-assault by Stalin's defenders, leading Soviet marshals and generals rewrote their memoirs to accommodate the more favourable view of the Generalissimo.[7]

Once again, the bland and faceless formulae of party leadership of the wartime effort replaced historical research that had begun to offer an alternative voice to the Stalin-era orthodoxy; sensitive issues such as wartime collaboration, repatriated prisoners of war, or panic and desertion, rarely made it past the censors and only in the form of fictional accounts.[8] All the while, several long-term trends in Soviet

[4] See Matthew P. Gallagher, *The Soviet History of World War II: Myths, Memories and Realities* (New York, Praeger 1963) for the history of conflicts between writers and military men during the Khrushchev era. See also Graham Lyons, ed., *The Russian Version of the Second World War* (London, Cooper 1976); Andreas Hillgruber and Hans-Adolf Jacobsen, 'Der zweite Weltkrieg im Spiegel der sowjetkommunistischen Geschichtsschreibung (1945–1961)', in B. S. Tel'pukhovskii, *Die sowjetische Geschichte des Grossen Vaterlaendischen Krieges* (Frankfurt, Bernard & Graefe 1961), pp. 13–94.

[5] Interested readers will find very capable summaries of the history of writing about the war in the aforementioned work by Gallagher, in Bernd Bonwetsch, 'Der "Grosse Vaterlaendische Krieg" und seine Geschichte', in *Die Umwertung der sowjetischen Geschichte*, ed. Dietrich Geyer (Goettingen, Vandenhoeck & Ruprecht 1991), pp. 167–87; and in Robert Davies' survey, *Soviet History in the Gorbachev Revolution* (Bloomington and Indianapolis, Indiana University Press 1989), chapter 8.

[6] A. M. Nekrich, *22 iiunia 1941* (Moscow, Nauka 1965); for the critical review that set the tone for all later comments, see G. A. Deborin and Major-General B. S. Tel'pukhovskii, 'V ideinom plenu u fal'sifikatorov istorii', *Voprosy istorii KPSS* 9 (1967), pp. 127–40. For Nekrich's account of the campaign, see his *Forsake Fear: Memoirs of a Historian* (Boston, Unwin Hyman 1991), chapters 7 and 8.

[7] See Seweryn Bialer, *Stalin and His Generals. Soviet Military Memoirs of World War II* (Boulder, Colorado, Westview Press 1984), esp. pp. 15–44.

[8] See Ales' Adamovich, *Voina i derevnia v sovremennoi literature* (Minsk, Nauka i tekhnika 1982) for an analysis of Soviet writers' use of the settings of wartime and the countryside

society prepared the way for a decisive break with the orthodox narrative of the war, including the unpopular and unwinnable Afghan war, the emergence of an anti-nuclear and disarmament movement, the steady decline in status of military careers, and, significantly, the rise of a new generation of political and cultural elites who no longer had direct wartime experience. Once the debate about the war was resumed in 1987 when the General Staff and Political Administration gave approval for posthumous publication of the writer Konstantin Simonov's interviews with the late Marshal Zhukov,[9] it quickly transgressed the previous boundaries, even those slightly wider ones permitted under Khrushchev. Just as the armed forces themselves were forced to hear criticisms of military policy from civilians, 'pacifists' and 'draft-dodgers', so too civilians and even civilian women[10] began challenging the former monopoly of military men over their own past.[11]

The revisionists went to the heart of the matter almost immediately, raising fundamental questions about the nature of the Soviet victory and its costs. The harshest critics indicted the entire Bolshevik-Soviet leadership for the miserable performance in World War II and viewed the wartime tragedies as only the culmination of a system fundamentally wrong from its inception in October 1917.[12] Indeed, the military purges were no longer viewed merely as a significant departure from the modus operandi of the Bolshevik leadership; rather, they were considered as one more manifestation of the generally inhumane attitudes that prevailed among those leaders.

to pose otherwise taboo moral questions. Among the works, for example, that treated wartime collaboration of Soviet citizens, Vasil' Bykov's novel, *Sotnikov*, was made into a powerful film, *Voskhozhdenie* (The Ascent; a reference to Calvary). A film by director Aleksei German, *Proverka na dorogakh*, based on his father's short story, deals with hostile attitudes toward returning or escaped prisoners. Eventually, a non-fictional treatment of POWs and MIAs appeared in E. A. Brodskii, *Oni ne propali bez vesti* (1987). A more honest account of partisans, the suspicions with which they were regarded, and their tremendous losses due to lack of professional leadership, was first raised in a fictional story by D. Gusarov, *Znamia* 5 (1988), pp. 3–65.

9 Davies argues that this approval marked a turning point, *Soviet History*, p. 103. Another signal of the expanded space for discussion of the war was the publication of Simonov's 'Uroki istorii i dolg pisatelia: Zametki literatora', *Nauka i zhizn* (June 1987; originally written 28 April 1965).

10 For a collection by women war veterans that was controversial for its frank descriptions, see Svetlana Alekseevich, *U voiny ne zhenskoe litso* (Minsk, 1989).

11 For the widespread interest in the history of the war and popular challenges to the orthodox version, see A. M. Samsonov, *Znat' i pomnit': Dialog istorika s chitateliami* (Moscow, Politizdat 1988).

12 The most radical revisionist account to date is that of Boris Sokolov, *Tsena pobedy. Velikaia otechestvennaia: neizvestnoe ob izvestnom* (Moscow, Moskovskii rabochii 1990). See also the 'conversation' of historian Gennadii Bordiugov and journalist Aleksandr Afanas'ev, 'Ukradennaia pobeda', in *Komsomol'skaia pravda* (5 May 1990), pp. 1–2; and the harsh reactions of the Institute of Marxism-Leninism and Soviet war veterans, *Komsomol'skaia pravda* (31 August 1990), p. 2. I thank Markus Wehner for this reference.

In response to the attack on the legacy and values of the military-industrial complex, high-ranking soldiers produced new data to defend their claims that, despite the ravages of the purges in the army and despite the constant political meddling of the party leadership in military affairs, the armed forces performed not only heroically but with considerable native military talent and with largely domestic (as opposed to Lend-Lease and other foreign aid) material resources.[13] The orthodox publicists and historians reformulated their position in favour of a 'balanced' view of Stalin's role in the war; in practice this meant downplaying the disastrous opening months of the war and the catastrophes in 1942 at Kharkov and in the Crimea and instead highlighting the victories at Stalingrad and Berlin, everywhere attributing considerable strategic wisdom to Stalin himself. The purges also were passed over lightly, one suspects, because many of the older military men who defended the orthodox version owed their career advances to the terror of the 1930s.

Standing somewhere in between the orthodox defenders and the 'radical' critics of the Soviet system of values have been those scholars who adhere to a third position, namely, that an anti-Stalin Leninist tradition existed in the Army similar to the anti-Stalin alternatives in the Party and economy. The arguments of these authors, many of them once associated with the embattled Institute of Military History, resembled those of Soviet historians writing and lecturing about other aspects of the post-revolutionary past, namely, a school that upheld 'alternatives to the Stalin system'.[14] For military historians who adhered to the 'alternative' thesis, the key figures are the executed Tukhachevsky, Uborevich, Yakir, Bliukher, and Gamarnik; but also the earlier deceased Frunze, some military specialists, and, in some cases, Trotsky. For these historians, the Stalinist clique of Voroshilov, Budennyj, Mekhlis, and others is viewed as a false tradition or as a rupture in Soviet military tradition, and one to be decisively extirpated. They, in contrast to the preceding two groups, have focused considerable attention on the purges and the system of terror in general as the major cause of the

---

[13] For surveys of the debates over military history, see the excellent accounts by Hans-Henning Schroeder, 'Die Lehren von 1941. Die Diskussion um die Neubewertung des "Grossen Vaterlaendischen Krieges" in der Sowjetunion', in *Der Zweite Weltkrieg: Analysen, Grundzuege, Forschungsbilanz* ed. Wolfgang Michalka (Munich, Piper 1989), pp. 608–25; and his 'Weisse Flecken in der Geschichte der Roten Armee', *Osteuropa* 5 (1989), pp. 459–77; and Bernd Bonwetsch, 'Georgij Konstantinowitsch Shukow – Heerfuehrer und Memoirenverfasser', *Osteuropa Archiv* (1988), pp. A327–36. In response to the polemics about wartime losses, the Military Publishing House released a volume that reproduces statistics from previously classified archives, *Grif sekretnosti sniat: Poteri vooruzhennykh sil SSSR v voinakh, boevykh deistviiakh i voennykh konfliktakh* (Moscow, Voenizdat 1993).

[14] See my essay in this volume on the Stalin question.

241

disastrous performance of the first wartime months. The 'alternativists' thereby do not throw out the whole Soviet past, but they argue that a more genuinely socialist non-Stalinist path of development was cut off or diverted by 'betrayers of the Revolution'.[15]

Owing to a reservoir of support among some wartime veterans and political groupings on the nationalist right end of the current Russian spectrum who defend Stalin's reputation as wartime leader,[16] the orthodox view of the war tenaciously holds on, but it is now clearly a minority position and its adherents are ostracised in the 'liberal' and 'democratic' media. Even the 'alternativists' appear to be on the defensive now that the Stalin question has 'infected' the entire Soviet period in popular consciousness and the media. Among the negative consequences of this swing has been a widespread willingness to accept even the most extreme claims about the Stalinist leadership and a fascination with the machinations of Stalin and his henchmen at the expense of more complicated historical explanations. An illustration is the persistent popularity of Viktor Suvorov's *Icebreaker*, in which the author revives Hitler's official justification for attacking the Soviet Union in June 1941, namely, that Stalin himself was planning to attack Germany and that 'Operation Barbarossa' was only a preventive, defensive war.[17]

The opposite side of the coin has been that many previous taboos have been broken and almost no subject is too sensitive to broach, although authors can count on frequently vitriolic responses. Part of the breaking of the taboos has been a belated recognition by post-Soviet historians of the topics and interpretations of non-Soviet historians.[18] In fact, many of

[15] This is the central argument of Dmitrii Volkogonov's two-volume biography of Stalin, *Triumf i tragediia*; and also the thesis of Anatolii Rybakov's novels *Children of the Arbat* and *39-yi i drugie gody* ('*39 and Other Years*). For a representative work on the purges of the military, in this case, of the officers of the Kiev Military District, see Dmytro Tabachnyk and Oleksandr Sydorenko, *Za standartnymy zvynuvachenniamy* (Kiev, Politizdat 1990).

[16] In answer to the veterans who hold on to their faith that Stalin 'led us to victory in the war', Igor Bestuzhev-Lada penned a powerful critique of Stalin as the great war leader, *Nedelia* 5 (1988).

[17] Suvorov, the pseudonym for a Soviet intelligence officer who defected to the West, offers no new evidence in support of his claims, which are no longer accepted by any but a fringe group in the German academic establishment. Hitler's preventive war thesis did, however, resurface in the German *Historikerstreit*. For a devastating critique of the Russian-language version, *Ledokol*, see A. N. Mertsalov and L. Mertsalova, '"Nepredskazuemoe proshloe" ili prednamerennaia lozh'?', *Svobodnaia mysl'* 6 (1993), pp. 45–54.

[18] Among the works most often cited are the classic two-volume history by John Erickson, *The Road to Stalingrad* (Boulder, Colorado, Westview 1984); and *The Road to Berlin* (Boulder, Colorado, Westview 1983); Alexander Dallin's *German Rule in Russia: A Study of Occupation Policies* (London and Basingstoke, Macmillan 1981); Alexander Werth's, *Russia at War, 1941–1945* (New York, Carroll & Graf 1984); and John Armstrong, ed., *Soviet Partisans in World War II* (Madison, Wisconsin, University of Wisconsin Press

the most revisionist arguments being put forward today are borrowed or adapted from long-banned 'bourgeois falsifiers'. What this has meant is that historians of the war inside the former Soviet Union have changed their stance vis-à-vis the international historical community and that the 'Great Fatherland War' is gradually being transformed and integrated into the broader history of the Second World War.[19]

The general battle history of the war has been pieced together by non-Soviet historians who based their accounts largely on captured German documents and testimony, Allied intelligence, and the voluminous published Soviet documents and interviews with Soviet officers and soldiers.[20] But major questions remain about even the military campaigns, from the role of Stalin at various times and in various fields, to the functioning of the war machine itself. At a more fundamental level, the process of integrating the Soviet experience of war has been marked by some tentative reconsiderations of the socio-spatial and chronological boundaries, beginning with the starting point of the war. Because the official historians of the 'Great Fatherland War' described a defensive war against the German aggressor, for them the starting point was, of course, the German invasion on 22 June 1941. But beginning in September 1939, Soviet army troops were involved in combat on the western and southern frontiers, as Stalin joined Hitler in the dismemberment of Poland according to the terms of the Nazi–Soviet agreements of August 1939. After the campaigns in what became western Ukraine and Belorussia, Soviet troops also seized northern Romania and fought a short but very costly war with Finland.[21] Of course, the character of these largely aggressive military campaigns was very

1964). Among the appreciative Soviet reviews, see Andrei Mertsalov, 'O kritike burzhuaznoi istoriografii vtoroi mirovoi voiny', *Voprosy istorii* 1987 (12), pp. 35–50.

[19] Of course, Soviet historians attended international conferences on World War II before the recent revisionist developments, but their participation was generally confined to countering what was then called 'bourgeois falsifiers'' accounts that distorted the true history of the Soviet Union's contribution to the war. In the new environment, post-Soviet historians often seem to be trying to outdo the most critical non-Soviet historians in their portrayals of the shameful and seamier sides of Soviet wartime behaviour.

[20] On the occasion of the fiftieth anniversary commemorations of the war's major battles, especially German historians organised conferences to which Soviet and post-Soviet counterparts made important, pioneering contributions. Because of the central role of the German–Soviet war in German history and its relationship to the Nazi period generally, German historians have written some of the most authoritative accounts of the war. The Military History Institute at Freiburg has been the primary intellectual force behind these projects. For some recent conference volumes, see Gerd Ueberschaer and Wolfram Wette, eds., *Der deutsche Ueberfall auf die Sowjetunion "Unternehmen Barbarossa" 1941* (Frankfurt a/M, Fischer 1991); Bernd Wegner, ed., *Zwei Wege nach Moskau* (Munich and Zurich, Piper 1991); and Wette and Ueberschaer, eds., *Stalingrad: Mythos und Wirklichkeit einer Schlacht* (Frankfurt a/M, Fischer 1992), the last two volumes with Soviet participants.

[21] V. Petrov, 'Byla takaia voina', *Argumenty i fakty* 39 (1988).

different from the war of defence against German aggression that began in the summer of 1941, but at least as far as the line-up of allies and enemies of the Soviet Union after 1941, these campaigns certainly played an important role (both Finland and Romania chose to ally with Germany against the Soviet Union); moreover, the frequently poor performance of Soviet troops in these campaigns forced the Stalinist military and political leadership to consider and institute major reforms in the final months before the German invasion.

Closely related to the controversies surrounding the more narrowly military history of World War II has been a critical reevaluation of pre-war Soviet foreign policy, especially the Soviet–German nonaggression pact and its secret clauses. Here too a few very outspoken critics, notably Viacheslav Dashichev and Mikhail Semiriaga, denounced the pact as morally heinous and politically wrong.[22] Both Dashichev and Semiriaga earlier tied their critique of the Stalin–Molotov foreign policy to an appeal for Gorbachev's 'common European home' orientation under Shevardnadze, that is, an orientation toward the West European democracies and against continued ties to Third World military dictatorships, who, by analogy, were aligned with the Axis powers of an earlier period. They too were publicly attacked by more 'establishment' diplomatic and military historians who defended the pact with the traditional argument: after Soviet overtures to the Western governments went unheeded, Stalin had no choice but to try to delay the inevitable German invasion. Conservative nationalists resisted Gorbachev's rhetoric of 'a common European home', viewing Shevardnadze's foreign policy as capitulationist and deleterious to Soviet national interests.[23] But what is important about this discussion is that the military history of the war is not as compartmentalised as it had been previously and isolated from, for example, the international behaviour of the Soviet state and international relations generally in the years leading up to the war.

In other key areas, the military history of the war is being integrated with political, social, economic, and cultural history. In the past, especially, Soviet historians have generally approached their subject from a narrowly military vantage-point and have viewed the army as

---

[22] For Dashichev's position, see his 'Vostok – zapad: Poisk novykh otnoshenii. O prioritetakh vneshnei politiki Sovetskogo gosudarstva', *Literaturnaia gazeta* (8 May 1988), p. 14; for Semiriaga's, see '23 avgusta 1939 goda. Sovetsko–germanskii dogovor o nenapadenii: byla li al'ternativa?', *Literaturnaia gazeta* (5 October 1988), p. 14. For a more conventional rethinking of the pact, see A. S. Iakushevskii, 'Sovetsko–germanskii dogovor o nenapadenii: vzgliad cherez gody', in *Stranitsy istorii sovetskogo obshchestva* (Moscow, Politizdat 1989), pp. 254–74.

[23] This certainly was the major political line in such conservative journals as *Voenno-istoricheskii zhurnal*, *Nash sovremennik*, and *Molodaia gvardiia*. The split has continued to characterise efforts to forge foreign policy in post-Gorbachev Russia as well.

somehow isolated from the society and political regime it served.[24] But even non-Soviet historians often wrote as if they assumed that politics were suspended for the duration of the war and that key military and political issues were arrived at unanimously by the Stalinist leadership in the Kremlin. It is here that the two papers by Bernd Bonwetsch and Jacques Sapir offer a refreshingly alternative approach. Bonwetsch focuses on the relations of Stalin and his military commanders and describes the political culture of the high military and political command. Without any access to new Soviet archival material, but rather by a careful reading of available published sources, Bonwetsch character- ises the pathology of decision-making in which 'civilians', most often high-ranking NKVD officers, meddled in military affairs. The result was frequently faulty diagnosis – catastrophes were attributed to lack of will and to treason – and mistaken strategic decisions emerging from an atmosphere of suspicion, intimidation, and irresolution. That atmos- phere itself was the consequence of the recent terror in the army and society.[25] An overwhelming predilection for the offensive among those military and civilian leaders who composed Stalin's entourage made the costs of waging war unnecessarily high in manpower and *matériel*.[26] In this sense, military campaigns differed little from the Soviet practice of extensive industrialisation and mass, forced collectivisation. Bon- wetsch concludes, 'however Stalin changed during the war, the victory was achieved with genuine Stalinist methods'.

Jacques Sapir's contribution challenges Bonwetsch's conclusions in part and poses a revisionist view of the operation of the Soviet political economy during the war. For a regime that has been characterised by many as a command economy and highly militarised,[27] surprisingly

---

[24] Despite slogans that affirmed the unshakable unity of Party and Army, or Army and People, in fact Soviet historians wrote about social and economic developments in virtual isolation from politics. See A. P. Nenarokov and O. V. Naumov, 'Glazami amerikanskogo istorika', *Voenno-istoricheskii zhurnal*, 12 (1990), pp. 60–6.

[25] For a review of the recent literature on the impact of the terror on the military and a view that diverges from Bonwetsch's, see Roger Reese, 'The Impact of the Great Purge on the Red Army: Wrestling with Hard Numbers', *The Soviet and Post-Soviet Review* 19, 1–3 (1992), pp. 71–90.

[26] This is also the conclusion of Boris Sokolov, *Tsena pobedy*. Sokolov describes the preference for symbolic captures of 'heights' especially in time for some important commemorative holiday; also the widespread practice of reconnaissance in force (*razvedka boem*), that is, sending small detachments of soldiers to draw out the enemy instead of employing less costly intelligence means. For other perspectives on the high command and political leadership of the war, see Seweryn Bialer, *Stalin and His Generals* (Boulder, CO, Westview Press 1984); and the revealing interviews of Konstantin Simonov, published posthumously as *Glazami cheloveka moego pokoleniia: Razmyshleniia o I. V. Staline* (Moscow, Pravda 1990).

[27] See Oscar Lange's classic description of the Soviet economy as 'war economy sui generis' in *Papers in Economic and Sociology* (London–Warsaw, PWN and Pergamon Press 1970), pp. 101–2. Soviet 'militarism' was one of the commonplaces in the

little has been written about the origins of the military-industrial sector, its evolution, or the relationship between the defence sector and other key parts of the Soviet political economy during the Stalin years. The history of the wartime Soviet Union itself has been even more focused on the purely military events;[28] historians assumed, as Bonwetsch's conclusion suggests, that Stalin won the war with Stalinist methods. Sapir argues, paradoxically, that only by demilitarising the 'war economy', better characterised as a mobilisation economy to distinguish it from the performance of wartime itself, was victory possible. The wartime crisis forced reforms in the planning process that might have produced a very different post-war Soviet Union had they not been reversed in the reaction that set in after 1948. The reforms meant a far greater resort to economic mechanisms rather than administrative fiat. Ultimately, Sapir's essay raises the issue of the reformability of the Stalin system and of alternatives that emerged during the wartime crisis. Memoirists and fictional writers as well have frequently called attention to the freer atmosphere of the war years, the disappointed hopes for post-war liberalisation, the relationship of these developments to post-Stalinist reformism.[29]

Perhaps the most interesting development in the history of the war is the first step toward investigating what might be called the wartime social psychology of the Soviet population. In the Soviet and post-Soviet debates, this has meant parting with the old formula of 'spiritual unity of the Soviet people', but even in general histories of the war written by western scholars, similar clichés had often substituted for more thoughtful analysis. By contrast, European historians of the war in Europe describe a far more complicated picture of attitudes ranging not

ideological arsenal of Cold War perceptions, with the Soviet Union inheriting the mantle of the Nazi war machine that was defeated in 1945. For a characteristic work in this vein, see Albert and Joan Seaton, *The Soviet Army: 1918 to the Present* (New York, New American Library 1986). See the exchange between William Odom ('The "Militarization" of Soviet Society', *Problems of Communism* 25, 5 (1976), pp. 34–51) and David Holloway, ('War, Militarism and the Soviet State', *Alternatives* 6 (1980), pp. 59–92).

28 Recent exceptions to the long-time silence include: John Barber and Mark Harrison, *The Soviet Home Front 1941–1945: A Social and Economic History of the USSR in World War II* (London and New York, Longman 1991); Mark Harrison, *Soviet Planning in Peace and War, 1938–1945* (Cambridge, Cambridge Press 1985); William Moskoff, *The Bread of Affliction: The Food Supply in the USSR During World War II* (Cambridge, Cambridge Press 1990). For a model study on the European war, see Alan S. Milward, *War, Economy and Society, 1939–1945* (Berkeley, University of California Press 1977).

29 The war was perceived to have brought a sense of freedom and relief through the common cause and common adversity; the chaos and confusion allowed some temporary escape from repressive control. Among the often-cited texts for these themes are Boris Pasternak's *Doctor Zhivago*, the memoirs of the writer Marietta Shaginian, *Chelovek i vremia* (Moscow 1980), and those of the physicist Andrei Sakharov, *Memoirs* (New York, Knopf 1990), ch. 3.

surprisingly from defeatism and collaboration with the enemy to heroic self-sacrifice. What this means for a start is that historians of the Soviet war need to disaggregate the wartime experience and abandon such vague and probably meaningless generalisations as 'the Soviet people'.[30]

At a minimum we might refer to Soviet peoples. After all, for many of the Soviet peoples, their experience of the war was Nazi occupation; but even here the experience was far from uniform; Soviet citizens had to make painful, often fatal, choices among collaborating with the Nazi occupiers, joining the anti-Nazi resistance, or several alternatives between these extremes. For peoples deported by Stalin during the war to Siberia or Kazakhstan, their attitudes can be reasonably expected to have been hostile or resentful. Even for the millions who lived in cities that were not occupied but were not far from the fronts, and for the millions of men and women who served in the armed forces, the official version has highlighted only formulaic heroism because it has treated the choices open to Soviet citizens in black-and-white terms of heroism or treason. Both the heroes and the traitors have been removed from history to the realm of the mythical, where superhuman forces of good and evil battled over the destiny of the Soviet people.

Up until recently, Soviet historians ignored this area of the wartime experience not only because of the narrow constraints on permissible problematics; available sources also precluded much research into new areas. Memoirs were generally unreliable because of censorship; archives were closed.[31] Today, by contrast, historians have access to new sources that contain a wealth of contradictory materials that have only begun to be sorted out by researchers: citizens' letters to newspaper editors and party organs, questions addressed to lecturers from the party's Agitation and Propaganda Section, and reports of rumours and overheard conversations from the NKVD informers (seksoty), to name only the most popular sources. But what has become clear, even at this initial stage, is that the population did not passively believe all that was told them, but that millions read between the lines of official reports and

---

[30] Beyond disaggregating the wartime populations and geographical regions, historians have begun to distinguish periods within the wartime experience better, rather than viewing the war as a chronological monolith.

[31] Even a recent series designed to offer the perspective of the ordinary soldier, Poslednie pis'ma s fronta (Moscow, Voenizdat 1991), highlights heroism, bravery, solicitude for loved ones, and patriotism, while avoiding panic, doubt, and disloyalty. Of course, the military censorship may have been very effective in discouraging such sentiments in soldiers' letters, but these source problems are not addressed by the editors of these largely patriotic volumes. See the critical remarks of A. M. Samsonov, '1941–1945. Na podstupakh k istine', in Istoriki sporiat (Moscow, Politizdat 1989), pp. 333–4; and a former soldier's account of the Battle of Stalingrad by Vladimir Shubkin in Literaturnaia gazeta (23 September 1987).

made their own sober conclusions about the situation at home and at the front. Many citizens found ways to subvert what they felt were unreasonable orders from above and devised their own strategies of survival and resistance. Others were so embittered against their own government that they expressed hopes for its defeat at the hands of the Nazis.[32] In short, the documents on popular attitudes reveal a picture of dynamic change and diversity across social groups and geographic regions over the course of the war years.

As the history of the war is rewritten and investigated anew, historians will begin to approach as well the question of the meaning of World War Two in the context of twentieth-century Russian and Soviet history. On the one hand, the tremendous social upheavals and economic transformations will pose new questions about the impact of the war on post-war Soviet society; among the many possible questions are the redistribution of industry and population, the consolidation of the military-industrial sector, the change in the Party's social composition and political culture, religious and cultural life, and interethnic and gender relations in the aftermath of the resettlements.[33] On the other hand, the emergence of the Soviet Union from World War II as a victorious superpower can be compared and contrasted to the collapse of the autocracy in World War I and the emergence of the Soviet state from the Civil War.

Neither in the Soviet Union nor in the West has the Russian experience in World War I been the subject of much investigation;[34] in general, this can be explained by the 'shadow of 1917', the domination of the writing of early twentieth-century history as a foreshadowing of the February and October Revolutions.[35] Soviet historians steered away

---

[32] See the pioneering articles by Tamilla Toman, '1941–1942: dni velikikh bedstvii v soznanii sovremennikov', in *Trudnye voprosy istorii* (Moscow, Politizdat 1991), pp. 158–73; G. A. Bordiugov, 'Velikaia otechestvennaia: podvig i obmanutye nadezhdy', in *Istoriia otechestva* (Moscow, Politizdat 1991), pp. 257–83. Almost simultaneously with the appearance of these studies in Moscow, western scholars too have taken up this topic. See John Barber, 'Popular Reactions in Moscow to the German Invasion of 22 June 1941', and my 'Soviet Soldiers and Officers on the Eve of the German Invasion: Towards a Description of Social Psychology and Political Attitudes', in a special issue of *Soviet Union/Union Soviétique*, 'Operation Barbarossa: The German Attack on the Soviet Union, 22 June 1941', 18, nos. 1–3 (1991).

[33] An early effort along these lines is the volume edited by Susan J. Linz, *The Impact of World War II on the Soviet Union* (Totowa, NJ, Rowan & Allanheld 1985).

[34] The only recent work by a non-Russian historian has been Norman Stone's *The Eastern Front 1914–1917* (London & Sydney, Hodder and Stoughton 1975). Before that, General N. N. Golovin wrote a study that focused very much on the military aspects of the war, *The Russian Army in the World War* (New Haven, Yale University Press 1931).

[35] As Allan K. Wildman explains in the preface in his magisterial study of soldiers' politics in 1917, historians generally divided on the place of the war in relation to the 1917 Revolutions. One group saw the basic social contradictions of autocratic Russia leading to a revolution that the onset of the war served only to delay. Their opponents saw the

248

from the topic because of the officially critical attitude toward the late Old Regime and the highly restricted access to state and military archives for the period. But with the relative demotion of 1917 as a watershed for post-Soviet historians, the Great War has begun to reemerge from its scholarly oblivion.[36] A comparison of the performance of the Old Regime and its successor (as well as comparisons with the performance of contemporaneous belligerents in both wars) under the strains of 'total war' might raise questions about the relative levels of state penetration of society, the transformation of the societies of the territory of the Soviet Union, the differing characters of the wars themselves, and the evolution of warfare generally.[37]

Finally, studies of the Civil War that was waged on the territory of the former Russian Empire have produced a richer historiographical tradition with which to compare the new perspectives that will emerge about the Soviet experience of the Second World War. Though vastly different from the Great War which had preceded it, the Civil War was also a war of total mobilisation and one which gave the eventually triumphant Bolsheviks their first lessons in politics and state-building. The later propaganda campaigns during the Second World War frequently invoked themes from the Civil War and (at least superficially) similar institutions were often improvised by a leadership that still remembered their Civil War experience. But surprisingly, historians have not investigated the two conflicts with an eye to answering larger questions about the place of military conflict and societal mobilisation in twentieth-century history. Such questions of continuity and change should be kept in the background as historians rewrite the histories of these international and civil wars.

Reviewing the recent trends in the rewriting of the war's history in the successor states, as yet no new national myths have emerged to replace the Stalinist orthodoxy; rather the volatile national political struggles that pit advocates of opposing visions of the post-Soviet future are reflected in the multiple versions of the past, especially the recent past of

1905 Revolution as having put Russia on a western path of reform, which the war 'tragically' derailed, producing the anarchy of 1917. In his own challenge to these extreme positions, Wildman devotes only chapter 3 of his two volumes to the war itself, *The End of the Russian Imperial Army*, 2 vols. (Princeton, Princeton University Press 1980 and 1987), pp. xv–xvi.

[36] In the past years, Russian historians and military history enthusiasts have commemorated the outbreak of the war and the major battles.

[37] Gottfried Schramm raises these issues in a synchronic comparison of the Imperial Russian Army with its French and German counterparts. See his 'Militaerisierung und Demokratisierung: Typen der Massenintegration im Ersten Weltkrieg', *Francia* 3 (1975), pp. 476–97; and 'Die russische Armee als politischer Faktor vor der Februarrevolution (1914–1917)', *Militaergeschichtliche Mitteilungen* 18 (1975), pp. 33–62. See also a conference organised by the Historial de la Grande Guerre and Trinity College, Dublin, 'Mobilising for Total War: Society and State in Europe, 1914–1918', 23–25 June 1993.

the wartime. If we focus on Russia, there the struggle over the nation's orientation between some new version of Slavophiles and Westerners will make it difficult to forge a consensus. In one corner, for those historians who turn to western Europe and the United States, the wartime alliance and cooperation, the hopes for post-war reform as a consequence of the limited intellectual and cultural liberalisation, and the struggle against Nazi tyranny and expansionism, offer the potential for reintegrating the wartime experience into an eventual liberal narrative of Russia's past. In another corner, the national(ist) (and often anti-western) conservatives can highlight many of the traditional themes of Allied reluctance and delay in opening the second front, the disproportionate contribution of the Soviet peoples to the finally victorious struggle, and the authoritarian political order that withstood the Nazi onslaught. A far-right constituency, in a paradoxical mirror image of the old totalitarian identity of Nazi and Stalinist systems, might even find in the Nazi–Soviet collaboration a 'positive' history of authoritarian nationalist systems in league against the bourgeois democracies and international Zionist conspiracies that they fear are currently in control of the Russian state.

In Ukraine, to take another example that has analogies in all the German-occupied territories of the former Soviet Union, at least two mutually opposed constituencies have supported different versions of the war; on one side are the veterans of the Soviet Army and their descendants, whose preferred narrative comes closer to the orthodox version of the war's history, while on the other side are the adherents to the cause of the anti-Soviet (and at least temporarily Reichswehr collaborationist) partisan movements. These two versions compete for public attention in state-sponsored ceremonies and media coverage; elsewhere, in the Baltic states, Croatia, and Slovakia, for example, the occasionally and more decidedly collaborationist resistance movements have won a form of moral victory over the internationalist orthodoxy of the Soviet period. Rewriting the history of the war has not been easy for any of the belligerent powers or the societies who lived at the mercy of those powers; similarly, the struggle for power and a new post-Soviet order will shape the intellectual context of professional historians as they enter the archives to rewrite the narrative of the 'Great Fatherland War'.

11

German exceptionalism and the origins of Nazism: the career of a concept
George Steinmetz

Every national historiography seems to have its own 'exceptionalism' thesis. The underlying structure of these theories is roughly similar: one's own history is shown to deviate from a standard model of development in ways that produce some unique outcome. But most exceptionalism theories become visible to a non-academic public for only a brief moment, and are otherwise only interesting for a narrow circle of specialists. Discussions of the 'open frontier' or the 'absence of socialism' in the United States are not likely to quicken the pulse of the contemporary reader. Debates over France's 'delayed' economic development probably seem even more recondite. By contrast, the thesis of the German *Sonderweg*, or special path to modernity, has continued to capture the imagination of a much wider audience, seemingly impervious to the waves of criticism directed against it.

The Sonderweg can best be understood as a complex and changing field of discourse held together by certain core ideas and texts, rather than a single, unified statement. At the core of most contemporary discourse on the Sonderweg is a problem and the outlines of an answer. The central question is: why did Nazism come to power in Germany, or, why did a system like Nazism come to power in Germany and not in other advanced industrial countries?[1] The basic

---

[1] Kershaw suggests that the Sonderweg approach has little to say about the specific character and cumulative radicalisation of Nazism, and is mainly a theory of the *origins* of Nazism (*Nazi Dictatorship*, p. 18). It is true that the critical exceptionalism approach has focused mainly on the Kaiserreich, and paid less attention to the Weimar Republic and the Third Reich. Yet the origins of Nazism are interesting to exceptionalists mainly because of the regime's longer-term effects. Key contributors to the Sonderweg thesis like Wehler clearly understand their project as one of working out the preconditions for Nazism, including the virulent antisemitism that culminated in the Holocaust (e.g. Wehler, *Deutsche Gesellschaftsgechichte*, p. 1293). As Wehler noted in the introduction to the English-language edition of *The German Empire*, 'The guiding question underlying this book has been to investigate why Hitler's National Socialist regime came to power some dozen years after the end of the monarchy; why this regime succeeded in establishing a system of unprecedented terror and barbaric mass extermination; and

answer focuses on the deviation of Germany's developmental path from its western neighbours. Germany is both part of the west and different from it. The notion of a German difference from the rest of the Occident has been around for centuries, of course, including strands which viewed Germany's distinctiveness in positive terms (see Part I). Since 1945, however, and especially during the past three decades, the exceptionalism 'thesis'[2] has been discussed extensively and refined. Earlier versions of the exceptionalism thesis often sought the seeds of Nazism as far back as the Reformation (cf. McGovern, *From Luther to Hitler*) or Romanticism (Butler, *Roots of National Socialism*; Kohn, *Mind of Germany*), while more recent contributors have located the decisive turning-points in the mid-nineteenth century (1848) and unification periods (1866–71), and have focused especially on the Kaiserreich (1871–1918). The most influential statement of the Sonderweg thesis during the past two decades has been Hans-Ulrich Wehler's *The German Empire* (1973), which focused attention on the final third of the nineteenth century. The recently published third volume of Wehler's encyclopaedic *Deutsche Gesellschaftsgeschichte* (1995), revisits in much greater detail Germany's fateful branching off from the West between 1849 and 1914.[3]

The exceptionalist historiography has hardly gone uncontested. David Blackbourn and Geoff Eley have criticised the exceptionalists' reading on both theoretical and empirical grounds. There are also various alternative explanations of Nazism which downplay the importance of historical continuities (see Ayçoberry, *Nazi Question* and Kershaw, *Nazi Dictatorship*). One of the most significant developments since the 1980s has been a 'normalising' German historiography that offers a positive reading of the Empire and of 'traditions and patterns worth cherishing'.[4] Yet despite these criticisms and counter-trends,

why it proved capable of conducting a second total war' (*German Empire*, p. 7; see also Wehler, *Deutsche Gesellschaftsgeschichte*, p. 461).

[2] I use the term 'exceptionalism' *thesis* rather than 'exceptionalism' *theory* deliberately in this paper to refer to the subset of Sonderweg discourse that tries to account for Nazism. On the distinction between *theories*, which are concerned with underlying causal mechanisms, and *explanation*, which deals with actual events, see Bhaskar (*Realist Theory*; *Naturalism*; *Scientific Realism*); also Wright ('Reflections'); Steinmetz ('Regulating the Social', pp. 16–17; 'Bhaskar's Critical Realism').

[3] The third volume of Wehler's *Gesellschaftsgeschichte*, which appeared as this volume was going to the editor, is discussed briefly below. Wehler does now acknowledge several arenas in which Imperial Germany was quite modern, but still emphasises the importance of the negative 'exceptional conditions' for the country's longer-term development – i.e. the rise of Nazism.

[4] Michael Stürmer, quoted in Kershaw (*Nazi Dictatorship*, p. 201). This 'upbeat' view of the Kaiserreich and German history more generally permeates the ongoing exhibition at the German Historical Museum in Berlin (cf. Stölzl, *Bilder*; also Kramer, 'Letter').

exceptionalist discourse has continued to proliferate beyond the universities, in a wide variety of texts and contexts.

Several factors seem important in understanding the broad resonance of Sonderweg discourse in Germany.[5] One has to do with the growing public interest in the Nazi period, and in German history more generally, since the early 1980s.[6] Despite the efforts by German politicians and intellectuals to 'historicise' the Nazi era,[7] to 'put the past behind us', the Nazi period has not yet been abandoned to the professionals. The question that seems to underlie much of the interest is still: 'How did this happen in the middle of Europe in a "civilised" century?'[8] Yet a broad interest in trying to understand Nazism cannot explain the appeal of any particular approach to that problem, such as exceptionalism.

One general reason for the robustness of the Sonderweg is its proven strategic usefulness.[9] The Sonderweg thesis has been used repeatedly to legitimate the post-war German states, especially (though not exclusively) the Federal Republic.[10] The exceptionalism narrative suggested that

[5] As discussed below (see note 10), exceptionalist discourse was quite restricted in GDR historiography and even more so in East German public opinion. So 'Germany' here refers mainly to pre-1989 West Germany and post-1989 Germany.

[6] I am referring here to the growth of phenomena like the History Workshops, mass-circulation history journals, and high-school research projects on the local area during the Nazi era. For an early overview, see *Der Spiegel* No. 23 (1983), pp. 36–42, 'Ein kräftiger Schub für die Vergangenheit'.

[7] On 'historicising' the Nazi era, see Kramer ('Letter') and Broszat (*Nach Hitler*).

[8] Jens Reich, former leader in the East German citizens' movement, quoted in Kramer ('Letter', p. 63).

[9] This is not a functionalist *explanation* of the prevalence of exceptionalism theory. To point to the usefulness of an idea is not to explain its genesis, i.e., a description of functions is not the same as a functional explanation.

[10] The GDR's position vis-à-vis the exceptionalism thesis is quite complex. Some eastern Marxists (most importantly Lukács, *Die Zerstörung*, and Abusch, *Der Irrweg*) proposed a variant of the exceptionalism narrative that indirectly legitimated the GDR as having successfully overcome feudalism, irrationalism, and the Prussian aristocracy. The difficulty was that the Sonderweg account made it difficult to attack West Germany politically as the heir of Nazism, since the Federal Republic had broken even more decisively with the Prussian-agrarian past, even in crudely geographical terms. Moreover, the connotations of the 'east' within exceptionalist discourse were almost entirely negative. Official East German ideology quickly settled on a simple equation of capitalism with 'fascism', of West German politicians and capitalists with crypto-Nazis. Another factor in the rejection of the Sonderweg by the early 1950s was the effort to define the 'nascent East German state . . . as the heir of a progressive, democratic tradition' (Iggers, 'Forward', pp. 16–17). But if the exceptionalism approach in its integral form was marginalised, elements of it crept back into East German historical writing through a reception of Marx's and Engels' own proto-exceptionalist view of nineteenth-century Germany. The interpretative incoherence that resulted from combining Marxist textual orthodoxy with political necessity is glaringly evident in much East German historical writing on the Bismarckian state. Especially in the 1980s, GDR historians offered internally contradictory readings of the Kaiserreich as both a modern capitalist state and an agrarian-Junker state (see Steinmetz, *Regulating the Social*, pp. 252–3). The complexity of the relationship between the Sonderweg thesis and

post-war Germany had eliminated the main source of Nazism: the agrarian Junker class, with its political and cultural power, and its inhibiting effects on liberalism. The Sonderweg thesis also diverted attention away from an array of possible alternative causes of Nazism which could be seen as surviving in post-war Germany: capitalism, economic crises, deep-rooted psychological structures or cultural forms, etc. According to the Sonderweg perspective, the roots of Nazism are 'history'.[11]

Since 1989, the Sonderweg trope has been deployed with increasing frequency in German political debate as a rhetorical weapon (see Part IV). The 'Sonderweg' has been uncoupled from the specialised historiography, and has started to accrue new meanings. Nonetheless, the historical writing continues to provide the concept with its power, through its claim to account for Nazism. The Sonderweg also retains its core reference to German deviation from the west. By accusing one's political opponent of steering Germany back onto an 'exceptional', non-western track, it is possible to raise the spectre of Nazism indirectly without engaging in libel. And a speaker who embraces the Sonderweg perspective is still aligned with the forces of liberalism and western social science.

This bring us to an additional set of reasons for Sonderweg theory's strength, having to do with the sociology of the German historical profession, cultural capital, and the ways in which exceptionalism theory meshes with certain understandings of serious social science.[12] However embattled its defenders may feel, the Sonderweg approach still has excellent credentials within the German academic field. It is associated with distinguished[13] historians at major German universities and research institutes. Two of Germany's leading periodicals, *Der*

---

the GDR has been further compounded since 1989, as several historians have described East Germany itself as a continuation of the German Sonderweg (see Part IV below).

[11] Since the Sonderweg thesis is critical of Germany's past it might seem paradoxical to emphasise its legitimatory function. Kramer ('Letter') seems to miss this point, counterposing the view of German history as 'bad until 1945' (Habermas) against the German Historical Museum's staging of a positive continuity in German history. In fact, *both* views are normative and legitimating, even if they valorise different things.

[12] Some forms of discourse are 'profitable' within a given cultural field while others seem awkward and foreign. The latter may neglect or contradict taken-for-granted assumptions in a given cultural context, or seem to lack taste or seriousness. A discourse about history that fails to 'fit' in this way may remain marginal *despite* its potential usefulness. Bourdieu's work (cf. especially 'Forms') theorises the way in which variable amounts of cultural capital accrue to different positions within a cultural field. In the current case, contending interpretations of Nazism can be seen as conferring differing amounts of cultural capital upon their adherents. In Germany, 'academic', 'scientific', and 'rationalistic' discourse is still more powerful than alternative forms of discourse (the outcome of the 1980's 'Historians' Conflict' is a good illustration of this).

[13] See Wehler ('Nationalismus', p. 74), for the use of the term 'distinguished' in this context; also Bourdieu, *Distinction*.

Spiegel and *Die Zeit*, turn to Wehler frequently for book reviews and commentary on German politics. Exceptionalism has a prestigious international and 'western-liberal' lineage among exile historians in Britain, the USA and elsewhere. Politically and morally, exceptionalism theory takes the side of modernity against tradition, liberalism against conservatism, reason against irrationality.[14] Methodologically, exceptionalism is associated with 'structural' approaches in the social sciences, which are still coded as scientific, serious, liberal, and Anglo-American. Many of the rival explanatory accounts of the rise of Nazism, by contrast, are associated with approaches seen as 'unscientific', less serious, or even politically suspect.[15] Exceptionalism theory is a well-established account of nineteenth-century German history and the genesis of Nazism. Reports of its death have been highly exaggerated.

This does not mean that the Sonderweg approach is currently hegemonic among German historians, even if twenty years ago it seemed to have become a 'new orthodoxy'.[16] The Sonderweg thesis is rooted in a form of modernisation theory which, along with other structural theories and historical 'metanarratives', has been sharply challenged by the turn to cultural and post-modern theories.[17] An equally significant challenge to the left-liberal Sonderweg thesis has come from the steady growth of a neoconservative 'intelligentsia' in Germany since the late 1979s, and from the changes in political culture

[14] The very 'will to explain' exemplified by the Sonderweg approach might be seen as an implicit rejection within historiography of a tainted irrationalism, romanticism, and anti-scientism, which exceptionalists have associated with the ancestry of Nazism (see Kohn, *Mind*).

[15] Such alternative include the 'evil genius' or 'great man' approach, focused exclusively on Hitler; 'mass society' theory, which since the 1960s has seemed suspiciously conservative; Nolte's view of Nazism as a radicalised mimesis of Stalinism (cf. Nolte, *Bürgerkrieg*; *Streitpunkte*); and any explicitly Marxist approaches (although, as I will argue below, the critical Sonderweg thesis is inextricably related to a certain form of Marxism). In addition to these unpopular forms of analysis, recent years have seen a huge proliferation of fragmented research projects on 'every conceivable aspect of Nazi rule' (Kershaw, *Nazi Dictatorship*, p. 211). Like the various culturalist, anthropological, and post-modern approaches, however, these have not yet resulted in a synthetic revisionist account of Nazism. See Reichel (*Der schöne Schein*) and NGBK (*Inszenierung*) for interesting moves in this direction. (One possible exception is the formerly unfashionable concept of 'totalitarianism', whose academic capital has skyrocketed since the collapse of the GDR and the Soviet Union.) The most promising new approach sees Nazism as a 'hegemonic project', one in which Hitler and the Nazis successfully bundled together and radicalised a variety of traditions and cultural materials, some of them quite old (like antisemitism), others traceable to the Kaiserreich period (eugenics and modern racism), and some originating in the post-World War I period (e.g. anti-Sovietism). For an interesting sketch of such an account, see Eley ('Fascism'). This approach has not been fully fleshed out, but is compatible with my discussion in Part III.

[16] James Sheehan, quoted in Blackbourn and Eley (*Peculiarities of German History*, p. 12).

[17] For an interesting analysis of these challenges to historical social science, see Wehler ('Selbstverständnis').

resulting from German unification, which have placed the critical exceptionalist approach 'even further on the defensive than it had already become during the *Tendenzwende* of the 1980s' (Kershaw, *Nazi Dictatorship*, p. 200). Wehler and other representatives of the Sonderweg thesis have been the object of conservative attacks.[18] German historians may thus have good tactical reasons for defending a view of pre-1914 German history as 'pathological' (Wehler, 'Westbindung', p. 141). On the other hand, as Wehler himself has noted, only two 'distinguished historians' (*'angesehene[n] Historiker'*; Wehler, 'Aufklärung', p. 191) were 'prepared to offer a feeble defense' of the *Tendenzwende* represented by Nolte and Hillgruber in the German 'historians' debate' of the late 1980s. In the context of this volume, however, there is no need to worry about providing ammunition to the far right, especially since the criticisms of the Sonderweg presented below are of a fundamentally different sort than those of the nationalist historians.

The first section of this essay traces the development of the discourse on German exceptionalism up through the consolidation of the 'critical' Sonderweg thesis during the 1970s. The second section focuses on the critique of this approach that emerged during the 1980s. David Blackbourn and Geoff Eley's pathbreaking books *Mythen deutscher Geschichtsschreibung* (1980) and *Peculiarities of Germany History* (1985) challenged the critical exceptionalism thesis on nearly every count, from its construction of Britain as a standard for comparison to its description of German middle-class behaviour in the later nineteenth century as 'feudalised'. An array of specialised historical monographs also contributed to the attack on the critical Sonderweg thesis, detailing various ways in which Imperial Germany's politics and culture resonated with capitalist industrialisation rather than contradicting it. The third section casts a critical eye on the terms in which this assault on the critical Sonderweg thesis has been framed. I argue that the critics share with their opponents a questionable set of assumptions about societies and social explanation. The fourth section discusses the development of Sonderweg discourse in the wake of the historiographic and political debates of the 1980s and early 1990s. Although many former proponents of the Sonderweg thesis have abandoned theory and explanation for the comforts of empiricism and straight narrative, the basic tenets of the Sonderweg remain quite influential among historians and within German political discourse.

[18] See, for example, Schöllgen (*Angst*, pp. 109–11); Zitelmann (*Westbindung*, pp. 11, 15, 184); and Weissman ('Der "Westen"'). The critical Sonderweg thesis is the obvious target of Nolte's hysterical polemic against a certain 'interpretation of National Socialism' which he views as the 'barely disguised motive' behind anti-racist and multicultural politics and the 'transformation of the German nation into a mixed-nationality population' (Nolte, *Streitpunkte*, p. 431).

In the conclusion I recommend that the concept of the Sonderweg should be redefined, since it is unlikely to disappear. German culture and politics have been indelibly marked by the exceptional crimes perpetrated by Germany during the years 1933–45. By arguing that German 'exceptionalism' *begins* with the Nazi era rather than culminating in it, we can reject the critical Sonderweg thesis without playing into the hands of those who would 'normalise' German history.

I. The many lanes in the 'German road'

The thesis of a 'special German road' originated long before – centuries before – the appearance of Nazism and theories of Nazism. An archaeology of this discourse must distinguish between a positive strand, which *praises* Germany's differentiation from the West, and a *critical* strand that codes this deviation as backwardness. Further distinctions within Sonderweg discourse concern the specific *explanation* offered for Germany's differentiation and the main *location* (politics, culture) of exceptionalism.

The positive understanding of German exceptionalism appeared as early as the Reformation in the self-understanding of the Protestant territorial rulers (Wehler, *Deutsche Gesellschaftgeschichte*, p. 462). As a result of the French Revolution and Napoleonic wars, this crystallised into a contrast between an authentic German 'culture' and a superficial French 'civilisation' (Elias, *History*, pp. 30–4). Later in the nineteenth century, and into the Weimar Republic, the ideologists of the 'German Path' celebrated Germany's unique combination of east and west, archaism and modernity (cf. Faulenbach, *Ideologie*; Olszewski, 'German Road'). Max Weber partially participated in the positive Sonderweg thesis with his sometimes idealised descriptions of the Prussian and German bureaucracy (Wehler, *Deutsche Gesellschaftsgeschichte*, p. 463; Weber, 'Bureaucracy'). The positive Sonderweg thesis then disappeared after 1945, only to resurface in neoconservative and far-right political discourse during the past decade (see Part IV below).

The *critical* contrast between Germany and its western neighbours may reach back as far as Tacitus' *Germania*, which constructed the Germans as backwards vis-à-vis the Gauls and the Romans in all respects other than military prowess.[19] The negative evaluation was expressed in the eighteenth century around the nobility's horror of the German language and its veneration of all things French (Elias, *History*,

---

[19] The militarisation of German culture is a perennial theme in negative exceptionalist discourse. To the contemporary reader, the combination of exoticisation and mockery in the *Germania* recalls nineteenth-century colonial anthropology. On the other hand, Tacitus' text has also been a favourite on the far right.

pp. 3–34). Heine (*Deutschland*) was only the most brilliant satirist of the *deutsche Misere* during the Vormärz (pre-March) period. In the 1860s, Marx and Engels ridiculed the Prussian 'Cabbage Junkers' and the *Spießbürger* who grovelled at their feet. After 1871, Engels continued to describe the Junkers as hegemonic, and saw Bismarck as organising 'the demolition of German industry, under the pretext of protecting it'.[20] This line of criticism was kept alive by liberals during the Kaiserreich. Weber (despite his partial adherence to a positive version of exceptionalism) argued in 1895 that 'an economically declining class' – the Prussian aristocracy – was 'politically dominant' in Germany (Weber, 'National State', p. 203).

The view of German society as dominated by an atavistic elite and an outdated culture was elaborated by Thorstein Veblen (*Imperial Germany*) during World War I and by the historian Eckart Kehr in the Weimar Republic (*Battleship Building; Economic Interest*).[21] Similar ideas were put forth in the 1930s by the unorthodox Marxist philosopher Ernst Bloch (*Heritage*) and the ex-Communist Franz Borkenau, who spoke in 1933 of a 'non-correspondence between national economic and political conditions' in the Empire ('Soziologie', p. 172). Trotsky suggested in 1932 that the emergent Nazi regime represented a 'dwindling majority' of Junkers (*Struggle*, p. 265). During World War II, Talcott Parsons (*On National Socialism*), Alexander Gerschenkron (*Bread and Democracy*), and the American anthropologist Robert Lowie (*German People*) continued in a similar vein.[22] Lowie focused on the nineteenth century, and the Kaiserreich in particular, as the key era for bringing out 'those features which distinguish Germany . . . from contemporary Western countries, and also to make clearer thereby the rise and maintenance of Hitler' (*German People*, p. 39). Among the central elements in Lowie's account of the rise of Hitler were the absence of a 'thoroughgoing revolution' (p. 39), Germany's late but explosive industrialisation (p. 54), the Junkers' dominant social status (p. 59), and a middle class that 'naively strove to attain the noble's status' by 'aping them' (pp. 59–60).

[20] Engels (*Origin*, p. 329) and 'Le socialisme' (n.d.). Increasingly, however, Engels described the Bismarckian state as allied with capital rather than the agrarian Junkers. On the shifts in Marx and Engels' views of Germany, see Steinmetz (*Regulating the Social*, Ch. 4).

[21] Kehr's work was quite influential in the development of the critical exceptionalist historiography during the 1960s and 1970s. See Eley (*From Unification*) and Puhle ('Zur Legende').

[22] Lowie, best known for his work on American Indians, lectured on German culture to US soldiers during World War II (cf. Lowie, *Toward Understanding Germany*, p. vii) and published the results of these lectures in 1945. A substantial reworking of the wartime material was published in 1954 after a research trip to Germany (Lowie, *Toward Understanding Germany*). I am grateful to Bernard Cohn for bringing Lowie's German work to my attention.

After World War II, a number of works based in disparate political and theoretical perspectives began to converge around a 'structural' variant of the critical Sonderweg thesis. This version explained German 'peculiarities', and ultimately the origins of Nazism, in terms of a fundamental disjuncture between the German Empire's rapidly modernising industrial economy and its 'traditional' political structures and/or cultural values. German history was seen as having been pushed repeatedly in destructive and anti-democratic directions by this clash between modernity and tradition. This structural argument about the non-contemporaneous levels of the German social formation was linked to a more specific focus on pre-1933 German liberalism as underdeveloped in comparison with western countries. Responsibility for this inadequacy was located with the German bourgeoisie, which was seen as having failed repeatedly to take the lead in promoting its supposed class interest in liberal democracy. In short, Germany failed to experience a 'bourgeois revolution'. The key moment in the narrative is 1848, when 'German history reached its turning-point and failed to turn' (Taylor, *German History*, p. 68). The middle class shared responsibility for the failure of liberalism and democracy with the Prussian nobility. The Junkers wielded undue influence within German politics and culture well into the twentieth century. The unnatural influence of the nobility was also reflected in the 'feudalisation of the bourgeoisie' and in the spread of anti-modern cultural values (conservative anti-capitalism, anti-urbanism, 'cultural pessimism'). Bourgeois weakness and aristocratic strength resulted in a fateful imbalance: while German industry grew swiftly, pre-modern values and political practices were preserved and reproduced well into the twentieth century. Germany's susceptibility to Nazism is ultimately explained by the social strains resulting from the coexistence of tradition and modernity.

Marxists such as Lukács (*Die Zerstörung*) and Kofler (*Zur Geschichte*) foregrounded Germany's lasting failure to embrace bourgeois modernity. Lukács claimed that the German bourgeoisie from the sixteenth century onward was 'characterized by a servility, pettiness, baseness, and miserabilism' which distinguished it from other European bourgeoisies (*Die Zerstörung*, p. 41).[23] As Lukács (*Die Zerstörung*, p. 80) put it:

> So, if we often hear the astonished question, how could great masses of the German people have accepted the childish myths of Hitler and Rosenberg, we can respond with a historical version of the question: how could the most educated and intellectually

---

[23] For even more official East German statements along these lines, see Alexander Abusch, *Der Irrweg*, and *Neues Deutschland*, 31 October 1947, Insert, Otto Grotewohl '30. Jahrestag der Sozialistischen Oktoberrevolution'.

advanced Germans have believed in Schopenhauer's mythical 'will', in the prophesies of Nietzsche's Zarathustra, in the historical myths of the Decline of the West?

Again, the primary source of Nazism was located in the absence of a bourgeois democratic revolution during the nineteenth century and the continuing weakness of liberalism and rationalism, along with the lack of synchronisation between economy, culture, and society.

During the 1960s, social scientists in the USA and Germany advanced similar explanations, often with only superficial variations in terminology.[24] The American sociologist Barrington Moore, Jr. emphasised the 'retention of a very substantial share in political power by the landed élite' (Social Origins, p. 438) in the countries that went fascist. However, his comparisons between fascist, communist, and democratic cases led him to recognise that the German bourgeoisie was at least strong enough to have been a 'worthwhile political ally'. If the bourgeoisie had been too feeble, a 'peasant revolution leading to communism' would have been a more likely outcome than fascism (Moore, Social Origins, p. 437). Dahrendorf (Society, pp. 381–96) analysed the Kaiserreich as riven by political and cultural atavisms.[25] Hans Kohn (Mind of Germany) argued that Germany succumbed to Hitler not 'because she had become part of modern western society' but 'because this modern society had been imposed on premodern social and intellectual foundations which were proudly retained' (Mind of Germany, p. 8). This surprising convergence of liberal and left-wing thought probably escaped most observers' attention due to the greater familiarity of popular-front style of interpretations of Nazism as the 'dictatorship of the most reactionary, the most chauvinistic, the most imperialistic elements of finance capital' (Dimitrov),[26] or Third International and SED slogans that simply equated fascism with capitalism.

There was also variation within the emergent critical Sonderweg paradigm in the relative emphasis placed on cultural as opposed to political backwardness. Like Lukács, Mosse (Crisis), Plessner (Nation), and Stern (Politics) stressed the prevalence of illiberal, anti-modern and idealist ideology in nineteenth-century Germany.[27] By contrast, the

---

[24] In 1973 Wehler praised Marxism's 'nearly unsurpassed' explanatory power (quoted in Weissmann 'Der "Westen"', p. 353). In addition to the texts discussed here, see also Hans Rosenberg (Bureaucracy) and most recently, Norbert Elias (Studien).

[25] Like some recent German historians, Dahrendorf also described Nazism as a modernising revolution (Society, pp. 381–96). See Kershaw (Nazi Dictatorship, pp. 203ff) on the more recent literature on Nazism as 'modernisation'.

[26] Dimitrov's 1935 report to the Seventh Congress of the Comintern, quoted in Ayçoberry (Nazi Question, p. 53).

[27] See also Brunschwig (Enlightenment); Hermand (Sieben Arten); and Greenfeld (Nationalism).

West German historians of the late 1960s and 1970s tended to emphasise politics – the autonomous Prussian-German state and the persistence of Junker domination of state and military (cf. Böhme, *Deutschlands Weg*; Stegmann, *Die Erben Bismarcks*; Wehler, *German Empire*). The most elaborate versions of critical Sonderweg theory stressed *both* cultural and political backwardness (e.g. Kohn, *Mind of Germany*; Dahrendorf, *Society*). Talcott Parsons' wartime essays ('Democracy'), for instance, discuss political peculiarities, especially the power and prestige of the Junkers and civil servants, alongside Germany's cultural 'atavisms' – the obsession with uniforms and titles, interpersonal formality, patterns of masculine superiority, underdevelopment of the 'romantic love' pattern, absence of economic individualism, and the old elites' con-tempt for everything 'bourgeois', including industry and trade, 'the bourgeois virtues', and 'liberal and humane culture'.

By the 1970s, many young historians had come to accept the thesis that 'the internal structure of the Kaiserreich was riven by a discrepancy between the political and social constitution' (Düding, *Der National-soziale Verein*, p. 15).[28] The notions of a 'feudalisation' of the German bourgeoisie, a 'failed revolution', and a causal chain leading forward to Nazism were also widely accepted. The influential culmination of this 'sociological' variant of the critical Sonderweg thesis was Wehler's *German Empire*. As Wehler summarised his argument about the origins of Nazism (*Nicht verstehen*, p. 70):

> The Prussian submissive mentality (*Untertanenmentalität*), Prussian reverence for authority (*Obrigkeitsdenken*), Prussian militarization of society, the unholy alliance of Prussian Junkers, politicians, and the military first brought Hitler to power . . . and then supported and consolidated the National Socialist system of domination.

The influence of this model has been extensively documented in the work of Eley, Blackbourn, Evans, and others.

By the end of the 1970s, however, this historical model was being subjected to a mounting barrage of theoretical and empirical critique. The most important event triggering this reevaluation was the publica-tion in 1980 of David Blackbourn and Geoff Eley's *Mythen deutscher Geschichtsschreibung*, followed by their *Peculiarities of German History* (1985), and a string of articles and monographs by other critics.[29]

---

[28] Another important turning-point in the rising influence of the critical view of the Kaiserreich was Fritz Fischer's (*Griff*) study of German elites' expansionist war aims in World War I.

[29] In addition to the essays cited above, see especially *Deutscher Sonderweg* (1982); Moeller ('Die Besonderheiten'); Grebing (Der 'deutsche Sonderweg'); Caplan ('Myths'); Aschheim ('Nazism'); and Fischer ('Anmerkungen'). For detailed accounts of the critique of the Sonderweg thesis, see especially Eley ('British Model'; *From Unification*;

II. Critiques of the German exceptionalism thesis

Geoff Eley articulated the most fundamental critique of the exceptionalism thesis, challenging its elision of socio-economic class locations with specific political/ideological positions. The assumption that bourgeoisie should 'normally' be in the forefront of liberal and historical change provides the standard by which exceptionalism theories judge the German middle classes and find them wanting (Eley, 'British Model', pp. 58, 75–90). Echoing Ernesto Laclau, (*Politics*), Eley insisted, however, that values and ideologies cannot be associated in a one-to-one way with social classes and modes of production. One cannot assume a necessary affinity between the bourgeoisie and parliamentary structures, liberal ideas, or democratic revolutions. The standards applied to nineteenth-century German liberalism are essentialist and anachronistic (Eley, 'Bismarckian Germany', p. 25):

> In maintaining the traditional view that German liberals failed – capitulated and denied the essential principles of liberalism in fact – historians like Böhme and Wehler bring an unrealistically twentieth-century standard of successful liberalism to bear on the problem, in which advanced criteria of liberal democracy, welfare statism and civil rights are used to evaluate the consistency and effectiveness of a mid-nineteenth-century liberalism.

A related criticism was directed against the implicit assumption that industrial capitalism as a system normally corresponds to democratic and liberal forms of politics and ideology (cf. Jessop, 'Capitalism'). Eley and Blackbourn also reject the idealised history of Britain (and the USA) which the critical exceptionalists used in their comparisons with Germany.

Another set of disagreements concerned the 'facts', or the interpretation of facts. Most political and cultural forms in Imperial Germany, according to Blackbourn and Eley, were quite serviceable for Germany's growing capitalist economy, even if they diverged from the norms of modernisation theory and liberal political philosophy. Various elements of the Kaiserreich which the Sonderweg model viewed as atavistic could be recast as modern and as compatible with capitalism. These included the Imperial German state, the legal system, liberalism, the Kulturkampf of the 1870s, and the norms and forms of everyday bourgeois life. The German unification settlement of 1867–71, for example, far from consolidating neo-feudal power

'Bourgeois Revolution'; 'German History'; 'Bismarckian Germany'); Evans ('Myth'); Faulenbach ('Eine Variante'); Groh ('Le "Sonderweg"'); and Kocka ('Der "deutsche Sonderweg"'; 'German history').

against the rising middle class, was 'an elaborate framework of capitalist enabling laws' (Eley, 'Bismarckian Germany', p. 28) comprising standardised markets, measures, and laws governing commercial transactions.

This counter-image of the German Empire as bourgeois and modern has been strengthened by recent studies of other areas, such as law (John, *Politics*), urbanism (Gall, *Stadt*; Ladd, *Urban Planning*), administrative change (Barmeyer, *Hannovers Eingliederung*), science policy (Feldman, 'Politics', pp. 259–63; vom Brocke, 'Hochschulpolitik'; Burchardt, *Wissenschaftspolitik*), and education (Blessing, *Staat*). The national system of poor relief promoted movement of labour power to sites of economic growth, and both national social insurance and municipal relief policies were attuned to the needs of industry and the logic of capitalism (Steinmetz, 'Myth'; *Regulating the Social*). Immigration laws were also adapted to German employers' labour needs (Herbert, *Foreign Labor*; Bade, *Deutsche*). Smith (*German Colonial Empire*) argued persuasively that German overseas colonial policy was driven less by the emigrationist goals favoured by conservative agrarian circles than by business concerns (even if few firms in the overseas colonies were actually profitable).[30] Various aspects of middle-class existence have also been reexamined, from fencing (Frevert, *Ehrenmänner*; 'Bourgeois Honour') to family life (Gall, *Bürgertum*), undermining the notion of a 'feudalised' German bourgeoisie (Blackbourn and Evans, *German Bourgeoisie*). Indeed, recent 'detailed studies seem to show that the aristocratic influence on the high bourgeoisie was not more but *less* pronounced in Germany compared with England or France' (Kocka, 'German History', p. 9). Wilhelmine Germany had a multifaceted discourse on modern sexuality and the largest gay liberation movement in Europe (Steakley, *Homosexual Emancipation Movement*). And the so-called 'primitivism' in German art at the beginning of the century is best interpreted not as literal cultural regression but as a distinctly modern appropriation of the 'primitive' in an effort to solve specifically aesthetic problems.[31]

Some exceptionalist historiography has depicted even the supposed-

---

[30] Detailed research on specific colonies has tended to reinforce these conclusions (cf. Sunseri, 'Social History'; Michel 'Les plantations'). Even in the German settler colony of South West Africa (Namibia) the tide turned against the German settler-farmers after the discovery of diamonds in 1908 (cf. Bley, *South-West Africa*, pp. 196ff). The settlers' displeasure with the administration of the colony, especially its land policies, can be seen graphically in pre-1914 South-West-African newspapers like the *Lüderitzbuchter Zeitung* and the *Keetmanshooper Zeitung*.

[31] See Lloyd (*German Expressionism*), who has argued against the standard view (Rubin 'Primitivism') that French cubism broke more decisively than German expressionism with older forms of visual representation in response to non-European art. See also Ekstein's study of German modernism (*Rites of Spring*, pp. 68, 80–9).

ly 'normal' stream of Imperial Government development, industrial expansion, as permeated by atavistic employer practices. German employers are said to have used repressive or paternalistic forms of industrial relations that are deemed 'traditional'. Recent studies have argued, however, that German capitalists were quite rational to employ such strategies (Crew, *Town*; Eley, 'British Model', pp. 108–10). On a related note, Biernacki (*Fabrication*) has shown that German managers and workers in late-nineteenth-century textile mills operated with more abstract ('modern') notions of time and labour than their contemporaries in British textiles.

One of the most powerful rebuttals of the critical Sonderweg approach has thus involved simply reversing the terms and emphasising elements of cultural and political modernity and *Bürgerlichkeit* in the German Empire. It is important to emphasise, however, that most of the critics are not returning to the views of conservative historians who *deny* the existence of connections between Nazism and pre-1914 German society. Only a few of the younger critics of exceptionalism have tried to send a 'good Empire' into battle against the 'evil Empire' of the Sonderweg theorists.[32] Instead, the central questions have been whether Imperial German institutions and practices were really so different from those of contemporary European societies, whether the 'evils' that undeniably existed in the Kaiserreich were an integral part of capitalist modernity or antithetical to it, and whether and how these evils are related to Nazism.

Opposition to the Sonderweg thesis is logically compatible with a number of different explanatory approaches to Nazism. Some of these alternatives concentrate on the Weimar period and deny the existence of deeper historical causes. Yet there is overwhelming evidence for various types of continuity between the Nazi era and earlier periods (cf. Kershaw, *Nazi Dictatorship*, pp. 143–7). Most critics of the Sonderweg thesis have not denied the existence of connections between Nazism and pre-1918 Germany, but have tried to be more specific about the exact character of 'continuity', about the varying historical depth of different causal strands, and about their interaction with factors originating during the 1918–33 period. The sources of Nazism and the practices and ideological elements that made up the Nazi repertoire cannot be seen as unchanged 'traditions'. As Eley writes 'the crucial problem becomes that of establishing how certain "traditions" became selected for survival rather than others – how certain beliefs and practices came to reproduce themselves under radically changed

[32] For an odd exception, see Dukes and Remak (*Another Germany*). Even the new conservatives have focused their energies on the Nazi era and have had less to say about the Kaiserreich, with a few important exceptions like Michael Stürmer.

264

circumstances, and how they became subtly transformed in the very process of renewal' ('Facism', p. 261).

Although the Nazis relied on elements of earlier ideologies rather than conjuring their policies out of thin air, they redefined these materials and combined them in unprecedented ways. The Nazi eugenics programme, for example, was the outcome of a continual radicalisation of the most reactionary elements of pre-1933 eugenics and the marginalisation of the 'respectable' (i.e. non-racist and non-repressive) sections of the eugenics movement (cf. Weindling, *Health*; Weingart, Kroll, and Bayertz, *Rasse*; Weiss, *Race Hygiene*). Before 1933, German eugenics was neither more extremist nor more successfully implemented than elsewhere.[33] One can see a similar mix of continuity and radicalisation in the policies concerning German youth (Peukert, *Grenzen*) and foreign workers (Herbert, *Foreign Labor*). Nazi race policies, 'colonisation' of Eastern Europe, and genocide were prefigured, albeit on a much smaller scale, in the pre-1914 colonial empire.[34]

An illustration of the way adherents and critics of the Sonderweg thesis give sharply different readings of the same apparent continuities in German history can be illustrated using the example of the disproportionate support for Nazism among the German petty bourgeoisie. Both sides may agree on the 'problem': As Walter Benjamin wrote in 1930, echoing other critics such as Kracauer (*Die Angestellten*) and Geiger ('Panik'), 'today there is no other class whose thoughts and emotions are more alienated from the concrete reality of its existence than the white-collar workers (*Gesammelte Schriften*, p. 220). The supposed paradox is that white-collar workers did not think and vote according to their 'objective' class position, which resembled that of the skilled working class. The exceptionalism narrative understands this 'alienation' partly in terms of the 'continuing presence [in Germany] of pre-industrial corporatist/bureaucratic traditions at advanced stages of industrialisation' (Kocka, *White Collar Workers*, p. 265; 'Class Formation', p. 78).[35] The critics might respond that sharp divisions between white- and blue-collar workers were not specific to Germany, but

---

[33] Indeed, eugenic sterilisation policies were first put into effect in the USA, and served as an inspiration to German eugenicists (Proctor, *Racial Hygiene*).

[34] Most significant are the urban land expropriation policies in the coastal city of Douala in German Cameroon (Eckert, *Die Duala*), efforts to repress racial mixing (Schulte-Althoff, 'Rassenmischung'), and the 'extermination order' against the Herero people by German troops during the 1904–7 war in South West Africa (Bley, *South-West Africa*).

[35] Kocka's (*White Collar Workers*; 'Class Formation') account of the different strength and location of the 'collar-line' in Germany is more multifaceted, of course, evoking *inter alia* the 1911 white-collar workers insurance law, which is not usually considered part of the negative exceptionalism syndrome.

common throughout Europe (Eley, 'Fascism', p. 260).[36] German white-collar workers' support for Hitler might have resulted less from any deep-seated mentality or habitus than from specific political and ideological processes, especially the left-wing parties' failure to respond productively to the shift to the Left by many white-collar workers in 1918 (Speier, *White-collar Workers*; Eley, *Fascism'*, p. 261). Thus even if the finding of white-collar over-representation among Nazi supporters was sustained – and there is increasing evidence that petty bourgeois supporters were less central to the Nazis' success than had previously been thought (Kocka, 'German History', p. 8) – the same facts may be constructed as continuity by one analyst and as change by the other.

In sum, German historians have pointed to serious shortcomings with the Sonderweg theory's overall comparative framework, its conceptual apparatus, and its evaluation of the evidence. Careful empirical work has chipped away at the image of the Kaiserreich as plagued by cultural atavisms and political backwardness. German politics were less demo-cratic than the rest of the 'West' in some respects but more advanced in others, such as the autonomy of municipal governments, universal male suffrage, and the strength of the socialist party. The state was possibly more independent of society than in France or Britain, but its policies were no less 'bourgeois' or 'modern'. German colonial policy was on average no more brutal or exploitative than French, Belgian, Dutch, Spanish, Portuguese, or Italian colonialism. In areas such as social and urban policies, education, science, and (after 1900) the arts, Imperial Germany was 'exceptional' only in a positive sense.

III. Transcending the social ontology of the exceptionalism debate

In response to these criticisms, proponents of the critical Sonderweg thesis were quick to insist on the differences between their respective positions or the non-existence of a distinct interpretive 'school' (Puhle, *Zur Legende*). Some even seem to have retreated into an ostensibly non-theoretical narrative historiography, with its more implicit forms of arguing through emplotment (White, *Metahistory*). Wehler's recent statements, however (see especially *Deutsche Gesellschaftsgeschichte*), explicitly reaffirm the main arguments of the 1973 book with respect to the political Sonderweg, while retracting some of the cultural arguments, which were less central in his account anyway. Wehler now places the term *Sonderweg* in quotation marks, preferring to speak of *Sonderbeding-ungen* – special or exceptional conditions (*Deutsche Gesellschaftsgeschichte*, p. 470). He still insists on the peculiar relationship of the Junkers to the

---

[36] The exceptional case calling for explanation might then be the United States and not Germany; see Kocka (*White Collar Workers*).

Imperial German state and on the German bourgeoisie's unusual 'striving for proximity to the state (*Staatsnähe*)', its 'submissive obedience to the state' (*Deutsche Gesellschaftsgeschichte*, p. 1268). Other 'special conditions' included Germany's authoritarian regime, powerful bureaucracy, and militarized form of nationalism, and the intensity of its antisocialism (*Deutsche Gesellschaftsgeschichte*, p. 1290). But Wehler now recognises that urban policy, education, and science in Imperial Germany were internationally advanced and acknowledges the untenability of the 'earlier formula of a "deficit of embourgeoisement" as a basic constituent of the "Sonderweg"' (*Deutsche Gesellschaftsgeschichte*, p. 1288).'' There was nothing unusual in comparative terms about the German bourgeoisie's 'imitation of the aristocracy' (*Deutsche Gesellschaftsgeschichte*, pp. 473, 719, 1270). Yet Wehler still insists that 'the German "Sonderweg" leading to National Socialism was deeply influenced by the Prussian aristocracy' ('Der Niedergang', p. 15).

None of this represents a revision of the basic model of society underlying the critical Sonderweg thesis, which is usually based implicitly (or, as in Wehler's case, explicitly – see Wehler, 'Modernisierungstheorie') on some version of modernisation theory.[37] Societies are conceptualised in terms of an array of subsystems or fields, each of which can be evaluated in terms of its relative degree of modernisation. Societies whose subsystems exhibit radically different levels of modernisation are subject to stress, crisis, or Durkheimian 'anomie'. Versions of exceptionalism based on Marxism are not much different in this regard. Marxists also emphasise the differential penetration of the various sectors of a social totality by the processes of commodification and capitalist rationality. Of course, Marxism has always seen social change as driven by contradictions between 'non-contemporaneous' forces – in the orthodox formulation, between the forward-pushing 'forces of production' and the outdated class relations that fetter the forces' further development (cf. Cohen, *Marx's Theory*).[38] Such contradictions are the very 'motor of history' within Marxism, and not some sort of unusual 'pathology'. Of course, traditional Marxism had difficulties making sense of the long-term coexistence of societal forms at radically different levels of capitalist development, or of 'superstructures' that

---

[37] On modernisation and political development theory, see the works published by the Committee on Comparative Politics of the US Social Science Research Council in the 1960s; also Huntington and Dominguez ('Political Development') and Inkeles (*Becoming Modern*). For the explicit connection to fascism and Nazism, see Scheuch and Klingemann ('Theorie') and the classic analysis of Parsons, who understood the juxtaposition in Germany of rapid industrialisation and urbanisation with cultural and political conservatism and leading to 'malintegration, tension, and strain' ('Democracy', pp. 236, 241).

[38] This is not to say that Marx himself necessarily understood social change in this way, even if some of his simpler formulations (such as the 1859 preface) support this reading.

diverged radically from their 'bases'. Non-orthodox Marxists, however, have been fascinated by such complexities, which they have addressed with such varying formulations as 'relative autonomy', 'Bonapartism', the 'articulation of modes of production', or *Ungleichzeitigkeit* (e.g. Althusser, 'Contradiction'; Poulantzas, *Fascism*; Wolpe, *Articulation*; Bloch, *Heritage*). Nonetheless, the sheer existence of Ungleich-zeitigkeit is usually seen as sufficient for explaining Nazism or other crises.[39]

Marxists and modernisation theorists thus share key ontological assumptions about societies, even if they have different views of the substance of the key historical process. Both assume that there *is* such a fundamental process, that all spheres of social life should be assessed in terms of the degree to which they have been seized by this process, and that unequal development is unstable and possibly dangerous. Black-bourn and Eley (*Mythen*; *Peculiarities*), for instance, do not challenge the assumption that correspondence among the levels of a social formation is a normal condition.[40] Instead, they set out to show that Imperial Germany was in fact characterised by just such contemporaneity, by redescribing various phenomena as modern and bourgeois.[41] More specifically, the critical Sonderweg approach shares the following assumptions theory with its critics:

(1) That all societies are composed of a predefined set of separate subsystems (typically called the political, economic, cultural, etc);

(2) That the level of development within each of the subsystems can

---

[39] At a deeper level, the similarity between Bloch's analysis of the effects of non-simultaneity and Althusser's ('Contradiction', pp. 114–16) analysis of Stalinism begins to crumble. Althusser's discussion of 'over-determination' suggests that simple non-contemporaneity of one social level vis-à-vis the rest of the social formation would not be enough to create an overall societal crisis, a 'ruptural unity', that could give rise to Stalinism or Nazism.

[40] My own study of social policy in Imperial Germany (Steinmetz, *Regulating the Social*) is not exempt from this criticism.

[41] A further problem is the impossibility of agreeing on what should be taken as 'modernity' or 'Bürgerlichkeit' within any given field. This undecidability is due in part to the different theoretical frameworks of the exceptionalists and their critics, but equally limiting are the features they both share as products of the same historical epoch. Thus, until recently, both Marxists and modernisation theorists regarded industrial concentration as the hallmark of economic modernisation or capitalist development. Within German historiography, this led both groups to focus on Germany's large, bureaucratic corporations. Gary Herrigel's study (*Industrial Construc-tions*), however, argues that the *Gewerbelandschaften* of highly specialised small and medium-sized firms have been a crucial component of German economic growth since the eighteenth century. Yet it has only become possible to perceive the modernity of these small firms in the past decade or so, *after* they had already emerged as the leading sector in the advanced capitalist world, and after the development of theories of post-Fordism and flexible specialisation. In other words, today's atavism may become tomorrow's avant-garde.

be measured in terms of some quality that applies across subsystems, like modernity or Bürgerlichkeit;

(3) That normal or stable societies exhibit roughly similar levels of modernity or Bürgerlichkeit in the different subsystems;

(4) That lack of correspondence across subsystems may lead to psychological, social, and political 'pathologies' (including fascism).

Much contemporary social theory, including the work of Luhmann (*Communication*) and Bourdieu ('Forms'; *Logic*), would reject these assumptions. Rather than comparing these theories in any detail, my goal here is to use their shared insights to criticise the way in which the Sonderweg debate has been framed. Contemporary social theory rejects the notion that one can determine a priori a 'normal' set of distinct social subsystems[42] for all modern societies, or that each of the subsystems should evolve in the same direction or at the same pace. Instead, the number of distinct subsystems, their character, and their degree of closure will vary as a function of contingent struggles, accidents, and histories. Each subsystem has its own autonomous forms of capital (Bourdieu) or operating codes (Luhmann), not to mention its own distinctive temporality.[43] For Luhmann, there is no common yardstick with which to compare the subsystems other than the simple fact of their closure or lack thereof. The *contents* of the subsystems cannot be compared; there is no 'superordinate standpoint of representation' for the entire system (*Communication*, p. 114).[44] In fact, Luhmann construes *convergence* in the logic of different functional subsystems as societal de-differentiation, hence regression (*Communication*, pp. 109–10). For Bourdieu, each field has its 'indigenous' forms of cultural capital and its own specific stakes. Economic capital cannot directly dominate each field, nor can economic scales of measurement be uniformly applied across fields – even if it is possible to translate 'cultural capital' into

---

[42] My use of Luhmann's term 'subsystem' in the following discussion rather than Bourdieu's 'field' does not express a preference for Luhmann or a denial of the massive differences between these theorists. Both theorists (as well as Laclau and Mouffe) fulfil the same critical purpose, however, with respect to the Sonderweg debate.

[43] On 'subsystem'-specific temporalities, see Braudel ('History'); Althusser (*Reading Capital*, pp. 91–118); Bourdieu (*Outline*).

[44] Against post-modernism, and in common with modernisation theory, Luhmann's theory does have a strong criterion of *progress*. The relevant difference from modernisation theory, however, is that progress has to do with the structural fact of subsystem differentiation and not with the specific contents of the various subsystems. A subsystem might well be based on a code that seems 'traditional', or on 'programming' that valorises the more 'primitive' pole of the binary code (cf. Luhmann, *Ecological Communication*, pp. 44–50 on 'coding' vs. 'programming'). For an assessment of the system's overall modernity, however, only the existence of autonomous (autopoietic) subsystems is relevant. On autopoesis, see Luhmann (*Ecological Communication*) and Jessop (*State Theory* pp. 320–31).

economic capital through more or less complicated and arduous processes (cf. Bourdieu, *Distinction*).[45]

The main point of these brief comments is that the condition of pervasive modernity cannot be held up as a 'normal' (or 'unexceptional') feature of modern societies. Historians interested in understanding the forms and nature of continuity in German history do not have to demonstrate the pervasive modernity or lack thereof in nineteenth-century Germany. The absence of modernity in some spheres, the existence of a *décalage* between structural levels, does not automatically explain the rise of Nazism. On the other hand, if it could be shown that the hegemonic projects of conservative groups were successful in the Kaiserreich, this would be an important place to look for continuities into the 1930s. Wehler's term 'special conditions', once stripped of its residual sense of comparison to an ideal-typical benchmark or baseline, seems to point in this direction. Who could deny, for example, that the autocratic and socially insulated character of the central state and politics in the Kaiserreich continued to shape Weimar politics, playing a role even in the abdication of power by the Reichstag and the collaboration with Hitler of state bureaucrats? The emphasis should be on exploring the actual institutions and ideologies, the fields of power and discourse, the successes and failures of hegemonic projects in German history, and then on showing how some of these materials eventually played a role in the rise and evolution of the Nazi regime.

Rejecting the critical Sonderweg thesis does not entail abandoning the notion of the singularity of the Nazi crimes, as some have implied (Faulenbach, 'Eine Variante'). Nor can the critique of the inherited Sonderweg thesis be equated with arguments (cf. Broszat, *Nach Hitler*) about the so-called 'historicisation' of Nazism. Indeed, the alternative approach proposed here is *more* open to the role of contingency and unique constellations of causes, and hence to *singularity*, than the exceptionalism approach.[46] The social-theoretical assumptions underlying the exceptionalism thesis suggest, somewhat perversely, the (potential) non-uniqueness of Nazism. By assuming the existence of a specific and delimited set of causal mechanisms determining macrosocial outcomes, the exceptionalism thesis implies that the 'outcome' in

---

[45] Economic capital thus operates across the social formation as a sort of abstract common denominator. This means that Bourdieu is able to handle societal-wide logics as well as field-specific ones, and, unlike Luhmann, does not need to construe the former as a threat to societal 'differentiation'. On attempts to reintroduce such society-wide codes into Luhmannian systems theory, see Rempel ('Systems Theory').

[46] See for example Eley's (1986) essay 'What Produces Fascism', which adumbrates a conjunctural causation model that points inexorably toward Nazism's uniqueness, as against the generalising 'theories of fascism'.

question could arise elsewhere. All societies have to traverse the 'crises of development' which produced the tensions leading to Nazism in Germany (cf. Wehler, *German Empire*, p. 239; Pflanze, 'Sammlungspolitik', pp. 158, 192). Whatever its ostensible emphasis on Germany's peculiarities, on a deeper level the exceptionalism thesis is based on a generalising model. But all recent philosophy of social science agrees that 'covering-law' models of social change are untenable in open systems like societies.[47] This does not invalidate the use of theory or comparison, only the search for general, repeatable explanatory models. Historical explanation is unavoidably conjunctural (Sewell, 'Three Temporalities').

As we will see in the next section, Sonderweg discourse is used so widely that we can hardly expect it to disappear any time soon. I will suggest in the conclusion that the Sonderweg should be redefined and not abandoned to the politicians and publicists. Rejecting general models of development does not require that we renounce the term 'Sonderweg' altogether. It does require that we leave the rarefied world of social theory and enter the terrain of ideas as 'weapons' (Kondylis, 'Sonderweg', p. 24).

IV. The Sonderweg as a political weapon

At the conference that gave rise to this volume, Eric Hobsbawm suggested that the Sonderweg thesis was 'no longer so burningly contemporary'.[48] This was also my initial reaction when I was asked to write on the Sonderweg for this volume. There is massive evidence, however, that while the critical exceptionalism thesis is on the defensive, Sonderweg discourse is alive and well. The notion of a German Sonderweg crops up in *New Yorker* articles (Kramer, 'Letter', p. 59) and in *New York Times* book reviews, where readers were recently assured that 'the roots of the Third Reich are to be found in Imperial

---

[47] More specifically, the ontology of both modernisation theory and its critics suggests that societies can be treated as quasi-'closed systems' (similar to experiments in the natural sciences; cf. Bhaskar *Realist Theory*; *Scientific Realism*), with a limited and predetermined set of 'independent variables' determining outcomes. But the causal mechanisms which produce social effects cannot be isolated as in a laboratory; human societies (like most natural systems as well) are unavoidably 'open systems'. As Bhaskar has shown, even many natural sciences cannot be understood in terms of single mechanisms or 'constant conjunctions of events', and therefore do not allow *prediction* but only post hoc *explanation*. The outcomes of natural evolution, for example, are the unpredictable result of interactions between diverse causal mechanisms, including not just random genetic mutations and natural selection, but also those mechanisms driving changes in the physical environment. If such natural events cannot be predicted or classified into a finite set of categories, why should historical structures as complex as 'German society' be amenable to such analysis?

[48] From the author's handwritten notes on the conference.

271

Germany'.[49] In this section I want to explore some of the sites of this proliferation, especially the increasing use of the Sonderweg as a rhetorical weapon in German politics.

As noted earlier, the critical Sonderweg thesis has been used 'politically' since its inception. This began in the context of World War I and crystallised during World War II in the Allied countries. United States Vice President Henry Wallace drew on a major theme of exceptionalism discourse in a national radio address in 1942:

> The German people must learn to un-learn all that they have been taught, not only by Hitler, but by his predecessors in the last hundred years, by so many of their philosophers and teachers.[50]

Talcott Parsons' wartime radio broadcasts, newspaper articles, and lectures in the military government training programme at Harvard's School of Overseas Administration were also based on an exceptionalism model (Gerhardt, 'Introduction'). The Sonderweg notion guided the western Allies' early policies in occupying Germany, as Berghahn ('Afraid') has recently recalled:

> When British and American soldiers advanced into Hitler's rapidly disintegrating empire in the spring of 1945, they carried with them mental images not only of a murderous dictatorship, but also of a backward Germany in which democracy and other benefits of modernity had never firmly taken root. As their officers and occupation manuals were telling them, this was a society run by a band of Nazi war criminals with the backing of authoritarian landowners, Prussian militarists and reactionary coal and steel barons, a society that had been swept by an irrational ideology into an orgy of destruction. There was also much serious talk about the peculiarities of the German mind.

By this time, the figure of the German Sonderweg had accumulated powerfully charged historical associations. The term 'Sonderweg' was also a 'multi-accentual' signifier, open to radically disparate uses by different actors.[51]

Since the 1980s, the boundaries between the political and intellectual uses of the Sonderweg theory have become increasingly blurred. The warning against an 'exceptionalist relapse' has been deployed in various settings, often with little connection to the original problematic

---

[49] Book review of Hannah Pakula's *An Uncommon Woman* by Olivier Bernier, *New York Times Book Review* (17 Nov. 1995, p. 22).

[50] Quoted in Gerhardt ('Introduction'), p. 40. Gerhardt also discusses the wartime participation of US academics and psychiatrists in government functions concerning Germany.

[51] On the notion of 'multi-accentual' signifiers, those bearing different meanings for different groups or speakers, see Hall ('Rediscovery').

(cf. Glotz, 'Sonderweg', pp. 333–4). In the early 1980s, Wehler evoked the Sonderweg in his polemic against the German peace movement's 'neutralism' (Wehler, 'Wir Brauchen'). After 1989, numerous historians and social scientists reached spontaneously into the exceptionalist toolkit when called upon to make sense of the collapse of the GDR and German unification (e.g. Offe, 'Wohlstand'). Jürgen Kocka, whose detailed explorations of the history of the German bourgeoisie in the 1980s led him to propose a much more limited application of Sonderweg discourse, fell back on the familiar category in 1990 (Kocka, 'Revolution'; 'Sonderweg'). The seminar of experts called together by Margaret Thatcher in 1990 to discuss German unification was organised around an exceptionalist question: have the Germans changed?[52] Wolfgang Mommsen ('Die DDR', p. 23) referred to the 'peculiar German path to modernity' and Germany's 'absence of an authentic democratic tradition' in accounting for the establishment of Communist rule in the GDR. According to Lutz Niethammer ('Erfahrungen', p. 114), the German Sonderweg not only led to the Third Reich but also conditioned the development of the GDR. Niethammer concludes ominously that 'we have landed once again in the track of the German Sonderweg, or perhaps in its *Ausläufer*'.[53]

German political actors have also latched onto Sonderweg terminology. In 1989 and 1990, warnings against efforts to retain a second, democratised German state in the East were often framed in terms of the Sonderweg.[54] Accusations of flirting with exceptionalism were used extensively to attack opposition to German participation in the Gulf War and other joint military missions.[55] Evoking exceptionalist

---

[52] Fritz Stern, 'Die Hoffnungen der Deutschen und die Sorgen der anderen', *Frankfurter Allgemeine Zeitung*, 26 July 1990.

[53] The word *Ausläufer* ambiguously suggests both 'offshoots', as if the Sonderweg was starting down a new path, and 'end portions', as if the Sonderweg were in its final stretch. Cf. Niethammer ('Erfahrungen', p. 115).

[54] For CDU statements explicitly equating opposition to unification with a German 'Sonderweg', see 'Kohl beruhigt die Verbündeten – Deutschland beschreitet keinen Sonderweg', *Frankfurter Allgemeine Zeitung*, 18 July 1990; 'Erfurt und Mainz sind eins', *Frankfurter Allgemeine Zeitung*, 4 December 1989. The Sonderweg was even broadened to include any condition provoking the 'scepticism of the western countries'. See 'Fallstricke. Die Vereinigung Deutschlands und die Europäische Integration'. *Gewerkschaftsreport* No. 1 (1991), pp. 14–19 (journal of the German industrial institute for labour union questions).

[55] See also: 'Sonderweg in die Sackgasse', *Süddeutsche Zeitung*, 16 June 1993; 'Am Ende des Sonderweges', *Süddeutsche Zeitung*, 13 April 1993; 'Deutschlands Bündnisrolle vor dem Richter', *Neue Zürcher Zeitung*, 3 April 1993; 'Germany's "Special Way"', *Washington Post*, 13 February 1991; 'Der Uno-Generalsekretaer am Rhein', *Neue Zürcher Zeitung*, 12 January 1993; 'Scholz: Deutschland muss Verantwortung übernehmen', *Süddeutsche Zeitung*, 3 Dec. 1992; 'Le retour de la "question allemande"', *Le Monde*, 23 December 1991; also the essays by Wolfgang Thierse and Jürgen Manthey discussed in Glotz (*Die falsche Normalisierung*).

arguments, far-left groups have tried to stop a resurgence of present-day 'Junkers'.[56] And while the idea of exceptionalism is usually negatively charged, far-right intellectuals and parties have revived the older approach which praises Germany's supposed deviation from the west rather than condemning it (Habermas, 'New Intimacy'). Franz Schönhuber, founder and former leader of the far-right Republican Party, rails against Germany's impure 'Vodka-Cola culture' and endorses a German 'third way' between East and West.[57] Fulminating against those who would replace the 'historical nation' with a 'supermarket civilisation', Ernst Nolte (*Bürgerkrieg*, p. 429) draws on this rich vein of anti-western exceptionalism.

The boundaries between the Sonderweg as formal historical hypothesis, as myth, and as political ideology have thus become extremely fluid. Social science again has become a part of the very reality it purports to analyse.

Conclusion: a post-Holocaust Sonderweg

I suggested above that the underlying sociological assumptions of the critical exceptionalism thesis might impair its ability to theorise 'singular' political outcomes. This becomes even clearer when we consider the exceptionalists' view of post-1945 German history. The standard position has been that 1945 marked the 'end of the Sonderweg', at least for West Germany (Kocka, *Revolution* 495–9; Winkler 'Mit Skepsis', p. 8). Some historians insist rather anxiously that the Federal Republic has overcome Germany's peculiar legacy by becoming an 'integral component of modern western civilisation' and 'a functional western democracy' (Sontheimer, 'Der "Deutsche Geist"', p. 238), and by acquiring an 'international face in the cultural arena' (Mommsen, 'Die DDR', p. 29). As Kocka remarked in an interview concerning German unification, 'West Germany had become a "post-Sonderweg" Germany ... Now we are getting a new mix.'[58] The Sonderweg thesis distracted historians from deeper continuities with the Nazi era in both West and East German political culture, leading them to underestimate the distinctiveness of post-war Germany.[59]

---

[56] The persistence of the anti-aristocratic theme was evident in 1993 when a group of left-wing 'Autonomists' burned the land registers in an east German town (Barby on the Elbe) in order to obstruct the return of expropriated land to its earlier owners. Their argument, which resonated unmistakably with the critical Sonderweg thesis, was that the 'Junkers' had been a key cause of Nazism and should be prevented from recovering their property. Cf. *tageszeitung*, 28 April 1993.

[57] *tageszeitung*, 25 May 1992. For an overview of fifty contemporary far-right publications in Germany, see Lange (1993).

[58] In Los Angeles *Times*, 2 October 1990.

[59] Certainly there were other reasons for this lack of attention to post-1945 continuities,

It is probably more realistic to argue that the gulf between the political culture of Germany and its neighbours has actually *widened* as a result of the unparalleled events between 1933 and 1945. Nazism has made it much more difficult for Germany – even a unified and democratic Germany – to be just another European country (cf. Fisher, *After the Wall*). One of the most striking signs of long-term continuity in German political culture, of course, was revealed by the unexpected ease with which many Germans in 1989–90 accepted the notion that East and West Germany 'naturally' belonged together, long after the separate exist-ence of the two states had been taken for granted.[60] Many observers have noted the extent to which post-1989 discussions of the GDR's past have been shaped by Nazism, to the extent that the Stasi debate has sometimes seemed a metaphor for discussions of earlier crimes (Haber-mas, *Past*, pp. 67–8). And if the movement of right-wing violence that erupted at the end of the 1980s is an international one, the specific constellation of victims and ideologemes in the German 'manhunt' (Enzensberger, 'Great Migration') can only be understood in terms of historical Nazism (Steinmetz, 'Die (un-)moralische Ökonomie').

I cannot discuss here the multiple ways in which contemporary Germany is still influenced by the Nazi past – although these include the strenuous and incredulous denials that contemporary Germany *is* deeply shaped by that past. Suffice it to say that these lasting effects make it more appropriate to use the concept of 'exceptionalism' for the post-war period, reaching into an indefinite future. There is then truly no need to worry about giving even indirect support to the programme of 'normalising' the German past, even if we then abandon the critical Sonderweg position. Positions in the battle over the Sonderweg are probably much too entrenched to hope for such a change. On the other hand, without a concept as powerful as the Sonderweg it will be difficult to recognise the extent of the lasting effects of the Hitler regime on German culture.

including West Germany's long-term political stability and public opinion polls showing declining levels of approval for Hitler during the decades after 1945. See Kershaw (1989, pp. 264–9); but see SINUS (1981).

60 This observation is based on my own conversations with German friends and acquaintances throughout the 1980s and then in late 1989 and 1990. Even during the allegedly 'neutralist' upsurge of the early- to mid-1980s peace movement, unification was a fringe theme. Military neutralisation was typically seen as compatible with the continuing existence of the two states. Of course there were often high levels of support for reunification in opinion polls (Zitelmann 1993, pp. 173–5), but it is difficult to assess the real meaning, if any, of such results. In 1989–90, everything changed. Acceptance of unification by a large majority of West Germans was suggested by the electoral outcome of 2 December 1990, in which 54.7 per cent of West German voters approved the CDU-led governing coalition (and thus its stance in favour of immediate unification, which was the main issue in the election).

275

References

Abusch, Alexander. *Der Irrweg einer Nation* (Berlin, Aufbau-Verlag 1946).

Althusser, Louis and Étienne Balibar. *Reading Capital* (London, Verso 1986).

Althusser, Louis. 'Contradiction and Overdetermination', in *For Marx*, pp. 87–129 (London, NLB 1977).

Aschheim, Steven E. 'Nazism, Normalcy and the German *Sonderweg'*, *Studies in Contemporary Jewry. An Annual* 4 (1988), pp. 276–92.

Ayçoberry, Pierre. *The Nazi Question. An Essay on the Interpretations of National Socialism (1922–1975)*. (New York, Pantheon Books 1981).

Bade, Klaus J, ed. *Deutsche im Ausland – Fremde in Deutschland: Migration in Geschichte und Gegenwart* (Munchen, Beck 1992).

Barmeyer-Hartlieb v. Wallthor, Heide. *Hannovers Eingliederung in den preussichen Staat: Annexion und administrative Integration, 1866–1868* (Hildesheim, A. Lax 1983).

Benjamin, Walter. *Gesammelte Schriften* Vol. III. (Frankfurt am Main, Suhrkramp 1972).

Berghahn, Volker R. 'Afraid of the 20th Century', *New York Times* (10 May 1992), Section 7; p. 9.

Bhaskar, Roy. *A Realist Theory of Science* (Brighton, Harvester Press 1978).
The Possibility of Naturalism (New York, Humanities Press 1979).
Scientific Realism and Human Emancipation (London, Verso 1986).

Biernacki, Richard. *The Fabrication of Labor: German and Britain, 1640–1914* (Berkeley, University of California Press 1995).

Blackbourn, David and Geoff Eley, *Mythen deutscher Geschichtsschreibung* (Berlin, Ullstein 1980).

Blackbourn, David and Geoff Eley. *The Peculiarities of German History* (New York, Oxford University Press 1985).

Blackbourn, David and Richard J. Evans, eds. *The German Bourgeoisie. Essays on the Social History of the German Middle Class from the Late Eighteenth to the Early Twentieth Century* (London, Routledge 1991).

Blessing, Werner K. *Staat und Kirche in der Gesellschaft: institutionelle Autorität und mentaler Wandel in Bayern während des 19. Jahrhunderts.* (Göttingen, Vandenhoeck & Ruprecht 1982).

Bley, Helmut. *South-West Africa under German Rule 1894–1914* (Evanston, Northwest University Press 1971 (orig. 1968)).

Bloch, Ernst. *Heritage of our times.* Translated by Neville and Stephen Plaice (Berkeley, University of California Press 1991).

Böhme, Helmut. *Deutschlands Weg zur Großmacht. Studien zum Verhältnis von Wirtschaft und Staat während der Reichsgründungszeit 1848–1881* (Köln, Kiepenheuer & Witsch 1966).

Borkenau, Franz. 'Zur Soziologie des Faschismus', in *Theorien über den Faschismus*, ed. Ernst Nolte, pp. 156–81 (Köln, Kiepenheuer & Witsch 1967 (orig. 1933)).

Bourdieu, Pierre. *Outline of a Theory of Practice* (Cambridge, Mass., Harvard University Press 1977).
Distinction (Cambridge, Mass., Harvard University Press 1984).

'The Forms of Capital', in *Handbook of Theory and Research for the Sociology of Education*, ed. J. C. Richardson, pp. 241–58 (New York, Greenwood Press 1986).

The Logic of Practice (Stanford, Stanford University Press 1990).

Braudel, Fernand. 'History and the Social Sciences: The *Longue Durée*', in *On History*, translated by Sarah Matthews, pp. 25–54 (Chicago, University of Chicago Press 1980).

Broszat, Martin. *Nach Hitler, Der schwierige Umgang mit unserer Geschichte* (München, dtv 1988).

Brunschwig, Henri. *Enlightenment and Romanticism in Eighteenth-Century Prussia* (Chicago, University of Chicago Press 1974).

Burchardt, Lothar. *Wissenschaftspolitik in Wilhelminischen Deutschland: Vorgeschichte, Gründung und Aufbau der Kaiser-Wilhelm-Gesellschaft zur Förderung der Wissenschaft* (Göttingen, Vandenhoeck und Ruprecht 1975).

Butler, Rohan d'Olier. *The Roots of National Socialism* (Faber and Faber 1941).

Caplan, Jane. 'Myths, Models and Missing Revolutions: Comments on a Debate in German History', *Radical History Review* 34 (1986), pp. 87–99.

Carsten, Francis. 'Der preußische Adel und seine Stellung in Staat und Gesellschaft bis 1945', in *Europäischer Adel 1750–1950*, ed. Hans-Ulrich Wehler, pp. 112–25 (Göttingen, Vandenhoeck 1990).

Cohen, G. A. *Karl Marx's Theory of History: A Defence* (Princeton, Princeton University Press 1978).

Crew, David. *Town in the Ruhr: A Social History of Bochum, 1860–1914* (New York, Columbia University Press 1979).

Czichon, Eberhard. *Wer verhalf Hitler zur Macht? Zum Anteil der deutschen Industrie an der Zerstörung der Weimarer Republik* (Köln, Pahl-Rugenstein Verlag 1967).

Dahrendorf, Ralf. *Society and Democracy in Germany* (New York, Norton 1967 (orig. 1965)).

Deutscher Sonderweg - Mythos oder Realität? (München, Oldenbourg 1982).

Düding, Dieter. *Der Nationalsoziale Verein 1896–1903* (München, R. Oldenbourg Verlag 1972).

Dukes, Jack R. and Joachim Remak, eds. *Another Germany* (Boulder and London, Westview Press 1988).

Eckert, Andreas. *Die Duala und die Kolonialmächte: eine Untersuchung zu Widerstand, Protest und Protonationalismus in Kamerun vor dem Zweiten Weltkrieg* (Hamburger Studien zur afrikanischen Geschichte; Bd. 2, Münster: Lit. 1991).

Eksteins, Modris. *The Rites of Spring. The Great War and the Birth of the Modern Age* (New York, Doubleday 1989).

Eley, Geoff. 'The British Model and the German Road', in *Peculiarities*, ed. Blackbourn and Eley (1985), pp. 39–155.

From Unification to Nazism. Reinterpreting the German Past (Boston, Allen and Unwin 1986).

'What Produces Fascism: Pre-Industrial Traditions or a Crisis of the Capitalist State?' in Eley, *From Unification* (1986), pp. 254–82.

'In Search of the Bourgeois Revolution: The Particularities of German History', *Political Power and Social Theory* 7 (1988), pp. 105–33.

Reshaping the German Right. Radical Nationalism and Political Change after Bismarck (Ann Arbor, The University of Michigan Press 1991 (orig. 1980)).

'German History and the Contradictions of Modernity' (Department of History, University of Michigan 1991).

'Bismarckian Germany', in *Modern Germany Reconsidered*, ed. Gordon Martel, pp. 1–32 (London, Routledge 1992).

Elias, Norbert. *The History of Manners*, Vol. I, *The Civilizing Process* (New York, Pantheon Books 1978 (orig. 1939)).

Studien über die Deutschen: Machtkämpfe und Habitusentwicklung im 19. und 20. Jahrhundert (Frankfurt a.M.: Suhrkamp 1989).

Engels, Friedrich. *The Origin of the Family, Private Property and the State*, in Marx and Engels, *Selected Works*, Vol. III, pp. 204–334 (Moscow, Progress 1970 (orig. 1884)).

'Le socialisme de M. Bismarck', in *Marx-Engels Gesamtausgabe*, I/25, pp. 188–94 (n.d).

Enzensberger, Hans Magnus. 'The Great Migration', *Granta* 42 (Winter 1992), pp. 15–51.

Evans, Richard J. 'The Myth of Germany's Missing Revolution', in *Rethinking German History*, pp. 93–122 (London, Unwin Hyman 1987).

'Wilhelm II's Germany and the Historians', in *Rethinking German History*, pp. 23–54 (London, Unwin Hyman 1987).

Faulenbach, Bernd. *Ideologie des deutschen Weges. Die deutsche Geschichte in der Historiographie zwischen Kaiserreich und Nationalsozialismus* (München, Beck 1980).

'"Deutscher Sonderweg". Zur Geschichte und Problematik einer zentralen Kategorie des deutschen geschichtlichen Bewußtseins', *Aus Politik und Zeitgeschichte* B33, August (1981) pp. 3–21.

'Der "deutsche Weg" aus der Sicht des Exils – Zum Urteil emigrierter Historiker', *Exilforschung. Ein internationales Jahrbuch 3* (1985), pp. 11–30.

'Die Frage nach den Spezifika der deutschen Entwicklung. Zu neueren Interpretationen des 19 Jahrhunderts'. In *Neue Politische Literatur* Sonderheft 3 (1986), pp. 76ff.

'Eine Variante europäischer Normalität? Zur neuesten Diskussion über den "deutschen Weg" im 19. und 20. Jahrundert'. *Tel Aviver Jahrbuch für deutsche Geschichte* 16, (1987), pp. 285–309.

Feldman, Gerald. 'The Politics of *Wissenschaft* in Weimar Germany: A Prelude to the Dilemmas of Twentieth-Century Science Policy', in Charles S. Maier, ed., *Changing Boundaries of the Political. Essays on the evolving balance between the state and society, public and private in Europe*, (Cambridge, Cambridge University Press 1987), pp. 255–87.

Fischer, Fritz. *Griff nach der Weltmacht; die Kriegszielpolitik des kaiserlichen Deutschland, 1914–18* (Düsseldorf, Droste 1961).

Fischer, Marc. *After the Wall: Germany, the Germans, and the Burdens of History* (New York, Simon and Schuster 1995).

Fischer, Wolfram. 'Wirtschafts- und sozialgeschichtliche Anmerkungen zum "deutschen Sonderweg"', *Tel Aviver Jahrbuch für deutsche Geschichte* 16 (1987), pp. 96–116.

Frevert, Ute. *Ehrenmänner: das Duell in der bürgerlichen Gesellschaft* (Munchen, Beck 1991).

'Bourgeois Honour: Middle-Class Duellists in Germany from the Late Eighteenth to the Early Twentieth Century', in *German Bourgeoisie*, ed. Blackbourn and Evans (1991), pp. 225–92.

Gall, Lothar, ed. *Stadt und Bürgertum im 19. Jahrhundert* (München, Oldenbourg 1990).

Bürgertum in Deutschland (Berlin, Siedler 1989).

Geiger, Theodor. 'Panik im Mittelstand', *Die Arbeit* 7:10 (1930), pp. 637–54.

Gerhardt, Ute. 'Introduction: Talcott Parsons's Sociology of National Socialism', pp. 1–83 in Ute Gerhardt, ed., *Talcott Parsons on National Socialism* (New York, de Gruyter 1993).

Gerschenkron, Alexander. *Bread and Democracy in Germany* (Berkeley, CA., University of California Press 1943).

Glotz, Peter. 'Deutscher Sonderweg? Aus dem Wörterbuch des wiedervereinigten Deutschland', pp. 33–41 in *Die falsche Normalisierung. Die unmerkliche Verwandlung der Deutschen 1989 bis 1994* (Frankfurt a.M., Suhrkamp 1994).

Grebing, Helga. *Der 'deutsche Sonderweg' in Europa 1806–1945. Eine Kritik* (Stuttgart, W. Kohlhammer 1986).

Greenfield, Liah. *Nationalism: Five Roads to Modernity* (Cambridge, Mass., Harvard University Press 1992).

Groh, Dieter. 'Le "Sonderweg" de l'histoire allemande: mythe ou réalité?', *Annales, ESC* 38, (1983), pp. 1166–87.

Habermas, Jürgen. 'The New Intimacy between Politics and Culture: Theses on Enlightenment in Germany', pp. 197–205 in *The New Conservatism: Cultural Criticism and the Historians' Debate*, ed. Shierry Weber Nicholson (Cambridge, Mass., MIT Press 1989).

The Past as Future (Lincoln, University of Nebraska Press 1994).

Hall, Stuart. 'The rediscovery of "ideology": Return of the repressed in media studies', pp. 56–90, in *Culture, Society and the Media*, eds. Michael Gurevitch, Tony Bennett, James Curran and Janet Woollacott (London, Methuen 1982).

Heine, Heinrich. *Deutschland. Ein Wintermärchen* in *Sämtliche Schriften* ed. Klaus Briegleb (Munich, Carl Hanser Verlag, 1968).

Herbert, Ulrich. *A History of Foreign Labor in Germany, 1880–1980: Seasonal Workers, Forced Labourers, Guest Workers* (Ann Arbor, University of Michigan Press 1990).

Hermand, Jost. *Sieben Arten an Deutschland zu leiden* (Königstein, Athenäum 1979).

Herrigel, Gary. *Industrial Constructions: The Sources of German Industrial Power* (Cambridge, Cambridge University Press 1995).

Horkheimer, Max and Theodor Adorno. 'The Culture Industry: Enlightenment as Mass Deception', in *The Dialectic of Enlightenment*, pp. 120–67, (New York, Continuum 1986).

Huntington, Samuel and Jorge Dominguez. 'Political Development', in *Handbook of Political Science*, Vol, 3. eds., Fred Greenstein and Nelson Polsby, pp. 1–114 (Reading, Mass., Addison-Wesley Pub. Co., 1975).

Iggers, George. 'Forward', in *German History in Marxist Perspective. The East German Approach*, ed. Andreas Dorpalen, pp. 11–18 (Detroit, Wayne State University Press 1988).

Inkeles, Alex. *Becoming Modern: Individual Change in Six Developing Countries* (Cambridge, Mass.: Harvard University Press 1974).

Jessop, Bob. 'Capitalism and Democracy: The Best Possible Shell?' in *Power and the State*, eds. G. Littlejohn *et al.*, pp. 10–51 (London, Croom Helm 1978).

State Theory. Putting States in their Place (University Park, PA.: Pennsylvania State University Press 1990).

John, M.F. *Politics and the Law in Late Nineteenth-Century Germany. The Origins of the Civil Code* (Oxford, Clarendon Press 1989).

Kehr, Eckart. *Battleship Building and Party Politics in Germany 1894–1901* (Chicago, University of Chicago Press 1973).

Economic Interest, Militarism, and Foreign Policy. Essays on German History, ed. Gordon A. Craig (Berkeley, University of California Press 1977).

Kershaw, Ian. *The 'Hitler Myth'. Image and Reality in the Third Reich* (Oxford, Oxford University Press 1989).

The Nazi Dictatorship. Problems and Perspectives of Interpretation, 3rd edn. (London, Edward Arnold 1993).

Kocka, Jürgen. *White Collar Workers in America 1890–1914. A Social-Political History in International Perspective* (London/Beverly Hills, Sage 1980).

'Class formation, interest articulation, and public policy: the origins of the German white-collar class in the late nineteenth and twentieth centuries', in *Organizing Interests in Western Europe* ed. Suzanne Berger, pp. 63–82 (Cambridge, Cambridge University Press 1981).

'Der "deutsche Sonderweg" in der Diskussion', *GSR* 5(3), (1982), pp. 365–79

'German History Before Hitler: The Debate About the German "Sonderweg"', *Journal of Contemporary History* 23 (1988), pp. 3–16.

'Revolution und Nation 1989. Zur historischen Einordnung der gegenwärtigen Ereignisse', *Tel Aviver Jahrbuch für deutsche Geschichte* 19. (1990), pp. 479–99.

'Nur keinen neuen Sonderweg', *Die Zeit* Nr. 43 (Oct. 1990).

Kofler, Leo. *Zur Geschichte der bürgerlichen Gesellschaft: Versuch einer verstehenden Deutung der Neuzeit* (Berlin, Dietz 1992 (orig. 1948)).

Kohn, Hans. *The Mind of Germany: the Education of a Nation* (New York, Scribner's 1960).

Kondylis, Panajotis. 'Der deutsche "Sonderweg" und die deutschen Perspektiven', in *Westbindung* ed. Zitelmann (1993), pp. 21–37.

Kracauer, Siegfried. *Die Angestellten aus dem neuesten Deutschland* (Frankfurt am Main, Frankfurter Societäts-Druckerei 1930).

Kramer, Jane. 'Letter from Germany. The Politics of Memory' (*New Yorker* 14 Aug. 1995), pp. 48–65.

Laclau, Ernesto and Chantal Mouffe. *Hegemony and Socialist Strategy. Towards a*

Radical Democratic Politics (London, Verso 1985).

Laclau, Ernesto. *Politics and Ideology in Marxist Theory* (London, Verso 1977).

Ladd, Brian. *Urban Planning and Civic Order in Germany, 1860–1914* (Cambridge, Mass., Harvard University Press 1990).

Lange, Astrid. *Was die Rechten lesen. 50 rechtsextreme Zeitschriften: Ziele, Inhalt, Taktik* (München, Verlag C.H. Beck 1993).

Lloyd, Jill. *German Expressionism. Primitivism and Modernity* (New Haven, Yale University Press 1991).

Lowie, Robert H. *The German People: A Social Portrait of 1914* (New York, Farrar and Rinehart 1945).

Toward Understanding Germany (Chicago, University of Chicago Press 1954).

Luhmann, Niklas. *Ecological Communication* (Cambridge, Polity Press 1989).

Lukács, Georg. *Die Zerstörung der Vernunft*, Vol. I (Darmstadt, Luchterhand 1973 (orig. 1954)).

Mann, Heinrich. *Der Untertan* (Leipzig, K. Wolff 1918).

Mann, Michael. *The Sources of Social Power*, 2 vols. (New York, Cambridge University Press 1986–1993).

McGovern, William Montgomery. *From Luther to Hitler. The History of Fascist-Nazi Political Philosophy* (Boston, Houghton Mifflin 1941).

Michel, Marc. 'Les plantations allemands du mont Cameroun', *Revue Française d'Histoire d'Outre-Mer* 57, 2 (1970), pp. 183–213.

Mielke, S. *Der Hansa-Bund für Gewerbe, Handel und Industrie, 1909–1914* (Göttingen, Vandenhoeck & Ruprecht 1976).

Mitchell, Timothy. 'The Limits of the State: Beyond Statist Approaches and their Critics', *American Political Science Review* 85(1) (1991), pp. 77–96.

Moeller, Robert G. 'Die Besonderheiten der deutschen? Neue Beiträge zur Sonderwegsdiskussion', *Internationale Schulbuchforschung* 4 (1982), pp. 71–80.

Mommsen, Wolfgang J. 'Die DDR in der deutschen Geschichte', *Aus Politik und Zeitgeschichte* B 29/30 (16 July 1993), pp. 20–9.

Moore, Barrington Jr. *Social Origins of Dictatorship and Democracy* (Boston, Beacon Press 1966).

Mosse, George L. *The Crisis of German Ideology: Intellectual Origins of the Third Reich* (1st edn) (New York, Grosset & Dunlap 1964).

Toward the Final Solution. A History of European Racism (Madison, University of Wisconsin Press 1985).

NGBK (Neue Gesellschaft für bildende Kunst). *Inszenierung der Macht. Ästhetische Faszination im Faschismus* (Berlin, Nishen 1987).

Niethammer, Lutz. 'Erfahrungen und Strukturen. Prolegomena zu einer Geschichte der Gesellschaft der DDR', in *Sozialgeschichte der DDR* eds. Hartmut Kaelble, Jürgen Kocka, and Hartmut Zwahr, pp. 95–115 (Stuttgart, Klett-Cotta 1994).

Nipperdey, Thomas. 'Die Deutschen wollen und dürfen eine Nation sein', *Frankfurter Allgemeine Zeitung* No 160 (13 July 1990), p. 10.

Nolte, Ernst. *Der europäische Bürgerkrieg 1917–1945. Nationalsozialismus und Bolschewismus* (Berlin, Propyläen Verlag 1987).

Streitpunkte: heutige und künftige Kontroversen um den Nationalsozialismus (Berlin, Propyläen 1993).

Offe, Claus. 'Wohlstand, Nation, Republik. Aspekte des deutschen Sonderweges vom Sozialismus zum Kapitalismus', in *Der Zusammenbruch der DDR* eds. Hans Joas and Martin Kohli, pp. 282–301 (Frankfurt am Main, Suhrkamp 1993).

Olszewski, Henryk. 'The "German Road" Ideology in Historiography', *Polish Western Affairs* 27(2), (1986), pp. 219–39.

Parsons, Talcott, *Talcott Parsons on National Socialism*, edited by Ute Gerhardt (New York, de Gruyter 1993).

'Democracy and Social Structure in Pre-Nazi Germany', in *Talcott Parsons on National Socialism* (1993), pp. 225–42.

Peukert, Detlev J.K. *Grenzen der Sozialdisziplinierung. Aufstieg und Krise der Jugendfürsorge von 1878 bis 1932* (Köln, Bund 1986).

Pflanze, Otte. '"Sammlungspolitik" 1875–1886; Kritische Bemerkungen zu einem Modell', in *Innenpolitische Probleme des Bismarck-Reiches* ed. Otto Pflanze (München, Oldenbourg 1983).

Plessner, Helmuth. *Die verspätete Nation. Über die politische Verführbarkeit bürgerlichen Geistes* (Kohlhammer 1959).

Poulantzas, Nicos. *Fascism and Dictatorship* (London, New Left Books 1974).

Prinz, Michael and Rainer Zitelmann, eds., *Nationalsozialismus und Modernisierung* (Darmstadt, Wissenschaftliche Buchgesellschaft 1991).

Proctor, Robert. *Racial Hygiene, Medicine under the Nazis* (Harvard, Cambridge, Mass. 1988).

Puhle, Hans-Jürgen. 'Zur Legende von der "Kehrschen Schule"', *Geschichte und Gesellschaft* 4, (1978), pp. 108–19.

'Deutscher Sonderweg'. *Journal für Geschichte* 4 (1981), pp. 44–5.

Reichel, Peter. *Der schöne Schein des dritten Reiches. Faszination und Gewalt des Faschismus*, 2nd ed. (München, Carl Hanser Verlag 1992).

Rempel, Michael. 'Systems Theory and Power/Knowledge: A Foucauldian Reconstruction of Niklas Luhmann's Systems Theory'. Paper presented at the 1995 meeting of the American Sociological Association in Washington, DC.

Rosenberg, Hans. *Bureaucracy, Aristocracy and Autocracy. The Prussian Experience 1600–1815* (Cambridge, Mass., Harvard University Press 1958).

Rubin, William. *"Primitivism" in 20th Century Art: Affinity of the Tribal and the Modern* (New York, Museum of Modern Art 1984).

Scheuch, Erwin and Hans D. Klingemann. 'Theorie des Rechtsradikalismus in westlichen Industriegesellschaften', *Hamburger Jahrbuch für Wirtschafts- und Gesellschaftspolitik* (1967), pp. 11–29.

Schoenbaum, Ronald. *Hitler's Social Revolution* (Garden City, New York, Doubleday 1966).

Schöllgen, Gregor. *Angst vor der Macht. Die Deutschen und ihre Aussenpolitik* (Berlin, Ullstein Verlag 1993).

Schulte-Althoff, Franz-Joseph. 'Rassenmischung im kolonialen System. Zur deutschen Kolonialpolitik im letzten Jahrzehnt vor dem Ersten Weltkrieg', *Historisches Jahrbuch* 105 (1966), pp. 52–94.

Sewell, William H., Jr. 'Three Temporalities: Toward an Evenemental Sociology' (1991). Paper presented at the 1992 meetings of the American Sociological Association.

SINUS-Institut München, ed. *Fünf Millionen Deutsche: Wir sollten wieder einen Führer haben. Die SINUS-Studie über rechtsextremistische Einstellungen bei den Deutschen* (Reinbeck, Rowholt 1981).

Smith, Woodruff D. *The German Colonial Empire* (Chapel Hill, The University of North Carolina Press 1978).

Sontheimer, Kurt. 'Der "Deutsche Geist" – Eine Tradition ohne Zukunft', *Merkur* 36(3), (1982), pp. 232–43.

Speier, Hans. *German White-Collar Workers and the Rise of Hitler* (New Haven, Yale University Press 1986).

Steakley, James D. *The Homosexual Emancipation Movement in Germany* (New York, Arno Press 1975).

Stegmann, Dirk. *Die Erben Bismarcks. Parteien und Verbände in der Spätphase des Wilhelminischen Deutschlands* (Köln, Kiepenheuer & Witsch 1970).

Steinmetz, George. 'The Myth and the Reality of an Autonomous State: Industrialists, Junkers, and Social Policy in Imperial Germany', *Comparative Social Research* 12, (1990), pp. 239–93.

Regulating the Social: A Historical Sociology of the Welfare State in Imperial Germany (Princeton, Princeton University Press 1993).

'Regulation Theory, Post-Marxism, and the New Social Movements', *Comparative Studies in Society and History* Vol. 36 (1994), p. 1.

'Die (un-)moralische Ökonomie rechtsextremer Gewalt im Übergang zum Postfordismus', *Das Argument* 203 (1994), pp. 23–40.

'Bhaskar's Critical Realism and its Significance for Historical Sociology'. Paper presented at the 1995 meetings of the American Sociology Association in Washington, DC.

Stern, Fritz. *The Politics of Cultural Despair. A Study in the Rise of the Germanic Ideology* (Berkeley, University of California Press 1961).

Stölzl, Christoph, ed. *Bilder und Zeugnisse der deutschen Geschichte* (Berlin, Deutsches Historisches Museum 1995).

Sunseri, Thaddeus. 'A Social History of Cotton Production in German East Africa, 1884–1915'. (Ph.D. diss., University of Minnesota 1993).

Tacitus, P. Cornelius. *Germania* (Wiesbaden, VMA Verlag 1990).

Taylor, A.J.P. *The Course of German History* (London, Hamish Hamilton 1945).

Trotsky, Leon. *The Struggle against Fascism in Germany* (New York, Pathfinder Press 1971).

Veblen, Thorstein. *Imperial Germany and the Industrial Revolution* (New Brunswick, Transaction Publishers 1990 (orig. 1915)).

Vom Brocke, Bernhard. 'Hochschul- und Wissenschaftspolitik in Preussen und im Kaiserreich 1882–1907', in *Bildungspolitik in Preussen zur Zeit des Kaiserreichs*, ed. Peter Baumgart, pp. 9–118 (Stuttgart, Klett-Cotta 1980).

Weber, Max. 'Bureaucracy' in *From Max Weber: Essays in Sociology* eds. H.H. Gerth and C. Wright Mills, pp. 196–224 (New York, Oxford University Press 1958).

'The National State and Economic Policy', in *Reading Weber* ed. Keith Tribe, pp. 188–209 (London, Routledge 1989).

Wehler, Hans-Ulrich. 'Wir brauchen keinen neuen deutschen Sonderweg. Antwort eines Historikers auf den Neutralismus der Friedensbewegung', *Frankfurter Allgemeine Zeitung* (15 September 1982).

'Nicht verstehen – der Preußennostalgie widerstehen!" in *Preußen ist wieder chic . . . Politik und Polemik in zwanzig Essays*, pp. 67–71 (Frankfurt/M., Suhkramp 1983).

'Vorzüge und Nachteile des deutschen Sonderwegs', in *Preußen ist wider chic.. . Politik und Polemik in zwanzig Essays*, pp. 33–6 (Frankfurt/M.: Suhrkamp 1983).

The German Empire 1871–1918 (Leamington Spa, Berg 1985 (German original 1973)).

Deutsche Gesellschaftsgeschichte Vol. III. (München, C.H. Beck 1995).

'Nationalismus als fremdenfeindliche Integrationsideologie', in *Das Gewalt-Dilemma* ed. Wilhelm Heitmeyer, pp. 73–90 (Frankfurt am Main, Suhrkamp 1995).

'Westbindung – oder Nationalismus und Großmachtsucht der Neuen Rechten?' in *Die Gegenwart als Geschichte*, pp. 138–58 (München, Beck 1995).

'Aufklärung oder "Sinnstiftung?"', in *Die Gegenwart als Geschichte*, pp. 189–201 (München, Beck 1995).

'Selbstverständnis und Zukunft der westdeutschen Geschichtswissenschaft', in *Die Gegenwart als Geschichte*, pp. 202–14 (München, Beck 1995).

'Der Niedergang einer Herrschaftselite', *Die Zeit* Nr. 45 (3 Nov. 1995).

'Modernisierungstheorie und Geschichte', in *Die Gegenwart als Geschichte* pp. 13–59 (München, Beck 1995).

Weindling, Paul. *Health, Race and German Politics between National Unification and Nazism 1870–1945* (Cambridge, Cambridge University Press 1989).

Weingart, Peter, Jürgen Kroll and Kurt Bayertz. *Rasse, Blut und Gene: Geschichte der Eugenik und Rassenhygiene in Deutschland* (Frankfurt/M.: Suhrkamp 1988).

Weiss, Sheila Faith. *Race Hygiene and National Efficiency: The Eugenics of Wilhelm Schallmeyer* (Berkeley, University of California Press 1987).

Weissman, Karlheinz. 'Der "Westen" in der deutschen Historiographie nach 1945'. In *Westbindung* ed. Zitelmann (1993), pp. 343–63.

White, Hayden. *Metahistory. The Historical Imagination in Nineteenth-Century Europe* (Baltimore, John Hopkins University Press 1973).

Winkler, Heinrich. 'Mit Skepsis zur Einigung', *Die Zeit* Nr. 40 (18 Sept. 1990).

Wolpe, Harold, ed. *The Articulation of Modes of Production* (London, Routledge and Kegan Paul 1980).

Wright, Erik Olin. 'Reflections on *Classes*', in *The Debate on Classes*, pp. 57–63 (London, Verso Books, 1989)

Zitelmann, Rainer, ed. *Westbindung: Chancen und Risiken für Deutschland* (Frankfurt a.M., Propyläen 1993).

Hitler. Selbstverständnis eines Revolutionärs (Hamburg, Berg 1987).

12

Stalinism and the politics of post-Soviet history[1]

Mark von Hagen

In spring 1993 an official in the Russian Ministry of Education responsible for humanities education explained that future elementary and secondary school history textbooks would 'eliminate all the excesses of our old history writing' and would emphasise a more harmonious view of the Russian past. When pressed further, the official promised that class struggle, wars, and revolutions generally, and the first half of the twentieth century (the Soviet period) in particular, would receive far less attention than they have in past curricula in favour of a more prominent place for nineteenth-century 'civilisation', by which he meant Russian culture and religion. One of the aims in the new privileging of the nineteenth century was to integrate Russian history into greater world historical processes and deemphasise what had been previously trumpeted in textbooks as the uniqueness of the Russian experience. For this official,[2] and for many other historians and citizens of the post-Soviet states, the Soviet period has become an aberration of Russian and human history. Rather than grapple with the painful facts of Stalinism, its origins and consequences, they prefer 'a more harmonious view of the past'. Indeed, a widely articulated desire to escape from the tragedies of the twentieth-century history has been one common response to the revelations about the Stalin period that have emerged since 1985 and to the debates about the meaning of those revelations.[3]

[1] I gratefully acknowledge the fellowship support of the Alexander-von-Humboldt Stiftung (Germany), the International Research and Exchanges Board, the National Council for Soviet and East European Research, and the participants in the Conference on Germany and Russia in Comparative Perspective, Philadelphia, 19–22 September 1991.
[2] Interview conducted by the author with Aleksei Vodianskii, head of sector for humanities education, Russian Ministry of Education, 16 March 1993.
[3] Other observers have focused on earlier periods and written more detailed chronologies of events; see the excellent accounts by Giuseppe Boffa, *The Stalin Phenomenon*, trans. Nicholas Ferser (Cornell 1992), especially chapter 12; R. W. Davies, *Soviet History in the Gorbachev Revolution* (Bloomington, Indiana, Indiana University Press 1989); John Keep,

Those frequently acrimonious debates have reflected the greater political struggles underway in society; the participants range from far right
to far left, however those categories may now be defined in the
post-Soviet landscape. A further consequence of the moral and psychological conundra with which the public discussion of the past has
confronted society has been demoralisation and disorientation. The
same Ministry official, when asked about the likelihood of a new
orthodoxy emerging in history textbooks along the lines of what he had
described, responded that orthodoxy was not the problem; rather, an
excess of pluralism and diversity has made impossible any sort of
orientation or consensus on values.

Although the debates that initially focused on Stalinism quickly
expanded to encompass the entire Soviet period, clearly Stalin and the
system over which he prevailed remain as a powerful symbol of the
central dilemmas for historians of modern history in Russia and the
other successor states to the USSR. The debates certainly bear comparison with the German *Historikerstreit*, with the Stalin period roughly
standing in for the much shorter Hitler period;[4] but the contrasts should
also provide cause for caution with any overly simple parallels. One
important difference is that in Germany and Italy, military defeat forced
political and intellectual elites to break radically with the Nazi and
Fascist regimes, whereas the reform process that transformed the Soviet
political system was initiated by its own leadership and has been far
more protracted. Despite the fact that the reforms were not initially
conceived as a repudiation of the entire Soviet experiment, they met
with determined resistance from powerful institutional interests – most
prominently in the security apparatus, the military and economic
bureaucracies, and the Communist Party elites. After Gorbachev,
beginning in 1987, made explicit the link between his reformist plans
and a revision of the prevailing narrative of the Stalinist past,[5] these
institutions asserted their legitimacy by defending that orthodox Soviet
version of the past.

'Reconstructing Soviet History: A New "Great Turn"?', *Studies in Soviet Thought* 38, no.
2, (1989) pp. 117–45; William B. Husband, ed., 'Glasnost' and Soviet Historians', *Soviet
Studies in History* 27:1 (Summer 1988); Donald Raleigh, ed., *Soviet Studies in History*, 27:
1–4 (Summer 1988–Spring 1989); Walter Laqueur, *Stalin: The Glasnost Revelations*
(Charles Scribner's Sons 1991); G. A. Bordiugov and V. A. Kozlov, *Istoriia i kon'iunktura*
(Moscow, Politizdat 1992).
[4] My understanding of the *Historikerstreit* is based largely on the accounts in Charles S.
Maier, *The Unmasterable Past: History, Holocaust, and German National Identity* (Cam-
bridge, Mass. 1988); and Ian Kershaw, *The Nazi Dictatorship: Problems and Perspectives of
Interpretation* (2nd edn London, Edward Arnold 1989).
[5] See Gorbachev's speech on the seventieth anniversary of the October Revolution,
October and Perestroika (Moscow 1987).

The contexts of the discussion

As a reflection of the powerful institutional interests at stake in the historical revisionism, the professional historical community has been, of course, an important – although, as will be clear below, not always the most important – arena for the struggles over defining and interpreting the national past. Professional historians were concentrated in the numerous and still large research institutes that were situated primarily under the aegis of the Academy of Sciences, Sector for Historical Sciences, to a lesser degree in pedagogical institutes and university history departments, and those institutes previously under the patronage of the Central Committee of the Communist Party and Ministry of Defence. Partly because the institutional setting of much history writing was closely affiliated with powerful establishment interests[6] and because of the special function that history has played for the legitimacy and self-image of all the neo-Stalinist regimes modelled on the Soviet state,[7] professional historians were slow to respond to Gorbachev's appeals for 'new thinking' about the past.

Because of history's privileged status in Soviet political culture, professional historians were further constrained by their close links to the hegemonic ideology of Stalinist Marxism. Those links, together with the tight control that Glavlit exercised in censoring intellectual life, resulted in the extremely low reputation of Soviet historians among the broader public. This was especially true for twentieth-century history, where the historians of the Communist Party of the Soviet Union set the research agenda and the range of permissible interpretations. Party historians worked in perhaps the most constrained environments; consequently, their writing characteristically was the least imaginative and most tendentious. Finally, Soviet historians who wrote about their own country's twentieth-century past suffered from virtual intellectual

---

[6] Here I have in mind the former central and republican Institutes of Marxism-Leninism and Party History, the Institute of Military History, and the central and republican branches of the Academy of Sciences. Perhaps not surprisingly, some of the most sensational 'revisionists' were affiliated with an institute that was not subordinated to these powerful institutional interests, the Moscow State Historical-Archive Institute (MGIAI, now part of the Russian State Humanities University). The Institute's former Director (and the new University's rector), Iury Afanasev, was in the forefront of the most radical, if not always the most intellectually responsible, rethinking of twentieth-century Russian history.

[7] For discussions on the political functions of contemporary history in the Soviet Union and accounts of several key intellectual-political battles, see Nancy Whittier Heer, *Politics and History in the Soviet Union* (Cambridge, Mass., the MIT Press 1971); John Keep, ed., *Contemporary History in the Soviet Mirror* (New York, Praeger 1964); Konstantin Shteppa, *Russian Historians and the Soviet State* (New Brunswick, N.J., Rutgers University Press 1962); John Barber, *Soviet Historians in Crisis, 1928–1932* (London and Basingstoke, The Macmillan Press 1981).

isolation from the international community, in that they rarely knew foreign languages and very few non-Soviet works were translated into Russian; as a result, major works by non-Soviet historians were accessible only in the hostile accounts of them under the rubrics of 'the fight against bourgeois falsifiers'.[8] Therefore, what narrowly defined debate actually occurred among Soviet historians on occasions when power struggles temporarily opened up political space for alternative approaches still did not reflect any of the often passionate discussions outside the Soviet Union. Thus even as Soviet historians gained unprecedented access to their national and regional archives and freedom to investigate new themes and periods, they initially limited their efforts to filling in 'blank spots', that is to correcting accounts of the past that were blatantly falsified or to chronicling previously ignored episodes. They were far less forthcoming with new conceptual models to explain the larger dilemmas of the Soviet period and its relationship to the longer durée of Russian Imperial and world history.

As a consequence of the nearly universal disdain in which Soviet historians were held and the related intellectual vacuum in the academic institutes, other actors on the contemporary scene stepped in to challenge the discredited professionals. From the beginning, fictional literature and journalism played an important role in setting the terms of the discussion.[9] Well before the professional historians began grappling with the Stalin question, Tengiz Abuladze's film *Repentance* (*Pokaianie*), Mikhail Shatrov's plays, and Anatoly Rybakov's novel *Children of the Arbat* (*Deti Arbata*) provoked impassioned polemics in the national media. And the influence of fiction extended well beyond living writers and filmmakers; the posthumous publication of previously banned works by Soviet, émigré and foreign writers often played an even more critical role than those of living ones in reshaping and reorienting historical discussions among intellectuals and the greater Soviet reading public.

The intellectual and cultural elite pushed professional historians into increasingly daring revisions, while the Gorbachev faction simultaneously stepped up pressure from above when it reestablished the rehabilitation process that had been started by Khrushchev and then

---

[8] Even the literature against 'bourgeois historiography' helped some Soviet historians develop alternative views, however. See Nikolai Romanovskii, 'Alternative Approaches to Soviet History', *World Marxist Review*, no. 11 (November 1989), pp. 89–92, at p. 89. I thank Thomas Sherlock for this reference.

[9] In Russian intellectual history, fictional literature traditionally has been the arena for the most important public moral and philosophical struggles; and unlike in the Anglo-American tradition, where political philosophy and especially political science for a long time shaped the intellectual environment of Soviet studies, in the contemporary Soviet Union that environment was shaped by writers, filmmakers, playwrights, and an important category of political journalists known as *publitsisty*.

halted under Brezhnev.[10] In addition to forming a special Commission of the Politburo to review the cases of repressed citizens, the Communist Party's Central Committee announced that another commission would be formed to write a new history of the Party. Still another source of pressure was the various civic organisations and so-called 'informals' that emerged after 1985 as alternative claimants to political legitimacy against the Communist Party and Soviet state. A key component of these groups' strategies in the political struggle was to construct alternative views of the past; they especially devoted their efforts to restoring the history of Stalin's crimes to national consciousness. The largest and most influential of these societies was *Memorial*, which grew out of a network of Brezhnev-era human-rights activists and dissident intellectuals.[11] While *Memorial* mobilised 'democratic' forces on the Soviet 'left', on the nationalist right still other 'informals', here characterised by the *Pamiat'* society and its intellectual allies, rallied to defend the Russian national reputation from what they charged were the nihilistic attacks of often 'cosmopolitan' besmirchers of the heroic past.[12] For *Pamiat'*, too, one's relationship to the past was key to their campaign of national repentance and renewal.

Other contexts deserve mention to complete the list of shaping influences and limitations of the ongoing debate. As Soviet readers and historians struggled to overcome the well-worn stereotypes and overly simplified historical narratives of the Stalinist 'Short Course', the publication of non-Soviet works offered alternative visions of the national past. In this category were the classics of Anglo-American Sovietology,[13] *tamizdat* and émigré accounts, and previously banned 'Soviet' accounts, most importantly the writings of Trotsky, Bukharin, the memoirs of Nikita Khrushchev, and the books of Roy Medvedev. Not only did these previously proscribed writings contribute to a widening of the intellectual horizons, but very often the authors themselves – one can mention here Stephen Cohen and Roy Medvedev as the most representative of this tendency – entered into the contemporary Soviet political fray.

---

[10] See Albert P. Van Goudoever, *The Limits of De-Stalinization in the Soviet Union* (London and Sydney, Croom Helm 1986).

[11] For more on *Memorial*, see Laqueur, *Stalin*, chapter 13 ('Memorial and Its Opponents').

[12] These views were most often aired on the pages of *Nash sovremennik* and *Molodaia gvardiia*. For a characteristic essay, see V. Kozhinov, 'Pravda i istina', *Nash sovremennik* No. 4 (1988).

[13] Among the translated works are: Alexander Rabinowitch, *The Bolsheviks Come to Power*; Stephen Cohen, *Bukharin and the Bolshevik Revolution*; Robert Tucker, *Stalin as Revolutionary*; Robert Conquest, *The Great Terror*; Richard Pipes, *The Russian Revolution*; and E. H. Carr, *History of Russia. The Bolshevik Revolution, 1917–23*.

The evolution of the Stalin debate

The combined impact of these several contexts was a rapid evolution of the debate over Stalin from a once parochial and still very Stalinist orthodox position to a remarkable range of thoughtful reflections that quickly replicated the most important debates outside the former Soviet Union, and all this despite the relative disadvantage that post-Soviet historians suffer when compared to their German counterparts, who now have a nearly fifty-year perspective based on scores of archivally based studies. What I characterise as the Stalin debate is not the same thing as the debate over the Nazi period in the important sense that the participants have not been authors of historical monographs, but rather of historico-philosophical essays; that notwithstanding, the intellectual agenda set forth in these essays is a rich and innovative one and will be the focus of the rest of this article.

The discussion actually started before the use of the term Stalinism had been sanctioned to describe the historical phenomenon. In adhering to this unspoken taboo, Gorbachev's early pronouncements on the 'command-administrative economy' and those of the publicists who took up his call for rethinking followed the practice of Khrushchev's earlier de-Stalinisation campaign in the 1950s. For Khrushchev the 'cult of personality' formula was intended to balance objective factors, the concrete historical conditions, with subjective ones, the personality of Stalin; but in fact the formula served more to personalise blame for the Stalin period after 1934.[14] The term 'cult of personality' was typically accompanied by such euphemisms as 'serious violations of Soviet legality', 'distortions of socialist democracy' and 'mass repression' to describe what was viewed as an aberration from the noble path of socialist revolution from Lenin to the present. However rife with contradictions this formula was, it represented the first compromised attempt to 'normalise' Stalinism while still acknowledging the 'crimes' against the party and people. For all the crimes, however, Khrushchev paradoxically concluded that the essence of the Soviet Union's socialist political and social system survived undamaged by the decades of arbitrary rule and mass murder.[15] For this reason, Khrushchev rejected the pejorative use of the term Stalinism and even refused to deny that he himself was a Stalinist. Unfortunately, however, historians in the 1950s and 1960s read these party pronouncements as a ban on the mention of

[14] See 'O preodolenii kul'ta lichnosti i ego posledstvii', *Spravochnik partiinogo rabotnika* (Moscow 1957); and the discussion in chapter 2 (Soviet Interpretation up to Gorbachev) in Boffa, *The Stalin Phenomenon*.

[15] This was the interpretation that informed Roy Medvedev's important underground classic of the period, *Let History Judge: The Origins and Consequences of Stalinism* (New York 1971). Unlike Khrushchev, however, Medvedev did use the term Stalinism to describe the multifaceted pheonomenon that was the subject of his book.

Stalin's name so the version of the Soviet past that emerged in response to Khrushchev's official revisionism was in many ways even more simplistic than that portrayed in the Stalin *Short Course*. Now everything that Stalin had done, short of the terror, was attributed to Lenin, including collectivisation (the fulfilment of Lenin's cooperative plan), industrialisation, and the building of a powerful state.

But there were important differences between Khrushchev's and Gorbachev's pronouncements as well that suggest the considerable distance that had been travelled in nearly thirty years. In sharp contrast to the scapegoating formula of 'cult of personality' that served to 'resolve' all the intellectual dilemmas of historians and ideologists after 1956, Gorbachev acknowledged that the Party too was culpable for the persistence of the 'command-administrative system' and the lack of democracy. In the context of the popular film, *Repentance*, Gorbachev's call for historical revisionism was also a call for society to examine its conscience and to repent for past 'sins'. No longer were all social and political ills blamed on Stalin and his entourage; rather, Gorbachev increasingly appealed to the intelligentsia in particular, but to society more generally, for a revitalisation and restoration to health. Of course, the international and domestic contexts of the mid-1980s made Gorbachev's task easier than had been the case for Khrushchev in the mid-1950s and early 1960s. Significantly, the Chinese, who had raised opposition to Khrushchev's campaign of de-Stalinisation, in the 1980s, were embarking on their own ideological revisionism and appeared little concerned with events in Moscow; furthermore, since the 1970s Eurocommunism had gradually distanced itself from the most paradoxical components of the Stalinist and Khrushchevian formulas. And, finally, but probably most important, the intellectual ferment that Khrushchev's initial revisions had catalysed continued to percolate in the 1970s and slowly crystallised in a variety of alternate political programmes and corresponding historical visions. Otto Latsis, onetime editor of the party's intellectual organ *Kommunist*, wrote that it was during the Brezhnev years that nearly all the contemporary antisocialist ideologies emerged (including monarchist, nationalist, and bourgeois-democratic ones), but that they had no chance yet for public articulation.[16] He also argued that after 1956, those Old Bolsheviks who had survived began to separate Leninism from Stalinism and thereby formulated alternative socialist platforms as well.[17]

The consequence of these developments and new circumstances was a

[16] Latsis, 'Stalin protiv Lenina', in *Osmyslit' kul't Stalina* (Moscow, Progress 1989), p. 217.
[17] One former Stalinist who broke with his past views after 1956 and wrote about this painful process with great eloquence is the writer Konstantin Simonov. See his posthumous memoirs, *Glazami cheloveka moego pokoleniia: Razmyshleniia o I. V. Staline* (Moscow, Pravda 1990).

rapid, if at first hesitant, emergence of a broad diversity of views about Stalinism and its relationship to Soviet, Russian, and world history. Though Gorbachev seemed reluctant initially to utter the world 'Stalinism' and preferred a variety of alternatives such as 'command-administrative system',[18] it and its more pejorative companion 'Stalinshchina' began to enter the discussion, in large measure thanks to the authority of former dissident/loyalist Roy Medvedev and the translation of foreign works into Russian. Stalin and Stalinism became a shorthand for all the tortured moral and political dilemmas that the past had laid at the doorstep of the current generations of Soviet citizens. The discussion about Stalinism reached a certain culmination point in two published volumes of collected essays, *Inogo ne dano* (There is no other way) and *Osmyslit' kul't Stalina* (Trying to Understand the Stalin Cult).[19] In these two volumes, authors representing a wide range of political platforms and opinions debated one another over the origins and consequences of Stalinism. The result was remarkably similar to the range of opinions that has been hammered out over the past six decades among scholars and political partisans in Europe and North America; furthermore, the authors arrived at these positions without much direct contact with their non-Soviet counterparts (it is true that Cohen's biography of Bukharin circulated in samizdat translations and some works of Trotsky were known to narrow circles of historians). The evidence and arguments marshalled in support of the divergent positions were original and derived from critical reflection of available knowledge (and before the archives had begun to divulge their secrets).

The two volumes demonstrate both the highest level of achievement and the limits of the debate (limits, incidentally, that have not been transcended in large measure by their non-Soviet counterparts as well). Nearly all the authors engaged in the exercise have much to say about the origins and consequences of Stalinism, but very few deem it necessary to define or discuss the phenomenon of Stalinism itself (despite a section heading in *Osmyslit' kul't Stalina* entitled 'Stalin and Stalinism as a socio-psychological phenomenon') beyond the sloganistic simplifications of 'administrative-command system' or 'mass repressions'. Here, it appears that professional historians and historically-minded publicists do not yet have the distance from the experience or the source base of archival documents to reflect profoundly on the character of the regime. And here it is that fictional genres, especially literature and film,

---

[18] This term was introduced by economist Gavril Popov in his review of the novels of Aleksandr Bek, especially *The New Assignment*, in *Nauka i zhizn'* 4 (1987), pp. 54–65; see also sociologist L. G. Ionin's review of Abuladze's film *Repentance* in *Sotsiologicheskie issledovaniya* 3 (1987), pp. 62–72.

[19] *Inogo ne dano* (Moscow, Progress 1988); and *Osmyslit' kul't Stalina* (Moscow, Progress 1989).

have captured at least provisionally the nuances and paradoxes of life under Stalin.[20] The most celebrated 'documents' at the beginning were the film *Repentance* and the novel *Children of the Arbat*. Gradually these works were superseded by the publication of long-banned novels by Vasilii Grossman, Alexander Solzhenitsyn, Mikhail Bulgakov, and Andrei Platonov.

But whereas the fictional accounts help to convey the complicated life of Stalinist Russia, these accounts are in turn unable to probe the questions of origins of the phenomenon. A persuasive proof of this observation is the highly sensational film of the perestroika period, *Tak zhit' nel'zia* (We Can't Live Like That), in which the director Stanislav Govorukhin attributes everything bad in the current Soviet world, especially its criminality, to the 'crimes' of Lenin. The film is of a peculiar genre, a sort of philosophico-documentary essay, but in its simple-minded rejection of everything in the Soviet past and the suggestions that the tsarist golden age was a loss to be lamented, it set a trend that has effectively postponed any intelligent discussion of Stalinism. As a consequence of the provisional triumph of such views as Govorukhin's, since the publication of the two aforementioned volumes, whatever historical attention the reading public has demonstrated has shifted to the tsarist period. Those publicists and historians who still write about the Stalin period have largely adopted Pipes' or, more often, Solzhenitsyn's interpretations of twentieth-century Russian history; in the best cases, they publish archival documents with extensive commentary and avoid any sweeping reinterpretations on the reasonable grounds that such generalisations would be premature.[21]

The Stalin debate: achievements and limits

Among the essays collected in the two volumes, the authors divide over several key issues of historical analysis that reflect successive stages in the evolution of the debate. A major tactic of the revisionists at an early stage was to argue a discontinuity between Lenin and the revolutionary

---

[20] It is telling, for example, that many of the publicists who attempt to capture otherwise elusive aspects of Stalinist political culture have resorted to the image of the 'mankurt' from Chingiz Aitmatov's novel, *The Day Lasts Longer than a Hundred Years*. The mankurts are slaves whose brains were desiccated by application of a shrinking cap on their heads; importantly, they are without memory.

[21] Of documentary publications, see the Novosibirsk 'Memorial' volume, *Vozvrashchenie pamiati: istoriko-publitsisticheskii al'manakh* (Novosibirsk 1992) and two volumes published by Moscow Memorial, *Zven'ia* (vol. I, 1991; vol. II, 1992); also *Dokumenty svidetel'stvuiut: Iz istorii derevni nakanune i v khode kollektivizatsii 1927–1932 gg.*, ed. V. P. Danilov and N. A. Ivnitskii (Moscow 1989); and a host of new journals devoted to archival publications, including *Istoricheskie arkhivy*, *Rodina* and its supplement, *Istochnik*.

tradition, on the one hand, and Stalinism, on the other. Historians and publicists deployed several concepts, including 'alternatives', 'turning points', and 'breaks'. Following the more favourable account of the New Economic Policy that Gorbachev outlined in his speeches, historical precedents for a more humane socialism than the victorious Stalinist version were most often identified with the moderate policies of NEP and the ideas of Nikolai Bukharin, who advocated a hybrid political economy that would harmonise elements of planning with a regulated market. Bukharin, not Stalin, became the 'genuine' successor to Lenin's legacy of 'revolutionary reformism'; publicists and historians 'reinter-preted' – often quite wilfully – Lenin's conception of socialism, especial-ly the so-called cooperative plan, in such a way that Lenin could serve the contemporary political agenda.[22] During the rehabilitation of Stalin's victims that was reactivated and extended by the reformist political leadership, the defeated members of political oppositions in the 1920s were cleared of all accusations of crime and treason and posthumously restored to Party membership and a place in the historical chronicle. Some feeble voices were heard to defend one or another part of Stalin's heritage, but generally a spirit of consensus reigned as the political leadership, intellectuals, and the articulate public worked in harmony to heal the wounds of Stalin's crimes. In order to save socialism, reformers put all or most of the blame on Stalin and tried to demonstrate that Stalinism and socialism were altogether different matters.

Contemporary 'alternativists' were generally affiliated with the reformist wing within the Communist Party and retained their loyalty to socialists ideals; in so doing they carried forward a tradition with both Soviet dissident (Roy Medvedev's *Let History Judge* and his journal *Politicheskii dnevnik*) and Western revisionist (here the work of Lewin, Cohen, and Tucker[23]) parallels, as well as sharing some affinity with earlier Trotskyist and Menshevik critiques of Stalinism. The most articulate and persuasive proponents of the Bukharin alternative to Stalin have been former *Kommunist* editor Otto Latsis[24] and the historian

---

[22] For some interesting observations on the importance of rethinking Lenin, see Markus Wehner, 'Auf der Suche nach der "Wahrheit"? Zum polemischen Streit sowjetischer Historiker und Publizisten ueber die 1920er Jahre und die Urspruenge des Stalinismus', *Osteuropa* 12 (1990), pp. 1129–44; and Lars T. Lih, 'NEP: an alternative for Soviet Socialism', in *The Soviet Union under Gorbachev, Festschrift for Robert C. Tucker*, edited by Stephen F. Cohen and Michael Kraus (forthcoming).

[23] See especially Stephen F. Cohen, *Bukharin and the Bolshevik Revolution* (New York, Random House 1973); Moshe Lewin, *Political Undercurrents in Soviet Economic Debates* (Princeton, NJ, Princeton University Press 1974) and *Lenin's Last Struggle* (New York, Random House 1968); Robert Tucker, *Stalin as Revolutionary* (New York, W. W. Norton & Co 1973).

[24] See his 'Perelom', *Znamia* 6 (1988), pp. 124–78; 'Stalin protiv Lenina', in *Osmyslit' kul't*

of collectivisation Viktor Danilov.[25] Because both contend that NEP, despite its crises, could and should have developed further, they focus on the end of NEP and on the defeat of its political and intellectual defenders. Danilov sees tragically lost opportunities not only in Bukharin's opposition to Stalin's murderous turn against the peasantry and toward breakneck industrialisation, but also in the spring 1929 variant of the first five-year plan, which, in Danilov's opinion, foresaw moderate and balanced economic growth.[26] Latsis concurs with Danilov's defence of a Leninist alternative and characterises Stalin's triumph at the end of the 1920s as an anti-Leninist political coup.[27]

More important, however, Latsis identified the greater significance of the 'alternative' tactic in its posing the relationship between 'the objective and subjective causes of Stalinism'. The alternativists have sought to break the spell of inevitability that reigned in previous Soviet accounts by stressing the options that were available in society and in the Party. Their focus has tended toward the 'subjective' in that they emphasise Stalin's wilful and violent termination of the market socialist experiment of the NEP. In the analogous debate over the Nazi dictatorship, Tim Mason has helpfully characterised the intellectual issues as ranging between 'structuralist' arguments that seek the roots of Hitler's dictatorship in the decision-making processes, the political economy, or the political culture, on one end, and 'intentionalist' explanatory schemas that focus more on the conscious intentions of the Nazi leadership, on the other.[28] The alternativists, with their emphasis on the voluntarism of the Stalinist leadership (Latsis at one point brands Stalinism as 'subjectivism'), fall within Mason's characterisation of the 'intentionalist' approach.

The general preoccupation with 'intentionalist' approaches can be

---

Stalina (Moscow, Progress 1989), pp. 215–46; and *Vyiti iz kvadrata* (Moscow 1989).

[25] For Danilov's views, see 'The Issue of Alternatives and History of Collectivization of Soviet Agriculture', *The Journal of Historical Sociology*, 2/1 (1989); and *Istoriia SSSR* 3 (1989). In addition to his advocacy of the Bukharinist alternative programme, Danilov played a key role in the rehabilitations of the agrarian economists Aleksandr Chaianov and Nikolai Kondrat'ev, as well as Trotsky.

[26] In support of Danilov's arguments, V. Popov and N. Shmelev, in their contribution to *Osmyslit'*, 'Na razvilke dorog: Byla li al'ternativa stalinskoi modeli razvitiia?', portray the NEP as a 'golden age' of sorts and argue that the NEP political economy was a very viable system. They tend, however, to focus on the consequences of the 'Great Break' in 1929, with its legacy of demographic losses and deformed social consciousness, rather than addressing either the origins or character of the Stalin phenomenon.

[27] G. Lisichkin, in his 'Mify i real'nost', is another contributor to *Osmyslit'* who defends Lenin and Lenin's Marxism against Stalin and argues that Stalin perverted Marxism, pp. 247–83.

[28] Tim Mason, 'Intention and Explanation: A Current Controversy about the Interpretation of National Socialism', in *Der 'Fuehrerstaat' : Mythos und Realitaet*, ed. Gerhard Hirschfeld and Lothar Kettenacker (Stuttgart 1981), pp. 23–40; and Ian Kershaw, *The Nazi Dictatorship*.

understood partly as the reaction to an official political history that long had been falsified. Much of the energy of serious historians has gone toward reconstructing the basic outlines of political struggles from long-denied Party and state archives. Furthermore, historians at this stage simply cannot draw on a body of solid social, economic, and institutional history that, for example, the historians of Germany have had available during their greatly more sophisticated debates about the nature of National Socialism. Despite a venerable Soviet tradition of multivolume histories of the peasantry, the working class, and intelligentsia, in fact the type of social history that Soviet historians wrote bore little resemblance to what non-Soviet historians usually meant by that term. Instead, these tomes were compilations of decrees and 'supporting' statistics that not only left the politics out, but failed to convey any sense of the very social groups whose histories they purported to be chronicling.[29]

Beyond constraints imposed by the absence of a solid base of social and institutional histories for the Soviet period, the sources of intellectual resistance among contemporary historians to exploring structuralist explanations might be similar to those for the persistent resistance among German historians to part with more narrowly intentionalist approaches. The structuralist approach, after all, 'extends the responsibility and culpability to groups and agencies in the Nazi State beyond the Führer himself'.[30] Conversely, a focus on Stalin's intentions not only implicitly privileges historical explanations based on intuited understanding of motives and intentions of leading actors in the drama and thereby ignores large issues of fundamental social, economic, and political change, but also, as Kershaw reminds us in the case of German history, 'whatever moral warning might be drawn from a study' of Stalinism is 'limited in its application'.[31] But after acknowledging these reasons for privileging an approach that focuses on high-level political actors, the intentionalist approach in Soviet history is additionally crippled in advance by the relatively narrow known source base (especially when compared to the richness of the German sources, such as the diaries of leading political, military, and economic leaders), which leaves the Soviet historian far more space where speculation must inevitably supplant real, hard data.[32]

[29] For the most recent 'monuments' in this tradition, see the multi-volume *Istoriia sovetskogo rabochego klassa* (Moscow, Nauka 1984–   ) and *Istoriia sovetskogo krest'ianstva* (Moscow, Nauka 1986–   ).
[30] Kershaw, *The Nazi Dictatorship*, p. 88.
[31] Kershaw, *The Nazi Dictatorship*, p. 69.
[32] The clearest example of such focus on matters of personality is Dmitrii Volkogonov's biography of Stalin, *Triumf i tragediia. I. V. Stalin: politicheskii portret* (Moscow, APN 1989). Volkogonov, who had access to a stunning range of previously classified archives

After the short-lived 'Bukharin boom'[33] of 1988, publicists began groping among a variety of more or less structuralist explanations and tried to identify longer-term and more deep-seated sources of Stalin's triumph and of the system he helped shape. As the search for the roots of the Stalin phenomenon went further and as the monopoly on political and economic reform began to slip from the central leadership, the early reformist consensus began to erode and sharp political differences to emerge. Beginning in 1988 a self-styled 'radical' political alternative formed to challenge Gorbachev's revolution from above and to demand more rapid democratisation and transition to a 'market economy'. These radical reforms by their nature entailed a rejection of the old model of Soviet socialism, rather than merely a reform within that system. All major existing institutions came under siege in the ensuing political struggles that pitted 'establishment' politicians against 'popular fronts' and 'democratic unions'. In place of the Communist Party's monopoly, the radicals proposed multiparty parliamentary democracy and even the dismissal of Communist officials from all state and social institutions. Calls to dismantle the security and police apparatus threatened the status of the KGB; projects to reform the army along the lines of a 'professional', volunteer, and much reduced force similarly alarmed the career military men and their allies in the industrial-defence bureaucracy. The proffered panacea of privatisation and market economy was accompanied by attacks on the planning and economic bureaucracies. And, finally, the swelling movements for national autonomy and, in places, for independence threatened the very fabric of the Union that formally held in place the multiethnic state.

All these challenges pushed the Stalin debate onto different grounds; by 1989 and especially during 1990, the 'radicals' had repudiated the entire Soviet period and impugned Lenin and Trotsky with no less vigour

and to the testimony of Stalin's co-workers and deputies, belongs – or at least belonged at the time he wrote his biography – rather unenthusiastically to the alternativist school. In fairness to Volkogonov, he readily admits to not having written a definitive history of the Stalin period, but rather preliminary sketches for a biographical portrait. But, as nearly all Stalin biographers have done in the past, so too Volkogonov constantly falls victim to the seduction of generalising about Soviet society from his central narrative about Stalin and his immediate entourage. And, in a practice long sanctioned by Soviet historians of the Party, Volkogonov and many of his colleagues continue to assume that signed decrees were forthrightly and unquestioningly implemented as policy down to the basic units of Soviet administration and society. Historians who share this assumption of the leadership's omnipotence and omniscience rarely think to raise issues of institutional, social, or cultural resistance and, consequently, Stalin's personality cult continues to hold them firmly in its grip, only now in its mirror version. Volkogonov's archival methodology has come under justified scrutiny by several historians. See A. Chechevishnikov, 'Istoriki i istochniki', *Svobodnaia mysl'* 14 (1992); and L. Maksimenkov, 'Eshche raz o kritike arkheograficheskikh priemov D. A. Volkogonova', *Svobodnaia mysl'* 3 91933), pp. 44–51.

[33] Bordiugov and Kozlov, *Istoriia i kon'iunktura*, chapter 2.

than their counterparts had attacked Stalin a year before.[34] The 'radicals' frequently reduced historical discussions to black-and-white stereotypes; in their calls to abandon the criminal Soviet period for a kinder and gentler tsarist past, they resembled the Stalinist historians who in their turn had dismissed the pre-1917 Russian past as dark and benighted in favour of an inspirational post-1917 pageant of proletarian progress.[35] The émigré, anti-Soviet version of this narrative preserved the radical caesura of 1917, but reversed the values assigned to the two periods. The anti-Soviet writers argued for an optimistic, if often rose-coloured view of pre-revolutionary Russia and an unmitigatingly bleak and denunciatory view of post-1917 developments, rarely distinguishing among Bolshevik leaders and viewing Lenin, Trotsky, and Stalin as mere faces of the same monster. The exemplar text for this narrative has no doubt been Aleksandr Solzhenitsyn's monumental literary-historical investigation, *The Gulag Archipelago*. For the millions of readers of Solzhenitsyn's moral indictment, the gulag became the dominant symbol of the Soviet Union, and Soviet citizens were ruthlessly divided into prison staff and prisoners. For those who propound such views, the moral stakes are high indeed; they have confronted fellow citizens with their tragic and criminal past in order to prevent the recurrence of such monumental bloodletting and terror in the future. They aim to commemorate the martyrs of this cruel system and purge the national consciousness of any attachment to the values of the Stalin regime.[36]

For all the excesses in the 'radicalisation' of the historical discussions, however, a breakthrough was achieved. The formerly impermeable boundary of 1917 was overcome, and historians now face the far more intractable issues that are tied up with the relationship of the Soviet period to its pre-revolutionary antecedents. The intellectual rehabilitations of Trotsky, the Mensheviks, and the religious-social thinker

[34] An early article that posed the question of Lenin's responsibility for much of the tragedy of Soviet history was Vasily Selyunin's 'Istoki', *Novyi mir* 5 (1988), pp. 162–89.

[35] Of course, with some important qualifications, the orthodox view that reigned in Soviet historiography until recently posited a fundamental continuity of post-1917 history and a more or less radical discontinuity between pre- and post-1917 history, with the October Revolution as the watershed of Russian, if not world, history. The Party leadership, united and unanimous, steered the Soviet peoples through the challenges of modernisation and defended the 'achievements of socialism' from domestic and foreign enemies. Here the exemplar text was Stalin's *Short Course*, first published in 1938 and republished in millions of copies.

[36] This version of the Soviet past has been reinforced both by the translated classics of Cold War Anglo-American Sovietology, such as Conquest's *The Great Terror*, and by the efforts of informal popular historical societies, such as *Memorial*. See the critical analysis of the Gulag narrative literature in Gabor Tamas Rittersporn, *Simplifications staliniennes et complications soviétiques: Tensions sociales et conflits politiques en URSS 1933–53* (Paris, Editions des Archives Contemporaines 1988).

Nikolai Berdiaev, have returned contemporary writers to the contradictions of Russia's backwardness and the revolutionary legacy of socialism.[37] Here several positions have emerged, many of them resembling the arguments worked out in painful struggles by generations of non-Soviet historians and Soviet exiles.

Some historians and publicists who reject the Soviet experiment but find the historical approach of the 'gulag perspective' unsatisfactory have searched in the pre-1917 period for the origins of Leninism and Stalinism. Aleksandr Tsipko, in a series of controversial articles and a book,[38] approaches his task in a manner that is difficult to situate in Mason's dichotomy of 'intentionalists' and 'structuralists'. Tsipko defines Stalinism as ultraleftist radical utopianism. He takes issue with those who view Stalinism as the natural child of Russian sociocultural backwardness and correctly argues that the nation's peasants were not to blame for the tragic collectivisation, nor did the cult of Stalin spread from the countryside to the city, but in the opposite direction. It is rather to the ultraleftist political culture of the urban populations, especially a part of the radicalised working class and leftist intelligentsia, that the historian should look for the source of Stalinism. He thereby shifts the centre of his causal argument from Stalin's personality and Russian autocratic traditions to the Bolshevik political culture that took shape during the Civil War and 1920s. For all his attempts to indict Bolshevik political culture, however, Tsipko remains in the realm of history of ideas, especially in his insistence on the Marxist influences on the Russian revolutionary tradition. He also rejects the radical discontinuity argued by the alternativists and sees little or no chance for a 'humane' socialism emerging in Soviet Russia. Ultimately, this type of argument comes very close to the influential view of Aleksandr Solzhenitsyn that

---

[37] Igor' Kliamkin's article, 'Kakaia ulitsa vedet k khramu?', *Novyi mir* 11 (1987), was an important precursor for the discussions of pre-and post-1917 history. He sympathetically explored the ideas of exiles, conservatives, and anti-Soviet writers, including Trotsky, the Menshevik Fedor Dan, and the *Smenovekhovtsy*. Recently, important collections of the Russian intelligentsia have appeared, including: *Vekhi* (Signposts) (1909; repr. Moscow, Novosti 1990); *Iz glubiny* (De profundis) (1918; repr. Moscow, Novosti 1991).

[38] Tsipko has published extensively in Soviet journals, the first articles, 'Istoki stalinizma', appearing in *Nauka i zhizn'* 11–12 (1988) and 1–2 (1989); an English-language summary of his views is available in *Is Stalinism Really Dead?* (New York, Harper Collins 1991); see my review of Tsipko in 'The Stalin Question', *The Nation* (25 March 1991), pp. 382–7. Often Tsipko, in his ideological determinism, comes close to the views of the Polish exile philosopher Leszek Kolakowski. The 'countryside' novelists (*derevenshchiki*), such as Boris Mozhaev in *Muzhiki i bab'i*, and agrarian economist Vladimir Tikhonov, actively promote the 'pro-peasant' views of Tsipko, who in turn cites their works as evidence for his own writings. See Tikhonov's remarks at a round-table discussion in *Istoriia SSSR* 3 (1989), pp. 20ff.

Marxism and Bolshevism were foreign – if not 'cosmopolitan' – bacilli injected into an otherwise healthy Russian peasantry.[39]

Among those who share Tsipko's antipathy for virtually the entire Soviet experiment, the widespread application of the term 'totalitarian', a characterisation enthusiastically borrowed from western Sovietology, signals little more than disapproval.[40] Just as the indiscriminate use of the concept has concealed a wide-ranging diversity of approaches in the Sovietological tradition of its origins,[41] so too in the Soviet debates little genuine consensus can be located among the authors who endorse the concept. For example, Gozman and Etkind, while defending the appropriateness of the adjective 'totalitarian' to describe the Soviet system under Stalin, argue that the collapse of the Khrushchev reforms in the 1960s demonstrated that Stalinism was more than terror and, in fact, could survive well without resort to mass terror. Furthermore, they argue that a political system emerged out of the terror in which the 'cult of personality' was far less important than a 'cult of power'.[42] Finally, they devote much of their article to the survival of genuine resistance to Stalinism throughout society, despite all the efforts to weld a monolithic unity through propaganda and terror.[43] M. Kapustin adopts a far more 'traditional' approach to totalitarianism by equating Stalin and Hitler

[39] Tsipko's analysis of Russian and world history is characteristic of many writers and thinkers who have emerged from a Stalinist Marxism toward something that might be called national or patriotic liberalism. Their critiques of Russian Marxism and Bolshevism in particular typically evolve from revisionist Marxism to the anti-Marxist writings of Russian turn-of-the-century religious conservatives such as Nikolai Berdiaev. The danger with the eclecticism, however, is clear from Tsipko's political agenda, which highlights a revival of Christianity, Russian national patriotism, law and order, and the authoritarian market. Because he identifies the Russian ultraleft – by which he most often means the Left Opposition that coalesced around Trotsky – as the major culprits in destroying native Russian initiative and Christian morality, Tsipko's arguments often resemble those of the more extreme Russian nationalists who have editorial control over several journals from which they espouse their virulent ideas about the responsibility of Jews and other non-Russians for the Soviet holocaust.

[40] See the articles in *Osmyslit' kul't Stalina* by L. Batkin, L. Gozman and A. Etkind, and M. Kapustin.

[41] A large literature on the shortcomings of the concept has proliferated, together with many recent defences. See Giovanni Sartori, 'Totalitarianism, Model Mania and Learning from Error', *Journal of Theoretical Politics* 5 (1) (1993), pp. 5–22, and Boffa's chapter 5 in *The Stalin Phenomenon*.

[42] This diverges from 'classical' totalitarian 'theory' as articulated in the study by Carl J. Friedrich and Zbigniew K. Brzezinski (*Totalitarian Dictatorship and Autocracy*, Cambridge, Mass. 1956) by eliminating both an all-powerful dictator and terror as two of the most important pillars of the regime. Gozman and Etkind do make a nod in the direction of T. Adorno's studies of the 'authoritarian personality', but find the studies insufficient for the Soviet case.

[43] See their 'Kul't vlasti. Struktura totalitarnogo soznaniia', pp. 337–71. Their analysis of Soviet totalitarian consciousness is characteristic of an intelligentsia 'culturological' critique well summarised in Andrei Sinyavsky's *Soviet Civilization* (New York, Arcade 1990).

(and, by the by, Ivan the Terrible) as models of authoritarianism. He tries, rather unsuccessfully, to raise his discussion above the level of the personal and biographical by pointing out the European-wide character of the phenomenon of the rise of paranoid and schizoid leaders.[44]

As summarised above, the adherents to these forms of the 'totalitarian' model fall more readily in the intentionalists' camp than in the structuralists'. Even though Kapustin, for example, focuses less on 'rational' political decision-making processes than on irrational features of Stalin's behaviour, he nonetheless privileges Stalin as a causal factor and thereby avoids discussion of culpability or enabling conditions in the several contexts in which Stalin operated. A variety of other approaches have attempted to identify some of those contexts and evaluate their roles in the emergence of Stalinism. One group of authors subscribes to a variety of Trotsky's argument of Stalinism as Thermidor.[45] The authors V. Popov and Nikolai Shmelev, in an article that otherwise comes closer to Danilov's and Latsis' defence of the NEP as a viable alternative to Stalinism, identify the gravedigger of the NEP as the bureaucracy.[46] They posit an insurmountable contradiction between bureaucracy and the market and see the first signs of serious difficulties as early as the scissors crisis of 1923. Terror is explained as the consequence of the bureaucracy's hunger for unlimited power.[47] Finally, Gennadii Bordiugov and Vladimir Kozlov tentatively seek to identify a social base for Stalin, though that is not the primary focus of their articles and books. They contend that Stalin's radical turn away from NEP found resonance among young workers who were infused with revolutionary impatience, or who came from the villages and brought with them a traditional patriarchalist understanding of politics, and who overwhelmed the Old Bolsheviks in the Communist Party by the end of the 1920s. Here Bordiugov and Kozlov come close to

[44] See his 'K fenomenologii vlasti. Psikhologicheskie modeli avtoritarizma: Groznyi-Stalin-Hitler', pp. 372–401. The equation of Hitler and Stalin, one of the commonplaces of original totalitarian 'theory', was popularised in Vasilii Grossman's novel about Soviet wartime experience, *Life and Fate* (*Zhizn' i sud'ba*). Grossman, as does Kapustin, suggests that the two leaders were manifestations of the same political syndrome. The psychological approach has been developed further by a St. Petersburg professor of psychology, A. E. Lichko. See his speculations on the diagnosis of Stalin by psychologist Bekhterev in *Literaturnaia gazeta* (28 September 1988).

[45] Trotsky's most comprehensive statement of the Thermidor thesis is in his *The Revolution Betrayed* (New York 1972; written between 1935 and 1936). See also Boffa's chapter 7 in *The Stalin Phenomenon* and Robert McNeal, 'Trotskyist Interpretations of Stalinism', in *Stalinism: Essays in Historical Interpretation*, ed. Robert Tucker (New York 1977).

[46] Popov and Shmelev, 'Na razvilke dorog', pp. 314ff.

[47] Even closer to Trotsky's theses are the writings of D. Dzarasov who traces Stalinism to the rise of a social class or group alien to socialism after Lenin's death, namely, the triumph of bureaucratism over democracy. See his 'Raboty nepochatyi krai', *Moskovskaia pravda* (31 January 1988); and 'Partiinaia demokratiia i biurokratiia: k istokam problemy', in *Inogo ne dano*, pp. 324–42.

Trotsky's argument for the roots of Stalinism in 'the domination of the petty bourgeoisie in the population as a whole, joining the working class and party' or, in other words, in Russia's backwardness.[48]

Many writers have taken up the question of Russia's backwardness, with or without Trotsky's related thesis of Thermidor,[49] and the fatally shaping character of the peculiar state-sponsored development that was undertaken to overcome that backwardness.[50] Mikhail Gefter introduces the theme of the Soviet experiment as the precursor to Third World revolutions of the mid-twentieth century.[51] A more developed 'modernisation' argument is made by V. Lapkin and V. Pantin,[52] who appeal to fellow anti-Stalinists to break the monopoly on 'objective' explanations which have been generally conceded to the defenders of Stalin. By remaining in the realm of ideas and high politics, they argue, the anti-Stalinists have in fact unwittingly perpetuated Stalin's cult. By contrast, the defenders of Stalin have identified those social forces they claim helped build the new society; they have strategically replaced Stalin with *us*. Instead, Pantin and Lapkin propose to place Stalinism in the history of Russian industrialisation. The state-directed industrialisation started under Finance Minister Witte was reinforced during World War I and the Civil War and by the world economic crisis that followed upon these wars. The 1920s are described less as a 'golden age' of market socialism than as the origins of an economic bureaucracy that came to promote superindustrialisation.[53] Forced industrialisation, coercive collectivisation, and the terror of 1937–8 become parts of one chain; Stalinism a stage in the development of society dictated by the choice of forced-pace industrialisation on a 'non-organic, non-market basis'. Lapkin and Pantin conclude their provocative essay with an acknowledgement of the moral dilemmas their argument raises; recognition of objective necessity is not to be equated with justification of the policies

---

[48] See their 'Vremia trudnykh voprosov. Istoriia 20-30-kh godov i sovremennaia obshchestvennaia mysl', in *Urok daet istoriia*, ed. V. G. Afanas'ev and G. L. Smirnov (Moscow, Politizdat 1989), pp. 232–67. This argument is developed further in the authors' chapter 3 in *Istoriia i kon'iunktura*.

[49] Trotsky's statement on Russia's backwardness is in his opening chapter, 'Peculiarities of Russia's Development', *The History of the Russian Revolution*, trans. Max Eastman (New York, Simon and Schuster 1932). This literature on Russian backwardness also owes much to the Menshevik historiography in emigration.

[50] See Boffa's chapter 6 in *The Stalin Phenomenon* for a summary of non-Soviet developmental approaches to Soviet history.

[51] See his '"Stalin umer vchera . . ."' in *Inogo ne dano*, p. 317.

[52] 'Chto takoe stalinizm?', in *Osmyslit'*, pp. 327–38. L. Gordon and E. Klopov make similar arguments in their contribution to *Osmyslit'*, 'Stalinism i poststalinizm: neobkhodimost' preodoleniia', pp. 460–96, and in their book, *Chto eto bylo? Razmyshleniia o predposylkakh i itogakh togo, chto sluchilos' s nami v 30–40-e gody* (Moscow 1989).

[53] Lapkin and Pantin follow the recently 'rediscovered' writings of Menshevik critics of Soviet economic policy during the 1920s, especially A. M. Ginzburg.

adopted.[54] Indeed, the moral stakes in the debate are such that authors still risk being charged as 'soft on Stalinism' if they tread too far away from the intentionalist mainstream; developmental or modernisation theories appear to their critics to 'historicise' or even 'normalise' Stalinism by making the phenomenon more comprehensible.[55]

Those historians and publicists who have gone farthest in suggesting what they see as the 'objective' socioeconomic or political preconditions of Stalinism have provoked fierce responses from their colleagues. Most of these authors have questioned the view of NEP as a viable alternative political economy and stressed instead the painful contradictions of the compromised and, in many senses, ill-conceived policies of the 1920s.[56] Admittedly, their critics have correctly chastised the would-be structuralists for a tendency to economic schematicism or overly deterministic formulas, but the attacks have gone beyond intellectual arguments to impute the moral character of the revisionist authors.[57] Moral sensitivities have remained so acute because ardent, genuine defenders of Stalin continue to make their case in popular journals and other forums. The emotional environment is thereby highly charged, and dispassionate analysis of the origins of Stalinism raises fears that the researchers want to rehabilitate the Communist despot. None of the younger revisionists looks to whitewash Stalin or his henchmen nor to diminish their criminality, but this is precisely what their critics suspect them of doing. Rather, the revisionists are trying to solve the riddle of the widespread

---

[54] 'Chto takoe stalinizm?', pp. 334–5.

[55] The debates over National Socialism have raised analogous moral questions among historians and publicists. See the discussion in Dan Diner, ed., *Ist der Nationalsozialismus Geschichte? Zu Historisierung und Historikerstreit* (Frankfurt/Main, Fischer 1987). In particular, advocates of a 'developmental' approach have been suspected of excusing too much of Nazism's murderous policies by focusing on modernising consequences, even when these were not necessarily the ones intended by the regime. See Kershaw, *The Nazi Dictatorship*, chapter 7; David Schoenbaum, *Hitler's Social Revolution: Class and Status in Nazi Germany, 1933–1939* (New York, W. W. Norton 1980); more recently Rainer Zitelmann, in *Hitler: Selbstverstaendnis eines Revolutionaers* (Stuttgart, Klett-Cotta 1991), argues that Hitler even conceived of his politics as modernising and revolutionary.

[56] See G. Bordyugov and V. Kozlov, 'Povorot 1929 goda i al'ternativa Bukharina', *Voprosy istorii KPSS* 8 (1988), pp. 15–23, and their other previously discussed works; V. A. Kozlov and O. V. Khlevniuk, *Nachinaetsia s cheloveka* (Moscow, Politizdat 1988); L. A. Gordon and E. V. Klopov, *Chto eto bylo?* (Moscow) 1989; and especially M. Gorinov, 'Al'ternativy i krizisy v period NEPa', *Voprosy istorii KPSS* 1 (1990), pp. 3–18. In arguing for the origins of Stalinism in the crises of the 1920s, these authors' positions parallel the German discussions about the crises of the Weimar constitution and the triumph of National Socialism. The fact that the Nazis defeated the ruling parties of Weimar, whereas the Stalinist faction triumphed over the anti-Stalinists within the ostensibly same Communist Party, of course, should caution us against taking this parallel too far.

[57] See, for example, the critical response to Gorinov's theses by G. A. Trukan, 'Vnutripartiinye raznoglasiia kontsa 20-kh godov: Sovremennyi vzgliad', *Voprosy istorii KPSS* 10 (1989), pp. 152–7.

involvement of large segments of the Soviet population in Stalin's campaigns, including his most murderous ones; but, importantly, they are also attempting to define the limits of Stalin's power vis-à-vis the bureaucratic structures, larger social and demographic processes, the international and domestic environments.[58] It is further revealing that the understandable reluctance to engage these painful moral issues that none of the historians who work on the post-1917 period has taken advantage of the excellent work done by Soviet and several non-Soviet historians of the pre-revolutionary period who have clearly taken a more structuralist approach based in historical materialism. These historians, in attempting to explain why the 1917 Revolutions occurred when and how they did (and implicitly their consequences), have written about 'the crisis of the autocracy' in the political, economic, social, and ideological realms.[59] After all, the Revolutions of 1917 addressed only the crisis in the political elites, if even that; the major social, economic, ethnic, and cultural dilemmas often assumed new forms, but certainly did not disappear. And it was these realities with which political actors at the top of the successor Soviet state had to contend. The structuralists in the Stalin debate come close to acknowledging a thoroughgoing structural crisis during the 1920s, but curiously fail to tie it to earlier periods.[60]

[58] Vladimir Zhuravlev, a historian at the former Institute of Marxism-Leninism, further warned that excessive attention to Stalin's paranoia or schizophrenia at the expense of broader social, economic, and political processes, 'the priority of the subjective principle' as he summarises it, 'inevitably leads to the idea of historical pessimism, when everything in socialism – in its past, present and future fates – depends on the personal qualities of the leader'. He reminds even those who ardently combat the Stalinist phenomenon that 'without understanding the reasons for the consolidation of the personality cult, we will not be able to work out a social mechanism that can guarantee society will be free from its repetition'. V. V. Zhuravlev, in a roundtable discussion about the 1930s, *30-e gody: vzgliad iz segodnia*, ed. D. Volkogonov (Moscow, Nauka 1990), pp. 10–11. Other commentators have also called for less categorical approaches to the Stalin period. See for example, G. Kh. Popov and N. Adzhubei, 'Pamiat' i 'Pamiat''', *Znamia* 1 (1988), pp. 188–203, esp. pp. 190, 201. Popov reminds his readers that 'in the culture of every people there are progressive and conservative elements. Both must be seen, both must be considered in their specific historical context. What was a clear weakness in one case begins to play a positive role in another situation. To suppress memory, to cut it up, to take only one part of it, means in fact to deprive oneself of all memory'.

[59] For a recent formulation of the thesis of a pre-revolutionary crisis, see the collective work, *Krizis samoderzhaviia v Rossii, 1985–1917* (Leningrad, Nauka 1948); see also the work of the Columbia University historian Leopold Haimson and his students.

[60] I cursorily outline some aspects of the possible continuities from the multifaceted 'crisis of the autocracy' to the 'crisis' of the post-tsarist order in 'The NEP, Perestroika, and the Problem of Alternatives', in *Socialism, Perestroika, and the Dilemmas of Soviet Economic Reform*, ed. John Tedstrom (Boulder, Colorado, Westview Press 1990), esp. pp. 7–11. For a similar structural argument about the origins of Stalinism, see Walter Suess, *Die Arbeiterklasse als Maschine. Ein industriesoziologischer Beitrag zur Sozialgeschichte des aufkommenden Stalinismus* (Berlin 1985). I thank Rosalinde Sartorti for this reference.

The 'national question' and the Stalin debate

Besides the continued preoccupation with intentionalist approaches and hostility to structuralist ones, another 'blank spot' that long persisted in the debates among largely Moscow-based intellectuals is suggested by the virtual silence in the two summary volumes (*Inogo ne dano* and *Osmyslit' kul't Stalina*) on the 'national question',[61] that is, on the sensitive topic of interethnic relations in the multinational Soviet state. Yet one of the most painful legacies of Stalinist politics has surely been the fate of national communities and cultures, including the Russians', in the Soviet multiethnic state. The emergence of a debate about these issues reflects many of the trends outlined above in the general discussions about Stalin, but it also illustrates other dilemmas about post-Soviet politics and history-writing.

During the 1920s and early 1930s, Soviet historians wrote very critically about the colonial and foreign policies of tsarist Russia, frequently bolstering their studies with the anti-tsarist attitudes of Karl Marx and Friedrich Engels. Their critical attitude toward Russian imperialism and their assertion of a radical discontinuity with the post-1917 period went hand in hand with a conscious effort to combat Great Russian chauvinism and chauvinistic nationalism in general and to promote 'proletarian internationalism'.[62] Beginning in the second half of the 1920s, however, Bolshevik Party leaders and some Marxist scholars (many associated with Mikhail Pokrovskii) attacked what was called 'national communism' (Sultan-Galievism in the Turkic and Muslim areas) and 'bourgeois nationalism' (the Hrushevskii school in Ukrainian history); although the Pokrovskii school did not intend it, the balance began to shift back in the direction of a privileged position for Great Russian interests. By the mid-1930s, after the Pokrovskii school had been crushed, the victors – now very consciously – resurrected the history of the Great Russian centralised state and banned discussion of historical alternatives to that narrative of centralisation, whether they be non-

---

[61] The national question is notably also missing from several of the early collections of revisionist essays and interviews, *Stranitsy istorii sovetskogo obshchestva* (Moscow, Politizdat 1989); *Urok daet istoriia* (Moscow, Politizdat 1989); *Stranitsy istorii KPSS* (Moscow, Vysshaia shkola 1989); *Istoriia otechestva: liudi, idei, resheniia* (Moscow, Politizdat 1991); *Istoriia i stalinizm* (Moscow, Politizdat 1991).

[62] For works characteristic of this critical trend see G. Safarov, *Kolonial'naia revoliutsiia: opyt Turkestana* (Moscow 1921); P. G. Galuzo, *Turkestan–koloniia (Ocherki po istorii Turkestana ot zavoevaniia russkimi do revoliutsii 1917 goda)* (Moscow 1929); on an interpretation of Ukraine as a tsarist colony, see Mykhailo Volobuev's writings, especially his 'Do problemy ukrains'koi ekonomiky', in *Bil'shovyk Ukrainy* (30 January and 15 February 1928). Even before Marxists in the 1920s began writing about tsarist colonialism, Siberian democrats had cast their appeal for greater Siberian regional autonomy in the genre of a history of colonialism; see N. M. Iadrintsev, *Sibir' kak koloniia* (Petersburg 1882).

Russian nationalist or federalist variants. All histories of non-Russian nations were subordinated to the history of the Great Russian people; non-Russians could no longer read textbooks devoted to their national histories until 1960. The dominant organising principle of Soviet history was the 'friendship of peoples', so that all friendly historical ties between Russians and non-Russians were highlighted and all such hostile ties were downplayed, ignored, or distorted in historical treatments.[63] Soviet historians' reevaluation of Russian–non-Russian relations paralleled a change in their treatment of Russian imperial policy; now they posited fundamental continuity of tsarist and Soviet diplomacy and nationality policy as progressive and liberationist phenomena.[64]

Once the histories of all non-Russian peoples were so coordinated with the history of the Russian people, so too were these histories rewritten to conform to a general scheme of periodisation and especially to parallel stages of class formation and struggle. Any researcher who suggested that Russian, and by extension Soviet, nationality policy had negative aspects could be and frequently was pilloried for 'nationalist deviations'. Especially, any discussion of anti-Russian revolts was viewed as fomenting interethnic hostility and thereby injuring the Soviet state. All mention of earlier appeals for greater sovereignty and autonomy for non-Russian peoples brought down the harsh hand of the censor and accusations that the author was a bourgeois secessionist and, at one period, an agent of British or other foreign imperialisms. Similarly, because the most populous non-Russian nations have always been located on the peripheries of the empire, of course, their ties with non-Russian and non-Soviet co-religionists or co-ethnics have been important; but here too these ties have been ignored or distorted in Soviet historical science and usually discussed under the rubric of 'the struggle against bourgeois falsification'.

In answer to the Stalin-era rewriting of the history of interethnic relations (and its further elaboration under Stalin's successors), a dissident canon emerged from *tamizdat*, *samizdat*, and émigré histories of several of the non-Russian peoples. That canon, in sharp contrast to the official Soviet narrative, focused almost exclusively on anti-Russian

[63] See the fascinating study of the concept of 'friendship of peoples' in Lowell Tillett, *The Great Friendship: Soviet Historians on the Non-Russian Nationalities* (Chapel Hill, N.C., The University of North Carolina Press 1969). See also the semi-autobiographical account of the transformation of the historical profession in Konstantin Shteppa, *Russian Historians and the Soviet State* (New Brunswick, NJ, Rutgers 1962).
[64] Not surprisingly, until recently Marx's and Engels' critical articles were not published or mentioned. Only in 1989 was Marx's highly critical account of tsarist foreign policy published in the Soviet Union. See Karl Marks, 'Razoblacheniia diplomaticheskoi istorii XVIII veka', *Voprosy istorii* 1 (1989), pp. 3–23; 2, pp. 3–16; 3, pp. 3–17; 4, pp. 3–19. (Also Engels' 'The Foreign Policy of Russian Tsarism'.)

social movements and anti-centralist intellectual trends.[65] Similar to the mirror-image relationship of the Gulag narrative to its Stalinist ortho-dox counterpart, so the 'captive nations' narrative accepts the funda-mental continuity of tsarist and Soviet nationality policy posited by the orthodox Soviet version, but simply reverses the values assigned to the continuity of imperial practice.

Against the background of these trends in nationality policy and history writing, the evolution of the 'nationalities' debate closely paralleled the general contours of the Stalin debate, as well as having repeated earlier stages in the writings about non-Russian peoples. In the context of Gorbachev's call for revising the federal structure of the Soviet Union, the intelligentsia responded with critiques of Stalinist nationality policy. The Georgian director Abuladze's film, *Repentance*, is set in a mythical Georgian town, and, among the other matters it treats, also poses the issues of survival of national cultures and intelligentsias. Fictional writers gingerly dealt with the tragedy of Stalin-era deport-ations of peoples and arrests of national intellectuals.[66] As professional historians had been reluctant to tackle the most difficult moral di-lemmas of Stalinism, so with the nationalities issues they entered the fray only after considerable delay. At first, historians joined in the rehabilitation of local and republican political leaders who had been purged and executed under Stalin.[67] Local social movements, such as *Sajudis* in Lithuania and *Ruch* in Ukraine, focused attention on other crimes of the Stalin period, such as the post-war deportations and the Ukrainian famine of 1932–3.[68]

In the spirit of the reformist faction within the Communist Party,

[65] By way of examples, for the history of Turkic and Muslim peoples, see the school of Alexandre Bennigsen (Helene Carrere d'Encausse, S. Enders Wimbush, Chantal Quelquejay); for Ukraine and Belorussia, see works by Hrihory Kostiuk, Yaroslav Bilinsky, Nicholas Vakar, Jurij Borys, Taras Hunczak, Basil Dmytryshyn, and Ivan Rudnytsky. Since the 1930s, Jewish history has also been taboo in the Soviet Union; meanwhile, the history of East European and Russian Jewry has gained solid academic legitimacy in Anglo-American universities. Among the most critical texts treating the nationality problems have been Robert Conquest, *The Nation Killers: The Soviet Deportation of Nationalities* (New York 1970); and Aleksandr Nekrich, *The Punished Peoples* (New York 1978).

[66] See, for example, the novel by Anatolii Pristavkin, *Nochevala tuchka zolotaia* (Moscow, Knizhnaia palata 1988), which treats the deportation of Northern Caucasian peoples during World War II through the perspective of a small boy, and the memoir-novel by Kamil Ikramov about his father, a prominent Uzbek Communist, who was executed along with Bukharin in 1938, *Delo moego otsa* (Moscow, Sovetskii pisatel' 1991).

[67] For typical rehabilitation volumes, in these instances for Ukrainian victims of the terror, see *Pro minule zarady maibutn'ogo*, ed. Iu. P. Shapoval (Kiev, Kiev State University Press 1989); Dmytro Tabachnyk and Oleksandr Sydorenko, *Za standartnymi zvynuvachen-niamy* (Kiev, Politizdat 1990).

[68] See the documentary volume, *Golod 1932–1933 rokiv na Ukraini* (Kiev 1990), published by decision of the Central Committee of the Communist Party of Ukraine.

historians rehabilitated a non-Stalinist alternative in Lenin's nationality policy of the early Soviet years. Previously unpublished stenographic records of Party Congress discussions of nationalities issues revealed a fierce struggle within the Party leadership over centralism and national autonomy, cultural and educational policy, cadre appointment policies, and many other issues.[69] Al'bert Nenarokov argued the historical possibility of a more genuinely federalist solution based on equality of nations and internationalism.[70] He saw that potential crushed by the triumph of the Stalinist faction in the mid-1920s. Nenarokov's arguments rehabilitated the critical intellectual legacy of the 1920s, but also reflected larger circles within the reformist wing of the party and intelligentsia that can be dated to the post-Khrushchev 'percolation' period; especially the banned writings of Ivan Dziuba in defense of a Marxist-Leninist nationality policy illustrate that organic link.[71]

Even these low-keyed critiques and moderate revisions of the Stalinist past provoked vitriolic campaigns from established elites and their intellectual spokesmen. On the Russian side of the struggle, the heavy hand of Zhdanov-era national chauvinism and xenophobia made itself felt in the often defensive attitudes of leading writers, publicists, and historians toward any suggestion that the Russian majority ill-treated non-Russian peoples or of significant foreign influences on and ties to Russian or Soviet culture. The labels of cosmopolitan, Freemason, Zionist, and especially Russophobe, poisoned many important discussions of the relationship of Russian and Soviet history to broader trends in European and world history. A further unfortunate development in these debates was the identification of non-Russians, most often Jews, as the source of what were viewed as major national catastrophes; notable has been the attention to Yakov Sverdlov, the Communist Party's first general secretary, and the persistent resistance to the full historical and political rehabilitation of Lev Trotsky,[72] but also to the

[69] See *Izvestiia TsK KPSS* 9 (1989), pp. 191–219, for the proceedings of a 1922 Politburo Commission on relations between the RSFSR and other republics; and *Tainy natsional'noi politiki TsK RKP: Stenograficheskii otchet sekretnogo IV soveshchaniia TsK RKP, 1923 g.* (Moscow 1992). See also Viktor Zotov, 'Natsional'nyi vopros: deformatsii proshlogo', *Kommunist* 3 (1989).

[70] See his *K edinstvu ravnykh: Kul'turnye faktory ob'edinitel'nogo dvizheniia sovetskikh narodov 1917–1924* (Moscow, Nauka 1991); also V. V. Zhuravlev and A. P. Nenarokov, 'Novye fakty i dokumenty iz istorii obrazovaniia SSSR', in *Istoriki sporiat* (Moscow, Politizdat 1989), pp. 191–227.

[71] *Internationalism or Russification?* (Anchor 1974; originally published in Munich, 1968 by Suchasnist Press). Dziuba wrote this work during the last months of 1965 and was arrested in 1972, after which he recanted his dissident views.

[72] For a recent review of the struggle over Trotsky's rehabilitation in historical literature, see Markus Wehner, 'Rueckkehr mit Hindernissen: Die "gebremste" Diskussion um L. D. Trotzkij in der Sowjetunion', *Osteuropa* 3 (1991), pp. 247–58; also Thomas Sherlock,

prominent role played by non-Russians in the Cheka and NKVD, especially Caucasians, Balts, and, again, Jews.

But much as the initial reformist measures in the political and economic realms failed to satisfy ever more radical political opponents, so too Gorbachev's belated response to the nationalities issues was increasingly viewed as half-hearted and timid. The demands for autonomy within a reformed Soviet Union gradually gave way to calls for secession and national independence. The Baltic popular fronts introduced new rhetoric into their critiques of Soviet policy, including 'Soviet imperialism' and 'occupation regime', that quickly spread to other republics. The non-Russian movements failed any longer to make the distinction between Russian and Soviet imperialism and vowed to end their 'colonial exploitation'. With the ascent of anti-Moscow popular fronts in many non-Russian republics and their subsequent secession and transition to sovereign statehood, the alternative narratives of the 'captive nations' won 'official' status. The more anti-Russian and anti-Soviet the version was, the greater chance it had of winning popularity. Contemporary 'democrats' and 'nationalists' mobilised these long-suppressed narratives, often heavily imbued with great doses of national messianic utopianism and often chauvinistic myth-making, in their struggles with the central authorities and their representatives in the peripheries.[73] Everywhere historians and would-be historians have been mobilised to articulate national interests for competing state and incipient state structures. Here, too, because of the moral-psychological climate and alignment of political forces, an even-handed version of the Russian imperial and Soviet pasts is proving as difficult to fashion as the painful state- and nation-building processes, not to mention the experiments with federal and confederal relationships among the former Soviet republics.[74]

'Politics and History under Gorbachev', *Problems of Communism* (May–August 1988), pp. 16–42.

[73] A good example of these trends is the transformation of historical consciousness in Ukraine. See, among others, Frank Sysyn, 'The Reemergence of the Ukrainian Nation and Cossack Mythology', *Social Research*, 58, no. 5 (Winter 1991); Bohdan Krawchenko, 'National Memory in Ukraine: The Role of the Blue and Yellow Flag', *Journal of Ukrainian Studies*, 15, no. 1 (Summer 1990), pp. 1–22.

[74] One notable exception to the general rule of increasingly and exclusively nationalist treatments is a collection of documents that sets the recent disintegration of the Soviet Union in historical perspective. *Nesostoiavshiisia iubilei: Pochemu SSSR ne otprazdnoval svoego 70-letiia?* ed. Albert Nenarokov *et al.* (Moscow, Terra 1992), traces the rise of the 'national question' at the beginning of the twentieth century through the federalist experiments of 1917 and the 1920s, the Stalinist reassertion of a unitary state, and concluding with the struggle for sovereignty of the successor states to the USSR. Alas, to date nothing in the post-Soviet historical communities comes close the masterful synthesis of Russian imperial nationality policy in Andreas Kappeler's *Russland als Vielvoelkerreich: Entstehung, Geschichte, Zerfall* (Koeln, Beck 1992).

In the short term, at least, many post-Soviet historians have turned to more primordial and essentialist narratives of their past, whether they be Russians ignoring their multiethnic empire in favour of Russian culture and civilisation, or Ukrainians who search for a 'pure' ethnic identity cleansed of Russian, Polish or Jewish contaminants. Still, in the chaotic conditions of the new publishing markets, these versions are forced to compete with a wide range of alternatives and the authors of school textbooks have been generally more responsible with the historical record.[75]

On balance, the publications and conferences of the past several years illustrate a wide-ranging discussion of alternative versions of twentieth-century history. But considerable obstacles to a reintegration of the Soviet period into a new Russian national past remain. Among them are the current triumph of the conception identified above with the nostalgia of film director Govorukhin and the Education Ministry official for the Russia of the tsars, the eagerness to personalise the 'blame' for the Soviet period and to resist any more or less structural explanations for the major transformations of the century, and the general post-Soviet tendency to 'ethnicise' history at the expense of a more 'internationalist' reading of the Russian and Soviet pasts. Despite, or perhaps because of, the rise of national(ist) elites to power in all the successor states, recognition of the dilemmas of multiethnic societies has little shaped the rewriting of national pasts. On the positive side, post-Soviet historians have begun to interact more regularly and on a new basis with the international community of historians concerned with their national pasts. If the professional historical community in the successor states is able to survive the devastation that all non-commercial sectors of the economy are now suffering; if their archival and library collections do not irretrievably collapse; and if the climate of intellectual pluralism is not crushed, historians will emerge with a challenging agenda that matches the intellectual excitement and moral intractability that twentieth-century Russian and Soviet history have laid at the feet of world history.

---

[75] As examples of more balanced approaches in Ukraine, a translation of Orest Subtelny's *Ukraine: A History* has sold tens of thousands of copies, and the historians M. V. Koval', S. V. Kul'chyts'kyi, and Iu. O. Kurnosova have authored a new text for tenth-and eleventh-grade students, *Ukrainy* (Kiev 1992).

13

Work, gender and everyday life: reflections on continuity, normality and agency in twentieth-century Germany

Mary Nolan

Until the mid-1970s the social history of the Third Reich was a terra incognita. Since then it has become an extensively explored but highly contested terrain. Everyday life in all its diversity and complexity has been thickly described and redescribed. We have innumerable studies of the changing nature of work and attitudes toward it, both official and unofficial. Working-class sociability on and off the shopfloor, the leisure activities of women and men, the changing face of village politics and office interactions, the experiences of those who joined Nazi organisations and those who distanced themselves from them have all been reconstructed. More recently the policies toward and experiences of women as well as the Nazis' preoccupation with gender issues have been investigated. While the initial body of work focused primarily on the period from 1933–1939, more recent studies concentrate on the war and immediate post-war era or span the years from the mid- and late 1920s to the mid-1930s.

The social history of Nazi Germany has been written primarily by leftists, feminists, and proponents of *Alltagsgeschichte* or the history of everyday life – three contentious and controversial groups. From its inception, the social history of Nazi Germany, understood as history from below, the history of the inarticulate and marginalised, the history of that which was unpolitical or not traditionally considered political, aimed to be methodologically unconventional, theoretically unorthodox, and politically provocative. From Tim Mason's pioneering study of the working class in Nazi Germany, through diverse efforts to specify the forms and meanings of opposition and collaboration, distancing and participation by men and women, to explorations of economic and social rationalisation, anti-feminism, and racism, from studies of the home and the home front to examinations of the Eastern Front, the social histories of the Third Reich have sparked vigorous debates.[1]

[1] Specific works will be referred to below. For an overview of German social history see

What then, have been the main controversies and what balance – if any – can we draw after two decades of research and dialogue? Let us look first at the principle paradigms and issues which have structured these debates and the main issues raised in them and then explore three substantive themes in which these issues are intertwined and for which different paradigms offer competing interpretations: work and the working class; women and gender; and politics and everyday life.

The debates

Class, race, and gender, that trinity of analytical categories, have structured approaches to the social history of Nazi Germany in ways that have often been highly contentious and mutually exclusive. Historians have argued for the primacy of class conflict or biological politics or the oppression of women more often than they have explored their interactions. The social history of Nazi Germany was initially written by left scholars, who analysed Nazi Germany in terms of fascism – and hence capitalism – and who privileged class relationships. Mason's pioneering study of the working class and social policy in Nazi Germany was followed by a host of studies which examined the persistence of class and the manifestations of oppositional attitudes and behaviours but also uncovered sources of integration, cooptation, and collaboration with the regime and its many organisations.[2] These scholars were seeking, if not a usable past, at least one in which National Socialism did not uniformly control all aspects of life and thought.

The primacy accorded to class was subsequently challenged from two directions. Feminist historians in Germany and abroad not only uncovered the history of women in Nazi Germany, but asserted the centrality of gender concerns and of misogyny and anti-feminism in Nazi ideology and policy.[3] Scholars working first on Nazi medicine

Geoff Eley, 'Labor History, Social History, *Alltagsgeschichte*: Experience, Culture and Politics of the Everyday – a New Direction for German Social History', *Journal of Modern History* 61 (June 1989), pp. 297–343; Robert Fletcher, *Journal of Modern History* 60 (September 1988), pp. 557–68. For an introduction to the social history of National socialism see Mary Nolan, 'The *Historikerstreit* and Social History', *New German Critique*, 44 (Spring/Summer 1988), pp. 51–80. For an introduction to studies of women and gender in the Nazi Germany, see Eve Rosenhaft, 'Women in Modern Germany', in *Modern Germany Reconsidered, 1870–1945*, ed. by Gordon Martel (London, Routledge 1992), pp. 140–58.

2 The main works in English are Timothy W. Mason, *Social Policy in the Third Reich* (Providence/Oxford, Berg 1993). This is a translation of his *Sozialpolitik im Dritten Reich: Arbeiterklasse und Volksgemeinschaft* (Opladen, Westdeutscher Verlag 1977); Detlev Peukert, *Inside Nazi Germany: Conformity, Opposition and Racism in Everyday Life* (New Haven, Yale University Press 1987).

3 The state of debate and research can best be gleaned from two old and one recent collection of essays. *Mutterkreuz und Arbeitsbuch: Zur Geschichte der Frauen in der Weimarer Republik und im Nationalsozialismus*, ed. by Frauengruppe Faschismusfor-

and Nazi doctors and then on biological politics more broadly came to see Nazi Germany as a quintessentially 'racial state', to borrow the title of Michael Burleigh and Wolfgang Wippermann's study of Nazi racism and racial policies.[4] Methodologically, the social histories of the Third Reich have been eclectic. Some drew heavily on the 'new' working-class history of the 1960s and 1970s and were explicitly informed by contemporary neo-Marxist debates about fascism. Others were concerned with the social consequences of state policies and with the popular responses to them. Still other works have been primarily informed by *Alltagsgeschichte*, which seeks to reconstruct everyday life and uncover subjective experience. Some rely primarily on sources generated by the Nazi regime, such as Gestapo reports, others on documents from firms and private organisations, and still others from memoirs, letters, and oral histories.

Whatever categories, methodologies, and specific subject matter they have chosen, the social historians of the Third Reich have grappled with three broad problematics. The first involves issues of continuity and discontinuity in twentieth-century German history. The second focuses on agency and power, or, more pointedly, on the question of who was an agent (*Täter*) and who a victim (*Opfer*) under National Socialism. The third concerns the implications of normality, of everydayness, be it in the factory, in the home or on the battle front, for understanding the social history of the Third Reich, popular attitudes toward it, and its place in German history.

German history is rife with debates about continuity from the Kaiserreich to the Third Reich, from the Weimar Republic to National Socialism, and from Nazi Germany to the Federal Republic and the German Democratic Republic. Social history has intensified these debates and injected new themes – work and social policy, economic and social rationalisation, leisure activities and reading habits, fertility patterns and family strategies.[5] It has examined more traditional topics – ideology, discourse, the army, and the shifting relationships between

schung (Frankfurt am M., Fischer 1981); *When Biology Became Destiny: Women in Weimar and Nazi Germany*, ed. by Renata Bridenthal, Atina Grossmann, Marion Kaplan (New York, Monthly Review 1984); *Töchterfragen: NS-Frauengeschichte*, ed. Lerke Grevenhorst and Carmen Tatschmurat (Freiburg i. Br., Kore 1990).
4 Michael Burleigh and Wolfgang Wippermann, *The Racial State. Germany 1933–1945* (Cambridge, Cambridge University Press 1991); Robert Jay Lifton, *The Nazi Doctors* (New York, Basic Books 1986); Robert N. Proctor, *Racial Hygiene: Medicine under the Nazis* (Cambridge, Harvard University Press 1988); Paul J. Weindling, *Health, Race and German Politics between National Unification and Nazism 1870–1945* (Cambridge, Cambridge University Press 1989).
5 In addition to the section on work below, see Anson Rabinbach, 'The Aesthetics of Production in the Third Reich', *Journal of Contemporary History* 11:4 (1974), pp. 43–74; Carola Sachse, Tilla Siegel, Hasso Spode and Wolfgang Spohn, *Angst, Belohnung, Zucht und Ordnung* (Opladen, Westdeutscher Verlag 1982); Marie-Luise Recker, *National-sozialistische Sozialpolitik im Zweiten Weltkrieg* (Munich, R. Oldenbourg 1985).

the public and the private – from the bottom up.[6] Questions of continuity and discontinuity have obvious implications for understanding the nature of the varied regimes that have occupied the shifting territory of twentieth-century Germany, for assessing the forces responsible for their creation and perpetuation, and for evaluating the relationships between state and society.[7] Did 1933 and 1945 mark breaks or were there significant continuities in elites and institutions, in social policies and class structure, in cultures high and low? Do the continuities discovered in the economic, social, and cultural realms imply that Nazi Germany was in certain respects normal, unexceptional, even uncontaminated by the regime's ideology and policies?

For social historians, issues of continuity and discontinuity have frequently been debated in terms of modernity and tradition. To what extent did the Third Reich initiate processes of modernisation, be they in work organisation, wages, women's workforce participation, family size and leisure activities? Or, to put the issue more precisely, how was the relationship between the 'modern' and the 'traditional' in both social life and in its conceptualisation in ideology and popular consciousness renegotiated in the Nazi era? ('Modern' and 'traditional' are admittedly elusive terms, but are preferable to 'modernisation', which more strongly implies a coherence, a uniform rationality, and a teleology that the combined, uneven, contradictory, and frequently irrational developments of Nazi Germany – and not just Germany – belie.[8])

Social historians have frequently sought out manifestations of opposition or *Resistenz*, terms covering a range of behaviours and attitudes lying between fundamental endorsement of the regime and wholesale and active resistance (*Widerstand*) to it.[9] They have listened for silenced

6 Major works include the multivolume *Bayern in der NS Zeit*, ed. by Martin Broszat, *et al.* (Munich, R. Oldenbourg 1972–81); Sarah Gordon, *Hitler, Germans and the 'Jewish Question'* (Princeton, Princeton University Press 1984); Ian Kershaw, *Popular Opinion and Political Dissent in the Third Reich, Bavaria 1933–1945* (Oxford, Oxford University Press 1984). For an introduction to the social history of the army see Omer Bartov, 'Soldiers, Nazis, and War in the Third Reich', *Journal of Modern History*, 63 (March 1991), pp. 44–60.
7 For an introduction to the voluminous debates about continuity and German peculiarity, see David Blackbourn and Geoff Eley, *The Peculiarities of German History* (Oxford, Oxford University Press 1984) and Hans-Ulrich Wehler, *The German Empire* (Leamington Spa/Dover, New Hampshire, Berg Press 1985). For an overview of recent works on continuities and discontinuities from the Third Reich to the Federal Republic, see Harold James, 'The Prehistory of the Federal Republic', *Journal of Modern History* 63 (March 1991), pp. 99–115.
8 For an introduction to debates on modernity and modernisation, see *Nationalsozialismus and Modernisierung*, ed. by Michael Prinz and Rainer Zitelmann (Darmstadt, Wissenschaftliche Buchgesellschaft 1991). See also Detlev Peukert, *The Weimar Republic: Crisis of Classical Modernity* (New York, Hill and Wang 1992).
9 Martin Broszat offers the most useful definition of these terms in 'Resistenz und Widerstand: Eine Zwischenbilanz des Forschungsprojekts "Widerstand und Verfol-

voices and suppressed alternatives, especially within the working class. Of particular concern have been the questions of how, when, and to what extent the traditional working-class milieus – of socialists, Communists, and Catholics as well as of the unorganised and unskilled – were destroyed or, more aptly, fundamentally restructured during the fourteen years of Hitler's rule. To what extent were attitudes toward work and leisure transformed and did such transformations serve Nazi goals?

Finally, social historians have explored how subjectivity and positionality shape perceptions about periodisation. Are the continuities and discontinuities which historians reconstruct also those which loom large in popular memory?[10] Do historians of structure and high policy posit a fundamentally different periodisation than those writing *Alltagsgeschichte* and women's history?[11] And whose popular memory should be central, for on issues of continuity and periodisation the memory of victims and perpetrators diverges as radically as their experiences did.[12] According to Andreas Hillgruber, for example, German soldiers remember the last years of World War II on the Eastern Front as a heroic and desperate defence of the fatherland against invading Asiatic hordes – and historians should view them from this perspective.[13] For concentration-camp inmates, such a defence meant continued genocide; its failure brought liberation.

Issues of continuity are closely related to those of normality, a complex theme that has been pursued by social historians in two rather different ways. Practitioners of *Alltagsgeschichte* and of women's history have explored the relationships, real and perceived, between continu-

---

gung in Bayern 1933–1945'", in *Nach Hitler. Der schwierige Umgang mit unserer Geschichte: Beiträge von Martin Broszat*, ed. by Hermann Graml and Klaus-Dietmar Henke (Munich, R. Oldenbourg 1987).

[10] According to Peukert and Reulecke, the origins of *Alltagsgeschichte* lay in part in an effort to bridge the gap between critical academic history and popular memory, for Germans did not see their experiences reflected in what historians were writing about the Third Reich: *Die Reihen fast geschlossen*, ed. by Detlev Peukert and Jürgen Reulecke (Wuppertal, Peter Hammer 1981), p. 13.

[11] Dan Diner, 'Perspektivenwahl und Geschichtserfahrung. Bedarf es einer besonderen Historik des Nationalsozialismus?' in *Der historische Ort des Nationalsozialismus*, ed. by Walter H. Pehle (Frankfurt am M., Fischer Taschenbuch 1988), p. 110.

[12] See Martin Broszat and Saul Friedländer, 'A Controversy about the Historicization of National Socialism', *New German Critique* 44 (Spring/Summer 1988), pp. 85–126; Ulrich Herbert, 'Die guten und die schlechten Zeiten! Ueberlegungen zur diachronen Analyse lebensgeschichtlicher Interviews', *"Die Jahre weiss man nicht, wo man die heute hinsetzen soll"*, ed. by Lutz Niethammer, Vol. I of *Faschismus-Erfahrungen im Ruhrgebiet. Lebensgeschichte und Sozialkultur im Ruhrgebiet 1930 bis 1960* (Berlin/Bonn, Dietz 1983), pp. 67–97.

[13] Andreas Hillgruber, 'Der Zusammenbruch im Osten 1944/45 als Problem der deutschen Nationalgeschichte und der europäischen Geschichte', *Zweierlei Untergang. Die Zerschlagung des Deutschen Reiches und das Ende des europäischen Judentums* (Berlin, Siedler 1986), pp. 24–5.

ities in the economic, social, and cultural realms across the period from the 1920s to the 1950s and the 'normality', real and perceived, of many aspects of Nazi society. They have reconstructed everyday life in all its often mundane repetitiveness; they have uncovered long-term secular trends that seem little influenced by Nazi policy even if they were either masked or packaged in new Nazi ideology. It is abundantly clear from oral testimonies that many Germans remember numerous aspects of life in the Third Reich as normal, and they claim to have avoided participation and ideological contamination by escaping into a purportedly unpolitical world of work or home or leisure. In both popular memory and the conceptual vocabulary of many historians, the normal and the unpolitical are seen as integrally related attributes. Precisely this association is problematic, for representations in memory do not necessarily reflect the reality of Nazi Germany. Historians must ask whether people were unpolitical and therefore uncomplicitous or whether all aspects of everyday life were politicised, blatantly or subtly? Were the words and categories in which everyday life was constructed and perceived tainted by the regime's antisemitism and racism, by its sexism and homophobia, by its draconian work ethic and rabid nationalism? Finally, how is one to weigh what is remembered as normal – the 1930s and the war on the western front, as opposed to what is repressed – the war on the eastern front and the Holocaust?

Other historians, who have sought to link the 1930s to the war years, the occupied territories to the home front, have explored how abnormal behaviour, i.e. racist and genocidal actions, came to be understood by those engaged in them as normal. Historians of Nazi medicine have traced the racialisation and radicalisation of eugenics and the reconceptualisation of the task of the doctors from curing the individual to curing the 'nation's body' (*Volkskörper*). These transformations were central to the planning and execution of compulsory sterilisation, euthanasia, and genocide, and to understanding the central role of doctors in them.[14] Others, such as Götz Aly and Susanne Heim, trace the work of economists and statisticians, population experts and urban planners, administrators and agronomists, arguing that they conceptualised and participated in deportations, population transfers, massive and involuntary labour deployments and eventually genocide, seeing it as part of the normal practice of rational economic and social modernisation.[15] Historians of the German army and of the war on the eastern front, such as Omar Bartov and Christopher Browning, have sought to explain why extreme brutality and racism became normal practice on the eastern

---

[14] See Lifton, *The Nazi Doctors*, and Proctor, *Racial Hygiene*.
[15] Götz Aly and Susanne Heim, *Vordenker der Vernichtung: Auschwitz und die deutschen Pläne für eine neue europäische Ordnung* (Frankfurt am M., Fischer 1993).

front and why participation in killing Jews and Russian POWs and civilians was considered routine.[16] The normality at the heart of these varied arguments is one of racism in high politics, intellectual and expert thought, and everyday life.

The implications of continuity and normality have been at the heart of bitter disagreements over whether National Socialism can be historicised, a term covering three closely interconnected but nonetheless separate issues. The first, and central, question involves the place of Auschwitz in the historical reconstruction of the Third Reich. Should Auschwitz be the central point to which all developments during the Third Reich must refer or does that distort parts of the Nazi era which can best be understood primarily with reference to non-Nazi traditions and developments.[17] A second issue involves whether the Nazi era is capable of being understood historically, as Martin Broszat has argued, or whether, as Dan Diner insists, Auschwitz is the central fact of Nazi Germany and represents 'a no-man's-land of understanding, a black box of explanation, a vacuum of extrahistorical significance, which sucks up attempts at historiographical interpretation'.[18] And if historical understanding is possible, can the historian of National Socialism employ the same methods as the historian of any other era? Should s/he abandon the distancing from the subject that has characterised most work on the Third Reich?

A third dimension of the debates about historicisation involves the place of National Socialism in twentieth-century German history. In the *Historikerstreit* of the mid- and late 1980s, conservative historians, such as Ernst Nolte, Michael Stürmer, Klaus Hildebrandt, and Andreas Hillgruber, sought to historicise and relativise National Socialism, to acknowledge but minimise the Holocaust by comparing it to other twentieth-century genocides. Nolte, going much further than his conservative colleagues, saw Auschwitz as an imitation of the Gulag and argued that genocide was undertaken to ward off an 'asiatic deed' by the Bolsheviks. These strategies contrast sharply with Broszat's insistence that Auschwitz was unique, even if many aspects of the Third Reich were uncontaminated by and explicable without reference to it. It is even more distant from those who see the Holocaust as unique, even

---

[16] Omer Bartov, *Hitler's Army: Soldiers, Nazis, and War in the Third Reich* (New York, Oxford University Press 1992); Christopher R. Browning, *Ordinary Men: Reserve Police Battalion 101 and the Final Solution in Poland* (New York, Harper Collins 1992).

[17] Broszat, 'A Controversy about the Historicization of National Socialism' (see note 18), p. 103 and Broszat, 'Pläydoyer für eine Historisierung des Nationalsozialismus', *Merkur* 39:5 (May 1986), pp. 373–85.

[18] Broszat, 'A Controversy about the Historicization of National Socialism'; Dan Diner, 'Between Aporia and Apology: On the Limits of Historicizing National Socialism', both in *Reworking the Past: Hitler, the Holocaust and the Historians' Debate*, ed. by Peter Baldwin (Boston, Beacon 1990), p. 144.

as they acknowledge continuities between Nazism and the preceding and succeeding regimes.[19]

If debates about continuity and normality raise the question of the place of the Third Reich in German history and its relationship to national identity, controversies about agency raise the question of moral and political responsibility for the multiple crimes of the regime. *Alltagsgeschichte*, with its careful reconstruction of people's ambivalent attitudes toward Nazi ideology and contradictory behaviour toward the policies and organisations of the regime, has successfully destroyed the neat categories of good resister (in the sense of *Widerstand*) and evil Nazi. People actively opposed some policies and programmes of the regime, distanced themselves intellectually or emotionally from others, but enthusiastically participated in still other aspects. Criticism of individual policies or political leaders coexisted with approval for Hitler.[20] The controversy is no longer about how people thought or behaved, but rather about the implications of their multiple and shifting identities. According to Dan Diner, social history explains 'how it really was' by studying the microscopic and stressing normality and continuity. But unlike the view from above, which emphasises the monstrous, the discontinuous, it fails to explain 'how it was possible'.[21] Others insist that there is a complex relationship between the opposition and acquiescence of workers, women or peasants on the one hand and racism, antisemitism, terror, and genocide on the other.

Agency is particularly troubling for social historians who have sought not merely to let the inarticulate speak but also to recover the voices of those who spoke a different language than those supporting the regime. Yet, the words, visions, and behaviour discovered were at best only partially 'alternative', and, as we will see below, seemed to become ever less so as the regime moved from full employment through *Blitzkrieg* to total war. Equally troubling is the relationship between intentions and consequences, between what people thought they were doing – retreating into the factory, seeking the comforts of domesticity, ignoring the

---

[19] The best English collections of documents from and articles about the *Historikerstreit* are *Reworking the Past*, ed. by Peter Baldwin (Boston, Beacon 1990) and *New German Critique* special issue on the *Historikerstreit*, 44 (Spring/Summer 1988). The major English analyses are Richard Evans, *In Hitler's Shadow: West German Historians and the Attempt to Escape from the Nazi Past* (New York, Pantheon 1989) and Charles S. Maier, *The Unmasterable Past: History, Holocaust and German National Identity* (Cambridge, Harvard University Press 1988). Among the major German collections are *Historikerstreit: Die Dokumentation der Kontroverse um die Einzigartigkeit der nationalsozialistischen Judenvernichtung* (Munich, Piper Verlag 1987); *Ist der Nationalsozialismus Geschichte? Zu Historisierung und Historikerstreit*, ed. by Dan Diner (Frankfurt am M., Fischer 1987); *Normalität oder Normalisierung? Geschichtswerkstätten und Faschismusanalyse*, ed. by Heidi Gerstenberger and Dorothea Schmidt (Munster, Westfälisches Dampfboot 1987).
[20] For a summary of this literature see Nolan, 'The *Historikerstreit*', pp. 53–60.
[21] Diner, 'Perspektivenwahl', pp. 102–3, 110–11.

most offensive aspects of the regime's ideology and politics – and what the consequences of such actions were – the stabilisation of the regime and the persecution of its many victims. In short, social historians and women's historians must decide whether ambivalence and indifference are to be categorised positively as *Resistenz*, negatively as complicity, or as some complex and shifting combination of the two. Did people tolerate and actively support antisemitism, racism, terror, and murder from fear, from a desire to survive, from pre-Nazi prejudices, or from ideological commitment to National Socialism? And how many moved from the former camp to the latter?

In exploring agency and responsibility, some social historians have even challenged prevailing definitions of victims and perpetrators. To be sure, many categories of victims remain appallingly clearly defined – Jews and Gypsies, Russians and Poles, 'asocials' and homosexuals, and politically active Communists and Social Democrats. But what of working-class men, or women of all classes? Both broad categories were in various ways relegated to subordinate social and economic, and, in the case of women, biological positions. Political persecution, wage discrimination, repressive pronatalism, and exclusion from high politics persisted throughout the Third Reich. Yet, both women and workers received benefits as well. Historians disagree about whether they benefitted from just the welfare and recreational aspects of the regime or also from participation in its multiple opportunities to exert power and control over others.[22] And how did such involvement affect both people's consciousness and behaviour and the survival and cumulative radicalisation of the regime?

These overlapping controversies about continuity, normality, and agency, and about the place of the Third Reich in twentieth-century German history, erupted with particular intensity during the *Historikerstreit* of the mid- and late 1980s and then subsided in the early 1990s for many reasons, not least because reunification dramatically altered the political context which spawned them. In both East and West Germany attention focused on coming to terms with the East's past. The experience of the GDR complicates the trajectories of class politics, workers' cultures, gender relationships, and social and political identities in twentieth-century Germany. It complicates the ongoing German effort to define its national identity for the twenty-first century based on its history in the twentieth. But it does not eliminate the need to reflect on National Socialism. However repressive, depressing, and oppressive the German Democratic Republic was, it was not a racist and genocidal

---

[22] For a discussion of these '*Herrschaftsbetriebe*', see Michael Geyer, 'The State in National Socialist Germany', in *Statemaking and Social Movements*, ed. by Charles Bright and Susan Harding (Ann Arbor, University of Michigan Press 1984), pp. 193–232.

regime like National Socialism, and it will not diminish the centrality of the latter in twentieth-century German history.

Work and workers' cultures

For the first three decades after the collapse of National Socialism, the history of the working class on and off the shopfloor was all but ignored. It was assumed that class and class conflict had ceased to exist, that politics and the state merited study, while economics and the factory were of distinctly secondary importance, that workers' cultures were destroyed as effectively as workers' organisations. Since the mid-1970s working-class history and *Alltagsgeschichte* have revealed the persistence of class, the waging of class conflict from above, the existence of oppositional behaviour, and the incomplete integration of workers into the Nazi *Volksgemeinschaft*.

This rich and persuasive body of local studies, firm histories, and analyses of leisure, reading, and attitudes toward work and skill, has shown equally clearly that the cultural and social expressions of class as well as class politics changed fundamentally. As the attention of historians has shifted from the 1930s to the war years, the evidence of opposition and of class as the central category has receded, while the manifestations of integration and the importance of race have emerged. And many of the changes initiated during the Third Reich persisted after 1945 as well.[23] These permanent changes, which contrasted rather markedly with the reemergence of pre-fascist forms of working-class culture and politics in post-World War II Italy, cannot be explained solely by the Nazis' repression of the Communist, Social Democratic, and Catholic workers' movements, important as terror and *Gleichschaltung* were in reshaping political organisations and attitudes.

More recent studies focus less on oppositional behaviour and attitudes than on the labour process, the composition of the working class, and Nazi and popular attitudes toward work. They suggest that the restructuring of work and the working class and the transformation of workers' cultures on and off the shopfloor played a crucial role in the remaking of the German working class. National Socialism picked up on, continued, and partially distorted processes of rationalisation that were initiated during the mid-1920s and continued in both the Federal Republic and the German Democratic Republic. Work, wages, skill

---

[23] Contrast, for example, Franz Neumann's *Behemoth* (New York, Harper Torch 1966) with such works as Mason, *Social Policy*; Peukert, *Inside Nazi Germany*; Sachse *et al.*, *Angst*; and Alf Lüdtke, *Eigensinn: Fabrikalltag, Arbeitererfahrungen und Politik vom Kaiserreich bis in den Faschismus* (Hamburg, Ergebnisse 1993).

hierarchies, and job training were transformed in fits and starts. These transformations were clothed in varied combinations of traditional and modern rhetoric, and were supported with varied degrees of enthusiasm by industry, the state, and, at times, even the workers' movements. An exploration of economic and social rationalisation will shed light not only on the fate of the German working class under Nazism, but also on the broader themes of continuity, modernity and normality.

During the 1920s, economic and social rationalisation were enthusiastically endorsed by industrialists and trade unionists, engineers, industrial sociologists and psychologists. Rationalisation was a slogan for productivity and efficiency, for science and prosperity, for ill-defined visions of modernity more broadly.[24] It was an umbrella term for the various means through which and levels on which this modernisation was to occur. Technological and organisational rationalisation referred to those changes most directly effecting production. Concentration mechanisation, flow production, the assembly line, standardisation, and various Taylorist measures, such as time and motion studies, fell under this rubric. Negative rationalisation was a euphemism for the ruthless closing of inefficient plants. And human rationalisation (*menschliche Rationalisierung*) referred not only to industrial psychology, personnel management, and vocational aptitude testing, but also to new skill-training programmes and a new and comprehensive range of company social and welfare policies, aimed both at tying workers to the firm and at creating a new worker and new working-class family, suited to the new rationalised work.[25] The Weimar rationalisation campaign was accompanied by an enthusiasm for Fordism, as the technical system and economic ideology associated with the Ford Automobile Company were called. The incompatible economic reform visions of industrialists and trade union functionaries, of engineers and politicians, were couched in terms of irreconcilable understandings of American econ-

---

[24] For a discussion of the many meanings of this term and an analysis of the Weimar rationalisation movement, see Mary Nolan, *Visions of Modernity: American Business and the Modernization of Germany* (New York, Oxford University Press 1994).

[25] Robert Brady, *The Rationalization Movement in German Industry* (Berkeley, University of California 1933) remains the best survey of technical and economic rationalisation in English, while the *Handbuch der Rationalisierung* published by the Reichskuratorium für Wirtschaftlichkeit is the most comprehensive contemporary survey in German. For Weimar rationalisation, see Thomas von Freyberg, *Industrielle Rationalisierung in der Weimarer Republik* (Frankfurt, Campus 1989) and Heidrun Homburg, *Rationalisierung und Industriearbeit* (Berlin, Haude and Spener 1991). Peter Hinrichs, *Um die Seele des Arbeiters: Arbeitspsychologie, Industrie- und Betriebssoziologie in Deutschland* (Cologne, Pahl-Rugenstein 1981) and Carola Sachse, *Siemens, der Nationalsozialismus und die moderne Familie. Eine Untersuchung zur sozialen Rationalisierung in Deutschland im 20. Jahrhundert* (Hamburg, Rasch und Röhring 1990) provide the best overviews of human rationalisation.

omic success and of the roles of mass production, mass consumption, and high wages in it.[26]

Rationalisation was not only widely preached but also widely practised during Weimar. In heavy industry, giant integrated firms such as Vereinigte Stahlwerk, Krupp, and Gutehoffnungshütte closed unprofitable operations, integrated production from the mining of coal to the construction of sophisticated machines, and invested heavily in reorganising plants and increasing productivity. Ruhr mining was extensively mechanised and flow production and an ever more minute division of labour spread in the finished goods sector.[27] And there were even elaborate campaigns to Taylorise the practices of the working-class housewife.[28]

During the 1930s and 1940s, rationalisation continued, but the enthusiasm for Americanism vanished. Even without the Nazi seizure of power, rationalisation measures would probably have continued. During the Depression, firms carried out rationalisation plans already embarked upon, even though that contributed to excess productive capacity, because only by so doing could they hope to reap benefits in the long run.[29] Under the Nazis, the need to revive the economy, the shortages of raw materials and foreign currency, and the primacy of rearmament all pushed concentration, work reorganisation and new technologies.[30] As Tilla Siegel has shown, the German Labour Front made the promotion of productivity its foremost ideological mission.[31] Although historians such as Heidrun Homburg, Thomas von Freyberg, and Rudi Hachtmann disagree about when and to what extent rationalisation entailed new technology and automation and to what extent it was, as in the 1920s, built around reorganising work while retaining flexibility and utilising skilled labour, they all acknowledge the prevalence of rationalisation efforts from the mid-1930s on.[32] Total war only intensified what rearmament and full employment had begun. As the macroeconomic context became ever

[26] Nolan, *Visions*, passim.
[27] See Brady, *Rationalization*, passim; Nolan, *Visions*, pp. 131–53. See also the multi-volume *Gesamtbericht des Enquete Ausschusses zur Untersuchung der Erzeugungs- und Absatzbedingungen der deutschen Wirtschaft* published by the Reichskuratorium in the late 1920s and early 1930s.
[28] Mary Nolan, '"Housework made Easy": The Taylorized Housewife in Weimar Germany's rationalized Economy', *Feminist Studies* (Fall 1988), pp. 549–78.
[29] Nolan, *Visions*, pp. 227–32.
[30] Ulrich Herbert, 'Arbeiterschaft im "Dritten Reich"', *Geschichte und Gesellschaft* 15 (1989); pp. 329–30.
[31] Tilla Siegel and Thomas von Freyberg, *Industrielle Rationalisierung unter dem Nationalsozialismus* (Frankfurt am M., Campus 1991), pp. 39–135.
[32] Siegel and Freyberg, *Industrielle Rationalisierung*, pp. 322–4; Homberg, *Rationalisierung*; Rudiger Hachtmann, *Industriearbeit im 'Dritten Reich'* (Göttingen, Vandenhoeck and Ruprecht 1989).

more irrational, the factory became ever more rationalised. As the state became ever less modern in the sense of bureaucratised, rational, and predictable,[33] production became ever more modernised in an organisational and technical sense.

What then were the effects of these rationalisation processes, which proceeded first in a democratic context which protected workers' rights, then in a fascist context which denied them, and after 1945 once again under both a democratic but less worker-oriented state and under a state socialist regime?

Rationalisation restructured both work and the relations among workers in factories and mines. We know most about this in the Weimar era, when rationalisation produced mixed results for capital and labour alike. In the chemical, mining, iron and steel, the metal-working industries, rationalisation intensified work, introduced new technologies, worsened working conditions and made supervision more pervasive and interventionist. Inefficient plants were closed and structural unemployment increased while in some sectors the number of unskilled and often female workers expanded. But rationalisation did not lead to extensive deskilling, for German industry continued to rely on specialised 'quality work' and the flexible skilled worker who produced it. Wages for those employed did not drop, but the gulf between the employed and the unemployed widened and working-class insecurity was pervasive. Rationalisation destroyed the 'quasi-institutions' and loose networks on the shopfloor that had united workers of varied political persuasions and worsened the possibilities of communication and informal organisation.[34]

This reshuffling and fragmentation of workers continued in the Third Reich as did a reorganisation of the wage system and greatly intensified pressure for productivity. The consequences of these processes were more divisive than in Weimar, for there were no workers' movements on the shopfloor to bring together what rationalisation split apart or to defend wages and social policy in the political arena. The restructuring of work and wages and the absence of trade unions fed into the individualised and often instrumental attitudes toward

---

[33] Martin Broszat, *The Hitler State* (London and New York, Longmans 1981) remains the classic study of the Nazi state; Hans Mommsen, 'Nationalsozialismus als vorgetäuschte Modernisierung', in W. H. Pehle, *Der Historische Ort des Nationalsozialismus* (Frankfurt am Main, Fischer 1990), pp. 31–46.

[34] Nolan, *Visions*, pp. 160–5, 167–78. Eva Cornelia Schöck, *Arbeitslosigkeit und Rationalisierung: Die Lage der Arbeiter und die kommunistische Gewerkschaftspolitik 1920–1928* (Frankfurt a.M., Campus 1977); Uta Stolle, *Arbeiterpolitik im Betrieb: Frauen und Männer, Reformisten und Radikale, Fach- und Massenarbeiter bei Bayer, BASF, Bosch und in Solingen (1900–1933)* (Frankfurt a.M., Campus 1980); James Wickham, 'Social Fascism and the Division of the Working Class Movement: Workers and Political Parties in the Frankfurt Area (1929–1933)', *Capital and Class 7* (Spring 1979), pp. 1–34.

work that Detlev Peukert among others has discerned.[35] Rationalisation may well have promoted a search for compensation and diversion outside of work, and those compensations and diversions were provided primarily by the Nazi Labour Front.

Rationalisation also created new divisions and hierarchies among workers. In the late 1920s the most important division was between those who retained jobs in rationalised industries and those who suffered from structural unemployment. The effects of the depression were so detrimental to the workers' movements because of the demoralisation and demobilisation that already existed from unemployment that had soared to 18 per cent in 1926 and hovered between 8.5 per cent and 9 per cent in the following two years.[36] By 1936 the Nazis were to eliminate unemployment and thereafter the regime was plagued by labour shortages, but the effects of the previous decade of economic insecurity and unemployment on workers were more lasting, as the Ruhr oral history project has shown so clearly. Younger workers were cut off from the experience of work and the workers' movement before 1933 and came to associate integration into wage labour and adulthood with National Socialism.[37] For young and old alike, perceptions of the 'good' and the 'bad' times were based more on the availability of employment and the prospects of security than on political events.[38]

Skill hierarchies and the sexual division of labour in industry were reshaped by rationalisation. Neither in Weimar nor in the Third Reich was there massive deskilling; rather, the universal skills of the *Facharbeiter* became more limited and plant specific, but industry continued to rely on the flexibility that skill provided.[39] Just as rationalisation in Weimar had created large numbers of low-paying assembly jobs, for which women were considered suitable due to their purported physical, mental, and emotional peculiarities, so too did National Socialism continue them. Its ideological opposition to women's waged labour notwithstanding, the regime found itself unable to force working-class women out of industrial jobs, even if it could limit the economic and professional activity of middle-class women. Indeed, the number of women workers increased steadily.[40]

---

[35] Peukert, *Inside Nazi Germany*, pp. 103–15, 171–4.   [36] Schöck, *Arbeitslosigkeit*, p. 155.

[37] See Niethammer, '*Die Jahre weiss man nicht, wo man die heute hinsetzen soll'*.

[38] Herbert, '"Die guten und die schlechten Zeiten"', *ibid.*, pp. 67–96.

[39] Von Freyberg has shown this most persuasively for the machine-tool industry in both Weimar and Nazi Germany. Freyberg, *Industrielle Rationalisierung*; and Siegel and Freyberg, *Industrielle Rationalisierung*.

[40] Annemarie Tröger, 'The Creation of a Female Assembly-Line Proletariat', in *When Biology Became Destiny*, pp. 237–70. Tim Mason, 'Women in Nazi Germany', *History Workshop Journal* 1 (Spring 1976), pp. 74–113 and 2 (Fall 1976), pp. 5–32. Stephan Bajohr, *Die Hälfte der Fabrik* (Marburg 1979). Dörte Winkler, *Frauenarbeit im 'Dritten Reich'* (Hamburg, Hoffmann and Campe 1974).

From the inception of the rationalisation movement in the mid-1920s, its capitalist proponents as well as many engineers and scientists of work attempted to tie wages to productivity, to introduce the *Leistungsprinzip* (performance principle). Individuals should not be paid according to the crude categories of skilled, semi-skilled, and unskilled. Nor should the 'political wage', that is the setting of wages by compulsory state arbitration, prevail. But precisely these two forms of payment did persist in Weimar, due to the power of the Social Democratic Party and the trade unions, and the pro-worker proclivities of the arbitration office of the Labour Ministry.[41]

After 1933 these obstacles to a recasting of the wage system were eliminated. Moreover, the 1934 Law for the Ordering of National Labour vastly increased the power of the firm over its employees. Although the law couched this increased power in the traditional or neofeudal terms of leader and follower, of factory community and loyalty, industrialists used their new authority in quite modern, rationalising ways.[42] As Tilla Siegel has shown, the state set maximum wages, but the firm had sole control over the wage form. And firms strove successfully to achieve the maximum differentiation so that occupation, skills levels, and sex would no longer be the sole determining factors. Wages were to depend as well on actual output, and any increases over the low base pay would come in the form of bonuses, overtime pay, and social benefits. While the regime and industry were not uniformly successful in increasing wage differentials, their efforts did contribute to disciplining workers and undermining any community of interests among them.[43]

Economic rationalisation fragmented the working class in multiple ways; human or social rationalisation suggested some of the ways in which it was being recomposed. As conceived in the mid- and late 1920s, the amorphous phenomenon of *Menschliche Rationalisierung, Menschenbewirtschaftung,* or *Menschenführung* included vocational aptitude testing, skill-training programmes, general worker education courses, company newspapers and company social programmes for both workers and their families. Engineers, sociologists and psychologists of work, and industrialists hoped to create a new worker, or

---

[41] Nolan, *Visions*, pp. 160–5. For an overview of discussions of the performance principle and performance wage, see Joan Campbell, *Joy in Work, German Work: The National Debate 1800–1945* (Princeton, Princeton University Press 1989).

[42] Tim Mason, 'The origins of the Law on the Organization of National Labour of 20 January 1934. An investigation into the relationship between "archaic" and "modern" elements in recent German history', in Mason *Nazism, Fascism and the Working Class* (Cambridge, Cambridge University Press 1995).

[43] Tilla Siegel, *Leistung und Lohn in der nationalsozialistischen 'Ordnung der Arbeit'* (Opladen, Westdeutscher Verlag 1989), and 'Wage Policy in Nazi Germany', *Politics & Society* 14:1 (1985), pp. 1–52.

rather several different kinds of new worker, differentiated by their sex, skill level, and employment sector. What these workers would share was a commitment to productivity, a belief in rationalisation, a sense of vocation (*Berufsethos*), and a heightened 'joy in work', however menial and meaningless that work might be. Workers were to develop a competitive and individualistic work ethic and simultaneously to see themselves as part of the factory community. They were to be loyal to their firm, but not their class.[44]

In the late 1920s and early 1930s, the proponents of human rationalisation were by no means idle propagandists. Rather, they astutely translated their new management and company welfare strategies into concrete programmes. To take one significant example, DINTA, run by the right-wing engineer Karl Arnhold and supported enthusiastically by Ruhr heavy industry, established apprenticeship training programmes and adolescent education schools in 100 to 300 major firms. By 1934 it published roughly 100 company newspapers with a circulation of over one million. It was also instrumental in establishing home economics education, kindergardens, and health and maternity care in the firms with which it worked.[45]

National Socialism by no means brought such efforts to an end. DINTA, for example, joined the Labour Front, becoming the Office for Vocational Education and Firm Leadership. By the late 1930s over two million workers had been through its courses and training programmes, which dispensed a mixture of skills training, work discipline, and Nazi ideology.[46] Carola Sachse has chronicled the diverse social-policy measures, ranging from housing and health programmes to family policy, undertaken by the Siemens electrotechnical firm and the conflicts between the firm on the one hand and the Labour Front on the other about who would control them and about the relative weight to be given to economic and labour-market needs as opposed to the racial goals of Nazi population politics.[47]

Whether or not these policies succeeded in altering workers' attitudes toward work and politics, they did succeed in making them more dependent on the firm – for training, for social benefits, for work and

---

[44] In addition to the citations in fn. 25, see Nolan, *Visions*, pp. 179–205.

[45] DINTA's accomplishments were chronicled in its own numerous *Tätigkeitsberichte* and special publications, as well as in Peter C. Bäumer, *Das deutsche Institut für technische Arbeitsschulung*, Schriften des Vereins für Sozialpolitik, 181/I (1930); and Rudolf Schwenger's two studies, *Die betriebliche Sozialpolitik im Ruhrkohlenbergbau* (Munich and Leipzig, Duncker and Humblot 1932) and *Die betriebliche Sozialpolitik in der westdeutschen Grosseisenindustrie* (Munich and Leipzig; Duncker and Humblot 1934).

[46] Ronald Smelser, *Robert Ley: Hitler's Labor Front Leader* (Oxford, Oxford University Press 1988), pp. 191–2.

[47] Sachse, *Siemens*, passim. See also Carola Sachse, *Industrial Housewives: Women's Social Work in the Factories of Nazi Germany* (New York, Haworth 1987).

leisure opportunities. The destruction of workers' organisations after 1933 and the specific wage policies of the Nazi regime reinforced such dependence. Simultaneously, many workers sought to take refuge from the larger society within the factory, for whatever its hierarchies and oppressions, it was a place where one could try to display one's skills and do quality work, where one would earn a living wage, where one could avoid politics in their most explicit forms.[48] War seems to have heightened the 'flight into the factory'.[49] On the one hand workers became ever more dependent on the firm for material and social support; on the other hand the factory was a source of continuity, a symbol of stability as cities were bombed, families were evacuated, and the Nazi regime crumbled. Both factors remained operative when the war ended and reconstruction began. Workers and factory councils looked first to the firm for help; formal organisations and informal networks were feeble in comparison.[50]

The specific Nazi contribution to the reconceptualising of work and the restructuring of the working class was racism. The Nazis were not the first to praise the virtues of work nor to preach the gospel of efficiency and individual productivity. Indeed, many of the most vocal propagandists of *Arbeit* (work) and *Leistung* (performance) in the Third Reich, such as Karl Arnhold of DINTA, had played a similar role in late Weimar. But Nazi ideology did make *Leistung* a central measure of an individual's worth and conceived of the *Volksgemeinschaft* as a pseudo-egalitarian association of those who were '*leistungsfähig*' and racially pure. The Nazis not only condemned but proved appallingly willing to punish and kill those deemed '*leistungsunfähig*', regardless of whether their alleged incapacity came from physical and mental handicaps, race, social circumstances, or attitudes.[51] On top of this composite hierarchy of race and productivity stood the skilled German quality worker (who

---

[48] Alf Lüdtke, 'Deutsche Qualitätsarbeit', 'Uebereinstimmung und Dissenz zwischen den Klassen in Deutschland', *Kommune* 7:4 (1989), pp. 62–6; '"Formierung der Massen" oder Mitmachen und Hinnehmen? Alltagsgeschichte und Faschismusanalyse', in *Normalität oder Normalisierung* 'Wo blieb die "rote Glut" : Arbeitererfahrungen und deutscher Faschismus', and '"Ehre der Arbeit" : Industriearbeiter und Macht der Symbole. Zur Reichweite symbolischer Orientierung im Nationalsozialismus', both in *Eigensinn*, pp. 221–350. See also, Herbert, 'Arbeiterschaft', pp. 339–40.

[49] For a long view of workers' increasing focus on the firm from late Weimar to late 1940s, see Michael Fichter, 'Aufbau und Neuordnung. Betriebsräte zwischen Klassensolidarität und Betriebsloyalität', in *Von Stalingrad zur Währungsreform. Zur Sozialgeschichte des Umbruchs in Deutschland*, ed. by Martin Broszat, Klaus-Dietmar Henke and Hans Woller (Munich, R. Oldenbourg 1990), pp. 469–549.

[50] We still lack studies of working-class neighbourhoods that would trace their restructuring from the late 1920s through the early 1950s. The Ruhr oral history project provides some suggestive material.

[51] Martin Geyer, 'Soziale Sicherheit und wirtschaftlicher Fortschritt: Ueberlegungen zum Verhältnis von Arbeitsideologie und Sozialpolitik im "Dritten Reich"', *Geschichte und Gesellschaft* 15 (1989), pp. 390–2.

was male, of course), in the middle ranks were less skilled German men and, below them, women, and at the bottom the less efficient, purportedly racially inferior foreign workers. Outside the hierarchy, but nonetheless central to its construction, were Jews on the one hand and on the other, the unproductive, a diverse and quintessentially Nazi category containing the 'asocials' and the 'eugenically unfit', the 'work-shy' and the undisciplined, the homeless and the handicapped.

As Germany moved from rearmament through *Blitzkrieg* to total war, the number of foreign workers, voluntary or coerced, increased exponentially even though their presence violated the Nazi desire for a racially homogeneous nation.[52] By the summer of 1941 there were 3 million foreign workers, by the autumn of 1944 7.7 million. By 1944 over one-quarter of all employees were foreigners; in the key sectors of mining, construction, and metals, the figure was nearly one-third and in agriculture almost one-half.[53] If foreign workers could not be dispensed with, in part because the regime was not willing to mobilise all women,[54] they could be classified by race, in a carefully graded hierarchy that placed Danes on top and Russians on the bottom. Wages and working conditions, food and housing, restrictions and punishments became ever harsher as one moved down the racial hierarchy. In factories and on farms, the invisible *Leistungsunfähige* were replaced by the ever present foreign worker, labelled inferior in race, efficiency and, if female, still further discriminated against. Many German workers moved into supervisory positions in this restructured workforce, elevated both by new tasks and by the elaboration of categories ostensibly inferior to themselves.

Racism and rationalisation were inextricably intertwined not only in the Nazi economy at home but in Nazi plans to restructure Central and Eastern Europe, economically and racially. Economists and population planners, agronomists and statisticians, working for the Four-Year Plan and a variety of other Nazi agencies, developed and implemented a blueprint to 'modernise' the economies of Austria, Poland, and Russia by eliminating inefficient productive units – many of which were Jewish – and by solving the problem of overpopulation. The methods sanc-

---

[52] See Ulrich Herbert, *Fremdarbeiter: Politik und Praxis des 'Ausländer-Einsatzes' in der Kriegswirtschaft des Dritten Reiches* (Berlin, Dietz 1989) for the debates about this at various stages of the war. The book also contains a detailed history of the treatment of foreign workers. An English summary of his findings appears in Herbert, *A History of Foreign Labor in Germany, 1880–1980* (Ann Arbor, University of Michigan Press 1990), pp. 127–92.

[53] Herbert, *A History of Foreign Labor*, pp. 155–6.

[54] Drafting all women would not only violate the regime's ideological precepts, but more importantly, might heighten male discontent and demoralisation, something Hitler greatly feared because he believed that dissatisfied civilians had stabbed a potentially victorious military in the back during World War I. Mason, *Social Policy*, pp. 19–40.

tioned to achieve this rationalisation included resettlement, evacuation, forced labour deployment, starvation, ghettoisation and, eventually, extermination.[55]

The effects of these transformations on German workers were uneven, contradictory, and extremely difficult to assess, but overall they seem to have encouraged the emergence of instrumental attitudes toward work and skill, isolated and individualistic attitudes toward co-workers and class comrades.[56] Even oppositional behaviour generally entailed a retreat into the private sphere, where individuals pursued higher wages, consumer-oriented leisure or isolated family life. A multiplicity of new, individualising and hierarchising work experiences were created in the two and half decades after the beginning of rationalisation in 1925. And after 1933 these were permeated by the racial categories of the regime. Once the workers' movements, which had offered a common analysis of different experiences, were destroyed, workers had to give meanings to their experiences individually or allow the regime and Nazi organisations, such as the Labour Front, to impose them.[57] It was neither the rationalisation movement of the 1920s nor the depression nor National Socialist recovery and rearmament nor World War II nor post-war reconstruction alone that fundamentally restructured work and the working class and eroded the basis of traditional workers' cultures, but rather the cumulative and reinforcing effects of each.

Women and gender

Until recently gender, women, and family have not featured prominently in discussions of fascism, war, and genocide, and in most analyses they still do not. Yet, these issues were central in Weimar and Nazi Germany – central to people's political consciousness, to state policy and to political ideologies as well as to the micropolitics of worker education and company social policy, of social work and the medical profession. In the turbulent years of the Weimar Republic the Nazis were not alone among political parties in propagating traditional ideas about women, gender, and family.[58] Nor were they alone in represen-

---

[55] Aly and Heim, *Vordenker der Vernichtung*, passim.
[56] Peukert argues this most strongly in his *Inside Nazi Germany*, pp. 103–25.
[57] Herbert, 'Arbeiterschaft', pp. 344–5. He asserts workers suffered less from a multiplicity of experiences than from the lack of a common working through of them. I think it was both.
[58] Uta Frevert, *Women in German History: From Bourgeois Emancipation to Sexual Liberation* (Oxford, Berg 1989), pp. 168–85; Renata Bridenthal and Claudia Koonz, 'Beyond *Kinder, Küche, Kirche*: Weimar Women in Politics and Work', in *When Biology Became Destiny*, pp. 33–65.

ting perceived social threats and anxieties in female or gendered terms, as Klaus Theweleit's analysis of the memoirs of Free Corps members shows so clearly.[59] The Nazis' anti-feminist, anti-emancipatory rhetoric was extreme, but their insistence on separate spheres and women's different nature was shared in many circles, including the bourgeois women's movement. Nazi concern with the birth-rate and women's roles as mothers built up a pervasive discourse about eugenics and motherhood – one that proved compatible with Communist and Social Democratic politics as well as with conservative and fascist ones.[60] And the contradictory and partial character of women's emancipation in Weimar made women susceptible to anti-feminist appeals long before women actually turned to the Nazi party or women's organisations coordinated by the Nazi state. Women, gender, and family, in short, were at the heart of political rhetoric and policy throughout the interwar period, even if those preoccupations were most evident under National Socialism.

The growing body of work on women and gender in the Third Reich has focused on three principle themes, the first of which involves modernity and tradition in Nazi ideology and policies. Did the regime's anti-emancipatory, misogynist rhetoric translate into policies which reversed long-term trends in women's waged work, political roles, and reproductive practices? The second issue concerns the relationship between gender and race and explores whether National Socialist biological politics, especially sterilisation, were directed primarily against women rather than men and whether their intention was primarily sexist rather than racist? The third, and most contentious issue is that of agency and responsibility. Was National Socialism both gendered and the responsibility of both genders or was it an affair of men (*Männersache*)? Were women – by which is all too often meant only ethnically German women – victims (*Opfer*) or perpetrators (*Täterinnen*)?

The first efforts to uncover women and recover the history of gender in the Third Reich, such as the essays in *Mutterkreuz und Arbeitsbuch*, Jill Stephenson's work on Nazi Women's organisations, and Tim Mason's articles on work and family, explored how National Socialism reshaped women's public political and economic roles and private fertility strategies. Rhetorically the regime promised to reverse the transformations in women's roles wrought by industrialisation, democratisation, and feminism and return women to the traditional realms of 'children,

[59] Klaus Theweleit, *Male Fantasies*, Vols. I and II (Minneapolis, University of Minnesota Press 1987, vol. I, and 1989, vol. II).
[60] Frevert, *Women*, pp. 185–93; Atina Grossmann, *Reforming Sex: The German Movement for Birth Control and Abortion Reform, 1920–1950* (New York, Oxford University Press 1995); Weindling, *Health*, pp. 399–440.

church and kitchen'. But in regard to women, as in regard to the petty bourgeoisie and small farmers, reality fell far short of the regime's reactionary promises. Certainly women were pushed out of all high political positions in state and party, but not out of all public roles. They could exert significant influence on social welfare and family policy within the vast Nazi women's organisations.[61] And the new Nazi public arena, with mass leisure and youth organisations, was certainly no more inhospitable to women than earlier forms. For some groups, such as adolescents in the League of German Girls, or women in isolated and traditional villages, Nazism even seemed to have opened new possibilities.[62]

Statistics on work reveal similar trends. From 1933 to 1939 middle-class women were pushed out of jobs in the public and private sectors and the number of women students dropped steadily. During the war, the universities became feminised, but middle-class women were still able to avoid waged work. Despite this, the Nazis never succeeded in reducing overall female labour-force participation. On the contrary, whereas 34.4 per cent of women worked in 1933, 36.7 per cent did in 1939 and a greater percentage were in trade, industry, service, and government than previously while the proportion of domestic servants declined. Moreover, the number of married working women increased by two million. Modern trends in women's labour-force participation could not be reversed for neither industry nor the state could dispense with a sex-segregated labour market. Manufacturing and clerical jobs that were considered 'women's work' before 1933 remained the preserve of women – ideologically and in practice – thereafter, and as full employment drew rural men into more lucrative factory jobs, agriculture became feminised.[63]

Whether a German woman worked or not, and whether she worked only as a youth or moved in and out of the labour force as she alternated paid employment and child bearing, or stayed in the factory or office life long, thus depended on her class position. It also – and increasingly – depended on her ethnicity and race. Labour-market politics and biological, population politics were inextricably intertwined from the early stages of the regime.[64] In the 1930s some women were to specialise

61 Claudia Koonz, *Mothers in the Fatherland* (New York, St Martin's 1987); Jill Stephenson, *The Nazi Organization of Women* (London, Croom Helm 1981).
62 Gerhard Wilke, 'Village Life in Nazi Germany', in *Life in the Third Reich*, ed. by Richard Bessel (Oxford, Oxford University Press 1987), pp. 17–24. Dagmar Reese, *'Straff, aber nicht stramm – herb aber nicht derb.' Zur Vergesellschaftung von Mädchen durch den Bund Deutscher Mädel im sozialkulturellen Vergleich zweier Milieus* (Weinheim and Basel 1989).
63 Frevert, *Women*, p. 218; Mason 'Women in Nazi Germany'; Tröger, 'Creation'.
64 Dagmar Reese and Carola Sachse, 'Frauenforschung zum Nationalsozialismus. Eine Bilanz', in *Töchter-Fragen. NS-Frauengeschichte*, pp. 81–2.

in reproduction, some in production, while still others were expected to alternate between the two; it all depended on the purported eugenic and racial value assigned to women by the regime and the eugenic policies it pursued.

During World War II, the links between race on the one hand and production and reproduction on the other were much more explicit, determining, and brutal as the German war economy came to rely heavily on foreign labour and increasingly slave labour. If imported labour from Western Europe was heavily male, slave labour from Eastern Europe included millions of women. Like their male counterparts, they were treated, or more accurately, mistreated, according to their place in the Nazi ethnic and racial hierarchy. Whatever that place was, they were expected to produce, not reproduce. Pregnancy would result in deportation back to the home country, dangerously late forced abortions, complications or death from lack of food and medical care, or the possibility that a baby deemed of racially 'good' stock would be taken away.[65] Thus while the Nazis failed to reverse long-term secular trends in women's work, they did mix racism and labour-market policies in ways that were new, explicit, and state sanctioned.

The effects of Nazi fertility policies were similar. Although the Nazi regime has traditionally been considered pro-natalist, some recent historians have argued that it was, in fact, anti-natalist, while others have more convincingly insisted that it was pro-natalist toward some women and anti-natalist toward others.[66] In regard to reproduction, race, ethnicity, and purported eugenic value were all determining, while class was relatively insignificant. Both the negative Nazi pro-natalist measures, such as the prohibition of birth control and abortion, and the positive inducements of marriage loans, maternity classes and mothers' crosses, applied only to those ethnically German women deemed to be politically acceptable and free of ostensibly hereditary defects and symptoms of asocial behaviour. These measures produced ambiguous results among their target group. Motherhood propaganda and marriage loans, aided by economic recovery, did lead to an upsurge of marriages in the 1930s, but they did not produce an increase in average family size. Despite the fact that contraception and abortion were illegal, people limited the number of children they had, continuing a trend toward the small nuclear family that had begun in earlier decades.[67]

What are we to make of the contrast between the modernity which statistics reveal and the traditionalism on which ideology insisted?

---

[65] Herbert, *A History of Foreign Labor*, pp. 169–72.
[66] For an introduction to these debates, see Atina Grossmann, 'Feminist Debates about Women and National Socialism', *Gender & History* 3:3 (Autumn 1991), pp. 350–8.
[67] Mason, 'Women in Nazi Germany', part I, pp. 101–5.

Three observations seem relevant. First, although ideology treated the category 'woman' uniformly, policy differentiated sharply among women by race, class, age, geographic location, and 'eugenic value'.[68] Second, the coexistence of traditional rhetoric and modern reality was hardly restricted to issues involving women; rather it was an essential characteristic of the regime in many areas. The emphasis on tradition masked the increasingly modern character of women's practices at home and outside and thereby may have made women's modern roles more palatable to men and women. Third, it is too simple to say that ideology was irrelevant given the statistically 'modern' trends, for we know too little about how women understood their roles in public and private, about the identities that they developed. We know too little about how this mixture of modern work patterns and traditional ideology was redeployed in the Federal Republic to push women out of the workforce and in the German Democratic Republic to keep them in it.[69]

The centrality of biological politics to labour-market policies encouraged feminists to turn their attention to the regime's racial and biological rhetoric and practices. Attention has focused above all on the intentions behind eugenics and compulsory sterilisation and their consequences for women. During the 1930s the Nazi state performed involuntary sterilisations on approximately 400,000 Germans, roughly half of whom were men. Historians of Nazi medicine, such as Robert J. Lifton and Robert Proctor, see compulsory sterilisation and the eugenic justification of it as a crucial foundation for the formulation of the Nazi regime's racial policies and a key preparatory stage for the policies of euthanasia and genocide that were to follow, albeit neither in a straight line nor inevitably.[70] Gisela Bock, who has reconstructed the formulation and implementation of the compulsory sterilisation programme at the top levels of the regime, likewise sees compulsory sterilisation as chronologically and logically prior to euthanasia and genocide, but she stresses gender rather than race in analysing its formulation and impact.[71] At the level of conceptualisation and high-level execution, Nazi racial policy in general and sterilisation in particular were the

[68] Rosenhaft, 'Women'; Tröger, 'Creation'; and essays in *Mutterkreuz und Arbeitsbuch*, all made this point, but it has frequently been forgotten in recent works which speak globally of German women.

[69] Robert Moeller, *Protecting Motherhood: Women and the Family in the Politics of Postwar West Germany* (Berkeley, University of California 1993) is a first step.

[70] Proctor, *Racial Hygiene*, and Lifton, *The Nazi Doctors*.

[71] Gisela Bock, *Zwangssterilisation im Nationalsozialismus. Studien zur Rassenpolitik und Frauenpolitik* (Opladen, Westdeutscher Verlag 1986). In an earlier article, she stressed the interaction of race and gender more than the primacy of one or the other. 'Racism and Sexism in Nazi Germany: Motherhood, Compulsory Sterilization, and the State', in *When Biology Became Destiny*, pp. 271–96.

work of men. As others have noted, however, at the level of reporting and selecting those to be sterilised and actually performing the sterilisations, women doctors and social workers, teachers and women's movement activists were deeply involved.[72] More provocatively, Bock argues that although compulsory sterilisation was performed on equal numbers of men and women, women were both its primary target and its primary victim. Women were more likely to suffer medical complications and death from sterilisation, and, even more importantly, they were denied the opportunity of motherhood, which was more central to their identity and social status than fatherhood was to men. Whereas in her early work Bock emphasised the complex mixture of pro-natalism and anti-natalism that characterised Nazi policy, a position still endorsed by many, she now argues for its anti-natalist character, citing both sterilisation and the payment of marriage loans to men instead of women.[73] Annette Kuhn spelled out the more general implications of this kind of argument by insisting that the seizure of political power by the Nazis cannot be separated from their seizure of women's bodies. For the Nazis, the solution to the 'woman question' was every bit as important as the solution to the 'working-class question' and the 'Jewish question'. Perhaps, she concluded, anti-feminism was even more fundamental to Nazi biological politics than racism.[74]

The debates about biological politics and gender confront us with the question that haunts all studies of women and National Socialism: were women, i.e. ethnically German women, victims or agents/perpetrators? Given that women were at best the second sex of the master race, given that they were excluded from the inner circles of state and party power, given that the regime undertook extensive efforts to control their reproductive activity, should they be considered *Opfer*? If so, how does their status as victims compare with that of Jews and Gypsies? To put women on a continuum of victimisation, as Bock does, is to ignore that the difference between being a live victim of sterilisation and a dead victim of genocide was total and absolute.[75] Yet, if women are to be considered *Täterinnen*, by virtue of what? Their real or imagined withdrawal into women's separate and unpolitical sphere? The pursuit of domestic normality, which soothed those who carried out the regime's atrocities directly? Their insistence that women were fundamentally different from rather than identical

---

[72] Reese and Sachse, 'Frauenforschung', p. 94.
[73] Frevert and Koonz both disagree. See Grossmann, 'Feminist Debates', p. 352.
[74] Annette Kuhn, 'Der Antifeminismus als verborgene Theoriebasis des deutschen Faschismus', *Frauen und Faschismus in Europa. Der faschistische Körper*, ed. by Leonore Siegele-Wenschkewitz and Gerda Stuchlik (Pfaffenweiler, Centaurus 1990), pp. 40–2.
[75] Reese and Sachse, 'Frauenforschung', p. 93; Grossmann, 'Feminist Debates', p. 352. The original formulation is Dan Diner's.

to men and could best serve their interests by emphasising difference?[76]

Historians, particularly German women writing the history of German women, are deeply divided on this issue.[77] Some historians see women – all women, up to and including those involved in the party and its genocidal practices – as victims of fascism's anti-feminism, misogyny and manipulation of reproduction. A second position sees women as co-conspirators (*Mittäterinnen*) but attributes this coagency to women's victimisation.[78] Women were involved in the regime, susceptible to its ideological appeals and material inducements, and willing to support its policies because they followed the lead of men, were dependent on them, and had been robbed of autonomy by patriarchy. In short, not their agency, but their lack thereof; not their pursuit of real or imagined self-interest or group interest, but their promotion of male interests, involved them in National Socialism. A third view, articulated most strongly by Lerke Gravenhorst, insists that during the Third Reich women were active and autonomous parts of a German collective agent (*Handlungskollektiv Deutschland*) and that feminist scholars today must accept that as a 'negative heritage'.[79] A fourth alternative, and by far the most persuasive, rejects the polarised terms of the debate, pleading instead for detailed historical reconstruction of the different experiences of different women, their particular forms of repression, their possibilities for action, and their degree of responsibility.[80]

Ethnically German women, like male workers, were targeted by the regime for subordinate incorporation into the *Volksgemeinschaft* rather than for persecution, wholesale exclusion or extermination. It is important to chronicle the multiple forms of discrimination to which they were subject, for the limits on what even these women could do were very real. But it is also important to investigate the ways in which these women, and differently by class, age, politics, and eugenic 'value', were incorporated and actively participated in Nazi society. It is important to explore which ideological goals they shared, which they rejected and

---

[76] Koonz has answered these questions affirmatively. Gisela Bock, review of Koonz, *Mothers in the Fatherland*, in *Bulletin of the German Historical Institute, London* 2 (1989), pp. 16–25. Angelika Ebbinghaus, *Opfer und Täterinnen. Frauenbiographien im Nationalsozialismus* (Nördlingen 1987).

[77] As *Töchter-Fragen*, Ebbinghaus and Bock's review of Koonz, indicates, this is an extremely acrimonious debate, which involves not only the past of German women, but the present of both German and American feminism and the advantages and dangers of arguing for rights and power by stressing difference rather than sameness.

[78] The term comes from Christina Thümer-Rohr, 'Aus der Täuschung in die Ent-Täuschung – Zur Mittäterschaft von Frauen', *Beiträge zur Feministischen Theorie und Praxis* 8 (1983), pp. 11–26.

[79] Lerke Gravenhorst, 'Nehmen wir Nationalsozialismus und Auschwitz ausreichend als unser negatives Eigentum in Anspruch?', in *Töchter-Fragen*, pp. 17–37.

[80] Reese and Sachse, 'Frauenforschung', p. 74.

whether this changed over the course of the Third Reich. The Nazi women's organisations, for example, were vast and among middle-class women popular; their popularity came in part from imitating what bourgeois feminist and religious women's organisations had previously done, especially around social work and motherhood education. Simultaneously, the Nazi women's organisations exposed women much more directly to the regime's eugenic and racial ideas.[81] Women shared, albeit very unequally, in the new leisure activities of the Strength Through Joy organisation, and the League of German Girls offered young females an appealing alternative to domestic drudgery and an opportunity to develop skills.[82] The regime did not just discipline and subordinate women; it also bribed and benefitted them. It denied motherhood to some women, even as it instrumentalised the idea of motherhood to mobilise others.[83]

Women, especially middle-class ones who could avoid waged work, sought to defend a separate women's sphere, a realm of domestic comfort that was ostensibly uncontaminated by Nazi ideology and policies. There is no simple way to assess the meaning and effects of such actions. Some may have avoided employment out of dislike of the regime, others from an aversion to waged labour. This avoidance of waged work helped stabilise and legitimise the regime, by aiding economic recovery before 1936, but contributed to the regime's labour shortages and the workers' higher wages thereafter. The Nazis' refusal to upset men by conscripting women undermined rearmament and limited Nazi Germany's economic mobilisation for war prior to 1940 but it also limited deprivations on the homefront and increased the regime's popularity. The same complex of forces that protected ethnically German women and men alike, however, led to the hyperexploitation of foreign workers – female and male – within Germany after 1940. Whether employed or not, ethnically German women were incorporated into the racial hierarchies that permeated and dominated wartime Nazi Germany.

The meaning of women's everyday life for the fate of the regime is also difficult to assess. Did women's traditional activities as mothers and homemakers represent an escape into a neutral, genuinely private sphere, or did Nazism eradicate any clear line between public and private by its invasive practices and ideological mobilisation? Did a retreat into domesticity – real or imagined – help create a refuge from

---

[81] Koonz, *Mothers*, pp. 218, 252–62.
[82] Hasso Spode, 'Arbeiterurlaub im Dritten Reich', in Sachse *et al., Angst*, pp. 275–328; Frevert, *Women* p. 242.
[83] As Grossmann correctly points out, the issue of motherhood is central to this debate. 'Feminist Debates', pp. 354–5.

the regime, or did retreat into that haven, like retreat into the workplace, help stabilise the regime? Was it one factor among many that enabled some individuals to ignore the crimes of the regime and others to perpetrate them, as Koonz has argued?[84] Or does that posit a collective guilt that blurs genuine responsibility and precludes an historically nuanced understanding of participation and distancing, of intention and outcome? Explorations of everyday life, which unfortunately often ignore gender, nonetheless suggest how we might answer such questions.

Politics, agency and everyday life

Two decades of scholarship on everyday life in the Third Reich raise troubling questions about politics and agency. The initial excitement of discovering *Resistenz* during the 1930s, which occurred at the same time that the polycratic rather than totalitarian character of the regime was being argued for, led historians to overestimate how much oppositional behaviour there was and how subversive its effects were. Similarly, efforts to discover an unpoliticised, a normal sphere of everyday life into which Germans could have retreated have proven elusive. Nazi policies and personnel, but, more importantly, Nazi attitudes, categories, and language seem to have been everywhere and contaminated everyone. Both *Blitzkrieg* and total war significantly worsened the situation, for they led to the creation of a multiplicity of racist structures and practices from which it was difficult to distance oneself, whatever one's attitude toward Nazi ideology. Let us look first at selected aspects of the 1930s and then at World War II at home and on the Eastern Front.

It is difficult to delineate the line between and the links between the public and private in any historical period, but in none more so than in the Third Reich. Few regimes have made as extensive an effort to penetrate, politicise and restructure the private, be it in terms of sociability, reproductive behaviour, family life, or attitudes toward the relationship of individual to state and society.[85] Yet, popular memory of the Third Reich – or more accurately the memory of those who were not victims of the regime – remembers the family and the factory as unpolitical refuges in which one could pursue one's own interests, cling to one's own attitudes, and distance oneself from the demands of the

---

[84] Koonz, *Mothers*, pp. 419–20.
[85] More systematic comparisons with both Fascist Italy and the family and welfare policies of other European countries are necessary before one could argue with precision about which policies were unique and which were an extension of policies adopted in other countries. Pro-natalism would be a good place to start.

regime.[86] Recent works, however, suggest that the private was transformed and politicised much more than memory acknowledges.

The private was impoverished and isolated on the one hand, but it was penetrated by selected Nazi categories and ideas (although not by the Nazi ideology wholesale) on the other hand.[87] Anson Rabinbach's study of reading habits in the Third Reich indicates one form of this penetration. Women who were surveyed by Strength Through Joy about how they preferred to spend their leisure time, stated unequivocally their wish to read. This *Lesehunger* revealed a desire for nonparticipation in Nazi organisations, just as it showed an individualisation of activities and the isolation of people in the private realm. But Rabinbach's analysis of what was read uncovered just how many Nazi ideas about race and gender, about the *Volksgemeinschaft* and the threats to it, structured the ostensibly unpolitical fiction that was preferred.[88] Heidi Gerstenberger's exploration of the public discourse around such issues as the homeless, reveals that people adopted new Nazi social science categories such as *Nichtsesshafte* in place of older, more picaresque ones, such as *Landstreicher* and in the process learned to see the homeless as part of an inferior group of 'asocials'.[89]

Works on eugenics and sterilisation suggest how pervasive acceptance of Nazi 'racial science' was, and not just among the medical profession.[90] To be sure, there were innumerable protests against individual sterilisation orders, but people did not object to the idea of sterilisation as a solution to social problems or to the categories considered for sterilisation; rather they questioned whether an individual in fact belonged to the category of, for example, the schizophrenic or the handicapped. It is impossible to know whether this was done from conviction or convenience, but in either case Nazi categories were legitimated even as individual exemptions were sought.[91]

Robert Gellately's study of the Gestapo revealed from a somewhat different perspective the complex intertwining of public and private.

---

[86] *Die Jahre weiss man nicht*. The recent oral history project of the former German Democratic Republic uncovered similar memories of the family as an unpolitical refuge. Lutz Niethammer, Alexander von Plato, and Dorothee Wierling, *Die volkseigenen Erfahrungen. Eine Archäologie des Lebens in der Industrieprovinz der DDR* (Berlin, Rowohlt 1991).

[87] Peukert, *Inside Nazi Germany*, pp. 209–23, 240.

[88] Anson Rabinbach, 'The Reader, the Popular Novel and the Imperative to Participate: Reflections on Public and Private Experience in the Third Reich', *History and Memory* 3:2 (Fall/Winter 1991), pp. 5–44.

[89] Heidi Gerstenberger, 'Alltagsforschung und Faschismustheorie', in *Normalität oder Normalisierung*, p. 44.

[90] Burleigh and Wippermann, *Racial State*, pp. 136–82; Proctor, *Racial Hygiene, passim*; Weindling, *Health*, pp. 489–564.

[91] For discussions of protests against sterilisation, see Bock, *Zwangssterilisation* and Koonz, work in progress on the Rassenpolitisches Amt.

His analysis of surviving Gestapo records in Lower Franconia showed that a high percentage of secret police investigations were initiated in the wake of denunciations by private citizens. Whereas Sarah Gordon saw Gestapo charges of violations of the racial laws as evidence of opposition to the regime's antisemitism and racism, Gellately, noting that there were many fewer convictions than charges, viewed them as evidence of a willingness by Germans to inform on neighbours and co-workers.[92] After reconstructing the complex reasons behind denunciations, which included neighbourhood and workplace feuds, a desire for personal gain, and, more rarely, ideological commitment, Gellately concluded that '. . . the question of the popularity of the regime is to a very large extent beside the point . . . Successful enforcement of Nazi racial policies depended on the actions of enough citizens, operating out of an endless variety of motives, who contributed to the isolation of the Jews by offering information to the Gestapo and other authorities of Party and state'.[93]

Alf Lüdtke's reflections on workers in the Third Reich suggest that a politicisation of the private occurred not only because of successful intervention by the regime or because of individual willingness to inform and thereby help criminalise private behaviour, but also because of the seductions National Socialism offered. For most workers the dominant concerns were survival for oneself and one's family and distancing oneself from authorities inside and outside the workplace. The effort to preserve and remain within the sphere of *Eigensinn*, of self-determined activities, led to an attitude of *Hinnahme* (acceptance) toward the regime – an acceptance that did work to stabilise the regime but that nonetheless stemmed from workers' own needs, interests and practices rather than from integration into or deep ideological commitment to the regime. Yet, as Lüdtke acknowledges, passive acceptance and distancing were accompanied by a certain attraction to the regime's ceremonies and symbols, by 'a wait-and-see curiosity' about the regime's promises to workers about improved social policy, leisure, and consumption.[94] The Nazis' endless rhetorical praise of work and *Leistung*, the repeated affirmations of 'German quality work' appealed to values with a long and honourable tradition, at least among older and more skilled workers.[95]

[92] Robert Gellately, *The Gestapo and German Society: Enforcing Racial Policy, 1933–1945* (Oxford, Oxford University Press 1990); Sarah Gordon, *Hitler, Germans and the "Jewish Question"* (Princeton, Princeton University Press 1984).
[93] Gellately, *Gestapo*, p. 214.
[94] Lüdtke, 'Wo blieb die "rote Glut"?'
[95] Lüdtke, 'Deutsche Qualitätarbeit', and Herbert, 'Arbeiterschaft', pp. 339–41. Peukert's work on youth gangs suggests that at least some of the younger generation rejected this older conception of work: *Inside Nazi Germany*, pp. 154–66.

A growing body of research on both the home front and the Eastern Front suggests that World War II marked a significant break in the relationship of everyday life to the institutions and racial policies of the regime. People's attitudes and behaviour on racial issues changed as did the context in which they lived. If many people could distance themselves from the regime's racial ideology and policies before 1940, it was much harder to do so thereafter both because of foreign workers within Germany and because of the antisemitic and racist policies of the army and SS on the Eastern Front and in occupied Poland.

As we saw earlier, rationalisation and racism interacted to reshape the structure of the working class and the organisation of factories and farms in wartime Germany. This wartime experience reshaped the consciousness of ethnically German workers. The presence of a large number of foreign, and often slave labourers, working with Germans but living in virtual apartheid, led German workers to reassess notions of hierarchy and to question the permanence of the preexisting social order.[96] Nationality proved a more important basis for solidarity than class, as the pervasive lack of concern shown by German workers toward the foreigners in their midst showed.[97] Workers, like the rest of the population, came to accept the racial ordering of work as given, and this racial ordering promoted passivity.[98] After 1941 morale on the home front was not notably high and the growing burdens of the war economy were not shouldered enthusiastically, but they were not resisted.[99]

Nor was there evidence of resistance on the Eastern Front, where the overwhelming majority of German soldiers fought. As Mason concluded, the army's morale was much higher than that of civilians; German soldiers displayed 'enthusiasm, commitment and discipline . . . Making war seems to have been experienced as a more positive activity than making munitions or mining coal'.[100] Why this was so and what this meant for the conduct of the war in the East has been the subject of intensive research by historians of the Germany army.

From Christian Streit's indictment of the officer corps for actively formulating the Commissar Order and annihilating Soviet POWs through Omer Bartov's study of the brutal behaviour of three frontline units to Theo Schulte's investigation of the actions of occupying forces behind the front lines to Christopher Browning's reconstruction of the

[96] Ulrich Herbert, 'Apartheid nebenan, Erinnerungen an die Fremdarbeiter im Ruhrgebiet', in *Die Jahre weiss man nicht*, pp. 233–67.
[97] Herbert, 'Arbeiterschaft', p. 332.
[98] Ulrich Herbert, 'Arbeiterschaft unter der NS-Diktatur', in *Bürgerliche Gesellschaft in Deutschland*, ed. Lutz Niethammer *et al.* (Frankfurt a.M., Fischer Taschenbuch 1990), p. 465.　　[99] Mason, 'Women in Nazi Germany', pp. 333–4.
[100] Mason, 'Women in Nazi Germany, p. 334.

participation of Reserve Police Battalion 101 in the Holocaust in Poland, a devastating picture of army behaviour has been painted.[101] As with assessments of everyday life on the homefront, controversy centres less on what the army did than on why it did it. Was the officer corps motivated by ideological conviction or by a professional ethic of modern industrial warfare?[102] Did junior officers and men plunder and pillage from fear, isolation, and limited resources, or from commitment to the regime's policy of domination and racial reconstruction in eastern Europe? Were loyalties to the 'primary group' rather than to the regime's ideologies?[103]

Recent works agree that the army on the Eastern Front must be seen not as a world apart, but as a microcosm of German society, in which more than half of all German male workers of military age served.[104] It was, in Bartov's words, 'the army of the people and a willing tool of the regime, more than any of its military predecessors'.[105] But they disagree about why that army of the people in all its ranks committed atrocities and participated in genocide. At issue is less agency than ideological motivation.

Browning insists that the men of Reserve Police Battalion 101 rounded up and killed Jews not from belief in the ideological race war that the regime was waging, but from peer pressure, conformity, careerism. As in the famous Milgram experiment, Browning argues that ordinary men could under certain circumstances torture and kill.[106] Their individual pasts, the 'everyday racism'[107] of the society in which they lived, the propaganda to which they were subjected in Poland, are all deemed insignificant in comparison to the situation in which they found themselves.

For others, it is precisely the character of the society from which they came, a society which shaped both the army and the type of war being

---

[101] For an overview of this literature see Theo Schulte, *The German Army and Nazi Policies in Occupied Russia* (Oxford, Berg 1989), pp. 1–28 and Bartov, 'Soldiers, Nazis, and War in the Third Reich'.

[102] Christian Streit, *Keine Kameraden: die Wehrmacht und die sowjetischen Kriegsgefangenen 1941–1945* (Stuttgart 1978) emphasises ideology while Michael Geyer explores the professional ethic of violence. See Schulte, *German Army*, pp. 16–17.

[103] Bartov argues that real primary groups rapidly disintegrated, but that the ideological construction of the idea of primary group loyalty played a significant role in motivating people. The conflict is between which ideological postulate people adhered to, not between ideology and a deideologized personal realm: 'Soldiers, Nazis, and War in the Third Reich', pp. 49–50.

[104] Bartov, 'Soldiers, Nazis, and War in the Third Reich', p. 8. Herbert, 'Arbeiterschaft', pp. 462–3.   [105] Bartov, *Hitler's Army*, p. 10.

[106] Browning, *Ordinary Men, passim*. For a critical review, see Daniel Jonah Goldhagen, 'The Evil of Banality', *The New Republic* (13 & 20 July 1992), pp. 49–52.

[107] The term is Peukert's, 'Alltag und Barbarei, Zur Normalität des Dritten Reiches', in *Ist der Nationalsozialismus Geschichte?* p. 57.

waged, that was crucial. As the war progressed those on the battlefront as well as those on the homefront were surrounded by racist structures and practices of domination. The many forms of *Resistenz* which had proliferated in the 1930s seem to have all but ceased after 1940. According to Michael Geyer:

> . . . by 1942–43 it needed an extraordinary effort and strong convictions to evade the emerging new society; for racism permeated every aspect of life in occupied Europe. It had ceased to be a matter of individually embracing racist ideologies. Rather, it was the established practice of social organization that was almost impossible to evade.[108]

This argument captures the prevalence of racism as the governing and structuring principle of wartime Germany, but it circumvents the issue of agency, of motivation. Did individuals, in fact, embrace racist ideologies?

Ulrich Herbert suggested that participation in conquest and occupation reinforced existing ideas of racial superiority (both Nazi and pre-Nazi) in the population at large.[109] Recently discovered correspondence from soldiers on the Eastern Front lends support to this. It was not merely that Wehrmacht officers on all levels preached antisemitism and racism, that they deified Hitler and dehumanised the enemy. The private correspondence of soldiers to their families and to their co-workers in factories in Germany reproduced this political and racial demonisation of the enemy. These letters contained repeated endorsements of the regime's hatred of those perceived as inferior 'others' – be they Jews, Poles, or Russians; they expressed unequivocal adulation for Hitler, and promised to fight to the death for the cause.[110] The line between public rhetoric and private perception was blurred, and the regime mobilised prevailing conceptions of masculinity and work for ideological race war. As Lüdtke concluded after reading many such letters from blue- and white-collar workers:

> many individuals perceived their masculinity in military terms and images. To these people, their original claim to perform a 'clean' job at home increasingly became linked to the efficient killing operations of the army. In the end, participation in the extermination of 'others' might appear to many as the ultimate fulfilment of those cherished notions of 'German quality work'.[111]

[108] Michael Geyer, 'The State', p. 218.   [109] Herbert, 'Arbeiterschaft', p. 353.
[110] Bartov, *Hitler's Army*, pp. 145–52. Alf Lüdtke, 'The Appeal of Exterminating "Others"': German Workers and the Limits of Resistance', *Journal of Modern History* 64, Supplement (December 1992), pp. S46–S67.
[111] Lüdtke, 'The Appeal of Exterminating "Others",' pp. S66–S67.

Afterthoughts
Ian Kershaw and Moshe Lewin

A volume of essays envisaged more as an experimental workshop than as a set of definitive statements cannot aim to arrive at firm conclusions. Tentative and provisional findings, together with hints at the possible future agenda for comparative research, are also necessarily a reflection of the fact that the historiographies of Germany and Russia have, until now, tended to bypass each other. It was striking that the historians of both countries attending the conference from which this volume has emerged met each other in most cases for the first time. Germanists came armed with many open questions derived in the main from applying to Russian development analogous argument from the German case. They found they had much to gain from the most recent uncovering of sources about the USSR. Experts on Russia and the Soviet Union had the opportunity to see how new, probing questions on their own areas of study could be raised and sharpened by better acquaintance with the rich literature and advanced research on German history. For it remains true that specialists in German history have, on the whole, not concerned themselves greatly with the problems of understanding the structural development of modern Russia. And, vice versa, the same applies by and large to experts on Russian history, for whom the extensive debates that characterise the historiography of modern Germany are for the most part *terra incognita*.

For these reasons alone, the preceding contributions have in most cases necessarily concentrated on the one country or the other, rather than explicitly comparing the two regimes and their societies. Nevertheless, they have suggested a number of 'afterthoughts' of a comparative kind on the dictators we have been examining and on the political systems they headed. Since crisis-ridden states and societies lurching into brutal dictatorship, and eventually – if in utterly different ways – emerging from them are not confined to the cases of Germany and

Russia, the comparison offered here might claim to have a wider relevance and application.

Nevertheless, there were features common to the Stalinist and Nazi regimes that separated them even from the many other despotic and dictatorial regimes of their time and since. In some ways, as Michael Mann began his essay in this volume by commenting, the Stalinist and Nazi regimes 'belonged together'. The unprecedented inroads into all walks of life attained in both systems through new techniques of mass mobilisation and new levels and types of repression and terror are crucial features that bracket these regimes together and distinguish them from other modern dictatorships. It amounted to a 'total claim' that both regimes made on their societies. How did this come about? How was it that these very different societies brought on themselves, almost simultaneously, regimes which, for all their contrasting elements, extended claims on their populations going beyond anything known in history beforehand, and were prepared to enforce those claims with new, untold levels of repression, persecution, and terror?

In its concentration upon the regimes themselves, our volume has not had the opportunity to explore in detailed, comparative fashion the structural conditions which led to the emergence of 'totalitarianism' in the two countries. One dimension which, however much it has preoccupied historians and political scientists studying either country, cannot be avoided in this context is that of 'modernisation'. The differing problems of modernisation in the two countries ought not, however, to be seen in isolation from the expansionist, hegemonic ambitions that each of them harboured, from the comprehensive systemic crisis brought on each of them by the first World War, and from the institutional and social fragmentation that inexorably ensued in both Germany and Russian.

I

The concept of 'modernisation' is, of course, highly problematic (if less so than that of 'modernity', often mistakenly used as a synonym). But however problematic the concept, it is difficult to avoid it and better to face up to its limitations, but also take into account its advantages, than to dismiss it altogether.[1] 'Modernisation' need not have connotations of 'improving' society, let alone of democratising it. In sociological, political, and historical writing, it has implied the process of long-term change that transforms a society resting on agriculture and its related

---

[1] See the compelling arguments for the general validity of the 'modernisation' concept in historical theory, in Hans-Ulrich Wehler, *Modernisierungstheorie und Geschichte* (Göttingen 1975).

political and social structures and cultures into an industrial society based on technological advancement, secularised culture, bureaucratic administration, and extensive (however shallow) forms of political participation. These changes were compatible with the emergence of quite different political systems – with varying forms of authoritarianism as well as with democracy. Both Germany and Russia aspired from the nineteenth century to become 'modernised' countries, seen above all in terms of rapidly advanced industrial development. This was regarded as the only way to expansionism and the attainment of great-power status.

Germany (or, more accurately, Prussia) 'took off' in earnest from the mid-nineteenth century. Russia's furious spurt came towards the end of the century. In both cases, coming 'later' than more advanced competitors offered some opportunities, but also caused significant problems and complications. The differences in pace, character, and methods applied during the accelerated industrialisation are worth exploring comparatively. They need to be seen in close connection with the related problems of state-building, national identity, and pressures to move to constitutionality.[2]

Despite the common determination to industrialise as rapidly as possible, the relative levels of economic development reached by Russia and Prussia/Germany before the First World War contrasted, of course, sharply. This, naturally, had social, cultural, and political implications. It was to lead to quite different manifestations of modernisation crisis. This in turn was to contribute to shaping the different trajectories into dictatorship.

Long before the First World War, Germany already possessed a modern (for its day) industrial economy, and advanced technology, and a highly developed 'organised capitalism'. Coupled with the sophisticated bureaucratic administration of a pluralistic and constitutional (though not democratic) state, this provided for techniques of control that in reality went a long way towards taming the revolutionary dynamism of the largest and best-organised working-class movement in Europe. One such technique – to exaggerate the threat to property and bourgeois order of Social Democracy – helped to build up the widespread anti-socialism and anti-Marxism which fed even before the war into the broader strands of counter-revolutionary ideology on the conservative and emerging radical Right. Colonial and imperialist aims,

---

[2] This linkage, in the context of comparative fascism, is suggested by Wolfgang Schieder, 'Faschismus', in *Das Fischer Lexikon: Geschichte* (Frankfurt am Main 1990), p. 180; and in *Totalitarismus und Faschismus. Eine wissenschaftliche und politische Begriffskontroverse. Kolloquium im Institut für Zeitgeschichte am 24. November 1978* (Munich/Vienna 1980), pp. 47–8. There seems no reason why the model should not be applied *pari passu* to the development in Russia, even though the political outcome was so different.

shored up by the shrill demands of nationalist pressure-groups, locked onto the same anti-Left ideology. An additional strand emerged from the anti-modernising ideas of those social groups that felt most threatened by modernisation and industrialisation. Unlike Britain, Germany combined a highly advanced economy with an extremely large agrarian sector. Most of Germany's population continued to live and work in rural or small-town settings. Evocation of the sentimentalised and idealised *Heimat* had no close parallels in the case of Germany's major industrial rival, Great Britain. The disturbance, upheaval, and anxieties caused by industrialisation not unnaturally produced resentment, anger, and distrust that could easily be seen – as it often was, for example, in the troubled 1890s – as a threat to 'traditional' ways of life. In truth, 'traditional life' had always been subject to change, and was changing rapidly under the impact of industrialisation. In many respects, rural society had itself been already modernised – or at the very least was deeply altered by the demands on capitalist production – by the time the reaction against modernisation set in. Backward-looking nostalgia for a romanticised, largely mythical, past coexisted, therefore, with the reality of a highly modernised society.

To some extent, of course, uneven development was common to most if not all developing societies. The lack of synchroneity of social development (Ernst Bloch), or 'combined development' (Trotsky) of modern and archaic traits in a society, was arguably more normal than exceptional during the process of industrialisation. The question is largely one of degree. In Germany the contrast was extreme not least because of the extraordinary speed of economic modernisation, the continued size of the non-industrialised sector, and the influence of the agrarian and *Mittelstand* lobbies. In addition, there was the contrived spread of a stridently anti-socialist political culture able to exploit exaggerated fears of industrialisation as a reaction against a numerically and organisationally strong, but in terms of actual radicalisation weak, working-class movement. But despite its anti-industrial 'agrarian myth', its *Mittelstand* nostalgia, and its strains of bourgeois cultural pessimism, Germany was a modern country on the eve of the First World War, not a society that had 'managed to miss the road to modernity and instead consolidated itself as an industrial feudal society'.[3]

Moreover, without the systemic crisis introduced by the war it

---

[3] Ralf Dahrendorf, *Society and Democracy in Germany* (London 1968), p. 64. For the most sustained criticism of this type of argument, see David Blackbourn and Geoff Eley, *The Peculiarities of German History* (Oxford 1987). Other references are provided in George Steinmetz's paper, above in this volume.

cannot be assumed that the tensions of an industrialising and modern-ising society would have predetermined a path to an authoritarian, let alone a fascistic, form of state.[4] In fact, until the early 1930s democracy had distinct chances of establishing itself, while the triumph of fas-cism seemed an unlikely proposition. What happened after the war might be seen, paradoxically, in some ways as a modernisation crisis within a modernised country.[5] The conflict-ridden 'Weimar experi-ment' produced what has been called a 'crisis of classical modernity' as every form of tension in the 'modern' versus 'archaic' expressions of culture, social values, and politics was taken to its extreme.[6] Bourgeois conservatism, petty-bourgeois reaction, and Nazi antisemi-tism united in associating the 'modern' and avant-garde with social-ism, internationalism, and revolution.[7] The fierceness of its rejection was enmeshed in the ideas of the neo-conservative as well as the radical Right. Any notion of a return to the pre-war bourgeois values was vehemently ruled out. Instead, there had to be a revolution where 'achievement' and 'heroic deeds', not birthright and formal qualifica-tions, offered the path to power and status. Without the political fragmentation and delegitimation that mirrored the profound and comprehensive socio-economic, cultural, and political crisis during the Depression years, the merging of the broad gamut of counter-revolutionary forces, non-Nazi as well as Nazi, into the Hitler dicta-torship could not have taken place.

During the dictatorship, while all significant autonomies outside state institutions were destroyed, and coordination, in so far as it took place at all, was at the level of the supreme leader, the reality was an enhanced level of institutional fragmentation (of party, state administration, 'secondary bureaucracies', armed forces, police administration) at state level. And the inchoate social motivations – part reactionary, part looking to the opportunities of a 'modern' society offered by 'national rebirth' – encapsulated in the propaganda vision of a classless and racially pure 'national community', were now channelled into spiralling aggression directed at 'enemies of the state', and above all racial minorities, then at external enemies and conquered 'Untermenschen'.[8]

Some rather fruitless debate has gone on about whether Nazism was

---

[4] The openness of the prospects for the *Kaiserreich* is stressed by Thomas Nipperdey, *Deutsche Geschichte, 1866–1918*, 2 vols. (Munich 1990, 1992).

[5] See Gerald Feldman, 'The Weimar Republic: A Problem of Modernisation?', *Archiv für Sozialgeschichte*, 26 (1986), pp. 1–26.

[6] See Detlev Peukert, *Die Weimarer Republik. Krisenjahre der Klassischen Moderne* (Frankfurt am Main 1987).

[7] Still valuable on this is George Mosse, *The Crisis of German Ideology* (London 1966).

[8] See on this the classical article of Martin Broszat, 'Soziale Motivation und Führer-Bindung des Nationalsozialismus', *Vierteljahreshefte für Zeitgeschichte*, 18 (1970), pp. 392–409.

'modernising' or 'reactionary'.[9] Of course, some modernisation did occur. In other areas, there was evident regression.[10] 'Archaic' and 'modernising' tendencies continued to coexist during the Third Reich.[11] But the Nazi regime, unlike Stalin's regime, cannot be regarded as a 'modernising dictatorship'. Its concern was with national rebirth and supremacy built on racial purification and regeneration.[12] What 'modernisation' took place was largely coincidental. Of crucial importance, though, was the way Nazi ideology allowed entirely 'modern' plans for 'social engineering' by doctors, eugenicists, population experts, and other 'modern' professional groups to take shape and flourish. Compulsory sterilisation of the 'unfit', the killing (under the euphemism of 'euthanasia') of those deemed to be a burden on society, the wiping out of Europe's Jewish communities, plans for the 'resettlement' of some twenty million Poles in Western Siberia: all were made possible not just by the ideological fanaticism of hard-core Nazis, but also by the enthusiastic collaboration of professionals and well-educated 'experts' in a system that gave them previously unimaginable scope and opportunity for power. The exponents of modern technology and modern social planning were only too willing to place themselves at the service of barbarism.

Where German capitalist development before the First Word War in certain ways strengthened the authoritarian state, such development in Russia weakened it. In Russia, the weakness of capitalism and the impact of a decaying absolutism produced, paradoxically, a radical working class and intelligentsia, as well as a land-hungry peasantry. These social groups were to bring Lenin to power as a consequence of the inability of the tsarist regime to cope with the scale of the agrarian problems or to manage the running of the war. Alongside the forced industrialisation in tsarist Russia, 'pre-industrial' attitudes were a

---

[9] The historiography is assessed in Ian Kershaw, *The Nazi Dictatorship. Problems and Perspectives of Interpretation*, 3rd edn (London 1993), ch. 7 and pp. 202–6.

[10] An essay collection essentially emphasising the modernising tendencies of Nazism is Michael Prinz and Rainer Zitelmann (eds.), *Nationalsozialismus und Modernisierung* (Darmstadt 1991). Emphatic in their rejection of such arguments are: Jens Albers, 'Nationalsozialismus und Modernisierung', *Kölner Zeitschrift für Soziologie und Sozialpsychologie*, 41 (1989), pp. 346–65; Hans Mommsen, 'Nationalsozialismus als vorgetäuschte Modernisierung', in Walter H. Pehle (ed.), *Der historische Ort des Nationalsozialismus* (Frankfurt am Main 1990), pp. 11–46; and Norbert Frei, 'Wie modern war der Nationalsozialismus?', *Geschichte und Gesellschaft*, 19 (1993), pp. 367–87.

[11] For an interesting illustration, see Timothy Mason, 'Zur Entstehung des Gesetzes zur Ordnung der nationalen Arbeit vom 20.Januar 1934. Ein Versuch über das Verhältnis "archaischer" und "moderner" Momente in der neuesten deutschen Geschichte', in Hans Mommsen, Dietmar Petzina and Bernd Weisbrod (eds.), *Industrielles System und politische Entwicklung in der Weimarer Republik* (Düsseldorf 1974), pp. 322–51.

[12] The correct emphasis is set in Michael Burleigh and Wolfgang Wippermann, *The Racial State. Germany, 1933–1945* (Cambridge 1991).

powerful presence. This was later to create problems for Soviet indus-
trialisers who resorted to extreme coercion and terror to eradicate
'pre-industrial' mentalities and inculcate habits of mind and behaviour
conducive to productive work in factories and *kolkhozy*. One of the
notable handicaps for the Soviet system was created by the catastrophic
backsliding away from whatever industrial discipline had already
existed and into archaic work patterns that had been prevalent during
the Civil War. This suggests that an emphasis upon 'pre-industrial'
attitudes characteristic of the '*Sonderweg*' thesis in Germany (which, as
the paper by George Steinmetz shows, can no longer carry the weight it
once did in German historiography) might be applied with greater
validity to the development in Russia.

Here, as Lenin, Trotsky, and a fine Russian-Soviet scholar of tsarist
Russia, A. M. Anfimov, pointed out, pre-capitalist relations still prevailed in the court, the bureaucracy, the noble estates (*sosloviia*), a poorly
developed middle class, and much of the peasantry. A dynamic and
fast-moving, but still narrowly based capitalist sector was insufficiently
powerful to turn Russia into a capitalist country, as the Russian
Marxists, notably Lenin (before his disenchantment after 1905) had
hoped. Rather, Lenin's regime after 1921 has to be regarded as the
product of the peculiar pre-capitalist situation in which the country
found itself after the Civil War. Had Russia already been a genuinely
capitalist country by 1921, what transpired thereafter would have been
impossible. Whatever degree of development in the direction of a
market economy based upon privatised landholding had spread among
the peasantry before the war was largely undermined by the Civil War.
Instead, there was a powerful reversion, stemming in part from the First
World War and in part from 'war-communist' policies during the Civil
War, to more archaic social and economic relations. This was, especially,
a genuine product of the peasants' own agrarian revolution, and of
're-communalisation' – that is, the return to the communal land-tenure
that was already weakening before the war. Its revival was accompanied by the elimination of much of the market- and production-
orientated agricultural sector that had, however haltingly, continued to
develop in tsarist Russia.

The forces that helped install Lenin and brought about the victory
of the Reds over the Whites posed no obstacle to the making of
Stalin's regime. On the contrary, they contained the necessary prerequisite for the emergence of a very Russian 'agrarian despotism'
that deliberately sought to legitimise itself by turning to the symbols
of tsars known both for development and cruelty. It could even be
argued that 'deep Russia' (*glubinnaia Rossiia*) – mostly *muzhik* country,
with sprinklings of semi-rural *bourgs* – took its revenge in a perverse

fashion by imposing on the new system some of its own mentality and values.

The first task of Lenin's regime was to improvise the creation of a new form of state, and to provide a modicum of economic recovery through the restoration of at least bare minimal living standards. This was done through the NEP. Finally, it was imperative to develop the country – something which neither the Weimar Republic nor the Hitler regime had needed to do for Germany. Where National Socialism in Germany could build upon a highly developed industrial, scientific, and technological base, the Russians had to create one practically from scratch.

Without revolution in the west, the Bolsheviks did not see their own backward country as fit for a programme of socialism. But a power-vacuum could not be tolerated. The rebuilding of the state could not wait. The workers in the October revolution were attacking a capitalism that was already starting to break up. But no less important was the peasants' action against the tsarist landowning class – a most powerful feudal 'left-over', as party theorists put it. Equally crucial was the support of the war-weary Russian soldiers, also predominantly peasants. The collusion of these largely plebeian forces was to end in a plebeian-bureaucratic system that passed through two stages: the first, a form of state arising during the Civil War, as the economy was collapsing; the second, during NEP, where the revival of the economy offered a prop for the state system. An immense problem for the regime was that the economy, outside the small industrial sector, still depended on small-scale peasant production – a position wholly different from Germany's – which itself rested on communal arrangements, often with ancient roots, now restored as the prevailing form of landholding in most of rural Russia.

The regime's spokesmen acknowledged that the aims of the huge peasant mass differed from those of the Bolsheviks. But they hoped that the compromise embodied in the NEP, together with effective methods of stimulation and control, would win over the loyalty of the peasants. The compromise did not last, and what was to become 'Stalinism' was to emerge from a clash between the state and a mostly pre-bourgeois mass (leaving aside the small market-oriented sector, among them the real petty-bourgeoisie who were to become the first victims of collectivisation).

These sketches demonstrate how the turning-points of 1929–33 had different origins in the two countries, and how sharply different social and economic structures conditioned the genesis of dictatorships whose ideological dynamic contrasted diametrically, but whose 'total claim' on the societies they came to dominate bears comparison.

II

If we turn from the structural preconditions and genesis of the Stalinist and Nazi regimes, to the regimes themselves, the essays included in this collection have perhaps highlighted some significant differences between the positions of Stalin and Hitler in their respective systems. The differences have roots in the relationship of Stalin and Hitler to their respective parties and, of course, in the disparate social structures and ideological motivations of those parties.

The sources of support for the dictatorial regime, and of opposition to it, have been extensively researched in the case of Germany, far less so for the Soviet system. However, we know that Stalin, like Hitler in Germany, enjoyed enormous popularity in the USSR. Meanwhile, information on opposition is beginning to filter out of personal diaries, kept well hidden for decades, as well as from archival sources. Will we discover that opposition and dissent were more widespread than we thought? There are certainly some pointers in this direction. But it is too early to say. There was more collaboration with the Nazis during the war in Russia than one might have expected. But the scope of both overt and concealed collaboration needs to be explored in future research. The approaches to consensus and dissent long since developed in the German case, notably, for example during the 'Bavaria Project', offer possible parallels for how work might take shape in the case of Stalinist society.[13]

Unlike initial Bolshevism, with its largely proletarian base, Stalinism managed to win the support of sectors of society beyond industrial workers.[14] The construction of a powerful industrial country, and the revival of patriotism, appealed to many. But whatever the other sources of support, the real social base, despite intense ideological indoctrination, was not provided by blue-collar workers but by a bureaucracy and the growing intelligentsia. A heterogeneous mass drawn from such sectors became increasingly visible and, finally, socially and politically dominant in the party membership and the regime as a whole. Here, too, the relatively sophisticated work on party membership carried out (and in progress) in the case of the NSDAP will both highlight contrasts in social structure and also offer methodological approaches that might fruitfully have application in the Soviet case.[15]

[13] For the methods and findings of the path-breaking 'Bavaria Project', see Martin Broszat et al. (eds.), *Bayern in der NS-Zeit*, 6 vols (Munich 1977–83).

[14] See Moshe Lewin, 'The Social Background of Stalinism', in Moshe Lewin, *The Making of the Soviet System* (London 1985), pp. 258–85.

[15] For the sociological structure of the NSDAP, see especially Michael Kater, *The Nazi Party* (Oxford 1983); see too the study of Detlef Mühlberger, *Hitler's Followers* (London 1991).

The first section of this volume, in particular, has indicated points of comparison, but especially of contrast, in the Stalin and Hitler cults. These formed both pivots of the respective regimes and also in many respects reflected the social motivations of the following.

The tissue of lies built into the artificially constructed Stalin cult served, in Lewin's phrase, as an 'alibi' for the fact that he was by no means the automatic or unchallenged heir to Lenin. Hitler, though his 'deification' was, of course, in large measure a carefully crafted product of Nazi propaganda, needed no equivalent 'alibi'. From 1921 onwards, he had never had a serious rival for the leadership of the NSDAP. The cult around him began very early – by the autumn of 1922, when it was initially stimulated by Mussolini's 'March on Rome'. And his followers were already speaking of him as Germany's 'saviour' even before he started to believe it himself.[16] On the refoundation of the NSDAP in 1925, the leadership cult was developed as the key instrument of party unity and ideological cohesiveness. It seems at least likely that this difference helps to explain – leaving aside personality disorder – Stalin's chronic insecurity and proneness to resort to terror against his own supporters, in contrast to Hitler's reliance (despite his distrustful and suspicious nature) on the personal loyalty of his paladins. This had nothing to do with *actual* security. There were several attempts (though none from his own entourage) to assassinate Hitler, even before the 1944 bomb plot, despite the dictator's elaborate security precautions; whereas, no one ever attempted to kill Stalin. Yet Stalin's paranoia transferred itself to a system where no one felt safe, and it suffused the political life of the country with a thick mist of moral decay.

In both cases the leadership 'myth' on which the personality cult rested was 'bought' in varying measures by extensive sections of the population. The erection and popularity of the cult were possible in each instance through the exploitation and distortion, in crisis conditions, of long-standing elements of an earlier political culture – traditions and ideologies of imperial statism in Stalin's case, pre-existing 'great man' expectations shored up by the German Right in Hitler's case. The personalisation by propaganda of the 'achievements' and perceived 'positive' features of each of the regimes – the association of Stalin with rebuilding the economy and national defence, of Hitler with recreating national pride and strength – helped to provide each of the dictators with the plebiscitary basis of support that formed a crucial component of their power.

In both cases, the leaders identified themselves with the state itself

---

[16] See Ian Kershaw, *The 'Hitler Myth': Image and Reality in the Third Reich* (Oxford 1987), ch. 1.

and did, indeed, expropriate and personalise state power. However, their power as leaders was exercised in different fashions.

Stalin was not content to remain aloof from the routine of political life. No detail was too small to be capable of grasping his attention. He felt compelled to lay his hands directly on institutions, transforming their functions and titles and emptying them in the process of institutional rationality. His dictatorship 'style' was to take over the chairmanship of more and more committees (as he did in the War), pile up impossible tasks on government agencies, and force them to cope (or pretend to cope), thereby making them vulnerable at all times to his personal displeasure and the corresponding tender mercies of the ubiquitous secret police. The result was inevitably the eroding – sabotaging from above might be a more correct description – of the machinery of state administration.

Hitler was less keen to become embroiled in day-to-day politics, and remained above the endemic in-fighting of his subordinates. Though less persistently interventionist than Stalin, and wholly unbureuacratic in the way he operated, the impact of Hitler's personal rule on the state apparatus was, as Mommsen's paper showed, at least as corrosive. Government agencies were left more or less intact; but the improvised establishment of extra-governmental 'plenipotentiary authorities' competing with the state ministries rendered the latter often almost redundant, and was certainly a recipe for organisation chaos. But, frustrated and irritated as ministers might have been with Hitler, they did not have to live daily, as Stalin's ministers did, with the threat of arrest and probable execution at the hands of the secret police.

III

This brings us back to the differing role and scale of terror in the two dictatorships.[17] It would be a grave error to personalise – and trivialise – the atrocities perpetrated by the regimes through attributing them solely to Hitler's paranoid race theories in the one case and Stalin's paranoid insecurity complex in the other. The widespread complicity of each society in the repression and terror practised by both regimes would be thereby both ignored and tacitly exonerated. Even so, the psychology of the dictators cannot be overlooked. Both Hitler and Stalin supplied themselves with, and were dependent upon, a powerful, demonised motivator that served to whip up and to justify their actions. What 'the Jew' was to Hitler, Trotsky and his real or supposed followers

---

[17] Some of the following remarks draw on the comparison made in Ian Kershaw, 'Totalitarianism Revisited: Nazism and Stalinism in Comparative Perspective', *Tel Aviver Jahrbuch für deutsche Geschichte*, 23 (1994), pp. 23–40.

were to Stalin. But where power is as personalised as was the case in each of the regimes, the 'psychopathology' of the dictator becomes pervasive – a legitimation for the many in both regimes prepared, for a variety of motives, to 'work towards' the Leader. Here, the role of denunciation, touched upon by Mary Nolan in her paper, would certainly merit detailed research in the case of Stalinism similar to that which it has already received in the historiography of Nazism.[18]

The different scale and function of terror in the two systems cannot, however, be reduced to personal pathologies, however significant those were. The different context in which the dictatorships took shape cannot be ignored. While Nazism arose from defeat in war, a relatively non-violent revolution, and a lengthy 'latent civil war', Stalinism emerged from a legacy of defeat in war, violent revolution, and a real civil war of untold horror and brutality. Compared with the level of violence in Russia between 1917 and 1920, the political violence and bloodshed in the 'latent civil war' of Weimar Germany pales into insignificance. Weimar Germany, for all its turbulence, remained a *Rechtsstaat*. In the Russian case, while the introduction of the NEP, against the backcloth of the Civil War, felt like a haven of peace and order, and appeared in some ways even 'liberal', Russia was and remained a dictatorship that kept expanding its power. With Stalin's takeover, the dictatorship entered into an era of extensive violence and brutality reminiscent of and in some ways surpassing the horrors of the Civil War.

After the drastic settling of scores which accompanied the Nazi takeover and consolidation of power in 1933–4, the level of repression within Germany actually dipped before rising again in 1938–9 in the wake of the expansion into Austria and Czechoslovakia. Moreover, it was directed primarily at the weaker, discriminated sections of society. Once the political opponents of the regime had been broken and destroyed, Nazism's main victims within Germany fell into identifiable groups, exposed to persecution on grounds of their alleged racial and eugenic inferiority.[19] For repression and persecution were, of course, not just aimed at the elimination of objective enemies of the regime, but were tools of the mission to attain the racial purification which was at

[18] See, for example, Robert Gellately, 'The Gestapo and German Society: Political Denunciation in the Gestapo Case Files', *Journal of Modern History*, 60 (1988).
[19] It goes without saying that many Germans outside these categories, often denounced by their neighbours, were persecuted for a multiplicity of minor alleged 'political' offences and that members of both major Christian denominations as well as the smaller Christian sects were also exposed to recrimination for opposition to anti-Church policy. But this does not invalidate the point that the main targets of persecution were fairly clearly defined: the Nazis' communist and socialist opponents, and groups singled out on racial and eugenics grounds.

the heart of the Nazi creed. This unending 'mission' meant that once the war had begun, the conquered populations of the occupied territories – above all those regarded as the lowest of the low, the Jewish minority – bore the brunt of the soaring levels of terror. The ultimate irrationality of the terror reflected Nazism's irrational goals.

The irrationality of Stalinist terror was of a different kind. Terror in this case was aimed less at external enemies than at enemies within – and these were mainly imaginary. Large and varying sections of the population were at risk in the quest to root out all presumed threats to Stalin's personal power. Whereas in Germany itself – though it was very different in the occupied territories – there was a certain horrific predictability to the terror, so that non-targeted groups were relatively safe as long as they kept out of trouble and retained a low profile, the very unpredictability of Stalinist terror meant that no one could feel safe. By the later 1930s Stalin had turned the terror against the party, the army high command, economic managers, the members of his own Politburo, and even the secret police itself.

Stalin's own paranoia about internal enemies on all sides had wider implications. It pushed the door wide open to personal and political score-settling on a grandiose scale by lots of 'little Stalins' within the party and the security police, as well as by thousands of ordinary men and women 'doing their bit' by denouncing neighbours and workmates for 'deviant' behaviour. Such willing cooperation (that was also of enormous assistance to the Gestapo and allowed it to operate – especially in the early years – on staffing levels far smaller than often presumed) did not prevent the bloating of the Stalinist repressive machinery. And though denunciation was both encouraged and utilised, the repression did not depend on denunciation since provable guilt was never a consideration in the persecution of victims.

Unlike Stalin, Hitler did not turn purges into a characteristic feature of rule. Nor did he create anything like the insecurity among the Nazi elite comparable to that which existed among the Soviet ruling groups under Stalin. However, the terrorising of specific groups within Germany and then, in the war, of whole populations regarded as 'racially inferior', was inseparable from the Nazi creed. In contrast, horrific though it was, the blood-letting in the Stalinist purges was not intrinsic to the Soviet system of rule. Mass terror against mythical enemies, the arbitrary imprisonment and shooting of countless individuals, and the use of slave labour in the hands of the secret police were all discontinued after Stalin's death, especially after the sensational debunking of his personality cult by Khrushchev in 1956. Though many conservatives, especially following Khrushchev's fall, tried hard to 'rehabilitate' Stalin, they failed. This alone shows that Stalin's particular brand of despotism could be, and was, replaced by a much more moderate form of authoritarianism in which repression could retract to a residual 'stick' with which the regime could beat dissidents rather than serve as a vehicle of revolutionary upheaval and social restructuring. What had been possible, and had even seemed acceptable, during a period of forced industrialisation, social crisis, and political turmoil, was not acceptable to, let alone needed by, the complex bureaucratic state and society which that industrialisation had produced, and which outlived Stalin.

IV

This returns us to a theme which in different ways has run through much of this volume: that of the self-destructive tendencies of the Stalinist and Nazi regimes.

A common element of inherent self-destructiveness, highlighted in several papers, was the irreconcilable conflict between the arbitrariness of personal despotism and the regulatory order needed by the bureaucratic administration of modern states. Such a conflict could be sustained over a period of upheaval, turmoil, and crisis; but not indefinitely. The 'contradiction of continuous revolution', as Michael Mann called it, had to end. And it could only do so by the end of despotism itself, and the survival of bureaucracy through a return to the predictability of 'system' and to 'politics' as the rationally expedient pursuit of limited goals. Both Stalin and Hitler had undermined 'system' and replaced 'politics' by ideological vision and unprecedented levels of state-sanctioned violence directed at the societies over which they ruled. In both cases, revolutionary dynamism went far towards destroying existing structures of rule, even where institutional forms remained intact. The norms of government had been replaced by 'will', underpinned by ideology, myth, and the untrammelled power of the secret police, itself justified by recourse to the ideological aims of the leader.

Beyond the inner structural contradictions lay the essential irrationality at the heart of each of the regimes.

National Socialism aimed at a war of limitless proportions for racial conquest and domination. This type of war could not be settled by compromise or limited gains. Its stakes were world supremacy or total destruction. Since the gamble involved taking on all the great powers, with resources far greater than Germany's, it can only be concluded that not only destructiveness on a gigantic scale, but also self-destructiveness was ingrained in the nature of National Socialism.

The self-destructiveness of Stalinism was of a different kind. The chronic fear and insecurity which the dictator's capricious and de-

356

ranged personality induced was scarcely a recipe for governmental efficiency. Absurdity was reached in the massive inflation of the security apparatus – which Stalin also regarded with acute distrust – in order to hunt down millions of invented enemies. Parts of the huge security machinery were, therefore, quite useless, acting against mythical threats, tracking down assassins and plots which had never existed. But the self-destruction went further than governmental dysfunction. During the 1930s, and again after the War, Stalin, aided by the readiness of thousands of 'little Stalins' to exploit conditions for their own careerist ends, went a good way towards the deliberate destruction of his own system. At the height of the lunatic purges, the fully irrational destruction of the state and party cadres had no other ultimate source than the dictator's power and security mania. The purges reflected the pathology of despotism. Attempts to discover a rationality in alleged power struggles between 'moderates' and 'radicals' have not proved convincing.[20] Stalin's killing involved moderates, radicals, those in between, and dedicated Stalinists as well. There is no rationality of an 'objective' kind to be found; merely the objective irrationality of Stalin's power.

The self-destructiveness of Stalinism carried the clear imprint of the dictator's imbalanced personality and actions. Other paths than those followed were available. The collectivisation policies of the early 1930s did irreparable damage to the economy of a heavily rural country. There had been alternative ways of industrialising which were ruled out on ideological grounds.[21] Similarly, as Jacques Sapir argues in his paper in this volume, the relative liberalisation of the economy that had proved both necessary and effective during the war was deliberately rejected in the reversion to rigid Stalinism after 1948. Another chance was lost. Once the system could 'shake off' Stalin and renounce his personality cult, as it did within such a short time after his death, the bureaucratic structures of the state could reconstitute and stabilise themselves in an essentially conservative authoritarian regime capable of functioning and reproducing itself until the mid-1980s. Whether self-destructive tendencies remained in the post-Stalinist Soviet state is a separate question, relating to its inability to produce the economic growth necessary to compete in an international economy dominated by capitalist production and in an international high-cost arms race.

After the collapse of the Third Reich, West Germany (with much help from the West) was able to build a highly modern capitalist economy

---

[20] See, as representative of this kind of approach, J. Arch Getty, *Origins of the Great Purges. The Soviet Communist Party Reconsidered* (Cambridge 1985).
[21] See Alec Nove and Janet R. Millar, 'A Debate on Collectivisation; Was Stalin Really Necessary?', *Problems of Communism* (July–August 1976).

and, on the basis of economic success, to establish the sound democracy which had been impossible in the Weimar Republic. Soviet reconstruction, on the other hand, simply returned to the pre-war model, mostly using pre-war technology, administrative planning, and management patterns. And, as regards political structures, Soviet triumphalism – in spite of the enormity of the material and above all human losses – ensured enhanced legitimacy for the system that had taken the USSR to victory in 'the Great Patriotic War'. Forty years later, the continued 'relative backwardness' of the Soviet economy and the inflexible political structures built on it could no longer be sustained. Russia had neither economic nor political models of its own to turn to. So Russia had to look to the West for models and inspiration. Today's Germany is among those models.

The specific conditions which produced Stalinism and Nazism will not recur. But the future is open, not least in the light of the continuing turmoil left by the decomposition of the Soviet Union, and we can never be sure what is over the horizon. The papers in this volume have tried to make a small contribution to a deepened understanding of two of the most terrible regimes ever experienced in the fervent hope that we shall never see their like again, in Europe or elsewhere. The hope may be a vain one. The massive sacrifice of human beings on the altar of political myth was not expected to reccur in an era of high technology and mass education. But it is becoming clear that this self-image of our own era is far too benign.

Index

Mann, Michael, 14–15, 138, 344, 356
Maoism, 144, 145
market, 297, 301
Marx, Karl, 258, 305
Marxism, 22, 39, 54, 72, 98, 140, 172,
   175, 258, 259, 267–8, 287, 299–300,
   311, 312, 313, 349
   see also Leninism
Mason, Tim, 295, 299, 311, 330, 340
Medvedev, Roy, 289, 292, 294
Mein Kampf, 7, 76, 113, 140, 149
Mekhlis, L. Z., 32, 187, 193, 196, 200,
   203, 241
Memorial, 289, 298n
memory, popular, 315, 316
men, 333–4, 335, 336
Mensheviks, 43, 110, 298
Michels, Robert, 66
Mikoyan, A., 32, 42, 49, 51, 59, 134, 203–4
Milgram experiment, 341
militarism, 141, 144, 148, 150, 151–2,
   261, 267
military theory, and economic policies,
   209–16
   see also operational art, Soviet
mining, 322, 323, 328
mobilisation techniques, 148–9
'mobilised' economy, 232, 246
modernisation, 4, 21, 46, 86, 88, 314,
   316, 321–7, 345–50
   theory, 255, 267, 302, 303, 344–5
modernity, 20, 21, 86, 107, 251, 255, 259,
   263–4, 266, 268, 269, 270, 314, 330,
   332–3, 347–8
Molotov, Viacheslav, 32, 33, 34, 42, 49,
   50, 51, 124, 125, 127, 134, 190, 199,
   204
Mommsen, Hans, 11–12, 14, 139, 140,
   146, 149, 152, 353
Mommsen, Wolfgang, 66, 273, 274
Moore, Barrington, Jr, 260
Moscow, battle of, 187, 189–91, 200, 218
Munich Putsch (1923), 78, 84
Mussolini, B., 80, 97, 136, 143, 144, 352

Narkomfin, 59, 60
national insurance, 263
national question, in Soviet Union,
   22–3, 29–30, 37–8, 41, 305–10
nationalisation, 57, 58, 66
nation-states, 140–2, 147–8, 149, 151,
   152, 153, 155
Nazaretian, A. M., 32, 33
Nazi–Soviet pact, 126–7, 243, 244
Nazism
   administrative methods, 146–9
   agency and responsibility, 318–19, 330

bureaucracy, 12, 75, 81, 90, 99, 106,
   139, 145–6, 265
charismatic nature of, 97–106
communication failures of, 81–2
compared to Stalinism, 4–5, 8, 12–15,
   18, 78, 83, 85–7, 88–97, 135–55, 225,
   295, 344, 351–8
and constitutional change, 77
destructiveness of, 82, 86, 87, 89, 95,
   105, 106
elite involvement in, 118–19
explanations of, 2–3, 75, 252–3, 255,
   258–9, 260, 261, 264–6, 270, 271
failed to reproduce itself, 106
foreign policy of, 169–73
and genocide, 173–7
historicity of, 317
and Hitler cult, 94–5, 97
inefficiency of, 139, 145–6
irrationality of, 96
internal conflicts in, 80
and Jews, 6, 354
labour policies, 325–8
lack of governmental programme, 81,
   92
lack of integration in, 78
legacy of, 275
medicine, 312–13, 316, 333
military failures of, 225
and modernisation, 347–8
and normality, 315–18, 337
opposition to, 94, 150, 170, 171–2, 314,
   318, 319, 320, 329, 337, 340, 342
political failures of, 86–7, 96
popular support for, 140, 141, 151–2,
   339
post-war attitudes to, 20–1, 22
propaganda, 84, 86
racism, 313, 316, 326, 327–9, 330,
   331–4, 338–9, 340–2
radicalisation of, 12, 13, 82–7, 89,
   95–6, 100–6
regime dynamic cycle, 153–5
renewal of, 84–5
and revolutionary nation-statism,
   140–2
revolutionary process of, 149–53
self-destructiveness of, 12, 14–15, 75,
   82–3, 87, 97, 106, 137, 139, 152, 155,
   356
and *Sonderweg* thesis, 251, 253ff.
and the state, 75, 76–9, 96, 139
structuralist and intentionalist
   theories of, 10, 12, 20, 22, 173–6, 296
and territorial expansion, 75, 83, 100
and 'time of struggle', 84
and totalitarian concept, 136–7